The

SAFARI
COMPANION

A GUIDE TO WATCHING
AFRICAN MAMMALS

Including Hoofed Mammals, Carnivores, and Primates

RICHARD D. ESTES

DRAWINGS BY DANIEL OTTE
FOREWORD BY KATHRYN S. FULLER

Chelsea Green Publishing Company
Post Mills, Vermont 05058

Published in South Africa by Russel Friedman Books CC, PO Box 73, Halfway House 1685, South Africa. ISBN: 0-9583223-3-3

Published in Zimbabwe by Tutorial Press, 16 George Silundika Avenue, Harare, Zimbabwe. ISBN: 0-7974-1159-3

The Safari Companion was designed and formatted by Electric Dragon Productions, Montpelier, Vermont.

LIBRARY OF CONGRESS CATALOGING-IN-PUBLICATION DATA

Estes, R. D.
The safari companion: a guide to watching African mammals / by Richard D. Estes; drawings by Daniel Otte.
p. cm.
Includes bibiographical references.
ISBN 0-930031-49-0
1. Wildlife watching—Africa, Eastern—Guidebooks. 2. Wildlife watching—Africa, Southern—Guidebooks. 3. Mammals—Africa, Eastern—Behavior. 4. Mammals—Africa, Southern—Behavior.
I. Title.
QL60.E84 1992   91-45014
599.096—dc20   CIP

To Runi, Lindy, and Anna
May this book lead to our African reunion

CONTENTS

FOREWORD

As a child, I dreamed of venturing into the heart of Africa. That dream came true after I finished college, and the person responsible was Dr. Richard D. Estes, one of the foremost authorities on the social ecology and behavior of African mammals, who invited me to join a research expedition to study wildebeest in Tanzania's Ngorongoro Crater.

My stay in that spectacular crater reinforced what is now a lifelong commitment to conservation. I was able to experience firsthand, with the guidance of an expert, the miracle and majesty of wildlife and wild spaces. At the same time, the pressures that could lead the fragile web of life to unravel were evident, spurring my determination to do whatever I could to make sure that similar profound experiences would be available to my children, and future generations.

That is precisely the mission of World Wildlife Fund—to conserve the abundance and diversity of life on earth. Now celebrating its thirtieth year, WWF has grown more sophisticated as it has come to understand the dimensions of the conservation challenge. Today, conservation is about much more than establishing parks and preserves. It is also about addressing human needs; it is about international economics and diplomacy; it is about the way we in the richer countries live our lives. However complex and varied the means have become, though, the ends have never changed.

The Safari Companion is written in the same spirit. It will foster a deeper appreciation of Africa's wildlife by teaching people on safari to be better observers and to understand how animals interact with each other and with their environment. The book is more than a field guide; it is a valuable tool for conservation.

An African safari is a remarkable experience that evokes two different yet equally powerful responses. A safari serves as a reminder of Earth's spectacular abundance of life while also illustrating its vulnerability. Successful and lasting conservation depends on both of these emotions: wonder at the natural world and a sober recognition of the challenges ahead. The Safari Companion will help inform the passion of the traveler in Africa and will help advance the cause of wildlife conservation around the world.

I hope your time in Africa is as inspiring and fulfilling as mine was. I also hope you return eager to join us in the fight to preserve natural wonders for generations to come.

Kathryn S. Fuller
President, World Wildlife Fund (USA)

PREFACE

This book was conceived in the mid-1960s, after completing my doctoral research on wildebeest behavior. While living for two and a half years in the wildlife paradise called Ngorongoro Crater, I had noticed that much of the behavior I found engrossing went unnoticed by visitors. Judging by what their vehicles did and did not stop to look at, I estimated that visitors were missing three-quarters of the interesting activities of the Crater's wildlife.

This was partly because drivers and guides were intent on finding a few glamorous species for their clients to look at and photograph, notably the big cats, wild dog, rhino, and elephant. But another, underlying reason became clear in conversations with visitors and guides: neither had access to information gained through scientific studies of the animals. There was, in fact, a vacuum waiting to be filled by a popular book that would explain the behavior of the common four-footed animals every visitor saw.

In the following decades I completed eight years of African fieldwork and led seventeen tour groups on safari. My experience in Africa and the courses and public lectures about the behavior of African mammals I gave in the United States reinforced my conviction that what safari-goers really needed was a behavior guide that would explain what the animals they came to see were doing.

I ended by producing two books. *The Behavior Guide to African Mammals*, a comprehensive reference work for researchers and students, was published in 1991. *The Safari Companion* presents the same basic information but is designed specifically to serve as a field guide for parks visitors who are assumed never to have studied animal behavior.

Readers should be aware that *The Safari Companion* is not a conventional field guide: most of the information in it cannot be found in conventional guides. The description of each species is brief and the black and white drawings serve to illustrate displays rather than simply show what an animal looks like. For those who feel the need of a regular field guide to identify the different mammals, the most popular ones are listed in the Suggested Reading section.

One of my main purposes in writing this book is to promote conservation of African wildlife and protected areas by increasing public understanding of the most spectacular array of land mammals remaining on the planet. The more one understands animals, the more one cares what becomes of them. It is my fervent wish that the experiences which have so enriched my life will still be possible for my grandchildren and for all future generations. How sad it will be if they have to live in a world without African wildlife.

I would like to thank the following individuals for reading one or another draft of the book and offering valuable suggestions: David Blanton, Eleanor-Mary Cadell, Russel Friedman, Geoffrey Kent, Lisa Linblad, Dick Mills, Sy Montgomery, Thomas and Caroline Spang, Elizabeth Thomas, Rick Thomson, Gabriel Whitehouse, Barbara Wilson, and Barbara Wood.

For permission to reprint illustrations, I am grateful to Richard Orr for his painting (Fig. 28.2) which first appeared in *International Wildlife*; and to Ippy Patterson for her drawing (Fig. 31.4) reprinted from A. Richard, *Primates in Nature* (New York: W. H. Freeman, 1985). In addition, Fig. 30.1 is based on a drawing in P. Charles-Dominique, *Ecology and Behavior of Nocturnal Primates* (New York: Columbia University Press, 1977); and Fig. 31.5 is adapted from a drawing in R. A. Mittermayer and J. G. Fleagle, "The locomotor and postural repertoires of *Ateles geoffroyi* and *Colobus guereza*, and a reevaluation of the locomotor category semibrachiation," *American Journal of Physical Anthropology* 45 (1986): 235-56.

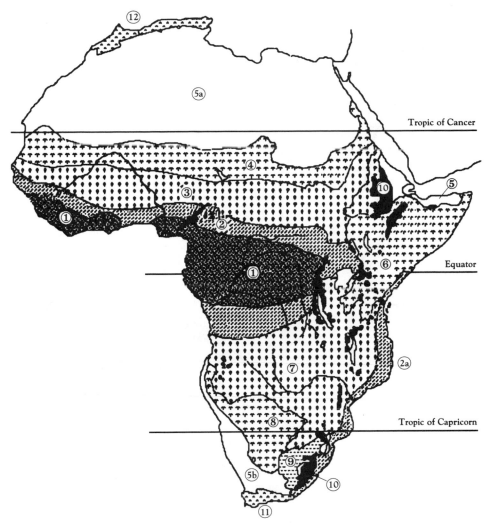

MAJOR VEGETATION TYPES

1. Lowland Rainforest
2. Forest-Savanna Transition and Mosaic
   a. Coastal Forest-Savanna Mosaic
3. Northern Savanna (including Guinea Savanna and part of Sudanese Arid Zone)
4. The Sahel (arid savanna and bushland)
5. Desert and semidesert shrubland
   a. The Sahara
   b. Namib Desert (Karroo semidesert)
6. Somali-Masai Arid Zone (dry savanna)
7. Southern Savanna (including wetter, broad-leaved deciduous *Miombo* Woodland Zone and drier acacia savanna)
8. South West Arid Zone (including Kalahari *sandveld* and drier Karroo dwarf shrubland)
9. *Highveld* temperate grassland and Karroo grassy shrubland
10. Afromontane vegetation (altitudinal zonation: montane forest, montane grassland, bamboo, heath, and alpine)
11. Cape and Karroo shrubland (Cape Macchia)
12. Mediterranean vegetation

Simplified from White, F. 1983. *The Vegetation of Africa*. Paris: UNESCO. Tucker, C. J., J. R. G. Townsend, and T. E. Goff. 1985. "African land-cover classification using satellite data." *Science* 227:369-75.

MAP OF EASTERN AND SOUTHERN AFRICA

1. Rwanda
2. Burundi
3. Lake Victoria
4. Lake Tanganyika
5. Lake Albert
6. White Nile
7. Lake Turkana
8. Mt. Kenya
9. Kilimanjaro
10. Mt. Meru
11. Lake Malawi (Nyasa)
12. Lake Kariba
13. Okavango Delta

MAIN NATIONAL PARKS AND GAME RESERVES OF EASTERN, CENTRAL, AND SOUTHERN AFRICA

FR (Forest Reserve) GR (Game Reserve) NP (National Park) NR (National Reserve or Nature Reserve)

KENYA 1. Sibiloi NP (left) and Marsabit NR. 2. Mt. Elgon NP. 3. Samburu-Isiolo (Buffalo Springs) and Shaba NR. 4. Nakuru NP. 5. Mt. Kenya NP. 6. Meru NP. 7. Aberdares NP. 8. Lambwe Valley NP. 9. Masai Mara NR. 10. Nairobi NP. 11. Tsavo NP. 12. Amboseli NP. 13. Shimba Hills NR.

TANZANIA 14. Kilimanjaro NP. 15. Arusha NP. 16. Serengeti NP (top), Ngorongoro Conservation Area, Manyara NP. 17. Tarangire NP. 18. Gombe NP. 19. Mahale Mts. NP. 20. Ruaha GR and Rungwa NP. 21. Mikumi NP. 22. Selous GR. 23. Katavi NP, Ugalla and Moyowosi GR.

UGANDA 24. Queen Elizabeth NP. 25. Kibale FR. 26. Murchison Falls NP. 27. Kidepo Valley NP.

ZAIRE 28. Garamba NP. 29. Virunga NP. 30. Kahuzi-Biega NP.

RWANDA 31. Parc de Volcans. 32. Kagera NP.

MALAWI 33. Nyika NP and Vwaza Marsh GR. 34. Kazungu NP. 35. Lake Malawi NP. 36. Lengwe NP.

ZAMBIA 37. Luangwa South NP. 38. Luangwa North NP. 39. Mweru Wantipa NP. 40. Kafue NP. 41. Blue Lagoon NP. 42. Lochinvar NP.

ZIMBABWE 43. Mana Pools NP. 44. Matusadona NP. 45. Zambezi and Victoria Falls NP. 46. Kazuma Pan NP. and Matetsi Safari Area. 47. Hwange NP. 48. Matobo NP. 49. Gonarezhou NP.

MOZAMBIQUE 50. Gorongosa NP.

BOTSWANA 51. Chobe NP. 52. Moremi GR. 53. Nxai Pan NP and Makgadikgadi Pans GR. 54. Central Kalahari GR. 55. Gemsbok NP.

SOUTH AFRICA 56. Kruger NP. 57. Pilansberg NP. 58. Suikerbosrand NR. 59. Mkuzi GR. 60. Hluhluwe and Umfolozi GR. 61. Golden Gate NP. 62. Willem Pretorius GR. 63. Giant's Castle NP. 64. Mountain Zebra NP. 65. Karroo NP. 66. Addo Elephant NP. 67. Tsitsikamma Coastal NP. 68. Bontebok NP. 69. Augrabies NP. 70. Kalahari Gembsbok NP.

NAMIBIA 71. Namib-Naukluft NP. 72. Skeleton Coast NP. 73. Etosha NP.

Chapter 1

USER'S GUIDE TO
The Safari Companion

GEOGRAPHICAL REGIONS AND ANIMALS INCLUDED IN THIS BOOK   This book includes the mammals that are commonly encountered by visitors to the wildlife preserves of eastern and southern Africa, specifically the parks and game reserves of Kenya, Uganda, Rwanda, Tanzania, Malawi, Zambia, Zimbabwe, Botswana, South Africa, and Namibia.

Rather than provide a little information about every species, *The Safari Companion* provides a lot of information about 86 species whose behavior is well known from field studies undertaken by scientists over the last 30 years. These are the same animals you are likely to see and hear on safari, and they include virtually all the large land mammals and most of the smaller ones. Rodents, rabbits, insectivores, and bats are not included. Although these orders include the majority of African mammals, most are nocturnal, small, seldom seen, and unstudied.

PREPARING TO WATCH ANIMALS BEHAVING   The first three chapters prepare readers who have never studied biology for the rewarding experience of watching and understanding the behavior of the animals they see on safari. Chapter 2 points out the unequaled variety of large mammals to be seen in Africa's parks; shows that the activities these animals perform are mostly basic and obvious; and singles out some of the more entertaining species to watch. Chapter 3 talks about the best times and places for game viewing; about how to approach animals with minimum disturbance; and about differences among and within species in approachability.

HOW INFORMATION IN PARTS I–IV IS ORGANIZED   The standard systematic arrangement used in field guides and mammal encyclopedias is followed: Members of the same order, family, subfamily, tribe, and genus are kept together in groups of progressively smaller, more closely related species. Groups that share a common ancestor are nested one inside the other like a series of Chinese boxes, the outermost being the order and the innermost containing species within the same genus (e.g., two jackals or two gazelles).

Each chapter introduces the family, subfamily, or tribe under consideration, in which various traits that distinguish the group are sketched, with emphasis on the kinds of social and mating systems that occur. This is followed by separate species accounts, in which the traits that make each species unique are brought out. In addition, separate chapters introduce Parts I, III, and IV, covering antelopes, carnivores, and primates, to provide more extensive background about these major groups.

INFORMATION IN CHAPTER INTRODUCTIONS The topics and headings listed below are used throughout the book to introduce families, subfamilies, and tribes (except for Chapters 9, 12, 14, 15, 17, and 21 that deal with only one species—these have little or no introduction). However, profound differences between ungulates, carnivores, and primates necessitate some variation in topics and their arrangement. How much or little information introduces any particular group depends on the number of species involved, the degree of variability among them, the complexity of their behavior, and how much is known about them. Supplementary subject headings are indicated by parentheses.

Each chapter begins with the name of the family, subfamily, or tribe followed by its Latin name. Next comes a list of all the African members. Species listed in the 1990 IUCN *Red List of Threatened Animals* as endangered or vulnerable are identified by superscript [en] or [v].

WHAT THEY ARE Includes information about the group's origins, its ecological place, and basic physical traits.

(FAMILY [OR SUBFAMILY] TRAITS) Introductions to major groups.

(WHAT THEY EAT) If particularly noteworthy.

SOCIAL/MATING SYSTEMS A summary of the different types that occur in the group, illustrated by standard symbols (see Table 1.1).

HOW THEY MOVE Gaits, postures (sleeping, sunbathing, etc.), swimming, climbing, digging, jumping ability.

(REPRODUCTION) Includes the same kinds of information usually given only in species accounts (see below).

(Mating behavior) Supplements information given in the Behavior Guide.

HOW THEY COMMUNICATE Sight 2, scent 1, sound 2. Numbers indicate which communication channels are preferred for sending and receiving messages. The example indicates that the group in question communicates primarily by scent and secondarily by sight and smell. A ranking of sight 1, scent 1, and sound 1 would indicate that all three channels are of primary and seemingly equal importance. More detailed information is included in introductions to families with especially elaborate communication systems (mainly primates and social carnivores).

TABLE 0.0 [FAMILY, SUBFAMILY, OR TRIBE] BEHAVIOR GUIDE Closely related animals not only look much alike, they also behave much alike. An inventory of behavior patterns shared by a group of related species therefore serves as a behavior guide to all the members. This is the arrangement used in *The Safari Companion*.

Each chapter introduction ends with a Behavior Guide, a table in which the displays and other visually distinctive behavior patterns common to the group are described and explained, along with associated calls or other sounds. The behaviors highlighted in the Behavior Guide are those that readers who stop and watch any representatives of the group can expect to see. Many of the basic displays and other visual signals are illustrated with silhouette or line drawings (icons) to make it easier to recognize them.

The different categories of behavior covered in the Behavior Guides are presented in the same sequence under standard headings used throughout the book: Self-advertising (including Territorial Advertising or simply Advertising Presence and Status); Aggression; Submission; Displacement Activities; Sociable Behavior; Courtship; Mother and Offspring; Play; and Response to Predators. In some carnivore chapters and in the primate section, calls are also catalogued separately.

INFORMATION IN SPECIES ACCOUNTS   Beginning with the common name of the animal (with superscript [en] or [v] if applicable) followed by its Latin name and an illustration, species accounts are presented under the following standard headings—again with some variation between sections dealing with animals as unalike as herbivores and carnivores.

(SUBSPECIES)   Listed only when distinctively different races exist in the regions this book covers. Those considered endangered or vulnerable are identified by the appropriate superscript.

WHAT IT IS   A brief description. Weight (wt) given in pounds (lb) and kilograms (kg). Shoulder height (ht), total length (tl), or head and body length (hbl), given in inches (in) and centimeters (cm) of adult males and females.

WHERE IT LIVES   Geographic, climatic, and altitudinal range.

Good places to see it   Popular game parks and reserves of eastern, central, and southern Africa where the species is numerous and/or notably easy to see and approach (emphasis on places I know firsthand). If places are too numerous to list, it is so noted, although one or more particularly good spots may be mentioned. In the case of animals that are rarely seen, this heading is deleted.

ECOLOGY   Habitat preferences and ecological niche; basic diet and foraging; water dependence or independence.

ACTIVITY   Whether day-active (○), night-active (●), or both (○/●). Daily ranging distance, time spent feeding, resting, moving, socializing, etc. when known.

SOCIAL/MATING SYSTEM   What I consider the most important information about the species is put in this section: whether it is sociable or solitary, territorial or nonterritorial, sedentary, migratory, or nomadic; sizes of home ranges and territories; social relations between females and between males; when young leave home; whether both sexes or only males disperse, etc.

Table 1.1.   *SOCIAL/MATING SYSTEMS: KEY TO SYMBOLS*

♂ ♀ ○   Symbols for male, female, and young.

♂ ♀   Territorial symbol: filled circle.

♂ ♀   Nonterritorial symbol: open circle.

Solitary Species

Solitary/polygynous system, both sexes territorial. ♂ territory includes 2 or more ♀ territories.

Solitary/polygynous system, both sexes nonterritorial. Adults have exclusive core areas but share the same home range.

Monogamously mated territorial pair.

Sociable Species

A group of associated ♀♀ and young that share a common home range.

Small and large groups of ♀♀ and young accompanied by a territorial ♂.

An all-♂ (bachelor) group.

♂ dominance hierarchy. Alpha ♂ monopolizes matings.

Small and large mixed groups (multi-♂, multi-♀).

Type of system is indicated by social organization symbol. Table 1.1 gives a few examples of commonly used symbols to illustrate the many different types and variations of social/mating systems described in this book.

(HOW IT MOVES)   Only if different from other members of its group as described in the chapter introduction.

FORAGING/PREDATORY BEHAVIOR   Included in carnivore accounts (Part III), describes how each species finds, secures, and consumes its food.

(FORAGING BEHAVIOR)   Included in some primate accounts when there is too much to include in Ecology.

REPRODUCTION   Whether seasonal or year-round; number of offspring; gestation length; minimum breeding age; intervals between births. Also in

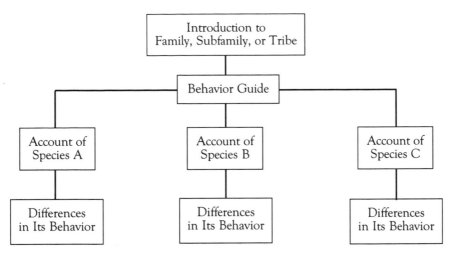

Figure 1.1. Chapter diagram.

some species accounts, mating behavior not covered in the Behavior Guide or Differences in Behavior.

OFFSPRING AND PARENTAL CARE   Behavior of mother and newborn, and any care given by father and other family members; weight and state of newborn; development stages; age at weaning, nutritional independence, and dispersal.

PREDATORS   Lists birds, mammals, and reptiles that pose a major danger to adults and young.

TABLE 0.0 DIFFERENCES IN [SPECIES] BEHAVIOR   Behaviors noticeably different from or additional to those described in the Behavior Guide to the group are described here, using the same format and headings. In general, differences between closely related species are limited to variation in the frequency or manner of performance of the same displays, so most supplemental guides are short.

So, to find a description and illustration of the display performed by a given species, use the Behavior Guide in the chapter introduction as the primary source, then go to the species account to learn how it differs from its relatives. The diagram in Figure 1.1 is included to make this arrangement as clear as possible.

MAKING YOUR OWN OBSERVATIONS   For the convenience of readers who want to make notes and sketches of interesting behaviors they see, there are extra pages in the back of the book, introduced by a brief lesson in how to go about it.

Chapter 2

GETTING STARTED

The number and variety of large animals on view out in the open in Africa's parks are unequaled anywhere else in the world. But the sheer numbers can be overwhelming and the variety bewildering. To sustain interest, the visitor needs to understand what he or she is seeing—otherwise, the novelty soon wears off. Given the keys to understanding animal behavior, watching animals becomes an ever more rewarding experience.

HOW ANIMALS SPEND THEIR TIME It is not certain that thought processes comparable to ours exist in other species. Yet studies of animal behavior continually affirm that the activities and "interests" of animals largely derive from basic needs—subsistence, safety, reproduction, which are also the basic needs of humans. Realizing this common denominator helps to demystify animal behavior, inspire confidence in one's ability to see the world through another species' eyes, and gain insight into what an animal is doing.

Any animal you stop and watch without disturbing is likely to be eating or searching for food, resting, scanning its surroundings to detect enemies or friends, or interacting socially, aggressively, or sexually with others of its kind. Herbivores have to spend a good half to two-thirds of their time just eating and digesting. Carnivores avoid much of this drudgery by eating the herbivores; the high-protein diet gives them more free time, which is devoted largely to loafing—or conserving energy, as ecologists and physiologists see it.

MORE AND LESS ENTERTAINING SPECIES The social and reproductive activities that captivate onlookers most occupy only about 10 percent of an animal's time—far less than eating and other behaviors related to nutrition and survival. However, there are major differences between and within species. Sociable species interact more frequently than unsociable species, especially those that live in family groups, harems, and larger groups.

Monkeys are the most active socially and sexually, and their eerie resemblance to people makes them particularly entertaining to watch. But there are also major differences between primate species. Chimpanzees, baboons, vervets, and other kinds that live in large, multimale troops have the most complex and interesting social and sexual relations. The leaf-eating primates that live in troops dominated by a single male, such as the gorilla and the black and white colobus monkey, spend much more time eating and less time interacting.

The same holds true for hoofed mammals. I find plains zebras, which live in harems and bachelor herds, the most entertaining of the plains game. Wildebeests, too, are almost always doing something worth watching, assuming you know what to look for. Impalas come next in my esteem; they have an extremely active social life and are always on the alert for lurking predators. Perhaps the herbivore that does least to reward the fascination with which nearly all visitors regard it is the giraffe: most of the time you spend looking at a giraffe it is standing there looking back at you. Elephants, in contrast, are totally fascinating to me, no matter what they're doing.

SEX AND AGE DIFFERENCES   Within species, the young and males tend to be more entertaining to watch than adult females. Young animals have far more time and inclination to play than adults do. Males, being preoccupied with rank and reproductive success, interact more often and more aggressively than do females, beginning in early youth. As the parent with sole responsibility for the feeding and care of offspring in most species, females are more careful, and they have to spend more time eating to keep producing milk. However, females interacting with their offspring are certainly interesting to watch, and so are the often subtle social interactions among females of the more gregarious species.

To understand the behavior of the animals you watch, the first step beyond recognizing species is to identify the actors by sex and age. It is not hard to distinguish adults, juveniles, and immature individuals, and determining the sex is usually easy—except in juveniles, where it matters least behaviorally.

WHAT YOU MAY ALREADY KNOW ABOUT AFRICAN MAMMALS   Many of the animals seen on an African safari are already familiar to visitors who have watched TV programs, perused coffee-table books about African wildlife, or read magazine articles and books about some of the more glamorous species like the lion, elephant, chimpanzee, and gorilla.

Moreover, the behavior of some of the commonest African animals is very similar to the behavior of related domesticated species. Anyone who knows dogs will find the behavior of jackals familiar and may note subtle differences in the African wild dog, which is less closely related. Those who have cats already know the African wildcat—and will recognize the very similar behavior of all the other kinds.

Zebras are not horses with stripes, but their behavior and social organization differ very little. Even though the African buffalo is unique, it belongs to the same tribe as all other cattle. Anyone familiar with domestic cattle will recognize the African buffalo's displays, calls, and cow-barn smell.

There are also many American, European, and Asian wild animals that have close kin in Africa. African jackals look and act much like American coyotes. Gazelles share many behavioral traits with the American pronghorn antelope. The African spotted-necked otter is closely related to the river otters of North America and Eurasia. The ratel reminds me of the related wolverine and the caracal looks quite a bit like a lynx.

REASONS TO STOP AND LOOK AT THE ANIMALS   Because herbivores spend most of their time eating and digesting, and carnivores spend most of their time sleeping, these are the activities you will most often see in an African park. But you may well witness dramatic and exciting events unfolding if you stop and watch the animals you meet. I have seen dozens of vehicles drive through a concentration of wildebeest in Tanzania's Ngorongoro Crater, completely unaware that three or four cows were calving at the time—the wildebeest calving season being one of the most spectacular annual events on the African plains.

Chapter 3

WHERE AND WHEN
TO SEE THE ANIMALS

THE DAILY ACTIVITY PEAKS   Whether I'm doing fieldwork or guiding a safari, I routinely go out at first light and spend several hours viewing wildlife before returning for a late breakfast. It's the best time to see lions and hyenas still on their kills or even hunting, to spot a leopard out in the open, to watch antelopes engaging in their morning frolics and skirmishes, and to tune in the dawn chorus of birds and beasts. Nothing surpasses the cool of early morning and the spectacle of an African sunrise.

Early morning and late afternoon happen to be the peak activity times for most animals. The transition from dark to light and light to dark—the most clearly defined events in the 24-hour cycle—triggers all kinds of action. Nocturnal species are still active as the diurnal animals leave their night refuges and resting places to begin foraging.

During the heat of the day there is relatively little activity; many animals avoid overheating and water loss by resting, preferably in the shade. Lions and other carnivores that eat big meals at long intervals are typically found asleep. However, many herbivores either remain or become active during the middle of the day, and so do baboons, other monkeys, and various diurnal carnivores, including cheetahs and social mongooses. It is a time when many animals go to water. Watching them coming to water is always interesting, vastly entertaining when elephants are involved, and sometimes dramatic when lions or crocodiles seize the opportunity to ambush prey when danger is least expected.

Most African parks have rules against night driving. Otherwise, night would be one of the most rewarding times for viewing wildlife. The big carnivores, except for cheetahs and wild dogs, do most of their hunting then. Diurnal antelopes and most other terrestrial herbivores have one or two night feeding bouts. And many strictly nocturnal creatures, such as the aardvark, porcupine, bushbabies, striped and brown hyenas, white-tailed mongoose, genets, and civet that are rarely seen in the daytime, are often encountered at night.

For most visitors the only way to see animals at night is to keep an eye out for them around game lodges and campgrounds. A variety of wildlife is attracted by the presence of nearby waterholes, salt licks, and garbage. Through habituation to people, many of these animals become remarkably tame. In addition to the nocturnal species already named, one can see—or more likely hear—the tree hyrax, fruit and insectivorous bats, owls, gecko lizards, and frogs and toads chorusing in the rainy season.

WHERE TO FIND THE ANIMALS   The chances of finding particular species you may want to see are greatly improved if you know where as well as when to look for them. Guides and drivers are generally expert in this department and keep one another informed about sightings of the most sought-after animals—especially leopard, cheetah, lion, and rhino. Nevertheless, you should be aware that although some animals have very particular habitat requirements, others tolerate a variety of habitat types and can be seen nearly everywhere.

Many carnivores, for example, are equally at home in wooded and open country. Leopards, however, will not go far from cover. Among herbivores, the elephant has the broadest habitat tolerance by far, ranging from rainforest to semidesert plains.

Among animals with more specialized habitat preferences, hippos must have water to submerge in and nearby grazing grounds. Wildebeests are specialized to harvest dense swards of short, palatable, and nutritious grasses. The sitatunga has elongated hooves and is otherwise adapted to live in swamps. Giraffes cannot subsist on open plains without trees or other woody plants they can browse. Rock hyraxes and klipspringers depend on cliffs and rock outcrops (called *kopjes*) as refuges from predators. The great majority of primates depend on trees for food and safety. Even such elementary knowledge can be put to practical use, if only to avoid wasting time looking for a species where it would never normally be. That is why habitat preferences are included under Ecology for each species included in *The Safari Companion*.

GETTING CLOSE—BUT NOT TOO CLOSE—TO WILDLIFE   If you're interested in watching animals behaving normally, you want to get close enough to see and hear clearly, but not so close that you disturb them. With binoculars, you can see anything bigger than a hare perfectly well from at least 100 yd. However, to get close-up pictures of anything smaller than a rhino, even with a 400-mm telephoto lens, you need to get closer than 100 yd. In fact, you can get and even stay within 100 yd of most wildlife without causing alarm if the animals are habituated to vehicles or to pedestrians.

Driving at speed straight toward an animal is *not* the way to make an approach. A slow, indirect approach is least disturbing. With animals that are blasé about cars, you can move right to the desired distance. Shy ones may have to be approached in stages, stopping if they act nervous or begin moving away, approaching again when they stop reacting. On the other hand, animals that live alongside highways present a special difficulty: they may ignore passing vehicles, but as soon as you stop, they take off.

The oblique approach works on foot, too, but it takes more time since most animals have been negatively conditioned to pedestrians. During foot approaches, you should avoid looking directly at the animal whenever it is watching you: staring is often associated with predators or aggression. Animals like antelopes, zebras, and warthogs, with laterally placed eyes and horizontally elongated pupils, can see all around, except directly to the rear, even while grazing. This makes it hard to sneak up on them—as every lion learns by experience.

The flight distance for a species depends partly on each animal's previous experience with vehicles and people, but other factors also play a role. Plains game is ill at ease and harder to approach when in or near cover. Conversely, cover-loving animals like bushbuck, reedbuck, small cats, and even leopards are likely to run away when encountered in the open.

Large groups are easier to approach and will allow vehicles (and predators) to come closer than will small groups or singles. There are also sex and age differences: females accompanied by young, especially newborn young, are the most reactive members of their species. Males are generally the least shy, especially males in the company of females or in bachelor herds. Finally, the time of day and kind of activity also make a difference. Most animals will let you get closer at night or under dim light conditions than by broad daylight. In the middle of a hot day, animals resting in the shade are reluctant to move and are more approachable. Some species have natural defenses that make them unafraid. The skunk's closest African relatives, the zorilla and striped weasel, rely on stink glands; porcupines rely on quills.

Lions and most other large predators are easily habituated to vehicles. Predictably enough, small herbivores and carnivores tend to be more alert and quicker to take flight than their predators. The antelope with the greatest flight distance is the eland, which is big enough to stand up to lions in defense of its offspring but unable to run fast or far. In most parks it will start moving away when a car comes within 300 to 500 yd. Other large herbivores that are big enough as adults to intimidate lions tend to worry less about cars than do the smaller kinds. Giraffes and buffalo bulls become exceptionally tame. Elephants occasionally attack cars, especially females with small calves.

FEEDING AND ANNOYING THE ANIMALS   The same animals that ignore an approaching car usually run away when approached on foot. Men on foot have been hunting African wildlife for maybe 2 million years, and the predatory image is still being reinforced outside, and too often inside, the parks. Since cars came onto the scene, most have had a clean record with the wildlife in national parks. People in vehicles, including boats, are not recognized as such: Animals see the whole ensemble, not the separate parts.

Around lodges and other facilities inside wildlife parks and reserves it is a different story. Here several factors combine to convince the animals that humans are harmless, if not their protectors and meal tickets. They find food, water, salt, and—in the case of small creatures such as bats, rats, mice, lizards, hyraxes, and numerous birds—shelter. Animals also find a measure of safety from large predators, which are often inhibited from hunting close to habitation.

The opportunity to see and photograph wildlife at close quarters on foot is a definite asset of wildlife lodges. Yet big animals that lose their fear of humans become potentially dangerous, especially when in quest of food. People who feed the animals contribute to the problem. It's a great treat to see superb starlings and other gorgeous birds hopping around practically at arm's length. But the novelty soon wears off when you find yourself hard-pressed to defend your breakfast. Feeding monkeys and baboons may be fun but has at least three undesirable results: it causes strife among the animals; it turns the monkeys into dangerous nuisances; and in the end the panhandlers have to be shot or trapped and translocated. Signs in Botswana's national parks read, "You feed them, we shoot them."

GIVING WILDLIFE A BREAK   Up to a point, the more cars animals see, the less they mind them. Animals are most approachable in the places where they are exposed to the most vehicles. However, the process can go too far when there is a constant succession of vehicles or so many of them around at once as actually to interfere with the animals' normal routine. To make it worse, the animals may undergo stress without obvious outward signs. Cheetahs, short of running or hiding, sit and gaze into the distance when stressed by a vehicle's close approach. The aloof cat look suggests they are completely ignoring you. But what they are actually doing is *looking away*, a behavior of cats attempting to appease the aggression of a dominant animal.

Since it is not always obvious when animals are disturbed, give them the benefit of the doubt and avoid crowding them. Etiquette, fortunately, favors the animals. It is good manners and better for the animals to wait in line rather than moving in on other vehicles and to move away once the desired close-up view and pictures have been obtained.

TIPS FOR VIEWING AND PHOTOGRAPHING WILDLIFE

BINOCULARS   Binoculars are essential for viewing wildlife. You need them to see small or distant objects clearly and they greatly increase your ability to observe the behavior of the large animals. In addition, binoculars enable you to see much better in dim light and will enhance your enjoyment by night: you can watch elephants, buffalos, hyenas, genets, porcupines, and many other animals from your lodge terrace or your room.

Binoculars of between 7 and 10 power are suitable for animal-watching. The higher the number, the greater the magnification. However, unless you have very steady hands, you may have trouble seeing clearly with 10-power binoculars. Binoculars have 2 specification numbers (7 × 50, for example).

The first number is the power of magnification. The second, usually from 30 to 55, specifies the diameter in millimeters of the objective lens (on the big end of the binoculars). The larger the objective lens, the more light it transmits, increasing the brightness of the image. At the same time, though, the field of view becomes smaller and the binoculars become bigger and heavier. Objectives of over 50 mm make the best night glasses, but objectives in the 30s are more convenient for general animal-watching because of their wide field of view. Some binoculars now on the market have objective lenses as small as 23 mm. I favor 7 × 35 and 8 × 32 binoculars. Yet 7 × 50 are also excellent; they gather twice as much light as 7 × 35 and cover a wider field than say, 8 or 10 × 50, since the field of view also decreases with increasing magnification.

A new prism design introduced in the 1960s made possible the present generation of very small but beautifully clear binoculars. The most famous of these, produced by Leitz and Zeiss, are also about the most expensive binoculars you can buy. But you can buy binoculars of similar design and acceptable clarity for under $100, which also holds true for conventional larger binoculars. Whichever binoculars you consider buying, make sure they focus sharply both on near and distant objects and that you see one image only through the viewing lenses. The lenses should be coated (giving a blue cast to the glass) to reduce the amount of light lost as it passes through the optical system's several components.

STILL PHOTOGRAPHY   What I say here about camera equipment and photography assumes at least an elementary familiarity with the subject. If your experience or interest goes no further than snapshots, it will not be worth your while to invest in the telephoto lenses and more complicated camera needed to get good wildlife photos. Unless you are serious about photography, you may be well advised just to forget about it on safari because having a camera and feeling you must use it at every opportunity can seriously interfere with your enjoyment of the experience.

Cameras and lenses   To take good close-up pictures of wild animals, you need a telephoto lens. And that means you need a camera that takes different lenses, preferably one with a bayonet mount for easy and quick changes. Assuming that you, like most professional photographers, have a 35-mm single-lens reflex camera, you need a telephoto lens big enough so that an animal the size of a wildebeest will fill the frame at a distance of 30 yd or so. Any lens smaller that 300 mm will only suffice for photographing bigger animals at shorter distances. I have always used a 400-mm lens and rarely feel the need for something bigger, except when trying to photograph birds and other small creatures.

The selection of 35-mm cameras and lenses is unlimited and bewildering. Computerized controls on the latest and most expensive models almost guarantee correct exposure and focus. However, many of the less expensive makes are well made and reliable, and offer the basics: one-stroke film advance and even a motor drive, through-the-lens light meter and automatic diaphragm control, and shutter speeds to $\frac{1}{1000}$ second.

Lenses are the most critical pieces of equipment. A really good lens produces pictures of such clarity and sharpness that I would prefer a used lens of high quality to a new one built to less rigorous standards. A simple, effective way of testing a lens is to take a few pictures of a newspaper (making sure the camera is firmly fixed and the lens is focused). Examine the results (negative or print) under magnification to make sure the type is sharp around the edges of the photograph as well as in the center. Most camera stores are willing to let customers try out a lens and may well be willing to make the test for you if you pay the costs of film and development.

Three different lenses should be adequate for your safari: the 50- to 55-mm lens that is standard on most 35-mm cameras, for landscapes, portraits, and snapshots; a 400-mm telephoto for wildlife photography; and a 135- or 200-mm telephoto to cover the intermediate subjects (portraits, landscapes, pictures of very close or very large animals). A zoom lens, in the range of 85 to 200 mm or 100 to 300 mm, is useful for composing pictures, but a good one is costlier than a single focal-length lens within the range covered by a zoom lens.

Dust can often be a problem on safari. To protect the camera and lenses you need to keep at hand, put them in a plastic bag.

Sharpness   A few people have such steady hands they can take pictures with a 400-mm telephoto at $\frac{1}{125}$ second that look perfectly sharp. But most of us need help. Although various types of pistol grips, gunstock mounts, chest and shoulder rests are useful when you're on foot with nothing solid on which to rest your camera, a sandbag or beanbag laid on a windowsill or roof is most convenient for photographing from a vehicle. A unipod, equivalent to 1 leg of a tripod, is another useful device, especially when you're afoot but also in a vehicle. Remember that photographing from a vehicle with a running engine—in motion or not—results in blurred pictures.

Films   Although fast films are necessary to take action pictures in dim light, the faster the film (the higher the exposure number or index) the grainier the transparencies and prints will be. The slower the film, the better the resolution and the sharper the image. Over 90 percent of the approximately 35,000 pictures I have taken are Kodachrome transparencies. I currently use Kodachrome 64, a film of moderate speed and good resolution that yields sharp images and realistic, durable color. For dim light, I use Ektachrome 200 or the new Kodachrome 200. For print film, I favor Kodacolor 100.

Part I

ANTELOPES AND OTHER AFRICAN RUMINANTS

ORDER ARTIODACTYLA, EVEN-TOED UNGULATES

SUBORDER RUMINANTIA, RUMINANTS

Families Represented in Africa	Species
Bovidae: antelopes, sheep, goats, cattle	75
Tragulidae: chevrotain	1
Giraffidae: giraffe, okapi	2

WHAT IS A RUMINANT?   Ruminants are even-toed ungulates that have four-chambered stomachs and chew the cud. In other words, these herbivores regurgitate food and rechew it as part of the digestive process. The earliest true ruminants became established some 37 million years ago and went on to replace nonruminants as dominant herbivores. Today, the bovid and deer families between them include ⅔ of all living ungulates.

Bacteria living in a herbivore's digestive system transform indigestible plant cellulose into digestible carbohydrates by the process of fermentation. The primary site of this bacterial digestion in most mammals is the cecum, a big pouch off the large intestine. In ruminants, however, fermentation occurs mainly in the rumen, the second and largest of the four stomach chambers; having this process occur before their food enters the true, acid-secreting stomach enables ruminants to transform cellulose more completely and efficiently than nonruminants can. They also gain a substantial protein bonus from digesting the constantly multiplying and dying rumen bacteria that reach the stomach intermingled with the processed plant material.

TEETH AND CHEWING   Ruminants have no upper incisors. In their place is a thick calloused pad. Grass or foliage is grasped between the lower incisors and the pad and is plucked or snipped, then chewed with rasplike cheek teeth. Grazers have broad incisors shaped like spatulas for gripping grass; browsers have more vertical, chisel-shaped incisors for snipping leaves and other, softer vegetation. While lying or standing and chewing the cud, mouthfuls of regurgitated rumen contents are ground between the molars with sideways movements of the lower jaw.

Chapter 4

INTRODUCING ANTELOPES
AND OTHER AFRICAN BOVIDS

FAMILY BOVIDAE	
Tribes Represented in Africa	**Species**
Duikers: Cephalophini	16
Dwarf antelopes: Neotragini	13
Gazelles: Antilopini	12
Reedbuck, kob, waterbuck: Reduncini	8
Rhebok: Peleini	1
Horse antelopes: Hippotragini	5
Hartebeest, topi, wildebeest: Alcelaphini	7
Impala: Aepycerotini	1
Bushbuck, kudu, eland: Tragelaphini	9
Buffalo, cattle: Bovini	1
Sheep, goats: Caprini	2
TOTAL	75

WHAT THEY ARE   Bovids are hollow-horned ruminants. Worldwide, the family includes 120 species, 84 of which are antelopes. This means that over ⅔ of all the bovids are antelopes. The remaining ⅓ are cattle, goats, and sheep.

Africa, the home of some 72 different antelope species, is antelope heaven. Very few cattle, sheep, or goats, which originated in Eurasia, ever got south of the Sahara on their own. One goat, the ibex, lives in the mountains of Ethiopia; the aouad or Barbary sheep inhabits mountains on the southern edge of the Sahara; and the African buffalo is the one indigenous bovine. So, all but 2 of the 12 chapters and 35 species accounts in Part I are about antelopes.

The bovid family tree is subdivided into subfamilies, tribes, genera, and species. To visualize this systematic arrangement, think of the family as the trunk. The primary branches are subfamilies, which divide into secondary branches known as tribes. The tribes divide into smaller branches—genera—and these divide into outer branches—species. Finally, the species subdivide into subspecies or races, which make the outermost branchlets of the family tree. These subspecies represent separate populations that have been genetically isolated long enough to develop distinctive differences. When subspecies become so different that they can overlap without interbreeding, they become full species.

16

Through this process of speciation, the amazingly diverse array of African bovids came into existence, beginning some 24 million years ago and reaching a peak during the last several million years of the Ice Age. To appreciate this diversity, consider that the 9 different tribes of African antelopes are as different from one another as sheep and goats (tribe Caprini) are from cattle (tribe Bovini). Accordingly, a separate chapter is devoted to each tribe.

FAMILY TRAITS   Bovids range in size from a 4-lb royal antelope to an eland, the largest antelope, buffalos, and wild oxen that weigh over a ton.

Horns: Bovid horns consist of an outer, horny sheath over an inner core of bone. Unlike deer antlers, they are never branched or shed. All bovid males and ⅔ of females are horned. In a few species (oryx, addax, eland), females' horns are as long or even longer, but female horns are invariably thinner and weaker because they don't have to fight for the chance to reproduce. Males do. Horn texture and degree of wear offer clues to the age of adult animals. Sharp points, smooth surface, and in species with ridged horns, wide grooves, indicate young adults. Worn-down horn tips, rough surface, and narrow grooves at the bases are signs of age.

Color: Ranges from mostly white to black, but shades of brown predominate. Sociable species that live in the open tend to have bold markings or a dark color which, along with conformation, help them to tell their own kind apart from all other species. Antelopes that rely on concealment to avoid predators are cryptically colored. The stripes and blotches seen on the hides of bushbuck, bongo, and kudu also function as camouflage by helping to disrupt the animals' outline.

Scent glands: Dense cluster of cells, generally flask-shaped, derived from hair follicles. Their chemically complex secretions convey information about the individual's identity, sex, age, and social and reproductive status. The names and locations of antelope glands are shown in Figure 4.1.

The most common and important scent glands are the hoof (interdigital) glands and the preorbital glands. The secretions of the hoof glands, exuding from the cleft between the hooves, leave a scent trace that helps antelopes follow one another. Preorbital glands are employed mainly for marking objects. Territorial dik-diks, klipspringers, and Thomson's gazelles, among others, place globules of black, tarlike secretion on twigs and grass stems to scent-post their property.

Form and Function: Antelopes vary in form almost as much as in size. With a little practice, and taking into account size, coloration, and movements, you can pretty well predict which ones are or are not adapted for long-distance running, bounding, or dodging—and the type of habitat for which a species is adapted. For example, small size, overdeveloped hindquarters, and cryptic coloration go together with dependence on cover and concealment, a bounding, dodging run, and a high-protein diet. Medium and large size, a level back, long, equally developed limbs, and conspicuous coloration go to-

Figure 4.1. Location of antelope scent glands. H, hoof gland (inset shows wildebeest forefoot with half the hoof cut away, exposing the flask-shaped gland). S, shin (carpal) gland (gazelles). P, preorbital gland. F, glandular forehead skin (impala). Sa, subauricular (below-the-ear) gland (reedbucks, oribi). D, dorsal gland (springbok). Pr, preputial gland (inset: g, glandular sac; u, opening of penile sheath). I, inguinal glands (inset shows reedbuck inguinal area: gl, gland orifice [cross-section shown in inset]; m, mammary; sc, scrotum). T, metatarsal gland (impala only). FH, false-hoof gland.

gether with avoidance of cover, open habitats (generally level ground), and reliance on speed and endurance to escape predators.

ECOLOGY   From the deserts to the lowland rainforests, from swamps to mountain moorlands, wherever there is vegetation there are antelopes to eat it. The great diversity of African antelopes reflects the wide variety of habitats available to terrestrial herbivores and the superior ability of ruminants to subdivide these habitats into narrow segments by specializing. Each species is adapted to a particular ecological niche by its size, anatomy, physiology, feeding technique, digestive system, dispersal pattern, and social and reproductive systems, enabling it to exploit a particular set of conditions more efficiently than any other ruminant.

Nevertheless, usually two or more species share some of the same resources and compete to some degree. One of the most impressive aspects of the African wildlife experience is the presence of up to a dozen different antelopes in the same area. Yet it was by taking measures to minimize competition—by becoming different species—that such a diverse array of antelopes came to exist in the first place.

WATER DEPENDENCE AND INDEPENDENCE   Antelopes that are water-independent can exploit vast areas that are seasonally or perennially waterless and therefore inaccessible to antelopes that have to drink regularly. In general, pure grazers are water-dependent and have to drink every day or two, particularly when subsisting on standing hay. Browsers can obtain enough water to meet their needs by eating green leaves, herbs, succulents, and other plants that store water in their tissues. But there's more to being water-independent than just substituting water-bearing plants. Antelopes that live in arid regions use various strategies—some behavioral others physiological—to minimize their need for water.

- They avoid overheating by resting in the shade during the hottest hours. Lacking shade, they align themselves with the sun to present the least surface. Their coats are light-colored and highly reflective.

- They feed during the coolest hours, in early morning or late at night, when vegetation has absorbed as much water from the air as possible.

- They concentrate urine and absorb water from their feces, producing barely moist pellets.

- They allow their body temperature to rise by as much as 10°F (6°C), simply storing heat rather than dissipating it by panting—and losing water in the process. The stored heat dissipates gradually in the cooler night air.

- When an antelope gets so hot that it has to cool down in a hurry, it does so by nasal panting—rapid, rhythmic breathing with mouth closed. Nasal panting cools blood flowing close to the surface in a rich capillary network; this blood then cools arterial blood flowing to the brain.

Adaptability to arid conditions varies from tribe to tribe and is not limited to desert species. Oryxes, springbok, Thomson's gazelle, and some other antelopes that live in waterless regions drink when water is available whereas gerenuk, Grant's gazelle, steenbok, and dik-dik have virtually never been seen drinking.

CHEMICAL DEFENSES OF BROWSE PLANTS   If you watch an antelope browsing, you may be surprised at how quickly it moves from one plant to the next, plucking only a small number of leaves from each bush or tree. Why is it so selective? Recent research has shown that many plants can actively defend themselves against herbivores by producing chemicals that make their leaves less palatable and digestible. Some infuse their leaves very quickly on being attacked, thereby limiting their losses to what a browser can consume within the first few minutes.

SOCIAL/MATING SYSTEMS   Whether antelopes lead solitary lives or live in herds depends largely on their habitat and food requirements. A simple rule applies: to stay together in a herd, antelopes need to see one another. With few exceptions, antelopes that live in dense vegetation are solitary. The more open the habitat and the more closely spaced the food plants, the larger the herds. An extensive plain closely covered with grass where herd members can graze shoulder to shoulder without hindrance can sustain the densest concentrations. Wildebeests and buffalos aggregate this way—one on shorter, the other on longer pastures. At the opposite extreme, a herd of browsers feeding on widely separated small bushes could not maintain close spacing. If numerous, a herd whose members were widely dispersed could not easily maintain contact and coordinate their movements, especially if vegetation obstructed their view.

Another rule that holds for all species is that the largest groups occur in the most uniform, open habitat. For plains antelopes such as gazelles, springbok, wildebeest, hartebeest, or topi, you will find the smallest herds where the grassland occurs in small patches separated by woodland, and the biggest aggregations on the most expansive grasslands.

THE FOUR BOVID SOCIAL AND MATING SYSTEMS Bovid social and mating systems are either territorial or nonterritorial, solitary or sociable. The four possible combinations are outlined below, along with the symbols representing each type.

SOLITARY/TERRITORIAL Both sexes become territorial as adults. Young of both sexes disperse as subadults, face equal risks, and survive in approximately equal numbers, leading to an equal adult sex ratio.

(♂♀) Monogamous pair: Male and female mate for life and each shares and defends the home range/territory against intruders of same gender. Examples: blue duiker, dik-diks, klipspringer, probably most other duikers and dwarf antelopes.

(♀♂♀) One male associated with 2 or more females (polygyny). Females live singly with dependent offspring on small home range/territories, 2 or more of which are included in the territories of the fittest males. Examples: bohor reedbuck, pygmy and Bates' antelopes (the 2 smallest bovids).

SOCIABLE/TERRITORIAL

(♂ ♀○♀○♀○) (♂♂♂) Adult males are territorial; females and young sharing the same home range associate in female herds. Female offspring remain in natal herd, whereas male offspring are evicted by territorial males in adolescence. Nonterritorial males associate in bachelor herds. Higher male mortality leads to adult sex ratio favoring females. Examples: The prevailing social/mating system among antelopes, including all sociable species except members of the bushbuck/kudu tribe.

SOLITARY/NONTERRITORIAL

(♂♀♀) Home ranges overlap to a large extent, but each adult has a small, exclusive core area. The largest social unit is a female with her dependent calf. Examples: The bushbuck is the only known representative.

SOCIABLE/NONTERRITORIAL

(♀○♀○♀) Females with a shared home range associate in herds.

(♂♂♂) Males compete directly for mating opportunities, end up in a dominance hierarchy based on size and seniority.

(♂♂♂) Subadult and adult males associate in loose bachelor herds, but mature males tend to become more solitary with age. Examples: spiral-horned antelopes (kudu, eland, etc.), cattle, sheep, and goats.

TRANSITION FROM SOLITARY TO SOCIABLE   The tendency to form herds can be seen in several of the "solitary" antelopes. In the oribi and common reedbuck, females band together after their grassland cover is removed by fire. Although these herds are temporary and loose, lacking the cohesiveness seen in many gregarious antelopes, sociability probably derives from this tendency to bunch together in the open.

BIASED MORTALITY RATES AND ADULT SEX RATIOS
The existence of female herds increases mating opportunities for males and therefore increases sexual competition among them: the larger the female herds, the more the fittest males stand to gain at the expense of less successful males. Primarily because of this male competition, adult sex ratios skewed in favor of females are characteristic of herding antelopes. But rivalry between males of the same age and social status is less punishing than the aggression of mature against immature males, which forces male offspring to disperse in adolescence; females are privileged to stay in their natal herd.

Male sexual competition also leads to higher mortality in more subtle ways. Males are often so intent upon one another that they forget to look out for danger, and bachelors are routinely forced into substandard habitat where there is more cover to conceal predators. As long as males remain in female herds, they benefit from the greater alertness of females—rigorously selected over millennia to be vigilant through lower survival of the offspring of inattentive mothers.

VARIATIONS IN SOCIABLE/TERRITORIAL SYSTEMS   Female herds normally contain no more than one adult male, the one who is the proprietor of the territory where the herd happens to be. The only lone animals are territorial males and females guarding concealed offspring. Even territorial males become sociable away from their own property. Although a herd of females may remain for an extended period in a single territory, the owner loses access to them as soon as they cross the boundary into a neighbor's domain. In fact, territorial males may be alone most of the time, particularly those with substandard locations. So, lone bulls of territorial species are simply males-in-waiting, not outcasts from the herd as often portrayed.

The willingness of territorial males to stay alone is explained by the difficulty of finding and winning a popular location in the first place, and the necessity to stay put and advertise ownership to keep it.

If the habitat is fairly uniform, a large area may be divided up like a patchwork quilt into a mosaic of occupied territories. Where the habitat is discontinuous and patchy, the territories of nearest neighbors may have no shared boundaries.

- Permanent, resource-based territories include the variety of vegetation types preferred by the species in all seasons.

- Seasonal and temporary territories are occupied only as long as other members of the species are present.

- Lek territories, where a number of males pack closely together on a breeding ground, have only been described in topi, kob, and lechwe (see those species accounts).

VARIATIONS IN FEMALE SOCIAL GROUPS   In contrast to the great differences between males of territorial and nonterritorial systems, the social and reproductive organization of females of these two systems is quite similar.

COMPOSITION   Herds may be closed or open to outsiders; cohesive and constant in composition or loose with variable composition; permanently resident, seasonally migratory, or constantly on the move. How often herd members associate varies from species to species and also in the same species, depending on environmental conditions. Composition is most constant in populations at low to medium density, where the animals are dispersed in discrete small herds each occupying traditional home ranges with minimal overlap. Such herds tend to be closed or semiclosed to outsiders; strangers attempting to join are subjected to aggression.

LEADERSHIP   One or more senior females usually take the lead during herd movements. Herds of closed membership have regular leaders, whereas any animal may become the leader in open societies—such as wildebeest or Thomson's gazelle aggregations—through the simple follow-the-leader tendency of social antelopes.

All-male herds, being less cohesive and lacking kinship bonds, may have no regular leaders, although younger animals tend to follow older ones. As a rule, individual spacing in bachelor herds is greater and more regular than in female herds.

RANK ORDER   In closed herds, look for a linear rank order, where number 1 dominates everybody, number 2 dominates everybody but number 1, and so on down to the lowest ranking individual, whom everybody is free to tyrannize. Between members of the same sex, rank is based on seniority; within the same age class, size and aggressiveness are decisive. By observing who threatens whom and, more subtly, who gives way when 2 individuals' paths cross, you can soon spot the top-ranked individuals. But when there are more than a few adults in the herd, it takes time and the ability to recognize group members individually to work out the whole rank hierarchy.

SOCIAL DISTANCE AND SOCIABILITY   Species differ in their tolerance for crowding. Spacing may be closest among females without horns. Yet even female impalas, which pack closer than other hornless females, are not true contact species like the buffalo, with horned females that often lie touching. If least individual distance is taken as the measure of sociability, species that tolerate contact are the most sociable.

SUBGROUPS   In large herds containing individuals of different age and sex, look for subgroups composed of like individuals. A mutual attraction between animals of the same gender and stage of development is most noticeable in species with annual calving seasons.

REPRODUCTION   A single offspring is the rule in all African antelopes, from the smallest dwarf antelope to the giant eland, and gestation ranges from 4 to 6 months in small- to medium-sized antelopes (up to gazelle size) to 8 or 9 months in the big ones.

Reproduction takes place during a time of food abundance. Antelopes that experience no extended periods of food scarcity breed throughout the year; females ovulate and conceive again within a few weeks after calving. But most of Africa has dry seasons lasting 3 to 8 months or more, and the reproductive cycles of the animals that live there are adapted accordingly.

Most antelopes breed during the rainy season. A gestation period of 8 to 9 months allows both conception and birth and/or peak lactation to occur during times of food abundance. However, carrying a calf to term has priority: mating peaks—called a rut if most mating occurs in a short period of intense activity—invariably occur at nutritional peaks when the animals are in top condition. Conditions at calving time vary greatly from year to year and are unpredictable. Over 90% of all adult females calve regardless, always prepared to take advantage of good conditions.

In equatorial regions where there are 2 rainy and 2 dry seasons and thus 2 nutritional highs, many antelopes breed twice, conceiving during the short and long rainy seasons. The secondary calving peak comes late in the long dry season, when the chances of calf survival are usually less favorable. However, there are a number of highly successful mammals, including the impala and topi, that produce young just before or at the beginning of the rains.

MINIMUM BREEDING AGE   Female antelopes up to the size of a Thomson's gazelle typically conceive before their first birthday. Among the medium-sized species, females breed as yearlings and calve by their second birthday. Mating and birth occur a year later in most large antelopes.

Males reach adolescence at about the same age as females but seldom get a chance to breed before they stop growing. As males grow bigger than females in all but the 2 tribes of solitary small antelopes, they also mature and breed later: a year later in territorial species of medium size (100–300 lb [45–137 kg]), and 2 years later in large antelopes (over 350 lb [160 kg]).

In nonterritorial bovids the difference in maturation rates of males and females is considerably greater than in territorial species because it takes longer for males in absolute-dominance mating systems to grow big enough to compete with their seniors. Greater kudu and eland bulls are 7 or 8 before they enter the ranks of breeding males, whereas females calve by the age of 3.

ESTRUS AND MATING   Estrus lasts for a day or less in territorial species, compared to at least several days in nonterritorial species. Extending estrus allows extra time for a top-ranked male to find and serve females. Copulation is brief in antelopes, occurring immediately after penetration and marked by a single ejaculatory thrust. Copulatory postures vary greatly but are much alike within tribes.

OFFSPRING AND PARENTAL CARE

HIDERS AND FOLLOWERS

Newborn young of nearly all antelopes go through a hiding stage lasting from a few days (impala) up to 2 months or more (reedbuck/kob and bushbuck tribes). An elaborate concealment strategy minimizes the chance that predators will find hidden calves. A calf's scent glands only begin secreting after the concealment stage, and body wastes are retained until the mother stimulates the calf by licking its rear end. (Note: you can tell a calf's sex by noting where the mother licks: between the legs of males, under the tail of females.) The flight response is suppressed in the newborn, but calves older than a few days will flee if discovered, then hide again at the first opportunity. Mothers with hidden offspring typically stand guard but stay away from the hiding place except to retrieve and suckle them, typically 2 to 4 times in a 24-hour period. Calves remain active for up to an hour, then go off alone with or without prompting and find a new hiding place, preferably in a clump of grass or other upstanding vegetation.

A number of bovid tribes have follower young, which do not go through a concealment stage but follow their mothers from the time they can stand. Members of the buffalo/cattle tribe, some sheep and goats, and some goat-antelopes have follower young, but this arrangement is rare in antelopes (see wildebeest accounts).

ANTELOPE BIRTHS   Pregnant females do not appear great with young until the final month of gestation and the udder enlarges only days before parturition. An important element of the hider strategy is isolation: calves dispersed singly are less vulnerable to discovery than are groups of concealed young. An expectant mother typically seeks seclusion several days before calving.

Birth is very similar in all antelopes. The fetus shifts toward the pelvic opening a few hours before labor begins, and the vulva bulges visibly shortly before the emergence of the white amniotic sac, which breaks sooner or later to reveal the yellow-tipped forefeet of the emerging calf. In addition to the distended vulva, a slightly raised tail is often the first sign that birth is imminent. Labor is under voluntary control and will not begin until the female is satisfied that there is no immediate danger from predators; she can interrupt the process at will until after the calf's head has emerged. Visible contractions occur only while a female is lying on her side. The legs are straightened and raised in hard labor. Bouts are interrupted frequently as the female rises to a kneeling or standing position to change sides and to maintain surveillance. She frequently examines the birthplace and consumes fluids and fetal membranes.

The average time from first appearance of the fetus to delivery is about ½ hour. As the calf finally slides completely out, either while the mother is lying or kneeling with hindquarters elevated, she turns and begins licking and cleaning it. Meanwhile the pair exchanges calls (bleats, baas, or moos), often beginning as soon as the baby's head has emerged.

Soon the neonate begins struggling to stand. It generally takes ¼ to ½ hour or longer for calves of hider species to gain their feet, compared to an average of 7 minutes for a wildebeest, the most precocious bovid. The afterbirth is retained usually for several hours postpartum, by which time the calf has usually gone into hiding. Unless disturbed, the mother consumes the afterbirth.

Once mobile, a calf begins seeking the udder, nuzzling and sniffing its way along the mother's body until eventually it locates a teat. Nursing begins the process of imprinting the calf on its own mother, which takes a day or two. Until this happens, a calf will approach and try to nurse any other member of its own species and often other species, including predators and people. Consequently the mother has to be close by whenever her offspring is active and must be able to identify her own if other young are present, discriminating initially by scent, later also by sight and sound. Mothers' efforts to prevent mix-ups are assisted by the tendency of females to reject offspring other than their own. Practically the only way for adoption to occur is through mistaken identity.

Although mothers suckle their young for at least 4 months in the smaller, early-maturing species and 6 to 9 months in the larger ones, calves begin sampling food plants within the first week or two and begin grazing or browsing and ruminating once they stop hiding.

CALF SOCIETY   Young antelopes spend surprisingly little time close to their mothers and, paradoxically, mother and young associate more closely in solitary species than in sociable species. After enduring the solitary confinement of the hiding stage, the only company available to solitary antelope offspring is the parents. In herding antelopes, calves usually have a choice and they prefer to associate with one another, as demonstrated by the peer subgroupings seen in large antelope herds. Except to nurse and in emergencies, when mother and offspring seek one another, calves spend their time together. This arrangement also gives mothers more freedom, and it is not unusual to find groups of quite small calves with few or even no adults in sight.

PARENTAL CARE   Males provide parental care only when paternity is assured. In the monogamous antelopes, fathers play a watchdog role, which includes surveillance, giving alarm signals, and even attacking small predators. In the polygynous species, the care and feeding of the young are entirely up to the mother, although males have been known to guard and defend young under conditions where a male remains associated with the same females for an extended period.

Mothers actively defend their offspring against predators, sometimes even risking their own lives. But cooperative defense, a characteristic of the cattle tribe, is rare among antelopes (see gazelle and eland accounts). Each mother is on her own.

RESPONSE TO PREDATORS   Many antelopes look formidable enough to defend themselves against their predators. So it is surprising to find that attempts at self-defense are rare and usually ineffectual. Antelopes caught by hyenas or wild dogs have normally been run to exhaustion; they are incapable of protecting their hindquarters and underbelly from their attackers' jaws. The big cats ambush their prey, taking them by surprise. Only if the hunter bungles the job does the prey have a chance to defend itself. Exceptionally formidable antelopes like the oryx and sable have been known to kill even lions, but antelope horns are designed and function primarily for reproductive competition between males—not as antipredator weapons.

To avoid being eaten, antelopes rely first on avoidance and second on flight. Like hider calves, antelopes that live in cover avoid detection by hiding and, if discovered, rush away and make for another hiding place. Open-country species depend on surveillance and membership in a group to keep a safe distance from predators and avoid being singled out. If chased, they rely on speed and endurance to outrun pursuers.

Table 4.1.   *ANTELOPE BEHAVIOR GUIDE*
Expect to see and hear ➤ *Usual context and meaning*

Self-advertising

Mostly by territorial and alpha ♂ ♂. ➤ Behaviors that call attention to the presence, high social status, and mood of the actor. Distinct from (but often combined with) aggressive and mating displays.

Showing oneself: adult ♂ standing or lying in conspicuous location and/or attitude, typically alone or apart from herd. ➤ For example, topi standing on mound advertises presence while keeping watch for rivals, ♀ ♀, and predators. Both territorial and nonterritorial antelopes show themselves.

ASSOCIATED ACTIONS

Calling and other sounds: snorting; sound of horns thrashing vegetation. ➤ Including alarm signals (alert posture, snorting, stamping, stotting, etc.) which also call attention to the performer. Wildebeest croaking; impala puffing/roaring; grunts of lechwe, kob, springbok; eland bulls' clicking knees.

Attention-catching movements: head-nodding, tail-flourishing, sideswiping, stamping, cavorting, etc.

Herding and chasing. ➤ Rounding up ♀ ♀ and chasing other ♂ ♂. Typical of territorial and alpha ♂ ♂.

SCENT-MARKING

Defecation on dung midden, ± urination, often emphasized by pawing. ➤ Doubles as a visual display, made conspicuous by posture and/or associated actions. Regularly performed by territorial ♂ ♂, typically along boundaries and at much-used resting places. Most territorial antelopes.

Daubing or rubbing preorbital-gland secretion on objects, ground, self, or others. ➤ Second in importance to dung as a way of scent-posting territory (duiker, dwarf antelope, gazelle, and hartebeest tribes).

Object-horning. ➤ Thrashing vegetation as an expression of aggressive mood, undirected to an individual; see also under Threat Displays. Universal, primarily ♂ ♂.

SELF-ADORNMENT

Mud-packing. ➤ Coating horns, face, shoulders with mud (hartebeest, topi, wildebeest, eland).

With vegetation. ➤ Carrying a load of grass or a branch on the head, picked up while thrashing vegetation (Grant's gazelle, wildebeest, eland).

Aggression

DOMINANCE DISPLAYS
Assertions of superiority without immediate threat of attack. All sociable species.

Erect posture. ➤ Neck and head raised more than the normal relaxed stance. Commonest of all dominance displays. Resembles alert posture.

Broadside stance. ➤ Standing broadside to opponent, head-to-tail (left) or head-to-head (right). Not a combat position for most antelopes. About as widespread as the erect posture and typically combined with it.

Confronting. ➤ Confronting opponent. Closer to combat position and thus more threatening than broadside stance. Opponents often look away. Less common than broadside stance.

Supplanting. ➤ Displacing a subordinate simply by walking toward it. Universal.

Slow, stiff approach, including high-stepping and prancing. ➤ Given in combination with dominance or threat displays (bushbuck tribe; courtship displays of topi, gazelles).

OFFENSIVE THREAT DISPLAYS
Actions that signal readiness to attack, usually performed from confronting position. Universal.

Medial-horn threat. ➤ Neck at about shoulder level, horns pointing upward. The commonest threat posture.

Kneeling position. ➤ Species that fight on their knees (hartebeest tribe, sable and roan).

Low-horn threat. ➤ Head lowered, chin in, horns pointing at opponent (duikers, dwarf antelopes, eland, oryx, wildebeest).

High-horn threat. ➤ Neck raised, nose angled downward (gazelle, kob, oryx/sable tribes).

Angle-horn threat. ➤ Head and horns tilted or aimed toward opponent, often from broadside stance (wildebeest, roan, sable, oryx, waterbuck, Grant's gazelle).

Staring. ➤ Looking directly at opponent. Universal.

Pronounced rhythmic nodding. ➤ Symbolic butting (topi, gazelles, kob).

Head-shaking or twisting. ➤ Rotating movements used in fighting by some species (wildebeest, topi, waterbuck, impala).

Aggression *continued*

Sideswiping. ➤ Abrupt head swing to shoulder or flank. Similar or identical to fly-shooing described under Displacement.

Feinted attack. ➤ Springing forward into combat attitude, without following through (gazelles, wildebeest, topi, etc.).

Rushing/charging. ➤ A real attack, usually directed at an inferior, as when an adult ♂ charges an adolescent ♂. Universal.

Chasing. ➤ Response of dominant to opponent that takes flight—e.g., after being charged or losing a fight. Universal. (Long post-fight chases common in topi, hartebeest, Grant's gazelle.)

Pursuit march. ➤ Driving inferior opponent at a walk, while displaying dominance. Probably all sociable species (especially Grant's gazelle bachelors).

Cavorting. ➤ Jumping, bucking, spinning, and similar antics signifying defiance or threat. Associated with high-intensity aggressive encounters. Especially common among territorial wildebeest and bachelor topi.

Vegetation- or ground-horning. ➤ A threat when addressed to a specific individual. ♂ ♂ of most species.

DEFENSIVE THREAT DISPLAYS
Displays associated with self-defense (including response in kind to offensive threats).

Head-low posture. ➤ Chin drawn in more or less, depending on direction of threatened attack; horns usually point upward. Nearly universal.

DEFENSIVE THREAT DISPLAYS BY HORNLESS FEMALES
Seen especially in response to ♂ courtship (bushbuck tribe, waterbuck, duikers).

Symbolic biting. ➤ Snapping, usually while facing away from opponent.

Pushing with snout. ➤ Usually without contact (bushbuck tribe).

Neck-winding. ➤ Writhing movements with neck and head raised (bushbuck tribe; see Fig. 13.2).

Submission

Responses to dominance and threat displays, or sexual harassment, which function to appease aggressor.

Head-low/chin-out posture. ➤ Chin lifted more or less depending on species, making horns lie back—the opposite of presenting horns. Practically universal.

Lying-out. ➤ Hiding behavior, display of complete submission in response to aggression or sexual harassment (sable, roan, wildebeest, dwarf antelopes).

Kneeling. ➤ As a preliminary to lying-out (wildebeest, sable, gray duiker).

Submission *continued*

Avoidance. ➤ Steering clear of more dominant individuals.

Passing behind. ➤ Response to a dominant animal blocking the way in broadside stance (wildebeest, horse antelopes).

Moving away. ➤ Withdrawal (walking or running away).

Turning aside. ➤ Moving out of the way of an approaching animal—i.e., being supplanted. Universal.

Displacement Activities

Everyday maintenance activities performed in tense situations. Universal.

Displacement-grazing. ➤ Neutral behavior, neither threatening nor submissive, common during encounters between territorial ♂♂ (wildebeest [see Fig. 11.4], topi, hartebeest; Tommy grazing duels).

Displacement-grooming. ➤ Grooming typical of the species. Universal.

Fly-shooing or sideswiping. ➤ Abrupt head swing to shoulder or flank (hartebeest and horse-antelope tribes; eland). Same movement is used to shoo flies and as an aggressive display, sideswiping.

Displacement alarm. ➤ Performed in the absence of danger, typically during aggressive interactions (wildebeest-topi tribe).

Sociable Behavior

MEETING AND GREETING

Nasal contact/sniffing. ➤ Friendly social interactions begin with nasal contact and sniffing. A universal identity-checking.

SOCIAL GROOMING

Two animals taking turns grooming one another. ➤ Relatively uncommon in antelopes; limited to head, neck, and shoulder area, thus distinct from sexual and maternal licking of genital area.

Licking/nibbling. ➤ Duikers, bushbuck tribe.

Scraping with lower incisors ± nibbling. ➤ Impala, dwarf antelopes.

Rubbing preorbital glands on partner. ➤ Scent-marking mate, offspring, in some cases adversary (duikers, wildebeest, gerenuk).

Courtship

PERFORMED MAINLY BY MALES

Lowstretch. ➤ Posture adopted when approaching or herding ♀. Most antelopes.

Urine-testing. ➤ The grimace and posture adopted after sampling urine, during which urinalysis is performed. Nearly all bovids.

Courtship *continued*

Pursuit. ➤ Early stages of courtship, when ♀ attempts to avoid ♂. Most hectic in solitary species.

Mating march. ➤ ♂ follows ♀ closely in premating and mating stage, while performing other courtship displays. Universal.

Foreleg-lifting. ➤ Performed by ♂ during mating march (members of duiker, dwarf antelope, gazelles, horse antelope tribes).

Prancing. ➤ Quick-stepping, high-stepping, or goose-stepping during mating march (gazelles, kob, topi).

Genital-licking. ➤ By ♂ while closely following ♀ (especially duiker, dwarf antelope, kob, and bushbuck tribes).

Empty-licking. ➤ Licking performed without contacting ♀ (impala, bushbuck tribe, otherwise uncommon).

Dominance displays. ➤ Erect posture and other dominance displays performed during mating march.

Nose-lifting and prancing. ➤ Abrupt raising of the muzzle while following ♀ in erect posture (Thomson's gazelle, kob).

FEMALE BEHAVIOR

Responsive urination and ♂ urine-testing. ➤ Reaction to lowstretch approach. Most antelopes.

Aggressive displays. ➤ Signs ♀ is unreceptive. Nearly universal.

Estrous Behavior

All species.

Coquettish behavior. ➤ Playful or skittish response to courtship.

Mounting behavior. ➤ Mounting or being mounted by other ♀♀.

Token avoidance. ➤ Slowly moving away, especially with tail extended or deflected.

Standing for mounting. ➤ Barely moving, standing or backing into ♂ attempting to mount, tail held out, up, or to one side.

Mother and Offspring

Lone adult ♀ guarding concealed calf. ➤ Standing in alert posture. If feeding, frequently looks up and scans surroundings. All antelopes with hidden young.

Calf lying-out. ➤ Prone attitude of calves during hiding stage (all antelopes but wildebeests and blesbok).

Mother retrieving hidden calf. ➤ Long, cautious approach, calf summoned finally by calling or head-bobbing. Applies to all hider species.

Mother and Offspring *continued*

INTERACTIONS OF MOTHER AND CALF
Applicable to all hider species.

Greeting and identity check. ➤ Sniff noses, mother sniffs calf's back.

Calf suckles while mother licks its anus and genitals. ➤ Licking causes calf to void wastes, which mother consumes.

Calf cavorts and frisks after nursing, follows, but runs ahead and lags behind if mother walks away.

Calf finds new hiding place. ➤ On its own initiative, while mother watches.

Play

Running, cavorting, excitement activities (stotting, alarm-trotting), sparring. ➤ Type of play varies with type of group (e.g., whether calves have playmates), age, and sex. ♂ ♂ more aggressive; spar and fight more than ♀ ♀.

Response to Predators

Alert posture and stamping. ➤ Standing with head raised while staring intently at a real or imagined predator. Sometimes combined with approach or circling. Universal.

Stotting or pronking. ➤ Stiff-legged bounding, typically with white rump patch or tail displayed (dwarf antelope, gazelle and reedbuck tribes, hartebeest, topi).

Style-trotting. ➤ High-stepping, springy trot (wildebeest, horse antelopes).

High-jumping. ➤ Leaping and scattering flight (impala, lechwe, eland, kudu).

Lying-out. ➤ In same prone attitude as hiding calves (small, cover-dependent species).

Standing in cover. ➤ Large antelopes that live in closed habitats (bushbuck tribe, kudu, gerenuk).

Skulking. ➤ Cover-dependent antelopes trying to sneak away from a disturbance (bushbuck tribe, lechwe, duikers, dwarf antelopes).

Freezing. ➤ Arrested movement, often with one leg raised (antelopes that hide: duikers, bushbuck tribe, gerenuk).

Chapter 5

DUIKERS
Tribe Cephalophini

Blue duiker, *Cephalophus monticola*
Maxwell's duiker, *C. maxwellii*
Aders' duiker, *C. adersi*[en]
Peters' duiker, *C. callipygus*
Red duiker, *C. natalensis*
(Harvey's red duiker, *C. n. harveyi*)[v]
(Weyns' duiker, *C. n. weynsi*)[en]
Black-fronted duiker, *C.nigrifrons*
(Ruwenzori duiker, *C. n. rubidus*)[en]
Red flanked duiker, *C. rufilatus*

Bay duiker, *C. dorsalis*
White-bellied duiker, *C. leucogaster*
Ogilby's duiker, *C. ogilbyi*[v]
Zebra duiker, *C. zebra*[v]
Black duiker, *C. niger*[v]
Abbott's duiker, *C. spadix*[v]
Jentink's duiker, *C. jentinki*[en]
Yellow-backed duiker, *C. silvicultor*
Common or gray duiker, *Sylvicapra grimmia*

Duikers in parentheses, treated here as subspecies, are considered full species by some specialists.

WHAT THEY ARE   A distinctive group of small- to medium-sized antelopes that dominate the rainforest, subsisting mainly on fallen fruits, the most abundant food resource on the forest floor. Africa is the only continent whose rainforests boast such a variety and abundance of ruminants. Throughout the African rainforest, duikers and other "bush meat" are the main source of protein.

Apart from differences in size (from 9–180 lb [4–80 kg]) and color, forest duikers are remarkably similar: sturdy build with short legs, rounded back, and massive hindquarters; big head with wide mouth, small ears. *Horns:* short, straight, back-slanted; present in both sexes, more or less concealed by an erectile hair crest. Females slightly larger than males. *Color:* concealing, from gray to black, commonly red-brown, with mostly inconspicuous markings; sexes alike; young either like adults or darker. *Scent glands:* preorbital glands in both sexes, opening into a horizontal slit on the muzzle; glands in all hooves; inguinal glands present in some species. *Teats:* 4.

SOCIAL/MATING SYSTEM   (♂♀) (♀♂♀)   Although only blue, Maxwell's, and bay duikers have been studied in any depth, all duikers are solitary and probably reside in permanent home ranges defended as territories. Blue and Maxwell's are known to live in pairs and evidence suggests at least two other forest duikers are monogamous, too. But possibly some duikers have a solitary/polygynous mating system.

HOW THEY MOVE   Carefully, with lowered head, in cross-walk; freeze in midstride when disturbed; rush from hiding and run, dodging and leaping, to disappear in nearest cover as abruptly as they appear—hence the name *duikerbok*, Afrikaans for diving buck.

COMMUNICATION   Sight 2, scent 1, sound 1.

Table 5.1.   *DUIKER BEHAVIOR GUIDE* *
Expect to see and hear ➤ *Usual context and meaning*

Territorial and Dominance Advertising

Placing preorbital-gland secretion. ➤ Scent-posting; especially ♂ ♂.

Tree-horning, after first sniffing and licking the spot, ± pawing ground afterward. ➤ Audible (horns grating on wood) and visual (gouges in bark) advertisement. Performed mainly near territorial boundary as pair and family activity; helps maintain social bonds.

Alarm-snorting and -whistling. ➤ Response to violation of individual or territorial distance.

Aggression

Low-horn threat. ➤ Same as combat attitude.

Pressing preorbital glands (see Fig. 5.1). ➤ Prelude to combat when performed by ♂ ♂.

Rushing, feinted attack; high-speed chases and attempted body-stabbing. ➤ Of trespasser or the loser of a fight.

OTHER ACTIONS ASSOCIATED WITH AGGRESSIVE DISPLAYS
Snorting, pawing, preorbital-gland marking, tree-horning. ➤ Performed especially by territorial ♂ ♂, with increasing frequency during aggressive interactions.

Submission

Head-low/chin-out posture. ➤ Submissive response to aggression.

Kneeling. ➤ Intention to lie prone.

Lying-out. ➤ Complete submission.

Distress cry and alarm whistle. ➤ Response to continuing harassment, as during courtship.

---

*Based on studies of only 4 species (Maxwell's, blue, bay, and gray duikers); how applicable this guide is to the rest remains to be seen.

Sociable Behavior

Mutual gland-pressing (see Fig. 5.1). ➤ A pair-bonding behavior second in frequency only to tree-horning.

 Social licking, elicited by approaching in head-low/chin-out posture and offering the desired spot for grooming. ➤ The most frequent form of social contact in a family, also used to appease aggression.

Short, soft groaning cries. ➤ A duiker seeking physical contact.

Courtship

MALE BEHAVIOR

Sexual pursuit. ➤ Very common during courtship, alternates with close following.

 Lowstretch. ➤ Posture of ♂ approaching and following ♀.

 Urine-testing. ➤ Checking ♀ reproductive status; mouth open but no pronounced grimace.

Aggressive behavior: biting ♀'s tail, hitting rump with horns, moaning and snorting. ➤ ♂ becomes increasingly aggressive as mate enters full estrus.

Close following while licking ♀'s rear end and marking her with preorbital glands (see Fig. 5.2). ➤ Posture of ♂ approaching and following ♀.

Foreleg-lifting. ➤ Performed during mating march.

Mutual gland-pressing. ➤ Prelude to mating.

FEMALE BEHAVIOR

Progression from avoidance to mating readiness.

Flight, circling, turning, buck-jumping, hiding. ➤ Avoiding ♂ advances.

Moaning, snorting, whistling, mewing.

Keeping tail clamped and moving out from under mate until fully receptive.

Mother and Offspring

See Mother and Offspring, Table 4.2.

Play

Running, jumping, rushing, circling, chasing, and fighting.

Response to Predators

Skulking into cover or freezing and sinking down in place.
➤ Response to predator by duiker that has not been detected.

Sudden flight and dodging run. ➤ After initial rush, duikers often stop in cover and try to see or smell what scared them.

Snorting. ➤ Short-range signal.

Distress cry. ➤ Elicits defensive response by adults of both sexes. Hunters imitate cry to lure and shoot duikers.

BLUE DUIKER, *Cephalophus monticola*

Figure 5.1. Male blue duikers pressing preorbital glands together during aggressive encounter.

WHAT IT IS   The smallest duiker and one of the smallest antelopes. ♂ wt 10 lb (4.6 kg), ht 13 in (32.5 cm); ♀ wt 12 lb (5.4 kg), ht 14 in (36.2 cm). *Head:* crest poorly developed. *Horns:* 2 in (5 cm), often absent in female. *Coat:* short, glossy. *Color:* inconspicuous blue-gray to maroon with bluish gloss on back, white underparts and haunches, and short tail with white underside.

WHERE IT LIVES   Most abundant and ubiquitous of all the rainforest duikers, replaced by the very similar Maxwell's duiker from Nigeria west. Ranges through East and southeastern Africa in various forested and closely wooded habitats.

ECOLOGY   Occupies the openest areas of the forest floor, shunning dense undergrowth except to hide. In bush and thicket habitat, it is small enough to pass beneath the clutter. A very choosy feeder, diet varies with habitat and season; subsists primarily on small fallen fruits in rainforest, supplemented by foliage, flowers, insects, and fungi.

ACTIVITY   ○ Strictly diurnal. Forages up to 7 hours and ranges about ½ mi (1 km) a day. Each duiker spends the night lying in a favorite resting place, only getting up to stretch and change position.

SOCIAL/MATING SYSTEM (symbol) Territories are small, averaging 6 to 10 acres (2.5-4 hectares). Monogamy very evident: couples stay close and synchronize their activities. They press their preorbital glands together and lick one another up to 6 times per hour, usually on the male's initiative.

REPRODUCTION In unhunted rainforest populations, pairs produce only 1 calf per year, in the driest months, and females calve first in their second year—late for such a small antelope. But where heavily hunted, females may start reproducing a year earlier and have 2 to 3 young per year, as this smallest duiker is the main source of rainforest bush meat, and gestation is only around 4 months.

OFFSPRING AND PARENTAL CARE (symbol) During 3-week lying-out period, mother suckles calf 3 times a day, otherwise stays 75 yd or so from its hiding place. As the baby becomes more mobile between 3 and 4 weeks and begins eating, it is suckled twice a day, morning and evening, then evenings only until weaning at 2.5 to 3 months. Mother and offspring associate most closely during second and third month, thereafter sleep separately.

PREDATORS Small size and preference for open forest make blue duikers particularly vulnerable to crowned hawk eagles. They are also preyed on by golden cat, leopard, and baboon. Close association of a mated pair and constant vigilance reduce the risks of being taken by surprise.

Table 5.2. DIFFERENCES IN BLUE DUIKER BEHAVIOR
Expect to see and hear ➤ *Usual context and meaning*

Sociable Behavior

Tail-flickering: regular up-and-down movement of the tail, making white undersurface flicker in forest gloom. ➤ Pretty automatic while active. Helps family members keep in visual contact.

Play

Blue duiker families are relatively playful.

Response to Predators

Stamping with rear feet. ➤ High-intensity signal. Other duikers respond with flight.

COMMON OR GRAY DUIKER, *Sylvicapra grimmia*

Figure 5.2. Common duiker courtship: close following during mating march.

WHAT IT IS   A medium-sized duiker modified for life in savanna wood-lands. Limbs longer, more evenly developed and back less rounded than forest duikers. ♂ wt 28 lb (12.9 kg), ht 20 in (50 cm); ♀ wt 30 lb (13.7 kg), ht 21 in (52 cm). *Horns:* males only, comparatively upright, 3 to 7 in (7–18 cm). *Color:* variable, grayer and lighter in arid zones; redder in wetter climates; dark facial blaze, head crest, and feet; paler underparts; young calves darker than adults.

WHERE IT LIVES   South of the Sahara virtually everywhere there is cover, except in rainforest and desert.

ECOLOGY   Most abundant in savanna and woodland, not found on open plains or distant from cover. One of the last antelopes to be eliminated by settlement. Varied diet of foliage, herbs, fruits, seeds, and cultivated crops; also known to eat resin, bark, insects, lizards, rodents, and birds.

ACTIVITY   ○/● Active day and night but largely nocturnal where heav-ily hunted. Each individual retires to a favored resting place to lie up and ru-minate. Females favor lower, denser cover than males, which prefer mounds and slopes as vantage points from which to guard their property.

SOCIAL/MATING SYSTEM   (⚯) (♀♂♀)   It is unclear whether bush duikers are monogamous or polygynous—or maybe both: the most suc-cessful males may be polygynous, the rest monogamous. In either case, males and females are sighted separately 2 to 5 times more often than in pairs and observers of wild bush duikers have rarely seen pair-bonding behavior. How-ever, a captive male and female social-groomed and pressed preorbital glands together like blue duiker couples; and each was aggressive to intruders of the same sex. Samples of different bush duiker populations suggest an equal adult sex ratio, and females are bigger than males—two more indicators of a monogamous species.

HOW IT MOVES   A conformation similar to steenbok or oribi suggests the bush duiker is faster with more endurance than forest duikers. It often outruns and outdodges dogs while dashing between hiding places.

REPRODUCTION   Develops faster and reproduces sooner and more often than most forest duikers. Females breed year-round, may calve at 1 year and produce 2 young per year. Gestation estimates range from 3 to 7 months; 5 to 6 months seems reasonable.

OFFSPRING AND PARENTAL CARE   Births have been observed only in captivity, as wild females calve in thick cover. Newborns can run within a day and after 3 days are hard to catch but hide for several weeks, except when summoned to suckle 2 to 3 times in a 24-hour day. By 6 months, calves are nearly as tall as adults.

PREDATORS   All meat eaters down to the size of martial eagles, which carry off young calves. Responding to a calf's distress bleats, mothers will attack small predators and have been known to butt a male baboon and an 8-foot python. Fathers also respond to distress calls.

Table 5.3.   *DIFFERENCES IN COMMON DUIKER BEHAVIOR*
Expect to see and hear ➤ *Usual context and meaning*

Territorial Advertising

 Placing preorbital-gland secretion. ➤ By ♂ only (in wild) but also by ♀ of a captive pair.

 Tree- and bush-horning. ➤ ♂ ♂ only.

Aggression

Snorting, wheezing. ➤ Snorting changes to wheezing at high intensity.

Courtship

MALE BEHAVIOR
Prancing alongside, tilting head from side to side. ➤ Invitation to press preorbital glands.

FEMALE BEHAVIOR
Mewing call. ➤ Response to being nudged.

Chapter 6
DWARF ANTELOPES
Tribe Neotragini

Royal antelope, *Neotragus pygmaeus*
Bates' pygmy antelope, *N. batesi*
Suni, *N. moschatus*
Kirk's dik-dik, *Madoqua kirkii*
Salt's dik-dik, *M. saltiana*
Piacentini's dik-dik, *M. piacentinii*[v]
Guenther's dik-dik, *M. guentheri*

Cape grysbok, *Raphicerus melanotis*
Sharp's grysbok, *R. sharpei*
Steenbok, *R. campestris*
Klipspringer, *Oreotragus oreotragus*
Oribi, *Ourebia ourebi*
Beira, *Dorcatragus megalotis*[en]

WHAT THEY ARE   Tiny (3 lb) to small antelopes, allied with the gazelles in the subfamily Antilopinae. Unlike duikers, the other tribe of small, solitary antelopes, dwarf antelopes are diverse enough to be placed in 6 different genera.

Neotragus and *Madoqua*, the smallest antelopes, are harelike, with hind legs much longer than forelegs. Steenbok and especially oribi are built more like gazelles. *Head:* narrow muzzle, bare or hairy nostrils, and prominent ears. *Horns:* in male only (but see klipspringer), short, straight spikes. *Tail:* short or rudimentary. *Color:* concealing, pale gray to dark brown with inconspicuous markings except for white rump patch or undertail. *Scent glands:* hoof glands in all feet; preorbital, inguinal, preputial, and shin glands. *Teats:* 4.

SOCIAL/MATING SYSTEM

(⚥)   Solitary/monogamous. The prevailing system among dwarf antelopes, known in dik-diks, klipspringer, oribi, and suni. Monogamy is probable in steenbok, therefore possible in the closely related grysboks.

(⚥ ♀)   Monogamous with an extra female (most likely a grown daughter that stayed home). Known in oribi and klipspringer.

(♀ ♂ ♀)   Solitary/polygynous. Royal and Bates' antelopes, the only 2 forest-dwelling neotragines. Male's territory encompasses smaller territories of 2 or more females.

(♂♂♀♀)   Territorial defense by a coalition of 2 or 3 adult males. Discovered in oribi, suspected in klipspringer. An arrangement previously unknown in solitary antelopes.

PAIR BOND   Behaviors associated with maintaining the integrity of the territory, performed together, function to maintain pair and family bonds. A dunging ceremony, frequently performed on established borderline middens, is the main pair activity of dwarf antelopes. It is typically triggered when the female crouches to urinate, bringing the male to check her reproductive status. Alarm calling in duet may also strengthen pair bonds in klipspringer and dik-diks. Social grooming, so important in duiker couples, is rarely seen in dwarf antelopes except during courtship.

MALE AGGRESSION   Males, ever the more aggressive sex, are generally more active than females in territorial demarcation and defense. Their stiletto horns can inflict mortal wounds and furious dwarf antelopes are more likely than bigger antelopes to stab to the body. Perhaps accordingly, rival males usually go through the motions of fighting without actually making contact (air-cushion fight).

HOW THEY MOVE   Dwarf antelopes make quick, nervous movements typical of delicate little antelopes. Remarkably long hind limbs enable *Neotragus* and dik-dik species to make jack-rabbit starts, sharp turns, and long leaps and bounds to evade pursuing predators. Steenbok and oribi have more evenly developed limbs and a more conventional running gait.

HOW THEY COMMUNICATE   Sight 2, scent 1, sound 1.

Table 6.1.   *DWARF ANTELOPE BEHAVIOR GUIDE*
Expect to see and hear ➤ Usual context and meaning

Territorial Advertising

Standing sentinel in alert posture. ➤ Usually a ♂, on vantage point where it can see and be seen to advantage (see klipspringer account).

Urinating and defecating in sequence on middens ± pawing before, during, or afterward. ➤ Dunging ceremony: the main territorial and pair-bonding activity in monogamous species (see dik-dik, klipspringer, oribi accounts).

Placing preorbital-gland secretion, often following or preceding dunging ceremony. ➤ Scent-posting property by both partners (dik-diks and klipspringer) or by ♂ only (steenbok, oribi).

♂ vegetation-horning. ➤ Advertises aggressive mood.

Alarm-calling, including duets. ➤ Triggered by appearance of predator, advertises presence of a mated pair. Comparable to duetting of pair-bonded birds (see klipspringer account).

Aggression

Erect or alert posture, both sexes. ➤ Exaggerated alert posture assumed at sight of possible territorial intruder.

Aggression *continued*

 Medial-horn threat. ➤ Commonest threat display.

 Low-horn threat. ➤ Same as combat attitude.

 Confrontation ± head-ducking. ➤ Prelude to air-cushion fight (fighting motions without contact) or real fight (rare).

OTHER ACTIONS ASSOCIATED WITH AGGRESSIVE DISPLAYS
Alarm calls, pawing, preorbital-gland marking, vegetation-horning.

Feinted attack. ➤ Jumping forward while rear feet stay planted.

Stotting. ➤ Bounding approach to trespasser by highly excited territorial ♂.

Chasing and attempted stabbing. ➤ By territorial ♂ of intruder or defeated rival.

Submission

 Head-low/chin-out posture. ➤ Response to aggression, most commonly by adolescent sons to aggressive fathers.

Kneeling. ➤ Intention to lie in submission.

 Lying-out. ➤ Hiding behavior, signifies total submission by defeated rival or frightened offspring.

Distress-bleating and alarm-whistling. ➤ Response to continuing harassment, as during courtship.

Displacement Activities

Feeding, grooming.

Sociable Behavior

 Greeting behavior. ➤ Between family members.

 Social grooming. ➤ Nibbling and licking, often associated with courtship behavior; otherwise not very common.

Courtship

MALE BEHAVIOR
 Lowstretch. ➤ Posture of ♂ approaching and following ♀.

 Urine-testing by ♂. ➤ Checking ♀ reproductive status; mouth open but no pronounced grimace (see Fig. 6.2).

Courtship *continued*

Close following while licking ♀'s rear end. ➤ Especially during mating march.

Foreleg-lifting. ➤ Performed during mating march.

Following in erect posture. ➤ ♂ dominance display.

FEMALE BEHAVIOR

Urination by ♀. ➤ Very frequent, prelude to dunging ceremony. Attracts ♂ (see Figs. 6.1, 6.4).

Avoidance: flight, moving away, circling, turning, buck-jumping, hiding.

Butting, poking. ➤ Aggression.

Submissive displays.

Holding tail out and squatting slightly. ➤ Response to ♂'s licking by receptive ♀.

Mother and Offspring

See Mother and Offspring in Table 4.2.

Play

Running, jumping, rushing, circling, chasing, and play fighting.

Response to Predators

Alert posture and fixed stare, stamping.

Stotting. ➤ A sign of excitement stimulated by sight of predator.

Skulking into cover, freezing and sinking down. ➤ Response to coursing predators when antelope is undetected.

Flight to refuge, followed by whistling alarm snorts. ➤ Response to ambush predators (cats).

Silence. ➤ Response to coursing predators.

SOUNDS OF ALARM

Whistling snorts; including duetting. ➤ See dik-dik and klipspringer accounts.

Distress bleat. ➤ Extreme fear, as when captured by a predator.

STEENBOK, *Raphicerus campestris*

Figure 6.1. Steenbok courtship: male sampling mate's urine.

WHAT IT IS   A small, brick-colored antelope that lives in patches of cover on the acacia savanna. Graceful build, long limbs with hindquarters bigger but not much higher than forequarters. ♂ wt 24 lb (10.9 kg), ht 20 in (50 cm); ♀ wt 25 lb (11.3 kg), ht same as ♂. *Head:* large rounded ears. *Horns:* sharp, upright spikes ringed only at base, 3.6 to 7.6 in (9-19 cm). *Coat:* smooth, glossy. *Color:* geographically variable, redder in East Africa, grayer in Kalahari; white underparts, rump patch, inside ears, pale eye ring, black triangle on nose including bare nostrils. Sexes alike, newborn has woolier coat but similar coloration.

WHERE IT LIVES   Two separate populations on either side of the *Miombo* Woodland Zone: from central Kenya through the southern part of the Somali-Masai Arid Zone; and from southern Angola and the Zambezi throughout southern Africa in suitable habitat.

GOOD PLACES TO SEE IT   Open habitats of southern Africa, notably in Hwange NP, Zimbabwe; Chobe NP, Moremi and Central Kalahari GR, Botswana; Etosha NP, Namibia.

RELATIVES   Sharp's grysbok replaces steenbok in *Miombo* Woodland Zone; they overlap in much of southern range, as in Zimbabwe, but grysboks prefer denser bush; they are darker, smaller, and more nocturnal.

ECOLOGY   Dry savanna wherever woody vegetation provides hiding places and forage. Southern population frequents more open habitat, probably because Sharp's grysbok monopolizes closed habitats. Northern steenbok has a broader niche, from sea level to 15,300 ft (4750 m), including denser cover in acacia groves and stony, well-wooded hillsides. A water-independent browser/grazer; eats foliage of various woody plants; forbs, seedpods and seeds, fruits and berries, and tender green grass. Digs up roots and tubers in Kalahari Sandveld.

ACTIVITY   ○/● Active day and night where undisturbed, becoming largely nocturnal near settlement. Withdraws into cover to rest and escape midday heat, using regular resting sites.

SOCIAL/MATING SYSTEM   (♂♀) Sighted far more often singly than in pairs, there is some doubt whether this slightly studied antelope is monogamous. However, there are no records of a male living with 2 females, and a captive male penned with 2 females mated with one and fought the other. Couples may share territories as small as 10 to 12 acres (4–5 ha) up to 0.4 mi² (1 km²) without staying close together. Maybe scattered clumps of cover separated by open ground, typical of steenbok habitat, make staying apart safer. When pairs are encountered, they tend to flee in opposite directions.

REPRODUCTION   Year-round with possible peak early in rains. Females can conceive at 6 to 7 months, calve at 1 year, and reproduce at 8-month intervals. Gestation estimated at 166 to 177 days. Males adolescent at 8.5 months, mature in second year.

OFFSPRING AND PARENTAL CARE   Young unusually precocious. A 2 lb (1 kg) calf was on its feet and nursing within 5 minutes, began nibbling vegetation at 2 weeks, and was weaned at 3 months. Nevertheless, calves are well-grown before beginning to accompany mother.

PREDATORS   Cheetah, wild dog, spotted hyena, leopard, caracal, and lion all prey on adults; young vulnerable to all predators down to the size of a martial eagle.

Table 6.2.   *DIFFERENCES IN STEENBOK BEHAVIOR*
        Expect to see and hear ➤ *Usual context and meaning*

Territorial Advertising

Urinating and defecating in sequence on dung middens. Steenbok paws before, during, and afterward, leaving covered piles. ➤ May not be pair activity. Both sexes make deposits in the same manner, but seemingly maintain separate middens.

Marking with preorbital glands. ➤ By ♂ only.

Response to Predators

Fast dodging run when flushed from hiding place, zig-zagging and bounding every few strides.

DIK-DIK, *Madoqua kirkii*

Figure 6.2. Dik-dik dunging ceremony: female defecating on border dung midden while mate tests her urine.

WHAT IT IS   A miniature antelope with a pointed, mobile snout, big eyes, and a duikerlike head crest of erectile hair. Very long hind legs, rudimentary tail. ♂ wt 11 lb (5.1 kg), ht 24 in (59 cm); ♀ wt 12 lb (5.5 kg), ht 25 in (62.5 cm). *Head:* snout like a little trunk. *Horns:* 3 in (7.5 cm), back-slanted, strongly ridged, concealed when crest erected. *Color:* upper body grizzled to gray-brown, crest, flanks and legs tan; pale eye ring and underparts. *Scent glands:* Preorbital glands prominent, opening into naked black spot.

WHERE IT LIVES   Northeast and East Africa in the Somali-Masai Arid Zone and adjacent savanna; the South West Arid Zone, in Namibia and southern Angola.

GOOD PLACES TO SEE IT   Meru and Amboseli NP, Samburu-Isiolo and Masai Mara NR, Kenya; Serengeti, Lake Manyara, and Arusha NP, Ngorongoro Conservation Area, Tanzania; Etosha NP, Namibia.

RELATIVES   Guenther's dik-dik (with an even longer snout) overlaps (and occasionally interbreeds) with Kirk's in northern Kenya. The other two species occur only in Somalia and Ethiopia, where dik-diks originated.

ECOLOGY   Adapted to arid conditions, dependent on cover but avoids tall herbage, preferring places with sparse grass, shrubs, and bushes. Often associated with rocky ground, around the bases of kopjes and hills, especially where clumps of sansevieria, thornbushes, and aloes interspersed with open glades offer a variety of food and secure hiding places. Bush encroachment creates favorable habitat for dik-diks.

Pure browsers, completely water-independent. The pointed snout, trunklike upper lip, and narrow incisor row enable dik-diks to pluck the most nutritious leaves, shoots, and fruits, if necessary standing bipedally to reach higher. The long snout also enhances the dik-dik's ability to cool off by nasal panting (discussed in Chapter 4); it provides additional surface area for evaporation and functions like a bellows to increase air pressure, while the slitlike nostrils minimize loss of water vapor to the atmosphere. But this cooling mechanism is only needed in extreme heat: dik-diks can tolerate temperatures of 104°F (40°C) for 8 hours before beginning to pant.

ACTIVITY   ● (○) More active at night, especially on moonlit nights. Serengeti dik-diks rest only 5 hours between 5 PM and 7 AM, spend half the time resting between 7 AM and 5 PM.

SOCIAL/MATING SYSTEM   (♂♀) Quite exclusively monogamous and closely associated. If you see one, chances are the other is nearby. Trios are not uncommon, the extra being a well-grown offspring. In prime habitat around a group of kopjes on the Serengeti Plains, 6 pairs of individually known dik-diks lived in territories ranging from 6 to 30 acres (2.5–12 ha), average 12 acres (4.8 ha). Three years later, 4 of the females and 2 of the males, now 6 to 9 years old, were still present in 5 territories. Two couples were still together and 2 widows had paired with new males; one of the couples and one of the remarried widows occupied the same properties as before. The other territories had changed in size and shape, as neighbors divvied up properties from which 1 or both partners had disappeared. Apparently pair bonds are more lasting than attachment to a particular location.

Offspring disperse between 6 and 9 months, males earlier than females because of paternal intolerance. Yearlings of both sexes join the adult population although horns only reach full size at 2 years.

PAIR BOND   The dunging ceremony is most important joint activity, followed by preorbital-gland marking, vigilance behavior, and possibly alarm-call duetting. Couples maintain 6 to 13 latrines located along boundaries. Middens of tiny pellets impregnated with urine are up to 7 ft (2 m) across and 4 in (10 cm) deep. Though females are slightly larger, males are more aggressive and dominant.

REPRODUCTION   Typically twice a year, coming into heat within 12 days of calving. East African dik-diks usually calve at the end of the long rainy and dry seasons. Gestation 6 months.

OFFSPRING AND PARENTAL CARE   Six calves born in zoos gained their feet in under 15 minutes and nursed within 2 hours. Wild mothers suckle offspring around sunrise, noon, sunset, and midnight. Within 10 to 15 minutes, the mother walks off, the calf follows a short way, then chooses a new hiding place.

PREDATORS   Jackals, eagles, leopard, spotted hyena, wild dog, and caracal prey on adults and fawns. Baboons and snakes take fawns.

Table 6.3.   *DIFFERENCES IN DIK-DIK BEHAVIOR*
Expect to see and hear ➤ *Usual context and meaning*

Territorial Advertising

Dunging ceremony: ♀ begins ritual, followed by offspring, if present; ♂ comes last, his droppings always ending on top. ♂ typically paws before and during elimination; often tests the ♀'s urine while waiting his turn (see Fig. 6.2).

Aggression

Hunched-back posture. ➤ Dominance display described in Salt's dik-dik.

Raising head crest. ➤ Sign of excitement, typical of threat and dominance displays.

Submission

Poking nose in flank or under neck, after approach in head-low/chin-out posture. ➤ Symbolic nursing: submissive response to aggression.

Courtship

FEMALE BEHAVIOR

Holding tail out and walking while whistling softly. ➤ Ready to mate; keeps walking during copulation.

KLIPSPRINGER, *Oreotragus oreotragus*

Figure 6.3. Male klipspringer standing lookout.

WHAT IT IS The only antelope that lives on kopjes and cliffs. Short body, massive hindquarters, and sturdy long legs. Stands on tips of truncated hooves. ♂ wt 23 lb (10.6 kg), ht 20–21 in (49–52.5 cm); ♀ wt 29 lb (13.2 kg), ht same as ♂. *Head*: wedge-shaped on short neck, with big rounded ears. *Horns*: wide-set, upstanding spikes, 4 in (10 cm). Occasionally present in females of East African race, *O. o. schillingsi*. *Coat*: rough, hairs air-filled, brittle, and loose (good insulation and padding). *Color*: nondescript, grizzled, yellow-brown or brown; ears with black border, white inside with radiating dark lines. *Scent glands*: Huge preorbital glands opening in bull's-eye of naked black skin.

WHERE IT LIVES Eastern Africa, from Red Sea hills to tip of South Africa, north to southern Angola; sea level up to 15,000 ft (4500 m), in climates ranging from arid and hot to wet and cold. More widespread in distant past, relict populations persist on isolated mountains in Nigeria and the Central African Republic.

GOOD PLACES TO SEE IT Tsavo, Aberdares, and Mt. Kenya NP, Kenya; Arusha, Kilimanjaro, and Serengeti NP, Tanzania; Luangwa NP (Muchinga Escarpment), Zambia; Nyika, Kasungu, and Lake Malawi NP, Malawi; Matobo NP, Zimbabwe; Augrabies and Kruger NP, South Africa; Namib-Naukluft NP, Namibia.

ECOLOGY   Depends on steep, rocky terrain as a refuge against predators and on adequate nearby food resources. Home may be a kopje on the open plain or an inselberg in the middle of a woodland. A hillside scree of loose rock, a cinder cone, even a level expanse of jagged lava rock are all places where the klipspringer's superior jumping ability and surefootedness enable it to escape terrestrial predators.

A water-independent browser of leaves, shoots, berries, fruits, seed pods, and flowers of evergreen shrubs and bushes, succulents (aloes, sanseveria, euphorbias), and herbs, plus a little new green grass.

HOW IT MOVES   Bounds up and down steep slopes and jumps from rock to rock, landing with all 4 feet together on the flat tips of its hooves; walks in a stilted manner and runs in jerky bounds even on level ground.

ACTIVITY   ○ (●?) Varies according to season and microclimate. Females spent 31% of the day foraging in the wet season, 24% in the dry season (Ethiopian study). Males stood lookout much of the time their mates were eating and resting, foraging only 18% and 9.5% of the day in the wet and dry seasons, respectively. Night activity remains unstudied.

SOCIAL/MATING SYSTEM   (♂♀) (♂♀ ♀) Unusually close proximity—average 4 to 15 yd—and the male's watchdog role distinguish klipspringer families. Both habits are adapted to open habitat where young and adults are exposed to eagles and ground predators. The female usually initiates and leads movements, followed by the male. By playing a watchdog role while his mate devotes the extra feeding time needed to bear and suckle young, the male protects his genetic investment against both predators and rival males. Where predation pressure is severe, pairs take turns feeding and standing guard.

Klipspringers may typically spend their adult lifetimes within the same home range/territory, which can be as small as 20 acres (8 ha) in lush climates, increasing to 37 acres (15 ha) in arid regions, up to 121 acres (49 ha) in subdesert. One adult male stayed 9 years on the same kopje. Families venture outside their territories only when drawn to new growth or a salt lick—as many as 9 adults have been known to gather on a greenflush. If fires burn off their cover and food, klipspringers will evacuate their territories and take up temporary residence in places they normally avoid.

Offspring usually disperse as yearlings, sons sooner than daughters, though without obvious parental prompting. Occasional extra females are probably daughters, which sometimes breed incestuously.

PAIR BOND   Although both sexes deposit dung in middens, a dunging ceremony remains to be described. Preorbital-gland marking seems more important pair activity. Synchronized and protracted alarm-calling may be equally or more important, possibly comparable to the duetting of pair-bonded birds.

REPRODUCTION Varies from seasonal in harsh climates to year-round in more equable conditions, with a rainy-season peak. Gestation: estimated at 5 (probable) to 7.5 months (long). Both sexes reach adult weight at 1 year.

OFFSPRING AND PARENTAL CARE After hiding for up to 3 months, calves stay close to mother, nursing twice a day for 7 to 8 minutes, during which father remains on highest alert. Weaning is complete at 4 to 5 months.

PREDATORS Leopard, jackals, and spotted hyena; calves vulnerable to eagles and baboons. Because klipspringers must often leave their refuges to forage, they are very alert to predators and to alarm signals of other species, react by fleeing to higher ground with or without first calling, the female leading. Once safe, they give whistling alarm calls in duet.

Table 6.4.   *DIFFERENCES IN KLIPSPRINGER BEHAVIOR*
Expect to see and hear ➤ *Usual context and meaning*

Territorial Advertising

♂ standing sentinel on promontory (see Fig. 6.3).

Dung middens up to 3 yd diameter, usually on flat ground along property lines. ➤ Unclear whether klipspringers urinate and defecate in sequence.

Both partners scent-posting property, every day or 2, ♀ leading. ➤ ♂ marks most and also overmarks ♀'s deposits. Look for black, shiny "pearls" on twigs.

Aggression

Medial-horn threat ± lowered forequarters.

Courtship

♂ makes faint humming sound while following and licking ♀'s rear end. ➤ During mating march.

Biting by ♀. ➤ Aggressive response to courting ♂.

Response to Predators

Bounding flight. ➤ Gait adapted to steep slopes.

Bounding in place. ➤ As during flight.

Whistling, especially in duet, ♀ calling right after the ♂. ➤ Synchronized calling, stimulated by predators, also serves to advertise couples' presence to other klipspringers and reinforce pair bond.

ORIBI, *Ourebia ourebi*

Figure 6.4. Female oribi standing in urination posture attracts mate to dung midden, where they engage in the dunging ritual.

WHAT IT IS   An antelope of tall grassland that resembles a small gazelle. Slender build, long neck and limbs; hindquarters rounded and slightly higher than forequarters. ♂ wt 30.8 lb (14 kg), ht 23 in (58 cm); ♀ wt 31.2 lb (14.2 kg), ht 23.6 in (59 cm). *Head:* narrow muzzle, large ears. *Horns:* thin, erect, 3.2 to 7 in (8–19 cm). *Color:* varies geographically; bright reddish to yellow-brown with extensive white underparts, including rump patch, chin, and eyeline; black pompom tail and bare, black spot below each ear (scent gland, similar to reedbucks'). Sexes alike, young calves darker brown.

WHERE IT LIVES   Discontinuous in moister parts of Northern and Southern Savanna: from Senegal to Ethiopia and south into western Kenya and Tanzania; coastal hinterland of East Africa; enclaves in southern Africa from Malawi and Mozambique to Angola and southeastern Cape Province.

GOOD PLACES TO SEE IT   Akagera NP, Rwanda; Lambwe Valley NP, Masai Mara NR, Kenya; Serengeti NP (Northern Extension), Tanzania; Kazungu NP, Malawi; Kafue NP, Zambia; Giant's Castle NP, South Africa.

ECOLOGY   Prefers open grassland tall enough to hide in but not too tall to see over, grassland sprinkled with bushes, interspersed woodland and grassland, or edge. Reaches highest density on floodplains and montane grasslands, especially in association with large grazers. Settlement, agriculture, and hunting have greatly reduced oribi habitat and range.

A grazer of green grass, switches to foliage, herbs, and other browse in the dry season, meeting water needs from green growth.

ACTIVITY   ○ (●?) Transvaal study shows 20 to 38% of daylight hours spent feeding. Night activity probable, but information sketchy.

SOCIAL/MATING SYSTEM   Surprisingly variable, depending on habitat conditions.

(♂♀) (♂♀ ♀) When grassland is tall enough to hide in, oribis live in monogamous pairs, defending territories of 74 to 247 acres (30-100 ha). But anywhere from 10 to 50% of territorial males live with 2 females.

(♂ ♀○ ♀○ ♀○) After annual fires remove cover, up to a dozen oribis band together. But unlike the cohesive herds of sociable antelopes, oribi groups are temporary and the members scatter when alarmed.

(♂♂♀♀) Cooperative territory defense by an alpha male assisted by 1 or 2 subordinate males has been documented for oribis of Serengeti NP. Coalitions have no more females than do unassisted males, but are less likely to be overthrown by outside rivals. The downside (from the chief honcho's viewpoint): satellite males sneak occasional copulations.

PAIR BOND   Couples associate less closely than dik-diks or klipspringers, perhaps partly because male oribis do all the patrolling and preorbital-gland marking without female assistance. Oribi couples and other family members do perform a dunging ceremony, initiated by the female, which is clearly important in maintaining social bonds. Wives also do their bit to defend the territory by chasing female intruders—suggesting that extra females in an oribi family are daughters, which are known to remain until nearly full-grown. Sons, however, are chased out when they reach adolescence.

HOW IT MOVES   More gazellelike and maybe fleeter than other dwarf antelopes (25-31 mph [40-50 kph]).

REPRODUCTION   Birth peak during rains but no strict breeding seasons. Gestation 6 or 7 months; females may conceive at 10 months, males at 14 months.

OFFSPRING AND PARENTAL CARE   A hand-reared male nibbled grass at 5 days, began to ruminate the fourth week, and marked with its preorbital glands and acquired adult coloration in its fifth week. In the wild, calves hide for about a month, begin spending full time with their mothers at 3 months, and are weaned at 4 to 5 months.

PREDATORS   Cheetah, leopard, wild dog, and spotted hyena prey on adults; these plus eagles and snakes prey on calves.

Table 6.5. *DIFFERENCES IN ORIBI BEHAVIOR*
Expect to see and hear ➤ *Usual context and meaning*

Territorial Advertising

♂ parading in erect posture. ➤ Seen during regular border patrol/marking rounds, with frequent pauses for scent-marking.

♂ marking with preorbital glands—up to 16 times/hr. ➤ Oribis in high grass prepare marking sites by biting off tops of grass stalks; sites marked only once.

Dunging ceremony, begun by ♀ assuming elimination crouch, bringing ♂ (see Fig. 6.4); he sniffs her rear, marks grass stem, paws, then adds his deposit. Other family/group members participate. ➤ Oribis do not maintain dung middens.

Rocking-horse run. ➤ ♂ territorial display, like exaggerated stotting, often performed during border patrols, showing white rump and black tail.

Aggression

Oribi horn threat. ➤ With chin out and ears cocked, tail erect, confronting or with head turned; abrupt upward head jerk precedes attack.

Chasing and counterchasing. ➤ Between neighbors during border skirmishes, often interspersed with air-cushion fights.

Courtship

Urination by ♀. ➤ Frequent as prelude to dunging ceremony, but ♂ seldom performs urine test.

Response to Predators

Rocking-horse run. ➤ Similar to stotting.

Whistling. ➤ A series of short blasts or a sustained shrill whistle.

Chapter 7

GAZELLE TRIBE
Antilopini

Thomson's gazelle, G. thomsonii	Dorcas gazelle, G. dorcas[v]
Grant's gazelle, G. granti	Soemmering's gazelle, G. soemmeringii[v]
Dama gazelle, G. dama[en]	Rhim or slender-horned gazelle, G. leptoceros[en]
Red-fronted gazelle, G. rufifrons[v]	Springbok, Antidorcas marsupialis
Atlas or edmi gazelle, G. cuvieri[en]	Dibatag, Ammordorcas clarkei[v]
Speke's gazelle, G. spekei[v]	Gerenuk, Litocranius walleri

WHAT THEY ARE   Medium-sized antelopes of arid regions, most of which live in or around the Sahara and the Horn of Africa (Somalia and Ethiopia). *Horns:* in both sexes (except gerenuk and dibatag), female horns much shorter to nearly equal in length. *Coat:* smooth, glossy. *Color:* shades of tan, with white underparts and rump patch; most species with dark side stripe and facial markings; sexes colored alike (except Grant's gazelle). *Scent glands:* hoof glands; preorbital glands, males only, undeveloped in some species; inguinal glands; shin glands (under tufts of longer hair) in most species. *Teats:* 2 (gazelles) or 4 (springbok, gerenuk, dibatag).

SOCIAL/MATING SYSTEM

  Large herd accompanied by a territorial male.

Small herd accompanied by a territorial male.

Maternal herd unaccompanied by territorial male.

Bachelor herd.

Large mixed herd, found in aggregations and during migration (in absence of territorial males).

Slightly (gerenuk) to highly (Thomson's gazelle, springbok) sociable. Herds open and fluid, with little aggression and no obvious rank order between females. Mothers with concealed young stay alone or in small maternity herds often unaccompanied by males. Unlike nearly all other antelopes, mother gazelles team up to defend young fawns against jackals, which often hunt in pairs.

Gazelles of different species often associate in the same herd, especially larger and smaller species, like Grant's and Thomson's gazelles.

HOW THEY MOVE   Among the fleetest antelopes, top speed of 50 to 55 mph (82–89 kph); dodge and turn sharply and make long (but not high) jumps to escape still-faster cheetahs. But overheating makes them vulnerable to distance runners (wild dog, spotted hyena).

HOW THEY COMMUNICATE   Sight 1, scent 2, sound 3.

Table 7.1.   *GAZELLE BEHAVIOR GUIDE*
Expect to see and hear* ➤ *Usual context and meaning

Territorial Advertising

Adult ♂ standing or lying, alone or apart from herd. ➤ Advertising presence and status.

Urination and defecation in sequence on dung middens, preferably located on bare ground. ➤ Visual display and scent-marking, characteristic of whole tribe.

Placing preorbital-gland secretion. ➤ Territorial display of scent-posting property. Look for black, shiny deposits on twig ends and grass stems (Tommy and gerenuk, not Grant's gazelle or springbok).

Bush-/grass-horning. ➤ Advertises aggressive mood and high status; often performed by territorial ♂ ♂.

Herding and chasing ♀ ♀ and ♂ ♂. ➤ To keep ♀ ♀ in, and rivals out, of territory.

Aggression

Standing in erect posture ± broadside stance ± nose raised or head turned away. ➤ Display of dominance, either undirected (as a display of territorial status) or directed to an individual of same or opposite sex (see Courtship Displays).

Walking in erect posture. ➤ Territorial ♂ on marking round, following inferior opponent in pursuit march, or ♀ during mating march.

Medial-horn threat. ➤ Commonest threat display in the tribe.

High-horn threat. ➤ Less common (see Thomson's gazelle).

Low-horn threat. ➤ See gerenuk account.

Angle-horn threat. ➤ Tilting head toward opponent, an aggressive display.

Head-low posture. ➤ Defensive threat, response of inferior to superior's threat.

Aggression *continued*

OTHER ACTIONS ASSOCIATED WITH AGGRESSIVE DISPLAYS

Head-ducking and -nodding. ➤ Symbolic butting, short step from fighting.

Head-shaking. ➤ Fighting movements.

Vegetation-horning. ➤ Redirected aggression. The message: "This is what I'd like to do to you."

Feinted attack. ➤ Jumping toward opponent while hind legs remain planted.

Air-cushion fights. ➤ Going through the motions without contact.

Submission

Head-low/chin-out posture. ➤ Submissive response to aggression.

Turning away and moving away. ➤ Avoidance of superior, when threatened or supplanted.

Lying-out. ➤ Complete submission.

Flight. ➤ Response of inferior or defeated rival to pursuit by superior or contest winner.

Displacement Activities

Grazing; scratching with hind feet; scratching with horn tips; scraping with incisors.

Sociable Behavior

Nose-to-nose sniffing and contact. ➤ Greeting behavior.

Nibbling and licking. ➤ Social grooming, mainly around preorbital glands and head; mostly associated with courtship and appeasing behaviors.

Courtship

MALE BEHAVIOR

Lowstretch. ➤ Posture of territorial ♂ approaching or herding ♀.

Urine-testing. ➤ Mouth open but no pronounced grimace in gazelle tribe.

Close following, ♂ in erect posture ± nose-lifting. ➤ Mating march: ♀ keeps moving even during copulation.

Nose-lifting and prancing. ➤ Abrupt raising of the muzzle and quick-stepping during mating march (e.g., Tommy).

Courtship *continued*

Foreleg-lifting. ➤ Performed during mating march by most species.

Vocal accompaniment: Sputtering or snoring noise emitted by ♂.

FEMALE BEHAVIOR

Urinates on demand. ➤ Response to ♂ approaching in lowstretch.

Avoidance: flight, walking away, circling, sharp turns.

Aggression: head-low posture, poking, erect posture.

Submissive displays.

Holding tail out. ➤ Readiness to mate.

Mother and Offspring

As described in Mother and Offspring, Table 4.2.

Cooperative defense of fawns. ➤ Two or more ♀♀ chasing and attacking jackals that hunt concealed fawns.

Play

Running, stotting, high-jumping, rushing, circling, chasing, and play-fighting.

Response to Predators

Alert posture, stamping, alarm-snorting, circling, other nervous behavior.

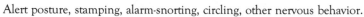

Stotting. ➤ Excitement behavior, most common in young, given in play as well as alarm.

Sidestripe flicker. ➤ Just as a gazelle starts to flee, the flank skin twitches up and down, creating a semaphore effect in species with side stripe.

Approaching and escorting predators. ➤ On open plains, gazelles often approach within 50 yd and even follow passing lions, in particular, as if fascinated; unworried while predator is in plain view and not stalking.

THOMSON'S GAZELLE, *Gazella thomsonii*

Figure 7.1. Thomson's gazelle in lowstretch posture.

WHAT IT IS   The common small gazelle of the East African plains. ♂ wt 37–64 lb (17–29 kg), ht 23–28 in (58-70 cm); ♀ wt 29–53 lb (13–24 kg), ht 23–25 in (58-64 cm). *Horns:* robust, parallel, strongly ridged in male, 10 to 17 in (25–43 cm); feeble, short spikes 3.2 to 6 in (8–15 cm) in female, more often broken, deformed, or absent than intact. *Color:* cinnamon; white rump patch smaller than in Grant's gazelle; bold black side stripe and facial markings, black tail.

WHERE IT LIVES   Somali-Masai Arid Zone and adjacent Northern Savanna, from northern Tanzania to northern Kenya; an isolated population in southern Sudan.

GOOD PLACES TO SEE IT   Masai Mara NR, Amboseli, Nairobi, and Nakuru NP, Kenya; Serengeti and Tarangire NP, Ngorongoro Crater, Tanzania.

ECOLOGY   A gazelle that left the sub-Saharan wastelands and invaded the savanna biome where more abundant food and water enable it to reach higher population densities than most gazelles. Along with wildebeest and zebra, it is 1 of the 3 migratory ungulates that dominate the East African grasslands. Half a million Tommies in the Serengeti population recall the former teeming abundance of African plains game. The main population feeds and reproduces on the short-grass plains during the rains and spends the dry season on the taller grasslands of the savanna woodland zone where the migrants have access to water and can capitalize on fire and occasional thunderstorms to find green pastures. In long grasslands, Tommies concentrate on pastures eaten down by the larger grazers, gleaning a living where bulk feeders would starve.

A grazer/browser, browsing shrubs and forbs when green grass unavailable. Goes to water every day or so in the dry season but water-independent when necessary.

ACTIVITY   ○/● Day and night, with usual peaks early and late in day.

SOCIAL/MATING SYSTEM   Gregarious, territorial, and resident in dispersed small herds contained in an established territorial network, or migratory, aggregating in large numbers on green pastures. Females and young live in open herds numbering 2 to 20 or more adults, among which there is no apparent rank order or individual social bonds. Where gazelles are concentrated, there are frequent exchanges between herds, despite vigorous shepherding by territorial males, whose efforts to round up and detain females on their properties create discrete, segregated groups of otherwise large, mixed aggregations. Spacing between territorial males of 300 yd down to 100 yd in concentrations is close for a gazelle. Territories may be as large as 495 acres (200 ha) at low density and as small as 6 acres (2.5 ha) in dense aggregations; but 25 to 75 acres (10–30 ha) is typical.

Pronounced gender differences in the horns cause territorial males to expel male fawns from female herds within 6 months, whereupon they join the nearest bachelor herd. But during migration and late in the dry season, when mating and territorial activity are minimal, aggregations containing both sexes and all ages are common.

REPRODUCTION   Gestation 5.5 to 6 months. Well-nourished females produce 2 young a year, conceiving again within 3 weeks after calving. Main birth peak after short rains (Dec./Jan.); secondary birth and main mating peak after long rains (June/July).

OFFSPRING AND PARENTAL CARE   Fawns hide in clumps of taller vegetation where available but are surprisingly hard to see even on bare ground. Mothers keep watch from a distance, associate in maternity herds if several fawns are lying-out in the same locale, otherwise remain alone.

PREDATORS   Jackals, spotted hyena, lion, cheetah, and wild dog. The preferred prey of cheetahs and wild dogs, the Tommy relies on vigilance, speed, ability to change direction suddenly, and the presence of other Tommies to elude capture. Cooperative maternal defense of fawns is effective against jackals hunting in pairs, which do well against lone defenders.

Table 7.2.   *DIFFERENCES IN THOMSON'S GAZELLE BEHAVIOR*
Expect to see and hear ➤ *Usual context and meaning*

Maintenance Activities

Tail-wagging. ➤ Metronome movement of black tail across rump patch is like a semaphore signal, saying in effect, here is a Thomson's gazelle; it helps Tommies recognize their own species at a distance.

Gazelles all lying facing same direction during morning rumination period. ➤ Sunning behavior; animals aligned to catch most direct rays.

Territorial Advertising

Herding and chasing ♀ ♀ and ♂ ♂. ➤ Territorial ♂ ♂ very active; behave like sheep dogs in herding ♀ ♀ away from border (see Fig. 7.1).

Aggression

Grazing duels. ➤ Territorial ♂ ♂ engage in protracted grazing duels during border encounters.

Courtship

Close following: Tommy ♂ keeps tail low. ➤ Mating march.

Prancing and nose-lifting. ➤ Following in lowstretch alternates with prancing, nose-lifting, foreleg-lifting, and mounting attempts.

Response to Predators

Racing vehicles and crossing over. ➤ Responding to vehicle as to a predator: crossing in front to avoid being overtaken and turned (as by wild dogs, cheetah).

GRANT'S GAZELLE, *Gazella granti*

Figure 7.2. Grant's gazelle males in mutual dominance display: standing in erect posture and flexing neck muscles.

WHAT IT IS   The impala-sized gazelle of the East African plains. Graceful build, with long neck and limbs. ♂ wt 143 lb (65 kg), ht 34–35 in (84–91 cm); ♀ wt 99 lb (45 kg), ht 30–33 in (75–83 cm). *Horns:* adult males distinguished by thick necks and long, strong horns, 20 to 32 in (50–80 cm); wide-set with bent-down tips west of Rift Valley (*G. g. robertsi* subspecies). Female horns thin, 12 to 18 in (30–45 cm). *Color:* pale to darker tan with extensive white underparts (note extension of the rump patch onto the hips); dark markings include vertical lines on thighs, face patches, and side stripe, which varies from well-defined to absent in females and young, and absent in adult males.

WHERE IT LIVES   The Somali-Masai Arid Zone, from southern Sudan and Ethiopia to northern Tanzania; and from the Kenya coast to Lake Victoria.

GOOD PLACES TO SEE IT   Tsavo, Amboseli, Nairobi, Sibiloi, and Meru NP, Masai Mara, Samburu-Isiolo, and Shaba NR, Kenya; Ngorongoro Conservation Area, Serengeti and Tarangire NP, Tanzania.

ECOLOGY   Inhabits subdesert, lowland thornbush, savanna woodland, open plains, and montane grassland up to 8200 ft (2500 m). Capitalizing on its water-independence, G. *granti* gleans a living in areas beyond reach of herbivores that have to drink. Some even migrate to short-grass plains in the dry season and the savanna woodland during the rains—opposite to the main migration. But large herds also share wet-season range and mix with the more numerous Thomson's gazelles.

A browser/grazer, Grant's gazelle rarely or never drinks. On short-grass plains, it browses microshrubs, sedges, and herbs.

ACTIVITY   ○/● Day and night, with usual peaks early and late in day.

SOCIAL/MATING SYSTEM

On open plains, large herds are often found in the vicinity of prominent landmarks such as hills and kopjes. Big herds—up to 400 members in the Serengeti—are mixed and include territorial males, each of which asserts dominance when the herd is on his property and reverts to bachelor status when it leaves.

Conventional 1-male herds, averaging 10 females (range 2–32), and separate bachelor herds averaging 4 to 5 (range 2–37) are also found both on open plains and in wooded savanna. The more closed the habitat, the smaller and more sexually segregated the herds. Female and bachelor herds average only 3 members in Tsavo NP.

Male offspring stay in female herds for a year or longer before being evicted and joining bachelor herds. They become territorial at 3 years. Territories are large, ranging from 1 to 3.9 mi^2 (2.5–10 km^2). Home ranges may be as large as 8 mi^2 (20 km^2).

REPRODUCTION   Perennial breeding with birth and mating peaks from December to February and August through September in East Africa. Gestation is 6.5 months and females conceive at 1.5 years, reentering estrus within weeks of giving birth. Males begin breeding at 3 years if they can win a territory.

OFFSPRING AND MATERNAL CARE   Expectant females leave the herd to calve in habitat offering secure hiding places for fawns, which lie-out for 4 to 6 weeks, then associate with other fawns in peer groups and begin to accompany mothers.

Maternal herds of 2 to 10 females may be encountered in zones of higher vegetation between territories.

PREDATORS   Spotted hyena, cheetah, leopard, and wild dog. Jackals prey on fawns only. Water-independence and perhaps greater height make Grant's less vulnerable to ambush than Thomson's gazelle.

Table 7.3. *DIFFERENCES IN GRANT'S GAZELLE BEHAVIOR*
Expect to see and hear ➤ *Usual context and meaning*

Maintenance Activities

Tail-wagging. ➤ Less conspicuous than in Tommy but fairly constant in relaxed, active animals.

Sunning during morning rest. ➤ As in Tommy; white underparts conspicuous.

Territorial Advertising

Grant's gazelle does not scent-mark with preorbital glands. ➤ Glands inactive.

 Bush-/grass-horning. ➤ Adult ♂♂ often "weave" horns in tall grass; sometimes a bundle lodges between horns.

Chasing ♂♂, rarely ♀♀. ➤ In open grasslands bachelor ♂♂ often mingle with ♀ herds, until resident ♂ chases them away.

Aggression

Mutual broadside display and head-flagging (see Fig. 7.2). ➤ Dominance display performed during display duels between adult ♂♂; abrupt head-turning advertises neck development. Common activity in bachelor herds.

OTHER ACTIONS ASSOCIATED WITH AGGRESSIVE DISPLAYS
Parallel marching and circling. ➤ Frequent during mutual broadside display.

Displacement Activities

Grazing during aggressive interaction. ➤ Uncommon in Grant's gazelle.

Courtship

 Following in erect posture, tail out with nose-lifting and prancing. ➤ Mating march features abrupt raising of the muzzle and quick-stepping by ♂.

SPRINGBOK, *Antidorcas marsupialis*

Figure 7.3. Springboks fighting.

WHAT IT IS   Southern African version of a gazelle. A fold of skin on the back housing a crest of white hair and skin glands distinguishes it from other gazelles. ♂ wt 90 lb (41kg), ht 31–35 in (77–87 cm); ♀ wt 81 lb (37 kg), ht 31–33 in (77–83 cm). Largest, northern race. *Horns:* male 14 to 20 in (35–49 cm), shaped like a stethoscope, with inward-pointing tips; female horns 10 to 30% smaller but similarly shaped (northern race). *Color:* cinnamon brown (paler in driest areas), with white head, underparts, backs of legs, tail, rump patch, and spinal crest. *Scent glands:* Glandular skin lining dorsal skin fold is unique to springbok. Preorbital-gland secretion is a clear oil.

WHERE IT LIVES   *Highveld*, Karroo, Kalahari *sandveld*, Namib/Karroo subdesert of South Africa, Botswana, Namibia, and southern Angola. The most abundant antelope of the South West Arid Zone, reintroduced throughout and outside its historical range.

GOOD PLACES TO SEE IT   Makgadikgadi Pans, Central Kalahari GR, Nxai Pan NP, Botswana; Kalahari Gemsbok NP, Oviston NR, South Africa; Etosha and Namib-Naukluft NP, Namibia.

ECOLOGY   Tolerates conditions ranging from desert to well-watered savanna with 30 in (750 mm) rainfall, from sea level to *highveld*, but avoids dense vegetation, mountains, rocky hills, and sand dunes. A grazer/browser, able to subsist without drinking as long as food plants contain minimum 10% water.

ACTIVITY   Unstudied, but seasonally variable. Springboks rest more (preferably in shade) by day and feed more by night in hot, dry weather.

SOCIAL/MATING SYSTEM   Comparable to Thomson's gazelle. Flexible grouping pattern adaptable to a wide range of conditions, including those listed below.

(♂♀○♀○♀○) (○♀♀○♀♂/♀○♀♀♀) (♂♂♂) Small to large female herds in an established territorial network, with nonbreeding males in segregated bachelor herds.

(♂♂♂♀♀♀) (○♂♀○♂♂/♀○♂♀♀♀) Small and large mixed herds in dispersed groups during dry season, and large mixed herds during migration and in concentrations on new grass.

(♀○♀○♀) Small maternal herds during birth peaks.

Reversing the usual wet-season dispersal/dry-season concentration movements, springboks aggregate on short green pastures in the rainy season and disperse in smaller units during the dry season; but they congregate on pastures revived by rain.

Males defend large territories of 67 to 173 acres (27–70 ha), where they energetically herd and chase other springboks during mating peaks. Female herds are open and loose although daughters may associate with mothers until they calve as yearlings. Sons have to leave earlier.

HOW IT MOVES   Clocked at 55 mph (88 kph), as fast as any gazelle, springboks trot more (including a flat, level gait and an exaggerated style trot) and perform a variation of stotting called pronking (see Response to Predators, Table 7.4).

REPRODUCTION   Seasonal, but season varies by up to 2 months from year to year, responding to variable climatic conditions. Main calving peak in spring at start of rainy season; secondary peak may occur in autumn. Gestation 6.5 to 7 months. Minimum breeding age is 6 to 7 months for well-nourished females. Males adolescent at 1 year, mature as 2 year olds.

OFFSPRING AND PARENTAL CARE   Reproductive synchrony within populations leads to the formation of sizeable maternal herds and crèches of fawns, which are sometimes left unattended.

PREDATORS   Black-backed jackal, spotted hyena, cheetah, wild dog, and lion.

Table 7.4.   *DIFFERENCES IN SPRINGBOK BEHAVIOR*
Expect to see and hear ➤ *Usual context and meaning*

Territorial Advertising

Territorial ♂♂ often lie in open, on middens or other bare ground, while other springboks seek shade. ➤ Middens are large patches strewn with dung.

Herding and chasing ♀♀ and ♂♂. ➤ Territorial ♂♂ very active during rut, grunt loudly while chasing rivals.

Aggression

Head-low posture ± head-jerking and snapping. ➤ Symbolic biting (may be unique to the springbok).

Courtship

MALE BEHAVIOR

Lowstretch with tail curled up, ears horizontal or cocked vertically, ± style-trotting.

Chasing with vocal accompaniment. ➤ Violent pursuit of estrous ♀, uttering deep, bellowing grunts.

FEMALE BEHAVIOR

Aggression: head-low posture with stabbing movement. ➤ Defensive threat.

Response to Predators

Style-trotting ± dorsal crest raised. ➤ Performed by mildly disturbed individuals, the usual prelude to pronking.

Pronking. ➤ Dorsal "flag" is flared when the full display is performed.

GERENUK, *Litocranius walleri*

Figure 7.4. Gerenuk courtship. Male rubbing preorbital gland on female.

WHAT IT IS   Stretch version of a gazelle, adapted for life in the arid thornbush. Very long limbs and neck, tail hock-length. ♂ wt 99 lb (45 kg), ht 35–42 in (89–105 cm); ♀ wt 68 lb (31 kg), ht 32–40 in (80–100 cm). *Head*: wedge-shaped and pointed with large, rounded ears. *Horns*: males only, 12.5 to 17 in (32–44 cm), thick and strongly ridged. *Color*: like impala, red-brown saddle on buff-colored body and limbs; white underparts and small rump patch; striking white eye ring and throat patch, contrasting with brown forehead and blaze.

WHERE IT LIVES   Somali-Masai Arid Zone: from central Ethiopia to northwestern Tanzania, from the coastal hinterland to the western wall of the Eastern Rift Valley, in arid thornbush country below 4800 ft (1200 m).

GOOD PLACES TO SEE IT   Tsavo and Meru NP, Samburu-Isiolo NR, Kenya.

ECOLOGY   One of the most desert-adapted antelopes; reaches highest density in arid bush beyond reach of more water-dependent herbivores. Prefers landscapes sufficiently open to permit free passage between shrubs and bushes, avoiding thickets and dense bush, tall woodland, and grassland.

Needle nose, flexible upper lip, slitlike nostrils, long legs and neck, and unequalled ability to stand erect and browse foliage 6 ft, 7 in (2 m) high enable gerenuk to feed selectively on leaves, shoots, flowers, and fruits of the thorn trees and bushes that dominate arid lowlands. Though virtually never known to drink, it depends on evergreen shrubs, bushes, and trees during an 8-month dry season.

ACTIVITY ○ (●?) Great variation from day to day in timing and duration of activities (Tsavo NP daytime study). No obvious peaks of feeding activity, but males spent 32 to 64% and females 51 to 68% of day feeding. Main rest period 10 AM to 1 PM, when most gerenuks stood or lay and ruminated; peak of standing and walking 3 PM to 6 PM, reflecting patrolling and scent posting by territorial males.

SOCIAL/MATING SYSTEM

(♂♀○♀○♀○) Territorial, sedentary, and semisocial, the gerenuk lives in herds averaging 3.2 animals in Tsavo NP and slightly more in the drier country of Somalia and adjacent Kenya. Rarely, up to 12 or more congregate. Single males and females account for some 42% of all sightings.

(♀♂♂) After separating from mothers at 1 to 1.5 years, subadult males associate in small bachelor herds that may accompany an adult female. Females often associate briefly but only mother and dependent offspring stick together. Home ranges in Tsavo are 346 to 840 acres (140–340 ha). Territories, averaging 519 acres (210 ha), are often isolated, without adjoining borders. Too large to be fully defendable, property owners use their preorbital glands to delineate the core area in current use. Mapped "black pearls" of one male were found to enclose 74 acres (30 ha) the first time and 30 acres (11 ha) a year later.

HOW IT MOVES Disturbed gerenuks usually trot away, gallop only in emergencies. Wedge-shaped hooves, powerful lower limbs, and modified lumbar vertebrae enable gerenuk to stand bipedally more securely than other antelopes.

REPRODUCTION Year-round; gestation 6.5 to 7 months; females reproduce at 8- to 9-month intervals. Minimum conception age 11 months for females, yearling males fertile but only competitive when mature at 3.5 years.

OFFSPRING AND PARENTAL CARE Mother and fawn exchange bleating calls, beginning at birth. Fawns start trying to stand bipedally at 2 weeks but take a month to become proficient.

PREDATORS Wild dog, cheetah, leopard, lion, and jackals (on fawns).

Table 7.5. *DIFFERENCES IN GERENUK BEHAVIOR*
Expect to see and hear ➤ *Usual context and meaning*

Territorial Advertising

Urinating and defecating in sequence. ➤ Typical, but established dung middens unknown.

Aggression

Rushing at opponent, with rumbling accompaniment.

♀♀ make empty poking movements and flap ears while head-shaking. ➤ In resisting ♂ advances, also in disputes between ♀♀.

Submission

Head-low/chin-out posture, with head at shoulder level, tail curled over back.

Sociable Behavior

Rubbing heads together ♀–♀; mother-offspring. ➤ Solicited by putting head under partner's chin and pressing upward.

Courtship

MALE BEHAVIOR

Foreleg-lifting. ➤ Exceptionally frequent and ritualized, often combined with nose-lifting.

♂ rubs preorbital glands on ♀ (see Fig. 7.4). ➤ During later stages of courtship.

FEMALE BEHAVIOR

Head-shaking. ➤ Defensive threat.

VOCAL ACCOMPANIMENT

♂ makes humming noise.

Response to Predators

Hiding. ➤ Freezing in alert posture is used by gerenuks to blend into background when standing in cover.

Stotting: Gerenuk folds legs at height of bound and holds tail low; rump patch is flared.

Chapter 8

REEDBUCK/KOB TRIBE
Reduncini

Bohor reedbuck, *Redunca redunca*
Common or southern reedbuck, *R. arundinum*
Mountain reedbuck, *R. fulvorufula*
Kob, *Kobus kob*

Puku, *K. vardoni*
Southern lechwe, *K. leche*[v]
Nile lechwe, *K. megaceros*[v]
Waterbuck, *K. ellipsiprymnus*

WHAT THEY ARE   A tribe of medium-sized to large antelopes that live close to water, especially on floodplains. Long necks and bodies, sturdy limbs, powerful hindquarters. *Horns:* males only, strongly ridged, short and hooked forward in reedbucks, long and recurved in *Kobus* species. *Coat:* smooth (kob) or shaggy (waterbuck, lechwe). *Color:* shades of tan to medium brown (reedbucks and female *Kobus* antelopes); male *Kobus* antelopes much darker. White underparts, rump, and facial markings. *Scent glands:* no hoof or preorbital glands (except kob); inguinal glands present in reedbuck and kob; reedbucks have a glandular bare spot below the ear. Many diffuse skin glands make the coat greasy and strong-smelling (especially waterbuck). *Teats:* 4.

SOCIAL/MATING SYSTEM   All species are territorial. Sociability ranges from solitary or slightly sociable (reedbucks) to two of the most sociable antelopes—kob and lechwe. But herds are unstable and often subdivide since relations between females are casual, without any clear rank order and rarely any aggression. Males do not scent-mark territories.

Monogamous pair. Example: common reedbuck.

Solitary/polygynous. Example: bohor reedbuck.

Sociable in small female herds accompanied by a territorial male, and segregated bachelor herds. Examples: mountain reedbuck, kob, puku, lechwe, waterbuck.

Sizeable female herds and separate bachelor herds. Examples: kob, lechwe, waterbuck.

Mixed herds. Female and bachelor herds around breeding leks and during migration. Examples: kob, lechwe

Lek or breeding arena. Territorial males cluster on very small territories and most females come to central "courts" to mate. Territories of conventional size surround arenas. Examples: kob, lechwe.

71

HOW THEY MOVE   Not designed for speed or endurance; most depend on cover or refuges (swamps) to escape predators such as wild dogs and hyenas. Even the swiftest reduncines, kob and puku, seek cover when hard-pressed.

HOW THEY COMMUNICATE   Sight 1, scent 2 or 3, sound 1.

Table 8.1.   *REEDBUCK/KOB TRIBE BEHAVIOR GUIDE*
Expect to see and hear* ➤ *Usual context and meaning

Territorial Advertising

 Adult ♂ standing or lying, alone or apart from herd. ➤ Advertising presence and status.

 Standing in erect posture. ➤ Either self-advertising when undirected, or a dominance display.

Whistling or grunting while standing in erect posture. ➤ Response of territorial ♂ (kob, lechwe, reedbuck) to disturbance, especially movements of its own species.

Bush-/grass-horning. ➤ Advertises aggressive mood and high status.

Herding and chasing ♀♀ and ♂♂. ➤ To keep ♀♀ in and rivals out of territory.

Aggression

Broadside stance in erect posture ± nose lifted or head turned away. ➤ Dominance display when addressed to an individual.

 Medial-horn threat. ➤ Commonest threat display in the tribe.

 High-horn threat.

 Low-horn threat.

 Angle-horn threat. ➤ Tilting head toward opponent during aggressive interaction, e.g., when 2 adversaries are displaying in broadside stance.

ASSOCIATED ACTIONS

Showing the penis. ➤ A trait of the genus *Kobus*, significance unknown (probably not a sign of sexual arousal).

Rhythmic nodding. ➤ Symbolic butting.

Head-shaking. ➤ Twisting movements of fighting.

Aggression *continued*

Ground-horning. ➤ Redirected aggression. The message: "This is what I'd like to do to you."

Parallel walking. ➤ By 2 ♂♂ displaying in broadside attitude (waterbuck, lechwe).

Rushing. ➤ Real or feinted attack.

 Head-low posture. ➤ Defensive threat, response of inferior to intimidation.

FEMALE DEFENSIVE THREATS
Poking, butting, snapping, charging.

Submission

 Head-low/chin-out posture. ➤ Submissive response to aggression.

Turning away and moving away. ➤ Avoidance of superior, when threatened or supplanted.

 Lying-out. ➤ Extreme form of submission.

Flight. ➤ Response of inferior or defeated rival to pursuit.

Displacement Activities

Grazing, scratching with hind feet, scratching with horn tips, scraping with incisors, alarm signals.

Sociable Behavior

 Nose-to-nose sniffing and contact. ➤ Greeting behavior. Seen also as prelude to horn contact in ♂ – ♂ aggressive encounters.

Incisor scraping/nibbling. ➤ Social grooming: unimportant in the tribe.

Courtship

MALE BEHAVIOR
 Lowstretch. ➤ Posture of territorial ♂ approaching or herding ♀.

 Approach in erect posture. ➤ Alternative to lowstretch (see kob account).

 Urine-testing by ♂. ➤ Routine check of ♀ reproductive status.

 Close following, with rubbing, nuzzling, licking of ♀'s rump, and many preliminary mounting attempts. ➤ Common behaviors during mating march.

Courtship *continued*

Foreleg-lifting ± nose-lifting and partial erection. ➤ Performed during mating march.

Prancing with nose-lifting. ➤ Display of kob and lechwe.

FEMALE BEHAVIOR

Urinating in response to ♂'s approach, typically in hunched posture, with tail raised. ➤ Stance similar to swan-neck posture.

Avoidance: flight, walking away, circling, sharp turns.

Aggression: head-low posture, butting, snapping, rushing.

Submissive displays: swan-neck posture. ➤ Mating stance assumed by ♀♀ in full estrus.

VOCAL ACCOMPANIMENT

Whistling following copulation (kob).

Mother and Offspring

As described in Mother and Offspring, Table 4.2.

Play

Running, stotting, high-jumping, chasing, and play-fighting. ➤ Mostly by juveniles, especially early and late in day.

Response to Predators

Skulking. ➤ Sneaking into cover in response to danger.

Alert posture, stamping, alarm-snorting, other nervous behavior.

Stotting. ➤ Excitement behavior, most common in young, given in play as well as alarm.

Style-trotting. ➤ Excitement behavior (waterbuck).

Hiding. ➤ By adults as well as young (reedbucks).

SOUNDS OF ALARM, EXCITEMENT

Whistling. ➤ Reedbucks, kob.

Snorting. ➤ Waterbuck.

Grunting. ➤ Lechwe.

REEDBUCKS, *Redunca* species

Figure 8.1. Male bohor reedbuck advertising territorial status by standing in erect posture.

WHAT THEY ARE   Three closely related species of tan-colored, cover-dependent antelopes that live in high grassland:

Common or southern reedbuck, *Redunca arundinum.* ♂ wt 132-209 lb (60-95 kg), ht 32-42 in (80-105 cm), horns 12-18 in (30-45 cm); ♀ wt 110-187 lb (50-85 kg), ht 26-38 in (65-95 cm).

Bohor reedbuck, *R. redunca.* ♂ wt 95-121 lb (43-55 kg), ht 30-35 in (75-89 cm), horns 8-16 in (20-41 cm); ♀ wt 80-99 lb (36-45 kg), ht 27-30 in (69-76 cm).

Mountain reedbuck, *R. fulvorufula.* ♂ wt 49-84 lb (22-38 cm), ht 26-30 in (65-76 cm), horns 5-15 in (14-38 cm); ♀ wt 42-77 lb (19-35 kg), ht same as ♂.

Hindquarters more developed than forequarters. *Tail:* hock-length and bushy. *Color:* bohor reedbuck, yellow-brown; common reedbuck, browner; mountain reedbuck, gray-brown. White throat patch and undertail; black fore-leg stripe in common reedbuck; mountain reedbuck plainest. *Scent glands:* Look for bare round spot below ear.

WHERE THEY LIVE   Bohor and common reedbucks occupy floodplain and drainage-line grasslands in the Northern and Southern Savanna, respectively; they overlap in southern Tanzania. Mountain reedbuck has interrupted distribution: hills and mountains of Ethiopia and East Africa; southern Africa; and Cameroon.

GOOD PLACES TO SEE THEM   Bohor reedbuck: Akagera NP, Rwanda; Lake Nakuru, Meru NP, Masai Mara NR, Kenya; most national parks and reserves of Tanzania. Common reedbuck: Kazungu NP, Malawi; Kafue, Lukusuzi, and Mweru-Wantipa NP, Zambia; Hwange and Matobo NP, Zimbabwe; Chobe NP, Moremi GR, Botswana; Kruger NP, South Africa. Mountain reedbuck: Aberdares and Tsavo NP, Kenya; Kilimanjaro NP, Tanzania; Willem Pretorius GR, Giant's Castle, Hluhluwe-Umfulozi GR, Doornkloof NR, Mountain Zebra NP, South Africa.

ECOLOGY   Common and bohor reedbucks need cover to hide in. The former is most common in drainage line grasslands; the latter is abundant on broad floodplains of the Northern Savanna. Mountain reedbuck occupies grassy hills and rocky slopes above 4900 ft (1500 m); common reedbuck uses similar habitat between East and southern Africa.

Grazers able to utilize grasses either unpalatable or inaccessible to most other herbivores, reedbucks browse foliage and herbs to some extent in the dry season. The mountain reedbuck is apparently water-independent, but the other 2 have to drink at least every few days late in dry season.

ACTIVITY   ● (○) All 3 species appear to be mainly night-active, but bohor and common reedbucks are often seen in open in late afternoon and for an hour or two after dawn—or anytime after fires have removed tall grass. Reedbucks subsisting on low-protein, high-fiber grass often feed and go to water by day; common reedbuck is known to spend more daylight hours foraging as the dry season advances.

SOCIAL/MATING SYSTEM

(♂-♀)   The common reedbuck lives in monogamous pairs in territories of 86 to 148 acres (35–60 ha). Pronounced gender difference in size and appearance, however, usually go together with polygyny, and pairs do not associate closely, social-groom with one another, or scent-mark their territory. Absence of keep-out signs could explain why territorial boundaries are vague, often trespassed, and subject to change. But self-advertising/alarm whistles in duet could denote pair bonds and advertise joint territory.

Male offspring are tolerated until nearly adult (in third year) whereas females, maturing a year earlier, leave in their second year. After fires remove cover, females and young associate in temporary herds.

(♀♂♀) (♂♂♂) (♂♀♂♂/♀♂♂♀♀)   Bohor reedbuck territories of 62 to 160 acres (25–65 ha) encompass the territories/home ranges of 1 to 5 females, which remain solitary as long as there is cover to hide in, but band together after cover is burned. Male offspring are evicted as young as 6 months, soon after their horns appear. Young males associate in twos and threes until full-grown, occupying border areas where persecution by territorial males is minimal. At high density on vast floodplains, bohor reedbucks form large mixed herds on flushes of new grass.

(♂♀○♀○♀○) The mountain reedbuck is sociable, living in small herds of 3 to 8 females and young. The ranges of females (89–188 acres [36–76 ha]) include the territories (25–69 acres [10–28 ha]) of several males.

HOW THEY MOVE   Run in a distinctive rocking canter, well-adapted to high grass and hillsides, displaying the white tail and whistling at every bound when excited. Reedbucks also perform an unusual variation of stotting (see Table 8.2).

REPRODUCTION   Not strictly seasonal, but the usual peak in rainy months. Gestation 7.5 months. Female mountain reedbucks conceive as young as 1 year and reproduce at intervals of 9 to 14 months. Females of the two larger species breed at 2 years, males at 4.

OFFSPRING AND PARENTAL CARE   Female common reedbucks isolate a month before giving birth and remain secluded during the 1.5- to 2-month calf concealment period. The previous offspring may rejoin mother soon after she calves.

PREDATORS   Lion, leopard, spotted hyena, cheetah, and wild dog.

Table 8.2.   *DIFFERENCES IN REEDBUCK BEHAVIOR**
Expect to see and hear ➤ *Usual context and meaning*

Territorial Advertising

A breathy, repetitious whistle, often given from hiding and during flight. ➤ Both sexes whistle, often in duet and especially at night. Loud whistling causes whole body to shake.

Rocking canter and stotting ± popping. ➤ Alarm signals that may also advertise territorial status, especially in combination with whistling and popping—possibly the sound of the inguinal sacs (arrow) popping open (and releasing scent) when the hind legs are thrown up at the height of a stotting bound (common reedbuck).

Defecation crouch showing white undertail.

No dung middens, but distinctive crouch (by adults of both sexes) could advertise territorial status visually; ♂♂ also defecate during aggressive interactions.

*The three reedbucks share the same display repertoire, although the frequency with which a display is performed may differ from species to species.

Submission

Head-low/chin-out posture with lowered forequarters. ➤ A more submissive variation of the usual submissive posture; e.g., adolescent ♂ to adult ♂.

Courtship

Foreleg-lifting. ♂ sometimes nudges, licks, and rubs head on ♀ after mating. ➤ Uncommon in reedbucks.

Mother and Offspring

Mother licking calf intently, from rump to head.

Calf touching noses with mother and offering the spot it wants licked. ➤ Mother no longer licks calves more than 4 months old, unless they solicit it.

Response to Predators

Variation on stotting. ➤ Shown under Territorial Advertising.

KOB ANTELOPE, *Kobus kob*

Figure 8.2. Kob courtship display: prancing in erect posture.

WHAT IT IS   An antelope of floodplains that looks like a heavyweight impala. Stocky build with hindquarters more developed than forequarters. ♂ wt 207 lb (94 kg), ht 37–40 in (90–100 cm); ♀ wt 139 lb (63 kg), ht 32–36 in (82–92 cm). *Horns:* S-shaped, strongly ridged, 16 to 27 in (40–69 cm). *Coat:* short and glossy. *Color:* golden to reddish brown, with contrasting white throat patch, eye ring, and inside ears; black-fronted legs. Adult males darker than females (male white-eared kob, *K. k. leucotis,* is ebony-colored).

WHERE IT LIVES Northern Savanna, from Senegal to southeast Sudan, south to Queen Elizabeth NP, southern Uganda. The very similar puku lives in the Southern Savanna.

GOOD PLACES TO SEE IT Murchison Falls and Queen Elizabeth NP, Uganda; Garamba and Virunga NP, Zaire.

ECOLOGY A grazer closely tied to floodplain grassland. Preference for tender green grass, dependence on water, avoidance of flooded ground and steep slopes limit it to green pastures in well-watered valleys. During rains, kobs concentrate on short pastures on higher parts of the floodplain; in dry season, they occupy greenbelts bordering marshland and pastures that produce a greenflush after annual fires.

ACTIVITY ○/● Day and night; peaks early and late in daytime, as usual.

SOCIAL/MATING SYSTEM

At average densities, kob populations live dispersed in small herds of 5 to 15 (up to 40) females and young within a permanent territorial network where males are spaced at least 100 to 200 yd apart. Female herds often exchange members and lack any obvious rank order.

When resident populations reach high densities, kobs form leks. These breeding arenas are permanent fixtures in resident populations, recognizable as lawns of bare ground or short grass 200 to 400 yd across, surrounded by taller grassland. An arena is shared by 30 to 40 adult males spaced only 15 to 30 yd apart, on territories of under 2 acres (0.8 ha), compared to a conventional territory of 100 acres (40 ha). Females and bachelor males congregate in hundreds in the vicinity, and 9 out of 10 females enter an arena on their day of estrus to mate with just a few of the centrally placed males.

Only the fittest males are up to the fierce competition for central courts and they last only a week or two before being replaced by bachelor males-in-waiting. Meanwhile, ⅔ of the territorial males occupy conventional territories that coexist with the arenas. Long tenures compensate these males for relatively few mating opportunities.

REPRODUCTION Breeds year-round in East Africa, females conceiving again 21 to 64 days after calving. First ovulation at 13 to 14 months; gestation c. 8 months. Males become territorial at 3 years. White-eared kob of southeast Sudan ruts seasonally during migration.

OFFSPRING AND PARENTAL CARE Calves lie-out in high grass for c. 1 month, relieved only by suckling intervals early and late in day. After hiding stage, juveniles form crèches, at 3 to 4 months begin accompanying their mothers. Daughters may remain attached until mothers calve again; sons join bachelor herds after weaning at 6 to 7 months.

PREDATORS   All the large carnivores. Kobs are slower, shorter-winded than most plains antelopes, but open range and large herds are hard for predators to approach undetected. Kobs make prodigious leaps when startled, and pursued by wild dogs or hyenas, seek refuge in water or reed beds.

Table 8.3.   *DIFFERENCES IN KOB BEHAVIOR*
      Expect to see and hear ➤ *Usual context and meaning*

Territorial Advertising

Standing in erect posture, often whistling or grunting. ➤ Standard attitude of arena ♂♂.

Herding and chasing ♀♀ and ♂♂. ➤ Common on conventional territories, rare on arenas—courts too small.

Aggression

Approach, grunting. ➤ Response by arena ♂ to trespassing neighbor.

Erect posture and abrupt looking away, tail-wagging. ➤ Mutual displays between territorial rivals. Looking away shows off white throat patch.

Courtship

Partial erection during courtship displays. ➤ Especially common on lek territories.

Approach in erect posture.

Prancing and nose-lifting, with erection. ➤ Especially common on leks, substituting for chasing and herding.

POSTMATING BEHAVIOR

♂ whistles repeatedly, standing hump-backed with penis still showing, then nuzzles/licks ♀'s genitals and udder as she stands in swan-neck posture.

LECHWE, *Kobus leche*

Figure 8.3. Territorial lechwes interacting on their common border; male on left stands in erect posture as rival approaches.

SUBSPECIES
Red lechwe, *K. l. leche*[v]   Black lechwe, *K. l. smithemani*[v]
Kafue lechwe, *K. l. kafuensis*[v]

WHAT IT IS   A sturdy, long-horned antelope that lives at the water's edge. Overdeveloped hindquarters, hooves elongated with wide splay and adjacent naked skin are aquatic adaptations. ♂ wt 227 lb (103 kg), ht 41 in (104 cm); ♀ wt 174 lb (79 kg), ht 38 in (97 cm). *Horns:* long, 18 to 36 in (45–92 cm), laid back, thin, strongly ridged. *Coat:* greasy with distinct smell, shaggy neck mane. *Color:* geographically variable; females and male red lechwe bright chestnut with white underparts, tail, throat, and facial markings; conspicuous black markings running down the legs, and black-tipped tail. Male Kafue lechwes darken with age and maybe seasonally; male black lechwes turn black-brown. *Scent glands:* Lacks usual scent glands.

WHERE IT LIVES   Southern Savanna on floodplains bordering marshes and swamps, from southeastern Zaire through Zambia, northern Botswana, and Angola. The most famous population is that of the Kafue Flats, which once numbered ½ million, now reduced to around 50,000, many of which live in Lochinvar and Blue Lagoon NPs.

GOOD PLACES TO SEE IT   Okavango Delta, Chobe NP, Moremi GR, Botswana; Lochinvar NP, Lake Bangweulu (black lechwe), Zambia.

ECOLOGY   The most aquatic antelope after the sitatunga, lechwes are literally an edge species that exploits the seasonally flooded meadows bordering rivers and lakes, a rich resource productive enough to sustain 2600 lechwes/mi^2 (1000/km^2). They feed in water up to their bellies and on the lush greenbelts exposed as floodwaters recede. At low water, lechwes venture miles from shore in swamps where there are hummocks and islands offering dry resting places, supported on the muck by their long, splayed hooves.

When annual floods arrive, lechwes and water advance together across the plains, migrating many miles on widest, flattest plains.

Lechwes graze grasses and sedges that grow in shallow waters and emergent ground, go without drinking during cool, dry weather while grass is green but go to water up to 3 times a day in dry, hot weather.

ACTIVITY   ○/● Day and night, usual early and late daytime peaks.

SOCIAL/MATING SYSTEM

A (symbols) (symbols) (symbols) B (symbols) H_2O Lechwe social organization varies from the conventional sedentary-dispersed pattern (A) to the mobile-aggregated pattern (B), in which most of the population is concentrated in waterside greenbelts; here some mature males stake out temporary territories during the annual mating peak.

(symbols)   Breeding leks occur within the densest aggregations on the highest, openest ground near water. A Kafue Flats lek typically includes 50 to 100 males clustered in a roughly circular area c. 500 yd across. The hub is marked by a cluster of maybe 10 to 20 females that have come unerringly to the "courts" of 1 to 2 superstuds. The arena is surrounded and roughly defined by an aggregation of nonbreeding lechwes.

Lechwes of the same sex and age tend to form subgroups within large aggregations. Females and calves stay nearest the water and are the first to plunge in when danger threatens. Mothers and dependent young associate consistently; otherwise, lechwe groups are completely loose and open.

HOW IT MOVES   Powerful hindquarters, elongated hooves, and an unusual bounding gallop are adaptations for running on flooded ground, and startled lechwes also make spectacular leaps and scatter in all directions like impalas. Disadvantage: its running gait is slow and clumsy on land, making lechwe depend on water as a refuge.

REPRODUCTION   A 2.5-month mating peak during the rainy season, typically coinciding with the onset of the flooding cycle (Nov.–Feb.); but ¼ of females breed outside the peak. Gestation 7 to 8 months, calving peak from mid-July to mid-September. Males adolescent at 1.5 years but only mature at 4. Females in good condition begin ovulating at 1.5 years.

OFFSPRING AND PARENTAL CARE   Females seek cover and dry ground for calving, where newborns spend c. 3 weeks in concealment, except for morning and evening suckling times, afterward join crèches of up to 50 young; juveniles act quite independently of their mothers most of the time—mothers and offspring even flee in different directions.

PREDATORS   Lion, leopard, spotted hyena, and wild dog.

Table 8.4.   *DIFFERENCES IN LECHWE BEHAVIOR*
Expect to see and hear ➤ Usual context and meaning

Territorial Advertising

Lechwes in erect posture giving whinnying grunts.

Aggression

Erect posture in broadside stance ± head-shaking and -turning. ➤ Dominance display commonest between arena ♂ ♂.

Approach in erect posture and whinnying grunts. ➤ Response by arena ♂ to trespassing neighbor.

OTHER ACTIONS ASSOCIATED WITH THREAT DISPLAYS
Displaying while walking parallel with adversary.

Courtship

Foreleg-lifting: lechwe does not straighten foreleg.

Following ♀ in mating march.

Response to Predators

Flight into water, leaping and scattering. ➤ Actions that make it harder for predators to single out a quarry.

WATERBUCK, *Kobus ellipsiprymnus*

Figure 8.4. Waterbuck appeasement ceremony: satellite male on right displays submission to territorial male giving angle-horn threat.

SUBSPECIES
Common waterbuck, *K. e. ellipsiprymnus*
Defassa waterbuck, *K. e. defassa*

WHAT IT IS   A big, shaggy antelope, females somewhat resembling deer. Stocky build, with long body and neck. ♂ wt 520 lb (236 kg), ht 51 in (127 cm); ♀ wt 409 lb (186 kg), ht 48 in (119 cm). *Horns:* 22 to 39 in (55–99 cm), tips curved forward, thick and deeply ridged. *Coat:* coarse-haired with a neck mane and ruff. *Color:* grizzled red-brown; lower legs black; white rump patch (defassa waterbuck) or elliptical ring around the rump (common waterbuck); white underparts, throat, hair inside ears, eyebrow line, and snout; males darken with age. *Scent glands:* Lacks usual scent glands but greasy coat emits musky smell.

WHERE IT LIVES   Northern and Southern Savanna. Defassa waterbuck lives west of the Rift, Luangwa, and middle Zambesi valleys; common race occurs in these valleys to the eastern seaboard. Hybrids occur where the two races overlap, as in Nairobi NP and Tanzania's Ngorongoro Crater.

GOOD PLACES TO SEE IT   Nakuru and Meru NP, Kenya; Moyowosi GR, Serengeti NP, Tanzania; Akagera NP, Rwanda; Queen Elizabeth and Murchison Falls NP, Uganda; Kafue and Luangwa NP, Zambia; Zambezi and Mana Pools NP, Zimbabwe; Kruger NP, Umfolozi-Hluhluwe GR, South Africa.

ECOLOGY   Living up to its name, the waterbuck has even less tolerance for dehydration than domestic cattle and has to stay within a few miles of water to drink every day or two. An edge species, it prefers grassland and firm ground adjacent to woodland. Habitats meeting all these requirements occur along drainage lines and within valleys, causing the typically patchy distribution of waterbuck. A grazer on medium and short grasses rich in protein; also eats herbs and foliage when green grass unavailable.

ACTIVITY ○/● Day and night. Foraging and resting times vary widely, reflecting seasonal and latitudinal differences, variations in pasture quality and growth stage, distance from water, sex, age, reproductive status, and predation pressure.

SOCIAL/MATING SYSTEM (♂♀○♀○♀○) (♂♂♂) (♂♂♂♀♀♀)
Sedentary and territorial but unusual in that bachelor males, which share the limited patches of suitable habitat with females and young, are tolerated close to and even in female herds by some territorial males. As long as they grovel on command, a territory owner may permit even adult males to reside on his property. Regular performance of an appeasement ceremony featuring the same submissive displays performed by females and young is the quid pro quo that enables up to 3 adult males to live as satellites—with occasional opportunities to sneak copulations and fair prospects of inheriting the territory.

Females associate so casually and range singly so often that one researcher decided waterbuck herds (typically 5 to 10 but up to 70 animals) consist of essentially independent individuals whose home ranges happen to overlap. Cows come and go, there is no established rank order or regular leader and no greeting ceremony or social grooming. Yet the same expert noted a positive social attraction between females, aggressive treatment of outsiders, and a tendency of certain cows to associate. Bachelor herds (average 5, up to 40 males) are exclusive and subject to a strict rank order although herd composition also changes hourly as members come and go. Male calves may be forced to join the bachelor contingent at 8 to 9 months, soon after their horns appear, remaining there until mature at 6 years.

Home ranges and territories vary in size, depending on the extent of preferred habitat, population density, and age (old animals have smaller ranges and territories than prime animals). In Queen Elizabeth NP, 10 cows had average home ranges of about 1500 acres (600 ha), a bachelor herd's range was 250 acres (100 ha), and territories were 133 to 557 acres (average 360 acres [146 ha]).

HOW IT MOVES Lacking speed and endurance, the waterbuck depends on cover as a refuge from predators such as hyenas and wild dogs. Trotting is an important gait; alarmed waterbucks both style-trot and stot.

REPRODUCTION Year-round near equator; once a year in higher latitudes, calving during rainy season. Gestation 8 to 8.5 months. Cows may calve at c. 10-month intervals, but rarely conceive before 3.

OFFSPRING AND PARENTAL CARE Females seek cover a couple days before calving, preferably in same locale they calved previously. Mother goes up to 550 yd from her calf's hiding place by day but stays close at night, retrieves and suckles it 3 times/day during 2- to 4-week hiding stage. Juveniles are often seen alone or in unattended crèches. Weaning complete at 6 to 8 months.

PREDATORS   Mainly spotted hyena, lion, leopard, and wild dog—the last 2 mainly on young. Waterbucks are thought to take refuge in cover at night, and mothers of young calves frequent woodland.

Table 8.5.   *DIFFERENCES IN WATERBUCK BEHAVIOR*
Expect to see and hear* ➤ *Usual context and meaning

Territorial Advertising

 Biggest, darkest ♂ with longest horns is the likely territory owner; to make sure, watch for interactions between ♂ ♂.

Aggression

 High-horn and angle-horn threat; neck arched, tail out, curved to side or up (see Fig. 8.4).

Submission

 Head-low/chin-out posture, tail out with champing. ➤ Submissive response to aggression, including chewing movements (see Fig. 8.4).

Courtship

MALE BEHAVIOR
Resting chin on ♀'s rump. ➤ Mounting intention.

FEMALE BEHAVIOR
Champing. ➤ Submissive response to ♂.

Sniffing ♂'s horns and penis. ➤ Receptive behavior.

Mother and Offspring

Mother summons hidden calf with bleat or moo.

Chapter 9

VAAL OR GRAY RHEBOK
Pelea capreolus
Tribe Peleini

Figure 9.1. Rhebok courtship: male foreleg-lifting.

WHAT IT IS   A medium-sized antelope with no close relatives, found in mountains of South Africa. Slender build with long neck and legs. ♂ wt 42–66 lb (19–30 kg), ht 28–32 in (70–80 cm); ♀ c. 10% smaller. *Head:* narrow snout with bulbous, bare nose, long, narrow ears. *Horns:* straight stiletto in male only, 6 to 10 in (15–25 cm). *Coat:* soft, rabbitlike fur. *Color:* gray, lower legs with dark front stripe, muzzle with dark blaze; skin of nose, palate, tongue, inside ears, penis, and eyes black; underparts light-colored; inner thighs and underside of bushy tail white; young often browner than adults. *Scent glands:* male preputial gland exudes strong-smelling black secretion.

WHERE IT LIVES   Only in South Africa, in montane grasslands above 3300 ft (1000 m), although some live among coastal sand dunes in Cape Province.

GOOD PLACES TO SEE IT   Karroo and Bontebok NP, Cape Province; Suikerbosrand NR, Transvaal; Giant's Castle GR, Natal; Sehlabathebe NP, Lesotho.

ECOLOGY   Prefers medium, well-watered *sourveld* pastures and scrub savanna of hills and mountainsides, where growing grasses are lush but become fibrous and unnutritious when dry. A mixed feeder, water-independent; grazes upland pastures during rains, browses herbs, leaves, and sprouting grass on lower slopes in dry season. Overlaps with mountain reedbuck but avoids taller grassland the latter prefers.

ACTIVITY   ○ Daytime. Seasonally variable, rheboks forage and rest equally in summer wet season, with the only predictable activity peak in late afternoon. In dry season, they spend ⅔ to ¾ of the day foraging, often in uninterrupted bouts.

SOCIAL/MATING SYSTEM   Herds are small, usually 3 to 5 females and young, sometimes up to 15, with 1 adult, territorial male. Territories big enough to support a resident herd give territorial males exclusive breeding rights (harem system). The home ranges/territories of a family of 4 animals and another of 6 animals were 81 and 101 acres (33 and 41 ha) in summer, increasing to over 185 acres (75 ha) in winter months of food scarcity.

Herds are closed to outsiders, including stray juveniles. Females only leave the herd during and after calving. Leadership and dominance, though rarely enforced by aggressive displays, are probably exercised by the oldest female. The male, having no need to keep his harem from absconding, trails behind them, but spends up to several hours a day patrolling and marking his boundaries.

Dispersing male offspring do not join bachelor herds but live alone in no-man's lands between territories until they mature at 1.5 to 2 years. After acquiring a territory, the newcomer has to wait for females to immigrate, as efforts to capture females from neighbors' herds seldom succeed. However, at least some female offspring emigrate, and settling down as the first wife of a newly established male is possibly the most desirable option. Such transfers occur mainly during the winter, when males are less vigorously territorial than during summer mating and calving seasons.

HOW IT MOVES   Quite similar to mountain reedbuck: a rocking canter interrupted by long bounds, with head and neck slightly lowered, during which the tail is rolled up to display the white scut and thighs; and stotting, with high bounds during which the hindquarters are thrown high. Rheboks also gallop at up to 40 mph (65 kph) without bounding, hugging the ground with ears back and tail curled. An ambling walk that changes to a cross-walk on broken ground.

REPRODUCTION   Seasonal, mating January through April, calving September through January after nearly 9-month gestation. Occasional twins make rhebok probably unique among African antelopes.

OFFSPRING AND PARENTAL CARE   Expectant mother reconnoiters good calving sites several weeks ahead of term, isolates 2 to 3 days before calving, rejoining herd 1 to 2 weeks afterward. During 6-week concealment period, mother comes no nearer to calf than 50 yd and may go as far as 500 yd; she retrieves and suckles calf for an hour early and late in day, in 3 to 7 bouts of 5 minutes, decreasing to ½ minute as the milk supply dwindles; weaning at 6 to 8 months. Juveniles associate in peer groups, but when danger threatens, each runs to its own mother and follows her closely. Adolescent males are not driven away by their fathers but disperse on their own initiative.

PREDATORS   Caracal and native dogs the main danger to adults (big cats rare); large eagles and baboons sometimes take small calves. Male rheboks are known to threaten and chase baboons.

HOW THEY COMMUNICATE   Sight 1, scent 2, sound 2. Rheboks detect movement at 400 to 500 yd, react to stationary animals or people at 100 to 200 yd, recognize own kind at 300 to 400 yd whether moving or standing. They can also track one another by scent.

Table 9.1.   *RHEBOK BEHAVIOR GUIDE*
Expect to see and hear ➤ *Usual context and meaning*

Territorial Advertising

Erect posture of territorial ♂. ➤ Visual display of territorial status.

Urination and defecation in the same distinctive crouch. ➤ A visual display of scent-posting. Patrolling ♂ ♂ mark at exposed locations and landmarks, but do not establish dung middens. Melanin pigment of preputial gland stains urine.

Snorting (also called "smacking"), stamping, and stotting. ➤ Reaction to territorial neighbor that approaches border.

Aggression

Territorial ♂ ♂ have borderline encounters but rarely go beyond air-cushion fights.

Erect posture in broadside stance or confronting ± looking away. ➤ Displays dominance.

Aggression *continued*

High-horn threat ± angle-horn threat.

Low-horn threat.

Stabbing movements. ➤ Especially during low-horn threats and air-cushion fights; also during chases of trespassers.

Racing and chasing. ➤ Trespassers are sometimes stabbed and killed.

♀ ♀ butting heads. ➤ Uncommon.

Head-low posture. ➤ Defensive threat/self-defense.

Submission

Lying-out.

Displacement Activities

Grazing, grooming. ➤ Especially during ♂ border confrontations.

Courtship

MALE BEHAVIOR

Staying close to ♀. ➤ Preliminary stage of 2–3 day estrous cycle.

Approaching ♀ in erect posture with erection while empty-licking.

Urine-testing.

Covers her urine with his urine and dung.

FEMALE BEHAVIOR

Urination. ➤ Prompted by ♂'s approach in lowstretch.

Unresponsive ♀ butts overly persistent ♂ in flank, tries to get away.

Responsive ♀ stands in head-low posture, urinates with tail curled up. ➤ ♀ may approach and stand before ♂, urinating, while looking back at him.

MATING MARCH

♂ foreleg-lifting (see Fig. 9.1). ➤ At practically every step, as ♀ keeps moving slowly forward.

♂ licks nose and ♀'s vulva, also her neck and head.

Copulation: a single ejaculatory thrust. ➤ After preliminary mounting attempts.

POSTMATING BEHAVIOR

♂ licks penis and both parties self-groom.

Response to Predators

Herd bunches, stands in alert posture.

Restless pacing, snorting.

Stotting.

Flight. ➤ Fleeing rheboks use hilly terrain to disappear from view.

Territorial ♂ attacking predators in defense of offspring. ➤ As certifiable father, ♂ rhebok protects his own genes.

Chapter 10

HORSE ANTELOPES
Tribe Hippotragini

Roan, *Hippotragus equinus*   Oryx/gemsbok, *Oryx gazella*
Sable, *H. niger*   Scimitar-horned oryx, *O. dammah*[en]
Addax, *Addax nasomaculatus*[en]

WHAT THEY ARE   Large, vaguely horselike antelopes of the savanna, arid zone, and desert. Male and female look much alike (except sable), with horns of nearly equal or equal length (though thinner in females); strongly ridged, scimitar-shaped except *O. gazella* (straight) and addax (corkscrew). Short upstanding mane. *Color:* nearly white to chestnut (to black sable bulls), with conspicuous black and white markings, especially on head. *Tail:* hock length or longer with horselike whisk. *Scent glands:* simple preorbital glands in roan, sable, and scimitar-horned oryx; hoof glands in all feet. *Teats:* 4.

SOCIAL/MATING SYSTEM

The conventional territorial system is represented by the roan and sable: territorial males, small to large herds of females and young, and herds of bachelor males kept segregated and celibate by the territory holders. But males are tolerated in the natal herd up to the subadult stage, unusually long. Until then, their resemblance to females keeps the aggression of territorial males in check.

Mixed herds. The similarity of females and males extends to the adult stage in oryxes and addax, enabling bachelors to remain in female herds—instead of kicking them out, breeding bulls settle for undisputed dominance. This arrangement is an adaptation to nomadism in arid environments, where these antelopes must continually search for vegetation revived by sporadic thunderstorms. Instead of investing in real estate, the fittest bulls in nomadic populations compete to be highest ranking in a male dominance hierarchy. But wherever conditions permit, bulls establish individual territories and assert mating rights over any herds that enter their domain.

Armed as they are with long, dangerous horns, female horse antelopes tend to be more aggressive than hornless female antelopes. Dominance hierarchies based on age and individual prowess are vigorously maintained in both sexes. Female herds, composed of animals sharing the same home range, are closed to outsiders. Herd members keep out of reach of each other's horns, making for individual spacing greater than in most species of hornless females.

HOW THEY MOVE   Oryxes are enduring but not particularly fleet runners, have a wonderful flowing trot, and an ambling walk. Galloping sable and roan are slower, bound higher and flex limbs more, trot less.

HOW THEY COMMUNICATE   Sight 1, scent 2, sound 2.

Table 10.1. *HORSE ANTELOPE BEHAVIOR GUIDE*
Expect to see and hear ➤ *Usual context and meaning*

Territorial or Dominance Advertising

Adult ♂ standing or lying, alone or apart from herd, in conspicuous location. ➤ Advertises presence and high social status. (Note: can be confused with lone bachelor ♂ ♂ in roan and sable.)

Lone adult ♂ patrolling in erect posture, pausing to defecate and thrash vegetation. ➤ Territorial sable, roan, and oryx.

Standing in erect posture. ➤ Self-advertising when undirected, and a sign of high status.

Defecation postures of oryx and addax (left), sable and roan (right). ➤ Note extreme crouch of oryx and addax.

Bush-/tree-horning. ➤ A visible and audible display of aggressive mood and high status. (May also deposit preorbital-gland secretion—except oryx.)

Herding and chasing ♀ ♀ and ♂ ♂, often combined with grunting (oryx, addax) or roaring (sable, roan). ➤ To keep ♀ ♀ from leaving and rivals out of territory, especially during courtship.

Aggression

Highly developed in this tribe.

Supplanting. ➤ Making a lower-ranked individual move aside by walking toward it. Enforced if necessary by threats (ducking, tossing, and hooking movements).

Pressing or rubbing horns on opponent's shoulder. ➤ Assertion of dominance between ♀ ♀; an invitation to spar when performed by immature ♂ ♂ (sable, roan).

Broadside stance in erect posture, tail out, ± nose lifted and head turned 45°. ➤ Display of dominance when addressed to an individual. During mutual displays of sable and roan, contestant with tail higher is the likely winner.

Parallel, head-to-tail stance. ➤ Position commonly taken during mutual dominance and threat displays.

Medial-horn threat. ➤ Commonest threat display in the tribe.

Aggression *continued*

High-horn threat. ➤ To deliver powerful downward blow.

Low-horn threat. ➤ Often performed from kneeling (combat) position by sable and roan.

Angle-horn threat. ➤ To stab sideways over or under the shoulder.

OTHER ACTIONS ASSOCIATED WITH THREAT DISPLAYS

Sideswiping (jerking head to shoulder or flank) ± tail-sweeping. ➤ May be threat (to stab) or displacement (fly-shooing) behavior.

Rhythmic nodding. ➤ Symbolic butting.

Head-tossing. ➤ Symbolic stabbing.

Ground- or vegetation-horning. ➤ Redirected aggression: The message:"This is what I'd like to do to you."

Rushing. ➤ Real or feinted attack.

Roaring or grunting. ➤ While pursuing fleeing ♂ or ♀.

Head-low posture. ➤ Defensive threat, response of inferior to intimidation.

Submission

Head-low/chin-out posture ± head-throwing. ➤ Submissive response to aggression (oryx).

Turning away. ➤ Avoidance of approaching superior.

Passing behind adversary and moving (often running) away. ➤ Conclusion of appeasement ceremony performed by subordinate ♂ ♂ in head-low posture when threatened by dominant ♂.

Fear-gaping. ➤ Combined with head-low/chin-out posture by intimidated ♀ ♀ and young ♂ ♂ (sable and roan). Probably shows intention to call out.

Distress cry. ➤ Loud braying of terrified ♀ or subordinate ♂.

Lying-out. ➤ Extreme submission, mainly seen as last resort of sexually harassed ♀ ♀ (especially sable).

Flight. ➤ Response of inferior or defeated rival to pursuit.

Displacement Activities

Grazing, scratching with hind feet, scratching with horn tips, scraping with incisors.

Sideswiping ± tail-sweeping. ➤ Insect-shooing gesture that may double as threat to horn opponent.

Courtship

MALE BEHAVIOR

Lowstretch (left: sable, roan) or erect posture (right: oryx). ➤ Posture of territorial or alpha ♂ approaching or herding ♀ ♀.

♀ urinating, ♂ urine-testing. ➤ Prompted by ♂'s approach in low-stretch. Testing is unusually common in this tribe, used by both sexes to assess ♀ reproductive status; pronounced lip-curl.

Driving and chasing ± roaring. ➤ Of sexually interesting but unreceptive ♀.

Close following in erect posture. ➤ Common behavior during mating march; often alternates with chasing and driving.

Foreleg-lifting. ➤ Very common during mating march; also used to force lying ♀ to get up.

Resting chin on ♀'s rump. ➤ Mounting prelude (oryx).

FEMALE BEHAVIOR

Flight, defensive threats, submissive behavior.

Courtship circling. ➤ To thwart close-following ♂.

Standing with tail out. ➤ Copulatory attitude.

Mother and Offspring

See Mother and Offspring, Table 4.2.

Crèches of calves that lag behind herd and may be alone, unattended by adults.

Play

Chasing, style-trotting, cavorting, and sparring. ➤ Mainly performed by the young in peak play periods during transition from one activity to another; especially common at start of morning activity peak.

Response to Predators

Alert posture, stamping, alarm-snorting, other nervous behavior.

Style-trotting. ➤ Excitement behavior, in response to predators and in play.

Alarm-snorting.

Flight.

ROAN ANTELOPE, *Hippotragus equinus*

Figure 10.1 Roan courtship: male foreleg-lifting, female fear-gaping.

WHAT IT IS   A big, roan-colored antelope with long, tasseled ears and a clown mask. Rangy build, high shoulders and powerful neck with upstanding mane. The fourth-largest antelope: ♂ wt 616 lb (280 kg), ht 50–58 in (126–145 cm); ♀ wt 572 lb (260 kg), ht within ♂ range. *Head*: long muzzle, wide gape. *Horns*: curve backward, massive, heavily ridged, 22 to 39 in (55–99 cm); 10 to 20% shorter in females. *Color*: varies from pale gray to rufous; black and white mask, sexes alike but male's mask blacker; calves tan, markings indistinct.

WHERE IT LIVES   Wetter parts of Northern and Southern Savanna (the broad-leafed, deciduous woodlands of the Guinea Savanna and *Miombo* Woodland Zone), and in montane grassland up to 7875 ft (2400 m). Formerly abundant in West Africa, less common in eastern Africa and mysteriously absent from the eastern *miombo* woodlands.

GOOD PLACES TO SEE IT   Ruaha NP, Tanzania; Nyika and Kazungu NP, Vwaza GR, Malawi; Kafue and Mweru Wantipa NP, Zambia; Hwange NP, Zimbabwe.

ECOLOGY   Tolerates more open savanna and taller grass than sable, also more at home on floodplains and at higher elevations. A water-dependent grazer/browser adapted to subsist on tufted perennial grasses growing on infertile soils of the interior plateau; 10 to 20% of its diet consists of foliage and herbs.

ACTIVITY   ○/● Day and night. Late risers, especially on cool mornings and in dew-wet pastures. Daily ranging seldom exceeds 0.8 to 1.5 mi (2–4 km). During afternoon activity peak, herds feed intensively until dark, then move some distance before settling down to ruminate for several hours.

SOCIAL/MATING SYSTEM The roan lives in small-to-medium herds of 6 to 20 females and young, although herds of 35 are not unusual. At its normally low density of c. 10/mi² (4/km²), it has a conventional sociable, territorial social organization. Females share a traditional home range averaging 600 acres (239 ha) that includes the territories of several different bulls. At very low density in substandard habitat, as in South Africa's Kruger NP, females may range areas as large as 23 to 39 mi² (60–100 km²) and be accompanied by the same bull, who, in the absence of resistance from territorial neighbors, defends a movable space around his own private harem.

Herd composition changes daily and seasonally: members disperse in small groups during the rains and concentrate in larger groups on the best available pastures near water in the dry season. The most cohesive groups are maintained by young of assorted ages, which cluster around the youngest calf and often lag behind the herd. Males stay in female herds for up to 3 years, then join and remain in bachelor herds until mature at 6.

REPRODUCTION Breeds year round, with minimum calving intervals of about 10.5 months. Gestation 9 to 9.5 months. Females conceive at 2 years; males begin breeding at maturity.

OFFSPRING AND MATERNAL CARE Cows rejoin herd c. 5 days after calving, but a mother stays within 500 yd of calf's hiding place, retrieves and suckles it in early morning and once or twice at night. Weaning by 6 months.

PREDATORS Calves vulnerable to spotted hyenas, leopards, and wild dogs; adults are large and formidable, and resident in regions of low-predator density.

Table 10.2. *DIFFERENCES IN ROAN ANTELOPE BEHAVIOR*
Expect to see and hear ➤ *Usual context and meaning*

Territorial Advertising

Ritualized defecation without pawing.

Submission

Appeasement ceremony. ➤ A very assertive bull aims downward blow at subordinate's rump as it passes.

SABLE ANTELOPE, *Hippotragus niger*

Figure 10.2. Sparring contest between two subadult sable bulls.

SUBSPECIES
Roosevelt sable, *H. n. roosevelti*[en]   Southern sable, *H. n. niger*
Kirk's sable, *H. n. kirkii*   Giant sable, *H. n. variani*[en]

WHAT IT IS   Rivals the greater kudu as most-handsome antelope, especially the male giant sable. Compact, powerful build, thick neck enhanced by upstanding mane, and sturdy legs. Resemblance of females and males holds up to 3 years or until males become darker and develop bigger horns. ♂ wt 517 lb (235 kg), ht 46–56 in (117–140 cm); ♀ wt 484 lb (220 kg); ht within ♂ range. *Head:* long muzzle with wide gape. *Horns:* massive and more curved in males, 32 to 65 in (80–165 cm); 24–40 in (60–100 cm) in females. *Coat:* short and glossy. *Color:* bulls black, females and young sorrel to chestnut (except southern race, in which females also turn brown-black); white "eyebrows" and muzzle divided by cheek stripe; white belly and rump patch. Calves under 2 months light tan with faint markings.

WHERE IT LIVES   Southern Savanna, from southeastern Kenya, eastern Tanzania, and Mozambique to Angola and southern Zaire, mainly in the *Miombo* Woodland Zone. The giant sable, isolated and vulnerable in central Angola, is one of the most endangered antelopes.

GOOD PLACES TO SEE IT   Shimba Hills NR, Kenya; Ruaha NP, Selous GR, Tanzania; Kafue and Mweru Wantipa NP, Zambia; Matetsi Safari Area, Hwange, Zambezi, and Kazuma Pan NP, Zimbabwe; Kruger NP, South Africa.

ECOLOGY   Preferred habitat combines savanna woodland and grassland; trees (fire-resistant, broad-leafed, deciduous) widely spaced with understory of sparse grasses utilized in rainy season. Drainage-line and floodplain grasslands that produce new growth after the annual fires keep sable in open during dry season. A grazer/browser, eats grasses supplemented by foliage and herbs, especially kinds growing on woodland termite mounds. Goes to water at least every other day and regularly visits salt licks (also chews bones to make up for mineral-deficient soils).

ACTIVITY   ○/● Traveling on average c. ½ mi (1.2 km) a day, sables are especially sedentary on dry-season pastures, when herds may spend weeks on the same field, leaving only to go to water or seek shade during hottest hours. But periodically herds move several miles and resettle on another pasture. Sables also regularly graze until dark, then move off before settling down to chew the cud, a tactic that makes it harder for predators to spot a herd's resting site and sneak up after dark.

SOCIAL/MATING SYSTEM (♂♀○♀○♀○) (♀○♂♀ ♀ / ♀○♀♀ ♀) (♂♂♂)   Herds of 15 to 25 females and young are typical but often represent only part of the residents (typically 30–75 sables in good habitat) sharing a common, exclusive home range of 4 to 10 mi² (10–25 km²), incorporating territories of 1.5 to 3.5 mi² (3.9–9 km²) of up to 5 bulls or more. Some herds or subpopulations have separate dry- and wet-season ranges miles apart. The general pattern in all populations is dispersal in small groups during the rains and early dry season, and dry-season concentration in large herds on available green pastures.

A female rank hierarchy based on seniority is continually reinforced by aggressive and submissive interactions. Males are subordinate to adult females until they grow bigger; by then obvious male secondary characters make them persona non grata to territorial bulls. Evicted from female society between 3 and 4 years, males live in bachelor herds until mature at 5, or stay alone, if no group is available, keeping out of the way of territorial bulls.

Territorial bulls often stay alone, even when a female herd is in residence, patrolling and scent-marking or just hanging out in some shady grove. Though conspicuous in a herd of brown females and young, lone bulls standing still in a clump of trees are easily overlooked.

REPRODUCTION   An annual calving season at the end of the rains (except perennial in Kenya's Shimba Hills). Season extends for several months and a few calves are born as much as 6 months out of phase. Gestation 8 to 9 months. Females conceive at 2.5 years; males adolescent by then but unable to compete for territories and mating opportunities until mature. Even in territorial class, certain prime bulls dominate their neighbors.

OFFSPRING AND MATERNAL CARE

Mothers stay secluded for first week or so of the calf's 3-week hiding stage. Cows with calves concealed in the same locale associate in maternal herds. Calves join cohesive peer group as they outgrow the concealment stage and seek mothers only to nurse; after weaning (6–8 months), calves have still less contact. Maternal-offspring bond is so weak that even small calves may be in different sections of a divided herd for days.

PREDATORS   Because it is big and inhabits regions with comparatively little wildlife, sables usually have relatively few predators. Lucky for them, as laggard young are vulnerable to spotted hyenas and leopards.

Table 10.3. *DIFFERENCES IN SABLE ANTELOPE BEHAVIOR*
Expect to see and hear ➤ *Usual context and meaning*

Territorial Advertising

 Scrape marks made by pawing identify dung deposits made by territorial sable. ➤ The only consistent difference between the dunging sites of patrolling sable and roan ♂♂ (differences in track and pellet size unreliable).

Herding and chasing. ➤ Usually when a herd approaches territorial boundary; otherwise territorial ♂ normally follows behind moving herd.

Submission

 Appeasement ceremony. ➤ As in roan (see Table 10.2).

Courtship

Urine-testing. ➤ All sables, including calves, test ♀ urine.

MALE BEHAVIOR

Driving and chasing ± roaring. ➤ Of sexually interesting, unreceptive ♀.

 Foreleg-lifting used by courting ♂ to prod lying ♀ into getting up. ➤ Behavior of persistent bull courting reluctant ♀.

FEMALE BEHAVIOR

Flight, including fear-gaping and screaming when chased hard.

Mother and Offspring

Lone sable emitting piercing, birdlike whistles. ➤ Separated mothers and young searching for one another.

ORYX/GEMSBOK, *Oryx gazella*

Figure 10.3. Waterhole confrontation between two gemsbok bulls. Bull on left giving offensive medial-horn threat, bull on right in defensive head-low posture.

SUBSPECIES
Gemsbok, O. g. *gazella*   Fringe-eared oryx, O. g. *callotis*[v]
Beisa oryx, O. g. *beisa*[v]

WHAT IT IS   Spirit of the desert embodied in an antelope. Compact build with deep chest; short, powerful neck with clipped mane; long, clean limbs, and a long, flowing horse tail. Sexes hard to tell apart, though males more muscular with thicker horns. ♂ wt 367–460 lb (167–209 kg), ht 46–50 in (115–125 cm); ♀ wt 255–414 lb (116–188 kg), ht same as ♂. *Head*: short and blunt; ears small. *Horns*: straight or slightly curved, average 42 in (105 cm; in East Africa, 30 in); record 48 in (120 cm). *Coat*: short, sleek. *Color*: pale gray to tan with black and white clown mask, black sidestripe and garters bordering areas of white.

WHERE IT LIVES   Somali-Masai and South West Arid Zones and adjacent dry savannas. The gemsbok of the Kalahari *sandveld* and Namib Desert of Namibia and Angola is biggest and most colorful. Beisa oryx lives in northeast Africa and Kenya's Northern Frontier District; fringe-eared oryx of southern Kenya and northern Tanzania is smallest and brownest, with relatively inconspicuous markings.

GOOD PLACES TO SEE IT   Samburu-Isiolo GR, Sibiloi, Meru, and Tsavo NP, Kenya; Kalahari-Gemsbok NP, Central Kalahari GR, Botswana; Etosha NP, Namibia.

ECOLOGY   Adapted for waterless wastelands uninhabitable for most large mammals, *Oryx gazella* is equally at home on sandy and stony plains and alkaline flats. It ranges over high sand dunes and climbs mountains to visit springs and salt licks. Depending on availability of forage and water (free or stored), the oryx ranges widely and nomadically or stays put in home ranges no bigger than a sable's or roan's in country accessible to water-dependent ungulates only in the rainy season.

A grazer/browser, it survives on tough, dry grasses when green grass unavailable, supplemented with foliage. Drinks regularly when water available but can get by on water-storing melons, roots, bulbs, and tubers, for which it digs assiduously. Endures extreme heat and desiccation by letting body temperature rise from 99.5° to 113°F (45°C) and using every means of conserving water (see Ecology, Chapter 4), cutting daily need to only 1.4 qt/100 lb (3 l/100 kg) body weight.

ACTIVITY   ○/● Day and night. Under extreme drought conditions, oryxes avoid exertion and direct sunlight, feed at night and very early in the morning, when plants contain the most moisture.

SOCIAL/MATING SYSTEM   (♂ ♀∘♀∘♀∘) (♀∘♀∘♀∘♂ ♂♂♂♂) Highly gregarious but pugnacious, the oryx forms mixed herds with semiexclusive membership, wherein each sex is ranked in a strict dominance hierarchy. Adult males are dominant over all females. Herds are led by a high-ranking cow, but directed and controlled by the alpha bull, who normally brings up the rear. Usually just 1 bull—but up to several in herds of 75 or more—is in breeding condition, recognizable by his behavior and large scrotum. Other males have a small scrotum and behave as submissively as females. The extras are simply bachelor males that continue to be tolerated with females as adults. In such vast, empty wastelands, males separated from their herd might wander indefinitely without finding other oryxes.

Although herds of up to 300 oryxes have been recorded, average group size is only 14 animals. Cows outnumber bulls 2 to 1. Where there is a dependable food supply and/or waterholes, 11 to 28% of the oryxes one sees are single males—most often individuals defending territories. In Botswana's Central Kalahari GR, known territorial males stayed year-round in ranges of 3.9 to 6 mi² (10–16 km²), while females circulated within home ranges averaging 49 mi² (127 km²). Daily ranging for such a supposedly nomadic animal was amazingly limited: females 1 mi (1.6 km) and bulls 0.6 mi (1 km). But in Serengeti NP a nomadic herd followed for a day covered 6.5 miles.

REPRODUCTION   Perennial breeding, although associated cows often calve within a period of several months. Gestation 8.5 months. Females as young as 2 years conceive, re-entering estrus a few weeks after calving. Males mature at 5 years.

OFFSPRING AND PARENTAL CARE   Calves hide up to 6 weeks, although crèches of younger calves are not uncommon and may be left unguarded for extended periods. Juveniles nurse perhaps 3 times in a 24-hour day. Peer groups of young persist for a year or longer.

PREDATORS   Lions and spotted hyenas regularly prey on oryxes, which surprisingly seldom succeed or even try to defend themselves, but rely on flight to avoid predators. They are strong and enduring runners. Leopards must occasionally take calves.

Table 10.4. *DIFFERENCES IN ORYX BEHAVIOR*
Expect to see and hear ➤ *Usual context and meaning*

Advertising Territory or Dominance

Adult ♂ displaying dominance to other ♂♂ and checking ♀♀ in a herd. ➤ The alpha herd bull or a territorial ♂ who joins a herd that has entered his territory.

Lone bull standing or patrolling in erect posture. ➤ Probably advertising territorial status.

Herding and chasing ♀♀ and ♂♂, often combined with grunting. ➤ Controlling herd direction and keeping members together.

Aggression

High-horn threat ± slow ducking motion. ➤ Strong threat to deliver downward blow.

Low-horn threat. ➤ Horn tips point at opponent: threat to rush and stab.

Submission

Head-low/chin-out posture ± head-throwing or head turned away. Chin is lifted abruptly in head-throwing motion, bringing horns to back. May carry over into scratching back with horn tips.

Moving away in knock-kneed or creeping walk. Combined with head-low/chin-out posture in display of extreme submission.

Courtship

♂ attempts to rest chin on ♀'s rump during mating march. ➤ Mounting-intention movement.

Response to Predators

Style-trotting. ➤ Particularly exaggerated in oryx: neck drawn to vertical with head swinging from side to side.

Chapter 11

HARTEBEEST TRIBE
Alcelaphini

Common hartebeest, *Alcelaphus buselaphus*
Lichtenstein's hartebeest, *A. lichtensteinii*
Topi, tsessebe, tiang, *Damaliscus lunatus*
Blesbok/bontebok, *D. dorcas*
Hirola, Hunter's antelope, *D. hunteri*[en]
Common wildebeest or gnu, *Connochaetes taurinus*
Black wildebeest or white-tailed gnu, *C. gnou*[v]

WHAT THEY ARE   Large and medium-sized antelopes of the savannas and plains, with high shoulders, long, thin legs, and elongated heads. Sexes much alike, except females have weaker horns and males turn darker. *Tail:* hock-length with bottle-brush tuft (*Damaliscus* and *Alcelaphus*), or horselike, reaching ground (wildebeests). *Color:* typically conspicuous and distinctive: dark with reverse countershading (darker below, lighter above) and/or contrasting markings; newborns of all species and adult Coke's hartebeest preserve ancestral tan color. *Scent glands:* preorbital glands developed in both sexes; hoof glands in forefeet only. *Teats:* 2.

SOCIAL/MATING SYSTEM

(♂♀∘♀∘♀∘) (♂♂♂)   The conventional resident/dispersed pattern: small and medium female herds accompanied by 1 territorial male and segregated bachelor herds.

(♂♀∘♀∘♂/♀∘♂♀♀)   Migratory pattern: aggregations of all classes.

(♂♂♂/♂♂♂)   Territorial arena or lek: topi only. All alcelaphines are sociable, territorial, and resident where and when conditions permit. As resident populations congregate in mixed herds on green pastures in the dry season, in the same pattern that distinguishes migratory/nomadic populations, the two grouping patterns are interchangeable.

Resident female herds are semiclosed associations between females that share the same home range, and a stable rank order is maintained. Territorial bulls enforce segregation of adolescent and older males, which live in bachelor herds in least desirable habitat on the fringes of the territorial network. However, bachelors manage to blend into aggregations, aided by resemblance to females. Away from their properties, territorial males revert to bachelor status; hence migrating animals intermingle freely. There is no rank order in aggregations and usually no lasting associations between individuals other than mothers and calves. Nevertheless, subgroupings of animals of the same sex, age, and reproductive status are usually discernible, stemming from the mutual attraction of like individuals.

HOW THEY MOVE   Fleet and enduring runners—especially topi and hartebeest. Also capable of moving long distances at a canter, assisted by their overdeveloped forequarters. Trotting is mainly performed as a display of excitement or alarm. Hartebeest and topi, but not wildebeest, also stot. All alcelaphines kneel when fighting and to rub their faces and horns in mud.

HOW THEY COMMUNICATE   Sight 1, scent 1, sound 1 to 2.

Table 11.1. *HARTEBEEST TRIBE BEHAVIOR GUIDE*
Expect to see and hear ➤ *Usual context and meaning*

Territorial Advertising

 Adult ♂ standing or lying apart from herd. ➤ Advertises presence of a territorial ♂, who is less conspicuous in a herd because of minimal gender differences.

 Standing in erect posture. ➤ Characteristic stance of territorial ♂ advertising status and keeping lookout. (Note: resembles the alert posture assumed by all classes.)

 Rocking canter. ➤ The way territorial ♂ ♂ meet approaching ♂ ♂ and ♀ ♀.

Defecation on stamping ground or latrine, usually preceded by pawing, sometimes by urinating. ➤ Bare patches strewn with dung are places where territorial ♂ ♂ regularly defecate, soil-horn, and rest.

Challenge rituals between territorial ♂ ♂. ➤ Daily repeated interactions between neighboring property owners, which serve to ratify and test the owners' territorial fitness.

Herding and chasing ♀ ♀ and bachelor ♂ ♂.

VOCAL ACCOMPANIMENT
Stimulated by movements of other ♂ ♂ or ♀ ♀, especially common during herding activity.

Croaking. ➤ Common wildebeest.

Quacking. ➤ Topi, blesbok, hartebeest.

Hiccoughing. ➤ Black wildebeest.

Alarm snorts. ➤ Deeper, louder snorts may also serve to announce territorial ♂'s presence.

Self-advertising

Actions also performed by nonterritorial individuals of both sexes, but most frequently and vigorously by territorial ♂ ♂.

Weaving: marking grass stems with preorbital glands. ➤ Topi, blesbok, hartebeests (see topi account).

Tree- and grass-horning ± rubbing preorbital glands. ➤ Advertises aggressive mood; performed by all adult ♂ ♂ and occasionally by ♀ ♀. See common wildebeest account.

Soil-horning ± mud-packing, head-shaking, and sideswiping or shoulder-wiping. ➤ Rubbing face and horns in and plowing dry or muddy soil, often in regularly used pits, from kneeling position. Typically precedes or follows defecation.

Rolling, usually after kneeling and soil-horning. ➤ Wildebeests only.

Aggression

CHALLENGE RITUALS BETWEEN ADULT MALES

The whole repertoire of aggressive, advertising, contact, and displacement behaviors is performed during challenge rituals. But the number, order, rate, and intensity of the actions are infinitely variable. Relatively few encounters lead to sparring or fights.

Approach and withdrawal, typically in grazing attitude (see Fig. 11.4).

Broadside stance in erect posture, ± nodding, head-casting, etc. (see Fig. 11.2). ➤ The primary dominance display in the tribe, varying slightly from species to species. Adversaries normally stand parallel, head-to-tail during aggressive interactions.

Angle-horn threat. ➤ Made while standing parallel, head-to-tail; signals intention to turn and face adversary.

Medial-horn threat, from kneeling (combat) position.

Low-horn threat (see Fig. 11.1 and 11.5).

Head-low posture. ➤ Defensive threat; response of inferior to intimidation (see Fig. 11.1).

OTHER ACTIONS ASSOCIATED WITH AGGRESSIVE INTERACTIONS

Rhythmic nodding. ➤ Symbolic butting.

Head-shaking. ➤ Levering and twisting movements of fighting.

Ground-horning. ➤ Redirected aggression. The message:"This is what I'd like to do to you."

Dropping to knees, rushing. ➤ Real or feinted attack.

Sideswiping ± tail-sweeping. ➤ Threat to hook and/or displacement fly-shooing.

Shoulder-wiping. ➤ By hartebeest and topi in particular.

Aggression *continued*

Cavorting: including running, jumping, bucking, spinning, head-shaking, style-trotting, tail-lashing, etc. ➤ Expresses defiance and excited, highly aggressive (or playful) state.

Displacement activities.

Submission

Turning away from approaching individual. ➤ Accepting dominance of supplanting individual.

Passing behind an individual displaying dominance. ➤ Declining challenge.

Head-in display of topi and hartebeest. ➤ Submissive response to a superior's approach or dominance displays.

Lying-out. ➤ Extreme form of submission.

Flight. ➤ Response of inferior or defeated rival to pursuit.

Displacement Activities

Scratching with hind feet, scratching back with horn tips, scraping with incisors.

Grazing. ➤ Prominent in challenge ritual, especially approach and withdrawal stage and while 2 ♂ ♂ stand parallel, head-to-tail (see Fig 11.4).

Sideswiping ± tail-swishing. ➤ Fly-shooing movement that may double as threat to hook opponent.

Alarm signals (alert posture, snorting, stamping) during pauses in challenge ritual. ➤ Adversaries scan surroundings for lurking predators, act alarmed without obvious cause.

Sociable Behavior

Touching/sniffing noses. ➤ Typical meeting behavior, prelude to friendly or aggressive interactions.

Neck-sliding. ➤ Hartebeest challenge ritual.

Rubbing face on partner's rump or shoulder. ➤ Wildebeest challenge ritual. Also ♀ – ♀ interactions (see wildebeest accounts).

♂-♂ urine-testing. ➤ See wildebeest challenge ritual.

Courtship

MALE BEHAVIOR

Lowstretch with ears cocked or lowered and tail out. ➤ Posture of ♂ approaching and while following ♀ in mating march.

Courtship *continued*

Urine-testing. ➤ Wildebeests only. Hartebeests and topi/blesbok show no interest in urine.

Following in erect posture while high-stepping; with ears lowered, tail raised. ➤ Topi, hartebeest.

Sniffing ♀'s rump.

Resting chin on ♀'s rump. ➤ Wildebeest.

Rubbing preorbital glands on ♀'s rump. ➤ Common wildebeest.

VOCAL ACCOMPANIMENT

Strangled bleat (topi, hartebeest), grunt (blesbok), or drawn-out bawl (common wildebeest).

FEMALE BEHAVIOR

Responsive urination. ➤ Prompted by ♂ approaching in lowstretch (wildebeests only).

Defensive threats, bolting and rapid tail-swishing, skittish or coquettish behavior, courtship circling. ➤ Evading contact and mounting attempts.

Lying prone like hiding calf. ➤ Unreceptive ♀ sexually harassed.

Holding tail out and deflected while standing in copulatory attitude (head up or down, ears back). ➤ Readiness to mate.

Mother and Offspring

Includes both hider and follower calves. ➤ See Offspring and Parental Care, Chapter 4 and Mother and Offspring, Table 4.2. See wildebeest account for description of follower-calf system.

Contact calls between mother and calf: quacking, mooing. ➤ Soft calls when close, loud when separated. Calf and mother recognize one another's calls.

Play

Chasing, style trotting, stotting, cavorting, sparring. ➤ Seen most often in early morning, initiated by calves.

Response to Predators

Alert posture, stamping, alarm snorting, other nervous behaviors. ➤ Response to perceived danger, chronically displayed by mothers of young calves.

Stotting. ➤ All species but wildebeests.

Style-trotting. ➤ All species.

Alarm-snorting. ➤ Loudest and deepest in blue wildebeest, thinnest and highest in hartebeest.

HARTEBEEST, *Alcelaphus buselaphus*

Figure 11.1. Red hartebeest bulls in challenge ritual. Bull on knees is soil-horning.

SUBSPECIES OF EAST AND SOUTHERN AFRICA
Coke's hartebeest or kongoni, *A. b. cokei* (Kenya, Tanzania)
Jackson's hartebeest, *A. b. jacksoni* (Uganda)
Lelwel hartebeest, *A. b. lelwel* (Uganda, west of Nile)
Red hartebeest, *A b. caama* (Botswana, Namibia, South Africa)

WHAT IT IS   A tall, tan or reddish antelope with bracket-shaped horns and elongated head, high shoulders and sloping back. Pronounced differences among subspecies in color and markings, horn shape, and size. From ♂ kongoni 312 lb (142 kg), 47 in (117 cm) up to ♂ western hartebeest (*A. b. tora*) 500 lb (228 kg), 57 in (143 cm). ♀ c. 12% lighter and slightly shorter than ♂. *Horns:* shape varies from kongoni's relatively simple brackets to recurved horns of lelwel and red hartebeests, from 12 in to (record) 26.75 in (30–67 cm). *Coat:* smooth, glossy. *Color:* varying from lion-toned kongoni, with lighter rump and almost no dark markings, to the gaudy red hartebeest, with white rump patch and belly, brown-black thighs and leg fronts, and black nose and forehead set off by white brow and lips. Males darker with more pronounced markings than females; calves pale tan without markings (barely distinguishable from topi calves by a line of longer hair between the eyes).

WHERE IT LIVES   Once the widest-ranging African antelope, hartebeests ranged from the Mediterranean to the Cape, and from Senegal to Somalia. Greatly reduced in numbers and range, but some 10 different populations distinctive enough to be considered different races still survive south of the Sahara. Lichtenstein's hartebeest, which occurs in the *Miombo* Woodland Zone, is considered a separate species.

GOOD PLACES TO SEE IT   Nairobi and Tsavo NP, Masai Mara NR, Kenya; Serengeti NP, Tanzania; Kidepo Valley NP, Uganda; Botswana game reserves and parks. Lichtenstein's hartebeest: Selous GR, Tanzania; Kafue NP, Zambia.

ECOLOGY   More tolerant of woods and high grass than other alcelaphines, hartebeests prefer the edge to the middle of open plains. Coke's hartebeest is closely associated with medium-length bush grassland growing on black-cotton soil dominated by red-oat grass and gall acacias. Most populations find the grasses they need at different seasons without moving long distances, but in Kalahari *sandveld* of Botswana hartebeests are nearly as mobile as wildebeests, tracking thunderstorms to find green pastures.

Among the purest grazers, hartebeests feed selectively in medium-height grassland; less water-dependent than other alcelaphines, but have to drink (or eat melons and tubers) when fodder is dry.

ACTIVITY   ○/●   Day and night, with usual peaks early and late in day.

SOCIAL/MATING SYSTEM   In Nairobi NP, when the kongoni reigned as dominant herbivore, female herds typically numbered from 6 to 15 members and resided within ranges of 896 to 1344 acres (370–550 ha), which overlapped 20 to 30 territories (average 77 acres [31 ha]). A herd spent from a few hours to a few weeks in any given territory. At low density in patchy habitat, cows have been known to stay indefinitely in a single large territory.

Competition for prime real estate is rigorous, especially at high density. Choice locations offer preferred grazing at all seasons, firm footing during the rains, and nearby water. Only prime bulls (4–7.5 years) can win central territories; these are passed on unchanged to successive occupants. A territory owner that leaves for even a few hours to drink and socialize risks finding his place taken when he returns. Bulls past their prime end up in marginal habitat, where they may control an expansive but empty estate.

Males often accompany their mothers until subadult (2.5 years) before joining bachelor herds. Three- to four-year-olds are mature enough to compete for territories—provided they have achieved high rank among their peers. Bachelor herds, numbering up to 35 members, may include males of 1 year up to old bulls and off-duty territorial males.

REPRODUCTION   Year-round with 1 or 2 extended peaks in the dry season(s). Females conceive as 2-year-olds; gestation 8 months; minimum interval between births 9 to 10 months. Mothers are followed by up to 3 offspring. Southern African hartebeests calve annually late in the dry season.

OFFSPRING AND MATERNAL CARE   Calves lie-out c. 2 weeks before joining mother's herd. Subadult male offspring hide behind mothers when harassed by a territorial bull; the mother will fight to protect son or leave the territory if the bull persists.

PREDATORS   Spotted hyena, lion, and leopard. Jackals occasionally prey on hidden calves.

Table 11.2. *DIFFERENCES IN HARTEBEEST BEHAVIOR*
Expect to see and hear ➤ *Usual context and meaning*

Territorial advertising

Territorial ♂ ♂ consistently stay c. 90 yd away from ♀ herds (in Nairobi NP).

Standing in erect posture on mound. ➤ Like topi, but less consistently.

Marking grass stems with preorbital glands. ➤ Uncommon compared to topi.

Soil-horning ± mud-packing, head-shaking, and shoulder-wiping; leaving black streaks on Coke's and Lichtenstein's pelts. ➤ Shoulder-wiping, usually performed from kneeling position after soil-horning, deposits preorbital-gland secretion (a nonstaining clear oil in other races).

Aggression

Long chases after fights. Look for open mouth. ➤ Significance of open mouth puzzling because hartebeests are notably long-winded.

Sociable Behavior

Neck-sliding. ♂ ♂ appear to sniff or nibble each other's head and neck. ➤ Greeting at beginning of challenge ritual.

TOPI/TSESSEBE, *Damaliscus lunatus*

Figure 11.2. Territorial tsessebes standing parallel, head-to-tail, in erect posture and head-casting during challenge ritual.

SUBSPECIES OF EAST, CENTRAL, AND SOUTHERN AFRICA
Topi, *D. l. topi* (SE Kenya)
D. l. jimela (East Africa, SW Kenya, NW Tanzania, NE Rwanda, eastern Zaire)
Tiang, *D. l. tiang* (southern Sudan to Lake Turkana, northern Kenya)
Tsessebe, *D. l. lunatus*[v] (SE Zaire to South Africa)

WHAT IT IS   A plains antelope like a smaller, darker hartebeest without the elongated forehead, with more ordinary-looking horns. Built for speed: lean body, clean-limbed. ♂ wt 286 lb (130 kg), ht 46 in (115 cm); ♀ wt 238 lb (108 kg), ht 45 in (113 cm). *Head*: long, narrow muzzle. *Horns*: male 12 to 24 in (30–60 cm); female 12 to 20 in (30–50 cm). Strongly ridged, simplest (new-moon-shaped), shortest, and thinnest in the tsessebe; thicker, shapelier, longer in other races. *Coat*: smooth, glossy. *Color*: tan to reddish brown with purple blotches on upper limbs, intensifying in hue from south to north and west to east, accentuated by reverse countershading (lighter above/darker below). Young calves tawny, without markings.

WHERE IT LIVES   Very extensive but patchy distribution in Northern and Southern Savanna and adjacent arid zones. Numbers and habitat greatly reduced by human hunting and habitat destruction although populations of

Serengeti and Southern Sudan ecosystems still abundant. The tsessebe is separated from the rest by the *Miombo* Woodland Zone.

GOOD PLACES TO SEE IT Akagera NP, Rwanda; Queen Elizabeth NP, Uganda; Masai Mara NR, Kenya; Serengeti NP, Tanzania; Moremi GR, Botswana; Kazuma Pan NP, Zimbabwe; Kruger NP, South Africa.

ECOLOGY Favors medium-length grasslands, ranging from vast treeless floodplains where the largest aggregations occur, to fields surrounded by open woodland. Found occasionally in rolling uplands below 5000 ft (1500 m). With long, narrow muzzle and mobile lips adapted for selective grazing, the topi harvests the greenest, tenderest growth, avoiding mature blades and stems; it has an advantage in pastures with old and new growth intermixed, but is less efficient than a bulk grazer on short pasture. Topis on green grass can go without drinking but drink every day or two when grass is dry. Most abundant where green grass is available the whole year, as on floodplains bordering rivers, lakes, and swamps. Where wet- and dry-season pastures are many miles apart, populations are migratory.

ACTIVITY O/● Day and night. A long rest period between morning and afternoon feeding peaks, broken by intervals of uncoordinated grazing. In early morning, spirited tournaments are frequent in bachelor herds.

SOCIAL/MATING SYSTEM Practically every form of territorial, sociable mating system known in antelopes is deployed by the topi/tsessebe under the appropriate environmental conditions.

The basic resident pattern, with small herds living in traditional home ranges contained in an established territorial network, prevails among resident populations in patchy habitat. Herds of 2 to 10 females and young of the year; some herds remain semipermanently on single territories of 124 to 988 acres (50–400 ha) that produce adequate amounts of the grasses preferred at different seasons.

The migratory pattern, adapted to large open plains where topis concentrate sometimes in thousands, allows a subpopulation to move together en masse. Whenever an aggregation settles down, even for a few hours, adult males establish small temporary territories and fragment the concentration into female and bachelor herds. Male competition is more intense than in resident populations, especially during the mating season.

At high density (122 topis/mi^2 [47/km^2]), breeding arenas or leks are established in some populations at certain traditional "hot spots" where lots of females regularly pass by, rest, or graze. On one large arena, 100 males were counted, spaced 100 to 250 yd on the outer fringes to as little as

25 yd near the center. Central males serviced nearly all the females from the large aggregation that circulated outside the lek, entering the arena alone or in small groups as they came into heat. A recent study indicates that central males are in fact the biggest, fittest males in the population, whereas the majority of arena males are actually smaller and perhaps unfit to claim either conventional or lek territories.

Resident herds of topi consist largely of related females which treat outsiders with hostility. When the resident bull is absent, cows sometimes give territorial displays to discourage trespassers. No rank order or regular association between females has been discerned in aggregations.

Male calves join bachelor herds between 8 and 16 months. Often yearling females also leave home and spend time in bachelor herds until bred in their second year.

REPRODUCTION   Annual in most regions, calving at the end of the dry season, but near the equator some populations have two peaks, and the Kenya *D. l. topi* north of the Tana River breeds year-round. Well-nourished females conceive at 16 months and males mature in third year. Gestation 8 months.

OFFSPRING AND MATERNAL CARE   Typical hider system in dispersed, resident pattern, but in aggregations calves that would normally hide for 3 weeks stay with the aggregation by day, go off to spend the night in hiding soon after dark. Calves past hiding stage associate in crèches. Weaning by 6 months.

PREDATORS   All the large carnivores, and jackals prey on newborns. But easier-to-catch game (wildebeest, zebra, warthog, etc.) are preferred prey when available. Nevertheless, enterprising spotted hyenas in the Masai-Mara NR sometimes catch lone territorial topis napping at midday.

Table 11.3. *DIFFERENCES IN TOPI BEHAVIOR*
Expect to see and hear ➤ Usual context and meaning

Maintenance Activities

Dozing attitude, with mouth resting on ground. ➤ Posture peculiar to topi.

Standing and dozing with eyes closed, while nodding. ➤ Seen regularly in groups during rest periods (especially ♂ ♂); significance unknown.

Territorial Advertising

Standing in erect posture. ➤ Topis and termite mounds go together. Territorial and also nonterritorial topis regularly stand on mounds.

Territorial Advertising *continued*

Rocking canter. ➤ Territorial ♂ coming to meet approaching topis.

High-stepping in erect posture, with ears lowered and tail out. ➤ Herding and courtship display made conspicuous by contrasting color patterns of legs. A territorial display occasionally mimicked by ♀ ♀.

Self-advertising

Actions performed by nonterritorial individuals of both sexes, but most frequently and vigorously by territorial ♂ ♂.

Weaving: marking grass stems with preorbital glands. ➤ Topi carefully inserts grass stem in orifice, wiggles its head to coat stem with gel-like secretion, then uses stalk to anoint horns and forehead with weaving motions. In high grass, topi prepares site by biting a stem in two.

Soil-horning, ± mud-packing, head-shaking, and sideswiping. ➤ After rain, topis seek muddy spots, rub their faces and then horn-plow the mud, followed by vigorous head-shaking and mud-slinging, ending by rubbing horns on chest and shoulders. Mudpack makes horns look more impressive.

Aggression

CHALLENGE RITUALS BETWEEN TERRITORIAL MALES

Head-casting during mutual display in erect posture (see Fig. 11.2). ➤ Pronounced nodding; exaggerated in tsessebe.

Other steps: touching/sniffing noses; other dominance and threat displays; soil-horning; pawing and defecating; sideswiping; cavorting; and confronting on knees ± horn contact. Encounters usually occur at the common border.

Courtship

Standing broadside or approaching in erect posture with high stepping. ➤ Posture of territorial ♂ as ♀ approaches.

♂ sniffs ♀'s vulva, but no urination or urine-testing follows.

Standing stiffly behind ♀ in erect posture with tail raised. ➤ Prelude to mounting.

BLESBOK/BONTEBOK, *Damaliscus dorcas*

Figure 11.3. Bontebok territorial male approaching female in lowstretch posture.

SUBSPECIES
Blesbok, *D. d. phillipsi* (the common race)
Bontebok, *D. d. dorcas*[en] (the isolated Cape Province population)

WHAT IT IS   A small, gaudier version of a tsessebe, with relatively level back and equally developed limbs. ♂ wt 143-176 lb (65-80 kg), ht 34-40 in (85-100 cm); ♀ wt 121-154 lb (55-70 kg), ht slightly shorter. *Horns:* simple S-shape, 14 to 15 in (35-50 cm); 10% bigger in male. *Color:* glossy dark red-brown with white blaze, belly, and lower limbs; bontebok has white rump and upper tail, glossier coat, with purple-black blotches on upper limbs and sides; blesbok's facial blaze is bisected by a brown band; newborns tan with dark blaze.

WHERE IT LIVES   One of 4 migratory herbivores that formerly ranged the South African *highveld* in uncounted thousands, the blesbok has recovered from near-extinction in the last century. Reintroduced on farms throughout and beyond its former range, but fences keep them divided into small, inbred units. The bontebok lives on the coastal plain (*strandveld*) of southwestern Cape Province. Isolated from the *highveld* for thousands of years by a belt of subdesert Karroo, it developed the distinctive differences noted above.

GOOD PLACES TO SEE IT   Bontebok NP (200-250 bonteboks). Blesbok: estimated population in hundreds of thousands, but only 2700 in nature reserves, especially Willem Pretorius GR and Tussen-die-Riviere Game Farm, Orange Free State, and Suikerbosrand NR, Transvaal, South Africa.

ECOLOGY   A selective grazer. More water-dependent and less efficient on short grass than springbok or black wildebeest, blesbok spent wet season on the medium-height *sweetveld*, went east into the taller, wetter *sourveld* during dry season where it could graze selectively more efficiently than the wildebeest. But to stay in good condition, it needed new growth stimulated by wildfires.

ACTIVITY   ○ (●?) Female bonteboks spend c. ⅔ of day feeding, ⅓ ruminating and resting, only 5% in other activities. Territorial males spend less time feeding and more time (13%) in other activities, mainly territorial and sexual in nature.

SOCIAL/MATING SYSTEM   (♂♀○♀○♀○) (♂♂♂) Fenced range imposes the resident pattern on existing blesboks. The population of 250 bonteboks living in the 11 mi² (28 km²) Bontebok NP is representative. When studied in the 1970s, the whole area was divided into territories of 25 to 99 acres (10–40 ha) owned by 25 to 30 bulls. The 87 adult females lived in semi-exclusive herds averaging only 3 cows and 1.5 calves (range 2–9). Most herds' home ranges included 2 to 3 territories, although territorial males, which consistently initiate and lead herd movements and keep the members together, did their best to keep a herd from leaving. Some herds actually spent over a year within a single territory.

Bachelor males and many yearling females associated in one large herd that was allowed to roam through the territories, as the owners only bothered to defend an activity zone of c. 175 yd radius representing the part currently in use. As many of the bachelors were mature males, small territories and frequent turnovers would be expected; but on the contrary, territorial tenure averaged nearly 2 years and one bull held the same property continuously for 5 years! To be worth defending year-round, territories have to incorporate the full range of preferred grassland types, and the advantages of ownership are so decisive that bachelors are only ready to try their luck at 5 years of age.

(♂♀♀○♂○♀♂♂) Most of the blesboks that ranged the unfenced *highveld* probably lived in large mobile aggregations like those still seen in high-density topi populations. A population of several hundreds on a large ranch, which does form mobile aggregations, illustrates the remarkable difference between resource-based territories in a resident population and temporary breeding territories in a migratory or nomadic population. Territories average only 5.7 acres (2.3 ha), and the density of territorial bulls during the rut is 417/mi² (169/km²), spaced 77 yd apart. Territorial behavior declines after the rut and all but disappears in the winter.

REPRODUCTION   Annually, calving season in early summer (Nov.–Dec.) after 8-month gestation. Well-fed females breed as yearlings; males mature at 3.

OFFSPRING AND MATERNAL CARE   The blesbok/bontebok has abandoned the hider-calf strategy. Females calve in small herds or in maternity bands in aggregations. Calves accompany mothers from the start; nursing calves are not licked to stimulate elimination. But blesboks are less precocious than wildebeests, needing more time to stand, to locate the udder, and to become strong, and they tend to lag behind rather than run beside their mothers.

PREDATORS   None bigger than a jackal, except in reserves where a few leopards and caracals may live.

Table 11.4. *DIFFERENCES IN BLESBOK BEHAVIOR*
Expect to see and hear ➤ *Usual context and meaning*

Territorial Advertising

Lowstretch, with tail curled up at high intensity (see Fig. 11.3). ➤ Herding and displaying to ♀ ♀.

Aggression

CHALLENGE RITUALS BETWEEN TERRITORIAL MALES

Looking away during approach (head-flagging); standing parallel head-to-tail, sniffing rumps—prompting tail-swishing and head-shaking; head-dipping; defecating; urinating; soil-horning; preorbital-gland weaving; and cavorting. ➤ Encounters average 6.5 min., usually begin with one ♂ invading a neighbor's territory. Some 30 different behaviors may be performed.

Standing facing or broadside in erect posture, with ears outspread. ➤ While watching territorial neighbor approach.

Submission

Head-low posture with tail curled up. ➤ Approaching with tail curled is response of intimidated blesbok to displaying ♂.

Courtship

Lowstretch ± tail curled up (see Fig. 11.3). ➤ Posture of territorial ♂ approaching ♀.

♂ sniffs ♀'s vulva. ♀ stands with tail out and ears back, then moves quickly away, wagging tail. ➤ Olfactory check of ♀'s reproductive status.

COMMON WILDEBEEST, *Connochaetes taurinus*

Figure 11.4. Displacement grazing during challenge ritual between territorial *C. t. mearnsi* bulls.

SUBSPECIES
Blue wildebeest or brindled gnu, *C. t. taurinus* (central and southern Africa)
Eastern white-bearded wildebeest, *C. t. albojubatus*
  (Kenya, Tanzania east of Gregory Rift Valley)
Western white-bearded wildebeest, *C. t. mearnsi*
  (Kenya, Tanzania west of Rift Valley)
Johnston's or Nyassa wildebeest, *C. t. johnstoni*
  (southern Tanzania, Mozambique to Zambezi River)
Cookson's wildebeest, *C. t. cooksoni* (Luangwa Valley, Zambia)

WHAT IT IS   A large, bearded antelope of the acacia savanna and short-grass plains. Deep-chested and short-necked, high shoulders and thin legs. ♂ wt 440–600 lb (200–274 kg), ht 50–58 in (125–145 cm); ♀ wt 370–516 lb (168–233 kg), ht 46–57 in (115–142 cm). Lower numbers are average for *C. t. mearnsi*, the smallest race. *Head:* broad, blunt muzzle. *Horns:* cowlike, smooth, with enlarged boss, wider and much thicker in male; 22 to 35 in (55–80 cm) in male; 18 to 25 in (45–63 cm) in female. *Coat:* short and glossy with vertical stripes of longer hair; a beard and lax or upstanding mane. *Color:* varies with subspecies, gender (males darker), season, and individually; ranging from slate gray to dark brown; lighter above/darker below; black face, mane, tail, and stripes, beard black (except white-bearded races).

WHERE IT LIVES   Eastern Africa from southern Kenya to the Orange River in South Africa, and from Mozambique to Namibia and southern Angola. Huge populations that once thronged the short-grass plains and bordering acacia savannas have dwindled drastically in range and numbers, except for the wildebeest of the Serengeti ecosystem, which may be as numerous (at 1.5 million) and nearly as wide-ranging as ever.

GOOD PLACES TO SEE IT   Most parks and reserves with suitable habitat within its range have small wildebeest populations, but the western white-bearded population, on view in Serengeti NP, Ngorongoro Conservation Area, and the Masai Mara GR, is by far the most impressive.

ECOLOGY   Wildebeests are equipped to take big bites of short green grass. A blunt muzzle and wide incisor row that prevent feeding selectively, combined with large body size demanding a bulk diet, are adaptations for harvesting swards of short green grass, where thousands of animals grazing close together can eat their fill. Short grasslands of this type occur on alkaline and volcanic soils unsuited for deep-rooted grasses. Grazing, trampling, and manuring by hordes of plains game stimulate new growth—as long as the ground holds moisture. Like other migratory populations, Serengeti wildebeests thrive on these grasslands during the rainy season, and withdraw to longer grasslands in areas of higher rainfall and permanent water during the dry season. Manmade wildfires and occasional thunderstorms often provide green pastures when most needed. Grasslands bordering alkaline lakes and pans, where colonial and annual grasses carpet the emerging ground, are also particularly favorable dry-season pastures.

A pure grazer which has to drink every day or 2 in the dry season, wildebeests are then limited to pastures within 10 to 15 mi (16–24 km) of water.

ACTIVITY   ○/● Day and night. Wildebeests observed in Namibia's Etosha NP spent ⅓ of 24-hour day grazing, c. ½ the time resting (including rumination). The balance was spent moving (12%) and in social interactions (1–1.5%). They grazed as much on moonlight nights as by day, but moved less. At night wildebeests bed down in columns which give individuals the security of being in a group while allowing everyone to run away without interference in emergencies.

SOCIAL/MATING SYSTEM

(♂♀○♀○♀○) (♂♂♂) Wherever conditions permit, wildebeests live in the resident pattern, in semiexclusive female herds typically averaging 8 cows, calves, and yearlings (range 2–25+), contained in an established network of territorial males. Nonbreeding males live in bachelor herds on the fringes in substandard habitat. Ngorongoro Crater's pastures are so productive in the growing season that 7 acres (2.8 ha) support a herd and as many as 3 resident territorial bulls.

(♂♀○♀○♂○) (♂○♀♂♀♂) The resident/dispersed pattern changes into the migratory/aggregated pattern when grass and water both dry up. If green pastures are available within commuting distance, resident herds and territorial bulls congregate on them by day and return home in the evening. But as drought deepens, more and more herds remain concentrated on available green pastures and soon lose their separate identities, while most territorial males remain in the bachelor contingent that intermingles with females and young in the same aggregations. Some bulls establish temporary territories within the aggregations.

The Serengeti population remains migratory and nomadic year-round. Up to 100,000 wildebeests concentrate within an area of 100 mi^2 (259 km^2). Such dense packing compresses territorial spacing to as little as 15 yd. Samples during the migration and rut showed that one square mile contained as many as 700 actively territorial bulls (270/km^2)! Yet no more than half the adult males in the population are territorial at one time even during the rut.

REPRODUCTION   The wildebeest's follower-calf system is tailored to its particular lifestyle. To stay mobile in aggregations on short grasslands where there is no place to hide, cows have to remain fully mobile, without providing a steady supply of calves to sustain hordes of predators. The wildebeest's solution, unique in the bovid family, is to produce 90% of their calves during a 3-week peak early in the rains; and each calf accompanies and depends solely on its mother for survival from the moment it can stand. Most females calve first at 3 years, after 8 to 8.5 month gestation. Males mature in their fourth year, but most need another year to become fully competitive.

THE SERENGETI RUT   The rut of this last great population is one of the world's most spectacular animal happenings. The coincidence of the rut with the migration off the plains intensifies the competition of 250,000 bulls to service 750,000 cows during a three-week peak. The noise made by thousands of bulls chorusing like so many giant frogs, the herding, chasing, fighting, and mating are indescribable. Needless to say, the groups of females each bull labors to collect and hold on his postage-stamp property—0.8 acre (0.33 ha)—are merely temporary. So are the territories: most bulls move on as soon as the stream of passersby thins out.

Late in the dry season, territorial behavior diminishes almost to the vanishing point.

OFFSPRING AND MATERNAL CARE   Cows like company while calving, whether in a small herd or on temporary calving grounds in migratory populations, where dozens of offspring are produced every morning during the calving peak. Probably the most precocious of all ungulates, wildebeest calves can stand and run in as little as 3 minutes (average 7 min.), within 2 days keep pace with a running herd. Maybe the most important advantage of a short calving season is to glut predators, but it also assures cover for newborns in maternity bands: older calves help keep predators from spotting first-day calves, giving them time to gain strength and become firmly imprinted on their mothers. Spotted hyenas and all the other large carnivores manage to kill many calves, but the more calves present, the better their chances: 4 of 5 calves born in aggregations survive the first month, compared to 1 of 2 born in small herds. Probably to allow more time for calves to gain strength before darkness brings increased danger, daily calving begins at dawn and ends by midday.

PREDATORS   Common wildebeest is the preferred prey of lions, but the chief wildebeest predator is the spotted hyena, which kills both fit and unfit adults and more calves than all other predators put together. Other large cats and the wild dog rarely take wildebeests bigger than yearlings.

Table 11.5. *DIFFERENCES IN WILDEBEEST BEHAVIOR*
Expect to see and hear ➤ *Usual context and meaning*

Territorial Advertising

Standing in erect posture. ➤ On stamping ground, rarely on mounds.

Calling. ➤ Western white-bearded wildebeest most vociferous; gives repetitive croaking call. Other races have a metallic call (sounds like *ga-noo*), rarely repeated over 8 times.

 Defecation on stamping ground, usually preceded by pawing. ➤ ♂ ♂ call attention to the act by first pawing. Bare patches strewn with dung are places where territorial ♂ ♂ and other wildebeests regularly defecate, soil-horn, roll, and rest.

Rolling, usually after kneeling and soil-horning. ➤ Unique to the 2 wildebeests among all antelopes. Bulls are the main performers; they roll onto their backs, almost never completely over.

Self-advertising

Actions performed by nonterritorial individuals of both sexes, but most frequently and vigorously by territorial ♂ ♂.

Tree- and grass-horning, often preceded by rubbing with preorbital glands. ➤ Tree-thrashing by adult ♂ ♂ in large populations damages and destroys many saplings, helps maintain preferred grassland habitat.

Aggression

CHALLENGE RITUALS BETWEEN TERRITORIAL MALES
May be brief or last up to 10 minutes, at low or high intensity, involve just a few or up to 30 different behavior patterns, including all the different self-advertising, marking, and aggressive (but no submissive) displays, social contact, displacement activities, and fighting.

 Angle-horn posture and urine solicitation. ➤ Made while standing parallel, head-to-tail; angle-horn signals intent to turn and face adversary. ♂ – ♂ urine-testing is possibly unique to wildebeests. Maybe they check one another's testosterone levels (higher in territorial than in bachelor ♂ ♂).

Aggression *continued*

Cavorting. ➤ Most spectacular in wildebeest, expressing defiance and excitement.

Displacement Activities

Sideswiping with tail-swishing. ➤ Fly-shooing movement that looks particularly aggressive in wildebeest.

♂ ♂ grazing during confrontation in combat position.

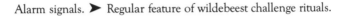

Alarm signals. ➤ Regular feature of wildebeest challenge rituals.

Sociable Behavior

Rubbing face on partner's rump or shoulder, ♂ ♂ during challenge ritual and between ♀ ♀. ➤ Deposits preorbital-gland secretion.

Courtship

Rearing on hind legs before ♀, with erection. ➤ Spectacular but rare copulatory display, performed by excited ♂ before uncooperative estrous ♀.

Vocal accompaniment: ♂ ♂ call at increased tempo during rut. ➤ Really excited bulls also foam at the mouth.

Mother and Offspring

Calves keeping beside mothers while walking or running.

Exchanges of loud mooing when mother and calf separated. ➤ Enables most pairs to reunite (calf and mother recognize one-another's calls).

Young calves resting together while mothers graze. ➤ Mutual attraction results in peer groups.

BLACK WILDEBEEST OR
WHITE-TAILED GNU, *Connochaetes gnou*[V]

Figure 11.5. Yearling black wildebeest responding to low-horn threat of territorial male by kneeling in head-low/chin-out posture.

WHAT IT IS   A small wildebeest specialized for life in the *highveld* and Karroo. Much smaller than the common wildebeest, with level back and equally developed limbs. ♂ wt 308–323 lb (140–157 kg), ht 44–48 in (111–121 cm); ♀ wt 242–268 lb (110–122 kg), ht 42–46 in (106–116 cm). *Head:* short with broad muzzle and protruding hair tufts. *Horns:* shaped like inverted meat hooks and equally dangerous, 21 to 31 in (54–78 cm) in male, with an expanded base shielding the skull; 18 to 24 in (45–60 cm) in female. *Coat:* short and sleek in summer, longer in winter; upstanding mane and luxuriant beard extending onto chest. *Color:* dark brown to black; lighter in summer, tail dirty white.

WHERE IT LIVES   Treeless plains in the temperate grasslands (*highveld*) and arid shrublands (Karroo) of South Africa. The black wildebeest, blesbok, springbok, and quagga once ranged there in the same manner and abundance as the white-bearded wildebeest, topi, Thomson's gazelle, and plains zebra still range the Serengeti ecosystem. Brought to the verge of extinction by hide hunters a century ago, the black wildebeest's numbers increased dramatically in recent decades (from 300 in 1938 to c. 10,000 in the early 1990s), thanks largely to restocking on private farms. Unfortunately, most of the herds are small and inbred, and there is no extensive part of their former range where *highveld* wildlife can live in a natural state.

GOOD PLACES TO SEE IT   Willem Pretorius GR and Tussen-die-Riviere Game Farm in Orange Free State, South Africa.

ECOLOGY   Adapted for the steppelike short-grass plains and dwarf shrublands of the South African temperate zone, with freezing winter and baking summer temperatures. The thick dark coat provides excellent insulation against heat and cold.

Possibly a grazer/browser, as the foliage of karroid bushes and shrubs made up ⅓ the diet of black wildebeests in one Transvaal nature reserve. But whether this is normal is debatable, as free-ranging populations spent the rains in the Karroo, attracted to short green grass, and the dry season in the *highveld*, where grasses predominate.

ACTIVITY   ○/● Day and night. Apparently similar to blue wildebeest, but no detailed data on activity.

SOCIAL/MATING SYSTEM   (♂♀₀♀₀♀₀) (♂♂♂) (♂♀₀♀♂)   Though never studied under natural conditions, all available evidence indicates a social/mating organization very like the common wildebeest's, with the main population migratory and nomadic in very large aggregations. Studies of enclosed populations of several hundred animals in Orange Free State game reserves indicate that territorial black wildebeests are more intolerant than their larger relative: spacing between resident bulls ranges from 0.5 mi (0.8 km) down to about 180 yd. But these are low-density populations—5/mi² (1.9/km²)—where resident bulls hold their properties indefinitely, seldom leaving them except late in the dry season, when some may sojourn a few days in bachelor herds. Presumably territorial spacing would be compressed in large aggregations during the rut.

Female herds in four reserves ranged from 11 to 32 cows and young, the average increasing with density. Resident herds seem more closed and strictly hierarchical than common wildebeest herds and strongly attached to home ranges that averaged 220 acres (89 ha) in Willem Pretorius GR.

The maternal bond lasts a year, until the birth of the next calf, after which yearling males join bachelor herds containing bulls of all ages. Although males mature at 3, they rarely compete for territories before age 4.

REPRODUCTION   Annual calving peak in November or December, 8 to 8.5 months after the rut.

OFFSPRING AND MATERNAL CARE   Calves about as precocious as common wildebeest calves, gaining feet within average of 9 minutes of birth. Grazing and ruminating at 1 month, weaning at 6 to 9 months.

Table 11.6. *DIFFERENCES IN BLACK WILDEBEEST BEHAVIOR*
Expect to see and hear ➤ *Usual context and meaning*

Territorial Advertising

Hiccoughing call. ➤ Sounds like the *hic* in a hiccough, carries up to 1 mile.

Rolling. ➤ Unique to the two wildebeests among all antelopes; bulls the main performers, roll onto backs, hardly ever completely over.

 Herding and chasing ♀♀ and bachelor ♂♂. ➤ Black wildebeests flourish their white tail.

Aggression

CHALLENGE RITUALS BETWEEN TERRITORIAL MALES
See description in Table 11.5.

OTHER ASSOCIATED ACTIONS
Nodding. ➤ Exaggerated as head-throwing in black wildebeest.

Cavorting: tail-lashing makes an audible swishing sound.

Submission

Kneeling in head-low posture ± head turned away, tail out or curled over back, and distress-bawling (see Fig. 11.5). ➤ Intention to lie down in submission.

Lying on side. ➤ The most extreme form of submission in the bovid family; explainable by this species' exceptionally dangerous horns.

Sociable Behavior

 Touching/sniffing noses.

Rubbing face on partner's neck or shoulder. ➤ During challenge ritual and between ♀♀. Deposits preorbital-gland secretion.

♂-♂ urine-testing (seen only during challenge ritual). ➤ As in common wildebeest.

Courtship

FEMALE BEHAVIOR
Bolting and rapid tail-swishing. ➤ Black wildebeest swishes tail across ♂'s face.

Holding tail up. ➤ Readiness to mate.

Chapter 12

IMPALA
Aepyceros melampus
Tribe Aepycerotini

Figure 12.1. Impala territorial male chasing juvenile male out of his female herd.

WHAT IT IS   A one-of-a-kind antelope. No close relatives. Graceful build, long neck, limbs evenly developed and slender. ♂ wt 117–167 lb (53–76 kg), ht 30–36 in (75–92 cm); ♀ wt 88–117 lb (40–53 kg), ht 28–34 in (70–85 cm). *Horns*: male only; S-shaped and wide-set, 18 to 37 in (45–91.7 cm), strongly ridged but comparatively thin; far larger in East African than in southern African populations. *Tail*: hock-length, bushy. *Coat*: smooth and shiny. *Color*: two-toned: tan torso and limbs with a reddish brown saddle; vertical black stripes down tail and thighs, hoof joints and ear tips black; white belly, throat, lips, line over eye, inside ears, and tail underside; sexes and young colored alike. *Scent glands*: on rear feet above hooves, marked by black tuft, and on forehead skin of adult males. *Teats*: 4.

WHERE IT LIVES   Southern Savanna, from central Kenya and Rwanda to northern Natal, west to Namibia and southern Angola. Highly successful antelope, dominant in its chosen habitat.

ECOLOGY   An edge species that prefers open woodland bordering short

127

to medium grassland, well-drained soil with firm footing and no more than moderate slope. Usually lives near water but can go without drinking. These requirements cause impalas to have an irregular and clumped distribution.

A grazer/browser: usually grazes while grasses are growing, browses on foliage, herbs, shoots, and seedpods when grasses are dry. Unusually adaptable, impalas can be primarily a browser in one area and a grazer in another, enabling it to thrive in places where overstocking and burning have caused perennial grasses to be replaced by bushes. In optimum habitat, reaches densities of $554/mi^2$ ($214/km^2$).

GOOD PLACES TO SEE IT   Most national parks and reserves within its range, notably Samburu GR, Nairobi Park, Masai Mara NR, Kenya; Serengeti, Tarangire, and Manyara NP, Tanzania; Hwange NP, Zimbabwe; Chobe NP, Moremi GR, Botswana; Kruger NP, Umfolozi and Mkuzi GR, South Africa.

ACTIVITY   ○ (●) Mainly daytime. Spends night resting in the most open available terrain, except one feeding bout starting before midnight and lasting until 3 or 4 AM. But highly active on moonlight nights during rut. Usual peaks of social activity and herd movements early and late in day.

SOCIAL/MATING SYSTEM   A strictly territorial animal when it counts: only landlords get to reproduce. Yet the very existence of territoriality in this species was long doubted by some researchers, mainly because of the dry-season attenuation or suspension of territorial behavior, when impalas are often found in mixed herds, and a rapid turnover of territorial males during the breeding season. The root cause of the confusion is the impala's naturally clumped distribution, with bachelor males in proximity to female herds at all seasons. In fact, male sexual competition is unusually intense in the impala because female impala herds tend to be large, giving owners of good territories many reproductive opportunities. From 6 to 20 females and young is a minimum average—herds of 50 to 100 are common.

Marking of 443 impalas in Zimbabwe's Sengwa Research Area led to the discovery that females there live in separate, stable clans of 30 to 120 individuals which occupy traditional home ranges of 198 to 445 acres (80–180 ha). Although clan ranges overlap as much as 31% late in the dry season and mixing sometimes occurs, very few females join a different clan—whereas virtually all males do, thereby avoiding inbreeding.

Female herds are notable for close packing, uniformity, synchronized activities, and lack of a regular rank order or leadership. There is little aggression and great variation in herd composition from day to day as clan members come and go.

Territory size varies with population density, season, habitat quality, location, and individual prowess. Holdings are smallest at high density in good habitat during the rainy/breeding season. They averaged 27 acres (10.8 ha) during the rutting peak in Sengwa, at a density of 129 to 176 impalas/mi^2 (50–68/km^2)–tiny compared to the average 143-acre (58 ha) properties Serengeti impalas defend in the dry season at a density of 83 impalas/mi^2 (32/km^2).

Actively territorial males spend up to ¼ of their time shepherding females, time that would otherwise be spent feeding and digesting. Keeping bachelor males away and cutting out juveniles whose horns betray their sex add to the energy they expend. In the East African populations, where breeding continues most of the year, few males last even three months before losing condition and being replaced. They join bachelor herds to recuperate and try again–but are only ready after rising to the top of the bachelor hierarchy. Impalas become attached to the place they first win a territory and when staging a comeback try to regain their former property, so more often than not, the male who replaces the current occupant is a former owner.

HOW IT MOVES   Famous jumpers, alarmed impalas high-jump 10 ft (3 m) and broad-jump 36 ft (11 m). To escape predators that stalk within pouncing range, a whole herd explodes in all directions. More rarely, impalas perform a unique and equally spectacular high jump (see Play, Table 12.1). As a runner, the impala is neither very fleet nor enduring; indeed, dependence on cover to escape spotted hyenas, wild dogs, and cheetahs may be important in its habitat preferences.

REPRODUCTION   Southern impala: 3-week rut end of the rainy season, apparently triggered by the full moon; beginning date varies by up to 20 days from year to year; vigorous territorial behavior limited to the few months preceding and following the mating peak. East Africa: breeding season more extended, although most females conceive late in the rainy season. More sustained sexual competition may explain the bigger horns of East African impalas.

Females conceive at c. 1.5 years; males, though adolescent as yearlings, only begin breeding after acquiring territories in their fourth year. Gestation 194 to 200 days.

OFFSPRING AND MATERNAL CARE   Late dry-season birth peak (Sept. or Oct). Some mothers bring fawns only 2 to 3 days old into the herd, where they associate with other newborns in crèches. Juveniles rest, move, play, and groom with one another, only seeking mothers to nurse or for protection. Weaning complete as early as 4 to 5 months; by then males' horns have emerged, exposing them to increasing aggression by breeding males. Males in East African populations all end up in bachelor herds by 8 months.

PREDATORS   Wherever abundant, impalas are a mainstay of all the large predators; fawns are small enough to be carried off by martial eagles.

Table 12.1. IMPALA BEHAVIOR GUIDE
Expect to see and hear ➤ Usual context and meaning

Territorial Advertising

Adult ♂ standing or lying, alone or apart from herd. ➤ Advertises presence of a territorial ♂.

Proud posture. ➤ Impala version of the erect posture (particularly statuesque).

Urination and defecation in sequence on dung midden. ➤ Visual display and scent-marking. Middens located on paths, roadways, other bare ground, and in the 15–30 yd neutral zone between adjoining territories.

Rubbing forehead on tree stem; often followed by horning. ➤ Visual display and scent-marking performed by territorial ♂ ♂ and top-ranking bachelors.

Vegetation-horning. ➤ Advertises aggressive mood and high status. Often performed by territorial males, especially during interactions with potential challengers.

Roaring display: tail raised exposing white underside, while giving 1–3 explosive snorts, followed by 2–10 deep, guttural grunts, audible up to a mile. ➤ Also produced while in motion, as when chasing intruding ♂ ♂ and driving ♀ ♀. Performance peaks during rut, by bachelor as well as territorial ♂ ♂.

Aggression

Standing or walking stiffly in proud posture, usually facing receiver ± head turned away. ➤ Display of dominance to rival ♂ ♂ or to ♀ ♀ trying to exit property.

Medial-horn threat.

High-horn threat. ➤ Presents forehead skin for inspection by inferiors; equals respond in kind.

Low-horn threat.

OTHER ACTIONS ASSOCIATED WITH DOMINANCE/THREAT DISPLAYS
Head-tossing, vegetation-horning, tail-raising/-spreading, displacement activities.

Aggression *continued*

Head-dipping. ➤ Exaggerated nodding.

Jumping toward opponent. ➤ Feinted attack.

Air-cushion fights. ➤ Going through the motions of fighting.

Yawning and moving jaw side-to-side. ➤ Seems to indicate tension, but significance unknown.

Tongue-flicking. ➤ Also seen in courtship.

Head-low posture. ➤ Defensive threat, response of inferior to superior's threat.

FEMALE AGGRESSION
Head-dipping, butting.

Submission

Moving away in head-low posture. ➤ Avoidance of superior, when threatened or supplanted.

Approaching and sniffing adult ♂'s forehead. ➤ Behavior of subordinate (checking skin-gland secretion)

Flight. ➤ Response of inferior or defeated rival to pursuit.

Displacement Activities

Grazing, scratching with hind feet, scratching with horn tips, scraping with incisors.

Sociable Behavior

Social grooming: tit-for-tat incisor grooming of the head and neck, between all classes, including adult ♂ ♂. ➤ After initial approach and nose-to-nose contact, a pair stands facing with heads turned 45°. One scrapes the other 4–8 times, then stops and waits for response in kind. Bouts typically include 6–12 exchanges before one or both move away.

Courtship

Lowstretch ± tongue-flicking. ➤ Posture of territorial male checking out ♀ ♀, often prompted by ♀ urination posture.

♀ urination posture, with tail spread. ➤ ♀ ♀ urinate when they feel like it, not in response to ♂ approach or display.

Urine-testing. ➤ Checking ♀ reproductive status; mouth open but no pronounced grimace.

COURTSHIP STAGES
Pursuit in lowstretch ± roaring, snorting, and wheezing. ➤ ♂ exerts himself to separate ♀ from herd.

♀ tries to hide in herd, circles back each time ♂ drives her out.

Courtship *continued*

Close following and tongue-flicking ± head-nodding. ➤ Mating march. ♀ ready to mate permits ♂ to lick her rear.

POSTMATING BEHAVIOR

♂ often chases ♂ ♂, herds ♀ ♀ and performs roaring display.

Mother and Offspring

Described in Mother and Offsrpring, Table 4.2.

Play

High-jumping. ➤ Series of soaring bounds, like exaggerated stotting, descending vertically and throwing hind legs high in air.

Chasing, cavorting, sparring.

Response to Predators

Alert posture, stamping, alarm-snorting, other nervous behavior. ➤ Impalas spend much time in bushy habitat, are unusually alert to possible danger.

Flight-intention movement: sudden upward head movement with neck stretched forward. ➤ Other impalas often react by taking flight.

Leaping and scattering. ➤ Startled herd members explode in all directions.

Chapter 13

BUSHBUCK TRIBE
Tragelaphini

Bushbuck, *Tragelaphus scriptus*
Sitatunga, *T. spekii*
Nyala,*T. angasii*
Mountain nyala, *T. buxtoni*[en]
Lesser kudu, *T. imberbis*

Greater kudu, *T. strepsiceros*
Bongo, *T. (Boocercus) eurycerus*
Common eland, *T.(Taurotragus) oryx*
Derby or giant eland,*T. derbianus*[v]

WHAT THEY ARE   A close-knit group of antelopes with spiral horns. They differ from all other African antelopes in having a nonterritorial social/mating system. Most depend on cover to avoid predators. Tragelaphine antelopes come in 3 different models:

Forest-antelope model: narrow body, deep chest; rounded back, hindquarters more developed and higher than forequarters. Bushbuck, sitatunga, nyala, and bongo.

Broken-ground/jumping model: tall and lean, with long, equally developed limbs, level back. Kudus and mountain nyala.

Oversize ox model: massive animals more like oxen than antelopes; slow runners but great jumpers. Eland.

Males take much longer to mature and grow much bigger and darker than females, developing secondary sexual characters to an extreme degree. All have a bare, moist nose and large, rounded ears (except common eland). *Horns:* males only—except bongo and elands—with 1 to 3 turns and 1 or 2 keels (ridges running the length of the horn), "ivory" tipped in most species. *Tail:* less than hock length, bushy and white underneath (except eland). *Coat:* short and sleek (except male nyala and sitatunga), with a crest of longer, erectile hair along the spine. *Color:* from light tan to dark brown or black with white markings: vertical stripes and spots on torso, spinal crest; chevrons, bars, and spots on head, neck, or chest. Males darken with age. *Scent glands:* foot glands located between false hooves on hind legs (absent in bushbuck, sitatunga, bongo); 1 pair of inguinal glands in most species (bushbuck, sitatunga, lesser kudu, mountain nyala). *Teats:* 4.

SOCIAL/MATING SYSTEM   From solitary to highly sociable; all species nonterritorial.

133

(♂♀♂♀) Solitary. Example: bushbuck.

(♀○♀○♀) (♂♂♂) (♂♂♂) Slightly to moderately sociable. Small herds rarely numbering over 6 females and young; females share a traditional home range with relatives (same clan). Males live separately from adolescence onward in even smaller bachelor herds, becoming increasingly solitary with maturity. Position in rank order is based on size and seniority. Examples: sitatunga, nyala, mountain nyala, kudus, bongo, Derby eland.

(♀♀♀♀♀) (♂♂♂) (♀♀♀♀♂♂♂♂) Highly gregarious. Herds numbering in the hundreds, containing numerous young and adults of both sexes are common; so are smaller all-female and all-male herds. Example: common eland.

Tragelaphine social groups of both sexes are characteristically loose and open, varying in membership from day to day, and notable for the low incidence of aggression. This and other tribes in the subfamily Bovinae, including cattle, have a male-dominance hierarchy instead of a territorial mating system.

(♂♂♂) The more rigorous reproductive competition in nonterritorial mating systems forces males to spend extra years maturing and to continue adding bulk even after maturation, resulting in dominance hierarchies based on size; senior males still in their prime do most of the breeding.

HOW THEY MOVE   Bushbuck type built for rushing, bounding, and dodging through the undergrowth—not for fast or sustained running. Kudus and elands are great high jumpers and the eland is a good trotter, but all lack speed and endurance. In flight the tail is raised to show the white flag as in reedbucks. Tragelaphines do not stot and rarely rise on their hind legs when browsing.

HOW THEY COMMUNICATE   Sight 1 to 2, scent 1 to 2, sound 1.

Table 13.1. *BUSHBUCK TRIBE BEHAVIOR GUIDE*
   Expect to see and hear ➤ Usual context and meaning

Advertising Dominance

Lone adult ♂ standing or lying in a conspicuous location, in relaxed or self-confident manner. ➤ Dominant ♂♂ are more likely to show themselves than are other classes.

Ground-and vegetation-horning. ➤ Advertises aggressive mood and high status.

Snapping branches with horns (often while vegetation-horning). ➤ Expresses aggression, but easily confused with branch-breaking while feeding (see bongo and eland accounts).

Advertising Dominance *continued*

Alarm-barking. ➤ Deeper, gruffer barks of ♂ ♂, heard especially at night, probably to identify an individual and advertise high social status.

Aggression

Supplanting. ➤ Making a lower-ranked individual move aside by walking toward it; reinforced if necessary by more aggressive behaviors.

Approach in stiff, deliberate manner. ➤ Display of dominance, often the prelude to broadside display.

 Broadside display, with head high or low and dorsal crest raised. ➤ Main dominance display in the tribe. Displays size and muscular development in profile. Mane, spinal crest, dewlaps (eland) increase apparent size.

 Confrontations; contestants often look away. ➤ Prelude to combat when combined with threat displays.

 Medial-horn threat.

 Low-horn threat. ➤ The more the chin is pulled in and the horns are aimed at the opponent, the stronger the threat.

 Head-low posture. ➤ Defensive threat.

OTHER ACTIONS ASSOCIATED WITH THREAT DISPLAYS

Upward thrusting movements. ➤ Stabbing threat.

Ducking head down and up. ➤ Symbolic butting.

Ground- and vegetation-horning. ➤ Redirected aggression. The message: "This is what I'd like to do to you."

Feinted attack. ➤ Jumping forward while hind legs remain planted.

Head-shaking and nodding. ➤ The mildest threats (slow head-shake is submissive in eland).

FEMALE AGGRESSIVE BEHAVIOR

Head-low posture.

Poking with the snout (mouth closed). ➤ Mainly hornless ♀ ♀, most commonly displayed during courtship.

Symbolic biting or snapping. ➤ Biting movements without contact (or rarely).

Symbolic or real butting.

Head-shaking.

Neck-fighting (rare). ➤ Hornless ♀ ♀ twine necks and may try to over-throw opponent by lifting from below.

Feinted attack.

Submission

Head-low/chin-out posture. ➤ Similar to ♀ posture during mating.

Nose-in-the-air ± neck-winding. ➤ Nose pointing skyward. When combined with neck-winding, indicates persistent resistance, usually against ♂'s sexual advances.

Turning away. ➤ Avoidance of approaching superior.

Flight. ➤ To escape pursuing superior or contest winner.

Displacement Activities

Activities of this tribe poorly known.

Grazing attitude, sideswiping, scratching with hind feet, scratching back with horn tips, scraping with incisors and licking.

Sociable Behavior

Nose-to-nose contact. ➤ Usual greeting and identity check on meeting.

Nose to genital area. ➤ Less common follow-up to nose-to-nose contact.

Social licking and nibbling. Head, neck, shoulders, and withers the primary targets; groomee presents place it wants groomed. ➤ Licking is the primary form of social grooming in the tribe. Grooming partners take turns but the prevailing direction is from lower to higher ranking. Postures assumed by groomee resemble dominance and threat displays.

Courtship

MALE BEHAVIOR

Tending bond: ♂ keeping close to ♀ and keeping other ♂ ♂ away. ➤ Not a display but an indication that ♀ is approaching estrus and being courted.

Dominance and threat displays. ➤ Common prelude to courtship, essential to impress and dominate ♀.

Lowstretch and drawing alongside ♀. ➤ Posture of ♂ approaching or driving ♀ (see Figs. 13.2 and 13.6).

Urine-testing. ➤ Grimace includes pronounced lip-curl.

Driving ♀ in straight line. ➤ No courtship circling during mating march.

Neck-pressing. ➤ Unique to this tribe. Possibly an expression of ♂ dominance, or simply a mounting-intention movement.

OTHER ACTIONS ASSOCIATED WITH MALE COURTSHIP

Mutual licking and nibbling, especially by ♂ in response to ♀ defensive tactics; rubbing cheeks on ♀'s hindquarters.

Courtship *continued*

Nuzzling udder. ➤ Nyala courtship.

Resting chin on ♀'s rump. ➤ Mounting intention (see Fig. 13.2).

VOCAL ACCOMPANIMENT

♂ utters infantile calls.

FEMALE BEHAVIOR

Responsive urination. ➤ Prompted by ♂ approaching in lowstretch.

Moving away.

Defensive threats.

Submissive behaviors, including nose-in-the-air ± neck-winding.

Mother and Offspring

Described in Mother and Offspring, Table 4.2.

Retrieving concealed calf: mother goes directly to hiding place, prompts it to rise by mooing, clicking, or smacking.

Hungry calves may block mother's path, perform aggressive displays, alternating nursing with vigorous jabs, butting, attempted neck-fighting and mounting.

Social licking between mother and calf.

Play

Performance of dominance and threat displays, fighting, running and chasing games, including cavorting. ➤ Mainly performed by the young, but running and chasing tend to be infectious.

Response to Predators

Alert posture, stamping, alarm-barking, walking in jerky manner.

Lowering head and neck. ➤ Investigating suspicious object.

Freezing in mid-stride. ➤ Startled response.

Abrupt flight ± high bounds. ➤ Escape tactic of kudus, bongo, eland.

SOUNDS OF ALARM

Loud, gruff barking.

BUSHBUCK, *Tragelaphus scriptus*

Figure 13.1. Bushbuck in broadside display.

WHAT IT IS   A colorful, sizeable antelope that hides in patches of woody vegetation all over Africa. Rounded back with powerful hindquarters. ♂ wt 88–176 lb (40–80 kg), ht 28–40 in (70–100 cm); ♀ wt 55–132 lb (25–60 kg), ht 26–34 in (65–85 cm). *Horns:* one twist, nearly straight, 10 to 22 in (26–57 cm). *Color:* individually and geographically variable: northern and western races reddest with best-developed stripes and spots; eastern and southern forms yellower with fewer markings; both sexes darken with age, males to chestnut; young reddish brown.

WHERE IT LIVES   Sub-Saharan Africa wherever there is cover to conceal it, from sea level to mountain moors at 10,000 ft (3000 m), from rainforest edge to patches of gallery forest and bush near water in the subdesert.

ECOLOGY   A forest-edge antelope dependent on concealment to avoid predators; ventures into open at night to feed; almost always found near water since the dense cover where it spends its days is most abundant along watercourses. A browser/grazer, eats tender green grass but mainly browses herbs and foliage of shrubby legumes; raids vegetable gardens. Fond of fruits and flowers, it often forages under trees where monkeys and hornbills are feeding.

ACTIVITY   ● (○) Mainly night, also day-active. Bushbucks observed in Queen Elizabeth NP ranged sizeable areas, averaging 51 acres (19.6 ha), because day and night ranges were entirely separate. Days were spent in or on the edge of the home thicket, resting 50% (often standing), feeding 38%, and moving 12% of the time. Shortly before dark, each bushbuck moved toward its night range, in open habitat, where it fed 25% of the time. When resting at night in the open, bushbucks usually lay down. All returned to their home thickets before dawn.

SOCIAL/MATING SYSTEM ⚥ ♂ The only solitary, nonterritorial African antelope, neither sex defends any part of its home range, and ranges may largely or completely overlap. But each adult's home thicket is an exclusive core area where it retires to rest and ruminate between bouts of foraging. Although bushbucks do not herd together, up to a dozen may feed peacefully in the same clearing in late afternoon. As bushbucks from the same neighborhood are all acquainted and often greet one another in a friendly manner, it would be more accurate to call this animal loosely and casually sociable, kept separate by feeding and antipredator strategies that favor separation of individuals.

In Queen Elizabeth NP, bushbuck density on the Mweya Peninsula was 67/mi^2 (26/km^2), equal to that of the Uganda kob in the same park. Exclusive core areas were as small as ⅓ acre for females and 1.25 acre (0.5 ha) for adult males.

REPRODUCTION   No strict breeding season in high-rainfall areas; birth peak during rainy season in arid regions. Gestation of 6 to 7 months enables females to reproduce nearly twice a year. Both sexes reach puberty at around 11 months, but males' horns only reach adult size at 3.

OFFSPRING AND MATERNAL CARE   Calves stay hidden for nearly 4 months before accompanying their mothers in the open. The maternal bond continues until the next calf is born or longer.

PREDATORS   All the larger carnivores. A bushbuck is not only effectively camouflaged while standing in cover, but also while lying down in the open at night. Hyenas and lions have been seen passing within 10 yd of bushbucks plainly visible through a starlight scope.

Table 13.2. *DIFFERENCES IN BUSHBUCK BEHAVIOR*
   Expect to see and hear ➤ *Usual context and meaning*

Advertising Dominance
Both sexes rub heads and necks on objects, especially the oily, scented area below and between the ears. ➤ Possible scent-marking.

Aggression

 Confrontation. At high intensity, bushbucks circle with tense, high steps, jump, chase, and clash horns. ➤ Outright fighting rarely observed and dangerous because of daggerlike horns.

Courtship

Aggressive behavior. ➤ If ♀ persistently resists ♂'s courtship, he pushes and drives her, snaps at and pokes her, even hitting her flanks with his horns.

♂ licking and nuzzling ♀'s genitals.

VOCAL ACCOMPANIMENT
♂ clicks and twitters.

SITATUNGA, *Tragelaphus spekii*

Figure 13.2. Male sitatunga, following closely in mating march, rests his chin on female's croup, preparatory to mounting; she responds with neck-winding.

WHAT IT IS A bigger version of the bushbuck that lives in swamps and is the most aquatic antelope. Forest-antelope build. ♂ wt 154–275 lb (70–125 kg), ht 35–50 in (88–125 cm); ♀ wt 110–124 lb (50–57 kg), ht 30–36 in (75–90 cm). Elongated hooves with wide splay and naked, padlike adjacent skin (pasterns). *Horns:* two turns, 18 to 36 in (45–90 cm). *Coat:* up to several inches long but thin, oily, and water-repellent. *Color:* females brown to chestnut; adult males gray-brown to dark chocolate; spotted and striped. Markings of adults partially obscured by long hair; white patches on neck but spinal crest often brown; calves rufous red, wooly.

WHERE IT LIVES Swamps and permanent marshes in the West African rainforest and wetter parts of the Southern Savanna. Coexists with the Nile lechwe in the great Sudd in southern Sudan, and with the common lechwe in Zambia, Botswana, and Angola.

GOOD PLACES TO SEE IT   Moyowosi GR, Tanzania; Busanda Swamps, in northern Kafue NP, Bengweulu Swamp, both in Zambia; Okavango Delta, Botswana.

ECOLOGY   Frequents the deepest parts of papyrus swamps and wetlands dominated by bullrushes, reeds, and sedges. Swamps are highly productive ecosystems that can shelter 142 sitatungas/mi^2 (55/km^2). A browser/grazer, often selects plants in the flowering stage. Feeds on swamp vegetation in water up to its shoulders, comes ashore to graze green pastures, and enters forest to browse woody vegetation. Will stand bipedally to reach high flowers, and males sometimes pull down and break branches with the backs of their horns. The long, mobile tongue is used to gather foliage into good-sized bites.

ACTIVITY   ● Sitatungas create broad highways and side roads through a swamp, including paths leading to onshore feeding grounds, where they emerge to eat under cover of darkness. Come out in daylight where protected from hunting, but usual daytime resting places are platforms of vegetation each animal prepares for itself by circling and trampling. Sitatungas also stand and ruminate in the water.

SOCIAL/MATING SYSTEM   (♀₀♀₀♀) (♂♂♀♀) (♂♂♂)   Although most sightings are of single animals, mothers often associate in twos and threes with their calves. Immature males associate together and with females; adult males avoid one another but often associate with females. Two-thirds of those seen in a Kenya swamp were accompanying females, including the largest group, which included 4 adult females and 4 young.

HOW IT MOVES   Slow and inconspicuous movements help the si-tatunga avoid detection. Though its plunging run is clumsy and slow on land, it can outrun predators in swamps, supported by its elongated, splayed hooves. It is also a good but slow swimmer.

REPRODUCTION   No strict breeding season, but most calving occurs in the dry season, and females reproduce apparently at yearly intervals, conceiving as yearlings. Males mature in fifth year. Gestation c. 7.5 months.

OFFSPRING AND MATERNAL CARE   Calves rarely observed out-side zoos. Even after lying-out a month, calves are only brought into the open when other sitatungas are present. After gaining aquatic competence, calves follow their mothers closely for some months, gradually breaking away beginning at 8 or 9 months. Young calves are suckled an average of 10 minutes.

PREDATORS   Lions and wild dogs occasionally prey on sitatungas, and leopards are a threat to sitatungas in the forest. Use of regular pathways makes it unusually vulnerable to human predators, which drive them into nets or deeper water with lines of beaters, or stalk them in dugout canoes.

Table 13.3. *DIFFERENCES IN SITATUNGA BEHAVIOR*
Expect to see and hear ➤ *Usual context and meaning*

Advertising Dominance

Alarm-barking by ♂ ♂ common at night, may continue intermittently for > 10 min. ➤ Gruff barks of 1 ♂ may be taken up by others. ♀ ♀ give a single, higher-pitched bark.

Aggression

Horn threats are rarely given from the broadside stance. Instead ♂ ♂ confront each other with heads turned away, or soil-horn.

Medial-horn threat.

Low-horn threat.

Soil-horning.

OTHER ACTIONS COMMONLY ASSOCIATED WITH THREAT DISPLAYS
Head-throwing (exaggerated upward movement).

Mother and Offspring

Mother can summon older calf by looking intently toward it while abruptly lowering and lifting her head.

CALLS
Calves bleat like sheep.

Low-pitched squeaks. ➤ Heard sometimes in feeding herds.

Response to Predators

Abrupt flight in plunging gallop. ➤ Escape tactic (see under How It Moves).

SOUNDS OF ALARM
Loud, gruff barking. ➤ ♀ bark is higher, more like a snort.

NYALA, *Tragelaphus angasii*

Figure 13.3. The nyala broadside display, one of the most spectacular antelope dominance displays.

WHAT IT IS   A dry-land, hairier version of a sitatunga, found only in southeastern Africa. Bushbuck body plan, with extreme gender differences. ♂ wt 216-275 lb (98-125 kg), ht 42 in (106 cm); ♀ wt 121-132 lb (55-60 kg), ht 36 in (92 cm). *Horns:* 24 to 33 in (60-83 cm) with 1.5 to 2.5 twists. *Coat:* short in females and young, long in adult males, including fringe from throat to hindquarters and longest spinal crest in the tribe. *Color:* females and young bright chestnut with 8 to 13 contrasting torso stripes, spots and chrevrons on chest and head; males dark charcoal gray upper body and limbs, tan lower legs; dark belly fringe and white spinal crest; stripes reduced or absent.

WHERE IT LIVES   Coastal plain of Mozambique and major river valleys extending into Malawi, Zimbabwe, and South Africa; range greatly reduced, especially in Mozambique.

RELATIVES   The so-called mountain nyala of the Ethiopian Highlands looks more like a greater kudu. *T. angasii* is closer to bushbuck and sitatunga.

GOOD PLACES TO SEE IT   Lengwe NP, Malawi; Gonarezhou NP, Zimbabwe; Hluhluwe GR, Kruger NP, South Africa.

ECOLOGY   Closely tied to thickets and densely wooded lowlands generally near water, with access to high-quality grassland. A grazer/browser.

Grazes fresh green grass during the rains; browses leaves, pods, various fruits, and herbs during the dry season, meanwhile drinking daily.

ACTIVITY   ● (○) Night and some day. Nyalas spend the day in or near cover, emerging at night to feed in grassland. During spring and summer months they spend the hottest hours in deep cover, typically standing motionless and almost invisible beside a tree. During cooler winter days they rest in light shade in the open. Most nyalas are inactive between midnight and dawn.

SOCIAL/MATING SYSTEM   (♀○♀○♀) (♂♂♂) (♂♂♂) The basic social unit is a female with her latest and next-to-latest offspring. Herds consist of 2 or more units, which in Natal's Hluhluwe GR typically number 5 to 6 nyalas. Only females guarding hidden calves stay alone. Although herds appear temporary and fluid, daughters tend to stay home and continue associating with their mothers after becoming mothers themselves. Female home ranges in Hluhluwe average 171 acres (range: 124–259 acres [50–105 ha]); male ranges average 207 acres (124–360 acres [50–146 ha]). Each range includes at least 10% forest and up to 28% open floodplain or other grassland.

Males 1.5 to 3 years old associate but even more casually than females, in twos and threes, rarely up to 9 males, and herd membership seldom remains unchanged for even 2 hours. Males become more solitary as they mature in their sixth year. The sexes stay segregated except when an estrous female is located, or when nyalas aggregate (up to 30, rarely up to 100) on a green pasture, at water holes, or fruiting trees.

REPRODUCTION   Year-round with conception peaks in spring and autumn. Estrus lasts 2 days, but females fend off suitors until final 6 hours. Females calve 7 months later, ovulate again within a week, but usually conceive only on the third try (3-week cycle).

OFFSPRING AND MATERNAL CARE   Calves hide 10 to 18 days. Yearlings often remain with their mothers after the next calf is born, but courting males drive adolescent males away when mothers reenter estrus.

PREDATORS   Lion, spotted hyena, leopard, and wild dog.

Table 13.4. *DIFFERENCES IN NYALA BEHAVIOR*
         Expect to see and hear ➤ *Usual context and meaning*

Advertising Dominance

Soil-horning. ➤ ♂ ♂ advertise aggressiveness by digging and tossing soil, preferably soft and wet; also horn and rub forehead on bushes.

Aggression

Approach in stiff, deliberate manner, lifting legs high. ➤ Prelude to broadside display.

Broadside display, with head low and dorsal crest raised (see Fig. 13.3); performed at variable intensity. ➤ Most spectacular display in the tribe; fringe and crest increase apparent size by 40%. ♂ that displays at highest intensity, with fluffed tail draped over rump and movements frozen, always wins.

Submission

Lowering crest and turning away. ➤ Loser of display duel.

Displacement Activities

Pretended feeding, scraping with incisors, sideswiping, head-flagging while backing away, alarm-snorting. ➤ Performed by losers during display duels.

Courtship

MALE BEHAVIOR

Urine-testing. ➤ Performed only when checking estrous ♀; routine checking consists of sniffing the ♀'s tail.

Nuzzling udder. ➤ ♂ pushes muzzle between ♀'s hind legs, sometimes lifts her hindquarters.

FEMALE BEHAVIOR

Standing in head-low or head-low/chin-out posture. ➤ Signals readiness for mounting. Courting ♂ sometimes tries to mount ♀ that is simply drinking, apparently regarding drinking posture as an invitation.

♀ uttering faint clicks while moving away. ➤ Significance unclear.

LESSER KUDU, *Tragelaphus imberbis*

Figure 13.4. Lesser kudu bulls engaged in ritualized horn-pressing fight, in which the stronger animal forces the weaker one's horns back upon its neck.

WHAT IT IS　An elegant miniature of the greater kudu. Narrow body and long legs; back relatively level. ♂ wt 202–238 lb (92–108 kg), ht 38–42 in (95–105 cm); ♀ wt 123–154 lb (56–70 kg), ht 36–40 in (90–100 cm). *Horns:* an open spiral with 2.5 (rarely, 3) turns, 20 to 28 in (50–70 cm). *Coat:* smooth; males have short white spinal crest but no beard. *Color:* females and young red-brown, males blue-gray, darkening with age. White markings: 11 to 15 white stripes, large throat and chest patches, nose chevron, and double cheek spots. Legs tawny with black and white patches. Tail black-tipped.

WHERE IT LIVES　Somali-Masai Arid Zone of Ethiopia, Somalia, Kenya, and Tanzania, below 3900 ft (1200 m).

GOOD PLACES TO SEE IT　Tsavo East and Meru NP, Samburu-Isiolo and Shaba NR, Kenya; both kudus are common in Ruaha NP and Rungwa-Kizigo GR, Tanzania.

ECOLOGY　Closely associated with *Acacia/Commiphora* thornbush, the lesser kudu depends on thickets for safety and seldom ventures into grassland or scattered bush. A browser, diet including up to 118 different plants, mainly foliage of the dominant trees and bushes, seedpods, seeds, fruits, vines, and a little green grass. Unlike the associated gerenuk, it seldom browses acacias and remains on all fours while feeding.

ACTIVITY　○ (●?) Day divided almost equally between feeding (33%), standing and lying (36%), and moving (29%). Idle hours mostly spent standing in thicket, virtually invisible unless a flicking ear or tail catches one's attention. Probably also active at night, but no published observations.

SOCIAL/MATING SYSTEM　(♀○♀○♀) (♂♂♂)　The existence of exclusive and long-lasting associations between females sets kudus apart from most other tragelaphine antelopes. In Tsavo NP, typical female herds include

1 to 3 cows and their offspring. There is no consistent leadership or rank hierarchy, nor any social grooming between females. Groups often merge but separate again without exchanging members. Herds tend to be larger in the rainy season but total at most 24 animals since population density is rarely greater than 3 kudus/mi² (1/km²).

Male offspring separate at 1.5 years when they begin to develop obvious male secondary characters (horns longer than ears, darker color, spinal crest). Subadult males often associate in pairs but frequently change partners. As they mature at 4 to 5, they avoid one another, even though 4 or 5 bulls may range much the same area and have no exclusive core areas. Male home ranges in Tsavo average 568 acres (230 ha), nearly the same as female ranges, whereas subadult males, the most unsettled class, have ranges averaging 741 acres (300 ha).

REPRODUCTION   Nonseasonal, despite poorer survival of calves born in driest months. Gestation 7.5 to 8 months and birth interval of 8 to 10 months between calves is normal for well-fed females.

OFFSPRING AND MATERNAL CARE   Females stand solitary watch over newborn's hiding place for several days after calving. During 2-week hiding stage, mother retrieves calf only for suckling, letting it nurse for up to 8 minutes during first month.

PREDATORS   Lion, spotted hyena, leopard, and wild dog; young calves also vulnerable to jackals. Like greater kudu, *T. imberbis* is adept at avoiding detection and at escaping capture by making tremendous bounds through and over the vegetation.

Table 13.5. *DIFFERENCES IN LESSER KUDU BEHAVIOR*
Expect to see and hear ➤ *Usual context and meaning*

Advertising Dominance

Ground- and vegetation-horning. ➤ Very common in lesser kudu.

Aggression

Horn-pressing (see Fig. 13.4). Confronting with heads lowered, contestants first touch noses, then bring foreheads together so that horn front surfaces meet, then press down in attempt to force opponent's horns back onto its neck. ➤ Ritualized test of strength and weight. Serious fighting, with horns forked together, is rare, but deaths resulting from locked horns are known.

OTHER ACTIONS ASSOCIATED WITH THREAT DISPLAYS

Ground- and vegetation-horning.

Head-tossing ± tongue-flashing.

Courtship

VOCAL ACCOMPANIMENT

♂ ♂ whine, gasp for breath.

Response to Predators

High-jumping flight with white tail displayed. ➤ Lesser kudus easily clear obstacles over 8 ft (2.5 m) high. ♂ ♂ raise chin high so that horns lie at shoulder level.

GREATER KUDU, *Tragelaphus strepsiceros*

Figure 13.5. Greater kudu bulls fighting with horns firmly engaged.

WHAT IT IS   The second-tallest antelope, with the most spectacular horns. Narrow bodied, long-legged. ♂ wt 418–693 lb (190–315 kg), ht 48–60 in (122–150 cm); ♀ wt 264–473 lb (120–215 kg), ht 40–56 in (100–140 cm). *Head:* proportionally small with huge, cupped ears. *Horns:* 2.5 turns (rarely, 3); average 48 in, record 72 (180 cm). *Coat:* smooth except spinal crest in both sexes and beard in male only. *Color:* red-brown to blue-gray; males turn darker with age; 6 to 10 torso stripes; prominent white nose chevron and small cheek spots; dark garters on upper legs; black-tipped tail with white underside.

WHERE IT LIVES   Over much of eastern and southern Africa, from Chad nearly to the Red Sea, south to Cape Province, west to Namibia and north to mid-Angola. Adept at concealment and catholic in diet (including garden produce), it is one of the few large mammals that thrives in settled areas (in the scrub woodland and bush that reclaims abandoned fields and degraded pastures). Still common in southern Africa but in East Africa its lowland habitat has been mostly expropriated, leaving only isolated populations on some mountains.

GOOD PLACES TO SEE IT   Selous and Ugalla GR, Ruaha NP, Tanzania; Luambe and Luanwga NP, Zambia; Hwange NP and most other Zimbabwe parks; Kruger NP and Natal reserves, South Africa; Etosha NP, Namibia.

ECOLOGY   Need for concealment limits habitat choices, partially offset by ability to live in waterless areas. Preferred habitat includes mixed scrub wood-land, acacia, and mopane bush on lowlands, hills, and mountains. A gourmet browser, it eats many kinds of leaves, herbs, fallen fruits, vines, tubers, succu-lents, and flowers, sometimes varied with a little new grass. Kudus studied in Kruger NP made extensive seasonal movements, dispersing in deciduous woodland in the rains and in the dry season clustering along rivers and the bases of hills where the most nutritious, evergreen growth is found.

ACTIVITY   ●/○ Night and day. Adult females studied in Kruger NP spent 50 to 58% of a 24-hour day foraging, 45% at night. Finding these ani-mals more active in daytime suggests the usual habit of hiding by day and coming out at night is imposed by human predation.

SOCIAL/MATING SYSTEM   (♀₀♀₀♀) (♂♂♂) (♂♂♂)   Herds typi-cally include 1 to 3 females and their offspring, but averages may vary season-ally, being smaller early and late in the dry season and larger in the rains. Kruger NP herds average 5 to 6 (up to 15), and are based on continuing asso-ciations of the same cows. Temporary mergers of cow herds are also common, forming groups up to 20 to 30 kudus. Two radio-tracked herds had home ranges of 889 acres (360 ha) and 1284 acres (520 ha).

Bachelor herds of 2 to 10 males are transient and may include mature bulls after the annual mating peak. Whether an established rank hierarchy ex-ists among local bulls is unclear, although individuals with overlapping home ranges have enough contact to know who's the boss. In Kruger NP, many bulls disperse singly during the rains but at least some return consistently to the same core areas after absences of 4 to 5 months. The home ranges of 2 radio-collared bulls were 2717 acres (1100 ha) and included the ranges of 2 to 3 cow herds, with which males associated only during the breeding season.

REPRODUCTION   Annual in southern Africa, calving February and March when grass is high. Near equator, mating peaks as rains end and calv-ing peaks during rainy season. Gestation 9 months; females may conceive at 2, a year before maturing. Males mature at 5 and keep growing.

OFFSPRING AND MATERNAL CARE   After hiding 2 weeks calves join maternal herd but continue to lie-out, at least at night, 4 to 5 weeks. Mothers suckle c. 7 minutes at a time until the calf is nearly 3 weeks old. Juveniles nutritionally self-sufficient at 6 months but stay in the maternal herd, females indefinitely; males disperse in second or third year.

PREDATORS   Lions and spotted hyenas kill adults, the other large carnivores prey on yearlings and calves; newborns also vulnerable to smaller carnivores.

Table 13.6. *DIFFERENCES IN GREATER KUDU BEHAVIOR*
Expect to see and hear ➤ *Usual context and meaning*

Advertising Dominance

Barking. ➤ ♂ greater kudu's gruff bark is one of loudest sounds antelopes make.

Aggressive Displays

Broadside display, with head up, low or turned away, back humped, dorsal crest and tail-bristling.

Locking horns during combat. ➤ Extremely rare, yet dead kudus with locked horns are occasionally found.

Submission/Surrender

Evasion: sidestepping, dodging behind obstacles. ➤ Response of subadult ♂ ♂ to displaying superior.

Courtship

Driving ♀ and drawing alongside.

Neck-pressing.

VOCAL ACCOMPANIMENT
♂ ♂ whine, gasp, cluck, grunt, hum.

Mother and Offspring

Retrieving calf, mother gives "smacking" call or signals visually by lowering and raising neck several times.

Other calls: ♀ hums, changing to a moo when mouth opened; calves give *u-u-u* distress call.

Social licking between mother and calf; other ♀ ♀ also social-lick calves.

Response to Predators

Sneaking. ➤ Kudu that sees an enemy without itself being seen often sneaks away.

High-jumping flight with white tail displayed. ➤ Obstacles over 8 ft (2.5 m) high easily cleared. ♂ ♂ raise chin high so that horns lie at shoulder level.

BONGO, *Tragelaphus (Boocercus) eurycerus*

Figure 13.6. Bongo male approaching female in lowstretch posture.

WHAT IT IS   The biggest, most colorful and sociable forest antelope. Built like a heavyweight bushbuck. ♂ wt 528–891 lb (240–405 kg), ht 44–54 in (110–130 cm); ♀ wt 462–557 lb (210–253 kg), ht slightly shorter. *Head:* wide, with enormous ears. *Horns:* 1 turn, 30 in (75 cm) up to 39 in (99 cm). Male's massive; female's thinner and more parallel. *Tail:* hock-length, with terminal tuft. *Coat:* smooth and glossy. *Color:* females and young bright chestnut above, darker below; males darken with age to blackish brown. Vivid white-yellow markings include 12 to 14 torso stripes, chest crescent, cheek patches, ear edging, and nose chevron. Legs banded black and white.

WHERE IT LIVES   Lowland Rainforest of West Africa and Zaire east to southern Sudan, and isolated populations in montane forests of Kenya.

GOOD PLACES TO SEE IT   Aberdare NP and Forest Reserve, Kenya.

ECOLOGY   Ground-level herbage in the rainforest exists only in forest clearings and secondary growth, which is where bongos are found. In the mountains, they frequent the cloud forest and bamboo zone. Bushes, herbs, creepers, and bamboo provide both cover and food. Browses the most nutritious leaves, flowers, and twigs of various shrubs and vines, thistles, and succulents, also cereals and garden produce. Uses its long, mobile tongue to grasp and bundle leaves and its horns to pull down and break hard-to-reach branches.

ACTIVITY   ●/○ Night and day. Although guests at Aberdare lodges see bongos which visit water holes and salt licks mainly at night, this proves only that they are night-active. Bongos may simply feel uncomfortable in the open by day. They move about in cover and feed early and late in the day, resting in thickets between 10:30 AM and 4 PM, longer in bad weather.

SOCIAL/MATING SYSTEM (♀∘♀∘♀) (♀∘♂♀∘♂)/(♀∘♂♀ ♀) (♂♂♂) A few related females that associate over a long time, casually joining and separating from other females and their offspring, may be the basic units in bongo society. The mean number of bongos observed drinking and eating salt at The Ark in the Aberdare Forest is just 2, and herds of over a dozen are considered large. Herds of over 5 or 6 animals usually include calves and smaller herds contain only adults (in southern Sudan). The biggest Aberdare herds (up to 50) are seen after the calving season, when mothers and young band together in herds of 9 or more—perhaps on the calves' initiative (see eland account).

Lasting associations between known cows, frequent aggressive interactions, and social licking all suggest a regular rank hierarchy. Also, senior cows seem to play leadership roles, appearing alone to check out a water hole, leaving and then returning with a herd in tow. Home range size may be over 39 mi² (100 km²) in the Aberdares, where bongos move up and down the mountain with changing seasons.

Adult male bongos are often solitary. Yet ⅓ of herds observed in Sudan that contained adults of both sexes included 2 or more adult bulls. During the mating peak in the Aberdares (Oct.–Jan.), though, usually a lone black bull accompanies or trails female herds.

HOW IT MOVES   The bongo's thick body, massive hindquarters, and short legs are designed for movement through dense vegetation. It is also an accomplished high-jumper. A clumsy, short-winded runner in the open, it skulks away silently in cover, or bolts suddenly from hiding, with nose out and horns laid back.

REPRODUCTION   Bongos in the Aberdares are known to breed seasonally, but nothing is known about populations living in its main lowland-forest range. A captive female that came into heat at 20 months, stayed in estrus for 3 days, and cycled at 3-week intervals may or may not accurately represent bongos in the wild.

PREDATORS   Primarily man, followed by spotted hyena and leopard. Bongos brought to bay by dogs grunt and stamp defiance, and mothers defend calves against hyenas.

Table 13.7. *DIFFERENCES IN BONGO BEHAVIOR*
Expect to see and hear ➤ *Usual context and meaning*

Advertising Dominance

Snapping branches with the horns, often in connection with vegetation-horning. ➤ By bulls and not followed by feeding on the broken branch.

Aggression

OTHER ACTIONS ASSOCIATED WITH THREAT DISPLAYS
Tree- and bush-horning ± snapping branches.

Grunting and snorting.

FEMALE AGGRESSION

Medial-horn threat. ➤ Offensive threat.

Head-low posture. ➤ Defensive threat.

Submission

Kneeling and lying. ➤ Avoidance of persistent suitor.

Courtship

♂ standing behind ♀ stiffly erect. ➤ Mounting prelude.

♂ bleats, clicks tongue, and licks lips.

Mother and Offspring

Social licking between mother and calf and between calves.

Play

Calves practice neck-fighting, head-shaking/throwing, nose-in-the-air, as well as chasing, etc.

Response to Predators

Style-trotting.

Laying tail over rump.

Snorting, distress-bleating, mooing.

COMMON ELAND, *Tragelaphus (Taurotragus) oryx*

Figure 13.7. Eland bull's low-horn threat causes lower-ranking bull to turn aside.

WHAT IT IS   An antelope in ox's clothing, the biggest African bovid. Ox-like characters develop in adult males, including thick neck and dewlap recalling Brahma bull; females slimmer and more antelopesque. ♂ wt 990–2072 lb (450–942 kg), ht 60–73 in (150–183 cm); ♀ wt 697–1034 lb (317–470 kg), ht 50–61 in (125–153 cm). *Horns:* 1 to 2 tight spirals; 17 to 26 in (43–67 cm) in male; longer in female (20–27 in [51–69.6 cm]) but much thinner. *Tail:* hock-length, cowlike, with terminal tuft. *Head:* short and broad; small ears; prominent dewlap. *Coat:* smooth except short spinal crest and dewlap tuft, plus a forehead patch and short neck mane in adult males. *Color:* basically tan but geographically and individually variable; redder with well-defined markings in north, fading to indistinct in South Africa. 10 to 16 torso stripes and white markings on legs; dark garters, spinal crest, dewlap, forehead, and tail tuft. Males turn blue-gray with age; young reddish brown.

WHERE IT LIVES   Arid zones and savannas from southern Sudan to South Africa, west to Namibia and Angola. Naturally low-density (fewer than 3 elands/mi^2 [1.2/km^2]). Disease (rinderpest), intolerance of human settlement, and poaching for its superior meat have resulted in drastic reductions of range and populations. But widely reintroduced on farms in South Africa and Zimbabwe.

RELATIVES   Giant or Derby eland, found west of the White Nile in the Northern Savanna. More colorful with far more impressive horns but no bigger than common eland. May represent intermediate stage between the common eland and greater kudu, which share a common ancestor.

GOOD PLACES TO SEE IT   Nairobi and Tsavo NP, Masai Mara NR, Kenya; Serengeti, Ruaha, and Tarangire NP, Ngorongoro Crater, Tanzania; Kagera

NP, Rwanda; Nyika NP, Malawi; Luangwa Valley and Kafue NP, Zambia; Hwange and Matobo NP, Tuli Safari Area, Zimbabwe; Kruger NP, Giant's Castle GR, Suikerbosrand NR, Tussen-die-Riviere Game Farm, South Africa.

ECOLOGY   One of the most adaptable ruminants, inhabiting subdesert, acacia savanna, *miombo* woodland, grasslands, and mountains up to 15,000 ft (4600 m). Avoids only swamps, forests, and deserts. Though less desert-adapted than gazelles or oryxes, eland uses the same water-conservation measures to cope in waterless areas, notably by letting body temperature rise as much as 13.5°F (7°C) on hot days. (See Water Dependence and Independence, Chapter 4.)

A browser/grazer, diet as varied as its habitat preferences. Browses mostly foliage, but also fruits, seeds, seedpods, herbs, and tubers. Rainy season diet 50 to 80% green grass. Elands access high foliage by breaking off branches with their horns.

ACTIVITY   ○/● Day and night. Elands feed long hours to sustain their bulk, but the schedule varies greatly with local conditions. In cool weather, they alternately feed and rest in daytime and keep feeding until late at night. In hot, dry weather, they rest all day in shade and feed all night.

SOCIAL/MATING SYSTEM

(♂♂♂) The common eland forms much bigger herds than other spiral-horned antelopes, but its groups are otherwise as open and changeable, with close bonds only between mothers and calves. Herds of up to 500 elands range the grasslands during the rains and invariably include numerous young, which associate in subgroups of similar age and same gender. On Nairobi's Athi Plains, groups containing calves averaged 48 animals, compared to 10 to 12 in mixed adult herds and only 3 to 5 in unisex herds.

Young calves form the most cohesive groups, maintaining an average distance of under 1 yd and resting in contact. Social distance increases with age and horn development to 11 yd in adults. The attraction between calves is what creates large eland herds: when groups containing young meet, the calves mingle, forming the nucleus around which mothers and other herd members are held in orbit.

The home ranges of females and young are very large: at least 67 mi² (174 km²) and up to 163 mi² (422 km²) on the Athi Plains. Bulls range only 19 mi² (range 5–23 mi² [13–60 km²]). Having no parental cares, males readily enter wooded areas avoided by cows with calves, which prefer open landscapes.

HOW IT MOVES   The slowest antelope, runs no faster than c. 25 mph (40 kph) and quickly tires, but can maintain a fast trot (13.5 mph [22 kph]) indefinitely. Startled elands display jumping prowess by leaping effortlessly over a companion's back. Youngsters can clear a 10-ft (3-m) fence from a standing start.

REPRODUCTION   No strict season but births peak end of dry season and most matings occur during rains, in large herds. Gestation 8 to 9 months; females can conceive at 2.5 years, 4 to 5 years before males mature. Estrus lasts 3 days.

OFFSPRING AND MATERNAL CARE   Calves either hide alone for 2 weeks or join a herd and crèche within days of birth. Juveniles stick together and will not go further than 50 yd from their companions even to nurse. Groups often lag behind the herd and can end up entirely alone, while mothers range singly or in splinter groups, especially after weaning calves at 4 to 6 months.

PREDATORS   Lion, spotted hyena. Mothers in groups and even singly confront lions, and bulls show little if any fear of predators. Yet the eland's flight distance from people and vehicles is longest of any African mammal: 300 to 500 yd or more even in parks. How come? Trading speed and endurance for bulk sufficient to cope with lions made eland vulnerable to firearms and pursuit in vehicles.

Table 13.8. *DIFFERENCES IN ELAND BEHAVIOR*
Expect to see and hear ➤ *Usual context and meaning*

Advertising Dominance

Ground-horning, including urination and rubbing forehead in urine, plowing and raking soil, mud, and piles of vegetation. ➤ Horning is linked with ♂ habit of rubbing forehead patch in urine (his own, another eland's, or another species') and other smelly substances.

Clicking sound, like castanets. ➤ Produced in foreleg tendons or joints, sound advertises presence of moving mature bull.

Aggression

Supplanting ± glance threat. ➤ Raising head slightly and looking at subordinate while ceasing any other activity.

OTHER ACTIONS ASSOCIATED WITH THREAT DISPLAYS
Ground-horning/plowing and forehead-rubbing, preceded by urinating. ➤ A threat when addressed to an individual.

Head-tossing ± wiping horn tips on withers. ➤ Strong threat.

FEMALE AGGRESSION
Medial- and low-horn threat, head-low posture, head-tossing and horn-wiping withers, sideswiping. ➤ Seen most commonly during courtship.

Submission

Slow head-shake while moving away. ➤ Response of intimidated eland to supplanting.

Displacement Activities

Most eland activities involve insect-defense movements expressed in social context.

Tail-wagging (while performing other displacement activities).

Sociable Behavior

Social licking of calves. ➤ All other classes lick calves but rarely each other, except as expression of submission. Calves also lick each other.

Courtship

Lowstretch and drawing alongside ± tongue-flicking.

Urine-testing. ➤ Grimace includes pronounced lip curl. All elands urine-test beginning at c. 3 months.

Slow head-shaking by ♂ in response to ♀ defensive tactics. ➤ ♂ responds submissively to ♀'s aggressive resistance.

Standing behind ♀ in erect posture. ➤ Mounting prelude.

VOCAL ACCOMPANIMENT
♂ bleats like calf.

Mother and Offspring

Retrieving concealed calf, mother calls it with sound like creaking door.

Faint bleating call heard when mother and calf are together.

Play

Performance of dominance and threat displays, sparring contests between subadult ♂ ♂, neck-wrestling between juveniles, mounting as a challenge, running and chasing games, including cavorting.

Response to Predators

Approaching and chasing predators in a group, or alone. ➤ Cooperative defense, as in buffalo (rare in antelopes).

Abrupt flight and high bounds. ➤ Emergency escape tactic.

SOUNDS OF ALARM
Loud, gruff bark.

Chapter 14

AFRICAN OR CAPE BUFFALO
Syncerus caffer
Tribe Bovini

Figure 14.1. Buffalo bull rubbing neck on ground, a self-advertising display of high status.

SUBSPECIES
Cape or savanna buffalo, S. c. caffer
Red or forest buffalo, S. c. nanus

WHAT IT IS   The only native African member of the tribe that includes wild and domestic cattle, American bison, etc., the latest and most advanced ruminants to evolve (in Asia within the last 7 million years). The African buffalo is not closely related to the Asian water buffalo, but its ancestry remains unknown. Though African livestock now greatly outnumbers wild animals, cattle remain poorly adapted to African conditions; without human intervention, they couldn't compete with wild hoofed animals.

Cape buffalo: massive build with short, powerful limbs, cow's tail. ♂ wt 935–1914 lb (425–870 kg), ht 60–66 in (150–165 cm); ♀ wt 1267 lb (576 kg), ht c. 10% shorter. *Head:* broad with wide mouth, bare, moist nostrils, drooping, fringed ears. *Horns:* size and shape reflect sex and age; broad base shielding forehead identifies mature males; width across horns up to 40 in (100 cm); length along curve 48 to 50 in (117–150 cm); 10 to 20% less in female, minus boss. *Coat:* short, thin, scant in old animals. *Color:* adults black to dark brown without markings, but old bulls often have grizzled heads; young calves black or dark brown, changing to dirty yellow-brown after sev-

158

eral months, then to reddish or chocolate brown. *Scent glands*: none described, but typical cow-barn smell. *Teats*: 4.

Forest buffalo: different enough to be considered a separate species—except the two forms interbreed wherever they overlap. Much smaller: ♂ wt 594–704 lb (270–320 kg), ht 38–43 in (97–108 cm); red-brown instead of black.

WHERE IT LIVES Formerly occurred throughout the Northern and Southern Savanna, in arid regions wherever there is permanent water and herbage, and from sea level to the limits of forest on the highest mountains. In the Lowland Rainforest buffalos inhabit clearings, swamps, floodplains, and secondary growth.

GOOD PLACES TO SEE IT A few of the parks where buffalos are both abundant and approachable: Masai Mara NR, Kenya; Ngorongoro Crater, Manyara NP, Tanzania; Kafue NP, Zambia; Hwange NP, Zimbabwe; Kruger NP, South Africa.

ECOLOGY Most abundant in well-watered savannas, swamps, floodplains, and montane grasslands and forests. Although herds can live in open woodland, the best habitat offers reeds, high grass, or thickets for cover. Grazer, including tall, mature grasses too coarse for most other ruminants to process. Massive cheek teeth, broad incisor row, and prehensile tongue that gathers and bundles grass before each bite enable buffalo to feed efficiently in longer grass. Herbs and foliage amount to 5% of diet, considerably more when grass is scarce or too unpalatable. Has to drink at least daily when pastured on standing hay.

ACTIVITY ● (O) Usually considered nocturnal, but herds protected from hunting spend 5 to 10.5 hours feeding at all seasons, night and day almost equally. Breeding herds range c. 2 mi (5.5 km) in the wet season, compared to ¾ mi (2 km) covered by stodgy bachelor herds. But buffalos daily commute up to 17 mi (27 km) between pasture and water in dry season.

SOCIAL/MATING SYSTEM

The buffalo is nonterritorial and extremely sociable, living in large, mixed herds that inhabit exclusive, traditional home ranges. At rest, members of the same clan often lie with backs touching, or with chin supported on a companion's back. Separate male and female rank orders are maintained, with adult males dominant over females. Bulls past their prime leave the breeding herds and associate in bachelor herds.

Herd size depends on habitat and pasture productivity; the more open and productive the range, the larger herds tend to be. On a broad floodplain in Kafue NP herds average 450 buffalos (range 19–2075), compared to 50 in the forests and glades of Mt. Meru, Tanzania. Home ranges vary from as small as 4 mi^2 (10.5 km^2) for a herd of 138 buffalos, to 114 mi^2 (296 km^2) for a herd of 1500. Bachelor herds of 5 to 10 up to 50 buffalos and solitary bulls have much smaller home ranges.

Buffalos that share the same home range may never assemble in the same herd. Although the majority aggregate during the rains, especially during the mating peak near the end, old bulls keep to themselves. In dry months, when good pastures are reduced to scattered patches, buffalos disperse in smaller units and prime bulls, along with subadult males, often form temporary bachelor herds .

Units consist of clans of a dozen or more related cows and their offspring that stay together as distinct subherds. They can often be spotted as separate columns of tightly clustered cows in a moving herd; 4 to 5 breeding (i.e., dominant) bulls consistently accompany each clan. Subdivision of large herds in the dry season is by clans. Each has its own trusted "pathfinder" that leads the way to pasture and water.

Males leave the clans as adolescents at 3 years and thereafter associate in peer subgroups that remain with the herd but keep clear of breeding bulls.

HOW IT MOVES   Gaits and movements like those of cattle. Though one of the slowest bovids, with top speed of 35 mph (56 kph), buffalos can outrun lions. But unable to accelerate quickly, they are comparatively easy for lions to ambush.

REPRODUCTION   Largely seasonal. With an 11.5-month gestation, longest in the family, birth peaks come early and mating peaks later in the rainy season. First calves at c. 5 years; intervals of c. 15 months between calves for cows in good condition. Estrus lasts 2 to 3 days. Bulls mature at 8 to 9 years.

OFFSPRING AND MATERNAL CARE   Despite long gestation and the ability of calves to gain their feet within c. 10 minutes after birth, they are too feeble to follow their mothers for several hours and need several weeks to keep up with the herd. Mothers that drop calves in the herd during a rest period are often left behind if the herd moves off, forcing the mother to go into hiding with her calf.

Females normally stop lactating in the seventh month of pregnancy, when the calf at heel is as young as 10 months. After the next calf is born, the mother becomes hostile to her last offspring, but yearlings continue following mothers for another year or more.

PREDATORS   Healthy adults are vulnerable only to lions; spotted hyenas are main predator of young, diseased, or injured adults.

Lions risk a herd mobbing attack when they catch a buffalo, are often treed, and occasionally trampled or gored. It is easier and actually safer to tackle bulls in bachelor herds. Buffalos fleeing from lions or hyenas often bunch tightly and run at much less than top speed, making it difficult for the predator to single out a quarry.

HOW IT COMMUNICATES   Sight 1, scent 2, sound 1.

Table 14.1. *AFRICAN BUFFALO BEHAVIOR GUIDE*
Expect to see and hear ➤ *Usual context and meaning*

Advertising Dominance

DOMINANT MALES

Position signal. ➤ Call given by high-ranking buffalos in herd, signals their presence and location.

Vegetation- and ground-horning; digging and tossing dirt. ➤ Advertises aggressive mood and high status, especially when performed in the presence of other bulls.

Kneeling and neck-rubbing. ➤ A display of aggressiveness peculiar to the bovine tribe.

Wallowing ± rolling and urinating. ➤ Dominant ♂♂ monopolize wallows. Urinating and rolling in wallow, plus other associated aggressive actions, indicate wallowing is more of a social than a maintenance activity.

Aggression

Supplanting. ➤ Making a lower-ranked individual move aside by simply walking toward it.

Approach in stiff-legged walk with head level or raised and chin pulled in. ➤ Display of dominance, often leading into broadside display.

Broadside display. ➤ Main dominance display. Advertises size and muscular development.

Circling during mutual broadside display. ➤ Equally matched adversaries end up circling slowly while performing broadside and other aggressive displays.

Confrontation ± looking away. ➤ Prelude to combat when combined with threat display, but may also be sparring invitation.

High-horn threat.

Medial-horn threat, in broadside stance.

Low-horn threat.

Head-low posture. ➤ Defensive threat.

Aggression *continued*

OTHER ACTIONS ASSOCIATED WITH THREAT DISPLAYS
Threatening when addressed to specific individual.

Vegetation- and ground-horning and dirt-tossing, kneeling and neck-rubbing, rolling.

Tossing and hooking movements. ➤ Threat to toss and hook opponent.

VOCAL ACCOMPANIMENT
Grunting and growling.

FEMALE AGGRESSIVE BEHAVIOR
Same as ♂'s but at lower frequency; ♀ ♀ rarely roll, neck-rub, or horn vegetation. ➤ Performed mainly to reinforce rank dominance.

Submission

Turning away. ➤ Avoidance of approaching superior.

Head-low, chin-out posture ± approaching and placing nose under dominant's belly. ➤ Infantile behavior derived from nursing.

Wheeling and running away, meanwhile bellowing with mouth open and tongue curled. ➤ Response to threat or attack.

Short grunt while bolting, followed by standing in exaggerated alarm posture. ➤ Scared buffalo on point of flight, after sudden attack.

Displacement Activities

Grazing, sideswiping, as in fly-shooing, scratching back with horn tips, scraping with incisors.

Sociable Behavior

Nose-to-nose contact. ➤ Usual greeting and identity check upon meeting.

Nose-to-genitals. ➤ Less common sequel to nose-to-nose contact.

Lying in contact.

Social licking. ➤ The primary form of social grooming; partners take turns but the prevailing direction is from lower- to higher-ranking.

HERD-COORDINATING CALLS
Low-pitched, 2–4 sec. call repeated at 3–6 sec. intervals. ➤ Signal to move.

Creaking-gate sound. ➤ Direction-giving signal emitted by herd leaders during movement.

Extended *maaa* call. ➤ Emitted by one or a few buffalos up to 20 times/min. before and during movement to water.

Calls made by grazing herd: brief bellows, grunts, honks, croaks. ➤ Help to keep herd going in same direction, signal that all is well, etc.

Courtship

MALE BEHAVIOR

Tending bond: ♂ keeping close to ♀ and keeping other ♂ ♂ away. ➤ An indication that ♀ is approaching estrus and being courted.

Dominance and threat displays. ➤ Common prelude to courtship, essential to impress and dominate ♀.

Lowstretch. ➤ Posture of ♂ approaching to check ♀ reproductive status.

Urine-testing. ➤ Grimace includes pronounced lip-curl.

Licking and resting chin on ♀'s rump. ➤ Mounting prelude.

FEMALE BEHAVIOR

Responsive urination. ➤ Prompted by ♂ approach and licking.

Moving away.

Defensive threats.

Submissive behavior.

ESTROUS BEHAVIOR

Standing still with tail arched, mounting of and by other cows, resting head on ♂'s rump or pushing muzzle under his belly.

Mother and Offspring

Nursing between ♀'s hind legs. ➤ Standard nursing position in buffalo.

Calves stay with mothers instead of forming crèches.

Vocal contact: croaking call by mother, higher pitched in calf, which calls only when separated.

Social licking between mother and calf.

Play

Running and chasing games, with tail arched, sparring. ➤ Mainly performed by the young.

Response to Predators

Alert posture, with tail arched ± advancing to investigate source of disturbance and head-tossing.

Wheeling and flight.

Stampeding in close formation.

Mobbing attack, stimulated by distress call, preceded by croaking calls and approach in alert posture, close-packed.

SOUNDS OF ALARM

Alarm snorts, *waaa* distress call.

Chapter 15

GIRAFFE
Giraffa camelopardalis
Family Giraffidae

Figure 15.1. Bull giraffes necking, thereby testing their strength and place in the male dominance hierarchy.

WHAT IT IS   The biggest ruminant and the tallest mammal. Very long neck with short, upstanding mane, high shoulders sloping steeply to hind-quarters; long legs nearly equal in length. ♂ wt 2420–4250 lb (1100–1932 kg), shoulder ht 9–11 ft (2.7–3.3 m), top of horns up to 18 ft (5.5 m); ♀ wt 1540–2600 lb (700–1182 kg), ht c. 2 ft shorter. *Head:* tapers to point; long, prehensile tongue. *Horns:* solid bone, skin-covered; a main pair in both sexes but female's thin and tufted; male's thick and bald on top, up to 5 in (13.5 cm). A median horn and 4 or more smaller bumps in males. *Tail:* hock-length, with long tassel. *Color:* brown to rich chestnut (old males darker, even black), dissected into intricate tapestry by patches and blotches of lighter hair, pattern unique in each giraffe. *Scent glands:* possible glands on eyelids, nose, lips; adult males have pungent smell. *Teats:* 4.

164

SUBSPECIES Eight recognized races, the reticulated giraffe (G. c. *reticulata*) of north Kenya most distinctive: its latticework of thin lines separating dark patches is also most unlike the markings of any other mammal. The familiar Masai giraffe (G. c. *tippelskirchi*) of East Africa has the most irregular pattern.

RELATIVES The rare okapi, *Okapia johnstoni*, confined to a small region within the Congo Basin and only discovered early this century, is a dead ringer for the rainforest ancestor of the giraffe.

WHERE IT LIVES Formerly throughout arid and dry-savanna zones south of the Sahara, wherever trees occur. Eliminated from most of West African and southern Kalahari range but still reasonably common even outside wildlife preserves.

GOOD PLACES TO SEE IT Too numerous to mention; most approachable along traveled roads in the popular national parks.

ECOLOGY Equipped to exploit a 6-foot band of foliage beyond reach of all other terrestrial browsers except the elephant. The 18-inch (45-cm) tongue and a modified atlas-axis joint that lets the head extend vertically further increase the height advantage. Giraffes can browse crowns of small trees; big bulls can reach 19 feet, a yard higher than cows. Feed mainly on broad-leafed deciduous foliage in the rains and on evergreen species at other seasons; menu includes 100 species but *Acacia* and *Combretum* trees are mainstays in most areas. Narrow muzzle and flexible upper lip, along with the prehensile tongue, enable this animal to harvest the most nutritious leaves in the quantity (up to 75 lb [34 kg] per day) necessary to sustain its great bulk. Drinks every 2 to 3 days when water available but also extracts water from green leaves; spends dry season near evergreen vegetation, as along watercourses, dispersing more widely in the rains.

ACTIVITY ○ (●) Females spend just over half a 24-hour day browsing, males somewhat less (43%). Night is mostly spent lying down ruminating, especially hours after dark and before dawn. Bulls spend about 22% of the 24 hours walking, compared to 13% for cows—the extra mileage goes into searching for cows in heat.

SOCIAL/MATING SYSTEM (♀○♀○♀) (♂♂♂) (♀○♂♀○♂♀♀) (♂♂♂)
The giraffe is nonterritorial and sociable, living in loose, open herds. At a given moment a giraffe may be in a herd composed of all males, all females, females and young, or of both sexes and all ages—or all alone if it is a mature bull or a cow guarding a new calf. There are no leaders and minimum coordination of herd movements.

The fluid nature of giraffe society reflects the need to spend most of its time feeding and to move independently between variably spaced trees, and size that makes it unnecessary to bunch together for mutual security. Also height and excellent eyesight enable giraffes to maintain visual contact at long distances: a dozen may be dispersed over ½ mi (0.8 km) of savanna and still be in a herd. In fact giraffes rarely cluster together unless they happen to be attracted to the same tree, nervous over the presence of lions, or aggregated in the open. Even at rest, herd members stay over 20 yd apart.

As usual, females are more sociable than males and rarely out of sight of other females. Mothers of small calves associate most consistently, at least partly because of a mutual attraction between youngsters that results in crèches of up to 9 calves. Average spacing between calves is usually less than 10 yd.

Males remain in maternal herds until they outgrow their resemblance to females at about 3 years, after which they join bachelor herds. They eventually leave their natal range, whereas females stay put. Home ranges of adults and subadults of the two sexes average 63 mi² in Tsavo NP (163 km²), but vary enormously—from 2 up to 252 mi² (5–654 km²). Once settled, bulls have smaller ranges than cows.

HOW IT MOVES   A giraffe has just 2 gaits: walk and gallop. The long legs and short trunk decree an ambling walk, with the entire weight supported alternately on left and right legs, as in camels. The long neck moves in synchrony to maintain balance. In galloping (top speed: 37 mph [60 kph]), forelegs and hind legs work in pairs like a running rabbit's.

To drink, a giraffe must either straddle or bend its forelegs. The same is true of the okapi, disproving the idea that the giraffe's extra-long neck and legs are the reason.

REPRODUCTION   Year-round, with rainy-season conception peak. First pregnant in fourth year, gestation 14 to 14.5 months; minimum interval between calves c. 16 months. Males begin competing for matings at 7 years but continue growing, giving seniors a decided weight and height advantage. Male's head also gains weight with age, through bone deposition—the process that creates the extra knobs on an old bull's head—enabling a bull to deliver ever heavier blows during contests. Combat is rare, though, as bulls from the same area all know their place in a rank hierarchy established through daily contests while maturing in bachelor herds. By the time a female in estrus is ready to mate, the local alpha male has usually supplanted all lesser rivals without ever coming to blows.

OFFSPRING AND MATERNAL CARE   If we assume Serengeti giraffes are typical, a cow returns to the same location each time she calves. The first week or so a calf lies-out half the day and most of the night, carefully guarded by its mother, which usually stays within 11 to 25 yd of her offspring for the first 2 weeks, although mothers may stay over 100 yd from a hidden calf and even leave it alone to go to water. The increased security of a maternity group guarding calves in a crèche allows a mother to go further and stay away longer. But calves are rarely left totally unattended; absent mothers usually return before dark to suckle their offspring and stay with them overnight. Although giraffes are weaned as yearlings and nutritionally independent at 16 months, the maternal bond lasts up to 22 months.

PREDATORS   From 50 to 75% of calves fall prey to lions and spotted hyenas the first months, despite hiding and the mother's determined defense. As adults are too big to be regular prey, a mother will stand over and defend her calf against lions, which run the risk of being kicked to death if they get within striking distance. Females never use their horns, and males only use theirs in contests with peers.

HOW THEY COMMUNICATE   Sight 1, scent 3, sound 4. The idea that giraffes are mute is a myth. Though normally silent, calves bleat and make a mewing call, cows seeking lost calves bellow, and courting bulls may emit a raucous cough. Giraffes also give alarm snorts, and moaning, snoring, hissing, and flutelike sounds have been reported.

Table 15.1. *GIRAFFE BEHAVIOR GUIDE*
Expect to see and hear ➤ *Usual context and meaning*

Male Advertising Dominance

A big bull walking confidently in the erect posture, head high, or urine-testing ♀ ♀. ➤ Observe behavior of other bulls toward such an animal, especially whether they discreetly move out of his path.

Aggression

CHALLENGE TO SPAR OR FIGHT
♂ ♂ only. ♀ ♀ do not spar or fight.

1. Challenger makes nonchalant approach, stands facing opponent in erect posture. ➤ Probable winner of a sparring contest can be foretold if one stands more erect or is taller than the other.

2. If opponent responds in kind, they have a confrontation.

3. They move stiff-legged into parallel position, or

4. March in step with necks horizontal, looking straight ahead.

5. They rub heads and necks ± twine necks (see Fig. 15.1) or lean against one another, ears flapping (low intensity), with pauses while gazing into distance. ➤ Assessing opponent's weight.

Aggression *continued*

 6. Contestants aim blows at rump, flanks, or neck either from head-to-head or head-to-tail position, damping impact by leaning away. ➤ Skillful rocking with blows avoids damage. The rare hard blow that lands solidly can down an opponent.

Standing broadside in erect posture.

Angle-horn threat from broadside stance. ➤ Aiming horns at adversary is intention movement or threat to strike a blow.

OTHER ACTIONS ASSOCIATED WITH THREAT DISPLAYS
Sideswiping, mounting, displacement activities.

Submission

Giving way: turning away from approaching individual; jumping aside. ➤ Yielding to displacing superior.

Head and ears lowered, chin in. ➤ Appeasement display.

Displacement Activities

Pretended feeding; scraping with incisors or licking.

Courtship

MALE BEHAVIOR
Following ♀ closely and keeping other ♂ ♂ away. ➤ Tending bond indicates ♀ approaching or in estrus.

 Urine-testing with pronounced lip-curl.

Contact: rubbing head on ♀'s rump, licking her tail, nudging, gentle butting, resting neck on her back.

Foreleg-lifting.

Standing immobile in erect posture behind ♀. ➤ Prelude to mounting.

FEMALE BEHAVIOR
Bolting and rapid tail-swishing.

 ♀ urinating in response to ♂'s approach and contact/sniffing.

Courtship circling.

Holding tail out and deflected while standing in copulatory attitude (head up or down, ears back).

 Mating. ➤ Male looks in danger of overbalancing..

Mother and Offspring

Young calves standing seemingly alone, just looking around.

Young calves in crèches.

Play

Racing around mother after nursing; calves gamboling; nose-to-nose greeting; older calves sparring. ➤ Especially early and late in day.

Response to Predators

Alert posture, head raised to maximum. ➤ Mothers of small calves especially vigilant.

Snorting. ➤ Rarely heard.

Kicking with front or hind feet. ➤ Response to close approach, especially ♀ with calf.

Part II

OTHER HOOFED MAMMALS

ORDER ARTIODACTYLA, EVEN-TOED UNGULATES

Family	African Species
Suidae: swine	4
Hippopotamidae: hippopotamuses	2

ORDER PERISSODACTYLA, ODD-TOED UNGULATES

Family	African Species
Rhinocerotidae: rhinoceroses	2
Equidae: zebras, asses, horses	4

ORDER HYRACOIDEA

Family	African Species
Procaviidae: hyraxes	11

ORDER PROBOSCIDEA

Family	African Species
Elephantidae: elephants	1

The 24 hoofed mammals in Part II belong to 4 different orders and 6 different families. About all they have in common is the fact that they are nonruminants. The plants they eat pass through the stomach before undergoing bacterial fermentation in the cecum, a large pouch off the colon. Elephants and hyraxes aren't even proper hoofed mammals—they're "near-ungulates" (Paenungulata) with toenails rather than real hooves.

Although their older digestive system is less efficient, nonruminant ungulates compensate by processing more food in a shorter time. And they are able to process tougher, more fibrous vegetation than ruminants can. The elephant, bushpig, warthog, hippo, and plains zebra are among the most successful large African herbivores.

Chapter 16

SWINE
Family Suidae

Wild boar, *Sus scrofa*
Bushpig, *Potamochoerus porcus*

Giant forest hog, *Hylochoerus meinertzhageni*
Warthog, *Phacochoerus aethiopicus*

WHAT THEY ARE   Even-toed ungulates of blimpish shape, with short neck and legs. *Head*: massive, nose a flattened disk, small eyes, and wartlike facial growths (warthog and giant forest hog). *Teeth*: canine teeth enlarged as tusks, lower pair honed razor-sharp against upper pair; molars low-crowned, simple as in humans (not serrated as in other ungulates). *Coat*: coarse and thin. *Color*: dull gray or brown-black without markings (except bushpig); piglets horizontally striped (bushpig and wild boar). *Scent glands*: hoof, carpal (bushpig), preorbital (warthog, forest hog), behind eyes (warthog). Also tusk/lip, salivary, chin, preputial, and anal glands. *Teats*: 4 (warthog) to 12 (wild boar).

SOCIAL/MATING SYSTEMS   Pigs live in family groups called sounders, which occupy traditional, but undefended, overlapping home ranges. Boars (adult males) keep growing bigger and enlarging their weapons, leading to a male dominance hierarchy based on seniority.

The basic unit of pig society is a sow with a litter of piglets. Two or more sows with offspring, likely mother and grown daughters or sisters, often join together to form larger sounders. However, two different grouping and mating systems exist in this family:

One-male harem system. One or more females and their offspring are led and guarded by a boar. Immature and unsuccessful adult males live alone or in small bachelor herds. Examples: bushpig and giant forest hog.

Segregated society. Sounders contain one or more females and young of the year; males solitary or associated in small bachelor groups. Example: warthog.

HOW THEY MOVE   Cross-walk and gallop; warthog also trots. Pigs lie down and get up by first sitting on their haunches (except warthogs), like dogs. Sleep on side with legs extended or on front with legs gathered and chin on the ground. All are good swimmers. Short necks and plump bodies prevent mouth-grooming backs or rumps, so they rub against objects and groom one another. Group members lie touching, a mark of sociability and a way for cold pigs to share body heat.

REPRODUCTION   Pigs are the only hoofed mammals that have multiple young: 4 to 5 in a typical litter, up to a dozen (wild boar, forest hog). Birth weight is only about 1% of the mother's mass, compared to 10% in antelopes. After a gestation of only 114 to 175 days, newborn piglets are born immature and helpless.

MATING   A lengthy process of 3 to 20 minutes in domestic pigs. Boars stand erect with trotters braced on the sow's back while pelvic-thrusting. They have a corkscrew-shaped penis and huge testes that produce 20 ounces of semen containing an estimated 290 billion sperm per ejaculation (domestic pig).

HOW THEY COMMUNICATE   Sight 2 to 3, scent 1, sound 1.

Table 16.1. SWINE BEHAVIOR GUIDE
Expect to see and hear ➤ *Usual context and meaning*

Male Advertising Presence and Dominance

SCENT-MARKING

Tusking and scent-marking trees (see Fig. 16.1). ➤ Boars reach as high as possible, scoring bark and depositing tusk-gland secretion. Biggest boars leave highest marks, one means of asserting dominance status.

Rubbing preorbital glands on trees and other objects. ➤ Warthog scent-marking.

Urination. ➤ Preputial gland gives ♂ urine a pungent odor.

Aggression

Strutting in broadside: moving in erect posture with mincing steps. ➤ Display of dominance, during approach to adversary.

Standing in broadside display (left): head raised, ears cocked, hair bristling. ➤ Dominance or threat display that shows size and power of displayer to best advantage. Hog on right responds with head-low posture (defensive threat).

Threat-circling and mutual broadside display. ➤ Prelude to fighting: slashing attacks to shoulders and neck by bushpig.

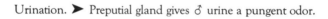

Confrontations. ➤ Normal combat position.

OTHER ACTIONS ASSOCIATED WITH THREAT DISPLAYS
Sideward and upward head movements. ➤ Snout-boxing and slashing-intention movements.

Tree-tusking ± scent-marking. ➤ A threat when addressed to specific opponent.

Aggression *continued*

Pawing the ground and rolling. ➤ Bushpig display.

Feinted attack.

Noises: grunting, growling, low-level squealing, gnashing tusks, and grinding molars.

Submission

Head low, ears flattened, backing away, and squealing. ➤ Inhibits attack, gives loser of a fight a chance to disengage and run away.

 Bolting. ➤ Boar chasing adolescent ♂.

Sociable Behavior

Physical contact with scent-marking and smelling.

Nose-to-nose and nose-to-mouth contact. ➤ Typical meeting behavior, prelude to friendly or aggressive interactions.

Lying in contact.

Social grooming with snout and incisors. ➤ Important in social relations between mother and young, among associated females, and in courtship.

Courtship

SIGNS OF ESTRUS

 Frequent urination by ♀.

Swelling of labia and mucous discharge, mounting and being mounted by other ♀ ♀.

Active interest in ♂ ♂, including nuzzling, playful biting, smelling and licking ♂'s genitalia.

Adopting rigid mating stance. ➤ In response to ♂ mating call, or even the odor of salivary or preputial glands.

MALE BEHAVIOR

Strutting with raised tail (shown under aggression). ➤ To impress and dominate ♀.

Urine-testing. ➤ Pigs sample urine but do not grimace.

Spraying urine over ♀'s urine.

Nuzzling, massaging, and scent-marking ♀'s sides and rear.

VOCAL ACCOMPANIMENT

Rhythmic grunting. ➤ Suid love song.Champing and foaming. ➤ Foam contains odors of salivary and tusk glands.

Clacking. ➤ Sound made by warthog.

Mother and Offspring

Nose-to-nose contact, ♀ and piglets.

Social grooming.

Suckling: piglets summoned by grunting and lying on side.

Piglets nose and poke teats to let down milk.

Play

Running games; play-fighting, including "boxing." Solitary play, including tail-chasing, make-believe scratching, digging, wallowing, tossing objects. ➤ Play common only among young.

Response to Predators

Warning grunt, bristling, mock or real charge, noisy flight with grunts and snorts, freezing and hiding by piglets.

Mobbing response. ➤ Concerted attack (bushpig, giant forest hog).

Sounds of alarm: loud grunts, squealing roars.

BUSHPIG, *Potamochoerus porcus*

Figure 16.1. Bushpig boar marking a tree, visually with tusks and with scent of tusk glands.

WHAT IT IS   African equivalent of the European wild boar, smaller and more colorful. Short, rotund body with rounded back. ♂ ♀ wt 119–253 lb (54–115 kg); ht 22–32 in (55–80 cm). *Head:* long, massive; males have bony shield and gristly pads on muzzle. Long tasseled ears. *Teeth:* 42; upper tusks barely project, functioning mainly as strop to hone lethal 3-in (7.5-cm) lower pair. *Coat:* coarse with long spinal crest. *Color:* varies geographically. Eastern and southern savanna forms dark brown to black with light head, ear tufts and spinal crest; overlapping and mixing in East Africa with the more colorful red river hog of the equatorial rainforest; piglets dark brown with rows of light spots. *Teats:* 6.

WHERE IT LIVES   One of the most adaptable ungulates, found throughout Africa south of the Sahel wherever there is adequate cover and water.

ECOLOGY   Lives in all kinds of wooded habitat and also thrives in swamps and marshes. An omnivore. Eats mostly roots, bulbs, and fallen fruits; also carrion, excrement, and small birds and mammals. Roots industriously with its hard snout, using tusks to dig deeper trenches and excavate roots. One of Africa's most serious agricultural pests, requiring stockade fences to protect crops such as manioc and maize, with great attendant destruction of trees.

ACTIVITY ● (○) Considered mainly nocturnal because bushpigs venture into the open at night. Where unpersecuted, they often forage actively in woods and thickets in daylight hours. Resting sounders may use regular day nests in mounds of litter, which they leave only if driven.

SOCIAL/MATING SYSTEM Families or harems consist of 1 boar and 1 to 4 sows plus offspring in sounders totaling up to 15 to 20 pigs. Aggregations of over 40 bushpigs have been recorded, presumably consisting of several different families, but usually sounders are mutually antagonistic. Depending on resource distribution and abundance, home ranges can be as small as 49 acres (20 ha) and as large as 2470 acres (1000 ha).

The boar leads and protects his family/harem. Offspring remain associated for a year or more, and some females may never leave. Littermates are inseparable companions for the first year or so. Males are eventually driven out by their fathers; at least some subadults associate in bachelor groups. Competition for food or access to wallows can lead to aggression, with adults pulling rank on immature classes. Sounders use communal latrines.

REPRODUCTION Year-round with peaks in the rainy season. First pregnancy as early as 21 months, a good 2 years before boars mature; gestation c. 4 months.

OFFSPRING AND PARENTAL CARE Sows farrow up to 6 young in nests prepared beforehand. For first 2 months piglets lie hidden while mother forages. Mothers readily join forces, forming sounders of over 20 bushpigs that include numerous partly grown offspring and several adults.

PREDATORS Mainly leopard and spotted hyena, followed perhaps by lion; down to eagles and snakes, to which piglets are vulnerable.

Table 16.2. *DIFFERENCES IN BUSHPIG BEHAVIOR*
Expect to see and hear ➤ Usual context and meaning

Aggression

Threat-circling and mutual broadside display. ➤ Can lead to slashing and biting fight, but much less common than frontal fighting.

Confrontations. ➤ ♂ ♂ push and box with their snouts crossed, engaging the bony shield and gristly cheek pads.

Sociable Behavior

Greeting bushpigs wheeze, blowing breath at each other.

Contact calls: soft grunts. ➤ Uttered by dominant individual in moving group.

Response to Predators

Freezing and hiding by piglets. ➤ Until spots fade at ½ year.

Sounder stopping to look back after initial flight.

SOUNDS OF ALARM

Loud grunts, squealing roars. ➤ Cornered pigs roar and squeal with nose to ground and mane bristling.

GIANT FOREST HOG, *Hylochoerus meinertzhageni*

Figure 16.2. Ramming fight between male giant forest hogs.

WHAT IT IS   The largest swine, an overgrown version of the bushpig. ♂ wt 319–605 lb (145–275 kg), ht 34–40 in (86–101 cm); ♀ wt 286–449 lb (130–204 kg), ht within ♂ range. *Head:* big with broad snout; inflated, padded cushions partially rim male's eyes; broad ears taper to a point. *Teeth:* 32 to 34; upper tusks to 12 in (30 cm), flaring outward. *Coat:* long, black hair over slate-gray skin; patches of lighter hair on face; babies straw-colored, un-striped. *Teats:* 4.

WHERE IT LIVES   Scattered populations along equator from Liberia to Kenya and Tanzania in various types of forest, from Lowland Rainforest to the bamboo and subalpine zones of East Africa's highest mountains.

GOOD PLACES TO SEE IT   The lodges in Aberdare NP and FR, Kenya.

ECOLOGY   Requires dense cover and year-round abundance of green herbage. Tolerance of temperatures from steaming lowlands to freezing upper slopes of Mt. Kenya may depend on thickets to ameliorate temperature extremes as much as for safety. Grasses, sedges, and other herbage it eats only grows in sunny locations, making second-growth forest, forest-savanna mosaic, and montane forests and glades the most favorable habitats. Seasonal movements between vegetation zones to find preferred herbage. Wide mouth and large, high-crowned molars adapted for grazing; inflated snout almost useless for rooting, which it rarely attempts and then only in soft ground.

ACTIVITY   ● (○) Mainly night. Only likely to be seen while grazing in the open, especially from dusk to midnight, the peak feeding period. The rest of the time they stay in the forest, remaining huddled in their beds on cold, wet days, but emerging to bask if the sun appears.

SOCIAL/MATING SYSTEM   The basic social unit is a sow accompanied by up to 3 successive litters and a boar that defends them from other boars and predators. Usually only males without a harem are solitary, and pairs are likely to be courting couples. Sounder may include up to 4 or 5 regularly associated sows. Different groups have overlapping home ranges —estimated at perhaps 4 mi^2 (10 km^2) in the Aberdare population—but exclusive core areas, including the thickets where they retire for rest and security. Hogs lie up in regular bedding grounds, recognizable as shallow scrapes beneath logs or between tree roots, screened by dense vegetation, with a nearby latrine. Different sounders also deposit dung in communal latrines located at the bases of trees on the commons where they graze.

Encounters between sounders at water holes, mineral licks, or on pastures often lead to temporary mingling, but only one boar is found even in large groups of 20 or more hogs. When two sounders meet, one boar leaves, either with or without his family, and usually without overt aggression. Boars, which undoubtedly know one another by smell and probably by voice, either assert or accept their respective places in the male hierarchy when they meet. Only when rank is unsettled do fights occur. Serious battles entail charging and ramming. When their hollowed foreheads meet precisely, air is compressed and makes a loud pop (see Fig.16.2). Despite reinforced skulls, healed impact fractures are not uncommon.

REPRODUCTION   Not strictly seasonal, but mating peaks late in rainy periods. Females can conceive as yearlings; males mature at least 2 or 3 years later. Gestation reportedly 125 days.

OFFSPRING AND PARENTAL CARE   From 2 to 11 young born in nest mother may prepare by carrying dry grass. She stays in dense cover with them for about a week, but they begin to accompany her within the first few days. In the open, piglets bunch beneath her.

PREDATORS   Though formidable and fiercely protective, giant hogs lose at least ½ their offspring, mostly to spotted hyenas and leopards.

Table 16.3. *DIFFERENCES IN GIANT FOREST HOG BEHAVIOR*
Expect to see and hear ➤ *Usual context and meaning*

Male Advertising Presence and Dominance

SCENT-MARKING

Tusking and scent-marking trees. ➤ Uncertain whether forest hogs have the habit or the tusk gland.

Rubbing preorbital glands on trees and other objects. ➤ Behavior that also needs further study. Readers' reports welcomed.

Aggression

Confrontations, leading to snout-pushing and snout-knocking, forehead-pushing, sometimes to ramming. ➤ After approaching with heads raised to horizontal and sniffing noses, contestants engage nose disks and push, followed by withdrawal of lighter animal.

Courtship

Signs of estrus: ♀ and ♂ consorting on their own.

♂ follows ♀ closely, grunting loudly, frequently urinates, pushes and butts her hindquarters with snout and forehead.

Copulation, lasting up to 10 min.

Mother and Offspring

Close contact, clustering beneath mother and walking in unison in open.

Play

Mainly play-fighting. ➤ Juveniles snout-box (deliver sideward blows to each other's head) and forehead-push by the hour, especially ♂ ♂.

Response to Predators

Frightened piglets lying still. ➤ Relying on straw-colored natal coat or brown and black juvenile coat to escape notice.

Loud grunts and snorts accompany flight and mock charges.

WARTHOG, *Phacochoerus aethiopicus*

Figure 16.3. Warthogs in frontal-pushing fight, with upper tusks engaged.

WHAT IT IS   Naked swine of the savanna. Slimmer than other hogs, with level back and comparatively long limbs. ♂ wt 150-220 lb (68-100 kg), ht 27 in (68 cm); ♀ 99-156 lb (45-71 kg), ht 24 in (60 cm). *Head:* large with flat face; prominent tusks, uppers average c. 8 in (20 cm) for male, up to 24 in (60 cm), lowers 4 in (10 cm); much shorter in female; prominent "warts" (thickened skin and gristle) below eyes, up to 6 in (13 cm) long in males, mere bumps in females and young. *Coat:* scattered bristles, whiskers, and a mane of long hair. *Color:* skin gray; mane and tail tuft dark; cheek whiskers white, shaped like tusks. Harderian glands in eye sockets leave dark stains on male's face. *Teats:* 4.

WHERE IT LIVES   Northern and Southern Savanna and adjacent arid zone, absent only from deserts, rainforest, and mountains above 10,000 feet (3000 m).

GOOD PLACES TO SEE IT   Common in virtually every park with savanna habitat, but opportunities to see approachable hogs on short pasture are limited. A few of the better spots: Nairobi and Amboseli NP, Masai Mara NR, Kenya; Arusha, Manyara, and Serengeti NP, Tanzania; Chobe NP, Botswana; Kruger NP, South Africa.

ECOLOGY   A true savanna dweller that avoids dense cover and forest but depends on burrows to escape predators and temperature extremes, especially in infancy. Although warthogs dig quite well, using snout as shovel, most holes they use have been excavated by aardvarks. Whether warthogs live in areas uninhabited by aardvarks is an open question.

Unequalled ability to exploit buried and highly nutritious rhizomes, bulbs, and such enables as many as 78 warthogs/mi^2 (30/km^2) to thrive in the best habitat, namely fertile alluvial soils with a good cover of palatable grasses or species with edible rhizomes. With molar teeth and jaw hinge mod-ified for grinding grass, warthogs graze when grass is green and use their hard-edged snout disk to uncover rhizomes of grasses and sedges, tubers, and bulbs in dry season; also eat some fallen fruits. They drink and in hot, dry weather use wallows daily.

ACTIVITY   ○ Strictly diurnal. After traveling an average 4.3 mi (7 km) in daylight, females and young retire before dark into 1 of up to 10 secure sleeping burrows dotted within their home range, emerging the next morn-ing—late in cold or rainy weather. Burrows are used by different sounders on a first-come, first-served basis. Boars are somewhat less diurnal, often remain ac-tive for an hour or so after dark, later on moonlit nights. They stay up late during rut to sniff out burrows occupied by sows in heat, returning to waylay them as they emerge next morning.

SOCIAL/MATING SYSTEM   (♀♀) (♀♀♀) (♂♂♂) (♂♂♂) Sows live in clans of related individuals that share the same resources. Mothers and daughters with offspring up to 2 years old may stay in the same group or in different groups that share a traditional home range (average 430 acres, range 158–924 acres [72–420 ha]). Sounders typically number 5 or less and include only 1 sow with her young of the year, but many contain 2 mothers with their combined broods; sounders with 4 to 5 sows occasionally number up to 16 warthogs. Associated mothers suckle one another's young—usually a reliable sign of kinship.

Males also remain in their natal home range. After parting from females they associate with their brothers or unrelated males until mature at 4 years. Adults only join female groups when a sow is in heat.

HOW IT MOVES   Top speed of 34 mph (55 kph) in emergencies, but warthogs in a hurry prefer to trot—characteristically with tail straight up like an antenna. They lie down and get up like ruminants, not swine, kneeling on forelegs in lying and raising the hindquarters first in rising. Feeding warthogs routinely graze and root while resting on their callused knees.

REPRODUCTION   A seasonal breeder wherever dry seasons are pro-longed, mating as rains end (3-day estrus) and farrowing 160 to 170 days later as rainy season begins (Sept.–Dec.) in eastern and southern Africa. In higher-rainfall equatorial regions, breeding is not limited to particular months. Both sexes fertile at 18 to 19 months, but few males breed before turning 4.

OFFSPRING AND MATERNAL CARE   Sows isolate to farrow, then stay underground nurturing 2 to 5 (rarely 6–8) tiny, hairless piglets for the first week. Except for brief excursions or to change dens, piglets remain in bur-row 6 to 7 weeks, after which they accompany their mother everywhere, filing

Figure 16.4. Warthog den with piglets in termite mound.

behind her in a fixed order. Begin grazing within 2 to 3 weeks but continue nursing briefly every 40 minutes or so from 3 to 6 weeks; weaned by 6 months.

PREDATORS   Being slower with less endurance than most savanna ungulates, burrows are essential sanctuaries when chased by cheetah, wild dog, or spotted hyena. However, cheetahs think twice before tackling adult warthogs, are often chased by mothers defending offspring. Fleeing juveniles pile headlong into a hole; adults reverse direction at last instant, can then use their tusks on pursuers that try to follow. Up to ½ offspring succumb to predators and other causes the first year.

Although burrows keep warthogs safe at night, emerging in the morning can be risky since lions are clever enough to sniff out occupied burrows and patient enough to wait in ambush at breakfast time.

Table 16.4. *DIFFERENCES IN WARTHOG BEHAVIOR*
            Expect to see and hear ➤ Usual context and meaning

Aggression

Fighting (see Fig 16.3). ➤ Ritualized pushing and boxing with blunt upper tusks and snout (no slashing or stabbing with lower tusks). Warts absorb blows, protect eyes.

VOCAL ACCOMPANIMENT
Grunting, growling, warning *woomph.*

Submission

Head low and mane lowered, ears flattened, backing away, squealing and squealing growl; bolting.

Sociable Behavior

Lying in contact. ➤ Especially in burrows and outside when it is cold.

Rubbing preorbital and tusk glands together or on partner's face and body. ➤ Often follows greeting.

Social grooming with snout and incisors: groomee solicits by lying prone or on side with legs raised. ➤ Directed particularly to neck and mane.

Courtship

SIGNS OF ESTRUS

Frequent urination, discoloring rear.

Adopting mating stance.

MALE BEHAVIOR

Following in a springy, hip-rolling gait, tail out and bent down, meanwhile clacking. ➤ Clacking is a chugging noise produced by clicking tongue or tusks, producing copious saliva.

Nuzzling, massaging, and scent-marking ♀'s head, sides and rear; resting chin on ♀'s rump.

Mother and Offspring

Nose-to-nose greeting, with explosive grunts.

Mother summons piglets from burrow with soft, low grunts.

Following mother in single file.

Squeaking and churring of small piglets. ➤ Expresses discomfort, distress.

Play

"Playful" interactions of littermates mostly involve sparring and aggressive displays. Rank order thereby established at early age.

Response to Predators

Trotting with tail vertical. ➤ Marks general arousal rather than specific response to predator.

SOUNDS OF ALARM

Single loud alarm grunt, growl-grunt, *woomph* (startled) call, distress squeal.

Chapter 17

HIPPOPOTAMUS
Hippopotamus amphibius
Family Hippopotamidae

Figure 17.1. Hippo bulls in mutual yawning threat display.

WHAT IT IS An enormous, amphibious mammal with smooth, naked skin. Inflated-looking body supported on short, relatively thin legs. ♂ wt 3529-7040 lb (1600-3200 kg), ht 56-66 in (140-165 cm); ♀ wt 1440-5157 lb (655-2344 kg), ht 52-58 in (130-145 cm). *Head:* huge muzzle, bigger in males; eyes, nostrils, and little ears placed high on head. *Teeth:* canines enlarged as tusks, lower pair up to 20 in (50 cm) in male, kept sharp by honing against short upper pair; middle pair of lower incisors elongated in male (12-16 in [30-40 cm]). *Tail:* a paddle, short and muscular with flattened sides. *Color:* brown to gray-purple with pink underparts and creases; short bristles on head, back, and tail. *Penis:* recurves backward and testes internal. *Glands:* mucous glands secrete an oily red fluid that protects skin from sunburn and drying, and perhaps infection; no scent or sweat glands. *Teats:* 2.

RELATIVE The pigmy hippo, *Choreopsis liberiensis*, a solitary, forest-dwelling native of the West African lowland rainforests, considered a living relic of the hippo's ancestor.

WHERE IT LIVES Formerly everywhere south of the Sahara where adequate water and grazing occur. Largely confined now to protected areas but still survives in many major rivers and swamps.

185

GOOD PLACES TO SEE IT   Almost any park and reserve with sizeable lakes and rivers bordered by grassland.

ECOLOGY   Hippos need water deep enough to cover them, within commuting distance of pasture. They must submerge because their thin, naked skin is vulnerable to overheating and dehydration. They avoid rapids, preferring gently sloping, firm bottom where herds can rest half-submerged and calves can nurse without swimming. At densities up to 81 hippos/mi^2 (31/km^2), hippo's local environmental impact is second only to elephant's. A grazer, it eats about 88 lb (40 kg) of preferably short grass nightly, mowing a 20-in (50-cm) swath with its muscular lips.

ACTIVITY   ● (○) Hippos walk 2 to 3 miles (3–5 km), at most 6 miles during nightly foraging. Paths from water to pastures start as broad highways but branch into inconspicuous secondary and tertiary tracks within a mile or two. After 5 hours of intensive grazing, hippos return to water beds before dawn to spend the day digesting and socializing.

SOCIAL/MATING SYSTEM ⚥ ⚥ ⚥ In the water or resting ashore, hippos tolerate even closer contact than pigs, regularly using neighbors as head rests. But on emerging at dusk, all except mothers and dependent offspring disperse singly since adults, being largely immune to predators, can afford to forage individually on their communal pastures.

The water part of the homeland is partitioned into individual mating territories by mature bulls (over 20 years), which defend from 50- to 100-yd sections of a river to 250 to 500 yd of lakeshore and shallows. Known individuals have held the same property for 4 years in rivers and at least 8 years in lakes; tenures of 20 to 30 years, the full adult life span, are possible. However, where prolonged dry seasons lead to overcrowding, territorial turnovers may occur every few months.

Herds typically number 10 to 15 hippos, but vary from 2 to 50 and up to 200 or more at highest density. Nonbreeding males are tolerated in the territories and even among the cows, as long as they behave themselves. But frequent savage attacks persuade some males to live in bachelor herds or alone in marginal habitat.

The organization of female herds remains unclear. Cows and calves associate in nursery schools, which guard babies against crocodiles and intruding bulls, but there appear to be no close ties between cows. Yet daughters stay with mothers until nearly grown, and a cow may be followed by up to 4 successive offspring, led by the youngest.

HOW IT MOVES   More agile than it looks: gallops at 18 mph (30 kph) in an emergency and half that speed in a jouncy trot, normally the fastest gait. Turns on a dime, climbs steep banks, but is unable to jump and won't even step over obstacles. Lies down and rises by first sitting down and up on haunches (like pigs). Seen underwater (rarely possible), hippos cross-walking on the bottom levitate like moonwalkers; their swimming movement is a gallop. As a hippo submerges, you can see its nostrils close and its ears fold into recesses. Resurfacing (usually in under a minute, maximum 5 minutes), the nostrils open as the hippo exhales and the ears spring erect, throwing off showers of droplets. Sleeping hippos rise to breathe, resurfacing as automatically as breathing itself.

REPRODUCTION   Most mating occurs in the dry season, always in the water, when populations are concentrated. Most calves are born in rainy months, after 8-month gestation. Females conceive typically at 9 years (range 7–15), calve at 2-year intervals; males become adolescent at 7 to c. 12 years.

OFFSPRING AND MATERNAL CARE   Cows isolate before calving, on land or sometimes in the water, stay alone with the tiny baby (48–121 lb [22–55 kg]) for 10 to 44 days before rejoining herd. Babies are programmed to nurse underwater, popping to the surface every few seconds to breathe; their ears fold and nostrils close while sucking, even on land. Serious grazing begins by 5 months, weaning at c. 8 months. Small calves are often left in crèches guarded by 1 to several cows while mothers go to pasture.

PREDATORS   Unprotected calves may become meals for lions, hyenas, and crocodiles. Staying close to mother is good security since hippo jaws are capable of biting a 10-foot crocodile in two. Trampling is probably the main danger to calves, during fights, chases, and stampedes, usually involving bulls. Mothers will mob bulls that create a disturbance in their midst.

Table 17.1. *HIPPOPOTAMUS BEHAVIOR GUIDE*
        Expect to see and hear ➤ *Usual context and meaning*

Territorial Advertising

Dung-showering on middens: bull backs up to heap, simultaneously urinates and defecates backward, meanwhile paddling excrement with its tail. ➤ Performed by bulls on land, especially along trails near water. Excrement of adult ♂ ♂ is smelly and interesting to other hippos.

Mutual dung-showering in the water. ➤ Frequent at territorial boundary. ♂ ♂ approach and stare at one another, then turn tail, elevate rumps, and let fly, afterward withdrawing.

Herding and chasing ♀ ♀ and ♂ ♂. ➤ Prerogative of breeding ♂ ♂.

Wheeze-honking. ➤ Vocal advertising, probably not limited to territorial ♂ ♂. Resonant grunts and wheezes make hippo among noisiest African animals (but away from water hippos rarely call).

Aggression

Dung-showering of social inferiors. ➤ Expresses dominance; performed mainly or exclusively by ♂ ♂.

Confrontations including yawning (see Fig. 17.1), rearing, lunging, jaw-clashing, and dung-showering. ➤ Prelude to, or substitute for, biting fights. Jaw-to-jaw encounters test size of gape, tusk development, and weight.

Position during serious fight. ➤ Slashing with lower tusks cuts deep gashes in 2-in (5-cm) hide.

Yawning display during confrontation in the water. ➤ The standard threat display, exposing the only obvious ♂ secondary characters: the spear-shaped central incisors and enlarged tusks.

Facing aggressor with mouth open. ➤ Defensive threat, most commonly by cows defending offspring against ♂ aggression.

OTHER ACTIONS AND SOUNDS ASSOCIATED WITH THREAT DISPLAYS
Water-scooping and head-shaking, charging and chasing.

Grunting, roaring, exhaling explosively above or below water.

Submission

Turning tail with slow tail-paddling and excretion. ➤ Submissive/appeasing behavior of ♀ ♀ and subordinate ♂ ♂. Performance includes urination ± defecation—maybe to stimulate urine-testing and thereby divert ♂ aggressor.

Approaching in crouch (on land or in shallows), head low ± genital-sniffing. ➤ Submissive display of subordinate to dominant hippo (especially juveniles and bachelors to territorial ♂).

Lying prone on land. ➤ Appeasing response to actual or threatened attack; ♂ ♂ that have disturbed nursery herd escape maternal wrath by lying prone.

Diving and flight. ➤ Response of inferior or defeated rival to pursuit by superior or contest winner.

Sociable Behavior

Lying in contact, social grooming.

Courtship

MALE BEHAVIOR
Urine-testing; no grimace, only evident when performed ashore.

Pursuit: ♂ drives estrous ♀ until she assumes prostrate position in the water, enabling him to mount. ♀ often submerged during copulation.

FEMALE BEHAVIOR
Urination on demand. ➤ See above, under Submission.

Courtship *continued*

Jaw-clashing. ➤ Self-defense against driving ♂.

Lying prone. ➤ Mating (and submissive) posture.

VOCAL ACCOMPANIMENT
Wheeze-honking.

Mother and Offspring

Nursery herds and calf crèches.

Social grooming: licking, nuzzling, scraping with lower incisors. ➤ By both mother and calf.

Disciplinary actions: nudging, sideswiping, or biting calf. ➤ Punishment of increasing severity if calf strays from maternal side (especially on land).

Calf responds by lying prone.

Getting between calf and danger, mother confronting ♂ or turning and slow tail paddling. ➤ Bulls often chase and sometimes kill small hippos, presumably ♂ ♂ still in mother's care.

Play

Calves in crèches engage in sparring matches and chasing.

Response to Predators

Diving and swimming away underwater. ➤ Reaction to people or vehicles by hippos exposed to shooting.

Explosive exhaling while submerged.

Wheeze-honking, yawning, water-scooping, head-shaking, feinted or real charge. ➤ Aggressive response to disturbance by people or other potential predators.

Chapter 18

RHINOCEROSES
Family Rhinocerotidae

Black rhino, *Diceros bicornis*[en]
White rhino, *Ceratotherium simum*

WHAT THEY ARE   Relics of an early era in the Age of Mammals, when odd-toed ungulates were the dominant herbivores, boasting dozens of families with hundreds of species. Adding the other 2 surviving families in the order Perissodactyla, horses and tapirs, the total of 15 living species is indeed a pitiful remnant.

Massive creatures with barrel-shaped bodies, supported on pillarlike limbs and 3-toed hooves. *Head:* big and weighty, with small, low-set eyes; prominent, highly mobile ears, and 2 medial horns on the snout. *Horns:* grow from the skin, consist of keratin (like hooves, nails, hair), and are unattached to skull. *Teeth:* no front teeth (incisors); cheek teeth high, broad, and strongly serrated. *Skin:* thick and creased at junctions, hairless except for fringed ears and tail bristles, plain gray to dark brown. *Penis:* recurved to rear and testes internal. *Scent glands:* possible preputial gland in white rhino. *Teats:* 2.

SOCIAL/MATING SYSTEMS   The white rhino is semisocial; males are territorial but unusually tolerant in that some allow satellite bulls on their property. The black rhino has long been considered solitary but sometimes forms groups and may or may not be territorial, depending on circumstances. Assuming variations are real, maybe rhinos tend to be solitary and territorial at low density in closed habitats and become more sociable at high density in open habitats, although not necessarily less territorial. (See species accounts.)

HOW THEY MOVE   Like other nonruminants, rhinos sleep soundly—either lying on their sides with legs to one side, on the brisket with legs gathered and chin on the ground, or standing. They move in a cross-walk, make haste at a fast, tireless trot, and gallop only in emergencies.

REPRODUCTION   Both species have breeding and birth peaks in rainy months. One calf, born after 15- to 16-month gestation. Females mature at c. 7 years, males at 10 to 12 years.

HOW THEY COMMUNICATE   Sight 3, scent 1, sound 1.

Table 18.1. *RHINO BEHAVIOR GUIDE*
Expect to see and hear ➤ *Usual context and meaning*

Territorial or Dominance Advertising

Dunging ceremony on dung middens: Rhino examines dung midden; sweeps and roots dung with forehorn (especially ♂ ♂); shuffles stiff-legged through midden; defecates and scatters dung with slow kicks of hind feet. ➤ Middens are located like signposts along rhino paths and territorial boundaries. Passersby of both sexes use them. Dung picked up by kicking leaves scent trail that other rhinos can follow or avoid.

Urine-spraying on bushes or shrubs (see Fig.18.2). ♂ backs up and sprays 2–5 times. ➤ Performed only by mature bulls; a sign of territorial status or rank dominance.

Aggression

Broadside display and stiff-legged walk. ➤ Dominance display showing size and power to best advantage.

Confrontations, typically with horn contact. ➤ Gentle nudging if friendly, horn-clubbing if aggressive.

OTHER ACTIONS ASSOCIATED WITH THREAT DISPLAYS
Horn threats: sideways clubbing and upward thrusting movements. ➤
In jousting contests, horns are used like staves to deliver sideways blows. In serious fights and against predators rhinos stab with upward thrusts.

Feinted attack (with puffing shrieks by black rhino).

Chasing (with gruff squealing by white rhino). ➤ After retreating adversary.

Head-low posture, silently facing aggressor (with ears back by white rhino). ➤ Defensive stance is same as offensive, putting animal in position to counter clubbing or goring attempts.

ASSOCIATED NOISES
Puffing snorts, shrieking, grunting, groaning.

Submission

Backing away.

Slow or rapid retreat (with chirping call by white rhino). ➤ Rapid retreat invites pursuit.

Displacement Activities

Grazing during confrontation. ➤ White rhino.

Sociable Behavior

Nose-to-nose meetings, nudging heads and gentle horn contact.

Staying together, especially resting side by side.

Courtship

The process of wearing down ♀'s resistance to ♂'s presence and contact is prolonged and risky in rhinos: takes 5–20 days in white rhino.

MALE BEHAVIOR

Urine-testing. ➤ Pronounced grimace with upper lip raised.

♂ attempts cautious approach, retreats before ♀ threats, but circles and returns.

Confrontations, including threat and fighting behavior (described under Aggression).

FEMALE BEHAVIOR

Frequent urine-spraying, mouthing (chewing) movements, threat displays, feinted or real attacks (with threat-snarling by white rhino).

CONTACT/MATING STAGE

Nudging ♀ with horn and head; rubbing muzzle on her sides and shoulders; resting chin on her rump. Preliminary mounts leading to copulation.

ASSOCIATED NOISES

Puffing, puffing snorts, squealing. ➤ Black rhino.

Mother and Offspring

Frequent physical contact.

CALLS

Squealing or squeaking. ➤ Distress signal, as when separated from mother.

Whining. ➤ Begging.

Panting. ➤ Contact call (white rhino).

Play

Solitary play: calves frolic; sometimes toss vegetation (black rhino calves and very young white rhinos). ➤ Black rhino calves rarely have play-mates.

Response to Predators

Rhinos react to churring calls of attendant oxpeckers.

Mock charge/real charge with puffing snorts. ➤ Especially black rhino.

Alarm-trot with tail curled over back.

Distress squeal of calves. ➤ Triggers maternal defense.

Flight.

BLACK RHINO, *Diceros bicornis*[en]

Figure 18.1. Male black rhinos confronting horn to horn, prelude to friendly or aggressive behaviors.

WHAT IT IS   The rhinoceros visitors used to see in parks of eastern and southern Africa. Long, low, powerful build. ♂ wt 2191–3000 lb (996–1364 kg), ht 56–64 in (140–160 cm); ♀ wt c. 200 lb lighter, ht c. 2 in shorter. *Head*: beaklike upper lip, pointed and flexible, employed as grasping tool. *Horns*: extremely variable in size and shape, front horn thinner and usually longer, 20 to 32 in (50–80 cm), rear horn 14 to 16 in (35–40 cm). *Color*: dark gray, often obscured by mud and dust in which it wallows.

WHERE IT LIVES   Formerly widespread in the Northern and Southern Savanna, Sahel, Somali-Masai and South West Arid Zones. Steady decline in range and numbers as humanity increased, suddenly accelerated in 1970s as increased demand for rhino horn in Arab and Asian countries (for dagger handles, medicine, aphrodisiac) made rhino horn more precious than gold. Now endangered everywhere—including South Africa, Zimbabwe, and Namibia where poaching used to be controlled, at least in most parks and reserves.

GOOD PLACES TO SEE IT   Ngorongoro Crater, Tanzania; Nairobi NP, Solio Ranch GR, Kenya; possibly Gonarezhou and Mana Pools NP, Zimbabwe; Kruger NP, Hluhluwe GR, South Africa.

ECOLOGY   Exploits a wide range of habitats, from semidesert thornbush to montane forest, and wetlands. Requirements include water, wallows, and mineral licks. Formerly ranged into quite open savanna, but only dwellers in the most impenetrable habitats and well-guarded preserves have survived recent persecution. Strictly a browser, known to eat over 200 different plants, especially leguminous herbs and shrubs. Feeds very selectively with its pointed, prehensile lip, uses molars to take big bites and pulp fibrous and woody growth; horns sometimes employed to break off high branches, remove bark, and dig up mineral earth. Rhinos can go 4 to 5 days without drinking; extract water by chewing succulents (sansevaria, euphorbias), but some travel 5 to 15 mi (8–25 km) every day to drink, and wallow almost daily, especially during hot weather. They dig for water in sandy riverbeds during drought.

ACTIVITY ●/○ Usually found eating or sleeping. They move and feed more at night; are most active early and late in daytime, least active in hottest hours.

SOCIAL/MATING SYSTEM   Black rhinos are solitary and territorial in some areas, semisocial and nonterritorial in others. My guess is that sociable tendencies are a response to crowding and open habitat. In any case, both sexes disperse from their birthplaces as subadults, then settle into home ranges where they spend the rest of their lives. Fidelity to place and predictability in daily and seasonal movements make the species particularly vulnerable to poachers.

(⚲♀⚲) (♂♂) In wooded habitat at unusually high density (2.5 rhinos/ mi² [1/km²]) in Natal's fenced-in Hluhluwe GR, males defend exclusive territories of 963 to 1160 acres (390–470 ha), which are included in or overlapped by undefended female home ranges of 1433 to 1900 acres (580–770 ha). Some territories include a second, adult satellite bull, which behaves submissively and keeps out of the way—the same arrangement as in white rhino.

(♀♀) (♀♂♂) (♂♂♂) In the mostly open grassland of Ngorongoro Crater, where over 100 different rhinos were identified on the 100 mi² (260 km²) floor in the 1960s (since reduced to c. 25 animals), bulls did not defend exclusive territories and females appeared to be about as sociable as white rhinos. Overlapping home ranges varied from 640 to 10,880 acres (259–4400 ha), depending on the distribution of food and water.

Relations between bulls with overlapping ranges were notably peaceful; individuals often associated amicably if briefly when they met at water or salt licks, and sometimes even went to sleep side by side. Yet outsiders that wandered onto the crater floor were invariably attacked. The presence of a cow in heat also led to aggression among resident bulls, though rarely to pitched battles—the biggest bull would end up serving the cow.

Though cows with calves are generally solitary, Ngorongoro mothers occasionally keep company for up to a year and sometimes take in subadult females or males that have been rejected by their own mothers. Temporary groups of 4 or 5 rhinos are not unusual; the largest recorded group was 13.

The arrangement in neighboring Serengeti NP, where density in 1976 was estimated at 0.14 rhinos/mi² (0.05/km²) in the best woodland habitat, was most representative of black rhino populations. Here both sexes were solitary and bulls were territorial. I use the past tense because poachers had shot all but a dozen of the estimated 700 rhinos by 1980.

HOW IT MOVES   Dismayingly agile for its bulk, it can turn in its own length at a full gallop, which is an impressive 31 mph (50 kph).

REPRODUCTION   Females conceive at 4 or 5, before maturity (7 years), calve at intervals of c. 2.25 to 4 years. As in rank-dominance mating systems, estrus lasts 3 days, during which bulls contend for exclusive mating rights.

OFFSPRING AND MATERNAL CARE   When expectant mothers seek isolation, they drive their previous offspring away. The rejects, still a bit young to face life on their own, do their best to find mother substitutes. Newborns are able to stand within 10 minutes of birth and thereafter follow their mothers very closely, pressing together rump-to-rump when facing danger.

PREDATORS   A lethal weapon (front horn), volatile temperament, and poor eyesight combine with speed and agility to make the black rhino unusually dangerous to predators—including people. It operates on the principle that the best defense is a good offense. Nevertheless, hyenas and lions sometimes manage to grab young calves if they fail to call out and/or the mother reacts slowly.

Table 18.2. *DIFFERENCES IN BLACK RHINO BEHAVIOR*
Expect to see and hear ➤ Usual context and meaning

Territorial or Dominance Advertising

Vegetation-horning, typically before or after dung-scattering or urine-spraying.

Aggression

Approach with upper lip curled giving screaming groans and puffing snorts. Head low, ears flattened, tail raised, and eyes rolling ± pauses for vegetation-horning. ➤ Threatening approach to stranger by resident. Intruder responds with defensive threat.

Courtship

Mating stage features several hours of preliminary mounting without erection.

Copulation lasts ½ hour.

Response to Predators

 Calves run behind mother.

WHITE RHINO, *Ceratotherium simum*

Figure 18.2. Territorial white rhino, spraying urine.

SUBSPECIES
Northern white rhino, C. s. *cottoni*en
Southern white rhino, C. s. *simum*

WHAT IT IS   A gentle giant, the biggest land mammal after elephants
(though outweighed by hippo). Almost double the weight of a black rhino,
with pronounced shoulder hump. ♂ wt 4488–4972 lb (2040–2260 kg), ht
68–73 in (171–186 cm); ♀ wt 3520 lb (1600 kg), ht c. 2 in shorter. *Head:*
massive with wide, square mouth, big ears. *Horns:* front horn average **24** in
(60 cm), longer but thinner in female; back horn much shorter, more triangular. *Color:* slate gray to yellow-brown.

WHERE IT LIVES   Formerly widespread in Northern Savanna west of
White Nile and Southern Savanna south of the Zambezi. Open habitat and
unaggressive nature made it especially vulnerable to human predation. In decline for several hundred years, southern race was wiped out in last century
except for a few hundred in Natal. Saved by effective protection and management in Umfolozi-Hluhluwe GR, surplus has been reintroduced over much of
its former southern range. Several thousand strong, it now outnumbers the
black rhino. But the northern white rhino has gone—except for a couple dozen
survivors in Zaire's Garamba NP.

GOOD PLACES TO SEE IT   Umfolozi GR, Kruger NP, South Africa;
Hwange NP, Zimbabwe; Garamba NP, Zaire.

ECOLOGY   A savanna form whose preferred habitat includes grassland with trees, water, and mud wallows. Perhaps the largest pure grazer that ever lived, the white rhino uses its wide mouth and muscular lips to graze a broad swath, feeding most efficiently in dense swards of short, green grass. Able to go 2 to 4 days without drinking, even in the dry season, but often drinks twice a day when water nearby.

ACTIVITY   ○/● Leaving aside seasonal, daily, and individual variations, white rhinos spend about ½ of a 24-hr day feeding, ⅓ resting, and the balance in walking, standing alert, wallowing, drinking, and socializing.

SOCIAL/MATING SYSTEM (♀♀) (♀o♀) (♀♂) (♂♂) The white rhino is the most sociable member of its family, largely because grazers can feed closer together than browsers and frequent open habitats. White rhinos in the main Natal reserves are also crowded, with over 12.5 animals/mi^2 (5/km^2), 3 times the density of the associated black rhino.

While females and young associate in groups, adult males are territorial and essentially solitary. They seek out cows to check their reproductive status and stick around only long enough to mate with any coming into heat. However, some territories include 2 and even 3 or 4 resident adult bulls, all but one of which turn out to be satellites that are tolerated as long as they kowtow to the owner. Since this situation occurs in fenced reserves where there are enough territories (200–600 acres [80–260 ha] in extent) for only ⅔ of the mature bulls, the arrangement may not be natural or normal.

Females and subadults are rarely alone. Cows in Umfulozi GR live in overlapping home ranges of 198 to 642 acres (80–260 ha), which take in 6 to 7 territories. Females are accompanied by their latest calf and often 1 or more unrelated juveniles whose own maternal ties ended abruptly after the birth of a new calf. Calfless cows associate in pairs and are especially tolerant of waifs; a couple may live with juveniles, which like to associate with peers of the same sex and age, in stable herds of up to 6 rhinos. Larger groups of up to a dozen are only temporary and likely to occur at midday when white rhinos converge on ridges to sleep in a cooling breeze.

HOW IT MOVES   A high-stepping trot is normally the fastest gait, timed at 18 mph (29 kph), which a rhino can maintain for at least 2 mi (5 km). White rhinos can gallop 25 mph (40 kph).

REPRODUCTION   See family introduction.

OFFSPRING AND MATERNAL CARE   Cows seek dense cover before calving, remain secluded several weeks before resuming accustomed home range and routine. Calves stand within an hour but remain unsteady for a couple days. They nurse 2 to 3 minutes on demand, begin grazing at 2 months, are weaned at 1 year.

PREDATORS   Newborns weigh only 143 lb, equal to 4% of mother's weight. Mothers are equipped to protect them against all predators but one.

Table 18.3. *DIFFERENCES IN WHITE RHINO BEHAVIOR*
Expect to see and hear ➤ *Usual context and meaning*

Territorial Advertising

Dunging ceremony. ➤ Territorial ♂♂ maintain 20–30 middens, which are also used by all passing white rhinos, but without kicking.

Urine-spraying (see Fig. 17.2): ♂ first horn-wipes bush or ground, then scrapes with all feet before spraying. ➤ Performed only by territorial ♂♂, on own property, c. 10 times/hr during boundary patrols.

Scrape-marking, as above but without spraying. ➤ Patrolling territorial ♂♂ scrape-mark every 30 yd or so, especially along boundaries.

Aggression

MAINLY BY TERRITORIAL MALES

Approach in erect posture, head raised, ears cocked. ➤ Territorial ♂♂ accost all passing rhinos, approach within smelling and viewing distance before deciding how to deal with them.

Confrontations. ➤ Standing in this position, territorial ♂ may simply silently stare or behave aggressively, depending on identity of intruder. All but territorial neighbors display active submission. As neighbors cannot afford to, they have to back away and defend themselves until off rival's property.

OTHER ACTIONS ASSOCIATED WITH THREAT DISPLAYS

Wiping horn on ground.

Head-low posture with ears back, combined with snarl threats and shrieking if attacked.

Sociable Behavior

Panting. ➤ Contact call common in groups and between mother and offspring.

Courtship

MALE BEHAVIOR

Keeping beyond distance at which ♀ behaves aggressively, gives hic-throbbing call during approach.

Blocking path or chasing while squealing or loud-wailing if ♀ tries to leave territory. ♂ shows remarkable restraint during extended courtship.

FEMALE BEHAVIOR

Curls tail and assumes rigid stance during ½-hour copulation.

Play

Social play: horn-wrestling matches ± prancing and head-tossing. ➤
Mostly by juveniles and adolescents, sometimes cows, usually involving
members of different groups.

Response to Predators

Mutual defense: group members stand rump-to-rump facing outward.

Calves run in front of mother during flight.

Chapter 19

ZEBRAS AND ASSES
Family Equidae

Plains or Burchell's zebra, *Equus burchelli*
Mountain zebra, *E. zebra*[v]

Grevy's zebra, *E. grevyi*[en]
Wild ass, *E. africanus*[en]

WHAT THEY ARE   Striped horses (plains and mountain zebras), a striped ass (Grevy's zebra), and the original donkey (the wild ass).

Horselike ungulates built for speed and endurance, with evenly developed limbs ending in a single hoof (the middle digit). Females c. 10% smaller than males but sexes look alike. *Teeth:* adapted for grazing, strong upper and lower incisors; broad, high-crowned, serrated cheek teeth; triangular-shaped canines in males only. *Tail:* hock length. *Color:* black and white stripes (individually unique) or plain gray (wild ass); brushlike mane. *Scent glands:* none described. *Teats:* 2.

Although equids stem from an ancient order and family, the genus *Equus* dates back only 2 million years, making current members of family as up to date as bovids, with which they compete on equal terms on the grasslands of Africa and Asia.

SOCIAL/MATING SYSTEMS   All equids are sociable and make extensive migratory or nomadic movements, but two very different mating systems and grouping patterns are represented.

Territorial system. A conventional territorial system, in which the fittest adult males hold property containing essential resources, like waterholes and good pasture. As territories are too large to defend in their entirety, bachelor males are tolerated. Females and bachelors form mixed herds on unowned land between territories and on migration. Examples: wild ass and Grevy's zebra.

Harem or family system. Instead of land, females are the property males compete to own (see plains zebra account). A more specialized system adapted for a nomadic existence, which enables males to have their cake and eat it, so to speak; females and young also benefit from the stallion's protectiveness of his wives and offspring. Aggregations of these zebras are composed of separate harem and bachelor herds. Examples: plains and mountain zebras; horse.

HOW THEY MOVE   Like horses. Same natural gaits: cross-walk, trot, canter, gallop. Broad backs enable most species to roll completely over, behavior associated with the habit of dust bathing; equids also regularly rub against objects (see Zebra Behavior Guide).

HOW THEY COMMUNICATE   Sight 1, scent 2, sound 2. All channels important but visual paramount; facial expressions and postures are equally important. Since equids bite and social groom with their mouths, attention naturally focuses on the mouth, which soft, flexible lips give considerable range of expression. Ear positions, neck angle, body posture, and tail movements have basically the same meanings in all equids. If you are familiar with horse displays, you can apply this knowledge to understanding zebras.

Table 19.1. *ZEBRA BEHAVIOR GUIDE*
Expect to see and hear ➤ *Usual context and meaning*

Maintenance Activities

Dust-bathing; rubbing against trees, rocks, termite mounds, etc.
➤ Zebras line up to dust-bathe (often on wildebeest stamping grounds) and scratch. Rubbing on isolated trees wears away bark; rocks worn smooth with grooved paths around them reflect centuries of rubbing.

Advertising Harem or Territory Ownership

Adult ♂ standing apart from ♀ herd or coming to meet an approaching herd or individual. ➤ A territory or harem owner (the former may also be all alone).

GREETING/CHALLENGE RITUAL

Greeting of equals. ➤ Meetings of equal adult ♂ ♂, at territorial boundaries (Grevy's zebra) or between their herds by family stallions (see Fig. 19.2). ♀ ♀ and young greet in similar fashion but with little or no aggression.

1. Both approach with heads outstretched and ears cocked, or 1 stands in erect posture watching other approach.

2. Contact and smelling: nasal contact and sniffing; rubbing cheeks; moving into head-to-tail position and sniffing penis, pressing and rubbing sides.

Resting/ pressing chin on partner.

3. Aggressive actions: biting, short squeal, kick threats, and kicking out with front feet (not at each other), often just before parting (parting jump).

Parting jump.

4. Dunging ceremony: Ostentatious defecation with tail raised, often preceded by nosing and pawing earlier deposit before over-marking the spot.
➤ Territorial interactions; less common between harem stallions.

Advertising Harem or Territory Ownership *continued*

5. Challenge rituals end with ♂ ♂ returning to their respective herds/territories, often in grazing attitude (displacement grazing).

HERDING AND HAZING BEHAVIOR

Herding/hazing posture. ➤ Controlling herd movements with threat displays.

Chasing. ➤ Especially of ♀ ♀ by amorous territorial ♂ ♂.

CONTACT/ADVERTISING CALLS

Braying (Grevy's zebra, ass); barking (plains, mountain zebras).
➤ Equivalent to neighing of horse. Not confined to stallions in the harem species, but ♂ ♂ are most vocal. Calls are individually distinct.

Aggression

Standing in erect posture with head high, ears pricked, tail arched.
➤ Dominance display.

High stepping (prancing).

Broadside display. ➤ Blocking way.

Head-low threat (ears back, snaking head movements). ➤ Illustrated above: herding/hazing posture.

BITING THREATS

Threat face: ears back; teeth bared; tail-swishing.

Biting-intention movements, ranging from head movements only, through rearing and rushing.

KICK THREATS

Lifting hindquarters (see Fig. 19.1) or forequarters in direction of adversary.

Rearing.

Chasing. ➤ Mainly between members of bachelor herds and during battles to abduct fillies in heat.

OTHER ACTIONS ASSOCIATED WITH THREAT DISPLAYS

Stamping and pawing, dunging ritual, short squeals.

FIGHTING TECHNIQUES

Biting and slashing: ears, neck, body. Look for bloodstains.
➤ ♂ canine teeth make superficial wounds.

Attempted leg bite, countered by dropping to ground.

Kicking out with hind feet. ➤ Dangerous, as kick can break leg or jaw.

Aggression *continued*

Kick threat or actual kicking with hind feet while moving away.
➤ Defensive threat.

Submission

Bachelor ♂ declining challenge of harem stallion by displaying submission: laying ears back and making open-mouthed chewing motions ± squealing. ➤ Resembles display of mare in heat. Ears back suggest threat but chewing is submissive—an intention movement to nibble-groom. Only immature animals and adult bachelor ♂ ♂ display active submission.

Moving away from threatening superior.

Grooming initiative. ➤ Appeasing behavior, as social grooming is initiated by lower-ranking individual.

Sociable Behavior

Nose-to-nose contact. ➤ Greeting behavior, prelude to friendly or aggressive interactions (as in challenge ritual).

Social grooming: scraping and nibbling partner's neck, shoulders, and back, performed by both partners at once. ➤ Most frequent between relatives, especially mother and foal.

Resting in pairs and mutual head-resting. ➤ Position enables pair to see in all directions and to brush flies off each other's face.

Blowing with loose lips (as in horses). ➤ Often heard in grazing herd; an "all's well" social-contact sound.

Courtship

SIGNS OF ESTRUS

Swollen, everted labia and mucous discharge; frequent urination; fighting and chasing among stallions; kick threats and kicking with hind feet in response to premature mounting attempts (see Fig. 19.1).

Mare-in-heat display: tail and neck extended, ears back, lips retracted and open-mouthed chewing. ➤ Similar to submissive display and to ♀ urination posture.

Mating posture (full estrus). Similar to mare-in-heat display, but with hind legs spread, mouth wide open, ± backing into ♂.

MALE BEHAVIOR

Chasing, nipping, mounting attempts (sometimes on the run).
➤ Rather violent, especially Grevy's zebra.

Urine-testing ± urinating on the spot afterward. ➤ Unusually conspicuous in equids, with pronounced lip-curl.

Dunging on ♀'s excrement.

Courtship *continued*

Nuzzling, social grooming; resting chin on ♀'s back or rump.

Preliminary mounting attempts without erection.

Parent and Offspring

Maternal protectiveness. ➤ Mother keeps other zebras, including last offspring, away from foal for first days, until maternal bond established and foal recognizes own mother.

Social grooming. ➤ Frequent, important for maternal and sibling social bonding.

Play

Running games, play-fighting. ➤ Common only among young and bachelors.

Response to Predators

Alert posture: standing with head high staring in one direction, stamping and snorting.

Flight.

Closing ranks around young and defense by herd stallion. ➤ Harem system.

SOUNDS OF ALARM

Snorting, *e-hah* gasp with open mouth.

Drawn-out squeal. ➤ Distress cry of captured or injured animal.

Qua-ha call of plains and mountain zebra. ➤ Contact call, given at highest intensity and frequency following disturbance.

GREVY'S ZEBRA, *Equus grevyi*[en]

Figure 19.1. Grevy's zebra mare threatening to kick stallion attempting to mount.

WHAT IT IS   A striped ass, also the largest wild equid, with massive head and big, rounded ears. ♂ wt 946 lb (430 kg), ht 56–64 in (140–160 cm); ♀ wt 849 lb (386 kg), ht within ♂ range. *Coat:* Stripe pattern like no other zebra: narrow with distinctive bull's eye pattern on rump, wider stripes on neck and chest.

WHERE IT LIVES   Restricted to the Somali Arid Zone of Ethiopia, Somalia, and Kenya. The only substantial population (several thousand) lives in Kenya's Northern Frontier District.

GOOD PLACES TO SEE IT   Samburu-Isiolo NR, Meru and Sibiloi NP, Kenya.

ECOLOGY   Less desert-adapted than the wild ass but tolerates arid *Acacia-Commiphora* thornbush country and barren plains of the Somali Arid Zone better than the plains zebra. Resident in areas with adequate water and pasture but where water is unavailable or grazing is poor in the dry season, Grevy's zebras migrate to areas of higher rainfall, including the foothills of Mt. Kenya. Subsists on grasses too tough for cattle to eat and digest, switches to browse when grass is gone. To obtain water, it digs and defends holes in sandy streambeds.

ACTIVITY   ○/● Unstudied, but like other equids grazes at night, though probably less mobile than by day.

SOCIAL/MATING SYSTEM   (♂♀○♀○♀○) (♂♂♂) (♂♀○♂♀ ♀○♂♀ ♀♀)   In the Samburu-Isiolo NR, stallions maintain territories of 1 to 4.6 mi² (2.7–10.5 km²) commanding the best pastures and watering points and the approach routes regularly taken by females. Ownership is so decisive reproductively that stallions remain on territories through the dry season whenever possible, while the rest of the population sojourns on distant greener pastures. This fidelity is rewarded when the others come back at the onset of the rains, followed shortly by a breeding peak.

Herds are larger in the wet season and smaller in the dry season since good pastures are reduced to scattered patches, but mixed aggregations of 100 to 200 zebras are not uncommon around water holes and during migration. Zebras of like sex and age form subgroups within these bands, which often include plains zebras where the two species overlap.

Mares associate with related individuals in clans that share the same home range. Although herd composition varies daily as members come and go, the same individuals are consistently found together. Maternal groups with young foals are most consistent and mothers with foals of about the same age associate in subgroups. Most zebras travel 3.5 to 5 miles (6–8 km) a day between pastures and water in the dry season, passing through several territories. Maternity herds of 2 to 5 mares are always found within a mile or so of water and often remain within a single territory for 3 months after foaling. Foals stay behind in crèches while their mothers go to water, guarded by a single adult—typically the resident stallion, who may also be their father (see under Offspring and Maternal Care).

Stallions don't even try to defend their large territories and even consort in a friendly if lordly manner with herds of 2 to 6 (rarely up to 10) bachelor males when no mares are around. They do patrol and demarcate territorial boundaries with dung middens and engage in challenge rituals with their neighbors—encounters which often seem more social than aggressive. However, when a mare in heat is at stake, the stallion with access is completely intolerant of territorial rivals, but conserves energy by simply keeping bachelors at a safe distance.

REPRODUCTION   With gestation of c. 13 months, both births and matings are concentrated during rainy season (Jul.–Aug. or Oct.–Nov.) However, 2-year intervals between births are common; estrus then recurs at monthly intervals, fueling male competition. Fillies begin ovulating at 1 to 1.5 years and typically foal at 3 years. Males mature at 6 years.

Females tend to return year after year to their birthplace to foal and mate—the basis for a matriarchal clan and a reproductive coup for lucky landlords.

OFFSPRING AND MATERNAL CARE   Adapted to harsh environment, Grevy's foals are unusually precocious: able to stand often within 11 minutes and run within 45 minutes (although so long-legged they have to straddle to nose the ground). Suckled at longer intervals than other equids but don't drink water until 3 months old. They begin grazing early, feeding by 6 weeks as long as horses of 5 months, are weaned by 9 months. Fillies separate when they start ovulating and being fought over by stallions, whereas colts stay with mothers until at least 3.

PREDATORS   Chiefly lions and spotted hyenas. Foals, normally well-protected in nursery herds, are sometimes left all alone or in an unattended crèche for hours if mothers have to commute long distances to water.

Table 19.2. *DIFFERENCES IN GREVY'S ZEBRA BEHAVIOR*
Expect to see and hear ➤ *Usual context and meaning*

Territorial Advertising

Dunging ceremony, often including urination. ➤ Performed on large dung middens established along territorial boundaries, which tend to follow topography.

GREETING/CHALLENGE RITUAL

Approach in erect posture, often braying, sometimes at a gallop.

Taking turns defecating and/or urinating on dung middens. ➤ Encounters between territorial stallions, along common boundary. Main steps listed in Table 19.1.

Aggression

Erect posture, often with braying. ➤ Dominance display.

Sociable Behavior

Social grooming. ➤ Most frequent between relatives, especially mother and foal; also between mothers and sometimes between territorial ♂ ♂.

Courtship

MALE BEHAVIOR

Often violent. Mating occurs only after stallion has subdued mare, in which dominance displays play a role.

Chasing away outside stallions by territorial ♂ with frequent loud braying.

Approach in erect posture with slow, measured tread, to sniff ♀'s rear end. ➤ Especially in response to sight of ♀ in urination posture.

Chasing, nipping, mounting attempts, sometimes on the run (see Fig. 19.1).

Mother and Offspring

Social grooming: frequent mouth-to-mouth nuzzling; mother rubs chin and neck over foal's back, nibbles its longer back hair.

PLAINS OR BURCHELL'S ZEBRA, *Equus burchelli*

Figure 19.2. Greeting ceremony/challenge ritual between plains zebra family stallions.

SUBSPECIES
Grant's or Boehm's zebra, *E. b. boehmi*   Chapman's zebra, *E. b. antiquorum*
Selous' zebra, *E. b. selousi*   Burchell's zebra, *E. b. burchelli*

WHAT IT IS   African version of the horse. Portly build. ♂ wt 550 lb (250 kg), ht 51–56 in (127–140 cm); ♀ wt 484 (220 kg), ht slightly shorter than ♂. *Color:* no gender difference; background white to buff color; striping varies geographically (and individually), most complete and bold in equatorial race (*E. b. boehmi*), decreasing toward southern Africa, where *E. b. antiquorum* and *burchelli* have unstriped lower legs and belly and shadow stripes between black torso stripes. Juvenile coat longer with brown stripes.

WHERE IT LIVES   From southeastern Sudan to South Africa and west to Angola, in Somali-Masai Arid Zone, Southern Savanna, and South West Arid Zone. The extinct South African quagga, striped only on head, neck, and back, was probably not a different species but a distinctive subspecies adapted to the temperate *highveld* and arid Karroo. Quagga, the Hottentot name, may come from the *qua-ha* contact call of the plains zebra.

GOOD PLACES TO SEE IT   Too numerous to list; 2 of the best places to get very close are Ngorongoro Crater, Tanzania and Etosha NP, Namibia.

ECOLOGY   One of most numerous and successful large herbivores, adapted to a broad range of grassland habitats. Though usually outnumbered by wildebeest where the two grazers occur together and equally water-dependent, tolerance for taller grass and more wooded savanna gives the zebra much greater geographical range.

A pioneer in the grazer community, first to enter tall or wet pastures, followed by wildebeests and gazelles after zebras have trampled and cropped the grass shorter; also crops short greenflush with its matched set of incisors and mobile lips much more efficiently than wildebeests and most other ruminants.

ACTIVITY   ○/● More active in daylight, spending nights preferably on short pasture relatively safe from ambush. Zebras graze individually an hour or so at a time at night but move about very little. Resting zebras often sleep soundly, but at least one herd member remains standing and alert. At daybreak in warm weather, herds begin filing to pastures of longer grass and may cover over 10 mi (17 km) before settling for another night. Mass movements between pastures and sleeping grounds, and to water at midday, are also peaks of social activity; stallions in bachelor herds are especially active and entertaining to watch.

SOCIAL/MATING SYSTEM   Harem masters have exclusive mating rights with 2 to 6 mares. Harems are so stable that mares remain associated for life; their foals gain added protection from the family stallion's readiness to defend his wives and offspring against all threats to their survival—and his reproductive success. On balance, it is a win-win arrangement. When members of the herd become separated, the family stallion goes looking and calling for them, and the whole herd will adjust its pace to accommodate sick or crippled members. Home ranges can be as small as 11 mi^2 (30 km^2) in the best habitat, to over 232 mi^2 (600 km^2) in migratory populations.

Harem ownership is about as safe as territory ownership: respected as long as the family stallion is fit enough to assert his rights. When a breeding male gets killed, severely injured, or too old to outface challengers, some lucky stallion stands to inherit his whole harem. But such luck is as unlikely as winning the state lottery: with a potential life span of over 20 years, stallions stay fighting-fit for some 15 years. The normal way to become a harem stallion is by abducting fillies in heat, one at a time.

Between 1 and 2 years of age, fillies begin ovulating and advertise estrus by adopting a distinctive posture (see Courtship in Table 19.1). Up to 18 stallions gather around a herd with an estrus filly and fight for her with the herd stallion and one another. This happens not just once but 5 days every month for about a year until the filly finally conceives. Abducting a filly from her father's herd is just the beginning of a recurrent ordeal, and the odds against a female bearing the offspring of the first stallion to steal her must be very low.

The fruits of conquest go to the inseminating stallion; the filly stays with him. After foaling, subsequent estrous periods are advertised so much more discreetly that rivals stay away—as long as the herd stallion is there to repel intruders. But newcomers are not welcomed by resident mares. The latest wife

must keep her distance, protected and herded by her consort, during a proba-
tion of several weeks. A strict rank hierarchy is enforced, the first mare to join
the harem and her offspring taking precedence over the second, the second
over the third, and so on down to the latest conquest. This order is strictly
enforced when a herd is filing. The stallion's usual position is behind his family, from where he can still direct the herd's movements when he sees fit.

Colts leave their families on their own initiative usually between 2 and 3
years to join a bachelor herd, there to remain until mature and ready to start
a harem at 5 years. Bachelor herds include 2 to 15 males, are usually led by a
young adult, and are quite stable, with a rank order based simply on age.

REPRODUCTION   Foals born in most months but a definite annual
birth/mating peak early in the rains (Dec.–Jan. in East Africa). Mares in good
condition conceive during the following "foal heat"; others reproduce at 2-year
intervals. First foals at 3 to 3.5 years.

OFFSPRING AND PARENTAL CARE   A mare labors lying on her
side, while the herd remains nearby and the stallion stands watch. Foals weigh
c. 70 lb (31–33 kg), are able to stand within 15 minutes and suckle in an
hour. The mother keeps all other zebras away for several days, much to the
distress of her previous offspring. But once the foal is imprinted on her, she
allows other herd members to contact it; its sibling can establish close ties
through mutual social grooming. However, the place closest to its mother is
taken by the newborn.

PREDATORS   Plains zebra a mainstay of lions throughout its range, but
spotted hyenas often hunt zebras in packs to overcome the close cooperation
of the group and the stallion's aggressive defense. In the Serengeti one wild
dog pack made something of a speciality of hunting zebras, but zebras are not
their usual prey.

Table 19.3. *DIFFERENCES IN PLAINS ZEBRA BEHAVIOR*
Expect to see and hear ➤ *Usual context and meaning*

Advertising Herd Ownership

GREETING/CHALLENGE RITUAL

Greeting of equals features open-mouthed chewing movements, but with
ears cocked, unlike submissive display (see Fig. 19.2).

Dunging ceremony. ➤ Resembles territorial boundary marking, as
though the herd and the space surrounding it is the territory.

Sociable Behavior

Mutual grooming and standing and resting in pairs. ➤ Most frequent
between relatives, especially mother and foal, but occasional between all
herd members. Also in bachelor herds.

MOUNTAIN ZEBRA, *Equus zebra*[v]

Figure 19.3. Greeting ritual between mountain zebra stallions; male on right rubs head on the other's shoulder.

SUBSPECIES
Cape mountain zebra, *E. z. zebra*[en]
Hartmann's mountain zebra, *E. z. hartmannae*[v]

WHAT IT IS   A zebra of the South West Arid Zone, much like plains zebra in appearance, social/mating system, and behavior. *E. z. hartmannae*: ♂ wt 656 lb (298 kg), ht 58 in (145 cm); ♀ wt 607 lb (276 kg), ht slightly shorter than ♂. *E. z. zebra* c. 100 lb lighter. Distinguished from associated plains zebra by a small dewlap under the chin, larger ears, and distinctive stripe pattern: absence of shadow stripes, fully striped legs, many narrow torso stripes, and a "gridiron" pattern of parallel stripes on the rump.

WHERE IT LIVES   Formerly inhabited the mountain ranges paralleling the coast from southern Angola to the Transvaal. Cape mountain zebra inhabits southwestern and southern Cape Province. Rescued in the 1930s, just in time, by creation of the Mountain Zebra NP, near Cradock. From a low point of 13 zebras in 1950, population increased to c. 474 by 1985, thanks to reintroductions of surplus stock to other protected areas, but genetic variability greatly reduced. Hartmann's race, estimated at 13,000 in the late 1980s, inhabits southern Angola and Namibia. Endangered if not extinct in Angola, where unprotected since civil war began in the 1970s.

ECOLOGY   Ranges barren, rocky uplands and arid plains. When rains rejuvenate plains, aggregates on best pastures, along with plains zebras. Penetrates the Namib Desert following rare downpours, even to the high coastal dunes. Lives in the mountains during protracted dry seasons, using network of ancient paths, some of which lead to springs and rainwater pools where herds come to drink once or twice daily. They also dig and defend their own wells in dry watercourses. Where fences haven't curtailed migration, they move a good 74 mi (120 km) between wet-and dry-season ranges.

ACTIVITY   ○/● Three feeding peaks early, middle, and late in day Hartmann's zebras generally drink early in the morning and after dark. Daily ranging of 0.5 to 2 mi (1–3 km) is typical, and they travel 3 mi (5 km) to water. Night activity unstudied.

SOCIAL/MATING SYSTEM Differences between plains and mountain zebras probably reflect the harsher conditions with which E. *zebra* must cope and a consequently much lower population density. Apparently less sociable than its savanna-dwelling relative, it also associates less frequently with other species. Breeding herds are a bit smaller, averaging 4.7 animals (2–8), with 2.4 mares (1–4). Herds range independently and rarely assemble in large bands, with interactions between herds and their stallions reduced accordingly. The *qua-ha* call is voiced infrequently and mainly as an alarm signal by the herd stallion, which often leads herd movements, especially to water. Herd members maintain wider individual distance than plains zebras and social-groom infrequently.

Offspring of both sexes leave their families at 13 to 27 months (mean age 22 months), often c. 4 months after the birth of a new sibling. Hartmann's mares can become so intolerant of their last offspring that they drive them from the herd after or even before foaling—up to ⅓ leave when only 14 to 16 months old. These preadolescent fillies and colts join bachelor herds which, unlike plains zebra male herds, include retired and injured stallions that have lost their herds.

Cape mountain zebras, living under less rigorous conditions, are more tolerant of offspring. Adolescent males are actually hindered in their efforts to join peer groups by good-shepherd fathers who try to prevent contacts with bachelor males and come looking for their escaped offspring.

Even in fenced reserves, mountain zebras have different summer and winter ranges but are notably sedentary between moves. The core areas of breeding herds average only 3.8 to 7.6 mi² (10–20 km²) on their winter range and less on their summer range.

REPRODUCTION   Breeding peaks during summer months, when pastures are greenest. Earliest recorded pregnancy at 26 months; average age at first foaling 5.5 years (range 36–105 months). One mother foaled again after only 375 days; another was still reproducing when 21 years old. Males reach maximum weight at 7 years.

OFFSPRING AND PARENTAL CARE   As in plains zebra—except for differences noted above under Social/Mating System. Birth weight 55 lb (25 kg). Up to 3 months, foals nurse at roughly hourly intervals during day, gradually decreasing to 1 to 3 times per day at 10 months, but foals occasionally suckle up to 20 months old.

PREDATORS   All the larger carnivores. A stallion has been known to kick a spotted hyena, the foremost predator, to death.

Table 19.4. *DIFFERENCES IN MOUNTAIN ZEBRA BEHAVIOR*
Expect to see and hear ➤ *Usual context and meaning*

Advertising Herd Ownership

GREETING/CHALLENGE RITUAL

Greeting stallions make chewing movements, but with mouth closed.

Chin-pressing. ➤ Leaning and chin-pressing are emphasized more than in plains zebra, and parting jump is rare.

Maintenance Activities

♂ ♂ roll in wet sand beside water holes they dig but are too narrow-backed to roll completely over.

Chapter 20

HYRAXES OR DASSIES
Order Hyracoidea
Family Procaviidae

Rock hyrax or dassie, *Procavia capensis*
Bush hyrax or yellow-spotted rock dassie, *Heterohyrax brucei*
Tree hyrax or dassie, *Dendrohyrax arboreus*

Eleven different species have been identified by specialists. But differences between species appear so minor to nonspecialists that only 1 species from each genus is included here—the 3 genera clearly are different.

WHAT THEY ARE Survivors of an ancient group of near-ungulates (Paenungulata) that lumps together such strange bedfellows as elephants, aardvark, and dugongs. Once dominant herbivores that included animals the size of forest hogs, the only hyracoids that survived the ascension of true ungulates were small forms able to subsist in uncontested niches—namely kopjes, cliffs, and trees. To turn mammals with hooves instead of claws into agile rock and tree climbers is no mean feat. It shows how natural selection can retool a structure evolved for one function into a form serving a totally different purpose.

Small, tailless creatures with long bodies and short legs that look more like rodents (woodchucks/marmots) than ungulates. Minimal gender differences (testes internal, a link with elephants): adult males have thicker necks, blunter snouts, and sharper, stronger tusks; also a bigger larynx and air pouches that amplify territorial calls. *Teeth:* Total 38; 2 upper incisors modified as tusks (as in elephants), 4 lower incisors modified as a comb used in grooming, cheek teeth rasplike with transverse ridges (another link with elephants) for grinding vegetation. *Feet:* 4 front and 3 rear toes tipped with rounded nails (like an elephant's) except for a scratching/grooming claw on the inside back toe; bare, moist, rubbery soles (providing traction for climbing). *Coat:* soft fur in tree and bush hyraxes, harsh in rock hyrax, sprinkled with long sensory hairs. *Color:* shades of gray and brown with or without white underparts. *Scent glands:* a large dorsal gland located in a bare spot 1 to 3 in (25–75 mm) long and surrounded by an oval of lighter-colored, erectile hair, conspicuous when fanned open, secretion an aromatic fluid. *Teats:* 2 in armpits (elephantlike; lacking in some tree hyraxes), 2 or 4 on belly.

SOCIAL/MATING SYSTEM

 Adult males of all species are territorial. Bush and rock hyraxes live in colonies typically composed of a male with a harem of several related females and their offspring. Often sharing the same rocks and even the same sleeping and sunning spots, these two species associate more closely than any other African mammals, except for some forest monkeys.

Tree hyraxes are solitary or live in families composed of a mated pair and their offspring. However, this hyrax also lives in colonies very similar to the other two high on certain mountains (see account).

Although hyraxes huddle together for warmth, social relations are often aggressive, and they do not engage in social grooming like other contact species.

HOW THEY MOVE   In a creeping walk—especially on cold mornings before sunbathing. They can jump-gallop c. 11 mph (18 kph) for up to 130 yards, are good jumpers and great climbers—the only ungulates that can scale smooth trees and rocks. Too long and low to sit up or walk bipedally, they crouch on all fours with back bowed, lie prone with forelegs extended and head resting between them, and extend hind legs with soles up to dissipate excess body heat.

HOW THEY COMMUNICATE   Sight 1 (tree hyrax 3), scent 1, sound 1.

Table 20.1. *HYRAX BEHAVIOR GUIDE*
        Expect to see and hear ➤ *Usual context and meaning*

Territorial Advertising

Adult ♂ on lookout point in distinctive posture, calling with head raised and jaws parted, and dorsal gland fanned open. ➤ Advertising calls of the 3 species are totally different (see species accounts). Calling bouts may continue for up to 5 min. and be repeated at intervals all night. Neighbors are often stimulated to reply.

White stains on vertical rock surfaces, created by hyrax urine. ➤ Rock and bush hyraxes both urinate at these sites, which advertise an active colony. Crystallized calcium carbonate makes the stain.

Aggression

Approach/stare.

Opening dorsal gland and bristling neck hair; secretion can be seen and smelled.

Raising head and shoulders (see Fig. 20.3).

Showing tusks by retracting upper lip.

Aggression *continued*

Grinding molars, growling, ± showing white membrane over eyes.

Snapping, biting.

Chasing.

 Confrontations. ➤ Face-to-face meetings provoke low-level threats (erecting dorsal gland fringe, showing tusks). Nonbelligerents avoid face-to-face meetings.

 Presenting rump, backing up. ➤ Defensive posture.

 Position during fights. ➤ Combatants back into each other, maneuver for opportunity to stab; open glands wide, exuding scent. Tusks can inflict fatal wounds.

Submission/Surrender

Closing dorsal gland, flattening ears, running from aggressor.

Sociable Behavior

 Sunbathing. ➤ Juveniles perch on adults (see Fig. 20.2).

 Orientation while huddling and sunbathing. ➤ Positioned to avoid confrontations.

Depositing droppings (rabbit-sized pellets) in communal latrine.

Mother and Offspring

Nursing offspring (see Fig. 20.1) switch between fore and aft nipples. ➤ Nursing attempts are often preceded by intense twittering.

Mothers whinnying while suckling, with tusks exposed.

Newborns uttering a 2-syllable twitter of distress; mothers respond with a lower, more guttural twitter while coming to their aid.

Play

Chasing and fighting games. ➤ Commonest during morning sunning sessions.

Response to Predators

Rapid flight and leaping across gaps; taking refuge in holes.

Playing dead, after being caught by predator. ➤ Hyraxes sometimes escape when predator dallies before feeding.

ROCK HYRAX OR DASSIE AND BUSH HYRAX OR YELLOW-SPOTTED DASSIE,
Procavia johnstoni and *Heterohyrax brucei*

Figure 20.1. Young bush hyraxes nursing.

WHAT THEY ARE   Two hyraxes of different size, appearance, and diet that live in the rocks and often associate. Rock hyrax: ♂♀ wt 4–12 lb (1.8–5.4 kg), hbl 16–23 in (39.5–58 cm). Bush hyrax: ♂♀ wt 3–5.3 lb (1.3–2.4 kg), hbl 13–19 in (32.5–47 cm). *Head:* rock hyrax has a blunter snout; bush hyrax sharper. *Teeth:* rock hyrax has high-crowned teeth adapted for grazing; bush hyrax's teeth are low-crowned, adapted for browsing. *Color:* rock hyrax is yellow-brown, underparts slightly lighter, with coarse fur; bush hyrax is gray or gray-brown, white underparts, with soft fur.

WHERE THEY LIVE   *Procavia* inhabits rocks all over Africa, except Lowland Rainforest, including mountains of Namib and Sahara Deserts. Main range of *Heterohyrax* is Southern Savanna but includes Namibia, sub-deserts of the Somali-Masai Arid Zone, and country between the Nile and Red Sea. In South Africa, elimination of natural predators enabled rock hyraxes to leave rocks and multiply into a major agricultural pest.

GOOD PLACES TO SEE THEM   Too many to list. Two particularly outstanding areas to see both kinds together: kopjes in Serengeti NP, including Lobo and Seronera Wildlife Lodges, Tanzania, and Matobo NP, Zimbabwe.

ECOLOGY   To be good hyrax habitat, a rock outcrop (kopje), cliff, or boulder scree must have numerous cavities big enough to admit hyraxes while excluding most of their predators, face away from strong prevailing winds,

Figure 20.2. Young rock hyraxes perched on mother's back, on her dorsal gland.

offer good lookout and sunning spots, and vegetation for food and cover. Hyraxes have little control over body temperature, depend on shelter against both heat and cold. Exposure to direct sunlight even at temperatures in the 70s (°F) results in heat stress within 2 hours. Like reptiles, they sunbathe to warm up in morning but avoid hot sunlight. Given feet useless for digging, hyraxes depend on existing holes to stay warm at night and cool by day. They also dust-bathe, and will bathe in and drink from rainwater pools.

Bush hyrax is a browser that feeds in trees and bushes; rock hyrax primarily a grazer. Differences in diet enable them to share the same sanctuaries with minimal competition. Need to venture up to 60 yd from safety to graze increases predation risk to rock hyrax. They compensate by bunching together (often with dorsal glands exposed—a stress symptom) and eat so rapidly (taking big bites with cheek teeth) that an hour of grazing satisfies daily need. The breeding male often stands guard; should he or a bush hyrax or a bird sound an alarm, the herd scurries back to rocks. When grass is unpalatable or scarce, rock hyraxes browse plants eaten by bush hyraxes, but can't climb as well or reach terminal branches accessible to the smaller species.

ACTIVITY ○ Rarely emerge before sunup, then spend an hour or more sunning before foraging; on cold, rainy days they stay indoors. Afternoon feeding periods are the most intensive. Both species move around and call on moonlight nights; territorial males move more, feed and rest less than other hyraxes.

SOCIAL/MATING SYSTEM Colonies consist of a territorial male living with a clan of related females and their offspring. Colony size depends on available resources and area of the home range. Kopjes in Serengeti NP are occupied by 2 to 26 rock hyraxes and 5 to 34 bush hyraxes. Sites smaller than 1 acre (4000 m²) are monopolized by a single colony with 3 to 7 females or held jointly by a colony of each species. Larger kopjes are shared among several colonies of the same species, which have overlapping home ranges but exclusive core areas defended as territories by harem males, averaging c. ¾ acre (2950 m²) for bush hyraxes and 1.2 acres (4800 m²) for rock hyraxes.

As females normally remain in their birthplace and reproduce in synchrony, one might expect cooperative care and cross-suckling of offspring as in many societies based on kinship, but hyraxes mothers care for only their own offspring. Females also occasionally disperse and are accepted in other colonies after an initially hostile reception. There is no dominance hierarchy, although older females usually lead and are most vigilant. The territorial male is top banana and plays the classic watchdog role that goes with breeding monopoly and assured paternity.

As usual, male offspring have to depart when they become adolescent (17 to 24 months); having to cross dangerous country between refuges makes dispersal unusually risky for hyraxes: minimum dispersal distance for Serengeti hyraxes is 1.2 mi (2 km). Worse still, chances are the nearest kopjes are all occupied by extremely unfriendly mature males. Small wonder that adult females outnumber adult males by at least 3:2 and often 3:1. The best most emigrants can expect is to reach a place big enough to accommodate peripheral males. Instead of associating amicably in bachelor herds, peripheral males defend exclusive sleeping holes and scuffle over status; if something happens to the territorial male, the dominant bachelor takes his place.

Relations between the 2 hyraxes are peaceful. They huddle together while sunbathing and sleeping, use the same latrines, and the young even play together. But the main reason they get on so well is the size difference: whenever there is any resource with limited access, such as a dust bath or pool of water, rock hyraxes always take precedence.

REPRODUCTION   Annual, with births during the main rainy season. In equatorial East Africa bush hyraxes respond to 2 rainy seasons with 2 peaks each lasting around 3 weeks. But each colony still only breeds annually: e. g., Serengeti babies are born March to May on one kopje and December to January on the one next door. Mating peaks (7 months earlier) are times of peak calling and fighting, promoted by testes weight increase to 20 times off-season size! Both sexes reach puberty at around 1.5 years but rarely conceive before 2.5 years; males may have to wait another year. Longevity 9 to 14 years. Differences in penises probably make matings between species impossible (see Courtship, Table 20.2).

OFFSPRING AND PARENTAL CARE   Bush hyraxes litter 1 to 3 young (average 1.6), rock hyraxes 1 to 4 (average 2.4). Born well-developed with eyes open, babies try to climb onto mother's back even before seeking teats; habit persists c. 5 months (see Fig. 20.2). Littermates divvy up teats, suck same ones throughout 1 to 5 month nursing period (see Fig. 20.1).

PREDATORS   The black or Verreaux's eagle specializes on hyraxes; martial eagle almost equally dangerous. Leopard, caracal, and snakes are other ranking predators.

Table 20.2. *DIFFERENCES IN ROCK AND BUSH HYRAX BEHAVIOR*
Expect to see and hear ➤ Usual context and meaning

Territorial Advertising

CALLS

♂ rock hyrax emits a series of spaced harsh yips, building to a climax and ending with guttural grunts. ➤ Impressive sound, suggesting bulk and power.

♂ bush hyrax emits a thin, high-pitched mewing. ➤ Weak sounding; far less impressive to human listener.

Courtship

FEMALE BEHAVIOR

No visible signs of estrus; aggressively resists mating attempts until ready to copulate.

Receptive ♀ backs into ♂, who maintains firm grip during copulation.

MALE ROCK HYRAX BEHAVIOR

Calls, then approaches estrous ♀ while weaving head, penis and dorsal hair both erect, and mounts.

Copulation after several thrusts, lasting a few seconds. ➤ Penis is much smaller and simpler than in bush hyrax, opening closer to groin.

BUSH HYRAX

♂ gives shrill cry during approach.

Pair performs dance as he sniffs vulva.

♂ rests chin on her rump preparatory to mounting.

 Thrusts without penetration while swinging head side to side ± mouth open, calling. Forces entrance after 3–5 min. ♀ jumps, turns, and bites, then chases him. ➤ Penis proportionally large (2.4 in [6 cm]) with cup-shaped glans and thin appendage at the tip, opening on the belly.

Response to Predators

Territorial ♂ or dominant ♀ defends herd's rear during flight; threat displays and possible mobbing of small predators. ➤ When rock hyraxes are caught away from rocks.

SOUNDS OF ALARM

Rock hyrax utters low-pitched squeak of variable intensity; bush hyrax utters a piping whistle. ➤ Both hyraxes respond to each other's calls.

TREE HYRAX OR DASSIE, *Dendrohyrax arboreus*

Figure 20.3. Male tree hyrax giving threat display.

WHAT IT IS   A nocturnal hyrax with an unforgettable call. About the size of rock hyrax but with a bigger head. Tree and bush hyraxes share a common ancestor, the former apparently more recent and specialized. ♂ ♀ wt 3.7–11 lb (1.7–5 kg), tl 13–24 in (32–60 cm). Coat: dense, soft fur. Color: geographically variable, dark brown to light gray-brown to pale gray; darker in wetter regions. Dorsal spot and underparts lighter, white stripe over eye and spots below ear and lip.

WHERE IT LIVES   Mainly in Lowland Rain Forest and montane forests of eastern Africa, also in evergreen forests of Natal and Cape Province.

GOOD PLACES TO SEE IT   Often heard, seldom seen. One good place to see it: roof of Mountain Lodge, in Kenya's Aberdare FR. Colonies in alpine zones of Mt. Kenya and Ruwenzoris hard to get to but easiest to see.

ECOLOGY   By exchanging rocks for trees as refuges and larders, improving temperature control and climbing skills, becoming nocturnal and solitary, this hyrax made itself one of Africa's dominant arboreal mammals, subsisting in hundreds per square mile of montane forest. Diet includes foliage, twigs, fruits, vines, and, in the alpine zone, grasses, sedges, forbs, tree lichens, etc. Feeds rapidly, consuming up to ⅓ its body weight each day.

ACTIVITY   ● (○: alpine colonies) Be prepared for 2 peak calling periods. Times vary, but first period often 2 to 3 hours after dark, the second after midnight (see Territorial Call, below).

SOCIAL/MATING SYSTEM

(♂♀♀) (♀♂♀) Forest dwellers live either as monogamous pairs, or in the polygamous solitary mode, in which a male's territory encompasses the smaller territories or home ranges of 2 or more females. The focal point of the territory is a den tree, recognizable by piles of droppings at the base. Hunters set foot nooses to snare tree hyraxes when they descend to use these communal latrines. Family members also use a regular network of arboreal pathways.

In alpine habitat up to 14,764 ft (4500 m), tree hyraxes live in colonies in the rocks and are largely diurnal, adopting the lifestyle and filling the niche occupied elsewhere by rock hyraxes. It is thus remarkably adaptable both socially and ecologically.

TERRITORIAL CALL   Male's call begins abruptly with a series of loud, measured cracking sounds, often compared to a huge gate with rusted hinges forced open, followed by a series of unearthly screams, ending in descending series of expiring shrieks. Especially common in dry season and on moonlit nights, calls may be repeated every few minutes for up to an hour and stimulate all territorial males within hearing to answer. Males appear to call from favorite perches. Females also call, but lacking air pouches and enlarged larynx, produce only a feeble imitation.

REPRODUCTION   May breed year-round in Lowland Rainforest. In East Africa mating activity and births both seem to peak during one of the two dry seasons.

OFFSPRING AND PARENTAL CARE   Litters of 1 to 3 young, born well-developed and furry, look like miniature adults.

PREDATORS   Crowned hawk eagle, leopard, golden cat, serval, python, even genets. Also hunted by humans for their hides, which are sewn into fur blankets or rugs (karosses).

Table 20.3. *DIFFERENCES IN TREE HYRAX BEHAVIOR*
Expect to see and hear ➤ Usual context and meaning

Calls

Banshee nocturnal call of the adult ♂ (see Fig. 20.3), crouching with head raised and jaws parted, dorsal gland exposed. ➤ See Territorial Call in text.

A neighing call given by agitated adults with raised head and open mouth. ➤ Develops from infantile distress call. Heard from individuals trying to escape and by courting ♂ ♂.

Screeching sound (like piglets). ➤ Mother's response to infant distress cry.

Flapping noise. ➤ Made by disturbed hyrax.

Piercing cry. ➤ Alarm call.

Aggression

Raising head and shoulders to vertical while showing tusks, with other aggressive displays.

Chapter 21

ELEPHANT
Loxodonta africana
Family Elephantidae
Order Proboscidea

Figure 21.1. Maternal herd in defensive ring around their young.

SUBSPECIES
Savanna elephant, *L. a. africana*[v]
Forest elephant, *L. a. cyclotis*[v]

WHAT IT IS   The largest land animal, Africa's true King of Beasts. ♂ wt 11,000 lb, up to 13,200 lb (5000–6000 kg), ht 9 ft 10 in to 11 ft (3–3.3 m); ♀ wt 6600–7700 lb (3000–3500 kg), ht 8 ft 4 in (2.5 m). *Head:* trunk, a muscular extension of the upper lip containing the nostrils, tip equipped with 2 fingerlike projections for handling small objects. Huge ears, up to 6.5 × 5 ft (2 × 1.5 m). *Teeth:* 6 sets of cheek teeth (2 upper and 2 lower) of increasing size that move into place as the animal outgrows/wears out previous set; upper incisors modified as continuously growing tusks averaging 134 lb (61 kg) apiece in males (maximum wt 287 lb [130 kg], length 7.7 ft [3.5 m]) and 42 lb (19 kg) in females at 60 years. *Feet:* 4 toes on front feet, 3 on rear feet. *Skin:* naked except for scattered bristles and sensory hairs; color gray or brown.

223

Genitals: open downward through skin flap between rear legs; penis invisible except when extended; testes internal. *Scent glands:* temporal glands near eyes, 3 times bigger in male, 6.6 lb (3 kg). *Teats:* 2 between forelegs.

FOREST ELEPHANTS Dwarfs inhabiting Lowland Rainforest would be considered a different species if the two forms didn't interbreed at the forest edge. Only 7 ft 10 in to 9 ft 2 in (2.4–2.8 m) tall, wt 3960 to 7040 lb (1800–3200 kg), with straight, downward-pointing, parallel tusks, more oval ears, front feet with 5 nails, rear feet with 4.

WHERE IT LIVES Formerly everywhere south of the Sahara where water and trees occurred. Range and numbers declined this century—first through uncontrolled ivory hunting, later accelerating with human population growth. Catastrophic decline began in 1970s and 1980s as soaring demand for ivory made poaching as profitable as drug dealing. Continental population estimated at 1.3 million elephants in 1981, mostly outside protected areas, fell to 750,000 by 1986. Losses up to 80% in most countries of eastern and central Africa convinced most conservationists that stopping ivory trade was the only way to stop carnage. Proposal opposed by the few states (in southern Africa) where elephants and other wildlife have been effectively protected. Their elephants *must* be culled to keep populations within ranges' carrying capacity, and sales of ivory and other elephant products help pay parks' operating costs. Thanks to aroused worldwide concern over elephants' plight, most major importing countries (Japan, India, Hong Kong, Singapore, United States) joined a moratorium on ivory trade, followed by dramatic drop in price of raw ivory in 1990 and a corresponding drop in poaching in East Africa. If trend and moratorium continue, elephants can make a comeback in protected areas—or at least hold their own.

GOOD PLACES TO SEE IT Amboseli NP, Masai Mara GR, Kenya; Tarangire and Ruaha NP (dry season), Tanzania; Kafue NP, Zambia; Mana Pools and Hwange NP, Zimbabwe; Chobe NP, Moremi GR, Botswana; Kruger NP, South Africa; Etosha NP, Namibia.

ECOLOGY Arguably the world's most versatile herbivore. Equipped with its unique nasal appendage—an all-in-one grasping, smelling, drinking, squirting, broadcasting tool—a big elephant feeds from ground up to 20 feet—higher than a giraffe can reach. The trunk can coil around and pull up grass, pick up peas, and tear off tree limbs. Tusks are also tools: for prying bark loose, digging pits and even caves in mineral earth to increase salt intake. Rasplike teeth grind up the toughest grasses, reeds, bark, and branches. Some bulls specialize in pushing over big trees.

Elephant dung consists largely of fiber that passes undigested through its comparatively small system. To compensate, adults consume and quickly process vast amounts: c. 330 lb/day (150 kg/day). Grass and herbs are mainstays in rainy season when elephants wander widely over the savanna; foliage and other browse are important in dry season when they feed more in forests, near water. Elephant trails that once crisscrossed the continent were the roadways used by human travelers. Many of today's highways are simply widened and paved trails engineered by elephants.

Second only to man in environmental impact, the elephant's good works have lately been overshadowed by devastation resulting when shrinking range and persecution force a population to concentrate. Tree destruction, normal and even beneficial when spread over a wide area, transforms and degrades habitats for many species besides the elephant itself when continuous in a limited area.

ACTIVITY   ○/● Feeds 16 and sleeps 4 to 5 hr/24-hr day, usually standing, sometimes lying on one side; drinks and bathes daily but can abstain several days while ranging up to 50 mi (80 km) from water source. Bulls drink up to 60 gal (227 l) a day, 26 gal (98 l) at a time. Bathing elephants roll and wallow in the shallows, often submerge completely in deep water. At small water holes, the trunk is used to shower, then dust- or mud-coat the body. After, they rub against trees, rocks, etc. Flapping ears on still, hot days helps cool blood flowing through network of veins on back surface.

SOCIAL/MATING SYSTEM   A matriarchal clan society, the basic units consisting of a mother with her dependent offspring and grown daughters with their offspring. Males live separately, alone or in bachelor herds. Being nonterritorial, mating success depends on size and weapons. Growth continues into old age; seniors are therefore the biggest tuskers and do most of the breeding.

COW HERDS   Typically number 9 to 11 elephants. Larger herds tend to split in two but continue occupying the same home range and associating at least half the time. These "bond groups," averaging 28 related elephants in 2 to 3 family units, usually stay under a mile apart, staying in touch through rumbling calls too low for people to hear. Different bond groups may share a home range; they may all belong to the same clan. Depending on primary plant productivity and resource distribution, home ranges can be as small as 5.4 mi² (14 km²) in a groundwater forest (e.g., Manyara NP, Tanzania) to over 1350 mi² (3500 km²) in arid savanna.

A herd's welfare depends on the matriarch's leadership, as demonstrated by the fact that cow elephants—like women but very few other animals—live long after ceasing reproduction (at c. 45 yr). The matriarch sets the herd's direction and pace and the rest of the herd follows, spreading out and feeding when she feeds, leaving off and closing up when she walks on. Even while browsing, herd members seldom stray further than 50 yd from a neighbor. Disturbances cause the herd to cluster around the matriarch (the biggest cow), with calves in the middle (see Fig. 21.1). Whether they flee or charge is up to her. Should something happen to her—like getting shot—the rest mill in blind panic. Rather than abandon her, they usually stay and get shot, too—a boon for poachers that also makes the standard management practice of shooting whole herds an efficient if sickening way of culling a surplus. The most touching proof of the cooperative nature of elephant society is attempts to raise and support a fallen group member, one on each side.

Under normal circumstances, a matriarch that becomes too sick or old (at 50-60 yr) to continue leading is replaced by the next-oldest cow; the feeble one either leaves the herd or is abandoned.

Persecuted elephants aggregate in herds numbering up to 200 animals including many young elephants. Animals from the same clan may often be involved, reunited in adversity and their common need for leadership. Aggregations of up to 1000 elephants used to form during rainy seasons and were often migratory. The presence of big bulls among the assembled cow herds indicated that mating activity was intensified in these assemblages.

BULL ELEPHANTS   Males leave cow herds at 12 years or later, depending on the onset of adolescent behavior and intolerance thereof by cows with young calves. Once on their own, bulls alternately wander solo and associate with other bulls, typically in herds of 2 to 14, occasionally over 35 and up to 144 bulls. Subadults tend to associate and interact in peer groups, but bachelor herds usually include various ages. Bulls wander further than cows but during periods of sexual inactivity most stay in small "retirement areas," often with 1 or more regular companions. Very old bulls, ponderous hulks with the biggest tusks, are the most sedentary. They end their days in swamps where they can still consume quantities of herbage as their last set of molars wears out.

HOW IT MOVES   Just one basic gait: an ambling walk; elephants cannot run or jump like other animals. Normal walking rate 3.7 to 5 mph (6-8 kph), increased to 6 to 8 mph (9.7-13 kph) by taking longer, quicker strides. Charging or fleeing elephants hit 25 mph (40 kph)—much faster than people can run. Elephants climb up and (sometimes slide) down precipitous slopes, sit on their haunches before lying down or getting up, can "sit up" like begging dogs, and stand semierect to reach food—or mount a female. Tuskless elephants practically stand on their heads to eat mineral earth.

REPRODUCTION   Not strictly seasonal, but most matings and births during rains. First conception at 10 to 11 years; gestation 22 months; interval between calves 4 to 9 years; twins extremely rare. Under crowded conditions or during droughts, elephants lower reproductive rate. Bulls of 25 and older begin competing reproductively, but normally bigger bulls over 35 monopolize matings. But onset of *musth*, a state of heightened aggressive and sexual activity, changes the odds. Musth bulls continually search for mating opportunities, are deferred to by other bulls, and preferred by cows in heat. (See Table 21.1, Male Advertising Presence/Dominance for signs of musth.)

MATING BEHAVIOR   Copulation complicated (as in spotted hyena) by unusual arrangement of genitalia. Preparatory to mounting, bull lays his trunk along cow's neck and head, rests his tusks or chin on her rump, and levers himself onto his bent hind legs, meanwhile bracing forelegs on her pelvis. His penis (turned back when merely extended), curving forward and upward when fully erect, probes for and finds the flap over the downward-opening vagina. Having gained entrance, the bull straightens on his hind legs and copulates in a normal-looking position.

OFFSPRING AND MATERNAL CARE   The tender loving care lavished on baby elephants is one of the species' more endearing traits (See Table 21.1, Mother and Offspring). Just to see a very young elephant (birth weight c. 265 lb [120 kg]) in a herd is breathtaking—how can these monsters avoid stepping on the tiny creature at their feet? Calves small enough to walk under mother (first year) remain in constant touch; if one strays over 20 yd away, it is retrieved. But gradually, the burden of staying close shifts to the calf—developing into the leader-follower ties that bind an elephant herd. A 9-year-old still spends half its time within 5 yd of mother's side, 5 to 6 years after weaning. Closely related females cross-suckle each other's calves; some cows keep lactating indefinitely. The bond between mother and daughter lasts up to 50 years.

PREDATORS   No land animal is safer from predators—excepting humans with firearms. Lions and spotted hyenas, perfectly capable of taking baby elephants, are treated as enemies; group defense and protectiveness of a maternal herd rarely give them opportunities.

HOW THEY COMMUNICATE   Sight 1, scent 1, sound 1, touch 1. All seem equally important, though eyesight is less acute than other senses.

Table 21.1. *ELEPHANT BEHAVIOR GUIDE*
   Expect to see and hear ➤ *Usual context and meaning*

Male Advertising Presence/Dominance

BULL IN MUSTH

Scent-marking with temporal glands: rubbing temples on trees, rocks, etc. at maximum stretch. ➤ Copious flow of sticky secretion stains cheeks. Pungent odor advertises musth condition; height of marks indexes size.

Swollen, partially extended penis dripping green secretion. ➤ Drips scent-mark route of musth ♂.

Male Advertising Presence/Dominance *continued*

Powerful low-frequency rumbles broadcast presence of musth ♂ to elephants miles away. ➤ Infrasound people can't hear. You might see vibrations of forehead when a bull is calling, or actually feel vibrations if very (too) close.

Aggression

Standing tall: head and tail raised, ears spread, trunk hanging. ➤ Dominance display. Similar to alert posture, but head is raised higher, making sharper angle with trunk.

THREAT DISPLAYS, FROM MILD TO SEVERE

Turning toward (body or just head) and approaching while nodding with ears half spread. ➤ Common displays between cows, reinforcing herd rank order.

Head-jerking and head-tossing: head abruptly raised, then slowly lowered. ➤ In tossing, head is first lowered, then jerked upward so that tusks describe an arc.

Head-shaking: head is twisted to side, then rotated side to side, making ears slap against face.

Forward trunk-swish: trunk is rolled up and abruptly unfurled like a party noisemaker, accompanied by trumpeting or air blast. ➤ Usually addressed to smaller adversary, including humans. Same gesture is used to rip up and throw objects (bushes, grass, branches).

Demonstration charge: rapid approach with ears spread, head high, tail out, trunk position variable, ± vocal accompaniment. ➤ Signs of uncertainty and ambivalence preceding charge, especially displacement activities, are indications of a demonstration rather than a real charge—but don't count on it!

Elephant stops short and moves away at an angle, looking back with head high and turned, back arched and tail raised. ➤ As in standing-tall dominance display.

SPARRING AND FIGHTING

Taking measure: confronting, heads raised as high as possible, tusks or trunk bases engaged. ➤ Prelude to challenge ritual, play, or serious fighting between ♂ ♂. One that stands taller usually dominates, especially if its tusks are also bigger. Equals may proceed to pushing and trunk-wrestling or—if ♀ in heat present—to serious ramming fight.

Trunk-wrestling.

VOCAL ACCOMPANIMENT

Growling, increasing to roaring; trumpeting; screaming.

Submission

Avoidance of superior: turning away, backing up, flight.

Submissive posture: flattening ears, arching back, raising tail.

Greeting ceremony. ➤ Described under Sociable Behavior.

Displacement Activities

Exaggerated feeding behavior: breaking off branches, tearing up and slapping grass against foot.

Touching temple gland.

Rubbing eye.

Swaying.

Foot-swinging.

Pawing.

Throwing dust.

Sociable Behavior

GREETING CEREMONY

Lower-ranking animal showing intention to insert trunk tip in mouth of approaching adult. ➤ Derived from calf's habit of putting trunk in mother's mouth.

Trunk-twining, touching, embracing, caressing, rubbing. ➤ Bonding behavior between mother/calf and herd.

Trumpeting, growling, urinating, and defecating. ➤ Intense greeting between bond groups.

Contact call: audible rumbling and growling that grades into inaudible infrasound. ➤ Voiced typically when a herd member has strayed; the matriarch usually answers. Growling is louder form of rumbling.

Flowing temporal glands, staining cheeks. Often seen in most or all herd members. ➤ Glands active in both sexes beginning in infancy; social function/significance unknown; possibly associated with stress.

Raising fallen herd member. ➤ Observed in ♂♂ as well as in ♀♀.

Courtship

MALE BEHAVIOR

Large ♂ accompanying ♀ herd.

Following and chasing ♀.

Placing trunk to ♀ genital opening or in her urine, then putting tip in his mouth. ➤ Using vomeronasal organ to test ♀ reproductive status (organ function explained in glossary).

Courtship *continued*

Competition between rival ♂ ♂, including supplanting, chasing, sparring, rarely fighting.

FEMALE BEHAVIOR

Infrasound calling. ➤ Broadcasts presence and location of cow in heat to elephants miles away.

Watchful, nervous behavior: moving quickly out of way, with head higher and eyes wider-open than usual.

Leaving herd and bustling away with tail raised, head turned to see pursuing suitor; circling and returning to herd.

Stopping when overtaken and contacted by bull.

Mutual touching, trunk-twining, caressing.

Backing into ♂ and standing for copulation. ➤ Fully receptive.

 Mating.

Excited behavior of other ♀ ♀: ear-flapping, head-shaking, backing toward courting couple while defecating and urinating; loud calling and milling. ➤ Signs of sexual stimulation.

Mother and Offspring

MATERNAL CARE OF SMALL CALF

Frequent touching with trunk, feet.

Helping calf to its feet using one foot and trunk.

Crooking trunk around calf's rump to help it up steep places.

Lifting it over obstacles or out of a wallow.

Pushing it under her to protect it from danger or hot sun.

Bathing calf: spraying water over and scrubbing it gently with her trunk.

Drawing water from her own stomach and spraying calf. ➤ During drought, to cool the calf—not an everyday event.

 Steering calf by holding its tail.

Calf following and holding mother's tail.

Calf distress call: squealing. ➤ Elicits immediate protective response from mother and other herd ♀ ♀.

Note babies' clumsy attempts to use trunk. ➤ Control develops gradually.

Play

Calves very playful, especially at water.

Solitary play by young calves.

Trunk-wrestling, shoving, butting, bullying other species. ➤ Usually ♂ ♂, beginning young and continuing to subadult stage. Contests with peers establish dominance order; bulls learn to assess adversary's fighting capability.

Response to Predators

Alert posture: standing with head raised, ears spread, tail raised, trunk raised or turned to catch scent.

Group defense: defensive ring around calves (see Fig. 21.1).

Demonstration or real charge. ➤ Illustrated under Aggression, above.

Flight.

SOUNDS OF ALARM, ANGER, PAIN

Trumpeting, screaming, growling, roaring.

Bellowing (growling with open mouth). ➤ Response to pain or intense fear.

Part III

CARNIVORES

ORDER CARNIVORA

Families Represented in Africa	Species
Viverridae: genets, civets, mongooses	34
Hyaenidae: hyenas, aardwolf	4
Felidae: cats	10
Canidae: foxes, jackals, wolf, wild dog	10
Mustelidae: weasel, zorilla, ratel, otters	7

CARNIVORE FAMILY TREE

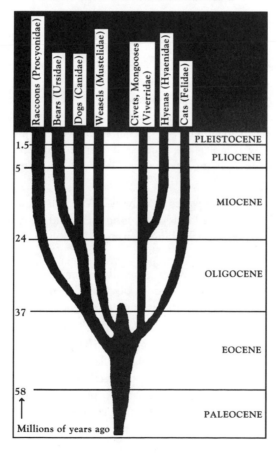

Chapter 22

INTRODUCING CARNIVORES

WHAT THEY ARE   An order of flesh-eating mammals that arose 40 million years ago from a family of small, mongooselike predators. Over the next 15 million years, all but 2 of 7 existing carnivore families evolved, including prototypes of dogs, cats, civets, mongooses, and others (see Carnivore Family Tree). The Carnivora divided early into 2 separate lines: the Feloidea, including cats and their allies, and the Canoidea, including dogs and their allies.

Carnivores evolved as predators of odd- and even-toed ungulates and rodents, which at the time were replacing more archaic herbivores that had been the prey of the carnivores' primitive ancestors. Interactions of predators and their prey cause each to improve their capabilities: by always taking individuals easiest to catch, predators promote survival of the fittest; as their prey becomes harder to catch, predators that improve performance are winners; their offspring pressure prey species to improve, and so on.

CARNIVORE TRAITS   Body long and supple; muscular limbs movable in all directions. *Feet:* 5 or 4 toes equipped with strong claws adapted for diverse functions (digging, climbing, holding prey, fighting). Most carnivores, including the best runners, walk on their toes with heel off ground. Skulls are reinforced to anchor powerful jaw muscles. *Teeth:* long canines adapted for gripping, slashing, stabbing; incisors chisel-shaped to strip flesh from bone; cheek teeth reduced in number, 2 specialized for cutting meat (fourth upper premolar/first lower molar—the carnassial teeth); back molars adapted for crushing. *Color:* concealing, except species with warning coloration and African wild dog.

SIZE   Of some 235 carnivores worldwide, Africa is home to 66 species, mostly small: 50% under 20 in (50 cm) long (head and body length [hbl]) and 90% under 3 ft (1 m). Weight ranges from 9 oz (268 g) dwarf mongoose to 400 lb (182 kg) lion.

GENDER DIFFERENCES   Males generally larger and more muscular with bigger canines, but differences seldom obvious. In monogamous species, females are as big or bigger than males (dwarf mongoose, jackals).

SENSES   All acute but variably developed, depending on ecological niche. Being nocturnal and descended from nocturnal ancestors, most carnivores have good night vision, including a light-reflective layer behind retina and a retina composed entirely of light-sensitive cells (rods). A few diurnal carnivores have color-sensitive cone cells that also provide maximum visual acuity, but most are presumed color-blind. Frontal placement of the eyes, particularly developed in cats and arboreal carnivores, also increases visual acuity by enabling animal to see in 3 dimensions. Smell and hearing are more important than vision for carnivores living in closed habitats.

WHAT THEY EAT   During long evolutionary history, carnivores have adapted to many different ecological roles. Strictly carnivorous species that prey mainly on vertebrates are greatly outnumbered by kinds that eat invertebrates, along with fruits and vegetables. Some, indeed, are insectivores and a few are primarily vegetarians. Most meat eaters prey on creatures smaller than themselves.

SPECIALISTS AND GENERALISTS   Carnivores limited to one type of habitat or feeding only on certain kinds of prey are specialized. Otters are aquatic; the wild dog a pack hunter specializing on medium-sized antelopes; the cheetah designed to outrun fleetest antelopes; the aardwolf with a diet of harvester termites.

Other carnivores—such as genets, ratel, jackals, and striped hyena are generalists, omnivores that eat whatever is available, from insects and earthworms to mammals their own size or larger. Species with widest geographical distribution (including Asia and Africa) are either omnivores or carnivores that can make do with whatever prey is available.

SCAVENGERS   Opportunism and conservation of energy are key ingredients of carnivore success. Scavenging is easiest way to get a meal but not reliable enough for any mammal to become as dependent as vultures. Indeed, vultures' near monopoly of daytime scavenging opportunities may be decisive deterrent. Jackals and hyenas are notorious scavengers but also active, capable predators, and lions and leopards scavenge nearly as readily as hyenas or jackals. So do omnivores like civet and ratel.

SOCIAL/MATING SYSTEMS   Summarized in Table 22.1; details given in family introductions and species accounts. A few generalizations are offered here:

- Most carnivores are solitary, territorial, and polygynous. The basic social unit is a female with offspring living in a home range/territory large enough to provide needed resources. Male and female associate only to mate although their ranges overlap, since males compete for access to females and the territories of the biggest, fittest individuals include part or all of several females' territories.

- Though relatively few carnivores are sociable, some of the most complex mammalian societies occur among those that are.

- Major factors underlying the evolution of social carnivores are surplus food, mutual security, and cooperative hunting. An excess of food removes pressure for offspring to disperse as soon as possible. Foraging in a group enables small or otherwise vulnerable day-active animals to leave cover and venture into the open. And hunting in packs often increases hunting success and food intake, thereby favoring the formation of social groups. But suppose varying conditions sometimes favor group hunting and solitary foraging other times? Just as some solitary species become sociable with a food surplus, some sociable species become solitary where prey species are very scarce or small.

• Most carnivore societies are based on kinship and descend in the female line; female offspring stay in the maternal group and males have to disperse. When group members are closely related, natural selection promotes cooperative care of offspring sharing the same genes. In societies where one couple monopolizes reproduction, as in the dog family and the dwarf mongoose, fathers play a parental role, and young adult offspring often postpone reproduction to help rear their parents' next litter. Since they share as many genes with full siblings (50%) as they would with their own offspring, helpers lose nothing genetically and the experience helps prepare them for parenthood.

PREDATORY WAYS   Ambush predators: lie in wait or stalk prey, taking victims by surprise (see Fig. 22.1). Fit and unfit individuals equally vulnerable.

Cursorial predators: run prey down in fair chase, often in packs, relying on superior endurance to exhaust faster quarry; most-vulnerable individuals selected as quarry (see Fig. 22.2).

Trackers: follow prey relentlessly by scent or sight, up and down trees or through underground passageways. Rare among African carnivores (see Fig. 22.3).

Pouncers: jump and land on concealed rodents and other small prey in their runways or hiding places (see Fig. 22.4).

Snatchers and grabbers: the most basic technique, employed by opportunistic foragers to capture prey flushed from or detected in their hiding places (see Fig. 22.5 and civet account).

HANDLING, KILLING, AND EATING PREY   Carnivores that grasp and handle prey with their feet and have special killing bites are most advanced. Cats kill small prey with precise neck bite and suffocate large victims. Canids and hyenas dispatch small prey with a "death shake" but simply "worry" large

Figure 22.1. Ambush predator (stalking lion).

Figure 22.2. Cursorial predator (running hyena).

Figure 22.3. Tracker (striped weasel).

Figure 22.4. Pouncer (jackal jumping).

Figure 22.5. Snatcher and grabber (civet eating rat).

victims to death: biting rear legs, tearing at underbelly, udder, or scrotum until the stomach cavity is opened, then pulling out entrails and internal organs. Civets, ratels, genets, etc. kill smaller prey with a crushing head bite, after first nipping and tossing victims that can fight back.

Feeding methods also vary with the carnivore and type of prey. Most use only their jaws in eating, whereas the most advanced (cats) hold food between their paws. Most carnivores start eating at head end, leaving skin, backbone and head of big game uneaten, but chew up and swallow small creatures whole.

REPRODUCTION   Typically nonseasonal. Litters of 2 (spotted hyena) up to 18 (wild dog); short gestation of 3 to 16 weeks. Carnivores are relatively slow to mature.

Estrus lasts several days to a week or more, allowing time for dangerously armed, normally solitary individuals to get together and condition females to accept male's proximity and finally, mating. Most carnivores seem to be induced ovulators—requiring repeated or continuous stimulation to ovulate. That would explain protracted courtship, prevalance of multiple or long-lasting copulations, and the penile bone present in all carnivores except hyenas.

OFFSPRING, PARENTAL, AND COMMUNAL CARE   Nearly all born at very immature stage, eyes and ears sealed, barely able to crawl (on forelegs only), with too little hair to protect them against cold or damp. To survive weeks of helplessness, they have to be kept warm, clean, and dry in a nest or den. Meanwhile, mother has to suckle them frequently and consume their body wastes. To become self-sufficient, many carnivores need practice or training in hunting techniques (see cheetah account).

Species in which father and other family members help mothers care for their young have large litters; wild dog offers most spectacular example of communal care of a single litter.

PREDATORS   Small carnivores are eaten by large carnivores. Even young big carnivores are vulnerable to adults of smaller ones.

HOW THEY COMMUNICATE   Preferred channels depend largely on a species' habitat and when it is active. Sight channel is least important in solitary nocturnal carnivores and diurnal species inhabiting dense undergrowth, but primary in diurnal, pack-forming species and other diurnal species living in open habitats. Nocturnal species rely primarily on scent and sound.

Scent is important in nearly all carnivores, including many visually oriented species. The variety of carnivore scent glands and prevalence of scent-marking implicate scent as the single most important communication channel. Glands are concentrated in the head and anal regions, areas virtually all carnivores inspect whenever two individuals of the same species meet. They rub or press glands against objects and often each other, to scent-mark paths, den sites, territorial boundaries, food, and family members.

Chemical analyses of carnivore glandular secretions disclose complex compounds capable of conveying a wealth of information: how long ago mark was made and depositor's identity, including gender and reproductive and social status. Feces and urine are also widely used, very commonly in communal latrines. Interest in feces may be promoted by anal-gland secretions.

GUIDE TO CARNIVORE VISUAL SIGNALS

FACIAL EXPRESSIONS   Carnivore facial expressions are very similar throughout the order and much the same as in primates. Anyone familiar with expressions of cats and dogs, and with associated postures and movements of the body, ears, and tail, is prepared to interpret carnivore displays. Because canine teeth are main weapons (as in primates), the mouth is a main focus of attention in social interactions. Friendly, aggressive, defensive, or fearful emotions cause changes in the normal relaxed position or expression of the lips, jaws, eyes, and ears—changes that are virtually the same across families and species. However, facial expressiveness is

Figure 22.6. Offensive threat (serval).

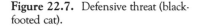

Figure 22.7. Defensive threat (black-footed cat).

Figure 22.8. Submissive posture (golden jackal).

variable, depending on differentiation of facial muscles, which is much greater in cats and dogs than in most other families. Civets, mongooses, and weasels have relatively stiff faces; difference between baring their teeth in anger or in play is hard to tell without other clues such as ear and tail positions, bristling hair, and vocal accompaniment.

POSTURES   The difference between an alert and confident animal and one that is fearful is obvious from their postures. With erect bearing and pricked ears, the former actively investigates its surroundings. The timid soul slinks or crouches and looks about furtively with ears down as though poised to bolt or hide.

THREAT DISPLAYS   To impress adversaries of their own or other species, carnivores display their fangs, bristle their coat to look as big as possible (many have manes and bushy tails that greatly enlarge their silhouette), and try to unnerve an adversary by sudden lunges, menacing growls, and explosive "spitting."

Table 22.1. THE MAIN TYPES OF CARNIVORE SOCIAL ORGANIZATION

Type	Dispersion Pattern and Mating System	Territorial Behavior	Offspring	Care and Feeding of Young	Foraging
SOLITARY/TERRITORIAL					
Polygynous (most carnivores: slender mongoose, serval, leopard)	♂ and ♀ associate only while mating; ♂ territory includes 1 or more ♀ ranges	Defense against outsiders of same sex	Disperse in adolescence; ♀♀ may settle in mother's range	By mother only	Solitary
Monogamous (aardwolf, ratel)	♂ and ♀ live as permanently mated pair	Joint marking and defense of pair territory	Both sexes usually disperse in adolescence	♂ shares parental duties; provisions offspring and/or mate	In pairs or alone
Monogamous family unit (jackals)	Pair with young of year and yearling offspring	Yearlings help defend family territory	One or both sexes defer emigration and breeding	Offspring help rear younger siblings	In pairs or alone, rarely in packs

SOCIABLE
(Clan or pack; group may include adults of both sexes.)

Type	Dispersion Pattern and Mating System	Territorial Behavior	Offspring	Care and Feeding of Young	Foraging
(dwarf mongoose)	Dominant pair monopolizes reproduction	Scent-marking mainly by dominant pair	Transfer or stay in natal pack	Communal care	Individual foraging in packs; no food-sharing
(wild dog)	Dominant pair monopolizes reproduction	Nonterritorial; scent-marking by dominant pair	Extra ♀♀ emigrate	Communal care	Pack-hunting; food-sharing
(lion)	All adult members breed	Individual and group territorial defense against same sex	♂♂ and some ♀♀ emigrate	Communal care	Individual and group-hunting; food-sharing
(spotted hyena)	Sizeable clans, separate rank orders, ♀♀ dominant; alpha ♂ sires most offspring	Aggression against outsiders ± territorial defense	♂♂ emigrate, ♀♀ remain in clan	No communal care, mothers rear own young unassisted	Individual and pack-hunting; food-sharing

Chapter 23

GENETS AND CIVETS
Subfamily Viverrinae
Family Viverridae

Common or small-spotted genet, *Genetta genetta*
Feline genet, G. *felina*
Large-spotted genet, G. *tigrina*
Servaline genet, G. *servalina*
Forest genet, G. *maculata*
Abyssinian genet, G. *abyssinica*
Angolan genet, G. *angolensis*

False genet, G. *thierryi*
Giant genet, G. *victoriae*
Johnston's genet, G. *johnstoni*
Fishing genet, *Osbornictis piscivora*
African linsang, *Poiana richardsoni*

African civet, *Civettictis civetta*

WHAT THEY ARE   A subfamily of small- to medium-size nocturnal carnivores considered to be the most primitive members of the order. Earliest fossils are barely distinguishable from immediate ancestors of the carnivore order; teeth and skeletons of living species have changed little in the last 40 to 50 million years.

Civets and genets belong to the Viverridae, the largest carnivore family, with 66 species, 7 genera, and 8 subfamilies. Mongooses and civets/genets are put in separate families by some specialists. Though different enough to be treated here in separate chapters, their common ancestry is best indicated by keeping them in the same family.

SUBFAMILY TRAITS   Long, narrow body with arched back, short legs, and long tail (except civet). *Feet:* 5 toes, wide; claws retractile in genets, not civets. *Head:* long and narrow, pointed or blunt muzzle; oval, catlike ears set high on head. *Teeth:* 38 or 40, adapted for carnivorous or omnivorous (civet) diet. *Coat:* smooth, with soft, dense undercoat (genets) or rough (civets); crest of longer hair along spine and tail. *Color:* dark spots, stripes, and blotches on light background; face mask; ringed tail. *Scent glands:* well-developed perineal glands in a pouch between scrotum and penis and below vulva; anal glands, and possible cheek and flank glands. *Teats:* 4.

SOCIAL/MATING SYSTEM   ♀♂♀   Probably solitary-polygynous mode typical of nocturnal carnivores that hunt small vertebrate prey and forage opportunistically for other animal and vegetable foods. But pending intensive field studies of African genets and civets, it is even uncertain they are territorial. If so, the outline of solitary-territorial social organization given in the carnivore introduction applies.

HOW THEY MOVE   Genets are agile climbers, using their short, curved, retractile claws to traverse branches upside down and descend trees headfirst. Genets and civets both jump well, have a slinking walk, trot (as transition between walking and running) and run in a diagonal stride, and jump-run with body alternately flexing and extending. They can sit up on their hind legs, and genets stand bipedally. They rest on their side or back and sleep in side curl (lying on side, nose to tail root), tail wrapping head and body. In grooming, they lick themselves, clean faces with moistened paws, nibble-groom, and scratch with feet. Genets sharpen claws on trees and grasp prey and adversaries with their paws. Civets usually eat without using their feet.

REPRODUCTION   Adolescent within first year but few species breed before 2. Thereafter produce 2 to 4 (range 1–6) offspring twice a year in equatorial regions; in more seasonal climates, reproductive peaks coincide with rains. Gestation 2 to 3 months.

HOW THEY COMMUNICATE   Sight 2, scent 1, sound 2. Sense of smell paramount, both in communication and foraging. Studies of captive genets indicate that familiar and unfamiliar individuals are distinguishable by their urine, feces, and perineal- and flank-gland secretions. Facial expressions poorly developed. Genet and civet visual displays emphasize body and tail postures and changing silhouette by raising and lowering spinal and tail hair.

Table 23.1. *GENET AND CIVET BEHAVIOR GUIDE*
         Expect to see and hear ➤ *Usual context and meaning*

Scent-marking

WITH PERINEAL GLANDS

Anal drag (as in mongoose—see Table 24.1). ➤ Practically any novel object is marked, including food. Secretion turns dark brown when dry. Musky odor permeates wood: genet's scent detectable after 4 yr.

Backing up against vertical objects.

Handstand-marking (see Fig. 23.1) of overhead objects. ➤ Rhythmic side-to-side motion spreads oily emulsion (genet).

OTHER FORMS OF MARKING

Rubbing flanks on objects. ➤ Usually associated with aggression.

Rubbing back, also cheeks, head, and neck on objects. ➤ Indicating possible presence of undescribed scent glands in these places (genet).

Urine-marking of various objects, mainly by ♂ ♂.

Defecation on latrines. ➤ Genets also occasionally leave scats on branches.

Aggression

Standing broadside in erect posture with coat bristling. ➤ Presenting maximum silhouette.

Staring. ➤ Common reaction when strangers meet. Whether offensive or defensive revealed by movement, posture, orientation.

Offensive threat: crouching and approaching; rushing. ➤ The one that stares more is likely to take the offensive (crouch and rush more) and win.

 Defensive threat: bowing the back and gaping, hair bristling. ➤ Usual response to approaching and staring adversary (genet).

Tail-flaring, usually while moving away.

 Head-darting: mouth opens wider with increasing intensity. ➤ Defensive threat. Common response to close approach by a stranger. The one that gapes wider and growls more is usually the loser.

Snapping. ➤ Bite threat.

VOCAL ACCOMPANIMENT
Growls, hissing and spitting, panting hiss (accelerated breathing with mouth open); screams at highest intensity (genet).

FIGHTING
Mutual head-darting and sparring; opponents toss and swing heads to avoid being hit. ➤ Bites to head, neck, and breast pull out hair but fighting is ritualized and basically harmless.

Submission

Turning away. ➤ Submissive response to head-darting.

 Lying down, turned at angle or sideways to aggressor. ➤ Effective in appeasing aggression (civet).

Courtship

MALE BEHAVIOR
 Grimacing after sniffing urine, musk deposits, or vulva. ➤ Urine-testing to determine ♀ reproductive status.

Close following and licking ♀'s genitalia.

FEMALE BEHAVIOR
Flight.

Elevating rear and holding tail aside when ready to mate.

After mating: ♀ rolls on back and anal-drags; both lick genitals.

Mother and Offspring

Kittens milk-tread while nursing.

JUVENILE CALLS

Whining with open mouth or meowing. ➤ Distress; elicits mother's aid.

Hissing, spitting. ➤ Alarm, fear.

Response to Predators

Offensive and defensive threat displays; feinted attack; flight.

Associated sounds: screaming, growling, cough-spitting.

FELINE AND LARGE-SPOTTED GENETS,
Genetta felina and *Genetta tigrina*

Figure 23.1. Large-spotted genet marking with perineal gland in handstand attitude.

WHAT THEY ARE Beautiful small carnivores with spotted and striped coats and ringed tails equal to body length; often seen along roads and near settlements at night. Long and low-slung, semiarboreal. Feline genet: ♂ wt 2–5 lb (1–2.3 kg), hbl 16–20 in (40–50 cm); ♀ slightly smaller. Large-spotted genet: ♂ wt 4–7 lb (2.3–3.2 kg), hbl 20–22 in (50–55 cm); ♀ wt 4–5.5 lb (2.3–2.5 kg), hbl 21 in (52 cm). *Feet:* sharp, curved, retractile claws. *Head:* pointed face with long whiskers; ears oval shaped, prominent, translucent. *Coat:* short except for spinal crest and fluffy tail. *Color:* darker in wet regions, lighter in dry; gray to reddish brown, markings rust-brown to black and individually unique. Spots arranged in rows; broad chevron on snout bordered by light fur; stripes on nape. Tail tip usually white in feline genet, black in large-spotted genet. Babies gray with faint markings.

WHERE THEY LIVE One species or another lives everywhere in Africa except Sahara Desert. *Genetta* species require close study to tell apart, and without their skins even experts can be stumped. However, G. *felina* and *tigrina*, the two commonest kinds, and several others overlap without inter-breeding, proving that at least some of the 10 recognized species are fully distinct. Feline genets live in the drier regions south of the Sahara, either side of the wetter savanna and forested regions inhabited by the large-spotted genet.

ECOLOGY   Genets subsist virtually anywhere there is food and cover. Preferences/tolerances for different habitats and life zones make for ecological separation of species. Feline and common genets are most desert-adapted; *tigrina* seldom ventures far from water and is most adaptable to human settlement. Diet includes wide range of animal foods plus fruits and nectar (from night-blooming trees pollinated by bats, bushbabies, genets, etc.). Vertebrate prey includes birds to chicken size, rodents, bats, bushbabies, lizards, snakes, frogs, and fish. Invertebrates: grasshoppers, crickets, moths, spiders, centipedes, scorpions.

ACTIVITY   ● Most active first half of night and more active than usual on moonlit nights. Radio-collared males traveled 1.9 mph (3 kph) while actively foraging.

SOCIAL/MATING SYSTEM   ♀♂♀ Typical solitary carnivores, except for uncertainty that males are territorial. In Serengeti NP at least 4 adults in a sample of marked genets used the same area. Elsewhere, radio tracking and retrapping marked animals showed males range areas as large as 1.9 mi^2 (5 km^2), whereas females may remain permanently within exclusive ranges 20 times smaller: 62 acres (25 ha). Females trapped and released up to 22 mi (35 km) away came back within days.

FORAGING/PREDATORY BEHAVIOR   Agile, versatile predators, genets hunt in trees and on the ground, alternately lurking in ambush and dashing at prey they flush while actively foraging.

REPRODUCTION   Seasonal at higher latitudes, otherwise perennial. Females can breed twice a year, producing 2 to 3 (1–4) young after 70- to 77-day gestation.

OFFSPRING AND MATERNAL CARE   After whelping in a hole or leaf nest, mothers spend first days nurturing offspring. Kittens' eyes open at 10 days (range 5–18), they start taking solid food at c. 6 weeks, and begin hunting between 11 and 18 weeks. By 6 months, having developed skill to catch and kill for themselves without instruction, they become independent; they begin scent-marking long before maturing at 2 years.

PREDATORS   No detailed information. Young are vulnerable to all predators down to size of hawks.

Table 23.2. *DIFFERENCES IN GENET BEHAVIOR*
Expect to see and hear ➤ Usual context and meaning

Scent-marking

Scent-marking with perineal glands and urine. ➤ ♀ ♀ mark 18–64 times/hr, mainly with their perineal glands and occasionally with urine. ♂ ♂ urine mark 8–10 times/hr, only 1 time in 10 with perineal glands. Marking rate increases with approach of mating peak.

Scent-marking with feces. ➤ Genets occasionally leave scats on branches.

Scuffing ground with hind feet while crouching (no urination); lying, rubbing, and rolling on the ground, especially when wet. ➤ Behaviors that may or may not involve scent-marking.

Aggression

Discharging stinking anal-sac secretions while urinating and screaming. ➤ By loser of a fight.

Lying on back. ➤ Defensive position, enabling genet to grapple and bite attacker while its own neck is protected.

Social Contact

Touching/sniffing noses, rear ends, backs. ➤ Typical meeting behavior and identity check.

Rubbing glands on ♀. ➤ During courtship.

Contact call: coughing, singly or in volleys. ➤ The commonest adult call (also voiced during courtship by ♂).

Courtship

MALE BEHAVIOR

Close following with grumbling and coughing calls.

Mutual sniffing of faces and genitals, rubbing cheeks together.

During 5-min. copulation, couple meows. ♂ sometimes bites ♀'s neck hair in final seconds.

FEMALE BEHAVIOR

Turning away, keeping tail and hindquarters low. ➤ Unresponsive.

Responding to calls, allowing ♂ to touch her. ➤ Responsive.

Mother and Offspring

Kittens purr while nursing.

Response to Predators

Discharging anal-sac secretions.

Flight, preferably up a tree.

CIVET, *Civettictis civetta*

Figure 23.2. Civet eating rat.

WHAT IT IS   Common nocturnal prowler, size and shape of a raccoon, with spots. Sturdy build; relatively long-legged; feet with doglike, nonretractile claws. ♂ wt 15-44 lb (7-20 kg), ht 14-16 in (35-40 cm), hbl 27-36 in (68-89 cm); ♀ 10-20% smaller. *Tail:* ½ hbl. *Head:* blunt muzzle, upstanding ears. *Teeth:* big and doglike with broad crushing molars. *Color:* varies regionally and individually, buff to dark or yellowish gray, covered with spots, blotches, and stripes; head lighter-colored with black robber's mask; nose, throat, ears, neck bands, and feet black; 4-in spinal crest of black-tipped hair from neck to tail tip. Juveniles dark brown with faint markings.

WHERE IT LIVES   African tropics almost everywhere except deserts and subdeserts, wherever cover is adequate, usually near water.

ECOLOGY   A remarkably unspecialized, basic sort of mammal. Being nocturnal, poorly equipped to climb or dig efficiently, and relatively slow-moving, civets need habitats with dense undergrowth, holes dug by other species, or other secure daytime refuges. Eats whatever is digestible: all sorts of invertebrates and vertebrates up to the size of newborn antelopes, carrion, and various vegetables, berries, and fruits.

ACTIVITY   ●

SOCIAL/MATING SYSTEM   ♀♂♀   Secretion of civet perineal glands, known as civetone, was so valuable as a fixative for flower perfumes before synthetics that African civets were kept in captivity for thousands of years. The pomade was spooned from the anal pouch 2 or 3 times a week—without damaging the animal! Yet to this day very little is known about the civet's natural history.

The frequency with which foraging civets scent-mark and the presence of latrines at the boundaries of adjacent ranges suggest the typical solitary-carnivore pattern, but studies of marked individuals are needed to determine whether either or both sexes are actually territorial. Aggressive behavior between captives, including littermates, suggests civets are loners.

HOW IT MOVES   Long legs propel it briskly when it chooses. Its jump-run is no match for a hyena or leopard, but civets are artful dodgers and jump over obstacles without breaking stride.

FORAGING/PREDATORY BEHAVIOR   Moves along in stealthy walk with head low, questing for food with nose and ears. Doesn't stalk or chase prey, but simply grabs hidden creatures it detects and ones that react too late to its shadowy approach. Uses only jaws for catching and killing; a feeding civet uses feet only to hold a carcass while tearing off pieces since it lacks shearing teeth (see Fig. 23.2).

Victims (e.g., snakes) that put up a fight scare civets. With crest raised, civet nips victim and retreats immediately; approaches, grabs, and throws it aside with a head-jerk, often leaping in the air right afterward. When satisfied the victim cannot fight back, civet grips it and gives it the death shake—so violently that backbones of snakes and large rodents may be broken in several places. Larger prey is finished off with a crushing bite to the skull.

REPRODUCTION   Apparently seasonal breeders, at least in southern Africa, with 1 to 4 young born early in the rains. Males adolescent by fifth month; females mate as yearlings. Gestation c. 80 days.

OFFSPRING AND MATERNAL CARE   Newborn unusually well-developed: eyes are already open or open within a few days, and they are able to crawl. Walk within 5 days but stay in hole for 2 weeks before making exploratory trips outside. By then, kittens have begun to play; run and jump within a month; react to danger by taking cover or freezing. Weaning begins when kittens start eating solid food at 1 month, complete within 14 to 20 weeks.

PREDATORS   No specific information on ranking predators, but spotted hyena prime suspect, not to mention man: civets are readily taken by nets, traps, and dogs.

Table 23.3. *DIFFERENCES IN CIVET BEHAVIOR*
Expect to see and hear ➤ *Usual context and meaning*

Scent-marking

Scent-marking with perineal glands: trees fronting paths and roads, pausing every 85 yd or so to back up and press everted gland against trunk.
➤ Thick yellowish grease deposited by both sexes, especially on fruiting trees eaten by civets.

Scent-marking *continued*

Defecation on latrines. ➤ Both sexes.

Urine-marking, by ♂♂ only, sprayed backward against bushes, grass, etc.

Neck-sliding on smelly substances, especially carrion.

Aggression

Standing broadside in erect posture. ➤ Raised crest increases silhouette by ⅓.

Mutual head-darting, directed at neck markings, no grappling. ➤ Ritualized fighting.

Courtship

MALE BEHAVIOR

Lying submissively in response to ♀ aggression.

Grips ♀'s neck if she meows and tries to move forward during 1-min. copulation, keeping all feet on ground and treading with hind feet.

FEMALE BEHAVIOR

Initially aggressive; remaining upright, thwarting mounting attempts. ➤ Unreceptive behavior.

Inciting pursuit by running past ♂. ➤ Receptive behavior.

VOCAL ACCOMPANIMENT

♂ gives *ha-ha-ha* contact call.

♀ in heat emits moaning and hoarse meows and a catlike meow during copulation.

Mother and Offspring

Nursing kittens tug at teats (like puppies), milk-tread (like cats), defend individually owned teats.

Coughing contact call. ➤ Causes littermates to cluster around calling kitten. Mother answers call to bring kittens to her.

Response to Predators

Seated posture of civet staring at possible danger. ➤ Alert posture.

Slinking into cover, with spinal crest flattened.

Running away, dodging and jinking to throw off pursuer.

Chapter 24

MONGOOSES
Subfamily Herpestinae
Family Viverridae

Slender mongoose, *Herpestes sanguineus*
Cape gray mongoose, *H. pulverulentus*
Ichneumon, *H. ichneumon*
Long-nosed mongoose, *H. naso*
Meller's mongoose, *Rhynchogale melleri*
White-tailed mongoose, *Ichneumia albicauda*
Black-legged mongoose, *Bdeogale nigripes*
Bushy-tailed mongoose, *B. crassicauda*
Selous' mongoose, *Paracynictis selousi*
Pousargues' mongoose, *Dologale dybowskii*

Marsh mongoose, *Atilax paludinosus*
Yellow mongoose, *Cynictis penicillata*
Dwarf mongoose, *Helogale parvula*
Banded mongoose, *Mungos mungo*
Gambian mongoose, *M. gambianus*
Liberian mongoose, *Liberiictis kuhni*en
Kusimanse, *Crossarchus obscurus*
Alexander's mongoose, *C. alexandri*
Angola or Ansorge's mongoose,
     C. ansorgei
Suricate or meerkat, *Suricata suricatta*

WHAT THEY ARE   A diverse group of small carnivores, most of which prey on insects and other invertebrates. The few predators on vertebrates (*Herpestes* species) are long, low, and sinuous (see slender mongoose and ichneumon accounts); the insectivores are squat. *Feet:* adapted for walking and digging (long claws, webbing between toes). *Head:* insectivores have broad skulls and short jaws. *Teeth:* 34 to 40, molars studded with sharp points for crunching up beetles, scorpions, millipedes, crabs, and such. *Ears:* inconspicuous, semicircular, low-set, and closable (adapted for burrowing). *Coat:* shaggy, with long hair on hindquarters and upper tail, hairs banded giving grizzled appearance. *Color:* light gray to dark brown. *Scent glands:* anal glands opening into a spacious anal pouch; also stink glands and cheek glands in some species. *Teats:* 4 or 6.

SOCIAL/MATING SYSTEMS   Both sexes territorial, repelling same-sex intruders.

(♀♂♀)   Solitary/territorial. Fittest males hold estates that incorporate several females' territories. Examples: most nocturnal and *Herpestes* species.

(♀♂♀♀)   One-male harem. One male lives with several related females which rear young communally. Example: ichneumon.

(♀♀♀♂♂♂)   Sociable/territorial: pack with single breeding pair. Only highest-ranking couple breeds. Other pack members, including unrelated individuals, cooperate in rearing young. Example: dwarf mongoose.

(symbol) Sociable/territorial: pack with several adults of each sex breeding in synchrony; young reared communally (banded mongoose, suricate).

HOW THEY MOVE   Mongooses with squat build and short legs are slow runners. Fastest gait the jump-run; also run and trot with diagonal stride. Ichneumon and slender mongoose have a slinking walk; excepting these 2, all mongooses are poor climbers that descend trees tail-first; most also poor jumpers but good diggers. Ability to manipulate objects not great (except marsh mongoose), but most mongooses smash eggs, millipedes, shellfish, etc., by hurling them between hind legs against rocks or tree trunks (see Fig. 24.7). They sit up on their hind legs (low-sit) and stand tiptoe (high-sit) braced by the tail (see Response to Predators, Table 24.1). Rest on side or back or spreadeagled on stomach; sleep seated, curled forward with forehead to ground.

REPRODUCTION   Birth peaks coincide with abundant food supply (rainy season). Social mongooses are slow to mature and breeding is suppressed in subordinate pack members.

HOW THEY COMMUNICATE   Sight 1, 2, or 3, scent 1, sound 1 or 2. Pivotal role of scent marking in mongoose social behavior and reliance on nose to locate food indicate scent is most important. Importance of sight, sound, and touch depends on social organization and activity cycle: important in diurnal social mongooses, less important in solitary nocturnal ones. Several diurnal species may have color vision (ichneumon, suricate).

Table 24.1. MONGOOSE BEHAVIOR GUIDE
Expect to see and hear ➤ *Usual context and meaning*

Maintenance Activities

Sunbathing postures: various lying, sitting, and standing attitudes.
➤ Diurnal species start day with sunbathing session, in postures that expose maximum surface to rays, with hair bristling to admit warmth.

Scent-marking

WITH ANAL POUCH
Chemically complex secretions identify individual, sex, age, and hormonal status. Practically any novel object is marked, including food and associates.

Anal dragging (see Fig. 24.5).

Backing up to vertical objects.

Handstand position (overhead objects; as in genet, see Fig 23.1).

Defecation on latrines. ➤ Located near dens, along territorial boundaries, or centrally.

Scent-marking *continued*

Urine-marking. ➤ Slender mongoose, yellow mongoose, ♂ suricate.

Rubbing cheeks on objects. ➤ Known in dwarf, banded, slender, marsh, yellow mongooses, and kusimanse.

Aggression

Erect posture: straightened legs, bowed back, bristling, and stiff-legged gait (slender mongoose shown). ➤ Display designed to make actor look bigger. Facial expressions poorly developed, limited to gaping (exception: slender mongoose). Orientation to opponent, tail and head carriage vary with species.

Staring (solitary mongooses). ➤ Common reaction when strangers meet. Whether offensive or defensive revealed by movement, posture, orientation.

Offensive threat: crouching and approaching; rushing.

Defensive threat: bowing the back and gaping.

Head-darting. ➤ Defensive and offensive threat, one-sided or mutual (see Table 23.1).

Snapping. ➤ Bite threat.

Mock mobbing attack by pack: jumping, rocking, running in place. ➤ Creates illusion of approach by single large, alarming foe; encounters with rival packs and small predators (banded mongoose).

MONGOOSE FIGHTING TECHNIQUES

Grappling and biting. ➤ Suricate.

Backing attack; curled up with mouth projecting between hind legs, or biting over shoulder (ichneumon shown). ➤ Defensive position (slender, marsh, dwarf, and banded mongooses; also offensive in suricate).

Lying on back, in position to hug and bite attacker (see Fig. 24.8). ➤ Defensive posture; inhibits aggressor's attack.

VOCAL ACCOMPANIMENT

Churring, growling, barking, screaming, clucking, cackling, explosive spitting. ➤ See species accounts.

Submission

Turning away from aggressor.

Crouching.

Lying on side (shown below, 1 pack member marking another). ➤ Appeasement display, effective in stopping aggression.

Sociable Behavior

Touching/sniffing noses and genitals. ➤ Typical meeting behavior, prelude to friendly or aggressive interactions.

Marking pack members with anal-pouch secretion. ➤ Pack members carry common scent; especially useful for home-team identification during encounters with other packs. Marking mutual or by dominant individuals in pack (banded mongoose).

Social grooming: nibbling and licking. ➤ As important for social bonding as for any hygenic effect.

SOCIABLE NOISES

Variety of churring, peeping, murmuring calls by social mongooses. ➤ "Conversational" sounds that keep pack members in contact and informed about each other's emotional state. Calls exchanged between mothers and offspring are the precursors.

Courtship

MALE BEHAVIOR

Close following.

Licking ♀'s genitals.

Mutual sniffing of noses and genitals; rubbing; social grooming.

Scent-marking ♀.

Gripping or mouthing ♀'s neck during lengthy copulation.

Licking genitals after mating.

FEMALE BEHAVIOR

Social grooming.

Crouching with rear elevated and tail deflected during copulation.

Licking genitals, rolling after mating.

Associated calls. ➤ See species accounts.

Parents, Helpers, and Offspring

Infants carried by nape, back, or head.

COMMUNAL CARE IN MONGOOSE PACKS

Guarding, provisioning, cross-suckling, retrieving, carrying, training, playing with young.

Play

Juveniles wrestling, play-fighting, chasing, ambushing, investigating holes, hiding.

Response to Predators

Low-sit posture (left: suricate); high-sit posture (right: slender mongoose). ➤ Alert postures of sentinel mongoose.

Alarm sounds: different ones for avian and ground predators. ➤ Social mongooses. Pack members respond appropriately to different signals.

Flight to refuge holes.

THREAT DISPLAYS

As in encounters with own species, displays function to make the animal appear bigger and more dangerous, inhibit attack.

Mock attack: running, jumping, rocking in place, coat bristling. ➤ Attempt to intimidate adversary by pretending to approach and appearing bigger.

Pack mobbing attacks. ➤ Real attacks against small predators (see banded mongoose and suricate accounts).

Spraying or dribbling anal-gland secretions. ➤ In extreme fear, as when captured. Potency of secretion varies with species.

Associated sounds: growling, spitting, screaming.

SLENDER OR BLACK-TIPPED MONGOOSE,
Herpestes sanguineus

Figure 24.1. Slender mongoose.

WHAT IT IS   Long, lithe mongoose with short legs and black-tipped tail, often seen darting across roads and paths. ♂ wt 18–28 oz (523–789g), hbl 13 in (32 cm); ♀ wt 13–20 oz (373–565 g), hbl an inch shorter than ♂. *Tail:* nearly as long, tapering to thin tip. *Feet:* narrow with short, curved claws (adapted for climbing, not digging). *Head:* narrow with pointed snout; wide, low ears. *Teeth:* adapted for meat-eating (large carnassials). *Coat:* relatively fine. *Color:* gray to dark brown (forest populations darkest); banded hairs give speckled appearance; eyes red.

WHERE IT LIVES   One of the most successful African carnivores, occurs everywhere there is cover in sub-Saharan Africa, except deserts.

ECOLOGY   Lives in all kinds of forest and savanna, preference for dense cover near water. Takes refuge and sleeps in holes, especially termite mounds. The most predacious member of the subfamily, tireless diurnal hunter of rodents, lizards, snakes, and birds, in trees and on the ground; also eats insects such as grasshoppers, crickets, termites, and fly pupae; sometimes fruits and berries.

ACTIVITY   ○ Often emerges only after sunup, sunbathes before going hunting. On cold dark days may stay in cover.

SOCIAL/MATING SYSTEM   ♀♂♀ In Serengeti NP mature males control territories of at least 123 acres (50 ha), which typically incorporate the territories of 2 females. Unlike resident females, breeding males tolerate smaller, subordinate mongooses of the same gender.

HOW IT MOVES   Unusually agile for a mongoose, moves with a sinuous, restless grace; travels at a quick trot, along regular paths, head low, long tail trailing with just the black tip raised, pausing to sniff and listen for prey. When pursued, changes from jump-run to a flat, undulating gallop; shifts direction in full flight—often by leaping at and ricocheting off trees; flips tail like a squirrel as it disappears. Easily makes vertical leaps of over a yard and moves backward surprisingly fast.

FORAGING/PREDATORY BEHAVIOR   Pounces on or chases prey flushed while foraging; sometimes catches grasshoppers in flight. Well-fed mongooses play with their victims, prodding or tapping them to make them run, then catching them again, finally dispatching them with a bite to head/neck area.

Birds and small mammals, which ignore most mongooses, react to this one as to a cat: give alarm calls, gather round, mob, and scold it.

REPRODUCTION   In equatorial regions females breed up to 3 times a year. A Serengeti slender mongoose whelped in March and again in July. Estrus lasts up to a week; gestation 58 to 62 days; usual litter 2 to 4. Females mature and conceive as yearlings, males probably later.

OFFSPRING AND MATERNAL CARE   Mothers attack much larger animals, even people that come too near babies. In captivity, males also show parental care; even carry babies, which curl up and become passive when picked up by head or neck. Eyes open at 3 weeks; leave nest at 4 weeks and begin taking solid food brought by mother; weaned at 7 to 9 weeks, usually become independent by 10 weeks and acquire second teeth by 24 weeks. However, one female still associated with 3 fully grown offspring; another reunited with a son 5 months after separating. A daughter inherited the territory of a mother that disappeared.

PREDATORS   Slender mongooses are alarmed by eagles but show little fear of snakes. Known to attack cobras and mambas, both major mongoose predators.

Table 24.2. *DIFFERENCES IN SLENDER MONGOOSE BEHAVIOR*
Expect to see and hear ➤ *Usual context and meaning*

Scent-marking

With anal pouch: anal-drag and handstand positions. ➤ By ♂ only, during mating season.

Urination and defecation on latrines, by both sexes.

Rubbing chest on another mongoose by ♀ in heat. ➤ Maybe deposits scent of an undescribed gland.

Aggression

Crouching with tail bristling, droning growl, spitting. ➤ Low-intensity threat (eg., defending food).

Crouching with body and tail hair bristling, breathy *hah*. ➤ High-intensity threat.

Staring and approaching, snarling/threat-gaping. ➤ Retracts lips vertically to show teeth.

Associated sounds: caterwauling. ➤ When 2 strangers meet.

Submission

Turning away from aggressor with submissive grimace: gaping with lips retracted horizontally showing pink gums, head lowered.

Submissive approach: slow, cringing, sometimes dragging body.

Courtship

MALE BEHAVIOR
Mounting attempts during mating march, whenever ♀ stops.

Copulation lasting c. 2.5 min.; ♂ gapes in response to ♀'s poking.

Mother and Offspring

JUVENILE AND MATERNAL CALLS
Whoo contact call, variable in volume and pitch. ➤ Mother to young, which respond in kind at 1 month.

Faint purring of newborn kittens nursing or sleeping.

Tsherr. ➤ Chirping distress call.

Play

Play with captured prey. ➤ Unusually playful species, including adults.

Haah-haah. ➤ Calls associated with play.

Response to Predators

Tschaarrr. ➤ Alarm call.

Flight to hole or up tree with tail raised high.

Bristling, wide-mouth gaping. ➤ Threat displays.

Spraying or dribbling pungent anal-gland secretions. ➤ Last resort.

ICHNEUMON, LARGE GRAY OR EGYPTIAN MONGOOSE, *Herpestes ichneumon*

Figure 24.2. Ichneumon eating a small rodent.

WHAT IT IS   Oversized version of the slender mongoose; the longest African mongoose. Long, sinuous body, long, tapering tail, and short legs. ♂ ♀ wt 5.3–9 lb (2.4–4.1 kg), hbl 19–24 in (48–60 cm). *Feet*: with long digits and long, slightly curved toes (better adapted for digging than climbing). *Head*: narrow with pointed snout and wide, low-set ears. *Coat*: wiry and long, overhanging legs. *Color*: speckled gray and brown in dry areas to dark red-brown in West African high forest; legs and head darker, snout and tail tassel black.

WHERE IT LIVES   Pan-African, throughout the savanna and arid zones; absent only from deserts and rainforest. Near East and Iberia (the only mongoose in Europe).

ECOLOGY   Ichneumon, Greek for tracker, earns its name: a restless, questing hunter of small vertebrates. Favors dense undergrowth bordering water, where prey is more abundant: rodents and other small mammals, birds, reptiles, frogs, and fish; also invertebrates like crayfish, freshwater crabs, and large insects.

ACTIVITY   ○ Believed to hunt most actively early and late in day, becoming inactive on very hot and cold days, windy and rainy weather.

SOCIAL/MATING SYSTEM   ♀♂♀   ♀♂♀   Usually seen singly in Africa and probably has the typical solitary-carnivore mating system. Studies in Spain and Israel show it can be sociable. Ichneumons observed in Spain lived in pairs or in groups of 3 to 7. In Israel, around artificial fish ponds that provided superabundant food, ichneumons lived in 1-male harems or families consisting of a male, 2 to 3 females, and their offspring. Whether the permanent home range maintained by each fish-pond family was defended as a territory is unclear; family members did maintain and share the same network of paths, latrines, scent posts, eating and sleeping places. Family females regularly associated and cooperatively reared their offspring, cross-suckling one another's kittens, and taking turns babysitting. They were assisted occasionally by the father and often by yearling offspring that had postponed emigration. In Spain, ichneumons are even known to forage in packs, meanwhile keeping vocal contact like social mongooses.

Presumably African ichneumons also have the potential to become sociable when resources exceed the requirements of 1 or 2 individuals. To produce this type of social/mating system, female offspring stay home instead of dispersing. Adolescent males would still be forced to leave.

HOW IT MOVES   Strictly terrestrial, a good digger and swimmer. Very active, quick reflexes. Trots while foraging but a slow runner, never venturing too far from a hole into which it can bolt if pursued.

FORAGING/PREDATORY BEHAVIOR   An opportunistic forager, dashes after prey it flushes and tries to grab it in jaws; kills large creatures with a neck bite and simply bites the head to kill small victims. Attacks snakes from the rear, jumping back before snake can retaliate. Breaks birds' eggs with standard backward throw. Reputedly digs up crocodile eggs and even lures birds within catching distance by performing strange antics, like chasing its own tail, twitching the black tail tassel, flopping over and rolling.

REPRODUCTION   Usually annual but more often when food abundant. Litters average c. 3; gestation only 60 days.

OFFSPRING AND PARENTAL CARE   Newborns' ears and eyes sealed. Eyes open within 2 weeks but remain milky looking through third week. Kittens react to sounds at 4 weeks and begin using noses within 7 weeks. Israeli ichneumons emerged from cover at 6 weeks and made excursions, always escorted by an adult; began eating solid food, provided by all family members, at 1 month. Weaned at 10 weeks but continued to be provisioned the first year even though foraging independently from 4 months onward.

PREDATORS   No information, except that all adults defend babies when ichneumons live in social groups.

Table 24.3. *DIFFERENCES IN ICHNEUMON BEHAVIOR*
Expect to see and hear ➤ *Usual context and meaning*

Scent-marking

With anal pouch, after first sniffing the spot. ➤ Family members use single communal site—e.g., a large stone or rock corner near regular trail. Young and old of both sexes perform equally; rate increases under stress.

 Latrines, located in partly open areas. ➤ Permanent, used by all family members.

Aggression

Gaping. ➤ Ichneumon has unusually wide gape.

Crouching nose to nose, chins on ground, preparing to spring.

Standing confronting, tails lashing.

 Snapping, lunging, jaw fencing, grappling, biting.

Backing attack: curled forward, mouth between hind legs.

Associated sounds: growling, clucking, cackling.

Sociable Behavior

O-o-o contact call. ➤ Voiced by members of foraging group.

Following nose-to-tail: snake-line procession of mother and young, each with nose "glued" to anal pouch of the one ahead. ➤ A very odd-looking formation that has reminded some observers of a giant snake. Possibly adapted to staying together while moving through dense undergrowth.

Courtship

MALE BEHAVIOR
Chasing when ♀ runs away.

Multiple preliminary mounting attempts, using chin to press ♀ into copulation crouch.

Mouthing ♀'s neck during 6–7 min. coupling.

FEMALE BEHAVIOR
Defensive threats, screaming after mating.

0-0-0 and pip contact call. ➤ Courtship calls.

Play

Both young and adults exceptionally playful.

Running games, including vertical leaps and caroming off objects.

Hiding and ambushing games.

Games with living and dead prey, in which incomplete segments of predatory patterns are performed.

Novelty games. ➤ Pets invent games.

Response to Predators

Sniffing to identify disturbance.

Freezing in prone position. ➤ Hiding attempt when surprised in open.

Backing attack.

Associated sounds: cackling, screaming, hissing, spitting.

WHITE-TAILED MONGOOSE, *Ichneumia albicauda*

Figure 24.3. White-tailed mongoose in defensive-threat display.

WHAT IT IS Africa's version of a skunk, often seen foraging at night in open grassland. Big, long neck and legs. ♂♀ wt 6.4–9.2 lb (2.9–4.2 kg), hbl 21–28 in (53–71 cm), tail 16–19 in (40–47 cm). *Feet:* equipped with long, curving claws. *Head:* long, pointed snout, wide forehead, large but low, rounded ears. *Teeth:* broad crushing molars, no shearing teeth. *Coat:* long and loose, up to 3.6 in (6.5 cm) on hindquarters and tail. *Color:* light undercoat overlaid with grizzled or gray-brown guard hairs; underparts and lower legs dark brown or black; tail usually white but variable. Newborns have light brown, wooly coat.

WHERE IT LIVES Just about everywhere insects are abundant, mainly savannas and arid zones, mountains up to 8000 ft (2500 m): absent from deserts and rainforest.

ECOLOGY Most abundant in grassland habitats with large populations of ungulates and plenty of secure daytime resting places. Uses 2 to 3 different dens a month for 5 to 15 days at at time. Feeds mainly on large insects and other invertebrates it finds on or close to the surface during nightly foraging. Harvester termites and ants are mainstay of Serengeti mongooses in late dry season; during rains they feed largely on dung beetles that mine manure of plains game. Unwary vertebrates up to hare size are taken occasionally.

ACTIVITY ● Forages actively up to 10 hours a night, resting briefly between bouts, increasingly in the early morning; retires underground before dawn. Spends almost no time interacting socially.

SOCIAL/MATING SYSTEM ⚲♂⚲ Mostly seen alone (87% of Serengeti sightings). Up to 9 adult-sized individuals sometimes seen in the same locality were temporary clusters of single mongooses attracted to a patch rich in insects, e.g., a termite swarm or dung-beetle concentration.

In areas of high insect productivity, supporting up to 10 mongooses/m^2 (4/km^2), offspring are slow to disperse and mothers sometimes tolerate grown daughters on their land. In Serengeti study area, up to 3 females and 5 juveniles shared home ranges of 96 to 291 acres (39–118 ha) and often doubled up in 1 of about 3 den sites per home range. There is little doubt that the additional mongooses were offspring of the resident female, as outsiders were always chased. Regular occupants never avoided one another or behaved aggressively when they met, but paused only briefly to sniff noses or genitals before going about their business. Adults and youngsters older than 9 months foraged singly and seldom came within 100 yd of one another.

The 4 adult males in the Serengeti study area had territories of 198 to 304 acres (80–123 ha) that typically included parts of 2 to 3 females' territories. Two or more males sometimes had pieces of the same female's property. Ranges of adjacent mongooses barely overlapped, border areas were scent-posted, and territories did not appear to change size or boundaries seasonally.

In areas with less abundant resources, mongooses have home ranges as large as 1976 acres (800 ha).

HOW IT MOVES Unable to outrun most carnivores, the white-tailed mongoose depends on stink glands as a deterrent. It ambles at 2.6 mph (4.2 kph) and trots at a brisk pace.

FORAGING/PREDATORY BEHAVIOR Head low, rump high, and tail trailing, foraging mongoose quarters ground at a walk or trot, with frequent pauses to poke or bite at something. Serengeti mongooses covered their whole home range every night, consuming c. 0.5 lb (230 g) of insects, equivalent to 3200 harvester termites. Digs for insects close to surface, without trying to catch airborne prey, but mostly picks insects off vegetation and uncovers beetles from dung. Occasional vertebrate prey includes poisonous snakes. White-tailed mongooses sometimes "mutter" while eating.

REPRODUCTION   Very little information; produces 1 to 2 young (rarely more), probably most born during rainy season.

OFFSPRING AND MATERNAL CARE   Born blind with sparse underfur. Females that share a home range may whelp at same time but don't cooperate in raising young.

PREDATORS   Presumably the stink glands, advertised by warning coloration and a spectacular threat display (see Fig. 24.3), effectively deter spotted hyenas and other large carnivores that could easily capture this mongoose. Or maybe not so easily—it runs fast for a mongoose and dodges with great agility when pursued. How far and effectively it can project its anal-sac fluid is unclear.

Table 24.4. *DIFFERENCES IN WHITE-TAILED MONGOOSE BEHAVIOR*
Expect to see and hear ➤ *Usual context and meaning*

Scent-marking

Anal-pouch secretion, deposited in anal drag. ➤ Marking rate increases to once in 2 min. during border patrols and aggressive encounters (e.g., between territorial ♂ ♂).

Urinating with arched tail, by both sexes. ➤ Distinctive posture calls attention to the act, but scent-marking or sexual function, if any, unknown.

Aggression

Erect posture with white tail, the most visible part of the animal at night, fluffed, arched, and waved (see Fig. 24.3). ➤ Meetings with friend or foe of its own and other species.

Courtship

Pairing up: ♂ and ♀ stay within 25 yd while foraging, for at least a few hours.

Repeated mounting attempts, interrupted by ♀ breaking away and circling, ending in copulation after ½ hr.

Whimpering, possibly purring. ➤ Courtship calls.

Mother and Offspring

Mother and young exchange whimpering calls.

Juveniles following mother keep tails conspicuously arched.

Play

Chasing, dragging objects to invite pursuit; somersaulting, cavorting with raised tail waving and switching against playmate.

Response to Predators

Freeze when disturbed, then run for cover after standing up to locate danger.

Tail and body hair bristling, tail raised; explosive grunts, deep growls, and clear, short bark. ➤ Threat display.

Shrieking and screaming in extreme fear, pain.

Spraying or dribbling anal-gland secretions. ➤ But Serengeti animals trapped and handled never discharged.

MARSH OR WATER MONGOOSE,
Atilax paludinosus

Figure 24.4. Marsh mongoose in high-sit attitude preparing to smash an egg.

WHAT IT IS   A big, dark mongoose often seen near water. Sturdy and lowslung, short legs. ♂ ♀ wt 5.5–11 lb (2.5–5 kg), hbl 25–26 in (62–64 cm). Tail: thick, tapered, 16 in (40 cm). *Feet*: long, un-webbed toes and naked soft palms. *Head*: broad between wide, rounded ears. *Teeth*: robust molars adapted for crushing shell-fish; long canines, upper set knife-edged. *Coat*: shaggy, with dense under-fur. *Color*: very dark brown, varying to lighter, speckled brown or red-brown.

WHERE IT LIVES   Sub-Saharan Africa, sea level to 8200 ft (2500 m).

ECOLOGY   As long as it has water and cover for concealment, the marsh mongoose tolerates a broad climatic range. Diet of freshwater crabs, crayfish, mussels, clams, snails, aquatic insects, fish, reptiles, birds and their eggs, frogs, and worms. Probably terrestrial insects as well.

ACTIVITY   ●/(○) Primarily, but not strictly, nocturnal.

SOCIAL/MATING SYSTEM   ♀♂♀   Unstudied but presumed to be similar to other solitary, nocturnal mongooses. Marsh mongooses seem to own sections of shoreline; they move along a network of well-beaten paths, scent-mark borders, and maintain latrines in open waterside spots.

HOW IT MOVES   Reputed to swim like an otter with undulations of its body and tail, despite absence of webbed feet and waterlogging of underfur. Commuting between lair and hunting grounds, it moves at steady trot.

FORAGING/PREDATORY BEHAVIOR   Wading in shallow water as it searches the bottom for prey, it gropes for and brings creatures caught with its dextrous hands to its mouth raccoon-style, crunching small items between the molars before swallowing them, dispatching slippery, struggling larger prey like fish or frogs with the canines and premolars. Mussels, crabs, and eggs (see Fig. 24.4) are opened by hurling them downward against rocks from a standing position.

REPRODUCTION   Perennial in wet equatorial regions. A birth peak early in the rainy season in more seasonal climates. Up to 3 young in litter.

OFFSPRING AND MATERNAL CARE   No information.

PREDATORS   Little information; probably hyena, lion, leopard, crocodile, python.

Table 24.5. *DIFFERENCES IN MARSH MONGOOSE BEHAVIOR*
Expect to see and hear ➤ *Usual context and meaning*

Scent-marking

With anal glands. ➤ ♂♂, in particular, handstand to mark undersides of logs and rocks.

Feces. ➤ Latrines usually located near water.

Aggression

Explosive bark-growls. ➤ Heard during fight.

Response to Predators

Low growl changing to sudden barking growl in higher range.

Escape into water: swimming away, diving, hiding underwater with only nose exposed.

SELF-DEFENSE
Counterattacking, especially in the water. One being bitten by a dog got its assailant by the throat and nearly drowned it, meanwhile discharging foul-smelling anal-gland secretions.

Backing attack: curling into ball, turning round and round, urinating, discharging anal-sac fluid. ➤ When cornered and terrified.

YELLOW MONGOOSE, *Cynictis penicillata*

Figure 24.5. Yellow mongoose scent-marking a rock in the anal-drag attitude.

WHAT IT IS   A plain-colored mongoose with a white-tipped tail. ♂ wt 1.3 lb (0.59 kg), hbl 12.4 in (31 cm); ♀ wt 1.2 lb (0.55 kg), hbl same as ♂. *Tail*: ¾ hbl, bushy, foxy-looking. *Head*: broad forehead, sharp nose, large ears that extend above the head. *Coat*: thick, wooly undercoat and long guard hairs. *Color*: tawny orange or yellow in South Africa to gray in northern Botswana; head grayer with white lips, chin, and throat.

WHERE IT LIVES   South West Arid Zone of southern Africa.

GOOD PLACES TO SEE IT   Widespread outside NPs, including suburbs of Johannesburg and other cities.

ECOLOGY   Inhabits dry savannas and open plains, especially the Kalahari *sandveld* but also the Karroo, floodplains, and, in the dry season, the edges of alkaline pans. Often shares dens with ground squirrels and sometimes suricates. Occasionally takes mice and reptiles, but mainly insects on or near the surface, especially harvester termites, beetles, grasshoppers, and crickets.

ACTIVITY   ○ Weather and temperature strongly influence both daily and seasonal activity patterns. Colony members rise before sunup in summer, first using the communal latrine and making a few tunnel repairs before foraging. They take cover from midday heat, reemerge in midafternoon, and forage until dusk. Cold winter days, colony members come up at sunrise to relieve themselves, go back inside until it gets warm enough to sunbathe. Up to 1.5 hours/day spent sunning and socializing, changing position and posture as sun's angle increases, hair on sunny side bristling to soak up warmth. By 9 AM pack finally gets started, but returns to the den while sun is still high enough to sunbathe some more before retiring.

SOCIAL/MATING SYSTEM   A mated pair lives either alone with their offspring or, more often, in a colony of about 8

(rarely up to 20) mongooses. Colonies include the breeding pair, their immature offspring, plus 1 or 2 young or older adults. Several other adults may live
on the fringes of the colony—probably dispersing young adults from the same
or a different colony. A dominance hierarchy is maintained, the alpha male
and female being number 1 and 2, followed by their dependent young, which
pull rank on the other adults and even dare to snatch food from their father.
He marks all members of his family daily with anal-pouch secretions.

Yellow mongoose family/colony home ranges are defended as territories,
primarily by the breeding males, which make daily border patrols to renew
scent marks, sometimes backed by the alpha female. A 44-acre (18-ha) island
inhabited by yellow mongooses was partitioned among 5 colonies. Each territory included a den or warren, located on rising ground, with numerous in-
tersecting tunnels. These mongooses can dig their own tunnels in sandy soil,
but more often adapt abandoned holes or move in on a colony of ground
squirrels.

FORAGING/PREDATORY BEHAVIOR   Unlike other sociable mongooses, *Cynicitis* forages individually and not in packs. An interesting, unex-
plained difference, particularly compared to suricate, with which it overlaps
both in range and diet. Yellow mongoose digs industriously in sandy soil for
buried beetle larvae, but suricate's superior digging ability gives it access to
wider range of invertebrate prey.

REPRODUCTION   Seasonal; litters of 2 to 4 early in rains (Oct.–Nov.).
Although subordinate females have been seen mating, alpha female somehow
represses their reproduction.

OFFSPRING AND PARENTAL CARE   Privileged status of young
ends at c. 10 months as they approach adult weight, followed by dispersal, apparently of both sexes.

PREDATORS   Large eagles, black-backed jackal, caracal, cobra, black
mamba.

Table 24.6. DIFFERENCES IN YELLOW MONGOOSE BEHAVIOR
Expect to see and hear ➤ *Usual context and meaning*

Scent-marking

With anal pouch: anal dragging and backing up to vertical objects. ➤
Territorial ♂ makes marking rounds before AM foraging, mainly along
border, anal dragging every 5–10 yd (see Fig. 24.5), at shorter intervals
and more intensively if rival neighbor nearby.

Alpha ♂ also marks pack members, first jumping over, then straddling
each mongoose with tail raised.

Scent-marking *continued*

Defecation on boundary latrine. ➤ Used by both neighboring territorial ♂♂.

Rubbing cheeks on grass tufts, etc. ➤ All colony members, especially around den and by territorial ♂ along boundary.

Rubbing back on grass and tree trunks, turning almost on side in the process. ➤ Territorial ♂ only, during marking round.

Aggression

After 2 mongooses meet in crouch, dominant rises higher and licks or bites subordinate's neck until it assumes submissive posture.

Holding tail out with tip above back. ➤ Posture of dominance.

Submission

Crouching, with tail tip down. ➤ Submissive attitude.

Lying on side. ➤ Surrender.

Screaming. ➤ By frightened animal if aggression continues.

Sociable Behavior

Approaching in crouch and sniffing cheek glands. ➤ Greeting and identity check, prelude to friendly or aggressive interactions.

Marking colony members with anal-pouch secretion by alpha ♂. ➤ All members share colony odor.

Courtship

Receptive ♀ approaching ♂ in submissive crouch, lies down when he sniffs her genitals.

♂ purrs, ♀ gets to feet and he mounts.

Copulation (up to ¾ hr). ♂ clasps ♀'s flanks and purrs, pausing between bouts of thrusting; ♀ keeps biting or licking his ears and neck.

Response to Predators

WARNING SIGNALS

Tail raised in S-curve and bristling. ➤ Alarm posture.

Short bark. ➤ Danger signal.

DWARF MONGOOSE, *Helogale parvula*

Figure 24.6. Dwarf mongooses nibble-grooming.

WHAT IT IS   The smallest African carnivore, size and color of a red squirrel. Muscular build with medium-length legs and 5-toed feet equipped with long claws. ♂ wt 11.4 oz (326 g), hbl 9.5 in (24 cm); ♀ 11 oz (315.5 g), hbl same as ♂. *Tail*: almost same as hbl, tapering to point. *Head*: short and broad with pointed nose, broad, rounded ears. *Teeth*: adapted for insect diet. *Coat*: smooth, glossy, uniform reddish brown to grizzled (rarely black); pink nose.

WHERE IT LIVES   Southern Savanna and adjoining Somali-Masai and South West Arid Zones, sea level to 6500 ft (2000 m), from Somalia and Ethiopia to South Africa and Namibia.

GOOD PLACES TO SEE IT   Common around wildlife lodges and dwellings inside national parks, as in Serengeti NP, Tanzania, and Tsavo NP, Kenya, both being places where this mongoose was studied.

ECOLOGY   Preferred habitat includes numerous termite mounds, woody vegetation in the form of thickets, open woodland, or scattered bush. Up to 80 dwarf mongooses/mi² (31/km²), highest density of any African carnivore. Diet mainly beetles, crickets, grasshoppers, termites, spiders, and scorpions; occasionally small rodents, snakes, lizards, and birds; also fruits and some vegetables. Water-independent but drinks when it can.

ACTIVITY   ○ Strictly diurnal, schedule subject to weather conditions. Packs begin and end day sunbathing and socializing at burrows.

SOCIAL/MATING SYSTEM Dwarf mongooses live in packs with 1 breeding pair. Their offspring are cooperatively reared by relatives and immigrants. In Serengeti NP, average pack size is 8.4 (range 2–18), including 2 to 3 adult males, 3 to 4 adult females, and 2 to 3 juveniles. Packs occupy permanent territories averaging 85 acres (34 ha), including 10 to 30 termite mounds used as refuges and dens. In dry tree savanna territories are as large as 395 acres (160 ha).

The breeding pair, usually the senior male and female, monopolize breeding as long as they remain dominant (several years). The female leads the pack; the male is most alert to danger and intrusions by rival packs. Other members feed and care for offspring, freeing the mother for extra feeding time she needs to keep producing milk.

Unrelated immigrants give the alpha pair's offspring the same quality care as blood relations give—a special exception to the rule that cooperative care is based on kinship. Reasons why:

- Limited options. Available habitat is usually fully occupied, sharply limiting opportunities to found a new pack. Offspring that try suffer higher mortality than those that stay home or join another pack.

- Nonbreeders waiting their turn to become dominant can often get into a shorter queue by transferring from their natal pack. Most transfers occur between 2 and 3 years of age, during the rains.

- The investment in rearing unrelated young is repaid in kind when immigrants start breeding.

Relations with neighbors are hostile and larger groups displace smaller ones when they meet—usually at a border, where next-door packs use the same termite mounds on a first-come, first-served basis.

HOW IT MOVES Very agile and active, this mongoose often moves at a fast trot, flees in the usual jump-run, high-jumps 1 yd, and climbs well for a mongoose.

FORAGING/PREDATORY BEHAVIOR In thornbush of eastern Kenya, an amazing association between dwarf mongoose and two bush hornbills (*Tockus flavirostis* and *T. erythrorhynchus*) has been documented. They forage together: hornbills catch insects, rodents, and other prey flushed by the pack and in return serve as lookouts, sounding alarm calls when avian predators are sighted. The association is so mutually beneficial that particular birds and packs associate daily; hornbills gather at termite mound where their pack spent the night and wait for mongooses to emerge (birds even give wake-up calls). If hornbills fail to appear, mongooses hesitate to leave refuge and begin foraging.

Dwarf mongooses uncover invertebrate prey by scratching like chickens in leaf and grass litter and around logs and trees. Pack forages on a front, every mongoose for itself, keeping in vocal contact.

REPRODUCTION   Seasonal, 2 to 3 litters of 1 to 6 young (average 2.9) during rainy season (Oct.–May) in Serengeti NP. Gestation 5 weeks; mother mates again within 2 to 4 weeks. Yearlings can breed but few reproduce before age 2. Subordinate females sometimes mate, typically when alpha's 4-day estrus stimulates them to come into heat. The alpha female also mates with other males if her mate loses interest near the end of estrus.

OFFSPRING AND COMMUNAL CARE   Subordinate females rarely become visibly pregnant, and those that do either abort or lose litters through infanticide. Extra lactating females help suckle alpha's offspring.

Babies emerge from den at 3 weeks, begin foraging with pack at 5 to 6 weeks. Until then, parents spend less time with babies than helpers, which take turns babysitting while pack forages. Weaning at 6 to 7 weeks.

PREDATORS   Birds of prey, particularly goshawks, and snakes. Even slender mongooses are a threat to babies; pack mobs any that prowl near den with young.

Table 24.7. *DIFFERENCES IN DWARF MONGOOSE BEHAVIOR*
Expect to see and hear ➤ Usual context and meaning

Scent-marking
Cheek-rubbing followed by anal-dragging. ➤ Secretions of anal pouch and cheek glands rubbed on objects, pack members, and sex partners, often in turn. Rate increases with excitement.

Aggression
Unusual, associated mainly with estrus, when alpha ♂ asserts dominance, and with attempted immigration, which same-sex residents resist. Acceptance takes 2 days–1 month; transferring ♂♂ are sometimes wounded or killed.

Rearing.

 Dominance mounting.

Hip-slamming.

Submission
Turning head during greeting.

Crouching low during approach, often with 1 leg raised. ➤ Lifting leg signals intention to roll onto side.

Sociable Behavior

CALLS ASSOCIATED WITH PARTICULAR BEHAVIORS

Peeping and churring. ➤ Contact call: 1–3 peeps/sec. Increases and fuses into *churr*, the "moving-out call" as pack begins general movement.

Excitement twitter: rapid call with abrupt shifts in frequency. ➤ Signals discovery of something unusual: strange animal or object, or another pack.

Tchee warning call: longer, frequency-modulated call. ➤ Signals presence of possibly dangerous creature, elicits alert behavior.

Tchrr alarm call (harsher, noisier than *tchee*). Call varies with identity and distance of stimulus. ➤ Predator sighted; pack runs for cover or hides. The harsher and shorter the call, the nearer the predator.

Courtship

MALE BEHAVIOR

Marking ♀ and objects. ➤ Rate increases when ♀ in heat, as does testes size.

Alpha ♂ chasing other ♂ ♂ away.

Soft twittering accompanying mutual grooming.

Copulation: duration up to 11 min.

Licking genitals after mating. ➤ Sign that ejaculation occurred.

FEMALE BEHAVIOR

Snaps and holds tail straight out to block mounting attempts. ➤ Unreceptive

Parents, Helpers, and Offspring

JUVENILE CALLS

Continuous nest chirp.

Purring and chirping. ➤ Contentment sounds (body contact, nursing).

High peeping calls. ➤ Distress, as when deserted.

Adult peep calling. ➤ Beginning at 3 weeks.

Play

ASSOCIATED CALLS

2 derived from contact peep by accelerating calling rate; 1 derived from excitement twitter.

Response to Predators

Flight to refuge holes. ➤ Dwarf mongooses do not bunch in open like bigger mongooses, but simply run and hide.

Threat displays and defense of young. ➤ Against slender mongoose or rival pack when babies are in den.

Warning signals: see Sociable Behavior.

BANDED MONGOOSE, *Mungos mungo*

Figure 24.7. Banded mongoose hurling millipede against a rock.

WHAT IT IS   A wide-bodied mongoose with stripes. The most commonly seen savanna species. Squat build, relatively long legs, feet with long claws. ♂ wt 2.2–4.4 lb (1–2 kg), hbl 13–16 in (33–41 cm); ♀ slightly smaller. *Tail:* ½ to ¾ hbl. *Head:* broad, tapering to point. *Coat:* coarse guard hairs over sparse undercoat. *Color:* grizzled brown with dark brown bands across back; tail tip and lower legs black; underparts light-colored; juveniles dark gray.

WHERE IT LIVES   Northern and Southern Savanna and neighboring arid zones. Gambia to Sudan, south to South Africa, north to Zaire. Absent from Lowland Rainforest and drier, more temperate regions of southwestern Africa.

GOOD PLACES TO SEE IT   Most of the major NPs with extensive savanna habitat. Easiest to spot on short pasture. A regular visitor to lodge garbage dumps.

ECOLOGY   Prefers savanna habitat where termite mounds provide refuges. Avoids closed woodland but likes patches of undergrowth; rarely ventures far onto short grassland. Eats beetles, crickets, grasshoppers, termites, ants, millipedes, spiders, and some other invertebrates; occasionally mice, birds and their eggs, snakes, lizards, and toads. Can live in waterless regions, but drinks sparingly when water available.

ACTIVITY   ○ Pack emerges cautiously from den well after dawn. Members relieve themselves at communal latrine, then scratch, nibble-groom, and play ¼ hr before beginning 2 to 3 hr of intense foraging. Rests in deep shade on hot days until heat subsides, then renews foraging until ½ hr before sunset. Arrived at shelter, pack socializes until dusk, then retires to sleep huddled together. Schedule varies with temperature and weather conditions.

SOCIAL/MATING SYSTEM With up to 35 adults and subadults (sometimes more), banded mongoose packs are the largest of any mongoose. Both large and small packs include up to 3 or 4 breeding females and as many breeding males. Five packs of 6 to 35 animals studied in Uganda's Queen Elizabeth NP had ranges of 94 to 321 acres (38–130 ha), the biggest pack occupying the largest, most open range. Packs are closed to outsiders and the members are ranked by age and individual temperament, not gender. Scent-marking objects and one another, social grooming, and vocal signals reinforce social bonds.

Interpack relations are hostile, especially between males. When neighbors meet at overlapping territorial boundaries, larger packs chase smaller ones, and packs of equal size sometimes have fierce, pitched battles. Yet male offspring usually transfer to another pack. Large packs eventually subdivide.

Den use is variable: some used only once, others revisited often, others occupied continuously for up to 2 months. Preferred den sites are old termite mounds with multiple entrances, situated on slopes and covered with thickets.

FORAGING/PREDATORY BEHAVIOR Daily ranging of 1 to 2 mi (2–3 km) in rich habitat, up to 6 mi (10 km) in dry savanna. Traveling pack moves in an undulating column, usually led by a senior female; foraging pack spreads out and moves slowly in the same direction, keeping in constant vocal contact. They scratch in litter like chickens, poking noses into every opening, using their claws to extract prey from narrow places and to dig up creatures detected underground. Each mongoose forages individually and jealously defends its finds—except from juveniles. Prey with stings or chemical defenses (spiders, scorpions, caterpillars, slugs, toads) are shaken, pawed, and rolled before eating.

Millipedes, beetles, dung balls, snails, and eggs are smashed by throwing them against rocks or trees (see Fig. 24.7). Food bonanzas—such as elephant dung loaded with beetles—are announced by the excited twittering and churring of the finder, bringing other pack members to investigate and unwittingly promoting food sharing.

REPRODUCTION Synchronized within but not between packs; most births during rains, up to 4 litters a year, 4 young/litter. Mothers usually ovulate within a week of whelping, mate with several different males during 6-day estrus. Gestation 2 months. Minimum breeding age 11 months. Over ½ young die in first 3 months.

OFFSPRING AND COMMUNAL CARE Eyes open within 9 days; young emerge from den for short foraging excursions at 3 to 4 weeks;

join morning foraging trips by 5 weeks; acquire adult coat by 6 weeks. Babies are suckled communally; 5 Queen Elizabeth NP packs averaged 2.4 lactating females; one pack had 4 to nurse 12 young. All adults groom, play with, and carry babies between dens. One or 2 babysitters guard den and youngsters mornings while mothers go foraging, returning to den after 2 to 4 hours to suckle and stay with offspring. Adult males do most babysitting and play a major role in socializing young, especially training them to forage, mainly through play.

PREDATORS   Banded mongooses intimidate predators the size of servals and jackals, even a large dog, by presenting a united front (see Table 24.1 under Aggression, mock mobbing attack, and Table 24.8, Response to Predators). Mutual aid is given to captured pack members: one alpha male rescued another male by climbing tree and forcing a martial eagle to drop it.

Table 24.8. DIFFERENCES IN BANDED MONGOOSE BEHAVIOR
Expect to see and hear ➤ *Usual context and meaning*

Scent-marking

Anal glands. ➤ Whitish musk dabbed on ground and objects around dens, also at waterholes, where mongooses rub and roll in damp soil.

Taking turns rubbing cheeks, also throat, belly on objects (including feces). ➤ Another way of distributing pack's scent.

♂ ♂ squirt "yellowish secretion" (urine?) over babies, also on objects, meanwhile treading.

Aggression

Erect posture: sidling stiff-legged around opponent, weight on hind legs, bristling.

Standing with foreleg over subordinate's shoulder and biting nape. ➤ Dominance behavior; may lead into nibble-grooming.

Ritual chasing: smooth, scurrying run after fleeing opponent, tail-dragging on ground.

Associated sounds: loud screeching, explosive chattering.

Displacement Activities

Digging and scent-marking.

Sociable Behavior

Mutual scent-marking with anal-pouch secretions. ➤ Pack members regularly anoint one another, rate increasing with excitement to frantic when confronting rival pack or predator.

 Lying on side before pack member, showing striped back. ➤ Solicits scent-marking; probably derives from submissive display.

Courtship

MALE BEHAVIOR
Chasing and play.

Close following, circling, nuzzling and pushing ♀.

Scent-marking ♀ between mounting attempts, ♂ with raised tail. ♀ also marks suitors. ➤ ♂'s anal pouch enlarged, secretes copiously.

Touching ♀'s neck with open mouth during 10-min. copulation.

Whining. ➤ Courtship call.

Parents, Helpers, and Offspring

Infants carried by skin or head. ➤ Frequent transfers between dens.

Communal care (see text, Offspring and Communal Care).

Play

Play invitation: lying down, head rolling, scratching at objects. ➤ Adult ♂ ♂ play more with juveniles than mothers do.

Holding food in mouth while rolling around and squeaking; scratching at hidden prey. ➤ Stimulates juveniles to forage, compete for food.

Response to Predators

High-sit and low-sit posture with hair sleeked.

Chirping. ➤ Alarm call.

Mock or real mobbing attack, meanwhile growling, churring, spitting, snapping. ➤ Described under Aggression, Table 24.1.

SURICATE OR MEERKAT, *Suricata suricatta*

Figure 24.8. Suricate adult and juvenile play-fighting.

WHAT IT IS   An odd-looking social mongoose of the South West Arid Zone. Thinner and longer-legged than other social mongooses. ♂ wt 1.6 lb (0.73 kg), hbl 11.2 in (28 cm); ♀ slightly smaller. *Tail:* ⅓ hbl, thin, pointed. *Feet:* 4 toes, long claws. *Head:* domed forehead, sharp snout, low, rounded ears. *Coat:* coarse, underside sparse, grizzled. *Color:* gray or tan with indistinct darker banding on back; buff or yellowish underside; dark eye patches, ears, and tail tip.

WHERE IT LIVES   Southwestern Africa: Angola, Namibia, Botswana, South Africa, in Kalahari, *highveld*, and Karroo, and adjacent dry savanna.

GOOD PLACES TO SEE IT   Kalahari Gemsbok NP (study site); most parks and reserves within its range with suitable habitat.

ECOLOGY   Inhabits driest, openest country of all mongooses. Particularly associated with hard ground, such as alkaline pans and stony river banks, less often with sandy soils, where it often shares dens peacefully with yellow mongooses and ground squirrels. Specializes in buried invertebrates: beetle larvae, crickets, scorpions, spiders, butterfly pupae and larvae, moths, and flies; also eats harvester termites, and small vertebrates: snakes, lizards, birds, and mice. Gains water in *sandveld* by eating tsama melons, roots, and tubers.

ACTIVITY   ○ Suricates leave den after sunrise, visit communal latrine, then sunbathe, groom, and socialize before foraging. After midday rest, pack forages again until late afternoon, ending up relaxing and interacting outside a burrow until dusk. They get up later on cold or rainy days, sun more in winter than summer.

SOCIAL/MATING SYSTEM (♀ ♀○♀♂♂♂♂) Very similar to banded mongoose, but whether suricates are also territorial remains uncertain. Predation and hostile relations between groups favor big packs: 10 to 15, up to 30 members. The mean composition of 8 packs numbering 9 to 17 members was 5.4 adult males, 4 females, 0.75 juveniles, and 1.1 subadults. A pack of 12 suricates had a home range of 6 mi^2 (15.5 km^2). Ranges include c. 5 burrows spaced 50 to 100 yd apart and used in rotation for months or years. These dens, slightly elevated due to excavated dirt and averaging 5 (up to 30) yd across, are a labyrinth of tunnels with c. 15 (up to 90) entrances. Suricates extend and repair the tunnels after rains soften the earth but usually occupy existing burrows, mostly prepared by ground squirrels.

Intrapack relations are notably peaceful and cooperative, with no indication of a dominance hierarchy, although males usually play the watchdog role and are most warlike when two packs meet. Despite intergroup enmity, apparently males routinely emigrate and try to join another unit. Sometimes females also transfer and participate in caring for the foster pack's offspring.

HOW IT MOVES Walking (on toes) and jump-running are the two usual gaits, but top speed is slower than a person can sprint. Poor climbers but superb diggers. Sunbathing postures—used to maximize exposure, especially of the thin-haired underside—include standing and seated while sun is low, sprawling on back or twisted to one side when sun is high. Sleep at night in seated groups, folded front to back, sharing body heat.

FORAGING/PREDATORY BEHAVIOR Acute sense of smell used to locate concealed and buried prey. Hearing no better than a human's; ability to spot avian predators at long distances and poor vision in dim light suggest possible color vision. Foraging pack maintains vocal and visual contact while each individual sniffs, scratches, probes, and digs for food. Irresistible urge to follow any pack member moving away keeps them together and headed in same direction. Suricates systematically hunt entire home range, taking different route every day. They rapidly dig trenches as deep as 1 ft (30 cm) in hard ground to unearth fat beetle larvae. Large or unfamiliar prey is battered with foreclaws before biting it tentatively, then hard, finishing with death shake. Rodents, lizards, and birds are dismembered by pulling down with claws while holding prey in jaws and pulling up.

REPRODUCTION Up to 3 litters a year, 3/litter, during rains. Gestation 11 weeks.

OFFSPRING AND COMMUNAL CARE Nonbreeding pack members babysit while mothers go foraging to keep producing milk. Mothers lick babies' genitals and anus to stimulate elimination, also lick-clean their faces and bodies. During weaning, beginning at 3 to 4 weeks, ending at 6 to 9 weeks, mother teaches juveniles to forage for themselves by running away from them while carrying food, using their newly awakened tendency to snatch and consume food without sharing, as adults do.

PREDATORS   Mainly hawks and eagles. Suricates rely on early warning by guard standing lookout from highest nearby vantage point while pack forages—lessening the danger of foraging in the open despite inability to climb well or run fast. Fail-safe back-up is an elaborate intimidation/threat display to deter ground predators (see below, under Aggression).

Table 24.9. *DIFFERENCES IN SURICATE BEHAVIOR*
Expect to see and hear ➤ *Usual context and meaning*

Scent-marking

With anal pouch. ➤ Concentrated on vertical and flat surfaces around den entrances; ♂ ♂ mark more often than ♀ ♀.

Urine-marking: by males, against uprights, cocking leg like a dog.

Aggression

Erect posture with hair bristling. ➤ Changes appearance from long, low animal to much bigger, dangerous-looking round object.

Mock or real mobbing attack: pack members bound high in place while growling, head-darting, and spitting. ➤ Creates impression of large, angry animal approaching.

Other aggressive sounds: clucking. ➤ Scolding "cross" sound; defensive threat as when defending food.

Sociable Behavior

CALLS

Murmuring sounds voiced during practically any activity. ➤ Group-cohesion calls voiced especially by ♀ ♀.

Wurruck-wurruck; soft trilling. ➤ Sound of contentment.

Courtship

Semiserious fighting; one gripping partner by muzzle. ➤ Prelude to sexual activity, sometimes provoked by ♀ nipping ♂'s cheek.

♂ responds by attempted mounting, gripping ♀'s nape if she resists. ➤ Grip induces passivity in ♀, as in juvenile when picked up.

No neck grip during coitus.

Parents, Helpers, and Offspring

Food sharing with juveniles. ➤ Privileged status ends once youngsters are able to feed themselves.

JUVENILE CALLS

Nest chirp. ➤ Birdlike call of newborn; sustained while awake.

High-pitched repetitive sharp call. ➤ Juvenile version of alarm bark. Signals distress; also functions to make littermates cluster together.

Babies purr, sometimes make treading motions. ➤ While nursing.

Play

Sparring. ➤ By all pack members during rest periods.

Play-fighting: juveniles grapple, standing and clasping one another, wrestle, paw, etc. (see Fig. 24.8).

Displacement digging.

Stiff-legged rocking. ➤ Rehearsing threat display.

Response to Predators

Alert postures and uneasy peeping. ➤ By lookout in particular.

SOUNDS OF ALARM

Pack members respond appropriately to different signals.

Clear, drawn-out note, varying intensity. ➤ Signals avian predator.

Waauk-waauk: gruffer, more abrupt call. ➤ Signals ground predator.

Alarm bark: repetitive, short, sharp call. ➤ Response to various disturbances, especially noises; given primarily by dominant ♂ ♂ (aggressive component).

RESPONSE TO ALARM SIGNALS

Juveniles run to mother, press close to her.

Flight to cover.

Threat displays and mobbing attack (see under Aggression). ➤ When pack caught in open far from refuge.

Adults seen to lie on juveniles to protect them from goshawk attack.

Chapter 25

HYENA FAMILY
Hyaenidae

Striped hyena, *Hyaena hyaena*
Brown hyena, *H. brunnea*

Spotted hyena, *Crocuta crocuta*
Aardwolf, *Proteles cristatus*

WHAT THEY ARE   Large, doglike carnivores related to civets and mongooses. The youngest and smallest carnivore family, dating back only c. 10 million years. Ancestors of striped and spotted hyenas separated early, evolving into forms quite like living species by 5 million years ago. Family may have originated in Asia where a number of *Crocuta* species lived during the Ice Age, but Africa never had more than one species of spotted hyena. The aardwolf, resembling a miniature striped hyena, is highly specialized as an insectivore.

HYENA TRAITS   Powerful build, shoulders higher than hindquarters, long neck and long legs; feet with 4 toes; bushy tail up to ½ head and body length; big ears. Sexes about equal in size (except spotted hyena) and appearance. *Head:* massive skull with prominent medial crest to anchor muscles that empower hyena jaws. *Teeth:* 32 or 34 robust teeth, including conical premolars designed for cracking bones. *Coat:* shaggy in striped and brown hyenas, short and thin in spotted hyena. *Color:* brown to black spots or stripes on a buff to dark-brown background; newborn colored like adults or nearly black (spotted hyena). *Genitals:* boneless penis very similar in whole family; female genitalia conventional except for spotted hyena's masculine-looking organ. *Scent glands:* sizeable anal pouch containing pastelike secretion of the anal glands; gland between front toes of hyenas. *Teats:* 2 (spotted hyena), 4 (brown hyena, aardwolf), or 6 (striped hyena).

WHAT THEY EAT   Exceptional ability to eat and digest bone, horns, and even teeth gives hyenas advantages over competitors, like sustaining milk production for a year or more. Also the only carnivores that eat hides, later disgorging indigestible hair. But popular view of hyenas as scavengers and undertakers is only partly true (see species accounts). Bottom line: hyenas utilize prey resource more completely and efficiently than other carnivores.

SOCIAL/MATING SYSTEMS

⟨❂⟩ Monogamous/territorial. Example: aardwolf.

⟨❂⟩ ⟨❂⟩ ⟨❂⟩ Sociable/territorial in family groups and clans of related females and males; communal care and cross-suckling of offspring. Examples: striped and brown hyenas.

(♀•♀○♀•♂♀♂) (♀♀○♀○♀ ♂♂♂♂) ♀|♀|♀ Sociable, more or less territorial in clans numbering up to 100 hyenas; communal den but no communal care. Example: spotted hyena.

Hyena society spans the extremes of carnivore social/mating systems, from the solitary/monogamous pattern of the aardwolf, to cooperative kinship society of brown and striped hyenas, to the unique spotted hyena system, in which females dominate males.

HOW THEY MOVE   Essentially doglike, especially resting postures and maintenance behavior (scratching, shaking, licking, nibble-grooming). More unusual are postures made possible by loose-jointed limbs: carpal crawling (kneeling and crawling on first joints, the way cubs negotiate narrow tunnels); lying with forepaws folded under; and running gait, in which hind feet are thrown out sideways (see Fig. 22.2). Another distinctive family trait: the deep elimination crouch with tail raised vertically, and the technique for scent-marking grass stems with the anal pouch (see Fig. 25.2).

HOW THEY COMMUNICATE   Sight 3 (2 in spotted hyena), scent 1, sound 1 or 2. Spotted hyena is one of the most vociferous African mammals; other hyenas are much quieter.

Table 25.1. *HYENA FAMILY BEHAVIOR GUIDE*
            Expect to see and hear ➤ Usual context and meaning

Scent-marking

The different forms and associated actions are often performed in series, especially along territorial boundaries.

 Pasting grass stalks with anal-pouch secretions. Marker sniffs previous mark, if any, then straddles stalk and walks forward, hind legs flexed, foreleg raised, holding/guiding stalk across everted anal pouch. ➤ Highly stereotyped performance, similar in all 3 hyenas, which smears 1–2 in length of stem with yellow or white pomade. Secretion informs other hyenas who made mark, its reproductive status, and how long ago.

Backing up to bush or other fixed object; smearing anal-pouch secretion at nose level with waggling movements.

 Defecation on latrines, in deep squat, tail erected. ➤ Bone residues turn hyena dung, dark when fresh, chalk-white, making latrines, often located along territorial boundaries, conspicuous.

Treading or trampling with hind feet. ➤ Often at conclusion of pasting and dunging rituals.

Scratching ground with forefeet, repeatedly and emphatically. ➤ Deposits secretion of scent gland between toes; often performed in aggressive and sexual context. May express frustration (common in spotted and brown hyenas).

Aggression

Erect posture: bristling, straightened legs, bowed back, pricked ears, erected tail, stiff-legged gait. ➤ Raised hackles of aardwolf, striped and brown hyenas increase apparent size up to 74%. Raising hackles is either offensive or defensive (see below, Response to Predators).

Hunched posture of striped and brown hyenas. ➤ Threat to bite legs.

Ritualized biting/shaking shoulder and neck. ➤ One-way aggression by dominant to subordinate (as by adult to subadult ♂; also between newborn spotted hyena cubs).

Fighting: muzzle-wrestling; biting shoulder, neck, rump. ➤ Mutual aggression.

Associated sounds: lowing, lowing-growling, grunting, roaring, yelling. ➤ Accompanies threat displays and fighting.

Submission

Turning away from aggressor.

Crouching while giving fear grimace, ears flattened.

Carpal-crawling: brown and striped hyenas present everted anal pouch while crawling, lying on brisket or side, or rolling on back ± pawing at superior's chin and squeaking (brown hyena). ➤ Displays of active submission, typically following greeting ritual; anal pouch is passed beneath dominant's nose.

Brown and striped hyenas in upright stance with lowered crest, turning head side-to-side, licking lips, and rolling eyes (see Table 25.2).

Vocal accompaniment: "laughing" (giggling), cackling, roaring, screaming, yelling, whining. ➤ Distress calls emitted when chased or bitten.

Sociable Behavior

GREETING CEREMONY

Touching/sniffing noses, mouths, necks, and genitals, standing parallel, head-to-tail, tails raised. ➤ Typical meeting behavior, prelude to friendly or aggressive interactions.

Everting and presenting anal pouch ± carpal-crawling. ➤ Submissive greeting, especially by young to adults (brown and striped hyenas).

Social grooming: nibbling and licking, especially neck and head. ➤ Among members of same family or clan, especially between close relatives. Reinforces social/kinship bonds.

Adults lying in contact. ➤ Probably close relatives—e.g., mother with grown daughter.

Contact and other social calls: whooping (spotted hyena); cackling howl (striped hyena). ➤ Variable rate and intensity convey emotional state. See spotted hyena account.

Hyena Courtship

MALE BEHAVIOR
Persistent following.

Mutual sniffing of noses and genitals.

Submissive behavior. ➤ Spotted hyena.

Pawing ground. ➤ When attempts to approach or mount ♀ frustrated.

Nipping or mouthing ♀'s neck during 2–10 min. copulation.

Licking genitals after mating.

FEMALE BEHAVIOR
Defensive threats (offensive in spotted hyena).

Copulatory stance: head low, back slightly arched, tail raised and deflected.

Parents, Helpers, and Offspring

Differs by species; see family introduction and species accounts.

Infants carried by nape, back, or head.

Young of different ages living in communal dens.

Long suckling bouts, including yearlings.

Play

Between young: jaw-wrestling, neck-biting, chasing, play with objects (bones, sticks, hairballs).

Response to Competitors/Predators

Craven behavior (crawling, lying down). ➤ Spotted hyenas waiting or approaching wild dogs; brown and striped hyenas to spotted hyena.

Threat displays.

Flight.

STRIPED HYENA, *Hyaena hyaena*

Figure 25.1. Striped hyena erecting crest in defensive threat, greatly increasing its apparent size.

WHAT IT IS   A lean, long-legged hyena with a big head, long mane, bushy tail, and prominent stripes. ♂ wt 55–99 lb (25–45 kg), ht 26–32 in (65–80 cm); ♀ slightly smaller. *Head*: broad, short muzzle, prominent, pointed ears. *Teeth*: well developed. *Coat*: shaggy, mane up to 8 in (20 cm) long. *Color*: tawny to gray with black muzzle and stripes on legs, torso, throat, and cheeks; juveniles like adults minus mane.

WHERE IT LIVES   From central Tanzania north through dry savanna, arid zones, and deserts to the Mediterranean and beyond (Asia).

ECOLOGY   Ranges arid wastelands except in East Africa, where it lives in woodland, favoring thornbush and scrub, leaving open plains and tree grassland to the dominant spotted hyena. Eats almost anything digestible, especially carrion; also fruit (figs, desert dates) insects, small vertebrates. Rarely kills anything larger than newborn antelopes.

ACTIVITY   ● Strictly nocturnal, spending days in secure lair. Radio-tracked Serengeti subjects rarely used same lair twice in a row. These hyenas foraged actively some 6 hours a night. A subadult male followed for 10 days covered nearly 12 mi (19 km) per night.

SOCIAL/MATING SYSTEM   Because striped hyenas forage singly, the species was long considered solitary. Studies showed that a number of individuals share and defend the same home range/territory.

Several presumably related females share a den and cooperate in rearing cubs, aided by grown offspring which babysit and bring food home. Accumulated bones in caves evince millennia of provisioning. Whether clans include several adult males as well as females, like the better-known brown hyena, is unknown.

In Israel, striped hyenas scent-mark and maintain latrines at regular feeding sites (garbage dumps) and along pathways. But in Serengeti NP, a radio-collared male and female, whose home range covered 17 and 27.8 mi² (44 and 72 km²), showed no such territorial tendencies.

FORAGING/PREDATORY BEHAVIOR   Foraging individual quarters the ground in zig-zag manner, poking nose into every bush, hole, and grass clump, following different route each night. Ignores herds of antelopes while actively pursuing large insects (moths, beetles, grasshoppers): running after, leaping for, and snapping at ones in flight. It makes occasional short dashes, at speeds up to 29.5 mph (50 kph) at such prey as hares, bat-eared foxes, gazelle fawns, dik-diks, and birds, but rarely catches any. Surplus food such as bones or pieces of skin are cached, pushed deep into shrubbery or grass clump, or else carried back to den.

REPRODUCTION   Nonseasonal; 1 to 6 cubs/litter; gestation 88 to 92 days. Begins breeding at 2 to 3 years. Estrus thought to last only 1 day.

OFFSPRING AND PARENTAL CARE   Communal care, including cross-suckling of cubs of different ages. All family members (possibly excepting adult males) carry food to the den.

Born deaf and blind, just able to crawl. Eyes open at 8 to 9 days; cubs emerge between 10 and 14 days. A Serengeti mother attended cubs soon after dark and often around midnight. They nurse for a year or more, begin accompanying mother foraging at 16 months.

RELATIONS WITH OTHER PREDATORS   Dominated both ecologically and behaviorally by spotted hyena, striped hyena surrenders food and runs away when chased; in turn it usually (not always) dominates leopards and cheetahs, appropriating their kills. Gives lions a wide berth.

Table 25.2. DIFFERENCES IN STRIPED HYENA BEHAVIOR
Expect to see and hear ➤ Usual context and meaning

Aggression/Submission

Raised hackles (see Fig. 25.1). ➤ Hackles rise when striped hyena is either aggressive or fearful.

Aggression/Submission *continued*

Hunched posture of dominant (right) and erect posture of subordinate hyenas. ➤ Nearly opposite to usual postures of dominance and submission: hunched posture and lowered head are threats to bite legs; standing upright and turning head offers neck to superior to bite, targeted by the black throat.

Fighting in kneeling position. ➤ Counters attempts to bite legs.

Sociable Behavior

CALLS

Cackling howl. ➤ Long-distance call; described but rarely heard.

Quiet *hoos*. ➤ Short-range contact call.

BROWN HYENA, *Hyaena brunnea*

Figure 25.2. Brown hyena pasting grass stalks with anal-pouch secretions.

WHAT IT IS   A dark, shaggy hyena that looks something like a German shepherd, southern version of the striped hyena. ♂♀ wt 86 lb (39 kg), ht 28–35 in (71–87 cm). *Head:* broad, short muzzle with big teeth; long, pointed ears. *Coat:* mantle of long hair along back overlying shorter-haired torso and obscuring markings. *Color:* dark brown with black stripes, legs yellow-brown, striped; mane straw-colored; juveniles gray, markings unobscured by mane.

WHERE IT LIVES   South of Zambezi River in Zimbabwe, Botswana, Namibia, and southern Angola. Exterminated in South Africa except northernmost Transvaal and Cape Province.

ECOLOGY   The dominant large carnivore in more arid parts of Kalahari and Namib Desert. It scavenges a living along the Atlantic shoreline, where it is called *strandloper*.

An opportunistic forager that prefers meat but makes do with fruits and vegetables, marine organisms, insects, and other invertebrates. Takes vertebrate prey up to size of young antelopes, but of some 58 different kinds of food identified in scats, vertebrate prey it had killed accounted for less than 6% by weight. In rainy season, when antelopes and zebras disperse over the Kalahari, remains of lion, leopard, and cheetah kills are major food source. In dry season, carrion in diet drops sharply while percentage of fruits and vegetables rises. Tsama and other melons are main source of moisture for 8 waterless months, but also eaten when hyenas are able to drink from rainwater pools.

ACTIVITY   ● During dry season brown hyenas actively forage nearly 10 of 12 night hours, gleaning mostly small food items while traveling up to 19 mi (30 km). During rains they forage and travel less.

SOCIAL/MATING SYSTEM   Multimale territorial clans, but females breed with nomadic males.

Six clans of brown hyenas studied in the subdesert Kalahari Gemsbok NP contained 4 to 14 members, including 1 to 4 adult females, 0 to 3 adult males, 0 to 5 subadults, and 0 to 4 young. These clans occupied huge ranges of 91 to 185 mi² (average 127 mi² [330 km²]). A clan of 13 hyenas studied in the less arid Central Kalahari GR occupied a range of 39 mi² (102 km²).

Female and some male offspring remain with their natal clan after maturing at 2.5 years. Male emigrants either join another clan (as do occasional emigrant females) or become nomads. Nomads, representing ⅓ of the adult males and 8% of the population, do most of the breeding; resident males rarely show any sexual interest in clan females.

A rank order keeps each clan member in its place, as indicated by displays of dominance and submission. All members scent-post and defend the territory against same-sex hyenas of neighboring clan, but show little antagonism to nomads. One clan of 3 males and 2 females made an estimated 145,000 anal-pouch deposits in a year throughout its territory, of which 20,000 would be potent at any given time.

FORAGING/PREDATORY BEHAVIOR   A foraging individual pursues small game it flushes but only a short distance; only 1 in 6 to 1 in 10 attempts to catch prey succeed. Sometimes stalks a bird or hare but rarely tries to move quietly. Hyenas that meet at carcasses of large animals are surprisingly tolerant—especially of the opposite sex. However, no more than 3 hyenas feed together; extras have to wait their turn.

Brown hyenas regularly cache surplus food, in a grass clump or hole 100 to 600 yd from the source, to be retrieved and eaten usually early the following night. Other scavengers rarely find caches, even though cacher scent-marks grass and bushes within 15 to 20 yd of cache sites. Alternatively, small scavenged items are carried an average distance of 4 mi [6.4 km] back to the den.

REPRODUCTION   Nonseasonal and unsynchronized within clans, resulting in offspring of assorted ages; typically 3/litter (range 1–4); gestation c. 90 days. Minimum breeding age 2.5 years. Females mate with different nomadic males during the second half of 2-week estrus.

OFFSPRING AND COMMUNAL CARE   Females isolate before whelping and spend up to 5 hours/night attending small cubs during 2 visits to natal den. After cubs start eating solid food at 3 months, mother brings them to communal den, which may be in continuous use for several years; thereafter attends cubs only once a night. Juveniles older than 8 months are left unattended for 2 to 3 nights. Communal suckling by all lactating females, on a first-come, first-served basis, and food brought to the den by helpers keep cubs from fasting. Brown hyenas nurse 25 to 30 minutes, continue to receive milk for at least 10 months, and are weaned completely only at 15 months.

Presence of older youngsters and small-bore tunnels make adult babysitters redundant. Youngsters too big to enter tunnels rely on defensive threat display. At 14 months they begin solitary foraging and may sleep away from den, but keep coming back through second year to socialize, play, and get free lunch.

RELATIONS WITH OTHER PREDATORS   See striped hyena account.

Table 25.3. *DIFFERENCES IN BROWN HYENA BEHAVIOR*
Expect to see and hear ➤ *Usual context and meaning*

Scent-marking

Pasting with anal pouch: two different secretions on same grass stem: the usual white pomade and a watery black secretion. ➤ Foraging hyenas paste grass and bushes 4–6 times/mi. White secretion is detectable by humans for at least a month, while black secretion odor fades rapidly. Apart from territorial function, marks identify individual and how long ago it marked, enabling clan members to avoid places another hyena has already foraged.

Aggression/Submission

Neck-biting: aggressor holding on and biting, while victim yells and growls but refrains from biting back. ➤ The usual one-sided aggression, most severe between territorial neighbors of same sex. Within clans, recurrent neck biting of subadults by same-sex adult ends with subadults emigrating.

Aggression/Submission *continued*

Jaw-wrestling fight. ➤ Develops from mutual efforts to neck-bite; usually seen only in play between immature hyenas.

Carpal-crawling and begging calls. ➤ Submissive behaviors often used to gain access to carcass where another hyena is feeding, or to induce a hyena carrying food to surrender it.

Sociable Behavior

Clan members socializing around communal den. Young of all ages lie in contact, social-groom, and play together.

Play

Play fights feature jaw wrestling and neck biting/shaking so rough that all cubs acquire neck scars.

SPOTTED HYENA, *Crocuta crocuta*

Figure 25.3. Spotted hyenas pulling down a bull wildebeest.

WHAT IT IS   A vaguely bearlike large hyena, the only one with spots. Sturdy build, high shoulders, and long muscular limbs. ♂ wt 123–138 lb (56–63 kg), ht 32–34 in (79–86 cm); ♀ wt 147–165 lb (67–75 kg), ht 34–35 in (84–89 cm). *Head:* massive; broad, rounded ears. *Teeth:* robust, outer incisors like small canines. *Coat:* rough, comparatively short. *Color:* reddish brown to tan, growing lighter and less spotted with age; yearlings gray and heavily spotted; natal coat nearly black and unspotted; tail pompom and nose black regardless of age. *Genitals:* boneless phallus 5.8 to 7.8 in (14.5–19.5

cm), equally developed in both sexes; female differences develop at puberty, when the urethral opening splits and teats enlarge.

WHERE IT LIVES   Everywhere south of the Sahara except rainforests and true desert, up to 13,000 ft (4000 m). Largely exterminated in South Africa.

GOOD PLACES TO SEE IT   Many parks in East and southern Africa; especially Ngorongoro Crater, Serengeti NP, Tanzania; Masai Mara NR, Kenya; Savuti Pan, Chobe NP, Botswana; Kruger NP, South Africa; Etosha NP, Namibia.

ECOLOGY   The most abundant large carnivore in areas where antelopes and zebras abound. More carnivorous than other hyenas, *Crocuta* is a formidable predator/scavenger that lives wherever animal resources are adequate. Eats vertebrates of all kinds, especially hoofed mammals; seldom eats invertebrates, fruits, or vegetables. Utilizes carcasses of large vertebrates more efficiently than other carnivores, which waste up to 40% of their kills. Eats everything but rumen contents and horn bosses of the biggest antelopes, even deriving nourishment from mummified carcasses. Bones, horns, hooves, even teeth are digested completely within 24 hours.

ACTIVITY   ● (○) Radio-collared female, followed in Ngorongoro Crater for 12 days, spent little time foraging and eating, but simply shared kills made by other clan members. She traveled less than 4 mi (10 km) in 24 hours, spending 84% of the time lying down. In Kalahari Gemsbok NP, where hyenas have to work for a living, clan members traveled an average of 16 mi during nocturnal foraging and remained active 31% of a 24-hour day.

SOCIAL/MATING SYSTEM   Lives in large clans and defends territory at high density, but differs from all other social carnivores:

- Clan members compete more and cooperate less than most social carnivores.
- Females are bigger than males and dominate them.
- Females compete for rank and food with one another; even close relatives do not cross-suckle offspring.
- Cubs are raised in communal dens, but seldom or never provisioned or guarded by clan members.
- Males play no parental role—only a privileged few are permitted anywhere near dens, where even juvenile offspring of high-ranking females dare to bully them.

In Ngorongoro Crater, where a resident population of 20,000 herbivores supports Africa's densest hyena population (c. 450 adults and their offspring),

7 different clans of 35 to 80 hyenas ferociously defend their sections averaging 12 mi² (30 km²) of the 100 mi² (260 km²) crater floor against their neighbors. At the opposite extreme, clans of 3 to 12 hyenas in subdesert Kalahari Gemsbok NP have ranges of 193 to 772 mi² (500–2000 km²)—much too vast to be defended as territories.

Members of a large clan seldom if ever all assemble at one place. However, a communal den shared by up to 10 females is a social gathering place for them and their dependent and older offspring. Each clan member knows its place in the hierarchy and behaves accordingly whenever clan members meet. Even without behavioral clues, dominant females are usually recognizable as the biggest, fattest hyenas, with swollen udders. Females not only dominate males at kills and other favored sites but also lead clan members on pack hunts, boundary patrols, and into battle.

Female offspring remain in their natal clan; males disperse at around 2 years. Sons of high-ranking females tend to emigrate later and, thanks to the large size and self-confidence gained as their birthright, are likely to become dominant breeding males in the clans they join. The ensuing reproductive jackpot is what drove females to compete for dominance. But to get there, they not only had to grow bigger than males, they also had to produce male sex hormones to become more aggressive. In the process, both their behavior and anatomy became masculine.

HOW IT MOVES   Ambling walk, rarely trots, lopes tirelessly at 6 mph (10 kph), and can gallop 25 to 31 mph (40–50 kph) for a couple miles at least. Top speed c. 37 mph (60 kph).

FORAGING/PREDATORY BEHAVIOR   Reputation as skulking scavenger, craven coward, and killer of young and sick animals applies to relations with humans. As scavengers around settlements, hyenas are persistent but remarkably craven when confronted. Similar caution combined with great patience is shown by hyenas awaiting the right moment to finish off sick or crippled large animals. Perfect opportunists, they always take the path of least resistance. Yet *Crocuta* is also the second-biggest and most formidable African carnivore, capable of running down and killing unaided a bull wildebeest 3 times its own weight.

How does the craven scavenger become transformed into the bold predator? Hunger drives a hyena to run down a large healthy ungulate—but only after failing to get a meal with less effort and risk. Predation also occurs spontaneously—e.g., when a daytime thunderstorm makes the ground slippery and antelopes easier to catch than usual.

Most hunting, like most foraging, is done alone. But clan members sometimes deliberately set off in packs to hunt specific quarry, such as zebras. More often, what look like pack hunts begin as chases by 1 or 2 hyenas that others passed en route join (see Fig. 25.3). Whenever 2 or 3 hyenas feed on the same carcass, they begin squabbling; by thus broadcasting the presence of meat, they unwittingly invite all pack members in earshot to the feast—and often enough, lions also get the message. Pitched battles between rival hyena clans are likely when kills are made near borders.

REPRODUCTION   Nonseasonal; 2 young/litter (range 1 4); gestation 4 months. Maturation at 3 years, females later than males.

The female's bizarre reproductive tract, entered and exited through the phallus instead of directly—the vagina entrance being blocked by a false scrotum and testes—makes copulation complicated. When hyenas mate, only the male has an erection—the female's phallus is slack, the prepuce a wrinkled ring around the enlarged urethra. The male has only to slide beneath the female to enter, an operation assisted by the upward angle of the fully erect penis; following which, he straightens into a normal mating stance (see Courtship, Table 25.4).

Female dominance imposes unusual diffidence and patience on males. Their obvious fear of female aggression makes courtship an often amusing spectacle (see Table 25.4).

OFFSPRING AND MATERNAL CARE   Communal denning but no communal care.

Long gestation results in unusually precocious offspring. Newborns weighing 2.2 to 3.6 lb (1–1.6 kg), already have milk incisors and canines, open (but unseeing) eyes, and capability of strong, directed movement on their forelimbs. Two to 6 weeks after whelping inside the entrance of an unused aardvark or other burrow, mother transports young to a communal den containing youngsters of different ages. Starting at 6 times/day, suckling is reduced to 3 times/day at 3 months, in bouts lasting up to 1.5 hours! Weaning takes several months beginning at 1 year, marked by frequent tantrums. Cubs of alpha female go to nearby kills and begin eating meat as early as 3 months, 4 to 5 months earlier than rank-and-file offspring. Yearlings tag along on hunts but rarely become competent before 1.5 years.

Beginning only hours after birth, siblings of like sex battle for dominance, employing their baby teeth and the same stereotyped neckbite/shake technique of fighting adults. The one that wins (firstborn has an obvious advantage) keeps the other from nursing until it weakens and dies. Because fighting occurs in the cubs' narrow tunnels, mothers are powerless to intervene. This sibling rivalry kills an estimated 25% of all hyenas in their first month. The surviving male grows faster and is likelier to achieve reproductive dominance; the surviving female eliminates a rival for dominance in her natal clan. There is no reproductive competition between siblings of opposite sex and consequently no killing.

RELATIONS WITH OTHER PREDATORS AND SCAVENGERS

LIONS   Very competitive; each tries to take the other's kills. Hyenas usually lose their kills and have to wait for lions to finish eating. However, hyenas in force often unnerve female and immature lions by advancing threateningly and noisily shoulder to shoulder, though rarely attacking. They get nowhere with big male lions.

WILD DOGS   Hyenas regularly try to profit from this predator's hunting efficiency, but even when greatly outnumbered, wild dogs usually stand off hyenas by mobbing and punishing one at a time. Lack of cooperative defense places hyenas at disadvantage.

LEOPARD AND CHEETAH   Spotted hyenas take their kills at every opportunity.

JACKALS   Often annoy hyenas successfully: dart in and steal tidbits from kills; mated couple outwits feeding hyena by moving in from both sides until hyena lunges at one, enabling the other to grab food and run.

VULTURES   Hyenas use vulture spotter network to find meat in daytime. When they see vultures volplaning to earth, hungry hyenas race to the spot.

COMMUNICATION

CALLS   Among the most vociferous African mammals, with 11 different, intergrading calls.
Groans and soft squeals   Often exchanged during greeting.
Whoop   Contact call, rising *o-o-o.*
Fast whoop   Rallying call given by excited hyenas (during border conflict or at a kill); brings clan members to the spot. Most whoops are emitted by males and apparently ignored by other clan members. When a female calls, her relatives and offspring react immediately.
Lowing   Expresses rising impatience and often leads into fast whooping; voiced by hyenas kept waiting at a kill.

CALLS ASSOCIATED WITH AGGRESSION

Grunting   Quiet, very low growl with mouth closed; accompanies aggressive behavior.
Giggling   High, cackling laugh, typically emitted by hyena being chased; expresses intense fear or excitement. The call of the "laughing hyena."
Growling   Deep, loud rumble, often with staccato vibration: defensive threat voiced by hyena under attack threatening to bite.
Yelling   Starts as scream, changing to a roar, voiced by hyena attempting to escape attackers; alternates with growling.
Rattling growl   Low-pitched, soft staccato grunts; given as an alarm call—e.g., by hyenas on kill at approach of a lion.

Table 25.4. *DIFFERENCES IN SPOTTED HYENA BEHAVIOR*
Expect to see and hear ➤ *Usual context and meaning*

Aggression

Parallel walk: two or more hyenas advancing shoulder to shoulder in erect posture, tails brandished over backs; accompanied by lowing and fast whooping. ➤ Prelude to mobbing attack on another hyena and attempts to intimidate lions.

Sociable Behavior

Phallic inspection: after mutual sniffing of nose, mouth, head, and neck, 2 hyenas stand head-to-tail and mutually sniff/touch extended phallus for up to ½ min., inside leg meanwhile cocked. ➤ Part of greeting ceremony between clan members, performed by both sexes beginning first month; but adult males rarely greet with females. Initiative usually taken by lower-ranking individual.

Social grooming: licking and nibble-grooming. ➤ Mothers and offspring. Rare between adults.

Hyena whooping. ➤ Contact and gathering call.

Courtship

Bowing display: standing behind reclining ♀ with penis extended, hyena abruptly lowers muzzle to ground, advances quickly, bows again, then paws ground close behind her. Retreats immediately if she responds aggressively. ➤ Performed by ♂ afraid to approach ♀ he is courting. Pawing deposits scent of the toe gland.

Mating: toward end of 4- to 12-min. copulation, ♂ rests head and body on ♀.

Mother and Offspring

Weaning tantrum. ➤ Thrown by a yearling whose mother refuses suckling.

Response to Competitors/Predators

Mobbing attacks. ➤ By spotted hyenas, against rival clans, also against lions, usually in attempt to appropriate or reclaim a kill.

AARDWOLF, *Proteles cristatus*

Figure 25.4. Foraging aardwolf.

WHAT IT IS   Like a miniature striped hyena that eats insects. Slender with long neck and limbs. ♂ ♀ wt 17.6–26 lb (8–12 kg), ht 16–20 in (40–50 cm). *Feet*: forefeet with 5 toes, hind feet with 4. *Head*: pointed, hairless snout and wide palate. *Teeth*: molars reduced to pegs, incisors normal, canines long and thin. *Coat*: 1 in long with dense underfur; mane 6 to 8 in (16–20 cm) long. *Color*: buff to red-brown with lighter underparts; vertical brown torso stripes, horizontal black stripes on upper legs; black feet, muzzle, ear backs, spinal stripe, and outer tail.

WHERE IT LIVES   From Ethiopia to central Tanzania in the Somali-Masai Arid Zone; and south of the Zambezi in the South West Arid Zone.

ECOLOGY   Not only an insectivore but consumer of a particular type of termite (genus *Trinervitermes*) that spends nights gathering dry grass and taking it into underground burrows. Aardwolves spend their nights scoffing up the termites with broad, sticky tongue. Specialization on harvester termites dictates aardwolf's geographical distribution and preference for open dry country with short grass, particularly areas that have been overgrazed by herbivores.

Aardwolf enjoys protein-rich diet obtained with relatively little effort or competition from other insectivores. Consumes up to 200,000 insects a night, or about 2.2 lb (1 kg). For variety, eats other insects: ants, moths, beetles, but mostly termites of other genera (notably the daytime harvester termite, *Hodotermes*). Also known to eat carrion, mice, birds, and baby tortoises.

ACTIVITY   ● During southern African winter, aardwolves emerge 1.5 hours before dark, sometimes sun at den entrance. Typically comes out abruptly and starts pasting or proceeds directly to the nearest latrine. Foraging routine includes irregular rest breaks ranging from a few minutes to over 1.5 hours, usually in or near a burrow.

SOCIAL/MATING SYSTEM (image) Preliminary evidence indicates that aardwolves live in pairs within territories of 247 to 494 acres (100–200 ha) or bigger in subdeserts. Bonds between couples seem loose, as individuals not only forage but usually sleep alone. Social grooming or even greeting ceremonies, elaborate in other hyenas, have not been reported; meetings between aardwolves are typically brief and either undemonstrative or aggressive. Yet males play a parental role, a good monogamy indicator, and unconfirmed reports of several females with offspring sharing a den suggest the sort of family group that develops in monogamous systems when daughters remain in the parental range.

Territoriality is shown by scent-marking along home-range boundaries and long chases of intruders ending in fights if one is overtaken. But when termites become scarce, up to 3 aardwolves from as many territories have been seen foraging on the same patch, sometimes within 100 yd of one another.

Territories include up to 10 dens, 1 or 2 of which are regularly used as daytime lairs 4 to 6 weeks at a time. Aardwolves rarely dig burrows they rest and take refuge in while foraging, but when ground is soft, may enlarge and adapt burrows dug by other animals.

HOW IT MOVES A slow runner but great dodger, using bushy tail as a rudder and to deflect attacks away from its torso.

FORAGING/PREDATORY BEHAVIOR Both aardwolves and aardvarks (*aard* means earth in Afrikaans) are termite specialists, but eat types that require totally different foraging techniques. Aardvark, the premiere African excavator, goes after wood-eating termites in their fortified mounds, whereas aardwolf simply licks up termites that come out of their burrows. To locate termite patches, it walks at c. 2 mph (3 kph) with head below shoulder level and ears cocked, listening for the sound of termites cutting or carrying dried grass (also audible to human ears). Where abundant, colonies are as close together as 25 to 50 yd; aardwolf moves from patch to patch lapping them up quickly. Hundreds of scurrying insects are left unconsumed—mostly soldiers that come pouring out of their holes to protect the helpless workers by spraying distasteful turpinoids. Aardwolf scats contain about equal numbers of workers and soldiers, indicating considerable tolerance for the repellent; their scats stink strongly of ammonia—which may be why they bury them.

REPRODUCTION Birth peak during rains and a defined mating season in South Africa. Average 2 to 3 young/litter (range 1–5); gestation 90 to

100 days. Territorial trespassing and disputes most frequent during mating peak, when males may have 1 or 2 fights a week to keep intruders from mating with their spouses.

OFFSPRING AND PARENTAL CARE   Though born with eyes open, babies are otherwise helpless, only emerge at 6 to 8 weeks. During 3 months at den, father spends up to 6 hours a night babysitting while mother forages. When ready to supplement milk diet, cubs forage with 1 or both parents; by 4 months often forage alone but sleep with mother. Adult size by 9 months; yearlings roam far outside the family range, preparatory to dispersing before next litter is out of the den.

Table 25.5. *DIFFERENCES IN AARDWOLF BEHAVIOR*
Expect to see and hear ➤ Usual context and meaning

Scent-marking

Pasting: Positioning itself directly over grass stem or bush, aardwolf smears a section with secretion by waggling its behind, causing erected tail to swing through 90° arc. Marks are concentrated around dens and latrines. ➤ Aardwolf technique differs from hyena drag-pasting technique. Aromatic-smelling secretions of Namibian aardwolves are dark brown or black; those of other populations are yellow ochre or orange.

Both sexes also post territorial boundaries, crouching and pasting every 50 yd or so. ➤ Boundary marking bouts last 5–20 min., during which aardwolf zigzags as when foraging but without feeding.

Aardwolves also scent-map their foraging routes by quickly wiping the anal pouch sideways against grass stems every 5 yd or less as they walk. ➤ Scent-mapping enables marker and other family members to avoid wasting time foraging the same area twice in succession.

Scats are buried in oval-shaped sandy latrines resembling giant litter boxes. Before defecating, an aardwolf digs a narrow trench, then squats low to make the deposit, afterward scratching dirt over it. Often urinates on the spot and scratches again before departing. ➤ Aardwolves deposit smelly scats up to 2 in (5 cm) in diameter and 8% of the animal's weight at one time; these consist 15–66% of straw, pebbles, etc. picked up along with termites on sticky tongue. Latrines seem to have no territorial significance but are often clustered, with up to 10 active ones in a territory.

Aggression

Kneeling threat display: in disputes between aardwolves, contestants often kneel with just neck mane erected.

Sociable Behavior

Mates exchange whistling calls, and a howl like a striped hyena's has been reported.

Response to Predators

Broadside threat display with cape raised, backed up with surprisingly deep growls, barks, and roars. ➤ Close to record for making itself look bigger, aardwolf enlarges silhouette by 74%. Same display used against potential predators and in fights between aardwolves.

Cubs said to make clicking sounds similar to warning clicks of termites.

Chapter 26

CAT FAMILY
Felidae

African wildcat, *Felis libyca*	Golden cat, *F. aurata*
Black-footed cat, *F. nigripes*	Swamp cat, *F. chaus*
Sand cat, *F. margarita*	Leopard, *Panthera pardus*
Serval, *F. serval*	Lion, *P. leo*
Caracal, *F. caracal*	Cheetah, *Acinonyx jubatus*[v]

WHAT THEY ARE   A family of carnivores genetically, anatomically, and behaviorally so like the domestic cat that the main differences are in size and coloration. The cheetah does stand apart from the rest, anatomically more than behaviorally, but big cats are just jumbo versions of *Felis*, distinguished mainly by a modification of the larynx that enables them to roar.

The family dates back some 40 million years; modern cats (subfamily Felinae) evolved along with ruminants and rodents and have been around for at least 24 million years. True cats of the genus *Felis* date back c. 6 million years, and the cheetah has been around 2 million years, but the other big cats became dominant only in the last half million years, during the Golden Age of Mammals.

FAMILY TRAITS   Typical build like domestic cat's, with long body and tail, muscular limbs ending in soft-padded feet equipped with hooked, retractile claws. *Head*: broad, with big, frontally placed eyes; prominent ears; short, blunt jaws specialized for killing and eating meat. *Teeth*: typically reduced to 30, including long, stabbing canines and narrow, sharp-bladed cheek teeth designed as meat shears (carnassials). *Color*: concealing, from pale gray to brown (sometimes black); most species spotted, striped, or blotched with darker markings, black or white markings on backs of ears, face, and tail. *Genitals*: short, barbed penis (with bone) just below testes, pointing to rear (for spraying urine backward). *Scent glands*: in foot pads, chin, and cheeks of smaller cats; paired anal glands.

WHAT THEY EAT   Mainly warm-blooded vertebrates. Cats are among purest carnivores: small ones prey primarily on rodents, other small mammals, and birds; big ones prefer antelopes and other ungulates but take all sorts of smaller creatures as opportunity affords.

SOCIAL/MATING SYSTEMS   All cats but the lion are considered solitary and territorial.

⚥♂⚥ The usual arrangement—in which females defend resources to support themselves and dependent offspring, and the fittest males defend the ranges of several females—has been documented for several cats. However, few of these secretive, nocturnal carnivores have been studied, and the one we know best, the domestic cat, has proved unexpectedly complex and variable. Apparently only part of the home range is defended, as different individuals share hunting grounds but avoid meeting, aided by scent marks that inform an arriving cat who was or is around. Adult males defend part of their ranges as territories, but often a number of tomcats gather around a female in heat, as in nonterritorial species. Furthermore, in situations where there is a food surplus, such as a garbage dump or fish packing house, feral domestic cats become as sociable as lions.

Whether these variations also occur in wild cats of the same and different species, living in completely natural conditions, is still unknown. Even in strictly solitary species such as the leopard, however, mothers often allow daughters to settle in their territories.

(♂♂)♀(♂) Unsociable, but some males form coalitions, like male lions, and jointly defend a territory; females usually solitary and considered nonterritorial, their large home ranges including parts of different male territories. Known examples: only cheetah.

(♀♂♀♂♂♂) Sociable/territorial. Related females occupy permanent pride territory, which male coalitions control until ousted by superior forces; young reared communally. Known examples: only the lion in nature; and feral domestic cats under conditions noted.

HOW THEY MOVE   Lithe and powerful, wonderfully quick reflexes; great jumpers; good swimmers and climbers (except cheetah and adult lions). Speed traded for power, massively muscled cats cannot run as fast as hares or antelopes—except cheetah, which is built like a greyhound. Cats also have relatively small hearts and lungs, giving them much less endurance than cursorial predators. They must use stealth to get close before quarry gets up speed. Despite their short-windedness, cats travel long distances at a walk or trot.

REPRODUCTION

MATING   Multiple copulations day after day are a felid trait, apparently necessary to induce ovulation and accomplish fertilization. Courtship is very similar in the whole family (see Table 26.1). The tendency of females to continue inviting copulation beyond their partner's desire to respond helps explain the frequent willingness of males to wait their turn instead of fighting each other.

HOW THEY COMMUNICATE   Sight 1, scent 1, sound 2. Scent plays a pivotal role in regulating felid social and sexual intercourse. The information contained in their scent marks keeps members of a community informed about one another's whereabouts, enabling them to choose whether to avoid or seek meetings. Glands in the chin and cheeks are rubbed on objects and on one another during the feline greeting ceremony, after which anal glands are inspected.

Visual communication is very important whenever cats can see one another. They have the most expressive faces of all carnivores, which, in combination with posture, ear and tail positions, backed up by vocal and other sounds, enable them to signal their feelings and intentions in redundant and unmistakable ways. A domestic cat and the African wildcat (which are the same species) use 25 different visual patterns, compounded of at least 9 facial expressions and 16 different tail and body postures. Positions and movements of the lips, eyes, and tail are highlighted by contrasting markings.

The unusually formidable combination of claws and long fangs could account for the elaborate felid visual repertoire—and for the surprising absence of submissive displays. Cats confronting a superior foe do not grovel like dogs, but inhibit attack by rolling on their backs, ready to use claws and teeth with devastating effect.

An impressive variety of sounds is produced by cats, for both long-distance and short-range signaling. Domestic-cat repertoire includes 8 calls; the lion's totals 13. As with visual signals, most cat calls are linked with aggression and produced in combination with visual displays—an offensive growl becomes a defensive snarl when a cat opens its mouth and bares its teeth. Of 6 calls small cats share—hissing, spitting, growling, screaming, purring, and meowing—all but the last 2 are hostile.

Table 26.1. CAT FAMILY BEHAVIOR GUIDE
Expect to see and hear ➤ Usual context and meaning

Advertising Presence and Status

SCENT-MARKING
Advertises territorial status, ownership of a kill, reproductive status (e.g., ♀ in heat) or simply the marker's right to be there. Rates go up during and after aggressive encounters.

Urine-spraying against objects at nose level or higher. Cat first sniffs spot intently, grimaces at predecessor's mark (if any), backs up and sprays; rubs head on spot before or after. ➤ The main form of scent-marking in the family.

Scuff-marking: rhythmic treading and forward kicking with hind feet ± urinating. ➤ Common in the bigger cats; scuffing makes visible mark; tracks carry urine scent.

Head-rubbing on objects: lips, chin, cheeks, head, and neck, preceded by sniffing, or licking and biting spot, ± grimacing. Cats often salivate, soaking chin and the spot. ➤ Stimulated by odors other than urine; deposits secretions of scent glands. Cats also rub cheeks and neck, roll and writhe on smelly things like carrion and dung.

Advertising Presence and Status *continued*

Defecating at landmarks. ➤ Many smaller cats bury their scats, but not big cats. Leopard and cheetah deposit scats at conspicuous locations.

Display claw sharpening: on trees, sometimes on ground, the same way domestic cats claw furniture. ➤ All cats sharpen claws. Makes visible marks and may deposit secretion of scent glands. Also functional: removes loose claw sheaths.

DISTANCE CALLS

Roaring of lion, sawing of leopard, chirping of cheetah. ➤ Territorial advertising and social calling (to relatives, consort partner). Distance calls of small cats are mainly mating calls.

Aggression

OFFENSIVE THREAT

Cat facial expression: mouth closed, eyes wide open, staring, small pupils; ears erect and turned outward (triangular shape in side view). ➤ Dominance and threat display, with no indications of ambivalence.

Approach in erect posture (domestic cat): slow, stiff-legged approach, tail down, tip twitching; when close moves head side to side, meanwhile growling and yowling. ➤ Similar in other small cats, with minor variations. Big cats crouch, head low, back stretched (but see lion-strutting display, Table 26.7).

Chasing/escorting. ➤ Seeing off same-sex trespassers by territorial individuals; pursuer keeps distance as long as invader keeps moving and departs.

DEFENSIVE THREAT

Facial expression: mouth open with teeth fully bared, eyes narrowed, staring, pupils large; ears flattened, presenting no silhouette. Crouching, meanwhile snarling, hissing, spitting. ➤ Totally defensive, with no offensive indications.

Forepaw raised to strike. ➤ Response to threatened attack. Leads into rollover if adversary continues to approach.

Rollover. ➤ Defense against imminent attack. Attacked cat grasps opponent with forepaws meanwhile raking belly with hind claws and biting. In fights, both cats perform these actions, meanwhile screeching, yowling, spitting, etc.

Offensive/defensive combination. ➤ A cat simultaneously and equally angry and fearful. Facial expressions and postures change with balance between the two emotions.

Back bowed, hair bristling, tail erect, ears more or less flattened; with yowling, growling, snarling, explosive spitting, hissing, meowing (small cats). ➤ Defensive threat especially against potential predator (classic cat-meets-dog display). Big cats do not bow back or raise tail vertically.

Signs of Intimidation

Looking away/around, meanwhile seated or lying. ➤ Cat looks into distance, apparently relaxed, but studiously avoids looking at adversary.

Slinking away. ➤ E.g., a lion at sight of a person afoot (in areas where fear of people persists).

Sociable Behavior

Meeting behavior: mutual sniffing of noses, head and neck extended, ears cocked; sniff and touch nape, flanks, finally under tail. ➤ Nonaggressive meetings. Friendly, relaxed cat holds tail high, allows anal inspection; fearful one keeps tail down and sidesteps, and pair ends up circling.

Greeting ceremony: sniffing noses, mouths, rubbing heads and often sides together (see Fig. 26.6), tail raised over back ± tip draped over partner's back. ➤ Affectionate meetings between members of same family/social unit. Resembles sexual presenting of estrous ♀. Reinforces social bonds.

Social licking, especially head and shoulder area. ➤ Mother and young, social bonding as distinct from cleaning; also consort pairs, and same-sex adults in lion.

Lying in contact. ➤ Mother and offspring, also same-sex adult lions.

CONTACT AND OTHER SOCIAL CALLS

Most of these are or derive from mother/young calls (see species accounts).

Meowing. ➤ Variable intensity; signals mild distress.

Purring. ➤ Contentment; heard also when adults greet and social-groom.

Courtship

Adult ♂ and ♀ keeping company. ➤ Solitary cats only consort to mate and lions prefer own gender except when mating.

MALE BEHAVIOR

Urine-testing. ➤ Grimace most pronounced in big cats.

Frequent urine-spraying.

Long mock pursuits, close following, patient waiting.

Frequent licking of erect penis.

Rubbing heads with ♀ (greeting behavior).

Real or symbolic neck grip while straddling ♀ during brief copulation. ➤ Small cats maintain grip, which induces passivity in ♀ (as in carried kitten). Big cats merely bare teeth or mouth ♀'s neck right after ejaculation.

Courtship *continued*

Licking genitals and grooming after mating.

FEMALE BEHAVIOR

Advertising onset of estrus: hyperactivity; calling; scent marking; rubbing against objects; rolling/writhing on ground. ➤ Alternately coquettish and aggressive response to ♂ advances.

Defensive threats: snarling, hissing, spitting, yowling, cuffing, rolling on back.

Sexual presenting and rubbing against ♂.

Copulatory crouch: rump elevated, tail deflected ± treading, head low, eyes narrowed, ears slightly back.

Turning over and cuffing ♂ at climax, then rolling/writhing on ground, followed by self-grooming.

Mother and Offspring

Infants carried by nape, back skin, or head. ➤ Mother readily changes cubs' hiding place if much disturbed.

Fierce maternal defense. ➤ Mothers may attack far larger animals.

Bringing live prey for offspring to practice catching and killing. ➤ Beginning while kittens still very young.

Milk-treading while nursing.

CALLS BETWEEN MOTHER AND YOUNG

Meowing. ➤ Signals mild distress, as when separated from littermates; mother responds by retrieving and licking cub.

Purring. ➤ Kittens, while nursing, being licked; also mothers suckling, licking offspring.

Hissing and slapping. ➤ Mother warning kittens to take cover.

Calling kittens from hiding. ➤ Summons to nurse or receive live prey.

Play

Stalking, ambushing, pouncing; neck biting; play fighting. ➤ Same patterns seen in domestic cat kittens.

Response to Predators

Offensive and defensive threats.

Slinking away; flight from feared predators, including climbing tree.

VOCAL ACCOMPANIMENT

Growling, woofing (lion). ➤ No special alarm call in most species.

AFRICAN WILDCAT, *Felis libyca*

Figure 26.1. African wildcat's refuge in the middle of a treeless plain.

WHAT IT IS   The wild prototype of a tabby cat. Distinguished from domesticated tabby by longer legs, more upright seated posture, and reddish, unmarked, translucent ears. ♂ wt 8–14 lb (3.7–6.4 kg), hbl 21–25 in (53–63 cm); ♀ wt 7–12 lb (3.2–5.4 kg), hbl 20.4–23 in (51–58 cm). *Tail:* ⅗ hbl. *Color:* variable; darker in wet, paler in dry regions; gray or tan, occasionally orange or black; dark garters on upper legs, fainter stripes on torso, indistinct spots on chest; tail ringed, black tipped; underparts lighter; young like adults. *Teats:* 8.

WHERE IT LIVES   All over Africa outside Sahara and Lowland Rainforest. Domesticated by Egyptians as early as 4000 BC. Commonest African cat, interbreeds freely with domestic cats.

ECOLOGY   Wildcats live wherever mice and rats thrive—including environs of towns and villages. As the densest rodent populations inhabit grasslands, wildcats are commonest in savannas, even living on treeless plains—e.g., Ngorongoro Crater floor, where they use holes dug by other animals as refuges from hordes of larger predators. Eat rodents mainly, supplemented by birds, lizards, snakes, and frogs; also large insects and other invertebrates. The biggest game taken by wildcats: hares and springhares.

ACTIVITY   ● Occasionally seen sunning outside burrow in morning, but strictly nocturnal in areas where game and other carnivores are abundant.

SOCIAL/MATING SYSTEM   ♀♂♀   Knowledge of the African wildcat rests on studies of the domesticated form (see family introduction), and on studies of the European wildcat (*F. silvestris*), which may be the same species in a slightly different form. Social and mating organization of the African wildcat is probably close to the European wildcat's.

Females fiercely defend a small core area within home range of perhaps 123 to 247 acres (50–100 ha). Mature tomcats include the ranges of up to 3 females in their territories. Undefended parts of the home range are the shared hunting grounds of all cats in the local population. Each cat that enters checks carefully to learn who's around, searching for and depositing in turn urine and glandular secretions, using vantage points to scan the neighborhood. If another cat is spotted, the later arrival waits for it to depart, although sometimes family groups and pairs of African wildcats have been seen hunting together.

FORAGING/PREDATORY BEHAVIOR   Unstudied but similar to a domestic cat's.

REPRODUCTION   Annual, 2 to 5 kittens most born during rains; gestation 56 to 60 days; females fully grown and breeding at 1 year; males mature at 2 to 3 years.

Domestic cats stay in estrus 4 days, ovulate day after mating. Several males have been seen accompanying an African wildcat in heat.

OFFSPRING AND MATERNAL CARE   Kittens born in hole in ground, hollow tree, cave, or nest in dense vegetation. Eyes open 10 to 14 days; mobile within a month; accompany mother hunting before 3 months, and become independent at 5 months. Two hand-reared females became antagonistic and fought for the same territory after littering. Yet each brought dead mice and birds as food offerings for the other's kittens, suggesting tendency to communal care.

Table 26.2. DIFFERENCES IN WILDCAT BEHAVIOR
  Differences from domestic cat, if any, have yet to be detailed.

BLACK-FOOTED OR SMALL-SPOTTED CAT,
Felis nigripes

Figure 26.2. Black-footed cat in skulking posture.

WHAT IT IS   A very small, beautiful cat of southern Africa. The small-est cat. Short body with relatively long legs. ♂ wt 3.3–3.7 lb (1.5.–1.7 kg), hbl 15–17 in (38–43 cm); ♀ wt 2.2–3.1 lb (1–1.4 kg), hbl 10.8–14.4 in (27–36 cm). *Tail:* ⅓ to ½ hbl, spotted, black-tipped. *Head:* wide with big, rounded ears. *Color:* cinnamon-buff (south) to tan (northern population); heavily spot-ted and barred: underparts pale, insides of thighs, chest, and chin white. *Teats:* 6.

WHERE IT LIVES   Botswana, Namibia, and South Africa in central South West Arid Zone, including Kalahari sands and Karroo.

ECOLOGY   Resident in open country dotted with bushes, scrub, and clumps of grass; hides in termite mounds or burrows dug by animals like springhares, suricates, and foxes. Preys on gerbils, mice, and other small ro-dents, small birds, lizards, and invertebrates (spiders, solifugids, beetles, and other insects), from which it meets its water needs.

ACTIVITY   ● Captives spend hours walking and trotting around cages at night, suggesting these cats hunt widely and actively for their prey.

SOCIAL/MATING SYSTEM   ♀♂♀   Unstudied in the wild. If being intractable and fierce in captivity, including ones taken and hand-reared before eyes open, is any indication, this is one of the most solitary and unso-ciable cats.

FORAGING/PREDATORY BEHAVIOR   Skillful and persistent dig-gers, likely preying largely on subterranean creatures, such as beetle larvae, spiders, and scorpions, as well as rodents and reptiles.

REPRODUCTION 1 to 3 kittens born in summer (rainy season), after 63- to 68-day gestation—a week longer than the larger wildcat. Estrus lasts only 36 hours, vs. 6 days in other small cats. A captive pair mated 6 times at intervals of 20 to 50 minutes.

OFFSPRING AND MATERNAL CARE Kittens more mature and develop faster than domestic kittens the first 5 weeks; eyes open at 6 to 8 days; leave nest at 4 weeks, start eating at 5 weeks, and capture mice at 6 weeks. A captive mother kept kittens from leaving the nest the first 3 weeks but thereafter hauled them out if they were slow to emerge. She tried to change nest sites every 6 to 10 days; began bringing home dead prey a little before they were ready to eat meat, followed shortly with live prey, which she simply released and kept from escaping while the kittens tried their predatory skills. Eventually they killed prey without ever seeing how it was done.

After becoming self-sufficient, black-footed cats mature much more slowly than domestic cats: a 15-month-old female was considerably smaller than an adult; another came into heat for the first time at 21 months—nearly twice the breeding age of a wildcat.

Table 26.3. *DIFFERENCES IN BLACK-FOOTED CAT BEHAVIOR*
Expect to see and hear ➤ *Usual context and meaning*

Response to Competitors/Predators

Frightened kittens scatter and lie motionless until mother sounds the all-clear: an unusual *ah-ah-ah* call accompanied by rhythmic up-and-down movements of the half-flattened ears. ➤ Instead of running for a hole or tree when frightened, as wildcats do.

SERVAL, *Felis serval*

Figure 26.3. Serval jumping.

WHAT IT IS   A long-legged, spotted cat with big ears. Tallest of small African cats; slender build with long neck. ♂ wt 22–40 lb (10–18 kg), ht 22–25 in (54–62 cm), hbl 27–40 in (67–100 cm); ♀ wt 19–27.5 lb (8.7–12.5 kg), ht and hbl within ♂ range. *Tail:* ⅓ to ½ hbl. *Color:* tawny to russet; darker in moister regions but bolder markings in arid regions; bars and blotches on neck, shoulders, legs, and tail, large solid spots on sides and legs; ears with black and white blotches; infants grayer with suffuse markings. *Teats:* 6.

WHERE IT LIVES   Throughout Africa's savanna zones, wherever grass grows and rodents live. Absent from rainforest and subdesert.

GOOD PLACES TO SEE IT   Often seen in Ngorongoro Crater and Lake Ndutu, both in the Ngorongoro Conservation Area. Common in montane and meadow grasslands; most likely to be seen along roads and beside waterways early and late in the day.

ECOLOGY   Prefers marshland, edges of gallery forest, montane grassland, and forest glades, often near water. Readily adapts to second growth and old cultivation sites near settlement. Specialized predator of common rats and mice, other rodents, and birds of tall grassland. Also takes snakes, lizards, frogs, fish, and insects. Long legs enable it to see better over tall grass and to jump high as it pounces; big ears used to pinpoint sounds made by prey. Larger prey includes flamingos, storks, and young of medium-sized antelopes.

ACTIVITY   ●/○ More day-active than most cats, especially early and late, longer on cool than on hot days. Two peak activity periods at night, the

first before midnight, the second from 4 or 5 AM into the morning. Ngorongoro servals cover an average 1.2 mi (2 km) in 24-hour day.

SOCIAL/MATING SYSTEM   ⚲♂⚲   Adults have exclusive core territories within larger home ranges shared with other servals. A male and female studied in Ngorongoro Crater hunted over a 4.7 × 2.5 mi (7.5 × 4 km)
meadow used by up to 5 other servals. Several of the females could have been
related, as female offspring are tolerated, whereas the mother and resident
adult males force adolescent males to emigrate.

FORAGING/PREDATORY BEHAVIOR   Exceptionally quick and
agile, a serval captures most rodent prey by pouncing. It leaps high in the air
and comes down with both front feet on its quarry (see Fig. 26.3), having first
pinpointed the location with its dish-antenna ears. Ngorongoro servals are
very efficient hunters: 40% of pounces by day and 59% at night were successful. Servals can swerve sharply while running full tilt, jump up and catch
birds in flight. Elongated forelimbs are used to reach into holes and snag mole
rats and hole-nesting birds like anteater chats. They wade to catch frogs and
fish, and dash into water after waders and waterfowl.

REPRODUCTION   Probably annual. Gestation 65 to 75 days; 1 to 5
young/litter. Male and female hunt and rest together several days, between
mating bouts, while female is in heat.

OFFSPRING AND PARENTAL CARE   Ngorongoro serval that had
2 litters in 2.5 years hid kittens in dense vegetation and changed hiding places
frequently. Instead of usual daytime activity pattern, she hunted and brought
food to her young kittens the whole day, only resting in late afternoon. Returning with a mouse, she started calling within 50 yd of kittens' hiding
place, stopped, listened, called again. The 3 kittens sat up, then ran to her
meowing when she called again. While one kitten ate the mouse, the mother
licked, then suckled the others, purring loudly. Later on, she had trouble
making kittens go into hiding so she could set off hunting; it took up to half
an hour of escalating growling and spitting to get away from them.

PREDATORS   Without cover to hide in, servals, which seem not to use
holes as refuges, would be vulnerable to larger carnivores, especially hyenas
and wild dogs. When servals see hyenas, they crouch and duck into cover and
wait for threat to pass. If hyenas come close, servals run in leaps and bounds
with sudden swerves, tails high.

Table 26.4. *DIFFERENCES IN SERVAL BEHAVIOR*
       Expect to see and hear ➤ *Usual context and meaning*

Scent-marking

Urine-spraying. ➤ ♂♂ spend more time patrolling and marking than ♀♀. ♂ followed 12 hours sprayed 556 times. No serval was seen to mark the same spot twice.

Rubbing chin and cheeks on grass stems and on ground, meanwhile salivating.

Aggression

OFFENSIVE THREAT

Serval nods instead of shaking head like most cats.

Prodding opponent with straightened foreleg.

CARACAL, *Felis caracal*

Figure 26.4. Caracal with rat.

WHAT IT IS   Africa's version of a lynx. Heaviest of the small cats. Relatively short in length, with long legs and big feet; hindquarters more developed than forequarters. ♂ wt 26-40 lb (12-18 kg), ht 16-20 in (40-50 cm), hbl 25-36 in (61-91 cm); ♀ wt 18-29 lb (8-13kg), 5-8% smaller. *Tail:* ½ hbl. *Head:* short, powerful jaws; long, tufted ears. *Color:* tawny to rufous with faint spots in whitish underparts; lips, ear backs, and tassels black; dark markings on cheeks and above eyes edged with white. Kittens like adults, with markings already formed and more distinct spots. *Teats:* 6.

WHERE IT LIVES   Arid zones and dry savannas of Africa including North Africa (also Asia).

GOOD PLACES TO SEE IT   Though rare, caracals are often active in daytime. South Africa's Mountain Zebra NP is one of better places to see it.

ECOLOGY   Prefers arid bush. Inhabits plains, mountains, and rocky hills, only venturing into open grassland at night; seems to need woody vegetation for cover; but avoids dense evergreen forest. An awesome predator for its size, regularly killing game its own size and larger: kudu calf, adult impala, sheep in South Africa, even ostrich. In Mountain Zebra NP (Cape Province), mountain reedbucks made up 70% by weight of caracal kills. The 25 caracals killed an estimated 190 mountain reedbucks and 2995 hyraxes a year. Other prey included springboks, steenboks, gray duikers, jackals, monkeys, mongooses, springhares, a few small rodents, and birds.

ACTIVITY   ●/○ Mainly night-active but also active by day and at twilight.

SOCIAL/MATING SYSTEM   ♀♂♀ Solitary, territorial but no detailed information. Of 57 caracal sightings in Mt. Zebra NP, 41 were of single adults; 11 were of adults in pairs.

HOW IT MOVES   Powerful hindquarters enable caracal to take long bounds and jump as high as 11 feet. A good climber, using its strong dewclaws to shinny up smooth tree trunks.

FORAGING/PREDATORY BEHAVIOR   More like a small big cat than a big small cat, preys on many of the same species as leopard, killing big game by strangulation; covers kills with leaves and grass or caches them in trees, returning repeatedly to feed. Exceptional jumping and climbing ability enable it to catch hyraxes more efficiently than probably any other carnivore. Takes sleeping birds from their perches, including fearsome martial eagle. Ambushes swift-flying sandgrouse, doves, and pigeons at waterholes: leaping up at birds in flight, it sometimes bats two from a flock with lighting paw strokes. Finicky eaters, caracals discard viscera of mammals, partially pluck the fur of hyraxes and larger kills, and avoid eating hair by shearing meat neatly from the skin. Yet it eats small birds feathers and all, and is as tolerant of rotten meat as any leopard.

REPRODUCTION   Year round with birth peak during rains. Litters: 1 to 4; gestation 62 to 81 days. Females begin cycling at 2-week intervals c. 4 months after littering, stay in estrus 3 to 6 days but mate only final 1 to 3 days. Puberty at 7 to 10 months, both sexes.

OFFSPRING AND MATERNAL CARE   Born in nest lined with hair or feathers, or in a burrow. Eyes open c. 9 days but kittens avoid light for

2 weeks and are very sensitive to noise. Begin walking at 9 to 17 days, and lick-groom selves at 11 days. The ears, folded at birth, only become erect after a month. Kittens utter twittering food calls at 12 days, leave nest and chase moving prey as early as 3 weeks, but only start eating meat at 1 to 1.5 months. Weaning in 4 to 6 months.

Table 26.5. DIFFERENCES IN CARACAL BEHAVIOR
Expect to see and hear ➤ *Usual context and meaning*

Visual Signaling

Striking black and white markings direct attention to facial expressions, making semaphore signals of every twist, turn, and flick of the tufted ears.

Looking around: pronounced side-to-side head-flagging and rapid flicking of the ears while 2 caracals avoid looking at one another. ➤ Movements and markings make "looking around" a conspicuous display. Interpretation: avoid meeting, interaction.

LEOPARD, *Panthera pardus*

Figure 26.5. Leopard safe in tree with springbok prey.

WHAT IT IS   The embodiment of feline beauty, power, and stealth. Long and low-slung with short, muscular limbs. ♂ wt 77–143 lb (35–65 kg), ht 24–28 in (60–70 cm); ♀ wt 62–128 lb (28–58 kg), ht 23–26 in (57–64 cm). *Tail:* ⅔ hbl. *Head:* wide, with short, powerful jaws. *Color:* tan to reddish brown with spots grouped in rosettes on torso and upper limbs; darker and more closely spotted (sometimes black with spots nearly obscured) in humid tropics than in arid zone; cubs: fuzzy coat, indistinct, close-set spots. *Teats:* 4.

WHERE IT LIVES   The most widespread wild felid: pan-Africa and Asia wherever cover and game exist.

GOOD PLACES TO SEE IT   Unpredictable. Often seen in Masai Mara NR, Kenya, and Lobo and Seronera in Serengeti NP, Tanzania, usually resting in trees. Some lodges put out baits to attract them (e.g., in Kenya's Samburu-Isi-olo NR).

ECOLOGY   Broadest habitat tolerance of any African carnivore, from Lowland Rainforest (the only large predator therein) to deserts, to highest mountains (leopard found entombed in Kilimanjaro icecap). Least specialized and most adaptable of the big cats, leopards persist even in settled areas, substituting domestic animals (and even people) for natural prey, which includes all forms of animal protein from beetles to antelopes 3 times its own weight. In Serengeti NP 30 different prey species were identified in scats, vs. c. 12 in lion diet; medium-sized antelopes and young of large species the mainstay, fleshed out with hares, birds, and several small carnivores. In another park with less big game, animals under 10 lb were the mainstay, 20% of kills weighed 10 to 90 lb, and 10% of the items identified in scats were invertebrates.

ACTIVITY   ● Lies up by day and part of night in trees or dense undergrowth, becoming active at dusk, often continuing couple hours after dawn. Radio-tracked Tsavo NP leopards ranged 15 mi (25 km) a night, traversing currently used range every few days; seldom used same resting places 2 nights running.

SOCIAL/MATING SYSTEM   ⧀♂⧀   A typical solitary cat, the leopard hunts and lives alone, associating with another adult only long enough to mate. Females and possibly males have overlapping ranges, while defending core areas as exclusive territories. Great differences in home-range size, even in same locale, were demonstrated in Tsavo NP, where 10 radio-collared leopards that were tracked for 3 years lived in areas of 3.5 to 24 mi^2 (9–63 km^2). Their ranges overlapped by up to 70%; each leopard used only ½ its range at a time. Male ranges may overlap several female ranges: in Serengeti NP an adult male and 3 females hunted the same 3-mile stretch of river, each independently.

Offspring become independent at c. 22 months, but remain in natal home range for some months and often get maternal handouts while struggling to become proficient hunters.

FORAGING/PREDATORY BEHAVIOR   The Prince of Stealth. Stalking with infinite patience and complete silence, a leopard tries to get within 5 yd of its quarry before pouncing, taking it completely by surprise. The maximum distance from which it will spring is 20 yd, and it quits within

50 yd if it misses, even though it can accelerate to 37 mph (60 kph). Tremendously strong, it can pull down and get a stranglehold on a 300 lb (136 kg) topi or subadult wildebeest; carry 150-lb impala up a tree; abduct a sleeping German shepherd without a sound. Yet a barking fox terrier can unnerve and tree a leopard in daylight. Such extreme boldness and timidity are both characteristic. For all its stealth, most leopard stalks seem to fail, at least in daytime.

REPRODUCTION   Unseasonal, 1 to 3 young/litter, at 2-year intervals. Gestation is 90 to 100 days. Females begin breeding at 2. Estrus lasts 7 days, recurring every 25 to 58 days until conception.

OFFSPRING AND MATERNAL CARE   Birthweight only 14 to 21 oz (400 to 600 g). Cubs hidden 6 weeks in dense thicket, cave, or hollow tree and moved periodically. Eyes open in 6 to 10 days; begin eating meat after hiding period. Weaned as early as 3 months but dependent at least a year. Mothers reduce range and spend 55 to 66% of time with cubs first few months but stay away up to 25 hours while eating and guarding large kills.

RELATIONS WITH OTHER PREDATORS   Ranks just above the cheetah in the predator peck order. Why a leopard allows hyenas to take its kills and chase it up trees is mystifying. Big leopards weigh more than striped and brown hyenas and more than most spotted hyenas, and they certainly *look* more powerful and dangerous. Inferiority complex is further evidence that confrontations are unnerving for the Prince of Stealth—but not always: a leopard with cubs is likelier to attack than flee from hyenas.

Table 26.6. *DIFFERENCES IN LEOPARD BEHAVIOR*
Expect to see and hear ➤ *Usual context and meaning*

Territorial Advertising

SCENT-MARKING

Urine-spraying and claw-sharpening: Passing leopard sniffs earlier marks, stretches out along trunk or branch and sharpens claws, finishes by spraying base of tree. ➤ Large trees with inclined trunks or big branches 2–3 yd overhead are favored marking sites. ♂ ♂ especially also spray bushes and other objects in the usual way during nightly roaming.

Feces. ➤ Leopards deposit smelly scats along pathways where other leopards are likely to encounter them.

CALLING

Sawing: emitted both while inhaling and exhaling, leopard gives 13–16 "strokes" in c. 12 sec. ➤ Equivalent to lion's roar, advertises presence and/or territorial status. Sounds like someone sawing wood; repeated every 6 min. or so during peak calling bouts, typically after nightfall and before dawn, often while leopard is walking.

Courtship

COPULATION CALLS

♂ growls, snarls, and gnashes teeth while symbolically biting female's nape. ➤ Thereby broadcasting copulation. Leopards mate as often as lions, with more sound effects.

Mother and Offspring

Visual signal: Leopard leading cubs arches tail over back, displaying conspicuous white tip. ➤ A follow-me signal, visible in dark; also emphasizes tail position and movement in social interactions.

CALLS

Urr-urr-urr. ➤ Contact call from cubs to mother.

Wa-wa-wa. ➤ Sound of contentment (equivalent to purring).

Purring. ➤ Mother summons cubs with loud, abrupt purrs.

Response to Competitors/Predators

Lions, hyenas, wild dogs: uses trees as refuge and larder for kills.

Cheetah: Leopard usually dominant; but I saw a cheetah with cubs tree a leopard.

LION, *Panthera leo*

Figure 26.6. Lions rubbing heads in greeting ceremony.

WHAT IT IS   Call of the African Wild, King of African Carnivores. Low but large and powerful, especially males. ♂ wt 416 lb (189 kg) (record: 572 lb [260 kg], Namibia), ht 48 in (120 cm); ♀ wt 277 lb (126 kg), ht 44 in (110 cm). *Coat*: short except for tail tuft and male's mane: appearing third year, maximum development at 5. *Color*: tawny with white underparts often faintly spotted (especially in East Africa); black tail tuft, ear backs, and lips; mane individually variable, from blond to black; cubs wooly with grayish, spotted coats, changing to adult coat by 3 months. *Teats*: 4.

WHERE IT LIVES   Sub-Saharan Africa except deserts and rainforest, wherever medium-sized and large herbivores survive. Still the most abundant large predator (after spotted hyena) in savanna and plains ecosystems. Formerly ranged Asia and Pan-Africa, but exterminated in North and South Africa by early this century (except for Kruger and Kalahari Gemsbok NPs and recently reintroduced in some Transvaal and Natal reserves).

GOOD PLACES TO SEE IT   Just about all the major NPs. The problem in more popular ones is finding lions unaccompanied by vehicles.

ECOLOGY   Savanna and plains habitats with greatest variety and biomass of hoofed mammals carry up to 1 lion/3 mi² (12/100 km²). Where prey density is very low, as in *Miombo* Woodland Zone or Sahel, there may be only 1 lion/50 to 100 mi². Commonest ungulates from impala to wildebeest and zebra in size are main prey. Different prides have different preferences and traditions. Some, hunting in groups usually including males, regularly kill buffalos, including biggest, oldest bulls; even bull giraffes are occasionally taken (caught lying down). Variety of smaller game also taken by hungry or curious lions, including rodents, birds, turtles, lizards, even fish, and ostrich eggs (by the few with knack of opening them). Another important source of food is scavenging. Lions respond to rallying cries of hyenas as readily as hyenas themselves and by day are guided to carcasses by descending vultures.

ACTIVITY ● (○) While prey is plentiful, lions spend 20 hours out of 24 conserving energy, becoming active in late afternoon when mothers retrieve, suckle, and socialize with young cubs and one another; hunt most actively early and late at night, carrying over for a couple hours after daybreak. But lions become active any time, day or night, hungry or gorged, that easy opportunities to catch prey present themselves.

SOCIAL/MATING SYSTEM

THE FEMALE PRIDE The basic units of lion society are prides of related females, each pride residing in a traditional home range/territory. Male offspring have to leave by 2.5 years. Resident adult males are immigrants that have gained custody of a pride range in competition with other males.

The number of adult females in a pride is adjusted to seasons of minimum prey availability and tends to be consistent over time. Surplus females have to disperse; if the membership falls below capacity, subadult nomads are accepted in the absence of recruits from within the pride. Home-range size also depends on prey density, being as small as 8 to over 154 mi² (20–400 km²).

In Serengeti and Kruger NP, a typical pride numbers about 13. The average composition of 14 prides totaling 181 lions was 1.7 (1–4) adult males, 4.5 (2–9) adult females, 3.8 subadults, and 2.8 juveniles and yearlings. Large prides, which can include up to 40 lions, may never assemble in one place. Members come and go unpredictably, alone and in groups, typically numbering 3 to 5 lions. There is no rank hierarchy among females and no 2 are likely to be found together more than half the time. But all residents are acquainted and whenever they meet, the lion greeting ceremony (see Fig. 26.5) reaffirms their social ties. A lion without the self-assurance to meet and greet sends a signal that it doesn't belong and is treated as an intruder. Each sex defends the part of the pride range in current use against intruders of the same gender.

MALE COALITIONS The opportunity to monopolize reproduction of a whole group of females is behind the pronounced sexual dimorphism seen in lions, alone of all cats. The advantages of large size and a showy (also protective) mane have also caused males to become so bulky and conspicuous as to reduce their hunting ability. Reproductive competition is so fierce that males form coalitions to improve their chances. Where lions are plentiful, a single lion has little chance of winning or holding a pride's territory. Once begun, the advantage of competing cooperatively should theoretically lead to bigger and bigger coalitions, ending up in gang warfare; yet coalitions of over 4 males are rare. Large groups have problems, starting with assembling and coordinating all the members. More important, a big coalition destabilizes lion society by taking over different prides then failing to defend them all, with fewer surviving offspring the end result.

Coalition partners are usually related males that left their pride as adolescents and stayed together as nomads until mature and ready to compete. Lone nomads also join forces and can form coalitions as cohesive as sibling teams.

Infanticide is another consequence of severe competition. Prime years for males are 5 to 9; even at 8 they are already losing weight and mane hair; few survive past 10. Having taken over a pride territory, often after a battle royal entailing severe injury and even death for the losers, the victors usually have only 2 years before losing in turn to a younger and stronger or larger coalition. Large coalitions of 4 to 6 males may last up to 4 years; losers don't get a second chance.

Given so little time to propagate their genes, sexual selection rewards males that kill all the suckling young of defeated rivals. When a nursing lioness loses her cubs, she comes into heat within a few weeks. Otherwise, the normal interval between births is 2 years—matching average male tenure. It is thus entirely understandable, though no less gruesome, that the first thing males do after a takeover is kill all the cubs they can catch. Lionesses may fiercely attack them, and in concert can sometimes stop infanticide, but mothers also get killed or have to flee with their offspring.

After a takeover, lionesses often come into heat every few weeks for 4 or 5 months without becoming pregnant. This interval of sexual hyperactivity turns out to be a form of insurance against desertion: newcomer males are likelier to become bonded to the lionesses and settle in their territory after months of feverish sexual activity than if the females conceived and stopped cycling the first time around. Birth control also allows time for the biggest and toughest male group to move in and take over. When the sterility period ends, pride females ovulate, conceive, and litter in synchrony. The cubs are then reared communally, improving the chances that a sizeable male coalition will eventually propagate their parents' genes.

FORAGING/PREDATORY BEHAVIOR   Like other cats, except for communal hunts. These usually involve 3 to 8 lionesses moving on a broad front in an attempt to drive quarry into an ambush or block the escape route of ungulates feeding in a cul-de-sac—as when wildebeests or zebras graze alongside a river or woodland edge. Males only hunt for themselves when no free lunch is provided by lionesses, hyenas, or other agencies.

Lions hunting in twos and groups have a success rate of c. 30%, compared to only 17 to 19% for lions hunting singly by daylight. But recent studies indicating that single hunters are about as successful as groups at night reopen questions about the primary reason lions became the only sociable cat. Maybe it was to control exclusive hunting grounds and share food with relatives, while protecting it against competitors, including other lions. But lions share food grudgingly; they often fight for places at a kill and prime males take the proverbial "lion's share"—up to 25% of their own weight. If the kill is small, the smallest and weakest lions lose out—hungry mothers won't share even with their own youngsters. High juvenile mortality rates during times of prey scarcity are the result. Nevertheless, when there is enough meat to go around, the whole pride prospers.

REPRODUCTION   Year-round but often synchronized within prides—perhaps mainly as a result of male takeovers and infanticide. Typically 3 cubs/litter, after 14 to 15 week gestation; 20 to 30 months between births. Females start breeding at 4, only a year earlier than males.

MATING   For every cub that survives to yearling stage, lions copulate an estimated 3000 times. Only 1 estrus in 5 results in progeny and estrus lasts c. 4 days, during which couples mate 2.2 times/hour. Surprisingly, coalition partners hardly ever fight over mating rights. The first to reach a female in heat becomes her consort—until and unless he has had enough. As partners are usually equals, fighting would impair their ability to withstand takeover attempts.

OFFSPRING AND COMMUNAL CARE   Weighing only 2 to 4.5 lb (1–2 kg) at birth, lions are helpless as any kitten. Eyes open at 3 to 11 days, walk at 10 to 15 days, run at 1 month. After 4 to 8 weeks in hiding, mother begins leading cubs to nearby kills. By 7 weeks they keep up with pride. Weaned at 7 to 10 months but remain dependent until 16 months at least. Mothers rarely bring live prey for cubs to practice catching.

Cub survival is highest when reproduction is synchronized, since communal suckling is most equable when there are no bigger cubs to hog the milk. Juveniles, often left alone for over 24 hours, are vulnerable to other predators that happen on their hiding place. Mothers won't wait for juveniles older than 5 to 7 months; when large prey is scarce and mothers grow thin, they often abandon weakened cubs unable to keep up, especially if there is only one.

RELATIONS WITH OTHER PREDATORS   Either competitive or predatory. Lions kill and often eat all the other carnivores, including leopards and cheetahs (but rarely hyenas—see spotted hyena account).

Table 26.7. *DIFFERENCES IN LION BEHAVIOR*
   Expect to see and hear ➤ Usual context and meaning

Advertising Presence and Social Status

SCENT-MARKING
Mainly in a territorial context.

Urine-spraying bushes, high grass, etc. ➤ Resident ♂ ♂ regularly patrol and spray bushes in currently defended part of pride territory. ♀ ♀ spray only occasionally.

Advertising Presence and Social Status *continued*

Scuff-marking ± urinating, by both sexes. ➤ Beginning at 2 yr.

CALLING

Roaring: usually standing or crouching but possible from any position and even while running. Roaring grades from soft *huh* to full-throated roars audible 5 mi. ➤ Multipurpose behavior: advertise territorial occupancy, contact pride members, strengthen social bonds (roaring in chorus); intimidate rivals during aggressive interactions. ♂'s roar deeper, louder than ♀'s, but sex and distance are both hard to judge.

Aggression

Strutting. ➤ ♂ dominance display, directed mainly to ♀♀.

Head-low threat: lion keeps head low, forelegs wide apart, shoulders higher than normal, gazing steadily at opponent with eyes and mouth as in typical offensive threat or while snarling (more defensive); ears twisted so that black marks face forward. ➤ Unlike threat posture of other cats. If tail is lashed up and down during display and the lion growls or coughs, a charge is imminent.

Sociable Behavior

Greeting ceremony (see Fig. 26.5): Lions moan softly and lean on one another so hard that when one is lying, the other often falls on top. ➤ Cubs more often rub against adults, and ♀♀ rub against ♂—the direction being from weaker to stronger.

♀♀ and ♂ coalition partners lying in contact. ➤ Characteristic; another sign of close social bonds.

CALLS

Humming. ➤ A sound of contentment, like purring, emitted during affectionate interactions and while cubs nurse.

Puffing, a faint *pfff-pfff* emitted with closed mouth as lions approach each other. ➤ Signals peaceable intentions.

Play

Including adult ♀♀. ➤ ♀♀ remain playful as adults, whereas ♂♂ lose the tendency at about 3 yr.

Response to Competitors/Predators

Woofing. ➤ Sound made by a startled lion.

CHEETAH, *Acinonyx jubatus*[v]

Figure 26.7. A coalition of 3 male cheetahs drinking.

WHAT IT IS   A cat with a grayhound chassis. Built for speed: light-boned, swaybacked, long, thin legs, and short neck. ♂ wt 77–143 lb (35–65 kg), ht 28–36 in (70–90 cm); ♀ wt c. 20 lb lighter, ht within ♂ range. *Tail:* long (26–32 in [65–80 cm]). *Feet:* small feet with blunt (except dewclaw) un-sheathed claws. *Head:* small, round with foreshortened face; relatively small teeth; low, broad ears. *Coat:* short except for ruff of longer hair framing face and short spinal crest; fluffy hair on chest and belly. *Color:* tawny, with small, solid black spots; white underparts; outer tail ringed black and white; black ear backs, lips, nose and distinctive "tear stains." Juveniles have long, silky fur—black with faint spots—and a cape of long, blue-gray hair. *Teats:* 10 or 12.

WHERE IT LIVES   Still widespread in sub-Saharan savannas and arid zones, wherever suitable prey occurs, though generally at very low density. Formerly ranged through North Africa and the Near East to India. An extra-ordinary lack of genetic diversity, suggesting that at one point it went through a genetic bottleneck (possibly all living cheetahs descend from one female), makes the species peculiarly vulnerable to disease.

GOOD PLACES TO SEE IT   Serengeti NP, medium- and long-grass plains, Tanzania; Masai Mara NR, Amboseli NP, Kenya; Etosha NP and private game ranches, Namibia.

ECOLOGY   Though range includes sparsely vegetated subdesert and steppe, the cheetah needs bushes, grass, or other cover to get within sprinting range of prey and to hide from larger predators. Specialized as predator on gazelles and springbok, the fleetest of plains antelopes; concentrates on impala, kob, lechwe, and reedbuck in wetter savanna; and takes smaller antelopes (oribi, bush duiker), calves and yearlings of all the larger antelopes, plus warthog, young zebra, and some small game like hares. Can go 4 days or more without drinking and easily goes 10 days in the Kalahari, where it eats melons.

ACTIVITY   ○ The most diurnal cat; seldom active at night and usually rests during heat of day. Average distance traveled in a day by female with cubs was 2.3 mi (3.7 km), compared to 4 mi (7 km) for males.

SOCIAL/MATING SYSTEM   ♂♀♂   Beginning with first estrus at c. 1.5 years, female cheetahs separate from their littermates and avoid contact with other cheetahs of either sex, except to mate. Cheetahs that live on migratory game have huge home ranges: c. 300 mi^2 (800 km^2) on Serengeti Plains.

Breeding males are territorial, competing for property in the hunting grounds traversed by most females. Serengeti males defend exclusive properties of 15 to 30 mi^2 (39–78 km^2). Male intruders are likely to be attacked and are sometimes killed, particularly if they cross the property of a male coalition. Most Serengeti adult males associate in coalitions: 40% in pairs and 19% in trios. Most though not all are brothers that have stayed together after separating from their mother at 17 to 23 months. Coalition partners are more standoffish than their lion counterparts and unequal: one is dominant and monopolizes most mating opportunities. But being number 2 or 3 is a better deal than being a solo number 1 in the Serengeti since only 4% of the single males ever win territories. Pairs have territorial tenures averaging 7.5 months and trios 22 months, compared to only 4 months for single males. Another advantage of coalitions is their tendency to kill bigger animals than single hunters.

Female cheetahs usually settle within their mother's home range, but most males travel long distances before maturing and settling down: over 124 mi (200 km) in the case of 9 males marked in Namibia.

FORAGING/PREDATORY BEHAVIOR   Hunting cheetahs employ several strategies to approach antelopes, depending on terrain, species, and behavior of the animals. Although top speed is an incredible 70 mph (112 kph), a cheetah can only sprint c. 300 yd before rising temperature and oxygen debt force it to quit. Average speed during a chase is under 40 mph (64 kph). So a cheetah tries to get within 50 yd and single out a particular quarry before launching an all-out effort; lone animals or group members at a little distance from the rest are often chosen.

When cover is available, a cheetah uses it like any cat and shows same ability to anticipate opportunities—like waiting crouched in ambush if game is moving in its direction. Lacking cover, a cheetah tries open but slow approach toward alert antelopes watching or even coming closer for a better look. If within 60 to 70 yd before they take flight, a cheetah gallops after them seeking a specific quarry, then accelerates to full speed. When a herd is grazing and unaware of its presence, a cheetah often tries a running approach to get within sprinting range before the animals take flight. A cheetah sprinting flat-out after a gazelle overtakes it with apparent ease. But then the gazelle turns sharply and the cheetah's greater speed keeps it from turning as sharply. If the gazelle manages to dodge its pursuer 3 or 4 times, the cat runs out of steam. But when a cheetah spots a young gazelle or other antelope that should be hiding, it runs up to 600 yd to claim a small but sure meal.

Cheetahs bring down quarry either by tripping it or knocking it off balance with a sideward or downward blow to its hindquarters. One running much slower or standing is pulled down by rearing and hooking its shoulder or flank with a dewclaw and yanking backward. Once the victim is down, the cat lunges for its throat, secures a vicelike grip on its windpipe, and proceeds to choke it to death, usually within 4 to 5 minutes. A cheetah then drags its kill into nearest cover, where it proceeds to eat up to 30 lb (14 kg), meanwhile keeping a lookout for hyenas and lions. Skin and bones and digestive tract are left uneaten; cheetahs do not return to their kills. Fully fed cheetahs can fast 2 to 5 days before killing again, but mothers keep much busier: one with cubs captured 31 gazelles and a hare in 35 days.

REPRODUCTION   Year-round with possible mating peak after rainy season; 3 to 4 (range 1–8) cubs/litter; gestation 90 to 95 days; first conception at 21 to 22 months; 18 months between births.

OFFSPRING AND MATERNAL CARE   Females give birth in cover and keep cubs hidden the first month. Newborns, weighing 5.2 to 10.5 oz (150–300 g), are blind but can crawl, turn head, spit explosively, and give soft churring calls. Mother of 10-day-old cubs moved them every other day, carrying them by the back. Cubs born in a zoo opened their eyes at 10 days, could walk by day 16, and got their milk teeth at 20 days.

Starting at 5.5 weeks, cubs are led to kills, thereafter follow mother except when she chases prey, often spoiling chances by playing or running ahead. At 3 months, already weaned, cubs stay behind, following slowly or waiting for mother's summons. Family feeds together with little squabbling, even on small kills. Afterward, mother licks cubs' faces clean, purring loudly. When cubs are ½ year old, mother begins bringing live gazelle fawns, hares, and such for them to practice catching and killing. Juveniles 9 to 12 months old hunt and capture hares and fawns but seldom master art of killing before 15 months.

RELATIONS WITH OTHER PREDATORS   Cheetahs are no match for other large carnivores, which appropriate at least 10% of their kills.

Lions kill cheetahs given the chance, and predators (including large eagles) take over half their offspring in first 3 months.

Table 26.8. DIFFERENCES IN CHEETAH BEHAVIOR
Expect to see and hear ➤ Usual context and meaning

Scent-marking

Crouching posture of a cheetah as it sniffs scent mark intently, followed by scuff-marking ± urinating; spraying urine; defecating; or (rarely) claw-sharpening. ➤ Cheetahs leave calling cards that tell who is/was in the neighborhood, on prominent landmarks: mounds and rocks (also used as observation posts), lone trees and bushes. Every passing cheetah meanders from landmark to landmark, receiving and leaving olfactory news.

Urine-spraying. ➤ ♀ ♀ spray less actively than ♂ ♂ except when coming into heat; both urine and feces of estrous ♀ attract all passing ♂ ♂.

Aggression

Offensive threat: stiff-legged approach with head below shoulder level, often in broadside stance. ➤ Black tear marks and ear backs show distinctly on lowered head.

Charging in offensive threat.

Defensive threat: sudden lunges, slapping ground and snapping, alternating with crouching and open-mouthed snarl.

Sociable Behavior

Greeting ceremony: contact limited to sniffing, face-licking, and cheek-rubbing.

CALLS

Most cheetah calls are unlike those of other cats.

Chirping and yelping. Sounds like bird's chirp and dog's yelp or yip; audible for over a mile at high intensity. ➤ Graded contact calls often given alternately and repeatedly.

Churring: a staccato, high-pitched growling sound, less audible than chirping. ➤ Mother calling hidden cubs, greeting or courting adults, and cubs at a kill.

Bleating. ➤ Sound of distress, equivalent to meowing.

Moaning: voiced along with bleating, growling, snarling, hissing, and coughing. ➤ Angry protest, as when hyena or lion has appropriated a cheetah's kill. Cheetahs make these more conventional sounds less often than other cats.

Purring. ➤ Friendly, contented cheetahs purr like huge domestic cats.

Courtship

Staccato purring. ➤ Voiced by a ♂ on the trail of an estrous ♀.

Mother and Offspring

CALLS

Whirring: changes to ferocious squeal at peak intensity. ➤ Made by cubs squabbling over a kill. May be equivalent to growling in other cats.

Nyam-nyam. ➤ Another sound cubs make while feeding.

Ihn-ihn. ➤ Mother summoning young, alternates with chirping.

Staccato purring. ➤ Sharp call by mother that elicits close following.

Short, high-pitched call. ➤ Makes cubs stay still.

Play

Chasing, boxing, wrestling, tug-of-war, king-of-the-castle, climbing trees, ambushing, stalking, pouncing. ➤ Cheetah cubs are particularly playful and acrobatic.

Chasing and slapping one another's hindquarters, the cheetah technique for downing prey. ➤ Becomes commonest form of play, beginning at 3 months.

Chapter 27

DOG FAMILY
Canidae

Fennec, *Vulpes (Fennecus) zerda*
Sand fox, *V. pallida*
Ruppell's fox, *V. ruppelli*
Cape fox, *V. chama*
Bat-eared fox, *Otocyon megalotis*

Golden jackal, *Canis aureus*
Black-backed jackal, *C. mesomelas*
Side-striped jackal, *C. adustus*
Simien jackal, *C. simensis*[en]
Wild dog, *Lycaon pictus*[en]

WHAT THEY ARE   Very successful carnivores that have been around 55 million years although the genus *Canis*, including jackals and the wolf/dog, evolved only within the last 2 million years. Differences in size, shape, and coloration among the existing 10 genera and 37 species are far less than occur in the different breeds of dog that humans have created from the one domesticated species.

FAMILY TRAITS   Weight range from 3 lb (1.5 kg) fennec to 176 lb (80 kg) timber wolf; males slightly to somewhat bigger than females but sexes look alike. Narrow but deep-chested body and long, thin legs. *Feet:* 5 toes on front, 4 on rear feet (except wild dog), equipped with strong but blunt claws. *Head:* long, narrow snout; upstanding prominent ears. *Teeth:* 38 to 50; long, sharp-edged canines, well-developed carnassials, sharp premolars, and wide molars adapted for crushing. *Tail:* bushy, hock length or longer. *Coat:* rough with dense underfur, longer, erectile hair on neck, shoulders, back, and tail. *Color:* from white to black, but mostly inconspicuous shades of gray, tan, or brown, often grizzled from banding of guard hairs; contrasting markings on face, ears, mane, throat, and tail. Newborns generally dark brown. *Scent glands:* mouth corners; probably other glands at base of long sensory hairs on nose, cheeks, forehead, and neck; anal glands, glands in vulva, and at least 3 kinds in the penis; a gland below the dark tail spot; glands between toes and in footpads. *Teats:* 6 to 14.

WHAT THEY EAT   All kinds of vertebrates and invertebrates, plus fruits and some vegetables. Mammals, especially rodents, hares, antelopes and other hoofed mammals, are main prey of most canids. All but the most specialized species (bat-eared fox, wild dog) readily scavenge. Highly opportunistic and intelligent, most eat whatever is available with least effort.

SOCIAL/MATING SYSTEMS

(♂♀⊙) The basic unit is a monogamous pair; most but not all canids are territorial. Whether a species is solitary or sociable depends on whether offspring disperse or stay with their parents.

(symbols) Solitary/polygynous. One male breeding with 2 or 3 females; extra females are usually daughters that fail to disperse. Example: fox.

(symbols) Monogamous pair with helpers. Offspring stay home and help rear younger siblings. Example: jackal.

(symbols) Sociable canids, most but not all territorial; groups composed of mostly related individuals that hunt in packs and rear offspring of the dominant breeding pair communally. Examples: wild dog, wolf.

Male parenting makes possible larger litters than a female could rear alone, and monogamy ensures that the male invests in his own offspring. Provisioning pups is a demanding task even for 2 parents; more offspring survive with the assistance of helpers, for whom the benefits equal or outweigh the costs when pups and helpers have the same parents.

To derive sociable from solitary canids seems as simple as having helpers stay with their parents instead of dispersing. The fact that solitary canids are capable of becoming sociable when there is a continuing food surplus suggests that is, indeed, how packs originated. When bat-eared fox daughters stay home and breed with their father, the mothers rear their offspring communally, including cross-suckling one another's pups. But truly sociable canids like the wild dog started along this evolutionary pathway a long time ago and have made various other adaptations for pack life:

- Social canids are bigger and females produce larger litters of smaller and more helpless young that require more care for a longer time. Big packs, with more helpers, reproduce more successfully than small packs.

- Retention of juvenile traits such as playfulness and submissiveness is an essential aspect of sociability. Whereas siblings of solitary species become increasingly quarrelsome and unsociable as they mature, social canids preserve close social bonds once their rank order is established.

- Subordination of other pack members to the alpha pair is based on prolonging parental authority. One consequence of subordination is reduced production of sex hormones, which suppresses reproduction of other pack members. (The occasional subordinate female that becomes pregnant is likely to lose her litter.)

HOW THEY MOVE   Canids are the premiere runners among carnivores, possessing both speed and endurance which large hearts and lungs and legs modified for efficient forward propulsion provide Traveling jackals and wild dogs move at a springy trot or a slow gallop (lope) of 7 to 10 mph (12–16 kph). The fastest pace is a bounding jump-run, with spine flexing and extending to achieve maximum stride length. Canids are good jumpers, and their blunt claws, useless for climbing, are well-adapted for digging.

REPRODUCTION

MATING   Preceded by an extended "engagement," often beginning months before estrus, during which pair bonds are formed or reconfirmed. Togetherness, cooperative hunting, joint territorial marking, social grooming, and a good deal of aggression are part of the process. Pair bonding assures the female that her mate won't desert, leaving her to rear puppies unassisted, and assures the male that the offspring he parents are his alone.

An unusual feature of canid reproduction is the copulatory tie, which locks a couple together for up to 30 minutes, depending on species. During this time they are vulnerable to predators or rivals of their own species although they can stand facing in opposite directions (see Table 27.1). A bulbous structure at the base of the penis balloons inside the vagina before the male ejaculates, preventing withdrawal until it detumesces. The exact function of the copulatory tie remains obscure.

HOW THEY COMMUNICATE   Sight 1, scent 1, sound 1.

SIGHT   Markings accentuate facial expressions and appendages, making visual displays conspicuous. Hackles, erected to increase apparent size, are highlighted by dark banding; conversely, white underparts accentuate lying in submission.
Facial expressions   More developed in some species than in others. Golden jackal can lift upper lip to display canines, whereas most other canids do no more than open their mouths slightly.

SCENT   Batteries of scent glands concentrated at both ends attest the importance of scent in canid communication. Checking identity, social and reproductive status through smelling glandular secretions is the primary function of the canid greeting ceremony. Glands in the feet automatically mark the route taken by each individual. Territories are defined by urinating; urine and vaginal secretions advertise the onset of estrus. Canids urine-test but without grimacing.

SOUND   Canids have the most elaborate calls of all carnivores. Distance calls, as usual, differ most between species, whereas short-range calls may be very similar.
Distance signals   Advertise territorial status, contact family members.

- Howling   Probably evolved from barking through fusion of rhythmic barks into continuous series of sound. Howling often begins with a series of yips. Howling sessions strengthen family and pack bonds.

- Barking   Universal canid warning signal. Differences in frequency, duration, rhythm, amplitude, and tonal quality not only identify species, but also the individual, its sex, and emotional state.

Short-range calls   Whining, growling, snarling, yelping, and luring call. Repertories of social canids most elaborate, featuring graded (variable) signals and combinations of different calls—e.g., submissive whining alternating with aggressive growling.

- Whining   Infantile call that elicits parental care, also used by adults to reduce social distance, express submission during aggressive encounters, courtship, and greeting.
- Cackling   Sound of extreme fear, emitted by jackals, foxes.
- Luring call   Faint, rhythmic call used to summon pups from den and during courtship.

Table 27.1. *DOG FAMILY BEHAVIOR GUIDE*
Expect to see and hear ➤ Usual context and meaning

Territorial Advertising

SCENT-MARKING

♀ urinating posture when marking low object. Uprights marked by backing up, also with raised hind leg. ♂ ♂ all lift hind leg like dogs. Marking is often followed by raking the ground while growling with raised hackles. ➤ Urine is the main form of scent marking. Couples advertise territorial status by marking in tandem, especially jackals, along territorial boundaries. Landmarks along regular paths are checked and marked by all passersby.

Handstand marking. ➤ Performed occasionally by wild dog and golden jackal.

CALLING
Barking. ➤ Bat-eared fox.

Howling. ➤ Jackals. During evening chorus, howling spreads from family to family.

Aggression

OFFENSIVE THREAT

Facial expression: mouth puckered, closed or slightly open, eyes wide, staring, ears pricked.

Posture and movements: body rigid, stiff-legged walk, hackles raised, back bowed, tail horizontal or vertical, stiff (wild dog) or lashed side to side (jackals), ± growling or snarling (golden jackal).

T-formation: Animal forming base of T may press against opponent's shoulder, stand up with forefeet propped on adversary's shoulder, and hip-slam or grab scruff, starting fight if other fails to yield. ➤ Aggressive interaction when dominance disputed (features also in pair formation).

Aggression *continued*

DEFENSIVE THREAT

Mixture of fear and aggression displayed by animal wanting to withdraw but prepared to defend itself if attacked. Aggressive and fearful elements combined or alternating.

Facial expression: lips retracted in snarl, teeth bared, ears flattened, eyes narrowed; alternately growls and whines; if pressed, snaps viciously but at empty air.

Posture: crouching, head low and muzzle raised, hair bristling, back bowed.

FIGHTING

Generally over status and rarely serious, ending as soon as one gives in.

Shoulder- and hip-slamming; kick with foreleg or hind leg (see Fig. 27.3); jaw or cheek wrestling, biting scruff.

Rearing and biting.

Defensive tactic: flourishing tail in opponent's face.

Submission

Looking away. ➤ Opposite of aggressive stare; avoidance of eye contact.

Raising a foreleg, turning head up, and flashing white chest; showing tongue. ➤ Raising foreleg and turning head up are intention movements to roll over. Showing white underside is submissive, tongue showing is licking-intention movement. Dominant may also look away and lick lips to reassure subordinate.

Submissive attitude: lips retracted in fear grimace, eyes narrowed, head turned away, ears flattened or spread sideways; crouching, tail between legs or on one side wagging weakly, hackles lowered. ➤ Behaviors opposite of aggressive.

Active submission (wild dog): inferior approaches superior in submissive attitude, licks its muzzle, and pokes corners of mouth, often whining. ➤ Ritualized begging, derived from juvenile food begging and possibly nursing (nuzzling, licking teats). Superior responds to overly persistent begging by seizing inferior's muzzle.

Passive submission: rolling on side and back, hind leg raised to expose groin. Immature individual may even dribble urine. ➤ Behavior derived from response of young puppies when nosed or licked in groin area to stimulate excretion.

Sociable Behavior

Mutual sniffing: whenever canids meet; first nose, mouth, cheeks, then anal and genital area. ➤ Self-confident animal raises tail to allow anal sniffing; one that keeps tail lowered, damping scent, shows timidity and inferiority.

Greeting ceremony: subdominant pokes and licks mouth corners of dominant, in the manner of a juvenile begging adult to disgorge food. Accompanied by whining and other juvenile behavior. ➤ Similar to active submission. Derived from ritualized begging. Promotes friendly relations between family or pack members, reaffirms rank order. Inferior becomes more actively submissive if superior reacts aggressively (see under Aggression).

Social grooming: nibble grooming, licking of head and neck. ➤ Between couples, mother and pups, littermates. Important in social and pair bonding.

Lying in contact. ➤ Mother and offspring, couples, pack members.

Contact and other social calls: barking, howling. ➤ To mate or group. Warning barks, howling in chorus.

Courtship

ENGAGEMENT PERIOD

Forming or renewing pair bond. Based largely on observations of golden jackal and probably applicable at least to other jackals.

Joint patrolling and scent-marking territory.

Displays of dominance and aggression, featuring T-formations, alternating with social grooming, infantile behavior (whimpering), and sexual behavior (licking genitals). ♀ holds tail out and angled to side, exposing distinctive genital pattern developed during mating season.

MATING STAGE

Lasting up to a week.

♂ follows ♀ closely, continually smelling and licking her swollen, bloody vulva, attempting to mount by clasping her with his forelegs and thrusting.

Copulatory tie of variable duration (minimum c. 4 min.).

POSTESTRUS

Renewed scent-marking and T-formations; couple stays further apart, sometimes going separate ways.

♀ often approaches ♂ submissively and performs the greeting ceremony; he responds by disgorging meat. ➤ Dress rehearsal for the ♂ role of feeding mate caring for newborn in den.

Parents, Helpers, and Offspring

Infants carried by nape, back skin, or head (wild dog). ➤ Mother readily changes cubs' hiding place if much disturbed.

One or more adults babysits pups at den, harasses hyenas or other predators that come near.

Adults arriving at den are surrounded by pups, which beg (lick, poke mouth, whine) until meat is disgorged. ➤ Dominant pups take precedence.

Play

Clumsy chewing, rolling, tail-biting (early play), progressing to tossing, chasing, pouncing, chewing, and tearing at toys; to stalking, chasing, and play fighting, leading to real fighting for dominance.

Play face: lips drawn back, open-mouthed grin, ears ± erect, eyes partially closed, slanted. ➤ Play face of less expressive canids (foxes, black-backed jackal) may be mistaken for defensive threat. Playful mood is recognizable by relaxed look and manner.

Play invitation: panting with tongue out; exaggerated looking away, violent head-shaking.

Play bow: lowering forequarters with rear and tail elevated, accompanied by whining and barking.

Response to Competitors/Predators

Offensive and defensive threats.

Cooperative attack, concentrated at rear end.

Associated calls: barking, growling.

BAT-EARED FOX, *Otocyon megalotis*

Figure 27.1. Bat-eared fox in alert posture.

WHAT IT IS A pale fox with enormous ears and robber's mask. Hindquarters rounded, more developed than forequarters; forefeet equipped with 0.8 inch (20 cm) claws adapted for digging. ♂ ♀ wt 7–11.9 lb (3.2–5.4 kg), ht c. 12 in (30 cm). *Head:* broad forehead and pointed snout; *Teeth:* 46 to 50, small, adapted for crunching insects; well-developed canines. *Color:* grizzled, with dark eye mask, muzzle, ear backs, lower limbs upper tail and tip; underparts, hair inside ears, and forehead band white to buff; newborns have sparse gray underfur, get adult coat by 4 to 5 weeks. *Teats:* 4.

WHERE IT LIVES Somali-Masai Arid Zone from Red Sea to central Tanzania and South West Arid Zone of southern Africa. Distribution matches that of the harvester termite, *Hodotermes mossambicus.*

GOOD PLACES TO SEE IT At normal or high density, often seen in parks with short-grass plains in low-rainfall areas: Masai Mara and Samburu-Isiolo NR, Amboseli NP, Kenya; Ngorongoro Crater and Serengeti NP, Tanzania; Nxai Pan and Savuti Pan, Chobe NP, Botswana; Kalahari-Gemsbok NP, South Africa; Etosha and Namib-Naukluft NP, Namibia.

ECOLOGY Occurs in light acacia woodland and plains, especially short grassland with extensive bare ground on volcanic, calcareous, or sandy soils—conditions preferred by the harvester termite, which cuts and collects dried grass night and day, thereby creating bare ground. Next in importance to this termite are adult and larval beetles, followed by grasshoppers, scorpions, vertebrates (small rodents and lizards), fruits, spiders, and millipedes. Diet varies seasonally and geographically, but insects encountered on the surface predominate during rains; foxes dig for other prey during dry season. Serengeti foxes eat eggs and young of ground-nesting birds; in neighboring Masai Mara NR, safari ants and a different kind of termite (*Odontotermes*) are important dry-season food.

ACTIVITY ● (○) 85% of activity at night. After hottest hours pass, foxes emerge from dens and thickets c. 4:30 or 5 PM and rest in open until dark. Activity begins with social grooming and play, after which foxes forage intensively until midnight, rest or alternately rest and forage from 1 to 4 AM, then forage again until dawn. Back at den, they bask and socialize until growing heat sends them to day beds. In cool weather, daytime activity increases; foxes of southern Kalahari are mainly diurnal in winter when freezing nighttime temperatures keep insects underground.

SOCIAL/MATING SYSTEM   ⚇   ⚇   Normally seen in pairs
or family groups, couples social-groom frequently and play together; sleep in same den, forage and rest together, often in contact, help and protect one another against enemies. Home ranges average 195 acres (79 ha) in Serengeti NP and 872 acres (353 ha) in adjacent Masai Mara NR.

Patches teeming with harvester termites and other insects are ephemeral, depending on rainfall, movements of large grazers, and other variables. Home ranges of bat-eared foxes have to change accordingly. Before each breeding season, couples prospect for the most productive foraging areas with nearby denning sites. Rich patches carry as many as 72 foxes/mi^2 (28/km^2), the highest density known for any canid; 1.3 to 8/mi^2 (3.4–21/km^2) is more typical. Home ranges overlap and dens are often clustered; families foraging on common ground mingle with little hostility.

Instances of a male living with 2 females are uncommon but recurrent. In one trio, the females (presumably mother and daughter) had 5 pups that they cross-suckled and reared together.

FORAGING/PREDATORY BEHAVIOR   Foxes must forage many
hours to fill up on termites and other invertebrate prey, using different techniques according to the quarry involved. Eating harvester termites is as simple as licking them up (see aardwolf). In contrast, a fox makes acrobatic leaps and midair turns to snap up grasshoppers and flying termites; catches lizards, gerbils, and birds with a sudden dash; and pounces on mice in the usual canid manner. Using bat ears like twin-dish antennae, it detects faint stirrings and pinpoints position of dung beetle larvae 6 in to a foot (15–30 cm) underground, then quickly digs them out through the hardest soil. Although foraging family keeps same direction and pace, each fox operates independently and only shares food with dependent young. Approach to a digging or eating individual is discouraged with growls and flattened ears.

REPRODUCTION   Once a year, beginning of rainy season; 3 to 6/litter;
gestation 60 to 70 days. First estrus at c. 18 months.

OFFSPRING AND PARENTAL CARE   When cubs emerge from
den at c. 17 days, litters average less than 3, indicating that 1 or 2 young often die in first 3 weeks. Infanticide is one possibility. More likely explanation (suggested by pronounced differences in birth weights that persist at 1 month):

large litters normally contain runts, which survive only in good years, enabling bat-eared foxes to capitalize on good conditions.

Cubs are rarely fed anything but milk, aside from occasional vertebrate prey parents kill and bring to den. Unlike other canids, this one rarely regurgitates food, probably because insect remains contain too much indigestible matter to be nutritious. But paternal babysitting and guarding allow mother to forage more and sustain milk production to c. 15 weeks, and cubs begin eating insects and foraging with parents relatively early. To offset increased predation risks, bat-eared foxes are particularly alert to danger and fiercely protective of their offspring. Young also reach adult size earlier than most canids, at 4 to 6 months.

PREDATORS   A whole host, including large eagles; even small eagles can take cubs. Breeding foxes attack jackals and even hyenas that prowl near den. Exceptional ability to zig-zag and change course while running full tilt toward the nearest hole helps this fox elude pursuers. The tail functions as a rudder, decoy, and shield that is flourished in the predator's face.

HOW IT COMMUNICATES

SOUND   Repertoire includes 9 different calls, 7 of which are used within the family group, audible only at close range.

Who-who   Birdlike whining or mewing; elicits following by cubs or mate.

Chirping or sibilant whistling   Distinctive, birdlike call given by cubs, in response to *who-who* and when separated or deserted; variable intensity (to loud and piercing). A long quavering version is adult contact call, given when mates become separated.

Woof, growl, hiss   Soft warning calls that send cubs running for cover.

Short whistle   Uttered during social-grooming, by either partner.

Growl, snarl, hiss   Defensive threat; rattling growl heard in play.

Snarl, yap   High-pitched sounds emitted during fights, also in play.

Scream/distress cry   The loudest call, given by hurt animal.

Short bark   Loud call of alarm, given when surprised or threatened.

High-pitched bark   Loud rallying call that brings mate and family to rescue, as when predator approaches den.

Table 27.2. *DIFFERENCES IN BAT-EARED FOX BEHAVIOR*
Expect to see and hear ➤ Usual context and meaning

Scent-marking

Infrequent; primary function may be in establishing pair bonds, as marking frequency is highest during period of pair formation, in tandem by couples unaccompanied by young.

Urine projected onto grass tufts and low bushes, rarely against trees, without raking ground before or afterward.

Scent-marking *continued*

Tandem marking: ♂ follows and covers ♀'s urine, after first smelling it.

Aggression

Offensive threat: tail arched, ears cocked, but no mouth pucker.
➤ Degree of tail-arching increases with aggressiveness.

Defensive threat: tail arched, head down, and ears pulled back.

Submission

Lying apparently asleep in proximity to vehicle with ears flattened.
➤ Not a sign of nonchalance but more likely of mild fear, an effort to avoid attention, like looking away in response to direct stare.

Sociable Behavior

Greeting ceremony. ➤ Uncommon—reflecting rarity of regurgitating food.

Simultaneous nibble-grooming (rarely licking). ➤ The predominant social activity between mates and parents and offspring.

Contact: pairs and family members often lie touching and huddle together for warmth on cold days.

GOLDEN JACKAL, *Canis aureus*

Figure 27.2. Golden jackals in howling session.

WHAT IT IS   The common jackal of the East African plains. Looks like a small coyote. ♂♀ wt 15–33 lb (7–15 kg), ht 15–20 in (38–50 cm). *Head*: long, pointed snout and big, pointed ears. *Color*: variable geographically, seasonally, and individually; usually golden to silver-gray; limbs redder than torso; hackles black-tipped in adult, fading in dry season; tail tip, nose, and mouth typically black; underparts and head markings white; eyes amber-colored; newborns nearly black. *Teats*: 4.

WHERE IT LIVES   From central Tanzania north and west through Somali-Masai and Sudanese Arid Zone, the Sahara, and North Africa. Same species as Asiatic jackal.

GOOD PLACES TO SEE IT   East African plains; notably Masai Mara GR, Amboseli, NP, Kenya; Serengeti NP, Ngorongoro Crater, Tanzania.

ECOLOGY   More desert-adapted than other jackals, inhabits waterless regions. Often the most numerous carnivore on the East African plains, a relatively luxurious habitat for this species. Eats carrion, the kills of other predators, and garbage whenever available, but primarily a predator on invertebrates and vertebrates up to the size of topi calves; also eats figs, desert dates, other fruits, and berries.

ACTIVITY   ●/○ Seen resting in the open, hunting and scavenging by day where fully protected, especially early morning and late afternoon. Often predominant among daytime scavengers, whereas black-backed jackals predominate at night kills.

SOCIAL/MATING SYSTEM   (♀○♠♀○♂)   Golden jackals of the Serengeti Plains defend territories of 518 to 1000 acres (200–400 ha) year after year. The living is easy during the rains, with even a food surplus, but so hard in the dry season that jackals dig up beetle larvae, spiders, solifugids, and ants to get by, with an occasional lizard, bird, or gazelle fawn. Yet couples leave their property only when tempted by a nearby large kill or to drink.

When food and golden jackals are both plentiful, young of both sexes often stay home up to c. 20 months instead of dispersing at 1 year. They gain a safe haven from which to prospect for mates and openings in the network of pair territories. Meanwhile they help their parents bring up the next litter— an altruistic act if they were unrelated or shared only one parent, but genetically self-serving when invested in full siblings. Helping also gives helpers valuable parenting experience.

Some Serengeti youngsters 6 months or older leave home during the dry season and sojourn in the nearest woodland—substandard golden-jackal habitat—and accordingly undefended. They return with the rains and food abundance, at the beginning of the whelping season.

FORAGING/PREDATORY BEHAVIOR   Under natural conditions, golden jackals obtain c. 80% of their food through predation. They forage for insects in the manner of bat-eared foxes: pouncing on or leaping up and grabbing them, nosing and scratching in dung to uncover dung beetles, excavating dung balls housing fat beetle larvae. They snap up small lizards and snakes, jump on concealed rodents, and forage beneath trees containing bird nests or ripe fruit. Large prey regularly hunted includes birds up to flamingo size, hares, and gazelle fawns. Jackals systematically search near maternal herds for concealed fawns; pairs often get fawns they find, despite team defense of gazelle mothers, which often thwarts single hunters. Animals their own size or larger are rarely killed unless debilitated, or when parents and grown young hunt occasionally as a pack.

RELATIONS WITH OTHER PREDATORS AND SCAVENGERS   Being strictly territorial, goldens are free to scavenge only on their own property, where they compete very aggressively with other scavengers, especially intruders of their own kind and black-backed jackals. Dominant over vultures, 1 jackal can keep dozens at bay. Though wary of lions, they steal meat from wild dogs and discourage reclaiming efforts with ferocious threat displays. Greater agility often enables them to rob feeding hyenas. One gambit of golden pairs is to move in from both sides until the aggravated hyena snaps at one; the other then darts in and snatches part or all of its food. As hyenas also rob jackals, pairs regularly dismember kills and eat separately some distance apart. If a hyena takes one's portion, they share the remainder.

Jackals regularly cache surplus food in holes or bushes, usually retrieving it within 12 hours. But the best insurance against loss is storing food in the stomach—which is why jackals bolt meat as quickly as possible, with minimum chewing.

REPRODUCTION   Annually during rainy season; up to 9 pups/litter; gestation c. 60 days. Puberty at 11 months (both sexes); minimum whelping age 1.5 years.

OFFSPRING AND PARENTAL/HELPER CARE   For first 3 weeks after whelping, 90% of mother's time is devoted to pups; suckling them c. 7 times in 24-hour day the first month. Pups' eyes open at 10 days; they begin exploring outside at 2 weeks if grownups present; start eating insects and disgorged meat and begin acquiring a golden coat at 1 month. After weaning (2–4 months), pups become increasingly adventurous, going 50 yd from den, resting in open, trying to follow parents or siblings setting off foraging. Sibling rivalry increases as juveniles compete for dominance. Rank order is settled by 6 months; biggest, toughest sibling gets to monopolize large food items like a gazelle leg—even to bury what it can't eat.

Mother brings more food to pups than either father or helpers. However, food she receives from them reduces lactation stress, and babysitting helpers free parents to hunt together, thereby increasing their ability to kill larger game and defend it against competitors. Pups at dens without helpers are left alone over 25% of the time, compared to only 6% of the time for those with helpers. Flooding of dens is a major cause of pup mortality.

PREDATORS   Larger carnivores; eagles and snakes prey on pups.

Table 27.3. *DIFFERENCES IN GOLDEN JACKAL BEHAVIOR*
    Expect to see and hear ➤ *Usual context and meaning*

Territorial Advertising

Contact call: a high, keening wail. ➤ Very different from associated black-backed jackal.

Aggression

Offensive threat: golden lifts lip to show canine teeth. ➤ The only jackal with this much facial mobility.

Sociable Behavior

Family members resting closer together, social grooming more, siblings fighting less, parents less assertive and quicker to intervene when pups do get into fights. ➤ Compared to other jackals.

Parents, Helpers, and Offspring

Babysitting, but not provisioning, by helpers.

BLACK-BACKED OR SILVER-BACKED JACKAL, *Canis mesomelas*

Figure 27.3. Black-backed jackal kicking opponent it downed with hip-slam.

WHAT IT IS   Handsome jackal with distinct saddle of black and silver hair; also known as silver-backed jackal. ♂♀ wt 15–30 lb (7–13.5 kg), ht 15–19 in (38–48 cm). *Color:* reddish brown to tan; redder on flanks and legs; saddle of mixed black and white hairs; black-tipped tail; underparts and throat white; young lead-colored with faint markings. Similar to other jackals apart from coloration. *Teats:* 6 or 8.

WHERE IT LIVES   Somali-Masai Arid Zone of northeastern Africa and the South West Arid Zone of southern Africa.

GOOD PLACES TO SEE IT   Most parks and reserves in east and southern Africa within its range.

ECOLOGY   In overlap zone with golden jackal, black-back prefers *Acacia/Commiphora* woodland, while the golden dominates the plains; they meet and compete along the woodland edge; in Ngorongoro Crater these 2 also overlap with side-striped jackals. In South West Arid Zone, where *mesomelas* is the only jackal, its range includes open habitats dominated by golden jackals in East Africa.

Diet is similar to golden jackal's (see account). Possibly black-back preys more on mammals, but the only consistent differences are in the species that occur in different types of habitat. In Serengeti woodland zone, the most important item on black-back's menu is a grass rat so abundant in years of good rainfall and dense grass cover that a square mile can carry 83,000 (32,083/km^2). In South Africa, black-backs take unguarded lambs and sometimes adult sheep, so they are gassed and poisoned just like coyotes in the western United States.

ACTIVITY   ● (○) Mainly nocturnal but often active by day.

SOCIAL/MATING SYSTEM   (♀○♂♀○♂) Like golden jackal with minor differences. Helpers are seemingly more important for pup survival, yet comparatively few offspring stick around and help; pup survival is consequently lower. The helper deficit could stem from more aggressive social relations of black-back families, which promote earlier independence and dispersal.

PAIR BOND   The pair bond lasts until one mate dies. Black-back couples do everything together, except when one has to babysit: marking and defending the territory, hunting, sharing food, calling and answering when separated, howling in chorus with their cubs, and social grooming.

Territories of Serengeti jackals average about 1 mi^2 (2.5 km^2) and are permanent but subject to change, becoming smaller during periods of food abundance as jackal numbers increase. There are always more jackals than territories anyway, and it takes both members of a pair, assisted by helpers if present, to hold property against constant probing by home-hunting couples. If 1 mate dies or is incapacitated, the news spreads as soon as a couple stops urine-marking together. The remaining jackal, along with any dependent offspring, is either killed or driven away in short order and the territory comes under new ownership.

Even with 2 defenders, black-backs are unable to keep out other jackals when a large animal dies on their land, as up to 6 other pairs converge on the carcass.

FORAGING/PREDATORY BEHAVIOR   Black-backs employ the same techniques as golden jackals (see account). Black-backs scavenge in larger numbers and more aggressively than goldens at lion and hyena kills. Perhaps greater competition between black-backs themselves leads them to take more liberties with the big predators, darting in to steal tidbits practically within reach of a lion's paw or a hyena's jaws. The 2 jackals also compete with one another at kills, apparently on equal terms.

REPRODUCTION   Annually in dry season; 3 or 4 (up to 6) pups/litter; gestation 60 to 65 days. Both sexes begin breeding at 1 to 2 years.

OFFSPRING AND PARENTAL/HELPER CARE   Development and care of the young as in golden jackal. Dens are often changed every 2 or 3 weeks, always on mother's initiative. Pups even a few weeks old are not carried but lured by the mother, which whimpers a promise to suckle them but stalls until they reach the new den.

Because black-backs often whelp when food is scarce, helpers can make a big difference. Average number of offspring reared to independence (14 weeks) by unassisted Serengeti parents was only 1.3; parents with 1 helper reared 3.3 cubs, and 2 families that had 2 helpers both raised 4˙cubs.

Unassisted parents have to work much harder to feed pups and themselves, meanwhile leaving den unguarded 40% of the time. Helpers provide up to 30% of disgorged food and litters with even 1 helper are alone only 15% of the time. Helpers spend 60% of their time at the den, enabling pups to spend much more time outside, socializing, playing, and learning. Meanwhile, parents can go hunting together and capture more large prey.

From 3.5 months on, pups become increasingly independent, foraging a widening area, learning to hunt and the limits of the territory, sleeping under bushes rather than in den. By 6 months they are fairly proficient hunters, but parents and older siblings continue to feed, groom, and play with them. In late afternoon, after resting separately all day, the family assembles in response to yipping calls that often develop into a group howling session. Between 6 and 8 months youngsters become self-sufficient and most leave the territory.

PREDATORS   Leopards, which have a well-known preference for dog meat, may be the ranking predator of adult jackals; eagles are constant danger to young pups around the den.

Table 27.4. DIFFERENCES IN BLACK-BACKED JACKAL BEHAVIOR
Expect to see and hear ➤ Usual context and meaning

Territorial Advertising

Urine-marking in tandem, ♂ first. ➤ Marking rate of patrolling pair is twice rate of single jackal.

Contact call: an abrupt, raucous yell followed by several shorter yelps. ➤ The Kiswahili name, *bweya*, is based on this call. In southern Africa, black-backs wail more like goldens.

Aggression

Defensive threat of jackal keeping vultures off kill. Back less humped than golden jackal's; tail whips from side to side. Jackal snaps, lunges, and leaps at any vulture that tries to land on the carcass.

Sociable Behavior

Siblings more quarrelsome, maintaining wider individual distance. Dominance asserted more tyrannically among siblings and by parents over same-sex offspring. ➤ Black-backs are more aggressive and less sociable than goldens.

SIDE-STRIPED JACKAL, *Canis adustus*

Figure 27.4. Side-striped jackal chased by female Grant's gazelle whose fawn the jackal is trying to catch.

WHAT IT IS   Jackal with a white-tipped tail, the only jackal in the broad-leaved wooded savannas. Blunter snout and smaller, rounder ears than other jackals. ♂ wt 16–26 lb (7.3–12 kg), ht 15 in (38 cm); ♀ wt 16–22 lb (7.3–10 kg), ht same as ♂. Zimbabwe population; up to 31 lb and 20 in (14 kg, 50 cm) in East Africa. *Color:* appears light gray or tan at a distance, with subdued markings except conspicuous white tip of dark tail; side stripe in some animals: white or off-white line edged with black from shoulder to tail base; underparts pale. *Teats:* 4.

WHERE IT LIVES   Broad-leaved deciduous woodlands of the Northern and Southern Savanna; bordering acacia savanna and forest-savanna mosaic to edge of equatorial rainforest.

GOOD PLACES TO SEE IT   Occurs at low density in most parks from central Tanzania to southern Zimbabwe. Two likely spots: the Ishasha Plain in Uganda's Queen Elizabeth NP; and along the Khwai River outside Moremi GR, Botswana.

ECOLOGY   Frequents a variety of wooded habitats; also bush, grassland, abandoned cultivation, and marshes offering good cover, up to 8900 ft (2700 m). Jackals trapped in Zimbabwe farmlands had eaten mainly wild fruits, small mammals, including mice, rats, and hares, and insects such as grasshoppers, crickets, beetles, and termites. Only 11% of stomachs contained carrion, reflecting the low density of wild herbivores in *miombo* woodland.

ACTIVITY   ● Seen occasionally in daytime; nightly activity peaks early and from before to 1 or 2 hours after dawn.

SOCIAL/MATING SYSTEM   (image) This jackal, still unstudied, is known to occur in pairs and family units of up to 6. Gatherings of 8 to 12 have been seen scavenging kills and offal around villages. Whether grown offspring help rear the next litter is unclear.

FORAGING/PREDATORY BEHAVIOR   Considered less predatory than other jackals but probably no clear differences in type of prey or hunting methods where equal opportunities exist. (See golden jackal, Ecology and Foraging/Predatory Behavior.) A free-ranging pet dug up and ate earthworms, millipedes, and crickets; chased down and jumped for grasshoppers and winged termites; and tried to catch small birds by dashing at them. An autopsied jackal had consumed over 3 lb (1.5 kg) of safari ant larvae mixed with adults—hundreds more were attached to its fur, mouth, and feet.

REPRODUCTION   Seasonally, just before or during rains; 3 to 6/litter; gestation 57 to 70 days.

OFFSPRING AND PARENTAL CARE   Termite mounds, aardvark holes, and hillsides are preferred den sites. Using preexisting dens, mother may dig a second tunnel off the nest chamber to serve as emergency exit. In 2 different excavated dens, the chamber was located 2 to 3 ft (0.75–1 m) below the surface and 6 to 9 ft (2–3 m) from the entrance. Development of the young and parental care appear very close to that of the other jackals (see golden and black-back accounts).

Table 27.5. *DIFFERENCES IN SIDE-STRIPED JACKAL BEHAVIOR*
Expect to see and hear ➤ *Usual context and meaning*

Territorial Advertising

DISTANCE CALLS

An explosive *bwaa*, usually uttered at night by lone animal.

Owl-like hooting. ➤ Side-striped jackal version of howling.

WILD DOG OR CAPE HUNTING DOG,
Lycaon pictus[en]

Figure 27.5. Wild dogs in stalking attitude.

WHAT IT IS A tricolored dog that lives in packs. A lean, long-legged canid built for speed and endurance. ♂♀ wt (East African dogs) 44-55 lb (20-25 kg), ht 24-30 in (60-75 cm). *Head*: blunt muzzle, huge rounded ears, dark eyes. *Coat*: thin, no underfur. *Color*: black, white, and tan, individually and geographically variable, only white tail tip and facial pattern (black muzzle, tan forehead) consistently present. Natal color black and white; tan patches start developing from black areas in second month. Dogs of the *Miombo* Woodland Zone and southern Africa are lighter, with more extensive white and tan patches, and bigger (up to 66 lb [30 kg]). *Scent glands*: a strong smell is characteristic of the species (see Family Traits).

WHERE IT LIVES Former range included Northern and Southern Savanna and adjacent arid zones. Persecution, disease, and reduction of wildlife habitats and populations have caused an alarming decline in wild dog numbers, raising fears that one of Africa's most interesting animals could soon become extinct.

The most carnivorous and one of the most specialized canids, as a pack hunter of antelopes. Preys mainly on the most abundant species between 30 and 100 lb (14-45 kg), but hunts game as small as hares and as large as adult zebras. Drinks regularly when water available but can go without for long intervals.

GOOD PLACES TO SEE IT   The only sure way to see wild dogs is while they are denning. Parks/reserves where wild dogs often seen: Serengeti and Mikumi NP, Tanzania; Masai Mara NR, Kenya; Hwange NP, Zimbabwe; Moremi GR, Botswana; Kruger NP, South Africa.

ECOLOGY   Known in East Africa as a plains animal, but ranges through all types of savanna, bush, and montane habitats: A climber met 5 wild dogs atop Kilimanjaro, at nearly 20,000 ft (6345 m)!

ACTIVITY   O As diurnal as cheetah, but often travels and hunts by moonlight. Where game is abundant, wild dogs spend only an hour or so in early morning and late afternoon hunting and eating, during which pack travels on average 6 mi (10 km). But where game is scarce, dogs routinely traverse home range in 2 to 3 days, trotting along at 6 to 7 mph (9–11 kph) and traveling 25 mi/day (40 km/day). One Serengeti pack that denned on the plains after game had migrated away made round trips of 43 mi/day (70 km/day) until the pups starved.

SOCIAL/MATING SYSTEM   By rights, the wild dog should be a very successful species. It is the most successful hunter of the most abundant large mammals and lives in large packs dedicated to rearing the largest litters of any carnivore (up to 18 pups). And yet it is in decline all over Africa, with maybe only a few thousand left in its whole vast range. No one knows why, although disease is the main suspect: wild dogs are highly susceptible to canine diseases, especially distemper and rabies, which wipe out whole packs. The clumped distribution of wild dogs and the fact that even widely separated packs make contact through transfers make them unusually vulnerable to epidemics.

Packs of 20 are common, up to 40 and possibly even 60 dogs have been counted, but the average (in Serengeti and Kruger NPs) is about 10. In the 1970s, when there were still a dozen or more packs vs. 2 or 3 nowadays, Serengeti packs typically numbered 6 adults, including 4 males and 2 females. A preponderance of males and emigration of female rather than male offspring are peculiarities of this species. However, in litters with 3 or more brothers, males also tend to emigrate and to disperse much further than females. If and when a male group meets up with a female, a new pack is formed; large packs also tend to split and a new nucleus pack of several males and 1 or 2 females can also form this way. As a rule, though, packs consist of closely related males and females unrelated to them.

Males and females have separate rank orders, headed by the breeding pair. One or the other is usually but not invariably the leader. Subordinate females have to emigrate if they are to reproduce. Daughters leave their natal pack by 2.5 years. Their chances of surviving are best when several sisters go together. However, once they meet up with a group of males, one of the females pairs up with one of the males, and the other sisters are stymied until they transfer again. Sometimes a subordinate challenges the alpha and manages to win, but this happens more often with males than females. Alpha females stay in the pack they first join and keep breeding for up to 8 years.

THE IMPORTANCE OF BEGGING Although dominance is despotic enough to inhibit breeding in subordinate pack members, overt aggression is so rare that the existence of a rank order was overlooked by early observers. Indeed, their normally close and peaceable relations set wild dogs apart from lions, spotted hyenas, or wolves. Peace and good will are maintained through ritualized begging, repeated in the canine greeting ceremony whenever pack members become active or meet after a separation, and by begging instead of fighting over food. In effect, pack members compete to be more submissive, using the technique that all young canids employ to make grownups stand and disgorge (see Sociable Behavior in Tables 27.1, 27.6). It continues to work for juvenile wild dogs after leaving the den; aggressive begging disguised as active submission enables them to displace adults at kills until they are a year old. Inducted then into the adult rank hierarchy, they finally lose their privileged dependent status.

HOME RANGES   Home ranges of 580 to 770 mi^2 (1500–2000 km^2) for the best-known Serengeti packs are far too big to be defended. The ranges of different packs overlap by anywhere from 10 to 80%. The area around a den is defended, though, and meetings between packs elsewhere are usually hostile—the larger pack chases the smaller one.

FORAGING/PREDATORY BEHAVIOR   Wild dogs catch some 85% of the animals they actually chase. Even their conspicuous color testifies to their hunting prowess: here is a predator that doesn't need to sneak up on its prey or hide from bigger predators. Speed and endurance, leadership and close cooperation are the keys to its success. Tactics vary to suit terrain and species hunted, but usually the leader selects the quarry and runs it down; the rest follow and show discipline by ignoring antelopes that run across their path. Members of large packs, though, often split during a chase and kill several different antelopes.

Top speed of about 40 mph (64 kph) is slower than a gazelle's best pace, but dogs can run 35 mph for at least 2 mi (3.2 km) and 30 mph (48 kph) for over 3 mi (5 km). Most antelopes are exhausted after a chase of 1 or 2 mi; if dogs can keep their quarry in sight, they usually overtake it within 3 mi or else give up. Often an antelope will run in a big circle or start zigzagging as it is overtaken, enabling dogs following the leader to cut across and either intercept or get closer to the quarry. The first dog to overtake prey the size of a Thomson's gazelle or wildebeest calf simply bowls it over or grabs a hind leg and throws it to the ground. Within a minute it is dismembered as other dogs grab hold and yank in opposite directions. They are less efficient at killing large prey like yearling wildebeests or zebras: while one holds it, other pack members "worry" it from the rear until it goes down, then proceed to pull out its internal organs. Spotted hyenas kill the same way, but wild dogs are only ⅓ their weight. Yet victims hardly ever put up a fight; already exhausted when caught, apparently they go into deep shock, a state in which they seem to feel no pain.

Wild dogs are selective hunters; the leader chooses the most vulnerable quarry. A hunting pack tests herds by running at them and scattering them. Injured, sick, or very young animals that run slower than their companions are quickly singled out by the leader. Wild dogs also try to get close before starting a chase by walking slowly toward a game concentration, the leader in the "stalking attitude" (see Fig. 27.5). Or, on rolling plains, a pack runs full speed over a rise, hoping to find and surprise antelopes on the other side.

REPRODUCTION   Year-round, with a birth peak during or after the rainy season. Average of 26 litters: 10 pups; gestation 69 to 73 days; interval between litters 12 to 14 months. Earliest whelping at 22 months; youngest mating by a male, 1.75 years; oldest, 7.5 years. Few wild dogs live beyond 10 years.

OFFSPRING AND COMMUNAL CARE   Pack may return yearly to favored denning area, sometimes to a particular den. Expectant mother chooses and does a bit of preparatory digging. (Note: the sight of wild dogs digging is not a reliable sign denning is imminent—dogs regularly prepare shady resting places by digging in holes or embankments.)

For 3 or 4 weeks after whelping, before pups emerge and begin taking solid food, mother stays at den while the pack goes hunting and often will not allow other dogs near the burrow entrance. In rare cases where a second female has whelped at the same time, the alpha bitch prevented her from attending her own offspring and/or killed the pups. When one wild dog produces so many pups that a large pack is needed to feed and rear them, such strict reproductive control is necessary.

Pups, weaned as early as 5 weeks, depend on meat disgorged by returning pack members, which also provision mother or babysitters that remain at den. Large packs supply more food and succeed in rearing more young than small packs. In the 1960s, all Serengeti packs that successfully reared young had over 11 adults.

Puppies lose their rotund shape and assume adult conformation beginning at 7 weeks. When pups are 8 to 10 weeks old, the pack abandons the den, after which the youngsters gain most of their food directly from kills. But for many more months they simply trail the pack without joining in chasing or killing. Until these laggards arrive, the adults gorge for all they're worth, then obligingly surrender the remains, with or without coercion.

RELATIONS WITH OTHER PREDATORS   Wild dogs show little fear of other carnivores, although they alarm-bark and move out of the way of lions. Relations with the spotted hyena (see account) are highly competitive because hyenas regularly try to steal their kills. It works when a tag-along hyena manages to arrive right after the pack leader catches its quarry and before other pack members arrive; or when a small pack is confronted by a large crowd of ravenous hyenas. Yet despite the size difference, hyenas are quite defenseless against wild dog mobbing attacks since they do not assist one another; a hyena set upon by several dogs is quickly routed, though rarely seriously hurt.

HOW IT COMMUNICATES

CALLS   Wild dogs have calls different from most canids.

Hoo   Long-distance call, bell-like hoot or coo that carries over a mile; voiced when pack members are separated.

Twittering   Birdlike, intense sound of excitement uttered during prehunt pep rallies, as quarry is overtaken, while competing for food, and while mobbing hyenas.

Deep, gruff bark   Usually one, uttered as an alarm signal.

Whining   Graded call uttered in different situations: plaintive whine of pup in distress; intense whine or squeal of dog attacked by superior; loud, abrupt whine by mother summoning pups from den; prolonged nasal whine of pups begging food.

Ultrasonic calls   Emitted by playing pups.

Table 27.6. *DIFFERENCES IN WILD DOG BEHAVIOR*
Expect to see and hear ➤ Usual context and meaning

Scent-marking

WITH URINE

Alpha ♀ marking around an occupied den, usually squatting with one leg slightly raised.

Handstand marking: ♂ aiming at exact same spot his mate is squat-marking. ➤ Being nonterritorial, wild dogs urine-mark less than most canids. Couples mark in tandem during pair formation and while mating, the ♂ overmarking the ♀'s urine.

Aggression

Offensive threat, with tail raised and ears cocked. ➤ Rare in this species, reserved for subordinate that forgets its place or challenges a superior.

Stalking attitude, with tail low, ears back or cocked. ➤ Posture of lead dog trying to approach game. Sometimes directed at other dogs as prelude to a mobbing action; may have an intimidating effect that reinforces rank dominance.

Submission

 Aggressive begging: 2 dogs holding onto the same meat trying to burrow beneath one another, lips retracted in a toothy grin, ears flattened, forequarters lowered, tails curled up, twittering excitedly. ➤ Competing for food by begging instead of fighting.

Sociable Behavior

Social grooming. ➤ Rare.

Lying in contact. ➤ Wild dogs regularly rest together in heaps, sharing shade and flies on hot days and body heat on cold ones.

 Pep rally: rousing after long rest, dogs rush about performing greeting ceremony, playing, and twittering. ➤ Like an athletic team pumping itself up before a game, pep rally brings pack members into hunting mood. Rally often includes mobbing of presumably low-ranking pack members, in much the same way they kill prey or gang up on hyenas, except biting is inhibited.

Chapter 28
WEASEL/OTTER FAMILY
Mustelidae

SUBFAMILY MUSTELINAE
Striped weasel, *Poecilogale albinucha*
Libyan weasel, *Poecillictis libyca*
Zorilla, *Ictonyx striatus*

SUBFAMILY MELLIVORINAE
Ratel, *Mellivora capensis*

SUBFAMILY LUTRINAE
Spotted-necked otter, *Lutra maculicollis*
Cape clawless otter, *Aonyx capensis*
Congo clawless otter, A. *congica*

WHAT THEY ARE   A diverse family of carnivores with 64 to 67 species (classifications disagree) and 26 genera in 5 subfamilies. Only the 7 listed species occur in sub-Saharan Africa. Mustelids branched off the carnivore main stem some 40 million years ago, in the form of small, long-bodied, short-legged predators resembling weasels, ferrets, and their kind (see Carnivore Family Tree, Part III). Many different forms have evolved since, including skunks, badgers, and otters, the last being among the most specialized carnivores.

FAMILY TRAITS   Five toes on all feet, claws of different shape and length according to use. *Teeth:* 28 to 32, including long, stabbing canines. *Ears:* low-set, round or triangular, closable. *Skin:* very tough and loose in many species, especially thick on neck, the main target during fights. *Genitals:* penis with well-developed bone, opening on belly as in dogs. *Scent glands:* compound anal glands, consisting of different layers and types of secretory cells that empty into a pair of anal sacs: both nauseating liquid, squirted or dribbled in self-defense, and musky secretions employed in scent-marking.

Mustelilds comes in various shapes and sizes, from weasels weighing a few ounces to a 77-lb (35-kg) sea otter; designed for a number of very different life styles. (See Chapter 22, Introducing Carnivores.)

Weasel type   Long, sinuous body and neck with very short legs, tubular head with short, powerful jaws and shearing cheek teeth. Strictly carnivorous, adapted for tracking and running down rodents, rabbits, and other warm-blooded prey (see Introducing Carnivores, Chapter 22).

Otter type   Muscular, streamlined shape, with long body and thick, tapering tail, short legs with or without claws; wide head with powerful jaws and broad molars adapted for crushing shellfish; protuberant, frontally placed eyes adapted for seeing underwater. Designed as predator of fish and other aquatic organisms.

Badger, ratel, wolverine type   Squat, wide body; strong legs (longer in ratel and wolverine, shorter in badgers), feet with long claws; short tail; massive

353

head with powerful jaws and broad molars. Adapted for digging and omnivorous diet.

Skunk type   Relatively short-bodied and long-legged with long digging claws, bushy tail; warning coloration. New World omnivores; zorilla closest African equivalent.

SOCIAL/MATING SYSTEMS OF AFRICAN MUSTELIDS

(♀♂♀)   Solitary/territorial system prevails in mustelid family. Females defend territories including resources needed to rear offspring; fittest males have territories including ranges of 2 or more females (zorilla; Libyan and striped weasels).

(♂♀♂)   Monogamous/territorial. A few mustelids live in monogamous pairs or family groups at least part of the year (ratel, possibly otters).

HOW THEY MOVE   Movements reflect variety of forms, including both swift and slow-moving species. Movements and postures common to the whole family:

- Running   Fastest pace is the jump-run; the back alternately flexes and extends as legs move in pairs; back most bowed in weasel type with very long body and very short legs.

- Swimming   Most mustelids swim well, though not compared to otters.

- Climbing   Most climb well, except otters and badgers.

- Sleeping posture   Side curl, nose to tail.

- Seated postures   Long, low-slung types (weasels, otters) can't sit like dogs or cats, but assume an S-posture (clawless otter) or simply crouch on all fours (spotted-necked otter).

- Alert postures   Low-sit (sitting up on haunches) and high-sit (standing on hind feet with forelegs dangling, braced by tail) postures, as in genets and mongooses.

- Dexterity   From slight (weasels) to nearly human (clawless otter).

REPRODUCTION   Seasonal in most species, with increased testes size and marking behavior during mating peak. Young born in extremely immature state after short gestation: 4 to 5 weeks in weasels to 2 months in otters. Yet most species breed only once a year.

MATING   Coitus of up to 3 hours. Ovulation is induced by copulation in at least some species; no delayed implantation in African mustelids (see Table 28.1).

HOW THEY COMMUNICATE   Sight 2 to 3, scent 1, sound 2.

SIGHT   Only aggressive and submissive displays have been described. Otters are decidedly myopic out of water and weasels are so scent-oriented that they pass close to motionless prey without noticing it, unless they smell it. Black-and-white color patterns that warn potential predators also facilitate visual communication at night.

SCENT Primary channel for nocturnal, solitary animals; used to demarcate territory, advertise reproductive status, identify individuals, and enable young to follow mother.

SOUND Eight different calls known in family. Distance calls apparently rare, except mating calls of some species. Growling, snarling, hissing, screaming, mewing, squeaking, and nest chirping are emitted in one form or another by most species. Smaller mustelids tend to be more vociferous during aggressive interactions.

Table 28.1. *WEASEL FAMILY BEHAVIOR GUIDE*
Expect to see and hear ➤ *Usual context and meaning*

Scent-marking

Scent posts at pathway junctions. ➤ Demarcate territory and also serve as message centers where animals with overlapping ranges or common borders (e.g., otters) leave calling cards.

With anal glands: backing up, anal dragging, or handstanding; technique depending on site. ➤ Similar to techniques of genet/mongoose family (see Table 23.1 and Figs. 23.1 and 24.5).

With feces (otters also dribble urine). Scats deposited on landmarks (sloping boulder, mound, log) along regular passageways. ➤ Scats black, shiny, smelly. Otter and striped weasel scats sticky, can be pasted on steep surface.

Latrines. ➤ Mostly located near dens.

Rolling/musking places: trampled, often bare areas beside water where otters roll and scent-mark. ➤ Otters roll and writhe both when drying off and to impregnate fur with odors—the way other carnivores roll in carrion, feces, etc.

Aggression

OFFENSIVE THREAT

Basic carnivore display, featuring staring, bristling, stiff-legged approach, snakelike weaving of body and head ± growling and other aggressive calls.

DEFENSIVE THREAT

Crouching or standing with bowed back, hair on end, neck raised, teeth bared; backing away hissing, screaming, or humming (ratel). ➤ Most impressive when addressed to other species (see Response to Predators).

Aggression *continued*

Crouching low, head and neck to ground, teeth bared.

Lunge-hiss or scream attack with snapping, neck-biting, followed by immediate retreat. ➤ Defensive nature of attack revealed by fearful calls.

Submission

Presenting neck with head turned away, upon meeting dominant individual. ➤ Spotted-necked otter.

Lying on back and waving paws ± squeaking. ➤ Can also be defensive (clawless otter).

Sociable Behavior

SOCIAL GROOMING

Nibble-grooming. ➤ Common between mother and young; rare between adults.

Lying on back or side before partner. ➤ Soliciting grooming. Black underparts of striped weasel, zorilla, and ratel are displayed in friendly and submissive interactions—opposite of black and white patterns displayed in threat.

Courtship

♂ pursues ♀, grips her neck, and drags her until she stops resisting. ➤ Characteristic of weasel subfamily, including striped weasel; neck grip induces passivity.

♀ in heat may utter enticing or begging calls which attract ♂♂.

COPULATION

Copulatory crouch: lying prone, neck extended, tail deflected. ♂ clasps ♀ and maintains neck grip.

Lying on side during extended copulation.

Parents and Offspring

Infants carried by belly or flank skin or scruff; large juveniles dragged.

Maternal nibble-grooming of offspring.

Nest-chirping of small infants.

Play

Aggressive play, exploratory play (creeping into holes), ambushing, and chasing are most characteristic. ➤ Most mustelids playful only when immature; otters playful as adults.

Playing with objects and prey.

Sliding (otters).

Response to Competitors/Predators

Defensive threat displays (see Aggression). ➤ Species without specialized stink glands also discharge anal sacs in extreme fear or pain (e.g., otters).

 Species with stink glands keep tail raised, dance, run in place, while displaying warning colors. ➤ Zorilla defensive threat.

Feinted or real attack + snarling, growling, grinding teeth, snapping, biting. ➤ See ratel account.

Playing dead. ➤ Reported in zorilla, ratel, otters caught by larger predator.

ZORILLA OR STRIPED POLECAT, *Ictonyx striatus*

Figure 28.1. Zorilla killing a rat, hair bristling as in defensive threat display.

WHAT IT IS   African approximation of a skunk. Sometimes confused with striped weasel, but much broader, bigger, and shaggier, with longer legs and long, curved foreclaws. ♂ wt 1.5–3.3 lb (0.68–1.5 kg), tl 23–27 in (57–67 cm); ♀ wt 1.3–2 lb (0.6–0.9 kg), tl 22–25 in (56–63 cm). *Tail:* bushy, ⅓ to ½ hbl. *Head:* comparatively small. *Teeth:* 34 with both shearing and crushing molars. *Coat:* long, silky, with fine underfur. *Color:* geographically and individually variable, predominantly jet black with pure white markings on upper side: 4 stripes along back; white ear backs; white mark between eyes and on each cheek (pattern individualistic), tail usually all white (varying to all black). Babies white, with future black areas shaded gray. *Scent glands:* well-developed stink glands. *Teats:* 4.

WHERE IT LIVES   Sub-Saharan Africa in savanna and arid zones; absent from forests.

ECOLOGY   Frequents dense woodland and savanna with undergrowth, also subdesert including coastal sand dunes of Namib Desert. Prefers grasslands kept short by large herbivores. Eats any vertebrates it can catch up to rabbit size but subsists mainly on insects, especially adult and larval dung beetles, grasshoppers, and crickets. Tame zorillas in feeding trials refused only stinkbugs, millipedes, slugs, snails, and crabs. Eats no vegetable matter.

ACTIVITY   ● Rarely seen before 10 PM and retires before dawn.

SOCIAL/MATING SYSTEM   Solitary, otherwise unknown. Mostly singletons and an adult with young are sighted. Observers of captives give contradictory accounts: one says males are mutually antagonistic and females avoid males except during estrus. Another claims different families can be kept together so amicably that they engage in social grooming.

HOW IT MOVES   At a springy trot, while foraging. Gallops faster than expected, swims well, and climbs if sufficiently pressed but is a poor jumper. Build and long claws adapted for digging.

FORAGING/PREDATORY BEHAVIOR   Foraging zorilla reverses and turns abruptly as it quarters, nose to ground, back arched, and tail horizontal. Sniffs audibly as it noses litter or dung to find insects; digs as deep as 1 ft (30 cm) to extract dung-beetle larvae. Snaps up large mobile insects or first pins them with a forepaw; follows flying ones and pounces when they land. Same techniques are used to catch vertebrate prey encountered above ground, after first stalking.

Zorillas kill rodents by wedging canine teeth between 2 vertebrae and breaking the spinal cord, or with a head bite that penetrates the skull. Rat-sized prey is dispatched with a throat bite. Bristles while attacking formidable prey, indicating a degree of fear (see Fig. 28.1). Kills snakes as mongooses do: biting snake repeatedly near the middle or tail and jumping back, then grabbing and delivering brief but vigorous shakes until the snake uncoils and retreats; finally pins it with forefeet and bites it behind the head until snake stops struggling.

REPRODUCTION   No information available for most of Africa. Breeds annually in spring and summer in South Africa (peak in Oct./Nov.). Testes size waxes and wanes accordingly. Gestation 36 days; 1 to 3 young/litter. A hand-reared female whelped at 10 months; a male bred at 22 months.

OFFSPRING AND PARENTAL CARE   Pink, nearly hairless babies only 5 in (12.5 cm) long weighing c. 0.5 oz (15 g) are unable even to crawl first week. By day 7 they can circle on forelegs and by day 10 crawl on all fours but still walk unsteadily after 39 days. Distinct black and white stripes develop in 19 to 21 days; eyes begin to open at 35 days. Zorillas 7 to 8 weeks old trot after foraging mothers, a week later perform complete defensive threat display. When lower canines erupt, several days before eyes begin opening, babies start eating soft parts of prey mother brings to nest, taking progressively more meat and less milk until weaned at 2 months. By then juveniles are accomplished diggers and catchers of insects. Soon after, they kill first vertebrate prey.

PLAY Zorillas begin playing a week after their eyes open, with increasing vigor as coordination increases. From 8 to 15 weeks, playing is the major outdoor activity, decreasing thereafter in intensity and duration.

PREDATORS No information. Squirts nauseating anal-sac fluid about a yard; producing a burning sensation in the eyes. Zorilla's coloration and impressive threat display give fair warning.

HOW IT COMMUNICATES
CALLS
Warning growl Combined with bristling hair. Response to disturbance, by own or other species.
Threat call Very loud, sudden, often combined with threat display and followed by fighting and spraying.
Release call High-intensity scream with descending pitch, uttered while squirting
Yapping Complex, high-frequency call, rising and falling. Voiced by submissive zorilla to appease aggression.
Greeting call Like submissive yapping but faster, stress on lower harmonics. Male courting female, meeting female and young zorillas; juveniles to mother. Signals friendly intent.
Mating calls Female calls almost continuously while mating: yapping and 2 calls similar to juvenile chirping and mewing.

JUVENILE CALLS
Nest chirp or squeak Rising and falling frequency. Distress call given first 2 or 3 weeks, when left alone.
Mewing Complex distress call emitted from weeks 2 to 8.
Contact Loud, rapid yapping uttered first 2 to 3 weeks when mother enters nest; precursor of adult greeting and submission calls.

Table 28.2. *DIFFERENCES IN ZORILLA BEHAVIOR*
Expect to see and hear ➤ *Usual context and meaning*

Submission
Lowered forequarters, head turned with cheek on ground, mouth open.
➤ Performed by estrous ♀ courted by ♂, and by juveniles in presence of adult ♂.

Sociable Behavior
Nibble-grooming or licking mouth. ➤ By adult ♂, responding to juvenile displaying submission (captive group).

Courtship
Unreceptive ♀ yaps and snaps when ♂ tries to sniff or mount.

Courtship *continued*

Receptive ♀ crouches and allows sniffing, sometimes in submissive posture.

Mating: during 106-min. copulation, ♀ yapped with growing frequency and volume.

Play

Play-fighting: wrestling, biting, rolling, and kicking while gripping cheek or neck skin; alternating with chasing games and play threats.

Response to Predators

Bolting for the nearest refuge. ➤ First line of defense.

Warning display: raised rear end aimed toward enemy, hair bristling, tail sticking straight up or curled over back, back bowed, head drawn in.

Feinted attack: springing forward and backward, growling or screaming loudly if cornered.

Discharging stink glands: hindquarters swing while squirting so that fluid covers an arc.

Playing dead. ➤ Last line of defense, in case squirting isn't enough. But if its enemy circles, zorilla flips over to keep back turned.

RATEL OR HONEY BADGER, *Mellivora capensis*

Figure 28.2. Ratel taking honeycomb from beehive to which a honey guide led it (*from a painting by R. Orr*).

WHAT IT IS African version of a badger. Powerful build, broad back and sturdy legs with wide feet; bearlike curved foreclaws nearly 1.5 in (35 mm) long, with sharp edges. ♂ ♀ wt 17.6–32 lb (8–14.5 kg), ht 9–11 in (23–28 cm), hbl 26–30 in (65–75 cm). *Tail:* short, 7 to 9 in (18–22 cm). *Head:* massive, with short, powerful jaws; small, dark eyes; external ears reduced to ridges of thick skin that close purselike when ratel digs or raids beehives. *Teeth:* robust, molars reduced to 4 per side, adapted for crushing. *Skin:* loose, thick around neck.

Coat: coarse with sparse underfur, anal and genital area thin-haired or naked.
Color: jet black except for gray or white (sometimes black) mantle extending

from crown to tail; young rusty brown. *Scent glands:* very large anal pouch resembling that of mongooses and hyenas. *Teats:* 4.

WHERE IT LIVES   Uncommon but widespread south of Sahara except in deserts and Lowland Rainforest. Ranges north to Morocco in West Africa (also widespread in Asia).

ECOLOGY   Lives in most life zones from very dry to very wet and up to 1 mi (1700 m) in montane forest. An omnivore that eats a wide range of invertebrate and vertebrate animals, from insects to the young of large mammals, and carrion, berries, and fruits. Second only to the aardvark as a digger, the ratel can reach prey too hard for most other carnivores to unearth. Social insects are an important food source, including termites, ants, and especially bees.

ACTIVITY   ●/○ Adaptable to local conditions, ratels living in rural areas may hide out in daytime, forage only at night. Elsewhere also active by day. Tame ratels are active for long periods day and night, with shorter intervals of rest and seclusion. Ratels use burrows, caves, and sometimes empty man-made beehives as lairs.

SOCIAL/MATING SYSTEM   (♂♀♂) Unstudied, but sightings of adults in pairs and similarity of the sexes suggest the ratel lives in monogamous pairs. Sightings of singles are most common, followed by duos and trios. Whether territorial or not is unknown.

HOW IT MOVES   Squat form, flat feet, and long claws make it a slow, clumsy runner, but it is able to maintain a lumbering, pigeon-toed trot indefinitely, covering up to 22 mi (35 km) in a night. Walks with a rolling gait and moves backward with agility; manages to climb rough-barked trees to reach beehives; instead of climbing down, often simply drops to ground. An unusual trait shared with otters is somersaulting down slopes, apparently for fun.

FORAGING/PREDATORY BEHAVIOR   A tireless hunter that pokes into every nook and cranny in food quest. Relies on sense of smell but also uses its ears, e.g. listening for movement after blowing vigorously into a hole. Avid digger, it unearths dung-beetle larvae, scorpions, spiders, estivating frogs, tortoises, turtles, and lungfish with apparent ease; preys on rodents in their burrows, termites in their mounds, and snakes, lizards, mongooses. etc. that shelter in ventilation shafts. Like bears, foraging ratels turn over stones and tear bark off dead trees. Shielded by rubbery, allegedly impervious skin, ratels catch and eat the deadliest snakes.

Particularly fascinating is the ratel's predation on bees and association with the greater honey guide (*Indicator indicator*), a bird with the unique ability to digest beeswax. The greater honey guide regularly invites people and a few other mammals (ratel, baboons, chimpanzees) to follow it to the nearest beehive. The ratel is the only animal that does, impelled by its own craving for honey and bee larvae. While neither bird nor beast depends on the other to find and raid beehives, cooperation must offer mutual benefits for the arrangement to exist; probably the ratel finds more hives with less effort when guided, and the greater honey guide gains entrance to otherwise inaccessible hives.

The greater honey guide attracts attention by calling to passersby with a cry like the sound of a shaken matchbox, then flies off a short distance with an initial downward swoop that shows off its white outer feathers and lands, resuming its urgent calling. If followed, the bird repeats the process until one of the many hives known to it is reached; then it falls silent and waits for its partner to spot the hive entrance, open it, and eat its fill. After, the bird claims its reward. Eyewitness accounts of ratels following honey guides report grunting and growling responses to the bird's calls.

Some honey hunters claim the ratel uses its anal glands to fumigate beehives the way people use smoke. Applying its everted anal pouch to the hive entrance hole, the ratel spreads secretion liberally while swirling its tail, sometimes in a handstand. The behavior itself is not unusual, since many carnivores scent-mark a food source, but the ratel's unusually copious secretion has been described as "suffocating," and beekeepers report piles of dead bees and a pervasive sharp smell in hives raided by ratels. Whether ratels really do fumigate hives or whether it is all a folktale remains to be seen.

Like other mustelids, ratels cache surplus food, including honeycombs.

REPRODUCTION   Information sketchy and contradictory. Gestation reported as 6 to 7 months, far longer than any other tropical mustelid; 1 to 4 young born in a leaf- or grass-lined nest. Survival of zoo specimens up to 26 years suggests it is an unusually long-lived animal.

RELATIONS WITH OTHER PREDATORS   Adults have no natural enemies. Though small, the ratel is incredibly powerful, with vicelike jaws, sharp claws, a ferocious temper, and impermeable skin so loose-fitting that a ratel gripped in a hyena's or leopard's jaws can twist around and bite back. Also, according to folklore and some anecdotal evidence, it goes for the scrotum when attacking large animals, including buffalo, wildebeest, waterbuck, kudu, and men. Injured ratels have been known to play dead and to dribble vile-smelling anal-sac secretion.

HOW IT COMMUNICATES

CALLS
Whistling hiss, bark-scream, rattling roar   Defensive threat accompaniment.
Breathy *hrrr-hrrr*   Talking to itself while foraging.

Grunting   Close-range contact call between ratels.
Fussy squeaking sounds   Emitted by nest-building female.
Plaintive whines and hiccuping   Distress call of babies.

Table 28.3. *DIFFERENCES IN RATEL BEHAVIOR*
  Expect to see and hear ➤ *Usual context and meaning*

Scent-marking

With anal glands: anal-dragging, handstanding, and backing up to uprights, while swirling tail. ➤ Anal pouch is reportedly everted whenever
ratel becomes excited.

With feces: deposited in hole it digs but leaves open. ➤ Tendency of
ratels to investigate holes enhances chances of another ratel finding scats.

Aggression

Defensive threat: crouching, gaping, bristling, attack, with aggressive
calls.

SPOTTED-NECKED OTTER, *Lutra maculicollis*

Figure 28.3. Spotted-necked otter
pursuing a fish.

WHAT IT IS   The smallest
African otter, with a light, speckled
throat. Typical otter shape; feet
webbed to ends of digit pads, each
with a claw. ♂ wt 10 lb (4.5 kg),
length including tail 34–42 in (85–
105 cm); ♀ wt 9 lb (4.1 kg), length
within ♂ range. *Tail:* c. ⅔ hbl.
Teeth: 36, adapted for cutting more
than crushing. *Color:* varies from
reddish- to chocolate-brown; some
otters with extensive white patches
(throat, upper lip, underparts) that
may increase with age; others with
little or no white patches. Young
darker, head especially, than old otters. *Teats:* 4.

WHERE IT LIVES   Sub-Saharan Africa in larger rivers, lakes, and
swamps. Absent from many apparently suitable lakes and rivers of eastern
Africa, notably Luanwga Valley and the Zambezi below Victoria Falls. Most
abundant in Lake Victoria and rivers and lakes of Zambia.

GOOD PLACES TO SEE IT   Clear lakes like Victoria, Kivu, Tanganyika,
Malawi.

ECOLOGY More aquatic and specialized as a fish eater than clawless ot-ters, coming ashore only to eat, sleep, sunbathe, and den. Limited ability to travel overland restricts it to permanent bodies of water, especially open water; yet sometimes common in mountain streams. Home range includes a network of regularly used trails and holts—holes in banks, rocks, or other cover used as sleeping places and dens. Eats fish, especially small, slow-mov-ing kinds, but up to 50% of diet consists of frogs and invertebrates (mussels, clams, crabs). Also eats waterbirds, eggs.

ACTIVITY ○ (●?) Variable. Otters observed at Bukoba, Lake Victoria emerged at first light, cruised aimlessly a while, then fished intensively for 2 or 3 hours, followed by basking and grooming, or withdrawal into holts until late afternoon. Active in moonlight but night activity unstudied. In Botswana waters, may be particularly active at twilight and dawn.

SOCIAL/MATING SYSTEM ♀♂♀ Studies of European and American river otters indicate that *Lutra* species conform to the basic solitary-carnivore dispersion and mating pattern (see Table 22.1). Whether the un-studied spotted-necked otter is like other members of its genus is unknown, but some observations suggest it is more variable and sociable. Though most sightings are of singles or a mother with offspring, larger groups are regularly seen where the species exists at relatively high density, as in Lake Victoria (1 otter/mi [0.6/km] of shoreline). Family groups including 2 adults and several young suggest these otters breed monogamously and share parental duties. Larger transient groups of up to 21, usually composed of same-sex yearlings, also occur. Schools of spotted-necked otters have even been reported to sur-round and drive schools of fish into the shallows.

The kind of water body and distribution of food resources influence the size and shape of an otter's home range and movements. Lake dwellers defend a stretch of shore and share fishing grounds. Stream dwellers can control a long stretch as an exclusive hunting/mating territory. Whatever the arrange-ment, otters have the reputation of ranging in a consistent pattern, creating worn paths by regular passage along the same routes, with frequent stops to renew scent marks.

HOW IT MOVES Best swimmer of the 3 African otters and the least mobile on land. Actually, it seems a rather slow, short-winded swimmer, going no faster than 2.5 mph (4 kph) and only staying underwater c. 15 sec-onds before surfacing. Usually dives no deeper than 7 feet (2 m). On land, walks and runs in a bouncy, diagonal stride at 3 to 4 mph (5-6.4 kph) and can jump-run nearly as fast as a man for a very short distance. Becomes over-heated and distressed, nevertheless, after only a short walk. Eats lying flat, tail outstretched, head low or slightly raised. Despite claws and webbing to finger-tips , it has considerable dexterity. Rests in the usual side curl, and high-sits to peer over high grass. While swimming sometimes rests floating on its back.

FORAGING/PREDATORY BEHAVIOR   A fishing otter searches visually and randomly for prey, diving repeatedly and briefly. Sighting a fish, it accelerates and soon overtakes slow kinds it prefers, grabs it in its jaws and bites it, then lands and eats it, holding catch under or between its paws. A nearly full otter continues to pursue and catch fish but will often toy with prey after crippling it, tossing it in the air or bunting it with its nose. A spotted-necked otter searching for frogs, crabs, and such probes under stones and in holes using its snout or hands.

REPRODUCTION   Annually late in the dry season; typically 1 to 3/litter; 2-month gestation. Females probably begin breeding at 2 years.

OFFSPRING AND PARENTAL CARE   Born in a hole, hollow tree, dense thicket, or reedbed, in a nest lined with grass and other plants. Mothers extremely intolerant of other otters until offspring leave the den and start swimming at 10 to 12 weeks. Father may then join his spouse and help bring up their offspring—assuming this is normal arrangement. Parental instruction in fishing has been witnessed: mother repeatedly dropping live fish beside her 3- to 4-month-old pup, which could not yet dive properly or catch fish.

Offspring remain with parent(s) a whole year until the next litter is born, then wander until they find places to settle down. Big yearling groups seen in Lake Victoria could consist of littermates that stay together awhile and join other yearlings in loose schools.

HOW IT COMMUNICATES

CALLS

Squeak or twitter   Commonest and most variable (graded) call. High-pitched squeak a begging or distress call. Tempo increases when frightened, changing to high-pitched trill when hurt. Lower, harsher trill produced in back of throat expresses rage.

Mewing   Challenge (aggressive), also emitted on land.

Squealing whistle   Sound of excitement given while play-fighting.

Chattering or rattling call   Compared to call of pied kingfisher but fuller and less piercing. Warning or scolding, usually given on land.

Gasping   Mild alarm, grading into spluttering snort at high intensity.

Hah!   Alarm snort.

Table 28.4. *DIFFERENCES IN SPOTTED-NECKED OTTER BEHAVIOR*
Expect to see and hear ➤ Usual context and meaning

Scent-marking

Sprainting: otters come ashore to deposit black, sticky scats on elevations, preferably rocks with flat, sloping tops. Latrines are established
near holts. ➤ Otters defecate and urinate at same time, crouching close
to ground, ♂ ♂ with tail vertical, ♀ ♀ with tail horizontal.

Aggression

Weaving head in snakelike manner while emitting trilling "battle cry."
Followed by sudden, vicious bite.

CAPE CLAWLESS OTTER, *Aonyx capensis*

Figure 28.4. Clawless otter eating a small fish.

WHAT IT IS   A very large, unspotted otter. Comparatively long legs,
forefeet like hands: unwebbed fingers with nails instead of claws, opposable
thumb, naked palms; hind feet webbed to outer joints, middle toe with
grooming claw. ♂ wt 40–62 lb (18–28 kg), hbl 29–36 in (72–91 cm); ♀ wt
29–42 lb (13–19 kg), hbl within ♂ range. *Tail:* 16 to 28 in (40–71 cm). *Head:*
massive, wide flat skull with broad, crushing molars and long canines;
whiskers especially prominent. *Color:* tan to chocolate-brown with variable
white or off-white markings on chin, cheeks, throat, chest, and belly; occasionally a mantle of white-tipped hair over forehead and shoulders. *Teats:* 4.

WHERE IT LIVES   Sub-Saharan Africa in streams, rivers, lakes, ponds,
swamps, and estuaries; also along Indian and Atlantic coasts in vicinity of
fresh water, in mangrove swamps and along rocky shores. Absent from various large rivers like the lower Zambezi and parts of the Limpopo. The smaller,
less specialized Congo clawless otter replaces it in Lowland Rainforest; they

overlap in Uganda, the southeastern Congo Basin, and parts of West Africa.

GOOD PLACES TO SEE IT   Tsitsikama Coastal NP, South Africa, one of the best. Viewable inside and outside many other parks, with luck or patient watching.

ECOLOGY   More amphibious and less aquatic than spotted-necked otter, cross-country mobility enables it to reach waters inaccessible to the latter, and less-specialized diet gives it a wider choice of habitats. As long as shores provide shelter, climate and vegetation type don't matter: clawless otters inhabit rain forest with 80 in (2000 mm) rainfall and subdesert with 4 in (50 mm), and mountain streams up to 9800 ft (3000 m). Diet depends on what is readily available: in Natal rivers, crabs are mainstay, followed by frogs, very few fish; in a Zimbabwe location with abundant tilapia and bream, otters eat mostly fish; along South African coast menu includes some 35 species of crabs, fishes, and octopuses. Here otters forage along vertical rock faces and recesses, also in tidal pools. Other prey includes turtles, snakes, waterbirds, mollusks, insects, and eggs of monitor lizards, crocodiles, and birds.

ACTIVITY   ●/○ Natal Province otters have activity peaks in late afternoon and early evening, while coastal population in Tsitsikama NP, is night-active, with a peak from 8 to 10 PM, inactive in daytime up to 3 PM.

SOCIAL/MATING SYSTEM   Unclear. The only study to date was the coastal marine population in Tsitsikama NP, which may be unlike most freshwater populations, except possibly on large lakes. An estimated 30 or 31 otters lived on the 36 mi (58.5 km) coastline. Four known males shared and perhaps defended a 7.4 mi (12 km) stretch like a clan territory, depositing their spraints (feces) in communal latrines near holts—shallow scrapes hidden in dense vegetation, averaging 3/mi (1.9/km) of the shore they shared. Three of the males took turns foraging together in pairs. The ranging pattern of females in this population was determined for only one known female: her home range extended along at least 9 mi (14.3 km) of coast, with a core area of 4.6 mi (7.5 km) where she spent most time.

In contrast, clawless otters on a Tanzania river appeared to have separate, exclusive ranges. Three different groups were known to reside on a 5 mile (8 km) stretch for at least 25 years. Other accounts say that clawless otters live in pairs and that males assist in rearing offspring.

HOW IT MOVES   Crouches in the S-shape common to long, low mammals; high-sits supported by tail. Walks at a leisurely pace but often jump-runs, humping less than spotted-necked otter. The webbed hind feet provide most of the propulsion when swimming, the tail serving mainly as a rudder.

FORAGING/PREDATORY BEHAVIOR   Captures nearly all prey with its hands, usually by feeling under rocks, in holes, and other hiding places. Rough skin on palms and fingers helps grip slippery frogs and fish. Foraging for hidden prey by feel is as productive in muddy water or at night as in clear water by day, whereas most fish are located and pursued by sight. Techniques also vary with conditions. An otter wading in a narrow mountain steam kept its head underwater, looking from side to side as it felt under rocks. One hunting in a pool dove to the bottom and probed under rocks for crabs and frogs, coming up with crabs or frogs in 23 of 37 dives. It ate while treading water (also underwater). A clawless otter after fish swam below the surface looking from side to side, staying under an average of 18 seconds. Spotting one, it accelerated and tried to grab it.

Otters can be left- or right-handed, like people, as shown in feeding (see Fig. 28.4) and in transporting prey, infants, and other items. Stones are used as anvils to smash freshwater mussels too hard for even their jaws; shell middens surround anvil rocks. After eating, otters wash face and paws in water in an elaborate ritual.

REPRODUCTION   Whether seasonal or not unclear; may vary with latitude, being less seasonal in equatorial regions. Has 2 or 3 young/litter; gestation 2 months.

OFFSPRING AND PARENTAL CARE   Two pups c. a week old weighed 9 oz (260 g) apiece. Born in a hole or a nest in dense vegetation, pups emit constant nest chirp. When eyes open at c. 1 month, they venture outside den while mother present.

RELATIONS WITH OTHER PREDATORS   Adults sometimes eaten by crocodiles; juveniles vulnerable to eagles. Otherwise, this mustelid is bigger and arguably even more formidable than the ratel, with equally tough, loose skin, a still more vicelike grip, more flexible and powerful body, and just as vicious when aroused. Mothers readily attack even people.

HOW IT COMMUNICATES

CALLS
Growls, snarls, screaming wail   Threats of increasing intensity.
Wow-wow-wow   Accompaniment to submissive lying on back, waving paws alternating with snarling. Equivalent to squeak of spot-neck.
Whack-o, whack-o   Loud, repeated 2-note chirp: greeting call.
Squealing, moaning, mewing, snuffling   "Conversational" sounds among family members.
Humming   Begging call, sounds like cat's defensive wail.
Whee-whee   Squeaky nest chirp, grading from soft to loud, short to long, expressing different emotions.
Hah!   Alarm snort.

Table 28.5. *DIFFERENCES IN CLAWLESS OTTER BEHAVIOR*
Expect to see and hear ➤ *Usual context and meaning*

Maintenance

 Sunbathing posture.

 Carrying fish under arm and walking on 3 legs.

Play

SOLITARY PLAY

Diving for pebbles: carries pebble out into water, drops and retrieves it before it reaches bottom. Variation: otter catches pebble on flat head, performs gyrations while keeping it balanced.

Chasing sticks: takes stick to bottom, releases and follows it to surface.
➤ Satiated otters play with prey same way as with inanimate objects.

Using tail to scoop objects within reach.

Sliding. ➤ A family group of 4 regularly took turns leaping and sliding down a grassy river bank, for up to ½ hr at a time.

Part IV

PRIMATES

ORDER PRIMATES

SUBORDER STREPSIRHINI: PROSIMIANS

Families Represented in Africa	Species
Lorisidae: bushbabies, pottos	9–11

SUBORDER HAPLORHINI: MONKEYS, APES, HUMANS

Families Represented in Africa	Species
Ceropithecidae: monkeys, baboons	40
Pongidae: great apes	3
Hominidae: humans	1

Chapter 29

INTRODUCING PRIMATES

WHAT THEY ARE   An ancient order with 4 major divisions: prosimians ("almost-monkeys"), New World monkeys, Old World monkeys (superfamily Cercopithecoidea), and apes and people (superfamily Hominoidea). Among the 185 living species with which we share common ancestors are creatures as unlike us as bushbabies and as incredibly like us as chimpanzees.

The skimpy fossil record indicates that primates were among the first orders to branch from the earliest mammals, a good 65 million years ago, evolving in tropical forests from arboreal insectivores similar to tree shrews. The first primates were small nocturnal creatures that leaped through the trees like frogs—quite like bushbabies. Monkeylike primates with large brains evolved at least 30 million years ago, and 2-legged hominids have been around for c. 4 million years.

PRIMATE TRAITS   Generalized skeleton, body, and limbs capable of varied postures, movements, and locomotor patterns. All primates can sit and stand and many can walk upright. Collar bone (clavicle) large for multidirectional forelimb mobility. *Hands:* used for both feeding and locomotion (except by hominids); 5 fingers and toes, tips protected by flat nails; at least 1 pair of digits opposable and able to grasp (usually thumb and big toe plus second digit). *Eyes:* surrounded by bony ring, placed frontally providing stereoscopic vision needed for judging distances accurately; diurnal primates have color vision and a central depression of sharp focus (fovea) in the retina, like ours. Well-developed pouch (cecum) off colon for digesting plant cell walls. *Genitals:* testes external in a naked or thinly haired scrotum; penis suspended (not attached to abdominal wall as in most mammals), often with bone. Female labia and often surrounding skin become swollen and colorful during estrus. *Teats:* 2 on the chest (extra pairs in some bushbabies).

Primate traits that show progressive development during evolution include a large, complex brain, manual dexterity, comparatively long gestation, late maturation, and long life span.

SOCIAL/MATING SYSTEMS   Span almost the whole range of possibilities, from solitary nocturnal prosimians like the potto to the most complex of all social systems: our own. Excepting the few solitary species, sociability is a primate characteristic. The great majority live in female-bonded social groups: female offspring stay in their mothers' group, while males have to emigrate and take over or join another troop before they can reproduce. Skewed adult sex ratios favoring females are characteristic of all such societies, helping to create and maintain polygynous mating systems.

A plausible scenario for the origin of sociability in higher primates is that the transition from nocturnal to diurnal activity caused ancestral bushbaby sleeping groups to forage together for mutual security.

The main social/mating systems of Old World primates are covered in the species accounts. An outline of types represented in African primates is given here, proceeding from simple to complex.

NOCTURNAL PRIMATES

Solitary/polygynous. Both sexes territorial. Female defends resources sufficient to support herself and offspring; fittest males defend territories including several female ranges. Examples: potto and other members of the subfamily Lorisinae.

Solitary/monogamous. Male lives with 1, sometimes 2 (bigamy), females in shared territory. Example: Zanzibar bushbaby.

Sociable/territorial. Female kinship group (matriline) with 1 breeding male. Adults forage individually but related females and young sleep together in day nests, often joined by male. Each matriline occupies a territory, but males may control several female territories. Examples: bushbabies.

DIURNAL PRIMATES All species gregarious. Individuals travel, forage, and sleep together, except peripheral males and chimpanzees (both sexes). Separate bachelor groups rare but occur in gelada and hamadryas baboons, patas monkey, and some black and white colobus populations.

Territorial troop with 1 resident breeding male—the prevailing system among higher primates. Examples: blue monkey, black and white colobus. Typically, 10 to 25 females and young live in a traditional home range small enough to be defended as an exclusive territory. Males compete for mastery of a female group; those that become *resident male* defend the territory along with the troop; they play a watchdog role, repelling rivals and guarding the troop against predators, thereby protecting their own genetic investment. Age-graded troops, a variation of this system in which subadult and young-adult males are troop members, normally have only 1 breeding male and only he performs the displays that go with the watchdog role (see black and white colobus account).

A bachelor bent on acquiring a harem normally has to oust a resident male to do so, after first testing different troops to find the easiest target. An easier way is to join a breakaway group from a troop that has grown too big for its territory, but this rarely happens; finding suitable, unoccupied habitat in which to settle is also problematic. Easiest and rarest of all is to find a troop that has lost its resident male.

 Nonterritorial troop with 1 resident male; unattached

males associate in bachelor groups. Example: perhaps only the patas monkey, a guenon that has adapted to terrestrial life by becoming a simian greyhound.

One-male harem, nonterritorial. Males compete for females instead of real estate, acquiring them one at a time, usually by conquest. Being unrelated, females tend to be more closely bonded to the male than to one another. Examples: gorilla, hamadryas baboon.

Multimale, nonterritorial societies. Characteristic of terrestrial but including some arboreal primates. Large troops range areas too extensive to be defended, overlapping with other troops. Males typically much larger than females and dangerously armed. Estrus is advertised by colorful, swollen genitals. Males and females organized in separate, steep dominance hierarchies. Troops compete for the same resources; larger groups with more males supplant smaller groups. Males guard troop against predators. Examples: savanna baboon, drill, mandrill (terrestrial species) and mangabey, red colobus (arboreal species).

Multimale territorial system. Example: the vervet, a guenon that lives on the woodland/grassland edge.

Communal territorial system. Example: chimpanzee. Males remain in and defend traditional home range cooperatively against neighbors, while females emigrate. Chimps often travel and forage alone. Females have exclusive core areas; social bonds between unrelated females are weak, whereas mother-son and fraternal bonds are durable.

FROM ONE-MALE TO MULTIMALE TROOPS   The account of a resident male blue monkey's inability to keep rival males from invading his troop while several females were in estrus shows how a multimale troop could evolve from a one-male system. If confronted with invasions by several different males at once, the resident male's only sustainable alternative may be to settle for dominance instead of exclusivity.

HOW THEY MOVE   Generalized skeleton and limb mobility enable primates to move any way they like. However, proportions of the limbs and shape of the body (narrow-bodied like monkeys or wide-bodied like apes) indicate the normal way of moving. Locomotion types of African primates are as follows.

- Vertical clinging and leaping: froglike jumps propelled by elongated hind legs, landing vertically and clinging to supports between jumps (bushbaby; see Fig. 30.1).
- Four-footed walking and running: hands and feet grasp supports while climbing.

- Slow-motion climbing, no leaping or running, 1 limb moved at a time (potto).

- Branch-walking and -running, including climbing, jumping, and doglike leaps: animals walk on palms, hands and feet usually grasp supports (guenon).

- Ground-running and -walking: walk on fingers on ground and often along branches (baboon, patas).

- Semibrachiation: during downward leaps between trees, arms held out to grasp foliage and to break fall on landing (colobus monkey; see Fig. 31.5).

- Ape locomotion: terrestrial knuckle-walking (chimpanzee and gorilla; chimps and juvenile gorillas occasionally swing by arms [true braciation]).

HAND COORDINATION   Prehensile hands, employed for climbing and eating, are the heritage of all primates. But manipulative skill varies, increasing progressively from prosimians to apes. Bushbabies are incredibly adept at catching insects, but their fingers close all together and cannot be operated singly. Higher primates have a precision grip: thumb and forefinger are used to pick up and manipulate small objects. But not all have a completely opposable thumb: colobus monkeys have only a stub. Maximum dexterity is attained by species in which the tips of thumb and forefinger meet at right angles, notably baboons and related macaques, and the apes, which rival humans in dexterity despite having to walk on their knuckles.

REPRODUCTION   Gestation is remarkably long in primates, being 4 months even in bushbabies no bigger than rats (gestation 3–4 weeks). It is 5 to 6 months in most monkeys, compared to c. 2 months in carnivores of comparable size. Slow to mature and long-lived, primates reproduce slowly and most, seasonally. Bushbabies are the only Old World primates that have more than one young at a time. Most monkeys breed only every other year, apes only every 4 to 5 years. Monkeys and apes have menstrual cycles of 20 to 35 days. Genitals of most primates flush and swell slightly during estrus, but only ones living in multimale troops have conspicuous sexual swellings. In many of these societies, copulation is not limited to estrus, whereas females are receptive only during estrus in most 1-male mating systems.

Chapter 30

BUSHBABIES OR GALAGOS
Family Lorisidae
Subfamily Galaginae

Greater or thick-tailed bushbaby, *Galago crassicaudatus* (including *G. garnettii*)
Zanzibar bushbaby, G. *zanzibaricus*
Lesser bushbaby, G. *senegalensis* (including G. *moholi*)
Needle-clawed bushbaby, G. *(Euoticus) elegantulus*
Small needle-clawed bushbaby, G. *inustus*
Demidoff's dwarf bushbaby, G. *demidovii*
Allen's bushbaby, G. *alleni*

WHAT THEY ARE   An exclusively African group of small, nocturnal primates that bounce through the trees like kangaroos or frogs. Family includes pottos and lorises (subfamily Lorisinae), very different creatures that move in slow motion.

Among living primates, bushbabies are most like earliest ancestors. Dwarf bushbaby teeth are almost identical to fossils 60 million years old. Bushbabies isolated when Madagascar separated from the African continent gave rise to lemurs, which fill niches similar to those occupied elsewhere by monkeys, while retaining the basic clinging and leaping form of locomotion.

SUBFAMILY TRAITS   Slender bodies with hind legs much longer and stronger than forelegs (froglike); tail longer than head and body length; size ranging from 2 oz (60 g) dwarf bushbaby to 3 lb (1.4 kg) greater bushbaby; males and females look alike. *Head:* rounded with short, pointed face; enormous, frontally placed eyes, immobile in sockets, reddish with black pupils that close to vertical slit; large bat ears, naked, transparent, and foldable. *Teeth:* 34 to 36; lower incisors and canines modified as a scraping/grooming comb. *Feet:* long, slender digits with padded tips and flat nails, except grooming claw on second toe; thumb and big toe opposed to other digits. *Coat:* soft, thick fur. *Color:* concealing, gray, reddish, or brown, with lighter underparts and subdued markings. *Genitals:* penis with bone; vagina sealed except during estrus. *Scent glands:* on scrotum and labia; lip and salivary glands; chest gland in greater bushbaby. *Teats:* 2 to 3 pairs of teats, located on chest, in armpits, occasionally on belly.

SENSES   Eyes designed to see and judge distances under conditions where only 1% of starlight reaches forest floor. Great size, protrusion, and frontal placement, a retina packed with light-sensitive rod cells, and a brilliant reflecting layer (the *tapetum lucidum*) enable bushbabies to jump between trees and

Figure 30.1. Clinging and leaping sequence of an Allen's bushbaby (*redrawn from P. Charles-Dominique*).

catch flying insects in what is pitch darkness to human eyes. Though eyes are immobile, bushbaby rotates head 180° and its protruding "fisheyes" cover a visual field over 50° wider than ours. All the other senses are also well-developed and important, both for locating food and predators and for social communication.

SOCIAL/MATING SYSTEM Basic units consist of a mother with offspring of assorted ages, occupying a permanent home range/territory. Males disperse in adolescence; the fittest ones have territories that extend through the ranges of several female groups. Related females and young sleep together in day nests, sometimes joined by the resident male, but adults all forage independently. Territorial males may tolerate subordinate adult males on their property, whereas ranges of breeding males overlap only slightly.

The Zanzibar bushbaby, formerly considered a subspecies of lesser bushbaby, has a social/mating system different from all other bushbabies. An adult male associates with only 1 or 2 females and their offspring in a shared territory.

HOW THEY MOVE Jumping techniques vary, depending on size and limb proportions, and whether the species lives in the forest canopy, middle layer, or undergrowth. Bushbabies capture flying, jumping, and scurrying insects by hand with a lightning-fast clutching movement in which the long slender fingers close all together on the palm. They lack neuromuscular co-ordination to move fingers individually; therefore cannot groom like higher primates, using their grooming claw and tooth comb instead.

REPRODUCTION   Forest bushbabies produce one offspring a year during the rainiest months. Greater and lesser bushbabies bear twins or triplets seasonally, the latter twice a year. Gestation (increasing with size): 112 to 126 days.

HOW THEY COMMUNICATE   Sight 3, scent 1, sound 1.

SIGHT   Postures and facial expressions relatively unimportant and undeveloped. Facial mime limited to opening mouth and furrowing brow. Ear and tail positions are most expressive and mostly linked with particular calls.

SCENT   Using urine and a variety of glands, bushbabies scent-mark their aerial pathways, borders, sleeping trees, and one another (see Table 30.1 and species accounts). The reproductive status of females is monitored through urine-testing (without grimacing).

SOUND   Repertoire of 10 or 11 different calls, some of which are similar in all species (greater and lesser bushbabies' calls listed in species accounts). Compared to higher primates, most prosimian calls are more stereotyped and invariable. Distance call of the greater bushbaby, which sounds something like a baby's wail, is by far the most powerful and familiar.

Table 30.1. *BUSHBABY BEHAVIOR GUIDE*
Expect to see and hear ➤ *Usual context and meaning*

Territorial Advertising

SCENT-MARKING

At strategic locations, especially border areas and sleeping sites. Social partners are also marked with urine and glandular secretions.

 Urine-washing: hand and foot on one side are raised while a few drops of urine are deposited on the hand, which then grasps and rubs urine on foot sole. Process repeated on other side. ➤ The most stereotyped of all forms of urine-marking: an automatic, repeated action of active bushbabies. Wetted hands and feet leave scent traces on everything touched.

Rhythmic urination: with hindquarters lowered, a few drops of urine are deposited on branch as bushbaby wriggles forward. ➤ Often performed in bouts.

With scrotal/labial glands: bushbabies brush gland against branches.

during or separately from rhythmic urination. ➤ Bare patch on ♂'s scrotum and surrounding ♀'s labia looks like waffle iron, contains scent glands.

Rubbing muzzle, lips, and cheeks on branches. ➤ Skin in these areas contains large saclike (apocrine) glands. Lesser bushbaby leaves saliva trail.

DISTANCE CALLS

See species accounts. ➤ Uttered during territorial encounters of both sexes, also to contact mates and family members.

Aggression

Offensive threat: ears cocked, eyes wide, round and staring, mouth wide open with tongue and upper canines visible.

Defensive posture: crouching with head raised, open mouth, teeth covered, ears widespread, often with hand held before body, uttering 2-phase growling call.

Defensive threat (greater bushbaby): cornered bushbaby stands like boxer with hands raised, ready to cuff or pounce and bite.

Submission

Cringing, head drawn in between hunched shoulders, ears folded, eyes narrowed.

Avoidance, retreat, flight while emitting submissive calls.

Sociable Behavior

GREETING

Nose-to-nose sniffing, nose-to-face contact. ➤ Meetings between individuals, prelude to other social interactions.

Genital-sniffing and contact.

Social grooming: licking concentrated on head, ears, chin, neck; tooth comb used only when fur matted. ➤ Second most frequent behavior on meeting. Important in maternal-offspring and social bonding between sleeping-group members. Also during courtship.

Grooming solicitation: presenting neck and armpit. ➤ Similar to soliciting of higher primates.

Lying in contact. ➤ Sleeping group in nest.

Courtship

Close following; sniffing/licking ♀'s genitals (see Fig. 30.3); urine-marking ♀; social grooming; calling.

Receptive ♀ crouches and deflects tail; unreceptive one withdraws and threatens.

♂ mounts as higher primates do, grasping ♀'s heels with feet.

Mother and Offspring

Mother jumping while carrying infant.

Mother licking and suckling infant; second baby in riding position.

Play

Running and jumping practice; littermates play-fighting. ➤ Babies begin playing very actively in week 2.

Response to Predators

Staring fixedly.

Alarm calls: series of increasing intensity.

Mobbing response of family group; following and harassing predator.

Parked infants react to movement of their perch by dropping to ground, uttering a distress call as they fall, taking a few jumps and lying still. ➤ Mother and other bushbabies gather and scold nearby predator or person until it moves away far enough for mother to retrieve infant.

GREATER OR THICK-TAILED BUSHBABY, *Galago crassicaudatus*

WHAT IT IS A giant bushbaby the size of a small cat with a sturdy build. ♂ wt 3.1 lb (1.4 kg), hbl 10.8–19 in (27–47 cm); ♀ wt 2.6 lb (1.2 kg), hbl within ♂ range. *Tail*: bushy, 13–21 in (33–52 cm). *Head*: foxy face with pointed snout and large, rounded ears. *Coat*: thick, woolly. *Color*: geographically variable; light gray with whitish tail to dark brown with black-tipped tail; underparts white to pale yellow or gray; face like body or lighter with light nose, dark marks on snout and around eyes. *Teats*: 1 to 3 pairs on chest, armpits, and/or groin.

Figure 30.2. Greater bushbaby.

WHERE IT LIVES Southern Sudan to southern Natal in eastern Africa; from Indian Ocean to Angola coast south of the Lowland Rainforest; from sea level to 5900 ft (1800 m).

ACTIVITY ● Awakens at twilight, starts foraging after dark; early and late night calling and activity peaks.

ECOLOGY Found in habitats where fruits abundant for at least half the year, mostly in dense evergreen forest and bush, also in different man-made habitats, such as plantations of exotic trees and suburban gardens. Tolerates temperatures down to freezing. Diet of fruit and gum, supplemented by seeds, nectar, and slow insects. Fig and other trees that keep fruiting, acacias and other gum-producing trees are favorite living places, carrying up to 285 bushbabies/mi^2 (110/km^2).

SOCIAL/MATING SYSTEM A local population studied in a Transvaal gallery forest visited many of the same gum and fruit trees and used the same aerial routes, but at different times. Traffic was regulated by the scent marks they left at strategic locations. Adults were permanently resident, whereas subadults either emigrated or died. Young adult males returned from time to time, and nonbreeding males which sometimes foraged together often engaged in social-grooming sessions. They avoided the resident breeding male, who was the oldest, biggest individual, although he tolerated subordinate males on his property. He controlled the ranges of 1 subadult and 4 adult females, which resided in 3 different territories.

Females from different ranges fought one another and scent-marked where their borders overlapped, yet they too sometimes social-groomed in the neutral zone. Even females from the same range had separate core areas and foraged singly, coming at different times to the same gum trees.

Another isolated group of 2 to 6 bushbabies that occupied a 17-acre (7-ha) range, consisting of a mother with her daughters and babies, associated over a period of years with the same male, often on a daily basis. Their territory was only part of his range, which varied seasonally along with his feeding grounds. He was with this family 20% of the time the group was observed, and found sleeping with or near them ⅓ of the days the animals were located in their nests. Presumably he divided his time between 2 or 3 different families.

SLEEPING QUARTERS Up to a dozen trees favored as sleeping and resting places are scattered through a territory. Several sites are usually clustered in particular trees, preferably forks or limbs among closely interlaced branches or tangled vines 15 to 45 ft (5–12 m) high. Greater bushbabies sometimes sleep on exposed branches. Nests, constructed only when females have small babies, consist of leafy platforms with a hollow in the middle.

HOW IT MOVES Differently from other bushbabies. Walks and runs along branches monkey-style, instead of hopping, making short jumps only while going fast. On the ground, either walks with hindquarters and tail elevated, hops like a kangaroo with forelegs dangling, or jump-runs. This bushbaby also has a slow, stealthy way of moving, sometimes while suspended below a branch, recalling pottos and perhaps also designed to escape predators' notice.

FORAGING BEHAVIOR Ranging habits comparatively regular, reflecting dependence on fruit and gum rather than insects. Spends several hours in a fruiting tree and keeps coming back as long as ripe fruits last; also makes nightly rounds of acacia and other productive gum trees. Ripe fruit, flowers, and oozing gum are located by scent. Figs and other small fruits are plucked by mouth, carried to a perch, and eaten from one hand. Chews away and discards the peel of large fruits, then licks or scrapes out the inside, using its tooth comb; licks fresh gum and chews older deposits, making incredible contortions to get at hard-to-reach goodies. As an insectivore, greater bushbaby lacks both agility and the quick-grabbing reflex of other galagos.

REPRODUCTION   Breeds annually in South Africa and coastal Kenya. Twins or triplets prevail in south, whereas single offspring is born in Kenya. Gestation c. 18 weeks.

MATING   During a mating season as short as 2 weeks in South Africa, female's genitals become red and swollen. Male's scrotum, normally fur-covered, enlarges and bare pink granular skin appears in the middle. Sexually stimulating secretions are produced at these sites. Two to 16 days later, female comes into heat for 2 to 10 days, cycling every 35 to 49 days if unbred. While resident males monopolize matings, young adults often surround and harass mating couples, provoking growling, grabbing, and spats.

OFFSPRING AND PARENTAL CARE   Unlike other galagos, foraging greater bushbaby mothers carry babies with them, once they are strong enough to cling to her broad back. For first 2 weeks while babies stay on a leaf nest or in a dense vine tangle, she carries them by mouth 1 at a time if moving necessary. At 25 days juveniles are capable of following mother; they begin licking gum by 5 weeks, but continue to ride and nurse until c. 10 weeks. Close association continues at least until they are subadult at c. 300 days, when they begin foraging independently.

PREDATORS   Genets and palm civets, the main mammalian predators, are no threat to adults, and only the largest birds of prey, mostly diurnal, are dangerous. They become vulnerable to larger predators while on the ground, however, and react very quickly to disturbances when there.

HOW IT COMMUNICATES

SCENT   Although it urine-marks in usual ways, secretions of the chest and scrotal/labial glands are apparently most important. No scent marking of partners reported during courtship. Analysis of chest-gland secretions shows they encode the time a deposit was made, and the sex, age, and individual identity of the marker, thereby enabling greater bushbabies to share a small area with minimal strife.

CALLS   Basic repertoire includes 10 to 11 calls, most very like lesser bushbaby's repertoire, but close-range calls more variable, reflecting more social contact between foraging greater bushbabies.

Loud calls

- Raucous cry   Theme song of the greater bushbaby, given by adults of both sexes, especially males during mating season. Besides territorial advertising, call doubles as family gathering cry. Voices are so distinctive even people can distinguish individuals.

- Hack, spit, scream   Offensive and defensive threat (contact-rejection calls). Staccato hack and spit sounds of varying intensity, emphasized by screaming of very fearful bushbaby.

- Sniff, knock, creak, squeak, whistle, whistle-yap, chirp, chatter, moan, rattle   Graded series of alarm calls, progressing from weak sniff through the list with increasing power and duration. Aroused bushbabies hold forth up to an hour.

- Yell   Distress call: a high-pitched, plaintive cry of extreme fear or pain, as when fighting or captured. Evokes mobbing response by other bushbabies.

Close-range calls

- Crack calls   Low-frequency grating sounds emitted by courting males, usually while following females and during social grooming.

- Buzz, click, squeak, and cluck calls   Contact-seeking calls between mother and offspring. Babies buzz, click, and squeak; mother clucks response.

Table 30.2. *DIFFERENCES IN GREATER BUSHBABY BEHAVIOR*
Expect to see and hear ➤ *Usual context and meaning*

Advertising Presence and Social Status

SCENT-MARKING

With chest gland, in highly stereotyped way, rubbing the skin against the support with an upward movement, after first sniffing the spot intently and often after making contortions necessary to get into position. ➤ Both sexes rub oily yellow secretion of the bare chest patch on scent posts strategically placed along aerial pathways. Gland is active in bushbabies older than 3 months, but dominant ♂ ♂ mark most. ♂ intruders were seen to glance around uneasily and quit the neighborhood after smelling the fresh mark of a resident male.

Foot-rubbing. Adult ♂ rubs first one foot then the other against supports, making scraping noise. ➤ Commonly performed along with urine- and chest-gland marking during social encounters and encounters with predators. Wartlike spines on the feet make scraping noise. Function unknown.

Advertising Presence and Social Status *continued*

DISTANCE CALLS

Raucous cry. Caller broadcasts with mouth slightly open, shaking violently, often from tall tree while turning head. ➤ The cawing and barking call that gives bushbabies their name (see under How It Communicates).

Aggression

Chest-gland marking. ➤ As a threat display to other ♂♂ during courtship.

Defensive threat: combined with hack, spit, and scream calls ± urinating and defecating.

Sociable Behavior

Social grooming: licking and combing one another (with tooth comb). ➤ Unusually frequent in this species, among associated animals of whatever sex and age (except males older than 2.5 yr), usually when individuals gather between feeding bouts and at sleeping trees.

Courtship

MALE BEHAVIOR

Also see text, under Reproduction.

Courting ♂ approaches and greets ♀, giving clucking call; tries to sniff her genitals, which receptive ♀ permits.

Mounting attempts: ♂ sometimes gently bites ♀'s back.

After intromission, ♂ pelvic thrusts 4–8 min., followed by ejaculation. Repeats process every 20 min. or so during copulation lasting several hr.

LESSER BUSHBABY, *Galago senegalensis*

Figure 30.3. Male lesser bushbaby following female during courtship.

WHAT IT IS   A bushbaby smaller than a squirrel. ♂♀ wt 6-8 oz (150-200 g), hbl 7 in (17 cm). *Tail:* 9 in (23 cm). *Head:* round with pointed snout and big, pointed ears. *Coat:* short, soft, woolly. *Color:* light to bluish gray with yellowish arms and thighs; dark cheek and eye patches; nose bridge white; underparts white to cream; feet white to gray. *Teats:* 2 on chest, 4 on belly.

WHERE IT LIVES   The most widespread and common bushbaby, found in all sorts of woodland outside main rainforest blocs, up to 5000 ft (1500 m).

ECOLOGY   Most at home in acacia savanna and *miombo* woodland. There may be 500/mi^2 (200/km^2) in acacia woodland—up to 1300/mi^2 in *Acacia karoo* thickets of Northern Transvaal. One studied population lived entirely on acacia gum, insects, and other arthropods; they were not seen to drink water or lick dew, even in dry weather.

ACTIVITY   ● Early- and late-night activity peaks; period between spent feeding, exploring, marking, traveling, grooming, and sleeping, without any set pattern as each bushbaby is independent. Foraging time averages 6 hours, varying seasonally with availability of insects and gum. Remain active even in heavy thunderstorms.

SOCIAL/MATING SYSTEM 🔵🔵🔵 Females with overlapping home ranges associate in daytime sleeping groups of up to 7 bushbabies, including offspring and usually 1, sometimes 2, adult males. Presumably these are related females, as adults maintain exclusive territories, from which sons disperse while daughters often stay home. The home ranges of 15 bushbaby groups averaged 7 acres (range 3–9 acres [1.2–3.7 ha]). Roads and open spaces often define boundaries, although size and shape tend to change over time. Core areas also vary seasonally, but all parts of the territory are usually visited at least once a week. Adult males' ranges overlap little if at all and there are frequent turnovers in the territorial network.

Social relations within a female group appear quite complex, but no rank hierarchy has been detected although the senior female chooses sleeping sites and builds nests. Alone at least 70% of the night, bushbabies are essentially solitary most of their waking lives. They sleep through the day in contact, and on waking lick themselves and each other, but even mothers of young infants spend little time social grooming. One by one they leave the nest, bouncing along communal pathways a short way before branching off in different directions to forage. They often call to one another the first hour, thereafter keep silent until the group reassembles before dawn near the sleeping site, to socialize till bedtime.

SLEEPING SITES   A group uses up to 13 different sleeping places in a year; some trees are used for generations. Nests are platforms made of soft, broad, fresh leaves, nest size corresponding to the number of occupants. The best sites offer concealment and shelter from temperature extremes; used more in hot than in cold weather, when bushbabies often sleep exposed and occasionally sunbathe. East African lesser bushbabies seldom use nests at all. Males are more likely than females to sleep alone.

HOW IT MOVES   Sees well by starlight up to 30 yd, judging jumping distances precisely. Preparing to leap a 5-yd gap, bushbaby rotates head up to 180° while checking in all directions and from all angles, ears meanwhile moving independently. Airborne, it holds arms overhead while the tail helps maintain balance and an upright attitude (see Fig. 30.1). Descends trees in any position, head- or tail-first. Sleeping postures vary, from side curl with head covered by hands and tail, forward curl with head resting on hands, to seated or lying on back. Ears of a sleeping bushbaby are folded to its head, conserving body heat.

FORAGING BEHAVIOR   Nightly round of seeking and eating gum exuding from bark through holes made by boring insects, revisiting many sites on successive nights to harvest gum in preferred fresh, soft state. Travels ¼ mi (1.2 km) and visits about 500 different trees per night. Insects are caught either by leaping and grabbing them, typically as they take flight, or by creeping within grabbing distance, snatching quarry with a movement too quick to follow, meanwhile reflexively shutting eyes and flattening ears to protect face from flapping wings or spurred legs of such prey as locusts and grasshoppers. Immediately after, bushbaby bites the quarry's head, then opens eyes and unfolds ears.

REPRODUCTION   Typically twins twice a year during rainy season, after 121 to 123 day gestation, reentering estrus soon after first birth. First conception at 200 days and birth at 1 year (1 baby the first time). Discharge of whitish vaginal secretion signals onset of estrus, as membrane covering vagina opens and labia and clitoris become red and swollen. Signs of estrus persist for 7 days, but female is only receptive 1 to 3 days. Cycle repeats at c. 32-day intervals. Males call and urine-mark with adult frequency at 1 year.

OFFSPRING AND MATERNAL CARE   Born with eyes open on a leafy platform, babies can crawl and cling tightly to mother's fur within an hour. By 4 days use hands like adults, begin grooming themselves at 1 week; twins lick-groom each other beginning second day and play at 6 days. Birth weight of 0.42 oz (12 g) doubles in a week, quintuples in a month. By 10 days the nest is an unrestful place for adults, as babies climb over them, wrestle, stand up, and practice jumping. They leave nest on excursions by 2 weeks and in another week run fast along branches. Juveniles developing jumping ability often lose balance but never their grip. Mother still has to carry 3-week babies across gaps, by mouth 1 at a time. She parks them on branches, separately or together, while foraging, returning at shorter or longer intervals but always in time to arrive home before dawn.

Babies begin eating gum by 3 weeks and capture insects within a month. Juveniles of 6 weeks go foraging on their own, jump 1-yd gaps and descend to ground for the first time. Though still suckled on rejoining family at sleeping tree, there is little maternal care after 6 weeks and weaning is complete by 10 to 11 weeks.

PREDATORS   Virtually any mammal, bird, or reptile larger than an infant. But bushbabies are so well-concealed by day and so hard to catch while active that they are only vulnerable on the ground. Bushbabies that have to travel cross-country between scattered trees live most dangerously.

HOW IT COMMUNICATES

CALLS   Repertoire of 10 to 11 discrete sounds, similar to greater bushbaby's. Combinations of some produce c. 25 recognizably different calls—none nearly as arresting as the greater bushbaby's raucous cry.

Loud Calls

- Bark   Territorial advertising; contact with family members.

- Sob, spit, spit-chatter, spit-grunt, rasp   Alerting and alarm calls of increasing intensity and pitch.

- Fighting chatter   Combination of 2-phase grunt and aggressive calls, given when attacked.

- Grunt, sneeze, shivering stutter, gerwhit, cluck, whistle, yap, wuff and wail, caw, explosive cough   Alerting and alarm calls; series of increasing intensity and pitch starting with hoarse grunt. Upset bushbabies perform the whole string for ¼–1 hour, e.g., when sleeping-group members are gathered before bedtime and mobbing a predator like scolding birds. Other times, intense alarm calls make bushbabies move higher and freeze.

- High-pitched, plaintive scream   Distress call of intense fear or pain. Brings other bushbabies, triggers mobbing response; also attracts small predators hopeful of a victim.

Distance-Decreasing Calls

- Clicks, crackles, squeaks, coos, soft hoots   Mother-infant calls. Babies call mother with high-pitched clicks (*tsic* calls) and crackles, grading into squeaks. Mother comes, answers with coos or soft hoots; also calls to elicit answer and locate "parked" infants.

Table 30.3. *DIFFERENCES IN LESSER BUSHBABY BEHAVIOR*
Expect to see and hear ➤ Usual context and meaning

Advertising Presence and Social Status

SCENT-MARKING

Urine-washing: mostly in sleeping trees at onset of nightly activity, thereafter only once or twice an hour, at no particular spot. ➤ Performed more frequently by ♂ ♂, especially territorial ♂ ♂. Rate increases during aggressive interactions, disturbance by a predator, presence in strange area, and genital-sniffing of another bushbaby. Lesser bushbabies do not make scent trails.

Rhythmic urination. ➤ Mainly ♀ ♀. Vaginal secretions may be deposited at same time or in similar posture.

Chin, lip, armpit, and chest rubbing: Adult ♂ ♂ rub these spots against branches and on females after genital-sniffing. ➤ Skin glands are present in these areas, but not in the bare spot on lesser bushbaby's chest, making chest-rubbing by this species a puzzle.

Courtship

Scent-marking: with urine, lip, chin, and armpit glands. ➤ ♂'s marking rate goes up most when courting estrous ♀. Apart from rubbing glands on her, much of the urine ♂ voids is dabbed on her.

Chapter 31

MONKEYS AND BABOONS
Family Cercopithecidae

WHAT THEY ARE   The family that includes all the Old World monkeys. Over half the 74 species are African, including baboons, mangabeys, and the extraordinary array of forest monkeys known as guenons. The other half are Asian, including the baboonlike macaques and most of the leaf-eating monkeys, of which Africa has only colobus species.

FAMILY TRAITS   Dog-shaped (narrow-bodied with deep chest), size from 2.6-lb (1.2-kg) talapoin to 90-lb (40-kg) baboon. *Tail:* longer than head and body length (guenons, mangabeys, langurs, colobus) to short stub (drill and mandrill). *Head:* projecting muzzle (especially baboons, mangabeys, macaques); face partially naked. *Teeth:* 32; upper canines with knife edge, honed against modified lower first premolar, both sexes or males only. *Cheek pouches:* pair extends beneath the neck skin, used to hold food gathered by hand (absent in leaf eaters). *Buttocks:* padded with a pair of calluses (callosities), bare and often colorful in baboons and macaques, small and hidden in most monkeys. *Color:* from drab, concealing tan or brindled yellow to the most colorful mammal: the mandrill. *Gender differences:* minimal to great size dimorphism; color differences limited to genitalia of some guenons, macaques, and baboons; manes and facial hair in baboons, macaques, and several guenons. *Scent glands:* known in only a few species (chest gland of vervet and mandrill; armpit glands of gray-cheeked mangabey). *Teats:* 2 on chest.

WHERE THEY LIVE   In rainforests, seldom seen by visitors, both because regions are off the beaten track and foliage obscures the view. The species given separate accounts in this book are the common ones seen in parks of eastern and southern Africa, including 2 guenons, 1 baboon, and 1 colobus.

ACTIVITY   ○ All species diurnal.

THE DIFFERENT KINDS OF AFRICAN MONKEYS AND BABOONS

SUBFAMILY CERCOPITHECINAE

Guenons   24 species. About half the primates in Africa, and 17 to 20 of them (depending on whose classification you follow) belong to the genus *Cercopithecus*. So alike genetically that probably most could interbreed, but strikingly different uniforms help them avoid mistakes. The only 2 members of the genus that live outside rainforest are the blue monkey and vervet.

Baboons   5 species: savanna and hamadryas baboons (*P. cynocephalus* and *P. hamadryas*), mandrill and drill (*Mandrillus sphinx* and *M. leucophaeus*), and gelada (*Theropithecus gelada*). All are large terrestrial monkeys with doglike heads that live in multimale troops and develop extreme sexual dimorphism.

Mangabeys   4 *Cercocebus* species. These large (up to 24 lb [11 kg]), leggy monkeys with long, semiprehensile tails, shaggy coats, and drab coloration move, behave, and sound a lot like baboons. Forest dwellers, two species are mainly arboreal and 2 are semiterrestrial.

SUBFAMILY COLOBINAE

Colobus Monkeys   6 species. Long-haired, long-tailed monkeys very different in appearance, movements, and temperament from the other subfamily. Reduction of the thumb to a little stub separates colobus from all other monkeys. A ruminantlike digestive system, featuring an enlarged stomach divided into chambers where food is fermented and predigested by bacteria, enables members of this family to live largely on leaves, including kinds that produce compounds poisonous to most herbivores. Necessity to consume large quantities of foliage and prolonged digestion are reflected in a rather bovine disposition and prolonged periods of inactivity. Superabundant food enables colobus to achieve much higher population density than omnivorous monkeys: a square mile of Uganda's Kibale Forest supports an estimated 777 red colobus (*Colobus badius*) (300/km^2).

HOW THEY COMMUNICATE   Sight 1, scent 2, sound 1. Color vision in 3 dimensions and vocal signals have replaced scent as the primary communication channels in the diurnal higher primates. Loss of the vomeronasal organ, which enables most mammals (including prosimians and New World monkeys) to monitor female reproductive cycles by testing their urine, attests the downgrading of chemical communication. Still, odors play a major role in the social and reproductive lives of Old World monkeys and apes. Visual cues, notably colorful sexual skin, track female reproductive status, but most monkeys and apes lack this form of advertising. The main olfactory organ must play an important role in reproduction as well as in communicating social status and individual identity. Social interactions involve contact with genitals and other odor-producing areas. Genitals of newborn monkeys and apes are examined and sniffed by all troop members that handle them. Several species have chest glands, greeting gray-cheeked mangabeys sniff one another's armpit glands, and a skin fold behind the head of guenons allegedly bears a characteristic odor that helps identify species and individuals.

STEREOTYPED (DISCRETE) AND VARIABLE (GRADED) SIGNALS
Relative importance of visual and vocal signals and their form depend on social organization and where a species lives. In rainforest, where most monkeys live in small, territorial troops whose members are often feeding out of sight,

vocal signals are at least as important as visual signals. Vocal and visual signals between troops are peculiar to each species and fixed in form—i.e., highly stereotyped. By using discrete signals unmistakable for those of other associated species, forest monkeys maintain clear communication channels with their own kind—just as associated birds have distinctly different songs and visual displays.

The visual and vocal signals of more complex primate societies are more variable in form. When one signal grades into another and elements of different displays blend together, expressing subtle changes of mood and intentions becomes possible. The changes in facial expression that mirror changing moods in apes and humans depend on elaboration of facial muscles and, of course, the face must be unobscured by hair. Prosimians can do little more than open their mouths; in guenons, hair of contrasting shades largely obscures facial expressions. Baboons, macaques, and mangabeys, living in multimale troops where facial expressions are important in regulating social relations, have bare faces and ears, light skin tones, and eyelids of contrasting color (emphasizing aggressive stares).

That said, the most remarkable fact about communication among higher primates is the similarity of their signal systems. Monkeys and apes share the same basic repertoire of gestures and facial expressions. Apart from their distinctively different (mostly male) advertising calls, many species have similar short-range calls, and distress and alarm signals. To avoid confusion among forest dwellers, selection has favored the development of visually distinctive patterns and movements that convey both the identity and message of the sender to distant receivers in dim light. That is why guenons wear masks that distinguish their species while obscuring their facial expressions.

Table 31.1. MONKEY AND BABOON BEHAVIOR GUIDE:
VISUAL SIGNALS
> *Expect to see* ➤ *Usual context and meaning*

Advertising Social Status

Look of confidence: relaxed manner, tail raised or trailing, looking around casually, walking with level back and limbs extended. ➤ Self-assured individual of high rank. Dominant ♂ ♂ walk, even sit, with a special swagger.

Look of anxiety: nervous glances, back hunched, limbs somewhat bent, tail low or curved downward; sits hunched over, head lowered. ➤ Low-ranking individuals.

Adult ♂ (vervet) stationed apart from group, in watchdog role ± displaying penis and calling. ➤ Behavior of resident (dominant) ♂. Genital display advertises mature ♂ status.

Aggression

Supplanting (displacing) a social inferior, which surrenders place as superior approaches in confident manner. ➤ Commonest and subtlest way of pulling rank.

AGGRESSIVE MOVEMENTS

Usually in combination with staring and open-mouth threat.

Head-bobbing; "pushups" (lowering and raising body by flexing and extending arms); branch-shaking; jumping in place. ➤ Designed to threaten distant adversary (including predators).

Jumping about: jumping, free falling, breaking branches, often accompanied by aggressive calls (see Table 31.2 and Colobus Territorial Advertising, Table 31.6). ➤ Performed by dominant ♂ threatening rival troop or individual, also predators.

Slapping and scrubbing ground; striking toward opponent, and feinted attack. ➤ Strong threats commonly made during hostile encounters at close range; these actions are performed during fights or while punishing subordinates.

FACIAL EXPRESSIONS

Staring: fixed, intense look at an adversary. ➤ Effect heightened by displaying colored eyelids (baboons, mangabeys).

Staring with open mouth: typically in O-shape, teeth covered, often with head-bobbing (guenons) or -lowering (baboons) and pushups (guenons).

Bared-teeth threat: mouth opened to display canines; linked with staring. ➤ Can be either offensive or defensive.

Threat-yawning: accompanied by eyebrow raising, ear flattening, and aggressive gestures. ➤ Distinguished from tension yawning by other aggressive behaviors. Common example: ♂ baboon harassing a rival preoccupied with an estrous ♀.

Submission

Rapid glancing: alternately looking toward and away from feared opponent. ➤ Response to stare or other threat.

Looking away: deliberately looking in opposite direction (visual cutoff), or pretending not to notice threat, or to be preoccupied (with grooming or some object). ➤ Comparable to a man, glared at by a stranger, saying to himself, "If I pretend not to notice, maybe he'll go away."

Fear grimace: lips retracted and turned up, showing clenched teeth; often accompanied by fearful calls. ➤ See grinning under Sociable Behavior in this behavior guide.

Submission *continued*

Social presenting: standing or crouching with rear pointing at receiver and tail deflected to show genitals. Receiver may ignore or respond by touching genitals or mounting (usually without erection or intromission). ➤ The most obvious and effective primate appeasement display. Closely resembles sexual presenting, including colors that mimic sexual skin of estrous ♀. Functions to channel aggressive into sexual behavior.

Displacement Activities

Tension or displacement yawning: scratching; pretended eating.

Sociable Behavior

Nose-to-nose contact. ➤ The usual greeting in guenons, prelude to other kinds of contact.

Mouth-to-mouth contact ("kissing"): often seen when 2 monkeys hold each other, especially adult ♂ ♂. ➤ Often combined with lip-smacking, tongue-clicking, and grinning.

Genital-sniffing: most frequent in response to ♀ presenting; also mutual genital-sniffing while two monkeys circle head-to-tail.

Touching (including touching and manipulating genitals). ➤ As a gesture of reassurance.

Social presenting. ➤ To reassure inferior or invite juvenile to climb aboard (see also under Submission).

Social grooming: using fingers and lips to remove skin particles, parasites; partners take turns (but ♂ ♂ give less than they receive—except when courting). ➤ Main form of social bonding, performed mostly among relatives, usually initiated by lower-ranking individual; often directed to mothers as a way of gaining access to their infants.

Grooming invitation: offering part to be groomed: seated facing or away, arm raised; lying offering back or front. ➤ Similar in all species.

Sitting, sleeping in contact, ± tail-twining.

Lip-smacking. ➤ Signals peaceable intentions, reassures approached individual. Common prelude to social grooming, infant handling, and copulation (limited mainly to grooming in guenons).

Grinning: similar to fear grimace, lips drawn back showing teeth, jaws closed. ➤ Reassuring or appeasing signal comparable to and often combined with lip-smacking.

Teeth-chattering. ➤ Similar to and probably derived from lip-smacking, but less common.

Courtship

♂ – ♀ consortship: ♂ keeping close to ♀ and keeping other ♂ ♂ away. ➤ In multi-♂ societies, dominant ♂ takes over when ♀'s sexual swelling reaches maximum.

Social grooming.

Sexual presenting by ♀, often with pout-face expression.

Copulation: (baboon) ♀ pouts and shows light eyelids. ➤ Identical stance in all species, but standing on ♀'s ankles not universal (e.g., not in colobus).

Care of Offspring

Clinging to mother's front. ➤ Infants and juveniles.

Riding astride (jockey position). ➤ Older juveniles.

Maternity groups, handling infants, social grooming.

Play

Play face: teeth bared as in bared-teeth threat, but eyes slitted or partially closed, never staring; combined with antic behavior. ➤ Play invitation.

Play with peers: wrestling, chasing.

Solitary play: with objects, with mother or other older animals.

Response to Predators

Head-bobbing, pushups, branch-shaking, jumping about. ➤ Threat displays (see above).

Mobbing, as in birds, or actual coordinated attacks (baboons).

Table 31.2.   *MONKEY AND BABOON BEHAVIOR GUIDE: CALLS*
Expect to hear ➤ Usual context and meaning

Advertising Social Status

MALE LOUD CALLS

Type 1: boom calls of blue monkey and several other forest guenons, grunt-roars of baboons. ➤ Most distinctive and audible calls in the species' repertoire, acquired at maturity; resonance enhanced by vocal sacs (blue monkey) or enlarged larynx (colobus). In 1-♂ troops, emitted by resident ♂, especially at beginning of day.

Type 2: *pyow* and *ka-train* calls of blue monkey, hack of vervet and red-tail monkeys. ➤ Response to any disturbance of the troop; calls develop in subadult ♂ ♂, not limited to alpha ♂; less unique than type 1 calls (calls of different species similar).

Aggression

Grunts and roars: short, deep calls (grunts of guenons, 2-phase grunt of baboons) increasing in tempo, grading into barks and roars with rising excitement. ➤ Response to rivals in same or another troop, and to predators. Adult ♂ ♂ bark or roar more often than grunt.

Low-pitched, rhythmic, noisy calls: *uh-uh* (baboon), chutters (vervet). ➤ Derived from juvenile distress calls (e.g., baboon yakking from chirping). Signal onset of aggressive interactions involving ♀ ♀ and immatures; calls make a bridge between aggression and flight (alarm) calls (next types).

Aggression/flight combination calls: shrill calls (fear) combined with low-pitched aggressive calls. ➤ A graded series, from pure aggression to pure fear; balance between types reveals which emotion is uppermost.

Submission/Fear

Special calls addressed to dominant individuals by subordinates (e.g., *woof-wa* calls of vervets). ➤ Friendly dominant ♂ ♂ respond with greeting grunts.

High-frequency whistles, squeals, screeches, screams of intense excitement, fear. ➤ Similar in practically all species, function to inhibit aggression and elicit aid of other troop members, especially of mothers and adult ♂ ♂.

Sociable Interactions

GROUP COHESION CALLS

Calls continually exchanged by moving troop members that keep them in contact. Applies to all Old World monkeys except possibly colobus.

PROGRESSION CALLS

Nasal grunts emitted as soon as a troop begins moving, rate and volume varying with activity and conditions (louder, more frequent when excited or when visibility poor). ➤ Given without change of expression, not directed to individuals but evoke automatic response from all troop members except adult ♂ ♂. Voices change (in pitch, rate, etc.) with age.

ISOLATION OR LOST CALLS

Shrill whistles or barks. ➤ Derived from progression calls, given mainly by infants and juveniles temporarily separated from mother, also by adults after losing contact with troop (baboons).

SHORT-RANGE CALLS

Often associated with lip-smacking and presenting. ➤ Quiet calls derived from cohesion calls, exchanged during friendly interactions.

Greeting grunts: faster or slower than progression grunts, emitted by adult males. ➤ Function to reassure approaching juveniles and subadults, or other social inferiors (baboons, mangabeys).

Courtship

Copulation calls. ➤ Special calls that indicate ♀ receptiveness (patas, mangabeys).

Mother and Offspring

Infant-mother exchanges: shrill calls (e.g., trill of infant blue monkeys), similar to cohesion calls in some species. ➤ By modulating frequency and varying intensity, infant calls can sound plaintive, questioning ("where are you?"), peremptory ("come here!"), or violent (tantrums). Mothers respond in kind or with progression calls.

Response to Predators

ALARM CALLS

High-frequency sounds of short duration uttered in rapid, sometimes long series (guenon chirps, shrill barks of baboons). ➤ Voiced by ♀ ♀ and young to same stimuli that elicit ♂ type-2 loud calls. Close structurally and probably derived from aggressive calls. Function to bring whole troop to same state of alertness.

Guenons have different calls for avian and ground predators. See vervet account.

BLUE OR SAMANGO MONKEY, *Cercopithecus mitis*

Figure 31.1. Blue monkeys social grooming.

WHAT IT IS   A big dark monkey with a very long tail. Sturdy build. ♂ wt 11–15 lb, up to 26 lb (5–7 kg), hbl 19–27 in (48–67 cm); ♀ wt 8–10 lb (3.5–4.5 kg), hbl 18–21 in (44–52 cm). *Tail:* 22 to 44 in (55–109 cm). *Coat:*

shaggy with a brow patch of bristling hair. *Color:* geographically variable, from drab to colorful; torso bluish to reddish; forelimbs and tail usually black; crown pure black to gray ringed by a white diadem in some populations; blue-black facial skin framed by grizzled hair; underparts light gray to black with showy white throat patch east of Rift Valley. Infants have thin dark gray or blackish coat with pink face, behind, and extremities. *Genitals:* uncolored, but male's pale blue-gray scrotum contrasts with dark thighs.

WHERE IT LIVES   The only forest guenon with an extensive range outside the Lowland Rainforest, inhabits various forest types of eastern and southern Africa.

GOOD PLACES TO SEE IT   Most parks and reserves in its range that have evergreen forest; often semitame (if not a nuisance) around lodges and campgrounds.

ECOLOGY   Inhabits evergreen forests of all kinds, from Lowland Rainforest and mangrove swamps through montane forest into the bamboo zone up to or above 9800 ft (3000 m), and forest patches surrounded by savanna. Highly arboreal, frequents middle zone (36-60 ft [12-20 m]) in primary forest, avoiding strong sunlight. Omnivorous diet, feeds opportunistically on most abundant available fruits, foliage, insects, and other invertebrates. Two troops studied in Uganda's Kibale Forest ate 93 different kinds of plants, but 10 different trees supplied nearly 66% of the fruits and foliage they ate. They concentrated on just 1 or 2 types of food a month at a time.

ACTIVITY   ○ Kibale Forest troops spend about 33% of the day eating fruits and foliage, 29% resting, 16.5% moving, 9% foraging for invertebrates, 6% grooming, and 6% in other social and miscellaneous activities. One closely monitored troop mostly traveled from 7 to 8 AM and 5 to 6 PM, and had a resting peak from 1 to 2 PM; ranging up to 1100 yd and covering a different area of 10 to 25 acres (4-10 ha) daily. Preference for certain tall trees to sleep in often resulted in the monkeys returning to the locale where they started the day. When a favored food tree was fruiting, the troop would feed until dark, then go to roost in a neighboring tree and return early next morning.

SOCIAL/MATING SYSTEM   Typical of forest guenons: a troop of related females occupying a permanent home range/territory over which a resident male exercises proprietary rights. Group and territory size are bound to vary greatly in an animal that lives in so many different places. In Kibale Forest, 5 troops averaging 17.8 (11-24) monkeys occupied spacious territories averaging 151 acres (61 ha). In the Kenya Highlands, 3 similar-sized troops had ranges of only 32 to 35 acres (13-14 ha).

Female offspring stay in their natal troop unless the number of monkeys comes to exceed available resources, whereupon part of the troop emigrates.

Males have to emigrate and compete with other have-nots to take over or found a harem. With 6 to 18 females in a harem, rigorous sexual competition has caused males to grow 50% bigger than females. And yet, with lone males continually roaming the forests looking for their big chance, most of the studied troops have proved remarkably stable over time.

SOCIAL DISTANCE AND LEADERSHIP Compared to vervets or baboons, blue monkeys maintain a wide individual distance and disperse over a wider area while foraging. Still, a troop is a cohesive unit, keeping in touch and synchronizing their movements through exchanges of progression and phased grunts (see Table 31.2, Sociable Interactions). Group movements are coordinated and can be initiated by several monkeys of any sex or age moving in the same direction; the troop often goes toward the male when he gives *pyow* calls; normally he brings up the rear.

ASSOCIATION WITH OTHER SPECIES Blue monkeys often associate with other monkeys, especially the red-tail (*Cercopithecus ascanius*) in rainforests, also with red colobus, black and white colobus, and mangabeys. In the savanna, blues associate mostly with vervets, and with black and white colobus in gallery and montane forests. In Kibale, 88% of interactions with other species were aggressive, mostly involving food competition.

REPRODUCTION Births peak during rainy season(s). Gestation c. 140 days. Minimum interval between births 15 months, but if offspring dies, mother begins cycling within 45 days. It therefore pays a male that takes over a troop to kill infants. This jump-start enables him to begin reproducing 7 to 13 months sooner than if his predecessor's offspring survived.

MATING During the 30-day estrous cycle, females give no visible signs of their reproductive state, but tend to mate in bouts, each lasting several days, toward the middle of the cycle. Pregnant blue monkeys rarely copulate.

OFFSPRING AND MATERNAL CARE Born at a relatively immature stage, infant blue monkeys are rarely out of touch with their mothers for the first months. At 2 months, infants begin to venture a little way on their own, and about the same time assume adult coloration. Mothers may leave juveniles briefly with other females and go foraging alone.

PREDATORS Crowned hawk eagle, leopard, chimpanzee. Relatively little predation apart from humans. Hawk eagles elicit intense alarm calls; mothers hide in dense foliage if one comes close.

HOW IT COMMUNICATES

CALLS Repertoire of 7 calls, of which all but 2 are discrete; only phased grunt and growling seem to intergrade. Call types and functions explained in Table 31.2.

Male loud calls

- Type 1   Distinctive, deep boom, amplified by air sacs. Penetrates forest canopy with minimum interference or distortion.

- Type 2   Loud, resounding *pyow*, emitted singly in a slow, regular rhythm every 8 sec. or so in series. Calls of different males individually distinctive, easily locatable. Rallies troop and warns other males to keep distance.

- *Ka-train*   An initial burst of sound followed by a train of pulses. Emitted as alarm call for predators (crowned hawk eagle in particular) and during aggressive interaction.

Table 31.3. *DIFFERENCES IN BLUE MONKEY BEHAVIOR*
Expect to see and hear ➤ Usual context and meaning

Courtship

Estrous ♀ following ♂ and soliciting copulation by approaching with tail raised, sometimes croaking, raising her chin, and shaking her head before presenting. If he fails to mount at once, she may look into his face, put her muzzle to his, and nuzzle his genitals.

Copulation: ♀ walks slowly forward while peering back at ♂ with pouting expression.

VERVET MONKEY, *Cercopithecus aethiops*

Figure 31.2. Mother vervet holding dark infant.

WHAT IT IS The common small monkey of the African savanna. Slender form and long tail. ♂ wt 12 lb (5.5 kg) up to 20 lb (9 kg), hbl 20 in (49 cm); ♀ wt 9 lb (4.1 kg), hbl 18 in (45 cm). *Teeth:* long, sharp canines present in both sexes. *Color:* varies geographically, from silver-gray to olive-, yellow-, or reddish green; white to yellow-white underparts; black face, ears, callosities, and often extremities; eyelids pale pink; scrotum pale blue and penis bright red in adult males. Infants born with dark, silky coat and pink face. *Teats:* close together on midline.

WHERE IT LIVES Throughout the Northern and Southern Savanna and adjacent arid zones, from Sudan to Cape. Some 20 different subspecies distinguished, a few as distinctive as races of savanna baboon.

GOOD PLACES TO SEE IT Just about every park with savanna habitat; vervets are frequently pests around lodges and campsites.

ECOLOGY Lives in nearly all kinds of woodland, especially along edge with grassland. One of the few guenons that left rainforest to forage in grasslands, but vervet's dependence on trees for safety keeps it from venturing very far. Often associated with riverine vegetation, especially groves of fever trees (*Acacia xanthophloea*), which provide both safety and sustenance year-round: gum, new leaves and thorns, flowers, pods and peas, even powdery bark and wood. Vervets eat the most abundant fruits, seeds, seedpods, new leaves, buds, sap, flowers, herbs, and grasses, along with invertebrates and some small vertebrates (lizards, birds eggs and nestlings). Insects, herbs, and grasses eaten mainly in the rainy season. Vervets help propagate their food plants by dispersing seeds in their droppings

ACTIVITY ○ The usual morning and late afternoon activity peaks, but daily ranging varies widely with habitat, predation pressure, distribution of food plants and water. Even neighboring troops can have consistently different routines. Vervets in Kenya's Amboseli NP go to water every other day, mainly in early afternoon, whereas vervets on Lolui Island, Lake Victoria, rarely drink. Daily ranging varies from 350 to 2600 yd, but one drought-stricken troop traveled 11 mi/day (18 km/day). A troop foraging on ground moves slowly on broad front, turning over dung and rocks, poking in holes for insects and such; travels purposefully in close single file when crossing between groves of trees.

SOCIAL/MATING SYSTEM (♂♂♂♀o♀o♀o) Vervets studied on
Lolui Island, a botanically rich mosaic of thickets, grassland, and forest, lived in troops averaging c. 11 monkeys: 2 adult males, 4 adult females, and 5 young, at a density of 230/mi² (89/km²). In Amboseli NP, troops based in groves of fever trees surrounded by grassland varied from 8 to 50 vervets (average 25), with 1 to 8 adult males, and maintained territories 2 to 10 times bigger than on Lolui (45–189 acres [24–76 ha]).

The basic units of vervet society are family groups of females and young that share and jointly defend a traditional home range. A number of attached males jointly defend the females and their land against males from other territories, while also competing with one another for social and reproductive dominance. A family rank order determines each female's social standing: the mother's rank predetermines her daughter's, beginning in infancy. Females of lower-ranking families have to kowtow even to juveniles of higher rank, or risk chastising by their mothers. First families take precedence at any resource in short supply. The lower classes literally curry favor with these aristocrats by vying to groom them, handle their babies, and enlist their support in disputes. But adult females restrict most of their social interactions to individuals close to themselves in rank, favoring close relatives.

Unlike females, male vervets transfer to another troop as they mature, ending 2 to 3 years of harassment by dominant males beginning with development of colorful genitalia in adolescence. Most transfers occur during the mating season. Changing troops is dangerous, for apart from predators possibly encountered en route, vervets of both sexes hate immigrants. Differences in size and weapons are so slight that an adult female vervet is more than a match for a barely adult male; females also gang up on male troublemakers, particularly newcomers suspected of infanticidal tendencies, sometimes with fatal consequences. So immigrants must avoid provoking a female or juvenile to chutter, rapid-glance, squeal, or scream, for fear of unleashing a mobbing attack.

Males can reduce the risks of emigrating by transferring with brothers or peers, or by joining a troop containing an older brother. Studies of Amboseli vervets showed that troops that exchange males are less hostile toward each other than those that do not. Males that fail to social-climb in the troop they join first usually transfer again, as often as not to a troop without relatives;

most thereby improve their rank. Perhaps to smooth the way, low-ranking males sometimes try to make friends with females during fracases with neighboring troops.

ASSOCIATION WITH OTHER MONKEYS   Vervets live among and use many of the same resources as baboons, also associate and compete with blue monkeys on the forest edge. Baboons always take precedence except on the smallest, outermost branches of food-producing trees but forage more in open grassland during dry season, thereby reducing competition. Male baboons prey occasionally on baby vervets, but lack the agility to catch older vervets in a fair chase.

HOW IT MOVES   Travels in a cross-walk both in trees and on the ground; runs in a bounding gallop. Vervets stand up straight, propped by the tail to peer over grass and spy-hop to get bearings in tall grass. Agile climbers, they rarely free-fall more than 1 yd but plummet up to 15 yd when displaying or diving for cover. Good swimmers, they sometimes enter water during flight.

REPRODUCTION   Seasonal, timing depending on climate. In Amboseli NP, mating occurs in the dry season, and births follow the short rains of October to December. Lolui Island vervets mate during short rains, have young beginning in long rains (Apr.) and continuing through dry season. Gestation 165 days; most females breed yearly, beginning at 3.5 to 4 years. Males begin at least a year later.

MATING   Vervets don't form consort pairs and copulate usually only once a day, mainly with dominant males. Periods of sexual receptivity range from 7 up to 66 days, but copulation not limited to estrus: females routinely copulate even during pregnancy. Usually there are no external signs of estrus, but in some populations estrous females develop sexual swellings colored like male genitalia.

OFFSPRING AND PARENTAL CARE   After a comparatively long gestation, vervet infants are more precocious and develop faster than other guenons. The first few hours, mother clutches baby and sits forward in a crouch; thereafter it clings securely to her front for at least ¾ of the day, fingers and toes gripping her fur and tail curled around her leg, tail, or back. Babies a few days old nurse sitting between mother's legs, sucking both nipples at once. Mothers let companions handle their infants, sometimes within hours of birth. Juveniles of both sexes and older females, strongly attracted to dark-colored babies, compete to touch, groom, cuddle, play with, and carry them. Adult males show no interest in infants.

Within a few weeks, babies begin expanding their network of playmates and babysitters, soon associating in cohesive subgroups with peers or older juveniles, but remain strongly dependent on mothers the first 3 months for food, warmth, and security. Then weaning begins: juveniles are forced to walk instead of riding on mother's chest by 4 months, and by 6 months forage and eat like adults, returning to their mothers only if bullied or for predator alert. When the next baby is born, yearling vervets are already established members of their troop, each closely associated with its own family.

PLAY   Vervet young spend much of their free time playing, beginning as early as 2 weeks, usually with other youngsters. Adults are rarely playful.

PREDATORS   Small size and ground foraging in the savanna make vervets vulnerable to more predators than any other African primate, keeping them from venturing over 300 yd from trees. Amboseli vervets have at least 16 potential predators but only a handful rate alarm calls: the 2 biggest eagles, leopard, serval, cheetah, lion, and snakes. Alarm calls for avian, mammalian, and snake predators differ (see How It Communicates).

HOW IT COMMUNICATES   Visual signals are more important for vervets than for other guenons, both because they live in relatively open, brightly lit habitats and in socially complex, competitive multimale and multifamily troops. At least 60 physically distinct gestures have been described, and their vocal repertoire includes no less than 36 distinct sounds. Most, however, are similar to the visual and vocal signals of other guenons.

CALLS   (Others listed in Table 31.2.)
Male loud calls   Absent from vervet repertoire (characteristic of 1-male territorial systems).
Dominance and threat
- Intertroop grunt   Similar to progression grunt; signals that sentinel male has sighted another troop.

- Long *aar*   Given with mouth slightly open and puckered, by females and young. Rallies troop to repel trespassers.

- *Chutter*   Staccato, low-pitched chattering emitted by females and juveniles; expresses aggressive threat and solicits support.

- Bark   Low-pitched, gruff call given by adult and subadult males running toward quarreling monkeys. Message: "Knock it off!"
Submission
- *Woof, wa,* and *woof-wa* calls   Given by subordinate males, increasing in intensity from *woof* to *woof-wa.*

- *Rraugh*   Emitted mainly by yearlings, mouth closed or partly open, teeth covered, during approach to older dominant vervets.
Response to predators
- *Uh*   Low-intensity response to minor predator.

- *Nyow* Moderate-intensity response to sudden disturbance or sight of minor predator.

- *Chirp* Short, sharp, low frequency call, far-carrying and source easily located. Given by females and young with mouth wide open and teeth exposed, in reaction to major mammal predator.

- *Rraup* Rough, short call given once, by females and young at sight of avian predator. Other vervets come out of treetops or run into thickets if on the ground.

- Threat-alarm bark Male equivalent of *rraup*; high-intensity alarm and aggressive threat, uttered repeatedly by adults and subadults. Tempo and volume increase with predator's proximity.

Infant and juvenile calls
- Lost *rrr* combined with pout face. Very distinctive and stereotyped, individually recognizable. Signals distress and identity to mothers. Experiments show that females recognize calls of other as well as own offspring.

Table 31.4. *DIFFERENCES IN VERVET BEHAVIOR*
Expect to see and hear ➤ *Usual context and meaning*

Territorial and Self-advertising

Scent-marking: begins with intent sniffing of marking place with arms wrapped around the branch; vervet then rubs chest on the same place. ➤ Both sexes scent-mark territorial boundaries by rubbing chest, and less often cheeks and lower jaws, against branches and other objects. A highly stereotyped performance that totally absorbs the monkey's attention.

Penile display: watchdogs often sit with blue scrotum and red penis displayed as they face toward a neighboring troop. ➤ The message: "A mature male is on guard. Keep out!"

Aggression

(Tail positions) Supplanting: self-assurance shown by confident walk, as indicated by posture and tail position. ➤ The more tail is looped forward over the back, the more confident the performer and the surer the receiver will give way. Horizontal tail position is fearful.

Red-white-and-blue display: Approaching in confident walk, performer displays his genitals by walking back and forth or around the receiver, stopping before him in presenting attitude, or by exhibiting while standing and walking bipedally. ➤ A stereotyped display of dominance between males of the same troop. If effective, the receiver responds submissively.

SAVANNA BABOON, *Papio cynocephalus*

Figure 31.3. Large male baboon being groomed by female and juvenile.

SUBSPECIES

Olive baboon, *P. c. anubis*	Guinea baboon, *P. c. papio*
Yellow baboon, *P. c. cynocephalus*	Chacma baboon, *P. c. ursinus*

WHAT IT IS   A big monkey with a dog (*cyno*) head (*cephalus*). Powerful build with shoulders higher than withers, and sturdy limbs. ♂ wt 59-97 lb (27-44 kg), hbl 29 in (72.5 cm); ♀ wt 31-37 lb (14-17 kg), hbl 24 in (60 cm). (Data for chacma; wt of ♂ olive baboon up to 110 lb [50 kg]). *Tail:* 22 to 34 in (56-84 cm), carried like riding whip (sharply kinked in yellow baboon). *Head:* close-set eyes below prominent brow ridge; sizeable, nearly naked ears; long muzzle and powerful jaws. *Teeth:* adult males armed with knife-edged canines 2.5 in (5 cm) long. *Hands, feet:* wide, with stubby digits, thumb and forefinger fully opposable with precision grip. *Coat:* coarse, varying from long in Guinea and olive baboons, including a cape in males, to short in yellow and chacma baboons. *Color:* brindled, olive-brown (olive baboon), yellow-brown (yellow baboon), reddish brown (Guinea baboon), or greenish brown with dark lower limbs (chacma baboon); nose, lips, ears, hands, and feet black; callosities, rump, and scrotum colored like face, shiny and often with purplish tinge in adults (pink in Guinea baboon). Juveniles lighter colored than adults; infants black with red faces and genitals. *Penis:* pink, with bone.

WHERE IT LIVES   The most widespread African primate, a tramp species found throughout savanna and arid zones wherever water and secure sleeping places (trees or cliffs) occur. Destruction of primary forest, agricultural expansion, and local extinction of predators have enabled it to expand its range.

GOOD PLACES TO SEE IT   Innumerable. Tanzania's Manyara NP has probably the highest baboon density of any park in Africa.

ECOLOGY   Monopolizes the niche for a monkey able to forage equally well in trees and on ground, and to range far from refuges. Hamadryas and gelada baboons are still more terrestrial and subsistent on grasses, but replaced by savanna baboon everywhere they formerly ranged except for most arid parts of northeast Africa (hamadrayas), and cold montane grasslands of the Ethiopian Highlands. Able to satisfy water needs largely from food and dew, but most troops drink regularly; dig wells in dry streambeds.

Diet includes an enormous variety of plants: grasses (the mainstay in typical savanna habitats), tubers, bulbs, roots, leaves, buds, flowers, fruits, seeds, shoots, twigs, bark, sap, aquatic plants, mushrooms, and lichens. Even when grasses are dry and so low in protein that ruminants lose condition, baboons, like warthogs, dig up and eat the nutritious corms and rhizomes.

Invertebrates such as grasshoppers, spiders, and scorpions are important dietary supplement, especially under arid conditions; also fresh- and saltwater shellfish. Vertebrate prey, taken opportunistically, includes lizards, turtles, frogs, fish, eggs and young of nesting birds, crocodile eggs, small rodents, hares, and antelopes still in the hiding stage. Only adult males take such large prey and rarely share it. In South Africa baboons can become major predators of young sheep and goats.

ACTIVITY   ◯   Unpredictable activity makes baboons unlike most African wildlife. Apart from rousing well after dawn, going to roost before dark, grooming and socializing mainly before and after daily foraging, a troop may be active at any time of day. Distance traveled and time devoted to foraging vary with location, season, and daily weather conditions. Rainfall is best predictor of daily ranging: journeys are longest (average 3.7 mi [6 km]) in dry season and shortest in wet (2.8 mi [4.5 km]); 3 to 4 mi/day (5–6 km/day) is normal in acacia savanna, half as far in lush habitats, and twice as far in arid regions (6 mi [10 km] or more). Members of foraging troop spread out but maintain contact and 90% of them do the same thing at the same time.

SOCIAL/MATING SYSTEM   A baboon troop is one of the most complex, subtle societies in the animal kingdom. Social relations are influenced by gender, by standing in the dominance hierarchy, by male-female and male-male alliances, by emigration and immigration—all mediated by a communication system nearly as elaborate as that of the great apes.

Perhaps most useful for understanding what goes on in a baboon troop is the knowledge that, internally, baboons are competing to attain and maintain dominance—females of different matrilines as well as males—and that externally, the troop has to compete with other troops for the same resources while defending itself against predators.

Baboon troops are as small as 8 and as large as 200 animals, but typically include 30 to 40 members, half of them immature. Adult females outnumber males 2 or 3 to 1. Troop ranges overlap widely and can be anywhere from 988 to 9880 acres (400–4000 ha), depending on the distribution and richness of resources. Different bands avoid one another unless forced to compete for scarce sleeping sites, water holes, or fruiting trees, in which case the larger troop prevails.

Family groups of females and offspring are the core of a baboon troop. Females spend their whole lives in their natal troop and home range, unless the troop outgrows its resources and subdivides. Males transfer, often repeatedly, beginning as subadults, after remaining in their family groups and subordinate to their mothers until age 4, when they begin a growth spurt and develop their dangerous fangs. The female rank order is family-based, strict, and stable: daughters inherit their mother's rank. Each mother heads a matriline, wherein offspring are ranked according to age, the youngest first. Initially, the deference due offspring of a high-ranking family is enforced, if necessary, by mother or older siblings, but by 2.5 years, a female's rank is fixed for life.

Long-term studies have disclosed what may be pair bonds between male and female savanna baboons. Although estrous females tend to be sexually receptive to dominant males, especially macho-male immigrants, those that associate with females regularly at other times enjoy privileged status. It turns out that each female has 1 to 3 favorite males she roosts with at night, social-grooms with, and stays near while foraging. When she comes into estrus, one or more of these favorites usually becomes her consort.

So it pays males to cultivate social bonds with females, particularly after transferring to a new troop to improve dominance status and reproductive success. It is a win-win arrangement, as associated males play godfather roles to the females' offspring, whether the real father or not. Holding, carrying, grooming, and food-sharing involving adult males and infants occur almost exclusively with socially bonded males. Godfathers are quick to come to the aid of juveniles bullied by other troop members and also provide protection for their mothers. Low-ranking females benefit most, as dominant females, attracted like all baboons to black infants, often handle subordinates' babies regardless of the mothers' or the infants' distress. The proximity of a big male inhibits them.

Males also exploit infant, juvenile, and female associates in disputes with rivals. A lower-ranking male can safely threaten and even dominate a higher-ranking one by holding out a black infant—it completely inhibits the other's attack tendencies. Alternatively, two adult males join forces to subdue one that dominates them separately.

All intratroop rivalries are suspended when the troop faces competition from a rival band or has to confront a predator far from any refuge. All the adult males join forces; their readiness to cooperate in defending the troop is the reason baboons can wander the savannas with impunity, even in the presence of lions.

REPRODUCTION   Nonseasonal, but conceptions peak during rains, when baboons are fittest. Gestation 6 months. Estrous cycles begin at 4.5 to 5 years; conception c. a year later, birth intervale 1.5 to 2 years. Mothers typically cycle 4 to 5 times before conceiving again, starting 10 to 12 months after giving birth. With a life span of 20 to 30 years, females spend half their adult lives caring for offspring, another third pregnant, and the balance menstrual cycling. Males need 8 to 10 years to achieve parity with mature males.

Color and size of the sexual skin track the estrous cycle. During 7-day prelude to estrus (proestrus), sexual skin is black with a pink tinge and beginning to inflate. Estrus stage of c. 10 days follows, when sexual skin is fully swollen and bright pink. In 2 to 3 days after ovulating, deflation begins and within 7 days sexual skin becomes flat and black again, remaining in this stage (anestrus) for 9 days, during which menstruation occurs, usually invisibly. Then the estrous cycle begins anew. Swellings of adolescent females are small, gradually increasing to full size at 5.5 to 6 years. Callosities and adjacent bare skin (not including the sexual skin) turn from black to scarlet within several weeks of becoming pregnant. Sexual skin of lactating females remains flat and black as in anestrus.

MATING   Females in proestrus invite copulation from practically any male, presenting while showing white eyelids and often lip-smacking. Subadult and large juvenile males have mating opportunities at this stage only, as adult males take over once the swelling is fully developed. Adult and especially senior males only respond to females with fully developed swellings, indicating that ovulation has occurred. Although presence of spectators during copulation evinces interest, adult males display surprisingly little sexual jealousy—maybe because of the sexual preferences resulting from social bonds between particular females and males.

OFFSPRING AND PARENTAL CARE   Births usually at night, accordingly rarely witnessed. Mother supports newborn with one arm and may have difficulty keeping up with troop. Infant's bright pink skin and black hair begin changing in third month; replaced by adult coloration at 6 months although males retain pink scrotum for another year or more. Babies move well at 1 month, climb well enough second month to clamber over logs and adult baboons, and develop manual dexterity to pick up objects with hands instead of mouths. They begin riding jockey style at 6 to 12 weeks.

In months 3 and 4 juveniles begin playing together in the subgroups formed by females with small young. Now feed on easily accessible foods and climb fairly well but still depend on mothers for food and transport. Yearlings are nutritionally independent but depend on maternal protection and guidance for another half year.

PREDATORS   Thanks to the cooperative defense of male baboons, a troop containing infants vulnerable to predators as small as eagles or jackals can safely forage on open plains where lions, spotted hyenas, and leopards are an ever-present danger. Large carnivores may be quick to pick off stragglers but very few try to penetrate a troop's defenses. When a troop is alerted to danger, adult males move toward source and demonstrate typical vigilance behavior. Sudden alarm sends the whole troop racing for cover, while males and sometimes adult females stay behind as rear guard. If necessary, they go on the offensive. Leopards are only a serious threat at night, and most baboons are smart enough to roost in places where they cannot be taken in their sleep.

Readers should note that roosting baboons also have a very effective deterrent to disturbers of their peace: showering them with liquid excrement.

HOW IT COMMUNICATES

CALLS   (Others listed in Table 31.2.)

Aggression
- Tooth-grinding   Audible when two males threaten each other at close quarters.

Fear and alarm calls
- *Yakking*   Short, sharp *yak* given with mouth open in fear grimace, by subadults and adults withdrawing from threatening dominant.

Courtship
- Muffled growl   Mouth nearly closed, cheeks puffing in and out. Female during copulation (chacma baboon).

Infant/mother
- Clicking   Chirplike *ikk* given by infants and juveniles, equivalent to *yakking.*
- *Ikk-ooer*   Two-phase call given by infants responding to maternal rebuff, expressing low-level fear or moderate distress.

Table 31.5. *DIFFERENCES IN BABOON BEHAVIOR*
Expect to see and hear ➤ Usual context and meaning

Submission

Fear-grimacing and ear-flattening, meanwhile averting gaze or staring into space. ➤ Compound display of fear and threat (ear-flattening), seen when a subordinate baboon passes close to a feared dominant,

Fear paralysis: a baboon cornered during a chase (e.g., large juvenile ♂ run down by adult ♂), crouches or lies flat, rigid with fear, meanwhile grimacing and churring.

Displacement Activities

Twitching (head, arms, shoulders), shoulder-shrugging, muzzle-wiping, and exaggerated grooming behavior. ➤ Shoulder-shrugging and muzzle-wiping are performed by a startled baboon—e.g., the sudden appearance of a snake.

Displacement Activities *continued*

Harassment of a consort pair by rivals causes consort ♂ to make rapid, sometimes frantic grooming movements and to hurry copulation.

BLACK AND WHITE COLOBUS OR GUEREZA,
Colobus guereza

Figure 31.4. Black and white colobus monkey holding white infant (*from a drawing by I. Patterson in A. Richard*).

WHAT IT IS Large, shaggy black and white monkey with a grim expression. Sturdy, pot-bellied frame, hind legs longer and stronger than forelegs, very large feet, hands with stub for a thumb. Gender differences minimal except in size. ♂ wt 20–32 lb (9–14.5 kg), up to 51 lb (23 kg), hbl 21–28 in (53.5–69 cm); ♀ wt 14–22 lb (6.5–10 kg), hbl 19–26 in (48.5–64 cm). *Tail:* 26 to 35 in (67–88 cm). *Head:* rounded, short muzzle, naked face, protruding nose overhanging upper lip. *Coat:* geographically variable in length and extent of white hair. *Color:* glossy black with white brow and full beard framing gray-skinned face; U-shaped mantle of long white hair along sides meeting across lower back; tail varying in different races from thin and black with white terminal tuft to all-white brush on Mts. Kilimanjaro and Meru. Newborns all white with pink face.

WHERE IT LIVES Across equatorial Africa and from northern Tanzania to Abyssinian Highlands, in forest habitats from sea level to 9800 ft (3000 m). Angolan black and white colobus (*C. angolensis*) also ranges into East Africa (Rwanda, southwestern and eastern Tanzania into southeastern Kenya). Distinguished from guereza by white shoulder tufts instead of U-shaped mantle and face framed with long white whiskers instead of white brow.

GOOD PLACES TO SEE IT Lodges in Kenya's Aberdare Forest; semitame colobus at Lake Naivasha; montane forests of Mt. Kenya, Meru, Kilimanjaro.

ECOLOGY Ability to subsist indefinitely on mature leaves of a few different trees enables guereza to inhabit a wide range of habitats, including secondary and riparian forest with very little species diversity and a prolonged dry season, unfit for other monkeys. Because its needs can be met within very small area, this colobus also persists in isolated forest patches on cleared land, clumps of gallery forest along rivers flowing through subdeserts, and in secondary woodland. The best colobus habitat, such as montane forest of Kenya's Kikuyu Escarpment and Tanzania's Southern Highlands, can support 1300 colobus/mi^2 (500/km^2).

The guereza prefers young to old foliage, and fruits make up to ⅓ of its diet in season, but its advantage over other monkeys, including red colobus, is the ability to digest mature foliage too fibrous, distasteful, or toxic for other monkeys (see Subfamily Colobinae in Chapter 31). In Uganda's Kibale Forest, 1 abundant tree provides 40% of guereza's diet; its mature leaves are shunned by the other 4 monkeys living there. On the shores of Kenya's Lake Naivasha, colobus subsist almost entirely on fever trees (leaves and unripe pods).

A guereza eats 25 to 33% of its weight in leaves per day (4.4-6.6 lb [2-3 kg]), yet spends less time feeding than associated vervets (30% vs. 47% of all activity time). Meanwhile, leaf eaters spend 99% of feeding time just sitting on a branch plucking leaves, long tails hanging down like the lichens that clothe the cloud forest.

ACTIVITY   ○ The different climates and habitats inhabited by guerezas make for similar variation in activity patterns. In simplest outline, a troop's daily ranging takes it along regular pathways from a central sleeping tree to sunning and forage trees and back. Troops of montane populations leave their sleeping tree well after sunup and travel to nearby high places open to sun and in view of neighboring troops. Troop members groom and sunbathe up to an hour before continuing at a leisurely pace to their current food trees, often pausing to snack en route. After feeding intensively till midday, troop assembles to rest, groom, and digest during hottest hours; resumes feeding to perhaps an hour before nightfall, then retraces route to sleeping tree, purposefully now and single file until home again. Then they relax, groom, and socialize some more before settling down to sleep at dusk. Cold, misty, or rainy days common in the mountains completely disrupt this schedule: guerezas sit hunched over like little old folk praying for the sun to appear.

SOCIAL/MATING SYSTEM   Troops typically number 6 to 10 individuals. The average in prime habitat is c. 9, including 1 adult male, 3 or 4 females, 2 subadults, 1 juvenile, and 1 infant. The maximum number of females is about 5 and the record troop totaled 19. Territories are remarkably small: from under 12 to 62 acres (5-25 ha).

Troops sometimes contain more than 1 adult male. Four of 21 groups accurately classified in Kibale and Budongo forests contained 1 or 2 extra males and 1 contained 4. The record was 6 big males in one group (but 2 were probably subadults). A male leaving his natal troop soon joins up with another male in like circumstances or becomes a peripheral male in another troop.

However, only the resident male is privileged to perform territorial displays and mate; others are subordinates or satellites. Minimal visible gender differences favor this arrangement since satellites can avoid provoking the resident male by behaving, as well as looking, like females and keeping a respectful distance from him and his harem.

The downside: tolerance increases vulnerability to an overthrow possibly followed by infanticide. Three of 7 Kibale troops were taken over in 4 years. In 2 instances 5 or 6 large males attached themselves to a 1-male troop some months before the overthrow; afterward, all but the new resident male left. Infanticide, deduced from circumstantial evidence, remains to be confirmed (but has been confirmed in red colobus).

How can a resident male cope with a whole gang of intruders? If he tries to keep them out and they keep coming back, he becomes exhausted; if tolerant, he encourages insolence that may lead to a takeover attempt. Maybe his only option is to exert himself just enough to keep the invaders intimidated. One proven way to do that is by redirecting aggression to the neighbors, from whom he has far less to fear, by vigorously performing territorial advertising displays (see Table 31.6).

Guereza troops are unusually cohesive. Even while feeding, members can sit close together as they pluck leaves. Females and young stay closest and subadult males stay furthest from the rest, a little further than the resident male. A remarkably low level of intragroup aggression, usually only supplanting by the adult male, and frequent social grooming and other friendly interactions, facilitate clustering. Troop movements are mostly led by the oldest female, after an exchange of soft grunts. Hostile encounters with the neighbors are initiated by the resident or sometimes by a subadult male.

HOW IT MOVES   With the bounding motion of a squirrel, at different speeds. A jumping guereza holds its elbows akimbo and lands on its oversized feet with legs together and flexed to absorb the shock (see Fig. 31.5), using the rebound of the branch to gain momentum and extra distance on the next jump. It swan-dives across wide gaps; launching spread-eagled with cape and tail billowing, it arcs over until it is falling headfirst, arms forward ready to clutch at branches and slow its fall. Shinnies up big trees, embracing trunk while propelling itself with alternating feet, climbs down headfirst. Very clumsy on the ground, progressing in froglike bounds. Walk is plantigrade (the whole foot on the ground) like that of other arboreal monkeys.

REPRODUCTION   Birth peak during rainy season but not strictly seasonal. Gestation 6 months; average interval between births 20 months. Females mature at 4, males at 6.

OFFSPRING AND PARENTAL CARE   Infants frequently handled by troop members, especially during first 2 weeks while faces remain pink. Usually after, but sometimes without first grooming mother, adult or subadult

Figure 31.5. Jumping sequence of the black and white colobus (*redrawn from R. Mittermayer*).

female takes baby even if the infant protests. A colobus holding two babies is not uncommon. During first month infants are often handled 3 to 5 times an hour in resting group. Their appeal wanes with white color; dark juveniles older than 4 months are ignored.

Newborn guerezas are comparatively precocious but develop slowly. Move about and begin sampling leaves and twigs by 5 weeks; at 2 months eat leaves in small quantities and start playing. At 4 months a juvenile explores, plays, and feeds on its own except when troop travels. Five-month infants often follow their mothers while traveling and spend hours playing with peers. Adults hardly ever play, but mothers tolerate playful attacks, even allowing juveniles to swing on their tails.

Mothers ignore offspring over 6 months old except during group progressions; by then juveniles are ⅔ adult size and nutritionally independent. Still, juveniles nearly 8 months old cling to mothers when it rains and sometimes need help to cross wide gaps or climb; even 10-month juveniles otherwise fully independent snuffle and squeal if left alone and yearlings may huddle with mothers at night.

PREDATORS   Juveniles are fair game for crowned hawk eagles, but resident male defends troop, rushing eagles that land near. Guerezas make aggressive displays to other predators, including people; but when thoroughly alarmed sky-dive into the undergrowth.

HOW IT COMMUNICATES

CALLS

Croaking roar   Rolling *rurr rurr rurr* audible up to a mile, emitted by territorial males, which have enlarged larynx and vocal pouches. Dawn chorus, given when sound carries furthest, while troops are still in sleeping trees, is one of the unforgettable sounds of the African wild. Calling often breaks out at other times, even at night, in response to disturbances. Encounters between troops seldom evoke roaring.

Snorting An explosive noise emitted by all colobus except infants as alarm signal; often the prelude to male's roaring.

Snuffling Sounds like rooting pig, emitted by females and young during disputes, signifying mild distress. Grades into or alternates with squealing (squeaking and screaming), signaling strong distress.

Tongue-clicking Prelude to aggression between adults; a lower level of arousal than snorting. Softer clicks are often given during approaches ending up in friendly interaction.

Purring Soft grunting audible at short range, general alerting call given as low-intensity alarm signal, often emitted as prelude to troop movement.

Table 31.6. DIFFERENCES IN COLOBUS BEHAVIOR
Expect to see and hear ➤ Usual context and meaning

Territorial Advertising

Croaking roar by resident ♂. ➤ Described in How It Communicates.

Jumping about: spectacular leaps through tree canopy by resident ♂, noisy landings emphasized by slapping branch; often combined with roaring (see Fig. 31.5). ➤ Also performed as threat against rivals and predators.

Troop display: sitting and sunning in high trees within view of neighboring troops.

Aggression

Stiff-legs display: seated animal with legs angled downward, knees slightly flexed, and feet unsupported for 1–30 sec. ➤ Given by all classes except infants, as threat. Often combined with displaying partially erect penis by adult and subadult ♂ ♂.

Sociable Behavior

SOCIAL GROOMING

Very important in colobus social relations, performed at higher rate than in most monkeys. Troop members expect, even demand to be groomed and sometimes to groom. ➤ Despite lack of a proper thumb, grooming is similar to that of other monkeys.

Soliciting grooming: stretching out in front of intended groomer. If ignored, solicitor may slap the other's cheeks lightly to make it pay attention, then try again.

Grooming intention: groomer comes up behind intended groomee and starts in; or making frontal approach, grabs the other's forelock and pulls its head down to the desired position. If groomee resists, groomer delivers a few light smacks to the head, followed by another tug.

Chapter 32

GREAT APES
Family Pongidae

Gorilla, *Gorilla gorilla*
Common chimpanzee, *Pan troglodytes*
Bonobo or pygmy chimpanzee, *P. paniscus*[v]

WHAT THEY ARE   Prohumans with superhuman strength. The superfamily Hominoidea includes three families: the exclusively Asian lesser apes (gibbons and siamang); the great apes, with 4 species; and people (Hominidae), with 1 species. Biochemical evidence, supporting anatomical and fossil evidence, indicates even closer kinship with African apes than looks and behavior suggest: we share 98 to 99% of the same genes. Gorillas, chimps, and humans are twice as different genetically from the orangutan; the 2 lines separated c. 12.5 million years ago, long before human and African ape lines parted company (c. 6.5 million years). Apes became distinct from other Old World monkeys 20 to 17 million years ago.

Gorillas and chimpanzees coexist in parts of the rainforest, yet rarely associate or even meet, as they prefer different habitats. Chimpanzees like primary forest with tall trees, upper slopes, and hilltops; gorillas frequent lush undergrowth and second growth along watercourses and clearings on the forest edge.

FAMILY TRAITS   Large, tail-less, hairy primates. Barrel-chested, width greater than depth (like humans). Forelimbs longer and more developed than hind limbs. Thumb and big toe opposable (enabling feet to grasp). *Head:* robust skull, vaulted cranium housing large brain, prominent brow ridge; bare, flattened face with small nose, features as individually distinct as humans' (including family likenesses). *Teeth:* powerful jaws with 32 teeth, males with large, dangerous canines sharpened by honing against lower first premolars. *Coat:* thin (except mountain gorilla); no undercoat; ears, hands, feet, face, and other areas (gorilla's chest, female chimpanzee's rear end) naked. *Color:* blue or brownish black to brown and ginger (some chimpanzees); skin black (gorilla) to tan or flesh-colored (some chimps). *Gender differences:* size dimorphism ranges from minimal in chimps to extreme in gorillas. Penis with bone. *Teats:* 2, enlarged only during lactation.

SOCIAL/MATING SYSTEMS   Outlined in Chapter 29.

HOW THEY MOVE   See Chapter 29 for details. Walk on all fours, forequarters supported on knuckles. All apes walk fairly well bipedally. They climb cautiously, using all 4 limbs to secure weighty bodies.

TOOL USE Only chimpanzees are known to fashion tools in the wild, although gorilla and orangutan show equal manipulative skill in captivity.

REPRODUCTION Slow breeders; reach adolescence as early as 8 years but females cycle several years before conceiving. Males rarely breed before mid-teens, becoming prime in twenties. Females are sexually receptive usually just during estrus. Sexual activity is sporadic in gorilla harems, whereas chimpanzees have frequent mating opportunities with females that advertise estrus with a massive pink swelling. The difference in sexual activity and male competition of these two species is reflected in testes size: the gorilla's are 70% as heavy as a man's; the chimpanzee's 200%, largest by far in the hominoid superfamily.

OFFSPRING AND PARENTAL CARE Apes develop more rapidly than humans, but infancy is still prolonged; young seldom weaned before age 5. Mothers bear sole responsibility for bringing up offspring although older sisters practice mothering and sometimes even adopt orphaned siblings. Males behave protectively toward infants and juveniles, but only a gorilla, with reasonable certainty of paternity, risks his life to protect wives and offspring.

HOW THEY COMMUNICATE Sight 1, scent 3, sound 1. Anyone skilled in interpreting the facial expressions and body language of people should feel right at home watching apes. Their facial expressions and many of their gestures look like ours and have the same meanings.

SIGHT Apes see in color and at least as well as we do. Their faces register anger, fear, sorrow, joy, surprise, and other emotions. Some facial expressions are linked with production of particular sounds, which change quality with the size and shape of the mouth and resonating cavities (sinuses). Putting these aside and considering only soundless facial expressions, the chimpanzee repertoire reduces to 6. The same expressions can be seen on a gorilla's face but, given very different physiognomies, are bound to look different and are therefore described separately (see Tables 32.1, 32.2, 32.3, and 32.4).

SCENT Body odors are important in ape social and sexual signaling, as evinced by genital examinations of infants and females. Undescribed scent glands are probable, notably armpit glands that produce the pungent smell emitted by excited gorillas, and odor compared to rancid human sweat has been noted among excited male chimpanzees.

SOUND Gorilla and chimp calls also sound very different. Although they have vocal repertoires of similar size and many of their calls are equivalent, the similarities are less noticeable than the differences. For instance, drumming on trees is the chimpanzee equivalent of chest beating by a gorilla, but also obviously different. Their charging displays are still more alike, but cannot be combined in a single description.

In apes, as in monkeys, distance calls are most acoustically complex and most distinctive of the species and individuals of that species. The gorilla's *hoot series* and chest beating and the chimpanzee's *pant-hoots* are amplified and made more resonant by air sacs, developed more in males than in females, connected to the larynx. As well as being long and drawn out, ape distance calls incorporate aggressive components that advertise a male's size and combative potential. A basic difference between the calls of chimps and gorillas is that most gorilla calls are emitted by adult males, whereas the species' whole repertoire is possessed by all individuals of the more independent and individualistic chimpanzees.

CONTACT   At least as important as in humans. Contact between mothers and infants is far closer and longer-lasting, especially compared to Western societies. As usual, social-grooming initiatives are taken by lower-ranking individuals and/or by one that wants something—to handle an infant or to mate. Apes also seek and give reassurance by touch, in the same manner as humans, and the places touched are the most sensitive areas: hands, face, genitals.

GORILLA, *Gorilla gorilla*

Figure 32.1. Silverback male gorilla chest-beating.

SUBSPECIES
Western lowland gorilla, G. g. *gorilla*   Mountain gorilla, G. g. *beringei*en
Eastern lowland gorilla, G. g. *graueri*en

WHAT IT IS   The largest primate. Robust build with big stomach, long, thick arms and short legs; wide hands and feet with thick digits. ♂ wt 352 lb (160 kg); maximum in wild 462 lb (210 kg), ht (measured as in humans) 4 ft 8 in–6 ft (1.4–1.8 m); ♀ wt 150–250 lb (68–114 kg), ht up to 5 ft (1.5 m). *Head*: massive; adult male with conical mass of bone and muscle; features individually distinct (especially nose); small ears. *Teeth*: big; sharp canines in adult males only. *Coat*: long and silky in mountain race; shorter and sparser in others. *Color*: blue-black to brownish gray, bare skin black (nose, lips, ears, chest, palms, soles); mature males with conspicuous gray or silver saddle. Newborn brownish gray. *Scent glands*: sweat glands in armpits.

WHERE IT LIVES   Western lowland gorilla: Lowland Rainforest of Congo, Gabon, Equatorial Guinea, Cameroon, Central African Republic. Minimum of 40,000, but in many isolated or semi-isolated populations. The smallest race.

Eastern lowland gorilla: Eastern Zaire and adjacent highland areas near Rwanda border. About 4000 survive in isolated pockets of rainforest. The largest race.

Mountain gorilla: Zaire, Rwanda, and Uganda border region. In 1992 c. 320 survived in or near the Virunga Volcanos and a separate population estimated at c. 300 inhabited the nearby Impenetrable Forest, in Uganda.

GOOD PLACES TO SEE IT Parks of Rwanda and eastern Zaire, especially Parc de Volcans, Kahusi-Biega, and Virunga NP.

ECOLOGY Nearly all gorillas live in humid equatorial rainforest, but few inhabit primary forest. Woody and herbaceous plants they eat grow only where sunlight reaches ground. Lush undergrowth lines waterways and swamps, but in narrow strips. Logged and cleared forests are much more extensive and productive; gorillas prefer regenerating secondary forest throughout their range.

Mountain gorillas live in forests between 9200 and 11,200 ft (2800-3400 m), visit alpine meadows up to 13,000 ft (4000 m). Mist and clouds often obscure sun and night temperatures can go below freezing. Massive trees of a few species dominate but do not shade more than 50% of the landscape, which has dense undergrowth of tangled vines, stinging nettles, wild celery, and other herbaceous plants.

Eastern lowland gorillas also live in mountains, northwest of Lake Kivu in tall, dense, variegated forest of Kahusi-Biega NP between 6600 and 8000 ft (2000-2500 m).

DIET Mountain gorillas of Rwanda's Parc de Volcans eat leaves, shoots, and stems of some 58 different plants in 7 different vegetation zones. But 9 mainstay species made up 80% of all feeding records, and just 3 species made up 60%: a scraggly vine (*Galium*), a thistle, and a kind of celery. Stinging nettles, blackberries, and a small *Vernonia* tree are also important foods. Roots, bark, grubs, snails, dirt, and dung are taken in small amounts to compensate for a diet deficient in vitamin B_{12}, potassium, and calcium.

Gorillas do not share food or use tools but are very skillful at opening and eating the palatable parts of each plant, whether roots, fruits, shoots, leaves, bark, pith, or grubs living in rotting wood.

ACTIVITY ○ Fairly regular daily pattern, varying from group to group, subject to greater daily variation in mountains (changeable weather conditions). Mountain gorillas huddle motionless in cold, rainy weather, and on sunny mornings often put off foraging to continue basking. On average day, a group spends 30% of time feeding, 30% traveling, and 40% resting, mainly at midday. Activities are closely synchronized, revolving around silverback leader. Daily ranging of Virunga gorillas, extremely variable, averages 380 to 600 yd (range 100-2700 yd). Gorillas of Kahuzi-Biega and Equatorial Guinea travel c. 1170 yd (1 km) a day.

NEST-BUILDING Gorillas build nests in trees or on ground to sleep in at night and most make nests for midday siesta. Group composition can be told by number and size of nests and the dung deposited in them. Construction takes at most 5 minutes, as seated or standing gorilla pulls in, bends over, or breaks off branches, placing them around and under body to form a crude platform or hollow with a roughly circular rim. Nests enable gorillas to sleep lying down, without falling from tree or rolling down steep slope.

SOCIAL/MATING SYSTEM Nonterritorial harem. A gorilla population consists of a number of silverback (adult) males, with or without harems of females and young. Annual home ranges are 1.5 to 3 mi² (4–8 km² in the Virunga Mountains and 7 to 9 mi² (20–25 km²) in lowland forest. Ranges overlap and change from year to year, have no sharp boundaries and are undefended. However, each group or lone male has a smaller core area where it spends most of its time, and different units normally avoid meetings—except when silverbacks are intent upon adding females to their harems.

A typical harem numbers 9 gorillas (range 2–20) in the eastern races, and only 5 (range 2–12) in the western race (Equatorial Guinea). The largest recorded group numbered 37. A mountain gorilla group typically includes 1 mature silverback, 1 young adult blackback son (8–12 years old), 3 wives, and 2-young (under 8 years). Different big groups of eastern gorillas have been known to contain up to 4 silverbacks (1 fully mature, the others grown sons), 5 blackbacks, 12 adult females, and 16 young.

TOUGH BUT OH SO GENTLE?   Before gorillas were studied in the wild, they were portrayed as about the most dangerous and savage of all wild beasts. Popular books and films based on studies of the mountain gorilla reversed that image, and the public now thinks of them as gentle, even pathetic giants driven to the edge of extinction by our species. This is the truer image: feeding and resting gorillas are as peaceful as cattle, and what remains of the mountain gorilla's range is literally mountain tops standing as islands in a rising tide of humanity. But mature male gorillas are another matter. The gorilla's legendary ferocity is based on the spectacular charging displays of silverbacks defending their families. Thanks to the strong nerves of gorilla observers, we now know that 99% of their charges are bluff—the silverback rarely follows through and clobbers intruders. But if the objective is to intimidate enemies and keep them at a distance, the display is outstandingly successful. And if pressed, silverbacks will follow through—so, many have died, overwhelmed by the guns and spears of poachers (and, not so long ago, by museum and zoo collectors).

Benign as they may appear within the peaceful family setting, silverbacks are nonetheless despots, perhaps as fearsome to females and young as to puny humans. The silverback's every wish is his troop's command. He leads and makes all the decisions, emits 92% of the group's calls, takes precedence whenever access to food or a mineral lick is limited, and can quell boisterous or quarrelsome behavior with a look, frown, or grunt. Each female is bonded to him and not to other females; he is the common link between them and their offspring, and his wives compete to groom and stay closest to him. The alpha female and her youngsters are the best-protected family members. If a group is left leaderless by the death of the silverback, it tends to disintegrate.

The reason male gorillas are so awesome has to do not with predators but with rigorous sexual competition. Like various animals with nonterritorial, polygynous mating systems (baboon, giraffe, elephant, buffalo, etc.), male gorillas mature much more slowly than females and continue growing into middle or old age, leading to a dominance hierarchy based on size and seniority. To compete for a harem, a male must have an established home range and the self-assurance to confront any rival. Few are mature and experienced enough before turning 15, maybe 4 years after becoming peripheral to and finally separating from their families.

A harem is acquired one female at a time, either by persuasion or conquest. Beginning in adolescence at around 8 years, females transfer to another group, usually at least twice; they become permanent members of the group in which they finally give birth. Some join large, established harems, but more elope with a lone silverback or join a small group. Since the first wife ranks highest and each newcomer has the lowest rank, lone silverbacks may be the best catch.

Females are neither abducted by force from their harems nor forcibly detained by silverbacks, which rarely show sexual interest in immature females. Yet over ⅔ of the transfers observed in the Parc des Volcans involved confrontations. Most occur when a group contains a female in heat; hostilities may continue intermittently for days and involve adult females as well as all adult and subadult males. The defending silverback tries to intimidate rivals with hooting, chest beating, and display runs; meanwhile, his armpit glands give off a pungent smell humans can detect at 25 yd. Broken canines and healed head wounds present in ¾ of found adult male skulls attest to violent encounters. When a bold intruder charges right into a family, females are also likely to be injured as they seek to defend their offspring from infanticide. Killing a rival's offspring is one way of competing for reproductive success—it also serves to make mothers sexually receptive again within days or weeks.

REPRODUCTION   Very slow. Average interval between births 4 years; first birth at 9 to 12 years; gestation 8.5 months. Given a mortality rate of 46% of live births, as in Parc des Volcans, a female that lives 40 to 50 years may leave 2 to 6 progeny. Males are infertile until they become silverbacks at 11 to 13 years, but a silverback with 3 or 4 wives that lives 50 to 60 years leaves 10 to 20 offspring. One grizzled patriarch, estimated to be 55 to 60 years old, had 19 known descendants and was still in charge of a harem.

MATING During 1 to 2 day estrus, copulation occurs at c. 3-hour intervals, usually initiated by female. Male clasps her around waist and either sits upright or leans forward, while she squats, arms wide, hands on ground or holding male's hands; or she rests on elbows with rump elevated. Rarely a couple copulates face to face. Both parties make thrusting motions and vocalize during the 1- to 2-minute act (range 15 sec.–20 min.). Copulation calls often attract attention of lone silverbacks; resident silverbacks become particularly irascible and vigilant when rivals are lurking in the undergrowth.

Female in heat often stimulates sexual behavior of other group members. Females mount other females and youngsters; young males mount and attempt to copulate with (usually female) peers. Group members keep away from a mature female in heat, but silverback may tolerate copulations with adolescent females.

OFFSPRING AND PARENTAL CARE Though weighing only 4.5 lb (2 kg), newborn has coat and clings to mother's front with hands and, less securely, with stubby toes. Gorillas develop about twice as fast as humans. An infant rescued from poachers crawled, bounced up and down, grinned, chuckled, and started to play at c. 8 weeks; walked and explored beyond arm's length at 4 months when it would normally begin riding mother's back. By 6 to 7 months a gorilla can already climb but continues to nurse until 1.5 to 2 years old. A growing youngster spends increasing time socializing and playing, mostly with its own siblings and parents unless there are playmates its own age. Older siblings and the silverback are gentle and protective—an orphaned juvenile slept in the same nest with the silverback. Juvenile females are permitted to groom and carry infants.

PREDATORS Leopards are the only large carnivore in gorilla country; crocodiles are potentially dangerous to lowland gorillas, although they seldom need go to water or swim. People are the danger, and where persecuted, gorillas flee for miles after a human encounter, their path strewn with liquid dung, a sign of panic. To face up to such fear and die defending one's family is nothing short of heroic.

Table 32.1. *GORILLA BEHAVIOR GUIDE: VISUAL SIGNALS*
       Expect to see ➤ Usual context and meaning

Facial Expressions

AGGRESSIVE
Staring: eyes fixed and hard, brows drawn down in scowl, lips pursed and slightly parted, head often tipped slightly down. ➤ Contrasts with normally bland expression of gorilla surveying surroundings without obvious attention.

Facial Expressions *continued*

Open-mouth threat face: staring with mouth partly to entirely open, lips curled back displaying gums and teeth. ➤ Expression accompanying charging display (see under Response to Predators).

FEARFUL/FRETFUL

Open-mouth grimace: resembles open-mouth threat, but instead of fixed stare, brow is raised, eyes shift nervously, mouth is opened wider and longer, corners drawn further back; head often tilted slightly back.

Lips pulled inward, mouth tightly compressed, eyes shifty (not looking directly at disturbance), head often tilted slightly up. ➤ Uneasiness.

Pout face: lips pursed or slightly parted, brows raised. Gorilla appears depressed and may whine. ➤ Typically seen in infants deprived of something they want.

PLAYFUL

Play face: open mouth, smiling but without showing teeth and gums; eyes relaxed.

Aggression

DOMINANCE

Supplanting: one gorilla getting out of another's way. ➤ Pulling rank by making inferior move aside or give up its place. E.g., silverback ousting ♀ from shelter during rain.

Strutting walk: body stiff, swayback, broadside stance, head turned away (but sneaking looks), arms bowed out at elbows, hair bristling, abrupt, short steps. ➤ Performed in a clearing or standing on a log where performer is visible to audience, rarely for more than 15 sec.

THREAT DISPLAYS

Display run (typically following hoot series). Rising on hind legs, grabs handfuls of vegetation and throws it into air; slaps chest (*pok-pok-pok*) meanwhile kicking one leg in air; runs sideways 1–2 yd; slaps undergrowth and tears off branches during or right after run; thumps ground with palm. ➤ Performed by silverbacks, especially in response to nearby rival. Actions performed as 1 continuous, violent motion finished in 5 sec. or less.

Displacement Activities

Tension yawning, grooming motions, pretended eating.

Sociable Behavior

Nose-to-nose greeting.

Embracing, touching (hand, head, genitals). ➤ Gesture of reassurance.

Social grooming. ➤ Mostly between mothers and offspring, ♀♀ with silverback ♂.

Sociable Behavior *continued*

Grooming invitation. Offering part to be groomed: seated facing or away, arm raised; lying, offering back or front.

Sitting, sleeping in contact.

Courtship

Hesitant, coquettish approach by ♀, to stand facing ♂ at a slight angle, waiting for a response. ➤ Soliciting by estrous ♀.

♂ opening or raising arms in clasping gesture. ➤ Signals readiness to mount.

♀ backing into ♂, looking back with pout-face expression. ➤ Sexual presenting.

Facial expressions during copulation: concentrated, ♂ with pursed, ♀ with compressed lips.

Play

Wrestling, climbing, rolling, practicing displays (chest-beating, strutting, etc.). ➤ With peers, older siblings, mother, father.

Solitary play: with objects.

Response to Predators

Charging display: rushing through undergrowth with vocal accompaniment (screams and roars), and threat face, usually stopping short.

Panic flight, leaving broad trail splattered with liquid feces. ➤ Gorillas subjected to hunting.

Table 32.2. *GORILLA BEHAVIOR GUIDE: CALLS AND OTHER SOUNDS* Expect to hear ➤ *Usual context and meaning*

Advertising Presence/Social Status

Chest-beating (see Fig. 32.1): alternate blows with open, slightly cupped palms. ➤ Practiced by all gorillas beginning in infancy, performed in any position—even hanging by one arm from a branch. Hollow-sounding *pok-pok-pok* is produced only by silverbacks (by air sacs sometimes visible as swellings either side of throat).

Hoot series: low-pitched but clear and distinct *hoo-hoo-hoo* that carries > 1 mi; repeated 2–20 times in series, volume increasing; hoots longer and plaintive-sounding toward end. ➤ ♂ advertising call, individualistic, typical prelude to chest-beating. Mouth parted and lips pursed. Usually given in response to sight or sound of nongroup members. Hard to locate, call also used as vocal probe by questing lone silverbacks.

Aggression

Roar of silverback ♂. Low-pitched, abrupt outburst, forced out through open mouth. Followed by aggressive displays, ranging from charging to short lunges. ➤ Among the most explosive sounds in nature, given only in situations of stress or threat, usually provoked by humans. Group responds by seeking protection behind silverback. Roars are individually distinctive.

Wraagh: explosive outburst, not as deep as roar, less shrill than scream. Never accompanied by aggressive displays. ➤ Call possessed by all adults, but voiced 9 times in 10 by silverback, in response to sudden stress, such as unexpected presence of people, alarm calls of other species, thunderclaps, wind. Group members respond by scattering.

Scream: extremely loud, shrill, prolonged up to 2 sec, repeated up to 10 times. ➤ May be given by all classes when group upset, but particularly associated with internal quarrels.

Sociable

Group cohesion calls: variety of intergrading, complex, soft grunting, rumbling, crooning, humming, purring, also wailing and howling sounds. ➤ Contentment sounds. Voiced mostly by stationary gorillas at end of long rest on sunny day or when surrounded by delicious food. Group about to resume foraging croons in chorus.

MILDLY AGGRESSIVE

Pig grunts: short, rough, guttural sounds. ➤ Warning, typically when gorillas dispute right of way or priority of access. Emitted mostly by silverback as assertion of authority.

Growl. ➤ Mild aggression in stationary group.

Pant series. ➤ Mild threat within group.

Copulation Calls

Calls by both sexes, building in intensity to longer, howl-like noises that cease abruptly when mount is broken.

FEMALE

Rapid, pulsating whimpers, lasting c. 20 sec.

MALE

Long grumbling noises lasting 5–20 sec.

Copulatory panting: low-pitched but loud *o-o-o-o* sounds produced almost continuously during intensive copulation.

Infant

Crying: sometimes building to shrieks and temper tantrums. ➤ Similar to wails of human infant. Gorillas rarely cry unless left alone.

Whining. ➤ Given when in danger of abandonment or injury.

Chuckling: rasping expirations. ➤ Emitted during play.

Alarm

Question bark: short call of 3 notes, middle note higher ("Who *are* you?"). ➤ 91% emitted by alpha ♂, signals mild alarm, as in response to branch-breaking by invisible animal or discovery of concealed observer.

Hoot bark. ➤ Alerting call expressing mild alarm. Group moves away.

Hiccup bark. ➤ Similar, but less alarm.

COMMON CHIMPANZEE, *Pan troglodytes*

Figure 32.2. Chimpanzee foraging in a tree.

WHAT IT IS   Our next of kin. Smallest great ape. ♂ wt 88 lb (40 kg; maximum in wild 121 lb [55 kg]), shoulder ht 31–37 in (77–92 cm), standing ht 40–68 in (1–1.7 m); ♀ 66 lb (30 kg), shoulder ht 28–34 in (70–85), standing ht same as ♂. *Head*: round or flat-topped, without crest, low brow; naked face, brow ridge, and big ears; small nose and nose holes; long, mobile upper lip. *Teeth*: larger than in humans, males with long, sharp-edged canines. *Hands, feet*: long hands and fingers, short thumb; big feet. *Color*: mostly black but varying from brown to ginger; coat length and thickness influenced by climate, age, and sex. Skin pink in infants, black to yellow in adults; often freckled, darkening with age. *Genitals*: females in estrus develop large, pink sexual swelling.

WHERE IT LIVES   From Guinea and Sierra Leone to western Uganda and Tanzania, north of the Zaire (Congo) River, in rainforest, savanna woodland, montane forest to 6600 ft (2000 m). Pygmy chimpanzee lives in primary rainforest south of Zaire River.

GOOD PLACES TO SEE IT   Gombe NP, Mahale Mts. NP, Tanzania; Kibale Forest, Uganda.

ECOLOGY   Adaptable, but most at home in rainforest, reaching densities up to 18/mi^2 (7/km^2), 10 times density in dry savanna. Chimps east side of Lake Tanganyika (Gombe and Mahali Mts. NPs) live in mountains covered with *miombo* woodland and evergreen forest; in Senegal's Niokolo-Koba NP they live in arid acacia savanna.

Opportunistic foragers, chimps wander alone or in small parties searching for edibles, gathering in larger parties to share bonanzas such as a fig tree in fruit. Annual diet of chimpanzees in Gabon rainforest consists of 68% fruits, 28% leaves, bark, and stems, and 4% animal food. Gombe NP chimps spend at least 4 hours a day eating fruit, and in growth season 1 to 2 hours eating young leaves, as well as flowers, pith, bark, and gum; seeds and nuts important in dry season. This population utilizes c. 230 different plants, while ignoring another 300 kinds. Each population and even each community has its own food habits and traditions; standard fare in one population may never be touched in another.

Around 5% of a chimp's time goes into foraging for invertebrate and vertebrate food, the latter including monkeys, bushbabies, nestling birds and eggs, and young bushpigs and antelopes.

ACTIVITY   ○ Fairly consistent daily pattern, with inevitable variation. Spend 45 to 60% of day feeding with morning and late afternoon peaks. Anytime between 9:30 AM and 3:00 PM but typically midday, chimps take siesta. They rest on ground or branch, sleeping up to half an hour, idly sitting, lying, grooming. Rainy days they build day nests and sit hunched over. Average day-ranging of females is 1.75 mi (2.8 km), males 2.5 mi (4 km).

NEST-BUILDING   Night nests slightly more elaborate than gorilla's, constructed in 1 to 5 minutes. Using fork, crotch, or crossing branches as foundation, chimp bends/breaks up to 6 sturdy branches and 10 smaller ones to make platform, using feet to secure each branch while crudely weaving them over and under one another. After adding leafy branches for padding, it lies down. Youngsters begin practicing as young as 8 months, really work at nest building between 2.5 and 5 years.

SOCIAL/MATING SYSTEM   Instead of staying in cohesive groups like gorillas and monkeys, this elfish ape goes its own way, bedding down wherever darkness overtakes it.

Chimpanzees live in communities of 9 to 120 animals, which may never all get together. Although gatherings of up to 70 chimps occur, groups other than a mother and dependent offspring are ephemeral. Minimum extent of a home range/territory is c. 2 mi^2 (5 km^2) in rainforest and averages 5 mi^2 (range 4–19 mi^2) in mixed savanna-forest habitat with an extended dry season. In Senegal chimps migrate within ranges of 77 to 150 mi^2 (200–400 km^2).

Chimpanzee territories usually have common borders and may even over-lap in prime habitat but are jealously guarded by community males, who exist in a state of hostility with their neighbors. In chimpanzee society, females emigrate while males spend their whole lives on their ancestral acres, associating together in a loose dominance hierarchy. Social relations are complex; high rank may be achieved through support of a maternal brother or friend, but associations are so casual that the ally may not be there when needed most. The alpha male stays on top by intimidating all his associates through frequent performance of the charging display (Aggression, Table 32.3). The main benefit of high rank is getting to inseminate the most females.

Adult females spend more time alone (50–80%, including dependent off-spring) than males do (2–54%). Each female has a core area of ¾ to 1.5 mi² (2–4 km²) where she spends 80% of her time. Community females are mostly unrelated and not necessarily on friendly terms. During adolescence (9–11 years), females range widely and mate freely but without conceiving. Nearly all end up transferring to another community, usually during estrus and just once, bearing young and settling down at 12 to 13. As resident females are hostile, an immigrant needs sponsorship and protection of community males to make a successful transfer; she also has to establish her own exclusive core area.

Contacts between mother and daughter cease with the daughter's transfer. Even before, their relations vary from affectionate to strained, whereas bonds between mothers and sons can last a lifetime (40–50 years).

BORDER WARFARE   Although relations between community males can be competitive to the point of fighting, encounters between males from neighboring communities can be deadly. Border patrols of up to 9 adult males sometimes spend up to 2 hours just listening and looking intently into enemy territory, clearly hoping to catch sight of some resident. If another male party comes into view, the 2 gangs give loud *pant-hoots* and perform threat displays without attacking. If 1 party is much smaller, it usually retreats—and in this way small communities lose ground to larger ones. But if a lone male—or even an old female—is spotted, the males may stalk, chase, capture, and then stomp, pound, and bite their victim so viciously that it dies within a few days.

FORAGING, HUNTING, AND TOOL USE   Foraging chimpanzees show impressive botanical expertise, an intimate knowledge of their range, and a detailed knowledge of where and when to find trees in fruit or flower. News of a food bonanza is broadcast by *pant-hooting* and *rough-grunting*, bringing all community members within hearing to claim a share. Such sharing was formerly considered altruistic; some even suggested individual foraging functioned to locate food sources that could then be shared communally. But it turned out that (a) only males give food calls and (b) chimps consume more food alone than in groups. Apparently males give food calls mainly to summon females for their own social and sexual ends; and chimps that respond are already in the know and simply anxious to get their share before it's all gone. So much for altruism.

HUNTING   A male prerogative, as in baboon and human societies. Like baboons, chimpanzees are opportunistic rather than systematic predators, although males must be on the lookout for opportunities, e.g., to cut off the escape of a nearby young baboon or red colobus. When opportunity knocks, members of a male party immediately take up positions and go into action like a trained team. Whichever male makes the kill has undisputed right to eat it; others come close and sit around with their hands out like panhandlers. Sometimes the owner hands out tidbits.

MANUAL DEXTERITY AND TOOL USE   Elongated hand and short thumb preclude a tweezer grip, but chimps can pick up small objects between thumb and side of the index finger, and are the only apes known to fashion tools in the wild. Leaves are wadded or chewed to make sponges for soaking up water from a tree cavity, sopping up blood and wiping out brains of prey, and wiping dirt off the chimp's fur. Sticks are used to collect swarming ants and bees, and grass stems to fish in termite mounds. Branches are waved in display, used to beat a predator such as a leopard, or thrown as missiles, as are rocks.

Rocks and wooden clubs are also used as nutcrackers. In West Africa, chimpanzees and man both consume *Coula edulis* and *Panda oleosa* nuts. A chimp puts a coula nut on a rock or root and smashes it with a club sought and carried for the purpose. Panda nuts are even too hard to crack with a club, so chimps bring stones to use as hammers. A study of nut-cracking showed that adult females and adolescents of both sexes consistently opened coula nuts with fewer blows than males, and that only adult females had the skill and patience to open panda nuts. Evidence of greater female manual dexterity and muscular control was the first distinct gender difference in tool-use technique and skill found in an animal.

REPRODUCTION   Slow: first birth at 13 to 14 years, then at 4- to 5-year intervals. Gestation 8 months. During menstrual cycles averaging 34 days, a huge pink swelling waxes and wanes, followed by menstruation. Maximum inflation lasts 6 to 7 days, during which female is most receptive and attractive to males. Breeding males only show interest in females after they begin menstruating at 8.5 to 10 years, when previously small swelling suddenly balloons. During ensuing 2 to 4 years of adolescent sterility, a female mates with all community males but only during the swollen stage. Mothers remain sexually unreceptive for 3 to 4 years, then cycle 1 to 6 times until again pregnant.

Sexually precocious, male chimps begin sexual activity as early as 2 years. During first week of estrus, females copulate c. 6 times a day with males of all

Figure 32.3a. Relaxed face.   **Figure 32.3b.** Grinning.

ages, normally without strife. But near the end of swollen stage, dominant males begin competing for priority and threaten or attack subordinates that try to approach. Although an alpha male has the advantage, apparently most pregnancies occur when a female elopes with a male for a week or longer, meanwhile avoiding contact with other chimps.

OFFSPRING AND PARENTAL CARE   Like humans, chimpanzees need an extended childhood and adolescence to gain essential subsistence skills and social graces, through observing role models and trial-and-error learning.

Total dependence lasts 6 months. Between months 5 and 7, baby takes first steps, begins riding jockey style, and starts eating solid food but remains milk-dependent for at least 2 years and is finally weaned only at 5 to 6. Some juveniles begin sleeping alone then, usually following a sibling's birth. Interest in mothering younger siblings is variable. Some adult males carry, protect, and play with babies, but most mothers fear males and keep other chimps away from offspring the first half-year.

Figure 32.3c. Play face.   **Figure 32.3d.** Rage.

Figure 32.3e. Pout face.

Juveniles of 5 and 6 years become frantic when separated from mothers (e.g., mothers in estrus), but become more independent after a series of episodes. Sons begin associating with all-male groups but rejoin mothers within a few days until 8 or 9. Daughters stay close even longer but begin joining male groups during estrus and eventually leave the community.

PREDATORS   Leopards live in all the places chimpanzees do and, judging from excited, aggressive reaction they arouse, must sometimes prey on chimps. Hard to imagine one foolhardy enough to tackle an adult chimpanzee unless it happened on one lying sound asleep. That's unlikely since chimpanzees nest in secure sleeping trees. Spotted hyenas are even unlikelier to be a serious threat. Lions, though present in savanna habitats, are now very scarce in areas inhabited by chimpanzees. So, they have nothing to worry about but people—who eat them in West Africa.

HOW IT COMMUNICATES   Complex communal society is served by an equally elaborate system of visual, contact, and sound signals. Maybe the noisiest of all African animals, lone chimps can maintain voice contact with associates. Unlike gorilla and most other primates, no calls are exclusive to one sex or age class. Despite gender differences in *pant-hoots*, for example, each chimp has the full deck. Both vocal and visual signals are finely graded, with one expression or call shading into another; and its extremely mobile face lets a chimp express the subtlest gradations of feeling and meaning.

Table 32.3. *CHIMPANZEE BEHAVIOR GUIDE: VISUAL SIGNALS*
    Expect to see ➤ *Usual context and meaning*

Facial Expressions

AGGRESSIVE

Staring or tense-mouth face: lips pressed tightly together, glaring.
➤ Expression before or while chasing/attacking subordinate, and while "ordering" a ♀ to copulate.

Open-mouth threat face: mouth more or less open: teeth covered by lips, glaring. ➤ Threatens subordinate or another species not much feared.

Rage expression (see Fig. 32.3d): mouth wide open, lips retracted showing teeth, accompanied by aggressive calls. ➤ Maximum intensity of tense-mouth face.

Facial Expressions *continued*

FEARFUL/FRETFUL

Open-mouth grin (see Fig. 32.3 b). ➤ Response to threat by superior or another, feared species; also to signal nonaggression during physical contact with other chimps.

Closed-mouth grin: lips retracted, teeth exposed. ➤ Signal of submission and fear, e.g., following attack by superior; equivalent to human polite or nervous smile.

Pout face (see Fig. 32.3e). ➤ Sign of anxiety or frustration, in response to strange object or sound; rejection of grooming; begging; infant searching for mother; response to threat or attack; juvenile temper tantrum.

PLAYFUL/SOCIABLE

Play face (see Fig. 32.3c). ➤ During playful physical contact.

Lip-smacking. ➤ While grooming another chimpanzee.

Aggression

MALE DOMINANCE/THREAT DISPLAYS

Bipedal swagger: side-to-side swaying by ♂ standing or walking upright with shoulders hunched, bristling, arms held out. ➤ Mainly a courtship display; also as threat between ♂ ♂ of nearly equal rank.

Quadrupedal hunch: head bent and drawn in between raised shoulders, back rounded. Performer may advance slowly, charge, and sometimes attack. ➤ High-intensity threat to rival ♂.

Charging display: incorporates most aggressive displays, especially arm-waving and running, dragging and throwing objects, drumming, stamping, slapping, swinging from branches, accompanied by pant-hooting and screaming. ➤ Conspicuous, noisy demonstration performed by adult ♂ ♂, especially upon meeting other chimps, also when stimulated by storms or other disturbance ("rain dance"). Inferiors that get in way risk assault.

AGGRESSIVE DISPLAYS NOT LIMITED TO MALES

Bipedal arm-waving and running: standing facing or running at opponent, arm(s) raised ± waving, accompanied by *waa*-barking or screaming. ➤ Bluff attack directed mainly toward another species—e.g., baboons competing for food.

Throwing objects, mostly at random, sometimes aimed. ➤ Usually to intimidate rather than deliberately hurt adversary.

Shaking and swaying branches with tense-mouth face. ➤ Response to disturbance, often by human observer, and accompaniment to body rocking of frustrated chimp.

Head-tipping: slight upward and backward jerk accompanying soft bark. ➤ Low-intensity threat, as when subordinate comes close to feeding superior.

Aggression *continued*

Hitting-away: motion with back of hand. ➤ Same context as the last; also as response to insect or snake.

Flapping: downward slap toward companion, accompanied by grinning, squeaking, screaming, or *waa*-barking. ➤ ♀ – ♀ squabbles.

Arm-raising: forearm or whole arm raised abruptly, palm toward adversary. ➤ Same context and often combined with head-tipping.

Submission

Social presenting: as in sexual presenting, crouching with rump presented to partner, ± screaming and open-mouth grin. ➤ Depth of crouch correlates with degree of fear; extreme crouch after severe attack; victim looks backward and backs toward aggressor. Even adult ♂ ♂ present to superiors.

Bowing: facing superior, arms bent more than legs, head lower than rump, often while panting. ➤ Subordinate, especially ♀, going to dominant ♂ that has made aggressive/courtship gestures. Bowing, bobbing, and crouching are comparable to human submissive behavior.

Bobbing: pushups while bowing, often with pant-grunts. ➤ Especially adolescent ♂ ♂ when high-ranking ♂ passes nearby.

Crouching: similar to presenting but different angle; associated with panting, squeaking, and grinning. ➤ Extreme form of bowing, same context but also after an attack.

Bending away: leaning away from another chimp with arm close to body and flexed at wrist or elbow, meanwhile soft-panting, or squeaking with closed-mouth grin. ➤ Reaction of youngsters to close passage of adult ♂ ♂, especially aggressive ones.

Creeping away, hiding, silent flight. ➤ Avoidance of feared superiors or humans.

Displacement Activities

Tension or displacement yawning, grooming motions, pretended eating, masturbation, temper tantrums, redirected aggression. ➤ Signs of conflicting tendencies, inhibition from attaining objective.

Courtship

MALE BEHAVIOR

Aggressive gestures: seated ♂ beckons to estrous ♀, with tense-mouth face, bristling, penis erect, sometimes waves branch or makes other aggressive displays. ➤ ♂ ♂ have individualistic courtship gestures.

FEMALE BEHAVIOR

Sexual presenting. ➤ Like social presenting except for estrous swelling.

Courtship *continued*

COPULATION

♂ in seated attitude, ejaculates after about 10 thrusts.

Response to Competitors/Predators

Aggressive displays (see above): Ground-thumping, branch-shaking, throwing objects, beating with hands or sticks, aggressive calls.

Hiding, sneaking off, fleeing.

Table 32.4. CHIMPANZEE BEHAVIOR GUIDE: CONTACT SIGNALS
Expect to see ➤ *Usual context and meaning*

Submissive, Appeasing, Reassuring

Extending open hand, palm up, often while whimpering, squeaking, grinning, or screaming. ➤ Mainly ♀ ♀ following sudden movement of nearby ♂, attack or threat, or when approaching a superior. Same gesture used in food-begging.

Wrist-bending: presenting back of flexed hand to another chimp's lips. ➤ Usually by adults and juveniles reaching out to infants, sometimes as submissive gesture by ♀ ♀ and juveniles to mature ♂ ♂.

Reaching and touching: head, back, rump, or nearest part with hand (sometimes foot). ➤ Submissive/appeasing; also by superior to reassure submissive inferior.

Patting: like human mother soothing child. ➤ Reassurance to distressed subordinate or offspring.

Chin-chucking. ➤ Of youngsters by grownups, especially ♂ ♂.

Kissing: pressing lips or teeth to body, usually groin, sometimes to face or mouth, often while bowing and crouching. ➤ Submissive animal kisses body, face, or a hand held out in reassurance; also dominant responding to submissive crouch, kiss, or extended hand.

Embracing. ➤ Maternal response to frightened or hurt infant; sometimes ♂ embraces frightened ♀.

Submissive mounting and pelvic thrusting. ➤ By both sexes, usually after being attacked.

Reassurance mounting: dominant to subordinate. ➤ Occasional response to screaming and presenting.

Social grooming: typical primate patterns, including lip-smacking and tongue-clicking. ➤ Between ♂ ♂, usually lower- to higher-ranking; also between members of same family.

Table 32.5. *CHIMPANZEE BEHAVIOR GUIDE:*
CALLS AND OTHER SOUNDS
Expect to hear ➤ Usual context and meaning

Advertising Presence/Social Status

Drumming: 1–3 double beats with the feet while jumping against a tree, by adult ♂♂. ➤ Associated with aggressive displays—e.g., given in response to distant group or when rejoining party. Louder even than pant-hoot, carrying 2 mi (3 km).

Pant-hoot: very loud calls uttered in series, produced while inhaling and exhaling, lips shaped into trumpet (hoot face). ➤ Distance call, stimulated by calls of group, reunion with other chimps, eating, and general excitement. Advertises caller's identity. Both sexes and all ages call, but ♂♂ most.

Aggression

Bark: loud sharp call of variable pitch; emitted most often by adolescent ♀♀. ➤ Annoyance or mild aggressiveness toward another animal, also during general excitement or as a threat to distant animals. This and following variations are emitted with mouth half-open, lips protruding, covering teeth.

Waa bark: More drawn out (0.5 sec. or longer) than bark, with tendency to rising and falling pitch; given singly or in series, by both sexes. ➤ Signals aggression combined with apprehension—e.g., a subordinate threatening distant superior.

Submissive/Fearful

Pant-grunt: like pant-hoot but quieter and faster. ➤ Submissive signal given by both sexes beginning in adolescence and increasing with age. Linked with grinning and other submissive signals (bobbing, crouching).

Squeak: short shrill cry, usually in series, given by all classes, especially adolescents. ➤ Distress following attack or approach of higher-ranking individual. Goes with closed-mouth grin.

Scream: high-pitched, far-carrying call, intergrading with squeaks; all classes, especially adolescent ♀♀ and ♀♀ with young. ➤ Distress resulting from social strife; signals submission, elicits reassurance, recruits mother's support against aggressor. Linked with open-mouth grin.

Whimper: soft, low-pitched sound, emitted by all classes; highest rate in juvenile and infant ♂♂. ➤ Varied circumstances: begging; seeing something strange; frightened infant clinging to mother or seeking nipple. Elicits food, reassurance, suckling, etc. Associated with pout face and with hoot part of pant-hoot.

Sociable

Grunt: soft, brief, low-frequency sound, emitted singly or in trains at varying rate, often grading into other calls (rough-grunting, barking, pant-grunting). ➤ Heard in various ill-defined situations: while feeding, during occasional excitement.

Lip-smacking and tooth-clacking. ➤ Social grooming.

Rough grunt: wide array of sounds ranging from squeaks to barks, but typically a pulsed grunt, distinctly slower than other grunting sounds (but tempo may increase with excitement). ➤ Relaxed adults emit groan-like trains of up to 10 pulses with a wide frequency range, e.g., while eating favorite food. Adults call most, especially older ♂♂. Jaws open slightly with each grunt.

Panting: rapid, soft, panting sound, emitted mainly by adults. ➤ Several situations: grooming, reunion of two chimps after separation, during peaceful behavior, and most loudly by thrusting ♂♂ during copulation. May indicate low probability of aggression.

Cough: like voiceless grunt, produced by rush of air from open mouth, given by adult ♂♂, adult and adolescent ♀♀, usually only once. ➤ Generally accompanies mild threat toward subordinate. Associated with threatening hand gestures.

Infant

Laughter: similar to human laugh, including steady exhaled laughter, chuckling, and wheezing. ➤ Commonest in young animals, during play and tickling sessions.

Crying: sometimes building to shrieks and temper tantrums. ➤ Similar to wails of human infant.

Whining. ➤ Given when in danger of abandonment or injury.

Alarm

Wraa: begins like *waa*-bark but ends in drawn-out howl lasting a second or more. ➤ Response to presence of humans, other predators, or strange animals. Combines elements of alarm and threat and may function as the chimp's only distance alarm call.

Thumping ground with hands. ➤ Threat to predator.

SUGGESTED READING

Altmann, J. 1980. *Baboon Mothers and Infants.* Cambridge: Harvard University Press.

Cheney, D. L. and Seyfarth, R. M. 1990. *How Monkeys See the World.* Chicago: University of Chicago Press.

Douglas-Hamilton, I. and Douglas-Hamilton, O. 1992. *Battle for the Elephants.* New York: Viking.

Doyle, G. A. and Martin, R. D., eds. 1979. *The Study of Prosimian Behavior.* New York: Academic Press.

Dunbar, R. I. M. 1988. *Primate Social Systems.* London: Christopher Helm.

Estes, R. D. 1991. *The Behavior Guide to African Mammals.* Los Angeles: University of California Press.

Fossey, D. 1983. *Gorillas in the Mist.* Boston: Houghton Mifflin.

Frame, G. W. and Frame, L. H. 1981. *Swift and Enduring: Cheetahs and Wild Dogs of the Serengeti.* New York: Dutton.

Gautier-Hion, A. et al., eds. 1988. *Evolutionary Biology of the African Guenons.* New York: Cambridge University Press.

Goodall, J. 1991. *Through a Window: My Thirty Years with the Chimpanzees of Gombe.* Boston: Houghton Mifflin.

————. 1986. *The Chimpanzees of Gombe.* Cambridge: Harvard University Press.

Haltenorth, T. and Diller, H. 1980. *A Field Guide to the Mammals of Africa.* London: Collins.

Hanby, J. 1983. *Lion's Share: The Story of a Serengeti Pride.* London: Collins.

IUCN. 1990. *Red List of Threatened Animals.* Cambridge: World Conservation Monitoring Centre.

Jackman, B. and Scott, J. 1983. *The Marsh Lions.* Boston: D. R. Godine.

Kavanagh, M. 1984. *A Complete Guide to Monkeys, Apes and Other Primates.* New York: Viking Press.

Kingdon, J. S. 1971. *East African Mammals.* Vol. 1 (primates). London and New York: Academic Press.

————. 1978. Vol. 3A (carnivores).

————. 1979. Vol. 3B (large herbivores).

————. 1982. Vol. 3C and 3D (bovids).

Kruuk, H. 1972. *The Spotted Hyena.* Chicago: University of Chicago Press.

Macdonald, D. W., ed. 1984. *The Encyclopedia of Mammals.* New York: Facts on File Publications.

Mills, M. G. L. 1989. *Kalahari Hyenas.* New York: Unwin, Hyman.

Mloszewski, M. J. 1983. *The Behavior and Ecology of the African Buffalo.* Cambridge: Cambridge University Press.

Moss, C. J. 1975. *Portraits in the Wild*. Chicago: University of Chicago Press.

————. 1988. *Elephant Memories*. London: Elm Tree Books.

Owens, M. J. and Owens, D. D. 1984. *Cry of the Kalahari*. Boston: Houghton Mifflin

Poole, J. H. 1987. Elephants in Musth, Lust. *Natural History*. Nov: 46–55.

Rasa, A. 1986. *Moongoose Watch: A Family Observed*. Garden City, NY: Doubleday.

Schaller, G. 1972. *The Serengeti Lion*. Chicago: University of Chicago Press.

Scott, J. 1985. *The Leopard's Tale*. London: Good Books Ltd.

————. 1991. *Painted Wolves: Wild Dogs of the Serengeti-Mara*. London: Hamish Hamilton.

Sinclair, A. R. E. 1977. *The African Buffalo*. Chicago: University of Chicago Press.

———— and M. Norton-Griffiths. 1979. *Serengeti, Dynamics of an Ecosystem*. Chicago: University of Chicago Press.

Skinner, J. D. and Smithers, R. H. N. 1990. *The Mammals of the Southern African Subregion*. Pretoria: University of Pretoria.

Smithers, R. H. N. 1992. *Land Mammals of Southern Africa: A Field Guide*. Johannesburg: Southern Book Publishers.

Smuts, B. et al., eds. 1987. *Primate Societies*. Chicago: University of Chicago Press.

Spinage, C. A. 1986. *The Natural History of Antelopes*. New York and Oxford: Facts on File Publications.

Stuart, C. and Stuart, T. 1991. *Field Guide to the Mammals of Southern Africa*. Cape Town: Struik Publishers.

Strum, S. C. 1987. *Almost Human*. London: Elm Tree Books.

Grzimek, B., ed. 1972. *Grzimek's Animal Life Encyclopedia*. New York: Van Nostrand Reinhold.

Van Lawick, H. and Van Lawick-Goodall, J. 1970. *Innocent Killers*. London: Collins.

Walther, F. 1984. *Communication and Expression in Hoofed Mammals*. Bloomington: Indiana University Press.

AFRICAN WILDLIFE ORGANIZATIONS

Following are some of the organizations active in African wildlife conservation. They accept donations.

African Wildlife Foundation   PO Box 48177, Nairobi, Kenya
or 1717 Massachusetts Avenue NW, Washington, DC 20036

The Conservation Foundation   1250 Twenty-fourth Street NW, Washington, DC 20037

East African Wildlife Society   PO Box 20110, Nairobi, Kenya

Fauna and Flora Preservation Society   1 Kensington Gore, London SW7 2AR, UK

Friends of Animals   11 West Sixtieth Street, New York, NY 10023

Greenpeace International   Keizersgracht 176, 1016 DW Amsterdam, Netherlands

Okavango Wildlife Society   PO Box 2362, Saxonwold 2132, South Africa

Owens Foundation for Wildlife Conservation   PO Box 53396, Atlanta, GA 30355

Sierra Club   730 Polk St., San Francisco, CA 94109

Tanzania Wildlife Conservation Monitoring   PO Box 3134, Arusha, Tanzania

United Nations Environmental Program   UN Headquarters, Rm DC 2-0803, New York, NY 10077

Wildlife Conservation International   Bronx Zoo, Bronx, NY 10460

World Conservation Society of Zambia   PO Box 30255, Lusaka, Zambia

World Conservation Union (IUCN)   Gland, CH-1196 Switzerland

World Wildlife Fund–US   1250 Twenty-fourth Street NW, Washington, DC 20037

Wildlife Society of Zimbabwe   PO Box 3497, Harare, Zimbabwe

GLOSSARY

ABBREVIATIONS

c.	*circa*, approximately
cf.	*confer*, compare
GR	Game reserve
NP	National park
NR	National reserve or (mainly in South Africa) nature reserve

METRIC EQUIVALENTS

cm	centimeter; 1 cm = 0.39 inch; 2.5 cm = 1 inch.
ha	hectare; 1 ha = 2.47 acres.
g	gram; 1g = 0.035 ounce
kg	kilogram; 1 kg = 1000 grams = 2.2 pounds.
km	kilometer; 1 km = 1000 meters = 0.62 mile; 1.6 km = 1 mile.
km^2	square kilometer; 1 km^2 = 100 ha; = 0.39 mi^2; 2.6 km^2 = 1 mile^2
l	liter; 1 l = 1.06 quarts
m	meter; 1 m = 1.1 yard = 39.4 inches.
mm	millimeter; 1 mm = 0.039; 25 mm = 1 inch

air-cushion fight   Fighting movements performed by two contestants without making contact—as though separated by an invisible cushion.

alpha   The top-ranking member of a dominance hierarchy, named after the first letter in the Greek alphabet.

amble   A walking gait in which the legs on the same side are moved together; also called *parallel walk* (cf. **cross-walk**).

aquatic   Applied to animals that live in fresh water. All aquatic mammals move readily on land, unlike most marine mammals.

arboreal   Referring to animals that live in trees.

artiodactyl   An even-toed ungulate (e.g., antelopes, cattle, sheep, deer, camels, pigs, hippos).

binocular vision   Vision that has depth of field; produced by the overlapping fields of view of 2 eyes. The frontally placed eyes of cats and primates have the most overlap and provide the best depth perception.

biome   Life zone; a major climatic-vegetation zone, such as the savanna or desert.

bipedal   Two-footed stance or locomotion.

bovid   A member of the family Bovidae, the hollow-horned ruminants, of which all but 3 of the African members are antelopes.

brisket   The part of the chest between and behind the forelegs in four-footed mammals.

browser   An ungulate that feeds mainly on plants others than grass, especially foliage.

calcrete pan   Soil permeated with calcium salts, forming a hardpan that holds rainwater.

canine teeth The usually long, pointed teeth—one in each quarter of the jaws—that are used for fighting and (especially in carnivores) for killing prey.

carbohydrates Various neutral compounds of carbon, hydrogen, and oxygen—such as sugars, starches, and cellulose—mostly formed by green plants.

carnassial teeth In carnivores, the fourth upper premolar and first lower molar, specialized for shearing meat and sinew.

carnivore A mammal belonging to the order Carnivora (e.g., dogs, cats, civets, mongooses, hyenas, weasels, and otters). Though nearly all eat animal food, a minority are purely carnivorous.

cecum A blind sac situated at the junction of the small and large intestine, in which digestion of cellulose by bacteria occurs in nonruminants.

cheek pouch A pair of deep pouches extending from the cheeks into the neck skin; present in most Old World monkeys (not the colobinae subfamily). Used for the temporary storage of food.

cheek teeth The row of premolars and molars used for chewing food.

concealing Color and markings that make an animal blend into its surroundings.

consortship Exclusive association with a female maintained by a male during estrus to keep any other male from mating with her (see **tending bond**).

contagious behavior An action that stimulates other animals to follow suit.

cross-walk A walking gait in which diagonally opposite limbs (forelimb and opposite hind limb) move together.

cud A mouthful of partially digested vegetation that a ruminant regurgitates, chews, insalivates, and swallows again while ruminating.

cursorial Adapted for running.

dewclaw A vestigial digit that fails to contact the ground; the inside (first) digit in carnivores.

dimorphism Refers to morphological differences between males and females (see **sexual dimorphism**).

discrete signal A call or signal that has no significant gradations; it is either on or off (cf. **graded signal**).

dispersal Movement of animals away from their natal home range, typically before maturity.

displacement activity A behavior that is displaced from its normal context; especially feeding and grooming behaviors performed under stress. Considered signs of indecision or frustration, as when two conflicting drives block one another (e.g., approach vs. withdraw, fight vs. flight).

display A behavior pattern that has been modified (ritualized) by evolution to transmit information by a sender to a receiver; a special kind of signal.

diurnal Referring to species that are primarily day-active.

dung midden A pile of droppings that accumulates through regular deposits, typically in connection with scent-marking. A latrine is similar, as an area where dung is deposited, but is not necessarily a pile of droppings.

ecology The scientific study of the interaction of organisms with their environment, including both the physical environment and the other organisms that share it.

ecosystem A community of organisms together with the physical environment in which they live.

edge Nontechnical synonym for *ecotone*—the transition zone between two different types of habitat.

edge species   Species that prefer the transition zone (ecotone) between different habitats (e.g., impala, waterbuck, sable, roan).

eocene   A geological epoch, from 58 to 37 million years ago.

erectile   Capable of erection. Refers mainly to hair, which fear and anger causes to bristle, making the animal look bigger.

estrus   Behavior associated with ovulation, being in most mammals the only time when females are sexually receptive.

Ethiopian Faunal Region   Africa south of the Sahara Desert.

false hooves   Vestigial hooves (digits 2 and 5) that persist in many ruminants on the fetlock above the hoof.

fetlock   The projection of the foot above the hoof in ungulates, and the adjacent joint (the pastern) itself.

flehmen   An obscure German term for the grimace associated with urine-testing.

flight distance   The space an animal maintains between itself and a feared presence such as a predator. A highly variable distance, depending on the individual's status, the identity and actions of the feared object, terrain, and time of day.

fossorial   Adapted for digging.

frugivore   An animal that feeds mainly on fruit.

gallery forest   Trees and other vegetation lining watercourses, thereby extending forested habitat into savanna and arid zones.

genotype   The genetic makeup of an organism.

genus (plural genera)   The next taxonomic level above species. In the Latin binomial system, the genus name comes first, the species name second. E.g., *Gazella granti* and *G. thomsonii* are two species of *Gazella*.

graded signal   A call or other type of signal that varies in intensity and/or frequency, thus being capable of transmitting subtle differences in the mood/intentions of the sender (cf. **discrete signal**).

greenflush   Renewed growth of dry grassland caused by precipitation or by burning.

group defense   Cooperative defense (usually against predators) by two or more individuals, as distinct from the more common defense by the mother alone (see **mobbing response**).

guard hair   The outer coat that overlies the shorter, softer hairs of the underfur.

Guinea Savanna   The northern equivalent of the Miombo Woodland Zone. Broad-leafed deciduous woodlands of the Northern Savanna, forming a long but narrow belt between the Forest-Savanna Transition and Mosaic and the drier acacia savanna to the north.

herbivore   An animal whose diet consists of plant food.

herd   A social group consisting of at least two same-sex adults; generally applied to sociable ungulates.

hierarchy   As applied to social groups, a usually linear rank order in which each member dominates all those of lower rank and is dominated by all indivuduals of higher rank.

highveld   Temperate grasslands of the South African interior plateau.

home range   The area occupied by an individual or group, determined by plotting the points where the indivudual(s) is seen over a period of time.

hoof glands   Scent glands situated in the cleft between the hooves of many antelopes.

inguinal glands   Pocketlike glands situated close to the udder in the groin area.

insectivore A mammal specialized to eat insects.

jump-run Running by alternately flexing and extending the body, with forelegs and hind legs working in pairs. Typical gait of long-bodied, short-legged carnivores such as weasels, otters.

juvenile An animal in the development stage between infancy and adolescence.

Karroo An arid part of the interior plateau in the temperate zone of southern Africa, dominated by dwarf shrubs and adjoining the Highveld grassland.

Karroid shrubs The dwarf woody plants that dominate the Karroo.

keratin The tough fibrous substance of which horns, claws, hooves, and nails are composed.

kin selection Selection that favors investing care in relatives. E.g., by promoting the survival of full siblings, older siblings stand to gain as much genetic benefit as they would through the survival of their own offspring, since both carry on average half of the same genes.

knuckle-walk To walk on all fours while bearing the weight of forequarters on the knuckles—as in chimpanzees and gorillas.

kopje (Afrikaans for *head*) A small hill, typically a rock outcrop, where various mammals find safety, shelter, and food.

latrine A place where animals regularly deposit their feces (see **dung midden**).

lek A breeding ground or arena where territorial males cluster around a central area, to which estrous females come to mate with a few of the most centrally located and fittest males (see kob, lechwe, and topi accounts).

lying-out The prone position, with head on the ground, assumed by infant antelopes in the concealment stage as well as by adults of some species that hide from predators, and by nonhider species when harassed.

matriline Group of related animals descended through the maternal line.

Miocene Geological epoch, from 24 to 5 million years ago.

Miombo Woodland Zone A distinctive vegetation zone within the Southern Savanna (see vegetation map) dominated by broad-leafed, deciduous, pinnately compound, leguminous trees, notably *Bracyhstegia* and *Julbernardia* species. Hot fires that sweep through this type of savanna every dry season select for fire-resistant trees. Guinea Savanna is the Northern Savanna equivalent.

mobbing response Cooperative attack by members of a group, triggered by behavior of the attacked animal or by a signal, such as a distress cry, from a group member.

monogamy Mating system in which most individuals have only one sexual partner; monogamous mammals tend to form permanent pair bonds.

montane Referring to African mountain habitats, including forest, grassland, bamboo zone, and moorland.

mopane A tree of variable growth forms. *Colospermum mopane* often forms pure stands in parts of the Southern Savanna and South West Arid Zone.

mopaneveld Savanna dominated by mopane trees or bushes.

Oligocene A geological epoch, from 37 to 24 million years ago.

opportunistic Referring to animals, notably carnivores, which capitalize on opportunities to gain food with the least expenditure of energy.

pair bond The social ties that keep members of a mated pair together, usually reinforced by mutual grooming, marking, calling, aggression toward outsiders, etc.

Paleocene Geological epoch, from 65 to 58 million years ago.

perissodactyl An odd-toed ungulates (e.g., rhinos, horses.)

plantigrade Flat-footed; applies to animals that walk on the whole foot (e.g., elephants, hyraxes, people.)

Pleistocene A geological epoch, from 1.6 million to 10,000 years ago.

Pliocene A geological epoch, from 5 to 1.6 million years ago.

polygamy A mating system in which an animal has more than one mate (cf. **monogamy**).

polygyny A mating system in which one male has reproductive access to two or more females.

preorbital Refers to area in front of the eye, where a gland occurs in many ungulates.

presenting The act of directing the hindquarters toward another individual, either in sexual solicition or as a gesture of appeasement derived from sexual presenting.

promiscuous mating Indiscriminate mating, as opposed to mating based on female choice, pair formation, or the outcome of male sexual competition.

pronking Special form of stotting.

race A subspecies.

rank order A hierarchial arrangement of the individuals in a group.

ritualization Evolutionary modification of a behavior pattern into a display or other signal, through selection for increasingly efficient and clear communication.

rumen The largest of the four chambers of the ruminant stomach, which is in effect a rumination vat.

ruminant An ungulate with a four-chambered stomach that chews the cud as part of the rumination process.

rut A defined mating period during which most conceptions occur, leading to an equally defined birth peak.

savanna Vegetation characteristic of tropical regions with extended wet and dry seasons. The ground layer is dominated by grasses, and the overstory, composed of predominately leguminous trees, ranges from broad-leafed deciduous woodland in the wetter savanna (rainfall up to 40 in [1000 mm]; dry season of 4 months or so) to grassland with scatted thorn trees and thorn bushes grading into subdesert (rainfall down to 10 in [250 mm] or less; dry season lasting up to 8 months).

scent gland Area of skin packed with specialized cells that secrete complex chemical compounds that communicate information about the identity and social and reproductive status of the animal.

selection pressure Any feature of the environment that results in natural selection through differential survival and reproductive success of individuals of different genetic types.

sex ratio The ratio of males to females in a population. Ratio at birth (natal sex ratio) tends to be 1:1 in most species and tends to remain equal in monogamous species. Yet adult sex ratios usually become skewed in favor of females (1:1.5, 1:2, 1:3, or even higher) in polygynous species, with increasing male sexual competition.

sexual dimorphism Differences in form between males and females, usually resulting from development of male secondary characters in response to sexual selection favoring larger size and showier display organs.

sexual selection Selection of genotypes through competion between members of the same sex (especially males) and mating preferences by members of the opposite sex (usually female choice).

siblings   Offspring of the same mother or father. Applies in this book to full siblings—i.e., siblings having both parents in common.

signal   Any behavior that conveys information from one individual to another, whether ritualized or not (cf. **display**).

sourveld   Afrikaans term for tall grassland that becomes unpalatable and unnutritious for livestock in the dry season, in contrast to sweetveld (see **sweetveld**).

species   Population(s) of closely related and similar organisms that are capable of interbreeding freely with one another and cannot, or normally do not, interbreed with members of other species.

spy-hop   Jumping into the air to scan surroundings; performed by an animal moving through vegetation higher than it is.

stotting   Also called *pronking*. A distinctive bounding gait in which the animal bounces off the ground with straightened legs, propelling itself by flexing the lowermost (pastern) joints. Performed by many antelopes when alarmed.

style-trot   Trotting exaggerated by lifting the legs higher than normal, often combined with defiant-looking head and tail movements. A sign of alarm/excitement in various antelopes, equivalent to stotting.

subspecies   A population that has been isolated from other populations of the same species long enough to develop genetic differences sufficiently distinctive to be considered a separate race.

sweetveld   Short and medium grassland in low-rainfall regions that cures quickly and retains nutritive value in dry season.

systematics   The classification of organisms based on their natural relationships.

tending bond   A male's attempt to monopolize mating with a female approaching or in estrus, by staying close to her and keeping other males away. Applies mainly to nonterritorial ungulates.

terresterial   Adapted to living on land.

territorial   Animals that defend a particular area against rivals (usually of the same sex) of its own species.

testosterone   A male hormone produced in the testes, which induces and maintains male secondary sex characters, and mediates sexual and aggressive behavior.

tsetse fly   Two-winged blood-sucking fly of the genus *Glossina* that transmits "sleeping sickness" (trypanosomiasis) to people (rarely) and domestic livestock (very commonly). The fly's presence in the woodlands of Africa south of the Sahara has helped to slow the pace of settlement and development, thereby preserving habitats for wild animals, which have a natural immunity to tsetse-borne diseases.

undercoat   The soft insulating underfur beneath the longer, coarser guard hairs of the outer coat.

ungulate   A mammal with hooves. Loosely applied also to such "near-ungulates" as elephants and hyraxes.

urine-testing   A nearly universal habit among mammals with a functioning vomeronasal organ, whereby female reproductive status is regularly monitored (mostly by males) through assaying hormone breakdown products in the urine. The testing procedure is most apparent in mammals that raise their heads, open their mouths, and retract their upper lips in a grimace as part of the testing procedure (e.g., see Courtship, Table 4.2).

veld (Afrikaans for *field*) Generally used in South Africa to describe habitats in which grasses are a dominant element; equivalent to savanna.

vomeronasal organ or Jacobson's organ A pair of narrow, blind sacs present in most mammals, situated on either side of the nasal septum, lined with sensory cells similar to olfactory cells. Part of a separate olfactory system dedicated to monitoring reproductive condition (see **urine-testing**).

yearling A young animal between 1 and 2 years of age (referring to species that take at least 2 years to mature).

withers The shoulder region.

INDEX

PERSONAL FIELD NOTES

TAKING NOTE OF THE BEHAVIOR YOU SEE If you wish to make notes about the animals you see, these pages will enable you to supplement or elaborate on the Behavior Guide tables throughout the book. When an animal you are watching does something noteworthy, put the date or a check mark in the Behavior Guide to its family or species beside the type of behavior you observe, then enter your own observations on these pages. A quick sketch or two may also help fix the event in your memory. If you're not sure how to classify the behavior, make an educated guess. You can always reclassify later. With practice, your insight and self-confidence will both grow. Who knows, you may even see something completely new—and that applies to even the most-studied species.

Record as little or as much detail as you like. The more closely you observe, the more details you will notice, and the more you will get out of watching animals. But don't overdo it—it should be fun, not a chore. Simply noting the date, place, time, and the species you saw performing a particular behavior you describe in a few words may be all you have the time or inclination to write. If you run out of pages, hopefully you have a notebook or journal in which you can continue making observations.

GOING BEYOND THE BEHAVIOR GUIDES As well as elaborating on the displays and other behaviors described in the Behavior Guides, you may want to make notes about other activities. For example:
MAINTENANCE ACTIVITIES

- Foraging and hunting behavior (how is it done?)
- Eating (kind of food, handling and eating techniques)
- Drinking (where, for how long; behavior of prey species going to water)
- Comfort behavior: grooming, wallowing, dust-bathing, sunning, keeping cool
- Sleeping (time, location, posture)

PREDATION Note sex and age of predator and prey, if you can; where and how the event unfolds, and so on.

OFFSPRING CARE Protectiveness of mother and other family or group members; suckling (duration); lying-out behavior (choice of hiding place; any tendency of juvenile to reveal its location by raising head, standing, etc.).

GETTING STARTED   The headings in the following note pages will serve as a reminder of the kinds of information you need to include along with descriptions of behavior, to help recall the events you recorded. If you want to add more details, notes on the weather, type and condition of habitat, sex and estimated age of group members are all useful.

To help you get started, here is a sample record of a behavior you would be likely to see if you stopped and watched a herd of impalas before or after their morning foraging.

Date, Place, Species, Type of Behavior	Description: Time, Activity, Context Note time, who does what to whom, and context (presence and activity of other animals; where event takes place, etc.)
3.4.93 Samburu GR Impala social behavior	8:35 AM 2 adult males (really big horns) take turns grooming one another, using lower front teeth. Male 1 scrapes 2's neck 4–5 times, stops, turns head, and waits for 2 to respond in kind—which he does. 8:37 AM Bout ends in fifth round when 1 walks off. Context: These males part of herd of bachelor males near Buffalo Springs, inc. c. 28 impalas of all ages. Some others also engage in mutual grooming. A few impalas still grazing, but most just standing around.

Date, Place, Species, Type of Behavior	Description: Time, Activity, Context

Date, Place, Species, Type of Behavior	Description: Time, Activity, Context

Date, Place, Species, Type of Behavior	Description: Time, Activity, Context

Date, Place, Species, Type of Behavior	Description: Time, Activity, Context

Date, Place, Species, Type of Behavior	Description: Time, Activity, Context

Date, Place, Species, Type of Behavior	Description: Time, Activity, Context

Date, Place, Species, Type of Behavior	Description: Time, Activity, Context

Date, Place, Species, Type of Behavior	Description: Time, Activity, Context

Date, Place, Species, Type of Behavior	Description: Time, Activity, Context

Date, Place, Species, Type of Behavior	Description: Time, Activity, Context

Date, Place, Species, Type of Behavior	Description: Time, Activity, Context

Date, Place, Species, Type of Behavior	Description: Time, Activity, Context

An Introduction to Agricultural Geography

Employing nearly on half of the world's workforce, agriculture is clearly of great economic and social importance. An incredible variety of methods is used globally; the Western world has the latest scientific and industrial advancements at its disposal, yet in some parts of the Third World a living is made using tools that have hardly changed in two thousand years.

David Grigg provides a comprehensive introduction to agriculture in both the First and Third Worlds, describing both human and environmental issues. Covering the physical environment, economic behaviour and demands, institutional, social and cultural influences, and the impact of farming upon the environment, the book explores the wide range of factors which influence how agriculture and agricultural practice differ from place to place.

For this new edition, the text, statistics, artwork and bibliography have been entirely updated and revised. In addition, two new chapters have been incorporated, on modernization and on the environment.

David Grigg is Professor in the Department of Geography, University of Sheffield.

An Introduction to Agricultural Geography

Second edition

David Grigg

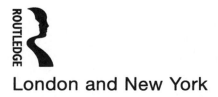

London and New York

First published 1984
by Unwin Hyman
Fourth impression 1989
Reprinted by Routledge 1993

Second edition first published 1995
by Routledge
11 New Fetter Lane, London EC4P 4EE

Simultaneously published in the USA and Canada
by Routledge
29 West 35th Street, New York, NY 10001

Typeset in Garamond by
J&L Composition Ltd, Filey, North Yorkshire
Printed and bound in Great Britain by
Biddles Ltd, Guildford and King's Lynn

British Library Cataloguing in Publication Data
A catalogue record for this book is available from the British Library

Library of Congress Cataloging in Publication Data
Grigg, David B.
    An introduction to agricultural geography/David Grigg. – Ed. 2.
        p.   cm.
    Includes bibliographical references and index.
    1. Agricultural geography.   I. Title.
    S495.G79 1994
    338.1'09–dc20   94–12681

ISBN 0–415–08442–3 (hbk)
        0–415–08443–1 (pbk)

For Jill, Susan, Catherine and Stephen, with much love

Contents

Figures

Tables

Acknowledgements

I am very grateful to Helen Doncaster, Sarah Harmston and Jean Walters, for their efficient and expeditious typing of my manuscript. Graham Allsopp and Paul Coles drew the maps and graphs, and to them, many thanks.

Michaelmas,
Snaithing Lane, Sheffield

Chapter 1

Introduction

Agriculture is by far the most important of the world's economic activities; it uses one-third of the total land surface and employs 45 per cent of the working population. Yet the study of agriculture receives relatively little attention from geographers. In Britain and the USA far more notice is given to manufacturing industry and the problems of urban areas. This neglect perhaps reflects the relative unimportance of agriculture in the economies of developed countries, in contrast to its predominance in the developing countries and the world as a whole. In Britain and the USA only 2 per cent of the employed population are engaged in agriculture, and it contributes a similarly small proportion to the national income. In many developing countries, however, over half the population depends upon farming for a living and it is the most important contributor to the national income. But even in developed countries agriculture is more important than these statistics suggest, for between 12 per cent and 30 per cent of disposable income is spent on food, while agriculture is the major user of land. In England, for example, four-fifths of the land surface is used for agriculture purposes.

Thus the study of agriculture geography is clearly important. The subject may be simply defined. Agricultural geography seeks to describe and explain spatial variations in agricultural activity over the earth's surface. The heart of this task is to explain the great diversity of agriculture. It has been estimated that there are over 250 million farmers in the world. Between them they grow many different crops – at least 1000 species are in use – and they raise these crops in a variety of ways. Thus on some British farms aircraft spray the land with pesticides and computers control the day-to-day running of the farm; yet in parts of the Middle East *fellahin* still raise wheat with implements little changed since biblical times. Equally great are the differences in organization and social conditions. Many farmers in Britain or the USA are rich and successful, owning their land; in parts of Latin America *peons* toil on land they do not own under conditions not far removed from slavery. Even more striking are the differences in productivity. One American farm worker can produce enough food to feed nearly fifty other people, yet throughout Africa and Asia many farmers are hard-pressed to feed themselves and their families.

A DEFINITION OF AGRICULTURE

Agriculture has been described as the purposive raising of livestock and crops for human needs. The word 'purposive' thus excludes hunters and gatherers who have not domesticated the plants and animals they use for food. Although forestry and fishing are often placed with agriculture in economic classifications, they are not considered here. It should be noted, however, that many Scandinavian farmers combine agriculture and forestry, while in parts of Asia coastal villages often practise both fishing and farming. Attempts to raise wild game for meat in parts of Africa form an interesting stage between hunting and pastoralism. It has been argued that some modern forms of agriculture, such as the broiler industry, are more akin to industrial operations than agriculture. But the fact that little land is used and that the technology and organization are modern and efficient cannot be allowed to exclude such activities; a rapid growth in the scale of organization and technical expertise is a distinctive feature of modern agriculture.

Some have argued that geographers have confined themselves solely to production on the farm; instead they should deal with the geography of the food system, and cover not only the production of food on farms but also the geography of input production – such as the manufacture of fertilizers and machinery – and the processing of the raw materials raised on farms, in flour mills, sugar refineries and breweries for example. Some would go further and include the distribution and consumption of foods as part of the system. This is a laudable aim, but as yet there is little written upon the subject, and the execution of this task lies in the future.

If agriculture is diverse, it is also remarkably complex, and there is a need to be clear what features of agricultural production the geographer is trying to describe and explain. Yet there is a long list of variables that give rise to diversity. Thus the differences between farming in Britain and the former Soviet Union are legion, but that of land tenure might spring first to mind, for in Britain farmers either own their farms or rent them from private landlords whilst in the Soviet Union all land was the property of the state, and indeed most still is. A study of Louisiana and southern Vietnam would show that rice is grown in both areas but the methods used and the efficiency with which the crop is raised differ greatly. Some comparisons would emphasize differences in the crops grown and the livestock raised. Thus a few miles to the west of Sheffield in northern England there are parishes where few if any crops are grown and no stock kept but sheep, which feed upon rough grazing and permanent grass. A few miles to the

Table 1.1 Characteristics of agricultural types

A Social attributes
1 Percentage of land held in common
2 Percentage of land in labour or share tenancy
3 Percentage of land in private ownership
4 Percentage of land in state or collective ownership
5 Size of holding according to numbers employed
6 Size of holding according to area of agricultural land
7 Size of holding according to value of output

B Operational attributes
8 Labour intensity: numbers of employees per hectare of agricultural land
9 Inputs of animal power in draught units per hectare of agricultural land
10 Inputs of mechanical power: tractors, harvesters, etc. per hectare of agricultural land
11 Chemical fertilizers: NPK per hectare of cultivated land
12 Irrigation: irrigated land as a percentage of all cultivated land
13 Intensity of crop land use: ration of harvested to total arable
14 Intensity of livestock breeding: animal units per hectare of agricultural land

C Production attributes
15 Land productivity: gross agricultural output per hectare of agricultural land
16 Labour productivity: gross agricultural output per employee in agriculture
17 Degree of commercialization: proportion of output sold off farm
18 Commercial production: commercial output per hectare of agricultural land

D Structural characteristics
19 Percentage of land in perennial and semi-perennial crops
20 Percentage of total agricultural land in permanent grass
21 Percentage of total agricultural land in food crops
22 Percentage of total agricultural output of animal origin
23 Animal production as percentage of total commercial output
24 Industrial crops (sugar, fibre, rubber, beverages) as percentage of total agricultural land

Source: J. Kostrowicki, *World Types of Agriculture* Warsaw, 1976, pp. 10–21

east sheep are unknown, rough grazing rare and grass is a small part of a land use pattern dominated by wheat, barley, sugar-beet and potatoes. There is thus a great variety of variables that must be discussed in order to describe spatial variations in agriculture. A Commission of the International Geographical Union has compiled a list (Table 1.1) of the principal variables which includes land tenure and size of farms, the use of labour and capital inputs, the degree of commercialization, the efficiency with which the inputs are used, the types of crops grown and the livestock raised.

APPROACHES TO DESCRIPTION

There are two contrasting approaches to the description of agricultural diversity.

First is the systematic analysis of the distribution of one variable. Thus it is useful to study the spatial variations in the growth of wheat. This can be done at any scale – the world or a British parish. Such a study tells us where wheat is grown, where it is absent, in what places it is a major crop, in what places it is of minor importance. It also suggests explanations of the pattern. The distribution of wheat growing may be related to rainfall or the presence of large urban markets. Valuable as such an approach is, it has its limitations. Wheat is not grown – or is rarely grown – as the only crop on a farm. Further, analysis of crop statistics may suggest that wheat is generally grown in characteristic crop combinations. In one region it may be commonly grown with sugar-beet and potatoes, in another area with barley and oilseed rape.

Second is the approach to description by means of the idea of type of farming map, or agricultural region. This can be best illustrated by amplifying the remarks made upon the distribution of wheat. The analysis of the distribution of crops requires statistics on the use of agricultural land, usually available only for administrative districts such as the British parish, the French commune, or in the USA, the county. But these figures are aggregates of the land use of a number of farms. If figures were available by farms, then it might be seen that not only are there spatial variations in the importance of wheat or in distinctive crop combinations containing wheat, but that these variations correspond to variations in other variables such as the size of farms or the presence or absence of dairy cows. An imaginary example may make this clearer. In the east of a country little wheat is grown, the farms are small, most of the farmers own their land and rely upon their family for labour. No sheep are kept and few beef cattle; most of the livestock are cows, and the main source of income is from the sale of milk. Moving westwards there are changes; more wheat is grown, sheep and beef cattle replace cows, farms are large and rented, and farmers hire labour. Maps of the distribution of wheat or dairy cows fail to capture the way in which a number of variables change spatially. It is clearly possible to classify farms into types on the basis of not one but several variables. Similarly, it is possible to see that some areas are characterized by a predominance of one type of farming.

Both the systematic study of spatial variations of a single variable, or the definition of type of farming area or agricultural region, are useful approaches to the study of agricultural geography. But they are only a beginning.

APPROACHES TO EXPLANATION

Description is essential to the understanding of the agricultural geography of an area, and it often suggests various ways of explaining spatial variations. There have been several approaches to explanation in agricultural geography.

Environment and agriculture

Agriculture deals with living plants and animals which thrive in some physical environments, but flourish less successfully or not at all in other environments. Not surprisingly students of agricultural geography have for a long time assumed that differences in the physical environment determine spatial variations in agricultural activity, and that regional differences in climate and soil give rise to distinctive agricultural regions or types of farming area. Thus the earliest regional descriptions of British farming, the Reports made to the Board of Agriculture in the 1790s, for the most part assumed that farming varied spatially largely as a response to differences between upland and lowland and between different soil types. Similar assumptions were made in many of the essays on the agriculture of the English counties published in the *Journal of the Royal Agricultural Society of England* in the mid-nineteenth century. It is a view which was still prevalent in the County Monographs of the Land Utilization Survey of Britain published in the 1930s and 1940s. In the USA a series of articles on the agricultural regions of the world, published in the 1920s and 1930s, all bore the assumption that climate was the principal determinant of world patterns of farming.

Such geographical determinism, or environmentalism – the belief that environment inflexibly determines human activities – was not confined to agricultural geography; it was a view attacked by Paul Vidal de la Blache in the early twentieth century. His studies of French *pays*, or regions, emphasized the mutual interaction of man and environment. But by the 1930s American geographers, reacting against environmentalism, were seeking explanations for agricultural differences everywhere but in the environment. After the Second World War this flight from determinism became apparent in Britain and Europe. This did not mean that there was no study of the relationships between crops and the physical environment; rather it was now left to agronomists, soil scientists, climatologists and botanists. Agricultural geographers had cut themselves off from their roots.

J.H. von Thünen, models and explanation

In 1826 J.H. von Thünen, a German economist, published *The Isolated State*. In this he argued that distance from the market was the prime determinant of what crops and livestock were grown and with what intensity.

He devised an imaginary world where all the other factors that could influence farming practice – such as soil type, or imports – were held constant. He thus devised the first economic model. When *The Isolated State* was translated into English in 1966, it had a profound impact on agricultural geographers and prompted many studies of the influence of distance on the farm, at the national level and the world scale. It emphasized one factor, assumed that economic forces were paramount, and largely discounted the significance of environment. It also led agricultural geographers to try and frame hypotheses and test them with rather more rigour than had hitherto been the case.

Behavioural approaches

In the study of agricultural geography the fundamental unit is the farm and the farmer. But most published agricultural statistics are available only at an administrative level that conceals farms by aggregation. Hence it has been difficult to explain agricultural variations in terms of individual behaviour. Yet clearly spatial variations in agriculture are a result of many decisions made by many individual farmers. Torsten Hägerstrand's studies of how Swedish farmers' adopted new farming methods have led to many studies of how farmers attitudes and assumptions affect decision-making on the farm. Such – and allied – studies led to a swing away from the economic determinism of which von Thünen was perhaps an unwitting forerunner. In recent years more emphasis has been put by geographers upon non-environmental and non-economic factors in explaining spatial variations in agriculture.

Internationalization, modernization and the political economy approach

In the 1980s the approaches outlined above became less common in agricultural geography, and there was a search for other modes of explanation. This was partly prompted by the growing importance of state intervention in the behaviour of farmers, and the inability to solve the problems of overproduction; and partly by the growing importance of food processers in the food production system. Some believed that the globalization of world food production was of paramount importance in understanding world patterns of production, and linked this to the rise of transnational food producers and processers. Others, concerned with much the same array of topics saw the growth of agribusiness – rarely precisely defined – as the key to understanding. Such theories are often described as the political economy approach. One advocate in the 1980s described these methodologies as being in their infancy, and it is perhaps not unfair to argue that they remain still more polemical than empirical; there are more calls to further research than reliable evidence. Such work as yet remains on the research frontiers of the subject rather than in an introductory text such as this.

PURPOSE AND PATTERN

The aim of this book is *not* to describe the agricultural geography of any one country, region or the world. This is a laudable aim and has been attempted by many. Nor is the purpose to take one explanatory factor and illustrate its significance. This is an introductory textbook, and it makes the assumption that it is highly improbable that one factor such as climate or distance from the market will explain spatial variations in all parts of the world. Instead those factors that have been suggested by geographers as important are reviewed. It should be emphasized that the aim is to show how a variety of variables can affect spatial variations in farming, not to discuss those variables *per se*. Thus differences in land tenure are a fundamental feature of the world's agricultural geography. But the concern here is only how differences in tenure influence variations in land use, productivity and farming structure.

The first part of the book deals with the biological characteristics of crops and livestock and the way in which the physical environment influences the farmers' choice of crops and animals. The second part deals with the economic behaviour of farmers and the behaviour of the consumers of food and fibre. The role of the state is considered, and also the consequences of the modernization of agriculture. This is followed by a consideration of the influence of the location of urban markets upon farming. Population density and labour availability are then discussed. The third part deals with institutional and social influences on agricultural geography. The role of land tenure, farm size, innovation diffusion and religion are discussed. A final chapter deals with the impact of farming upon the environment. It is not suggested that this approach is comprehensive or exhaustive; even less that this is the only way to approach the study of agricultural geography. The aim of this book is to emphasize that the remarkable diversity of the world's major industry requires an equal breadth of mind if its spatial variety is to be understood.

SOURCES AND FURTHER READING

J.P. van Aartsen, 'Agricultural geography', *Tijdschrift voor Economische en Sociale Geografie*, 1953, vol. 44, pp. 27–8.

B. Andreae, *Farming Development and Space: A World Agricultural Geography*, New York, De Gruyter, 1981.

P.J. Atkins, 'Redefining agricultural geography as the geography of food', *Area*, 1988, vol. 20 pp. 281–3.

O.E. Baker, 'Agricultural regions of North America', *Economic Geography*, 1926, vol. 2, pp. 459–93.

I.R. Bowler (ed.), *The Geography of Agriculture in Developed Market Economies*, Harlow, Longman, 1992.

I.R. Bowler and B.W. Ilbery, 'Redefining agricultural geography', *Area*, 1987, vol. 19, pp. 327–32.

R.O. Buchanan, 'Some reflections on agricultural geography', *Geography*, 1955, vol. 44, pp. 1–13.

J.T. Coppock, 'The geography of agriculture', *Journal of Agricultural Economics*, 1968, vol. 19, pp. 153–75.

A.N. Duckham and G.B. Masefield, *Farming Systems of the World*, London, Chatto & Windus, 1970.

W.C. Founds, *A Theoretical Approach to Rural Land Use Patterns*, London, Edward Arnold, 1971.

H.F. Gregor, *Geography of Agriculture: Themes in Research*, Englewood Cliffs, New Jersey, Prentice Hall, 1970.

D.B. Grigg, *Agricultural Systems of the World: An Evolutionary Approach*, Cambridge, Cambridge University Press, 1974.

T. Hägerstrand, *Innovation Diffusion as a Spatial Process*, Chicago, Chicago University Press, 1967.

P. Hall (ed.), *Von Thünen's Isolated State*, Oxford, Pergamon Press, 1966.

W.E. Hart, 'Problems and potentialities of the behavioural approach to agricultural location' *Geografiska Annaler*, 1980, vol. 62B, pp. 99–108.

D.W. Harvey, 'Theoretical concepts and the analysis of agricultural land use patterns in geography', *Annals of the Association of American Geographers*, 1966, vol. 36, pp. 362–74.

J.D. Henshall, 'Models of agricultural activity', in R.J. Chorley and P. Haggett (eds), *Models in Geography*, London, Methuen, 1967, pp. 425–58.

B.W. Ilbery, *Agricultural Geography, a Social and Economic Analysis*. Oxford, Oxford University Press, 1985.

P. Laut, *Agricultural Geography*, 2 vols, Sydney, Nelson, 1968.

R. Le Heron, 'Food and fibre production under capitalism: a conceptual agenda', *Progress in Human Geography*, 1988, vol. 12, pp. 409–30.

H. McCarty, 'Agricultural geography', in P.E. James and C.F. Jones (eds), *American Geography: Inventory and Prospect*, Syracuse, Syracuse University Press, 1954, pp. 259–77.

W.B. Morgan and R.J. Munton, *Agricultural Geography*, London, Methuen, 1971.

W.N. Peach and J.A. Constantin, *Zimmerman's World Resources and Industries*, 3rd edn, New York, Harper & Row, 1922.

J.T. Pierce, *The Food Resource*, Harlow, Longman, 1990.

J. Rutherford, 'Agricultural geography as a discipline: a suggested conceptual foundation for University work', *Jerusalem Studies in Geography*, 1970, vol. 1, pp. 37–105.

L.D. Stamp, *The Land of Britain: Its Use and Misuse*, London, Longman, 1948.

L. Symons, *Agricultural Geography*, Boulder, Colorado, Westview Press, 1979.

J.R. Tarrant, *Agricultural Geography*, Newton Abbot, David & Charles, 1974.

W. Van Royen, *Atlas of the World's Resources*, vol. 1, *The Agricultural Resources of the World*, New York, Prentice Hall, 1954.

Chapter 2

The biology of agriculture

The farmer – unlike the manufacturer – deals with living things. Plants and animals have inherent biological characteristics that determine their productivity; and they only function efficiently in environments to which they are adapted. Both these factors profoundly influence the nature and location of agricultural production.

FOOD CHAINS

All the energy on earth comes from the sun. The solar radiation received at the earth's surface is used by those plants that contain chlorophyll to produce, by photosynthesis, carbohydrates and protein. In addition the plant needs mineral nutrients that come from the decomposition of rocks and are taken into the plant in solution via its roots. Carbon dioxide, hydrogen and nitrogen are derived from the atmosphere, although the latter has to be fixed in the soil as a soluble nitrate before it can be taken up by the plant. But plants only use a minute fraction of the energy available in solar radiation. The energy contained in plants represents, at the very most between 1 and 5 per cent of the energy in the solar radiation incident at the earth's surface.

The amount of energy formed by plants is known as the Net Primary Product, and all other parts of the natural kingdom are dependent upon this source of food and energy. The natural vegetation provides food for herbivores, animals that graze on plants; they form the second level in the food chain. However, just as the plants contain a small fraction of the energy present in solar radiation, so there is a great loss of energy between the plants and the animals that graze upon them. A further level in the food chain is represented by the carnivores that prey upon the herbivores as does, for example, the lion upon the wildebeest. Again, there is a remarkable loss of energy between the herbivores and the carnivores.

These food chains also exist in agriculture. Solar radiation provides the energy for crop plants; these may be eaten directly by humans in his guise as herbivores, or by cattle and sheep as herbivores. They in their turn are eaten by humans as carnivores. The loss of energy through the chain is considerable. For example, on the open range of the south-western USA 800,000 kilocalories of solar radiation reach each square metre in a year. Of this, after respiration, transpiration and other leakages, only 800 kilocalories are available in the vegetation. Cattle graze this sparse scrub and grassland, but the meat produced by the herds is equivalent, in energy terms, to just 20 kilocalories per square metre; only 2.5 per cent of the energy available in the natural vegetation, and 0.0002 per cent of the energy in the solar radiation incident at the earth's surface.

The loss of energy between vegetation and animal is fundamental to the economics and geography of agriculture. The amount of food produced per hectare by plants is always far greater than that produced by animals. To put it another way, to produce a given number of calories for human food nearly always requires more land for animal food than for plant food. In the United Kingdom milk is the most biologically efficient of the animal products (Table 2.1) but its yield is only one-ninth of that obtainable from potatoes, and one-sixth of that derived from wheat. At the other extreme, beef cattle and sheep produce only 2–3 per cent of the energy per hectare obtained from potatoes. It is not surprising, then, that livestock products are more expensive than plant foodstuffs, or that in densely populated regions in poor countries food crops are dominant and livestock products rare. Perhaps more surprising is that, although the protein content of most plants per unit weight is below that of most animal foods (the protein content of wheaten flour is half that of an egg, that of manioc only

Table 2.1 Edible yields from animals and crops

	Energy (Mcal/hectare)	Protein (Kg/hectare)
Potatoes	24,000	420
Wheat	14,000	350
Cabbage	8000	1100
Peas	3000	280
Dairy	2500	115
Dairy and beef	2400	102
Pigs	1900	50
Eggs	1150	80
Broilers	1100	92
Beef	750	27
Sheep	500	23

Source: W. Holmes, 'Efficiency of food production by the animal Industries', in P.F. Wareing and J.P. Cooper (eds), *Potential Crop Production*, London, 1971, p. 224

a fifth), the protein output per hectare of land under most plants exceeds that of land used by animals (Table 2.1).

CROP PRODUCTIVITY

Botanists measure the productivity of natural vegetation by estimating the total weight of the biomass per hectare, which includes roots, stalks, stems, fruit, seeds and leaves. But the yield of agricultural plants is only the edible part of the crop, or in the case of fibres, the usable part. The yield of crops varies a great deal because of differences in climate, soil type and the amount of inputs such as fertilizer that are used, the amount of weeding, and the efficiency of protection against pests and diseases. But there are also inherent variations in the yield of different crops when measured by the weight harvested per hectare; the world average yield of potatoes (Figure 2.1) is twenty times that of millet, while maize yields are more than double those of sorghum. The yields of the tropical root crops – manioc, yams and sweet potatoes – are well above the tropical grain crops, and the main temperate root – potatoes – yields far more than the leading temperate grain, wheat. But these yields are not an adequate measure of the output of food per hectare, for crops vary in the number of calories they

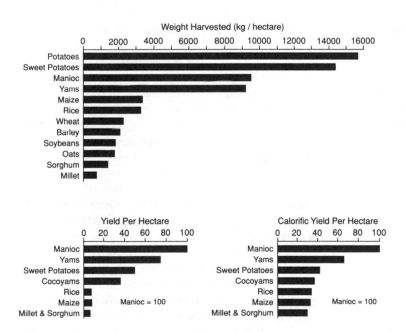

Figure 2.1　(a) Harvested yields of selected crops, world average, 1987–9
　　　　　　(b) Harvested yields and calorific yields of food crops in West Africa

supply per unit weight. For example, 100 g of millet provides 345 calories, but the same weight of manioc only 109 calories. Thus the calorific output of crops is not necessarily the same as the harvested weight, although even with lower calorific values the roots normally produce more calories per hectare than the grains. In Figure 2.1 the yield per hectare and the calorific output per hectare of the principal food crops of West Africa are compared. In both cases the crops are expressed, not in kilograms per hectare, or calories per hectare, but as a percentage of manioc. Although the root crop cocoyams gives a far greater *yield* per hectare than the cereals, its food output per hectare (and that of sweet potatoes) is little more than that of the grains. Thus, whereas manioc has a marked advantage as a food crop in West Africa, cocoyams has little advantage in food value over the grains, in spite of its greater harvested yield.

PERENNIALS AND ANNUALS

Crops can be classified in a variety of ways, but of particular importance is the distinction between annuals and perennials. Annual crops are sown and harvested within one year, and are resown the following year with seeds retained from the harvest or bought from a merchant. If the growing season is long, then double cropping and even triple cropping is possible in the tropics and sub-tropics, although generally irrigation is necessary. Perennials, in contrast, once planted yield annually for some years. A distinction can be made between the herbaceous perennials and the woody stemmed perennials. In the former the roots are permanent, but the herbaceous growth is cut at the harvest and later regrows; bananas and sugar-cane are the two important agricultural plants in this category. However, because sugar content declines with each succeeding cut, sugar-cane may be replanted at frequent intervals. In the woody perennials, both the roots and the stems above ground are permanent, and it is the fruit or leaves that are harvested. This group includes the temperate orchard trees such as apples and pears, grapes, olives, and tropical crops such as tea, cocoa and coffee. Rubber trees are cut to drain off latex.

The nature of these crops presents a number of difficulties to farmers. First, they do not bear fruit until some years after planting (Table 2.2), and take even longer to bear fruit suitable for sale. Thus many of these crops are grown on plantations where financial resources are great enough for this period without return to be borne. Alternatively, they are grown on smallholdings where, however, most of the land will be devoted to food crops. Second, once planted the crop yields each year regardless of the level of demand, and so problems of overproduction are very marked. Tea and rubber are exceptions to this generalization; latex is only yielded by the rubber tree if the bark is cut, while tea production requires the leaves to be picked; some control of output is thus possible. None the less, the

Table 2.2 Perennial crops: their length of life (years)

	Age when bearing begins	Commercial bearing	Maximum yield	Duration of yield
Apple	4–7	6–12	16–25	20–35
Orange	3–4	5–8	15–20	20–35
Grapes	3	4	5	30–40
Coffee	3–4	5–6	–	20
Coconut	7–10	10	–	60
Cocoa	5	10–12	–	–

Source: W.N. Peach and J.A. Constantin (eds), Zimmerman's World Resources and Industries, New York, 1972, p. 299

perennial crops have presented persistent problems of overproduction. Part of the reason for this is the expansion of planting when prices are high; there is of course no guarantee that prices will still be high five to ten years later, when the bushes or trees begin to bear commercial fruit. Coffee has proved particularly susceptible to these problems.

THE BIOLOGY OF LIVESTOCK

The differences between crops and livestock in terms of food output per hectare have already been noted. There are also important differences between the various animals used by people to produce meat, milk, wool and hides.

Note should be taken of the difference between the ruminants and the non-ruminants. Ruminants have micro-organisms in the gut that allow them to digest the cellulose in fibrous plants, particularly grass. In this way cattle, buffalo, sheep, goats and deer can feed upon grass and the leaves of trees. People, of course, cannot do this, nor can pigs and poultry which have simple stomachs and eat the same type of plant products as human beings. They are thus in competition with humans for limited food resources. However, as they can eat the residues of human food, they can be kept as scavengers and are particularly useful in densely populated regions; China for example, has 40 per cent of the world's pigs and 20 per cent of the chickens.

Cattle and sheep can feed on grass, which is very widely grown. This has two advantages. First, grass under temperate climatic conditions and good farming methods gives a higher dry matter, energy or protein yield than most crops, but it can only be converted into human food if grazed by ruminants. Second, grass and other plants containing cellulose can colonize large areas of the earth's surface which are too dry or too cold for crops grown directly for human consumption. This land could not be utilized if it were not grazed by ruminants. In the semi-arid areas sheep and goats are more tolerant of aridity than cattle, because cattle need 50 per cent more drinking water per unit of body weight than sheep. Sheep and goats, then, make up the greater part of the livestock of nomadic pastoralists who have for the most part been driven into the remoter arid regions by sedentary cultivators.

Some types of cattle can survive in dry regions, for they can range long distances in search of grass or bushes, but under such circumstances they put on little weight, and have to be shipped to areas of better grass, or grain must be purchased, to fatten them for market. There is often a distinction between areas (generally environmentally inferior) where cattle are reared, and where they are fattened. In Britain sheep are reared in upland areas, but fattened in lowland regions. In the USA, the pattern used to be for young cattle to be reared in the drier parts of the Great Plains and in parts of the Rockies, and then driven east to the lusher grasslands and grain-growing regions of the Midwest, where they were fattened for market. Now, however, cattle are often reared in the drier areas and then fattened on grain imported from further east. Dairy cattle have different requirements from beef cattle; they cannot move any considerable distance in search of food, and the quantity of milk they produce is controlled by the amount and quality of their fodder intake.

The way in which livestock are fed varies a great deal. In many parts of the world cattle and sheep can be kept on natural vegetation, although at very low densities; the interior of Brazil and Australia are examples. Grass plays a part in this vegetation, but is not sown by the rancher or treated in any way. In contrast, sown grass plays a significant role in the feeding of cattle in the Netherlands, New Zealand, Ireland and Britain, but here improved varieties of grass are sown and often irrigated and fertilized. Livestock may also be fed upon crops grown on arable land; a wide range of fodder crops are grown, including potatoes, cabbages, turnips and other fodder roots and various oilseed crops. In addition, grain is now widely grown as a feed for cattle; Europe still imports grain for this purpose.

Livestock densities vary a great deal owing to differences in the environment, but also to the differing feed requirements of the various species. Thus, in the United Kingdom, dairy cows have the highest feed requirement, sheep require only one-tenth of that, pigs one-half and poultry one-fiftieth. This reflects primarily differences in body weight, but livestock also differ in their biological capacity to convert feed into energy (Table 2.3). Pigs are the most efficient converters of feed into energy, beef cattle the least efficient; on the other hand, dairy cattle are the most efficient converters of feed into protein (Table 2.3, note 6). Other factors help to decide what livestock or combination of livestock will be kept. Differences in body weight mean that animals of different species will give very different amounts of edible meat. Cattle produce five times as much meat as pigs, but the latter twice as much as sheep. However, these

Table 2.3 Efficiency of livestock production

	Output[1] and feed ratio %	Output[2] energy and feed energy	Gross[3] feed energy to edible protein %	Crude[4] Protein (kg per hectare per yr)	Gross[4] energy (MJ per ha per yr)
Pigs	–	–	12	–	–
Pork	47.9	35	–	–	–
Bacon	38.5	35	–	105	14,438
Broilers	36.0	16	20	135	7071
Sheep	17.6–13.2	11–14.6	3	65	7486
Cattle	8.6	5.2–7.8[5]	6[6]	53–65	3924–4796[5]

Notes: 1 Output of carcase in relation to feed dry matter intake

$$\frac{\text{Carcase Kg}}{\text{Feed intake kg}} \times 100$$

2 Output of energy in carcase in relation to input of feed energy. Total energy in carcase divided by energy in total feed multiplied by 100.
3 Conversion of gross feed energy to edible protein in lifetime performance.
4 Under UK conditions.
5 Beef herd.
6 Beef herd; for dairy cows it is 23 per cent.

Source: C.R.W. Spedding, S.M. Walsingham, and A.M. Hoxey, Biological Efficiency in Agriculture, London, Academic Press, 1981, pp. 253–5, 303

differences are partly compensated for by the differences in gestation periods between cattle and sheep, and poultry and pigs, the former taking longer to produce marketable meat. Pigs and poultry produce far more protein per hectare than sheep or goats, and pigs produce more calories than other livestock (Table 2.3).

PESTS AND DISEASES

Biologists have shown how elaborate are the interrelationships between the flora and fauna of the natural world. Most plants and animals are food for some other plant or animal. Nor are the animals kept by humans, or the plants grown by them, any exception. Cattle may be savaged by tigers, sheep by dogs; less dramatically they provide a host for ticks, insects and parasites. Crops, too, provide food for birds, animals and insects. To the farmer these creatures are pests and diseases which must be eliminated, however natural their role. Despite advances in pesticides, pests and diseases still destroy a large proportion of the world's standing crop each year. The spread of disease has also had an important effect on the location of some crops. The banana provides a good example of this.

The banana in the Americas

The banana is widely grown as a food crop throughout the tropics, but in the last century it has been grown both on plantations and smallholdings in the Americas for export to the USA and Western Europe. It was first grown for this purpose in the late nineteenth century in Jamaica and the Caribbean coastal areas of Central America, at that time sparsely populated. The United Fruit Company developed railways and plantations in Honduras, Guatemala, Costa Rica and Panama. Some bananas were grown on the Pacific coast of Central America as early as 1906, but there the dry season meant that irrigation was needed, and production was thus more expensive than on the humid Caribbean coast. The latter region was closer to the north-east of the USA and to Europe, an important factor, for there should be no more than three weeks between cutting and consumption. However, in the 1920s the plantations of the Caribbean coast were invaded by Panama disease, a fungus that attacks the roots of the banana and destroys the plant. Fungicides were developed that would destroy the disease, but they were too expensive. In the 1930s a second disease, *sigatoka*, spread through the region; this attacked the leaves and reduced the quality of the fruit, but it could be controlled by copper sulphate sprays. In the 1930s the United Fruit Company abandoned its disease-ridden holdings on the Caribbean coast, and concentrated banana production on the Pacific coast. However, since the 1950s, the Caribbean areas have been revitalized by replacing the variety *Gros Michel* with *Cavendish*, which is immune to Panama disease; but the Pacific regions remain the dominant producers.

The tsetse fly in Africa

Africa has one-fifth of the world's agricultural land, but only one-seventh of its cattle. There are many reasons for this, including the poor quality of the natural grazing, the lack of suitable fodder crops and the limited local demand for meat, but of particular importance is the prevalence of a disease, sleeping sickness, which afflicts both man and cattle. In cattle the disease is called *Nagana*, and it is carried by a parasite endemic in the game animals of the continent. The tsetse fly bites both game and cattle to obtain blood, and so transfers the disease from game to cattle. The tsetse fly thrives only in areas with thick bush; it is thus not found either in densely populated areas where the bush has been removed for cultivation, or in drier regions where moisture is insufficient to maintain bush. But it does occupy a large proportion of Africa, and cattle are few in these regions (Figure 2.2). Various attempts have been made to eliminate the disease: in northern Nigeria pesticides have been used, but this has proved very expensive, as are curative drugs. As yet there is no means of immuniza-

Figure 2.2   The tsetse fly in Africa and the distribution of cattle
After A.T. Grove, *Africa*, Oxford, Oxford University Press, 1978

tion. The reduction of the tsetse fly, by whatever means, would greatly improve the productivity of the African savannas.

CONCLUSIONS

The biological aspects of agriculture have considerable significance for the agricultural geography of the world, yet they have been relatively neglected by agricultural geographers. Most of the work has been done by agronomists and, more recently, by biogeographers; it is to be hoped that agricultural geographers will build upon their example.

SOURCES AND FURTHER READING

T. Bayliss-Smith, *The Ecology of Agricultural Systems*, Cambridge, Cambridge University Press, 1982.
W.J. Carlyle, 'The marketing and movement of Scottish hill lambs', *Geography*, 1972, vol. 57, pp. 10–17.

A.N. Duckham, S.G.W. Jones and E.H. Roberts, *Food Production and Consumption: The Efficiency of Human Food Chains and Nutrient Cycles*, Oxford, North Holland Publishing Company, 1976.

C.F. Jones and P.C. Morrison, 'Evolution of the banana industry of Costa Rica', *Economic Geography*, 1951, vol. 28, pp. 1–19.

A.M. Jordan, 'Trypanosomiasis control and land use in Africa', *Outlook on Agriculture*, 1979, vol. 10, pp. 123–9.

G. Leach, *Energy and Food Production*, London, IPC Press, 1976.

R.S. Loomis, 'Agricultural systems', *Scientific American*, 1976, vol. 235, pp. 99–105.

R.S. Loomis, and P.A. Gerakis, 'Productivity of agricultural ecosystems', in J.C. Cooper (ed.), *Photosynthesis and Productivity in Different Environments*, Cambridge, Cambridge University Press, 1975, pp. 145–72.

R.S. Loomis, W.A. Williams and A.E. Hall, 'Agricultural productivity', *Annual Review of Plant Physiology*, 1971, vol. 22, pp. 431–68.

R. Lowrance, B.R. Stinner and G.J. House, *Agricultural Ecosystems*, New York, Wiley, 1984.

M. Pyke, *Man and Food*, London, Weidenfeld and Nicolson, 1970.

I.G. Simmons, *Biogeography, Natural and Cultural*, London, Edward Arnold, 1979.

I.G. Simmons, 'Ecological functional approaches to agriculture in geographical contexts', *Geography*, 1979, vol. 65, pp. 305–16.

I.G. Simmons, *The Ecology of Natural Resources*, 2nd Edn, London, Edward Arnold, 1981

C.R.W. Spedding, *The Biology of Agricultural Systems*, London, Academic Press, 1975.

C.R.W. Spedding, *An Introduction to Agricultural Systems*, London, Applied Science Publication, 1979.

P.F. Wareing and J.C. Cooper, *Potential Crop Production: A Case Study*, London, Heinemann, 1971.

Chapter 3

Climate and crops

All crops differ in their biological characteristics and their environmental requirements, while the physical character of the earth's surface varies greatly from place to place. A great many variables influence plant growth and development, including day-length, the amount of solar energy received, the amount of precipitation available for transpiration, temperature during the growing season and the level of mineral plant nutrients in the soil. Many of these variables, all critical for successful plant growth, can be modified by the farmer; in dry regions irrigation can supplement precipitation, fertilizers can add plant nutrients and temperature and day-length can be modified by growing crops indoors with heating and controlled lighting. But all these modifications of the natural environment are costly. There are, however, some parts of the earth's surface where a particular crop will grow best without these modifications, and a knowledge of such places helps to explain the distribution of crops.

OPTIMUM GROWTH

Plant requirements in terms of temperature, moisture and plant nutrients are rarely linear. For any plant there are (i) minimum requirements of temperature or moisture without which no growth will take place; (ii) maximum limits, beyond which growth ceases. Between these limits are (iii) environmental characteristics which give optimum growth and development; here are found the highest *yields*, the weight of the edible part of the crop per hectare. For example, in the USA in 1908, when little fertilizer was used, wheat did not grow at all with small amounts of rainfall; then, as annual rainfall increased so did yields, until the highest yields were found in places with an amount of rainfall between 625 and 875 mm. Further increases in rainfall led, however, to a decline in yields (Figure 3.1). It follows that one might expect there to be for any one crop areas of the earth's surface where yields are highest and variability is lowest. This is the *ecological optimum*. Away from the optimum area, environmental conditions

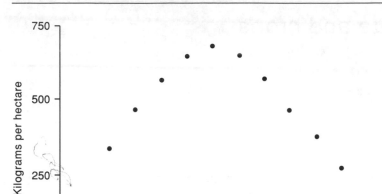

Figure 3.1 Mean annual rainfall and the yield of wheat, USA, 1908
Little fertilizer was used on wheat crops at this time
Source: O.E. Baker, 'The potential supply of wheat', *Economic Geography*, 1925, vol. 1, pp. 15–52

deteriorate so that yields fall and variability increases, until the point of minimum requirements is reached and the crop does not grow at all; this is the *absolute* limit to growth.

In an imaginary continent, the optimum conditions for a given crop are in the centre (Figure 3.2). Yields are 5 tonnes per hectare, but they decline away from this zone, and eventually climate conditions are so adverse that no growth occurs and the yield is zero. This is the absolute limit of cultivation. However, farmers are not likely to cultivate the crop near the absolute limit, for economic as well as ecological factors determine where a crop is grown. Suppose the price received for the crop is £100 per tonne, and the cost of production (the same everywhere) is £150 per hectare. Under these conditions production cost per tonne will increase with increasingly adverse climatic conditions (Figure 3.2), and profit per hectare will also decline away from the optimum zone. Indeed, when yields fall to 1.5 tonnes per hectare, the price received will equal production cost and income will be zero. Farmers will clearly cultivate the crop only within this economic limit. The economic limit, unlike the absolute limit, is not fixed. A fall in production cost or an increase in price would extend the economic limit out towards the absolute limit, while an increase in production cost or a fall in price would cause a contraction of the margin of cultivation towards the optimum area.

Figure 3.2 The economic and ecological optima and limits (Cost of production £150 per hectare, price per tonne £100)

OPTIMUM AREAS AND COMPETING CROPS

So far it has been assumed that only one crop is grown by farmers, but obviously this is not always so. Now, not only does the earth's surface vary greatly in the opportunities it affords for plant growth, but the environmental requirements of crops differ a great deal, so that the optimum areas and the absolute limits will vary as well. In some cases the optimum areas

Table 3.1 Polar boundaries of selected crops (degrees of latitude, northern hemisphere)

Coconut palm	15°	Soybeans	45°
Oil palm	16°	Millet, sorghum	45°
Sisal	19°	Olive tree	45°
Cocoa, arabica coffee	22°	Grape vines	51°
Bananas, manioc	23°	Beets, corn	51°
Rubber	25°	Rubber tree	52°
Sweet potatoes	35°	Tobacco	53°
Cotton	38°	Maize	54°
Sugar-cane	39°	Wheat	63°
Peanuts, tea	41°	Barley, potatoes	70°
Citrus fruit	42°		

Source: B. Andreae, *Farming, Development and Space. A World Agricultural Geography*, Berlin, Walter de Gruyter, 1981

of two crops – or two groups of crops – are mutually exclusive. Thus, tea and rubber are confined to the tropics because they require high temperatures and large amounts of rainfall throughout the year; they cannot be grown in the temperate regions (Table 3.1 and Figure 3.3). Conversely some cereal crops, temperate grasses and potatoes can be grown at the poleward limits, but their successful development needs a period of low temperature – vernalization – that never occurs in the tropics. Sugar-cane

Figure 3.3 The latitudinal limits of the principal crops (northern hemisphere only)

and sugar-beet well illustrate this mutual exclusiveness. Both require periods of high temperatures for sucrose to form in the plant, and both ideally require rainfall during the growing season, but a dry period at harvest. However, the risk of frost limits the northward expansion of sugar-cane, and the absence of a cold period prevents the growth of sugar-beet in the tropics. Only in a few regions – such as southern Spain – are sugar-cane and sugar-beet grown together, and then both are irrigated.

A more common situation occurs where two or more crops have a similar optimum area and compete for the zone where both crops give their highest yields, which diminish with increasing distance from the optimum area (Figure 3.4). This is a situation commonly found on the arid peripheries of humid regions in North and South America, Russia and south-east Australia. The position may be illustrated with reference to Argentina. Both maize and wheat give their highest yields in an area to the west of Buenos Aires, but maize is the predominant crop in this zone, because, with equal inputs, it gives higher yields than wheat (Fig. 3.4). Southwards rainfall declines, and so does the proportion of the cropland in maize, until wheat becomes the dominant crop. This is because maize yields fall off more rapidly than wheat yields as rainfall diminishes, for wheat is more drought-resistant than maize.

Figure 3.4 Optimum areas and competing crops

NET PHOTOSYNTHESIS

A variety of factors influence the location of crops, but the most important are photosynthesis, temperature and moisture. Photosynthesis is the process by which organic matter is formed in plants and is a chemical process triggered by sunlight. Potential net synthesis can be calculated from meteorological data on solar radiation and temperature, and is a reasonable guide to the potential rate of crop growth in different parts of the earth's surface. The amount of solar radiation received at different times of the year is influenced by day length and cloud cover. Figure 3.5 shows the net photosynthesis in grams per square metre per day for five of Koppen's climatic regions and for three different growing periods. Of these the eight-month season, which includes all the food grains, is the most important.

Net photosynthesis is highest in the mid-latitudes, (Fig. 3.6) including southern Europe, the Near East, much of Australia, the USA, southern Africa and southern South America. It is lower towards the equator, including the humid tropics, and poleward. Net photosynthesis is highest in the summer four months in northernly locations with long days, but there are few crops that can develop rapidly enough to benefit from this (Fig. 3.5). The tropics have lower potential growth than the mid-latitudes in all three growing seasons, but their disadvantage is least in the year long season, so that perennial crops are an efficient use of their growth potential. The calculation of net photosynthesis assumes that an adequate supply of water and plant nutrients is available, and so is not reliable as a safe guide to where crops grow best. Similarly many of the areas of highest net photosynthesis are in arid regions, and crop production can only take place with irrigation.

TEMPERATURE

Temperature is a principal determinant of the geography of crops. Most temperate crops will not grow until temperatures are above 6°C, and for

Figure 3.5 Net photosynthesis in grams per square metre per day for five climatic regions
Source: Jen-hu Chang, 'The agricultural potential of the humid tropics', *Geographical Review*, 1986, vol. 58, pp. 333–6

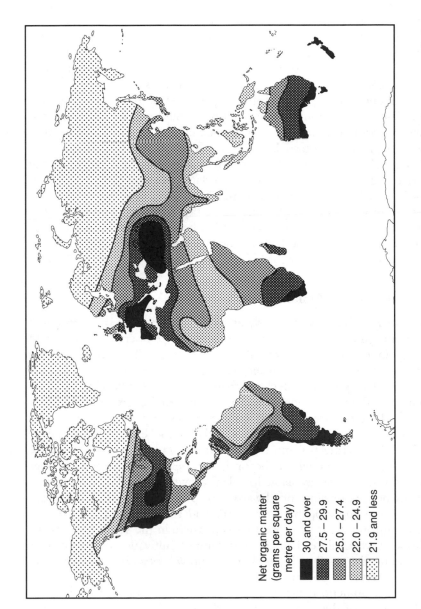

Net organic matter
(grams per square
metre per day)

■ 30 and over

▨ 27.5 – 29.9

▦ 25.0 – 27.4

▥ 22.0 – 24.9

⠿ 21.9 and less

Figure 3.6 World variations in net photosynthesis (net organic matter in grams per square metre per day)
Source: Jen-hu Chang, 'Potential photosynthesis and crop production', *Annals of the Association of American Geographers*, 1970, vol. 60, pp. 92–101

tropical crops this threshold is higher. Low temperatures are a hazard; in spring they can retard germination, and severe frosts may destroy a growing crop, whilst early frosts in late summer may damage the mature crop. Some autumn sown crops need low temperatures in winter in order to germinate in spring, a process called vernalization. Crops vary greatly in their thermal needs, as can be seen in Table 3.1. A number of crops such as the oil palm and cacao need high temperatures throughout the year, and this limits their cultivation to the tropics. However, barley, potatoes and some grasses can be grown in cool short summers as far north as the subarctic.

The distribution of crops has another aspect; just as tropical crops have a limited poleward extension, so many temperate and subtropical crops not only have a northern limit, but also do not extend to the tropics, partly because of high temperatures but also because of disease and excessive rainfall (Fig 3.3). Some crops have a remarkable latitudinal range; of the cereals rice and maize can be grown in lowland areas on the equator, but also north of 50° in the northern hemisphere. Rye, oats, sugar-beet and potatoes are grown north of 50° latitude in the northern hemisphere, but rarely south of 30°. However, these and other temperate crops can be grown in equatorial regions at high altitudes, where temperatures are lower than at sea level (see Chapter 5).

Crop distributions in Finland

Finland is one of the most northerly areas of cultivation in the world, and well illustrates the complex interrelationship of temperature, price and technology in explaining the distribution of crops. The length of the growing season and accumulated temperatures – a measure of the energy available for plant growth – declines from south to north. This has four consequences. First, the range of crops that can be grown diminishes northwards. In the extreme north only potatoes and timothy grass can be grown in the short summer; conversely in the extreme south-west, which has the warmest summer, the widest range of crops can be grown, including winter wheat. Second, the yield of each crop declines northwards as the energy available for plant growth diminishes. Third, farm income per hectare declines northwards, for production costs do not vary greatly for the same crop between north and south, although yields do. Fourth, the greater range of crops that is possible in the south reduces the risk of total harvest failure. The northern limit of cultivation of each crop is thus not simply the absolute limit where a crop will yield, but also where an adequate net return is obtained.

Neither environment, technology nor prices have remained unchanged. At the beginning of this century spring wheat was little grown in Finland, even in the south-west, but the introduction of hardier varieties enabled it to be grown on the Arctic Circle by 1946. The limit of other crops was

Figure 3.7 The northern limit of widespread cultivation of cereal crops in Finland in 1950 and 1969
After U. Varjo, 'Productivity and fluctuating limits of crop cultivation in Finland', *Geographica Polonica*, 1979, vol. 40, pp. 225–33

extended northwards in this period by the breeding of cold-resistant
varieties. Both this northward extension, and the increase in yields between
1920 and 1940, were presumably assisted by the rise in mean annual
temperatures experienced at this time, not only in Finland, but throughout
the northern hemisphere. Between 1950 and 1969 the northern limit of
barley and spring wheat retreated (Figure 3.7); but this was not due to the
slight fall in mean annual temperatures that occurred in the 1950s and
1960s. In 1969 crop yields were still higher in the south than the north, but
production costs were the same in each region, so that net return per
hectare was greater in the south. In the 1960s, however, the price of several

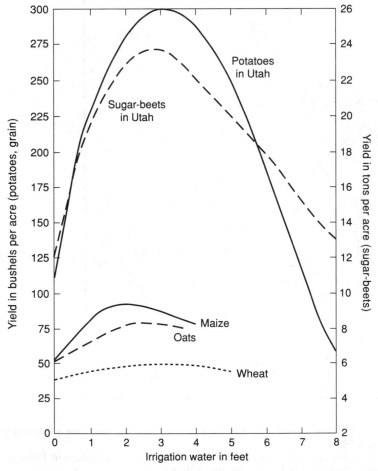

Figure 3.8 Crop yields and the water supply
Source: C.J. Wiesner, *Climate, Irrigation and Agriculture*, Sydney, Angus and
Robertson, 1970, p. 90

crops fell, while production costs rose. Thus, the cultivation of some crops – notably barley and spring wheat – which had been profitable in the north ceased to be so, and it is this that accounted for the southward retreat.

MOISTURE

Soil moisture is essential to plant growth for without water plants wilt and die, and plant nutrients cannot be taken up by the crop. Moisture affects crop growth in two ways. First, crops differ greatly in the amount of water needed to give optimum yields. Wheat and rye for example, can be grown in areas where annual rainfall is between 25 cm and 100 cm, but rubber needs over 178 cm and tea over 254 cm. As over half the earth's surface receives between 25 and 100 cm of rain in a year, wheat can be widely grown. In contrast only 10 per cent of the earth's surface has over 178 cm and 5 per cent has over 254 cm of annual rainfall, so that tea and rubber have a much more limited distribution. Second, as noted earlier (Figure 3.1) there is a relationship between water supply and crop yield, but it is not linear. The yield of wheat, oats, sugar-beet, maize and potatoes increases as water supply increases, but declines after an optimum yield has been reached (Figure 3.8).

The distribution of mean annual rainfall is not a reliable guide to the possible location of crops, because not all the water is available to the plant; some is evaporated, some transpired. Evaporation rates in the tropics are some four times those in north-west Europe because of temperature differences, and so mean annual rainfalls in West Africa have to be above those in northern Europe to give equivalent soil moisture availability. A map showing the difference between mean annual rainfall and potential evapotranspiration is a guide to the areas where soil moisture is limited (Figure 3.9). In arid areas crop production is impossible without irrigation; in semi-arid areas it is possible but only a limited range of crops can be grown, yields are low and variability is high; subhumid regions have similar but less pronounced problems.

A further problem concerns the seasonal distribution of rainfall; an apparently adequate rainfall may be concentrated in a very short growing season, therefore limiting the range of crops that can be grown, as in the Sahel (see below, pp. 35–7), or rainfall may be in the winter when temperature conditions determine that the effective growing season will be in the spring and summer. But the principal problems of rainfall and crop growth are in the semi-arid areas, where rainfall is low and highly variable from year to year.

Rainfall variability and the margin

Away from the area of optimum rainfall not only do crop yields decline, but variability from year to year increases. This is particularly so in the

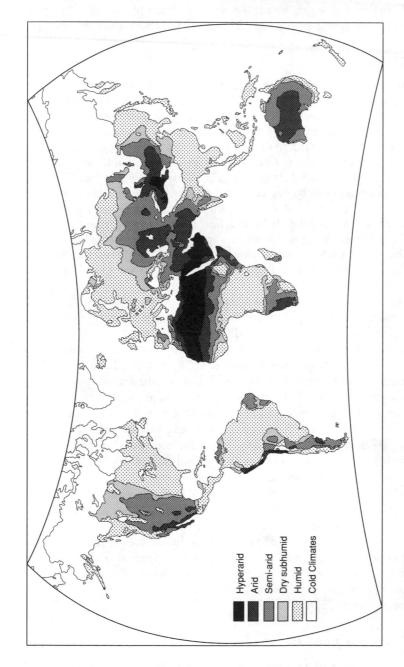

Hyperarid
Arid
Semi-arid
Dry subhumid
Humid
Cold Climates

Figure 3.9 Aridity zones of the world
Redrawn from a map in N.J. Middleton and D.S.G. Thomas, *World Atlas of Desertification*, United Nations
Environment Programme, Edward Arnold, London, 1992, p. 4

Table 3.2 Annual rainfall and percentage of harvests a total failure, Southern Great Plains, USA

Rainfall (mm)	Percentage of crop failures
482 and over	25
457–81	30
431–56	40
406–30	40
381–405	50
330–80	60

Source: K.H.W. Klages, *Ecological Crop Geography*, New York, Macmillan, 1942, p. 190

subhumid and semi-arid zones, where much of the world's commercial wheat is grown; such areas include the Prairie provinces in Canada, the Great Plains in the USA, and southern Russia. Thus in the Southern Great Plains, as rainfall diminishes, so the percentage of harvests that are total failures increases (Table 3.2). In areas of high variability, rain is often concentrated in one season, and brought by depressions whose tracks vary from one year to the next. In the Mediterranean basin for example, the eastward course of depressions in winter determines the amount of rainfall. In Tunisia, if the depression track extends southwards towards the Sahara, then much of the southern half of the country receives the 200 mm thought necessary for a wheat crop; more commonly the depressions run further north and only the coastal regions receive enough rain (Figure 3.10).

A very similar situation is found in northern Iraq, at the foot of the Zagros Mountains. Depressions from the west bring winter rainfall to the foothills and to the Asyrian plain, but as the route of the depressions varies from year to year, so the southern limit of the 200 mm isohyet fluctuates; there is a zone of uncertainty between the foothills, where 200 mm is always assured, and further south towards the desert, where 200 mm is rarely (if ever) reached. Farmers have settled only where there is a high probability of 200 mm in a year.

GRASS AND CEREALS IN ENGLAND AND WALES

Two examples of the distribution of crops, in England and Wales and West Africa, illustrate some of the complexities of explaining crop distributions. In 1989, crops occupied 47 per cent of the cultivated land in England and Wales, and grass the remainder. Three-quarters of the total cropland was cereals, and wheat and barley alone made up 70 per cent of the cropland. Although cereals can be grown in every part of the country except the wetter uplands, and there are few places where grass will not grow, there is a marked difference between the distribution of grass and cereals. West of a

Figure 3.10 The location of the 200 mm and 700 mm isohyets in Tunisia, 1944–7 and 1931–4
After D.B. Grigg, *The Harsh Lands*, London, Macmillan, 1970

line drawn north–south through the Isle of Wight, grass occupies at least half the cultivated area. Eastwards it is rarely more than one-quarter, and a large proportion of all wheat and barley is grown in eastern and southern England. Nor is this pattern new. The difference was equally marked in 1870, when reliable agricultural statistics were first available, and was probably as clear in earlier periods.

The predominance of grass in the west, and its lesser importance in the east and south, can partly be related to differences in environment. Grass is the cheapest fodder crop for cattle and provides grazing in spring and summer, and hay and silage for winter feed. Grass grows in England when mean daily temperatures exceed 5.6°C, so that the growing season is longer in the west and south than in the north and east, and longer in lowland than in upland regions. Rainfall is also necessary for growth, and empirical research suggests that grass will grow as long as the soil moisture deficit – the difference between potential transpiration and rainfall – is less then 50 mm. It is thus possible to calculate the number of days when growth will occur (Figure 3.11) For the period April to September there is a marked

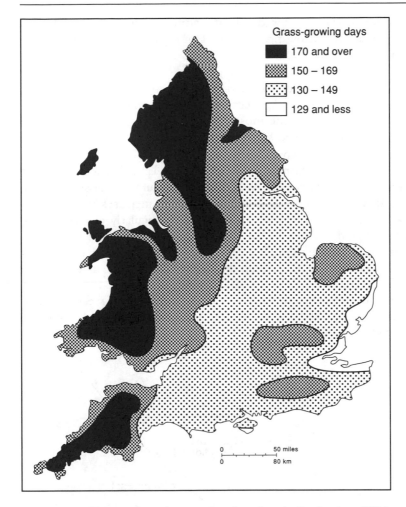

Grass-growing days

■ 170 and over

▨ 150 – 169

⬚ 130 – 149

□ 129 and less

0   50 miles
0   80 km

Figure 3.11 The number of grass-growing days in England and Wales. A grass-growing day is one when mean daily temperature exceeds 5.6° C and the difference between potential transpiration and rainfall is less than 50 mm
After G.W. Hirst, 'Grass-growing days' in J.A. Taylor (ed.), *Climatic Factors and Agricultural Productivity*, University College of Wales, Aberystwyth, Memorandum No. 6, 1963, pp. 25–9

difference between east and west. South and east of a line drawn from the Humber to the Exe there are less than 150 grass-growing days, west and north there are more than 150 days. As hay yields can be shown to be related to effective transpiration, Wales and western England have advantages over eastern England in producing grass. However this difference needs some qualification. Although the uplands of the north and west lose few days in the growing season due to moisture deficit, high rainfall gives poor quality grass (see below, pp. 51–3) so that the distinction between east and west refers only to the lowlands.

It is less easy to show that eastern England has advantages over the west in the cultivation of wheat and barley, for there is no clear regional difference in yield. This may be because the small amounts cultivated in the west are grown only in the most favoured regions, and receive more attention. There are, however, some points to be made.

The first relates to the preparation of the seed-bed. Winter wheat is sown in early autumn, and the farmer must prepare the land thoroughly, almost immediately after the previous harvest. During the summer most soils have a moisture deficit, but from early autumn rainfall increases the moisture content and makes them difficult to cultivate, particularly clay soils. The higher the rainfall, the earlier the land returns to field capacity. If this occurs in late summer or early autumn, it may not be possible to sow winter wheat at all, and the land will be fallow until the spring. The average date of return to field capacity is much later in the drier regions of the east, the south-east and the East Midlands (Figure 3.12) than in the north, south-west, the West Midlands and Wales, where the wet conditions make the sowing of autumn crops difficult.

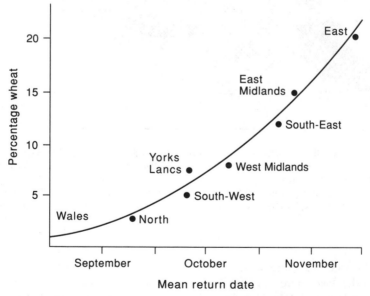

Figure 3.12 The mean date of return to field capacity and the percentage of land in wheat, 1969
After L.P. Smith, 'Assessment of the probable dates of return to soil moisture capacity in the autumn', ADAS Quarterly Review, 1971, vol. 2, pp. 71–5

Second, wheat yields in Britain are inversely related to summer rainfall, unlike grass yields which are positively related. The drier south and east thus has an advantage; indeed four-fifths of all the wheat in Britain is grown in areas where summer rainfall is less than 380 mm, and where accumulated temperatures exceed 1500 day degrees C. Third, most British barley, until recently, was sown in spring, ideally by mid-March. The later the crop is sown, the greater the loss in yield. Again the east and south have the advantage of a drier spring than the west, although not of course a warmer spring.

Thus, although wheat, barley and grass can be grown successfully in all but the higher altitudes, the east and south offer better conditions for cereals than for grass, while in the west grass has the advantage. Over the last hundred years the distinction between west and east has persisted. However, the relative area in grass and cereals has changed considerably in this time. In the 1870s a high proportion of the cultivated area was in cereals, but the fall of grain prices in the 1880s led to an increase in the area under grass, and a decline in the area under cereals with a low point reached in the 1930s. Since then, the cereal area has increased again. The greatest change in the relative importance of cereals and grass has taken place not in the driest or wettest areas, but in the climatically intermediate Midlands where both grass and cereals can be grown. It is price changes that determine whether grass or cereals are grown here.

There are other factors that help explain the differences between west and east. In England large farms predominate in the east and south, except in the fens and the London region, while the small farm is the dominant unit in Wales and the west and north-west of England. Modern grain production requires the use of machinery which, however, cannot be economically employed upon small farms. Nor can such machines be easily used in areas with steep slopes; eastern England has larger areas of level land than the west or Wales. Grain production has other drawbacks on the small farm. Returns per hectare are comparatively low; while the occupier of a large farm can make a good living from cereals, the farmer with less than 40 or 50 ha must choose an enterprise with greater returns per hectare. For example, in 1978 the gross margin per hectare for spring barley averaged £246 per hectare, for winter wheat £320, but for dairying £500 per forage hectare. It is this, in addition to the physical advantages of the west for grass, that makes farmers there choose dairying. This demonstrates that physical factors alone can rarely explain the distribution of crops.

CROP DIVERSITY IN WEST AFRICA

In the tropics temperature is a limiting factor for the growth of only a few crops, and it is more commonly the amount and seasonal distribution of rainfall that determines the limits and optimum areas for crop growth. This is well demonstrated in West Africa; a wide range of food and cash crops are grown. There are twenty-one crops that occupy 1 per cent or more of the harvested area of at least one of the seventeen countries. The principal food crops are cereals, millet, sorghum, rice and maize. Root crops such as manioc, cocoyams, sweet potatoes and yams are also important locally. Perennial cash crops include rubber, tea, coffee, oil-palm, coconuts and sugar-cane, while pulses, groundnuts, cotton and soybeans are also grown.

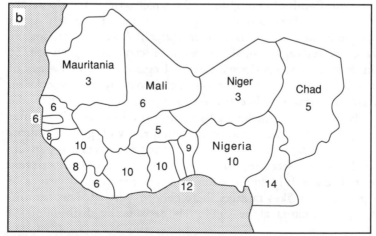

Figure 3.13 Crop diversity and water surplus in West Africa. (a) Number of days in a year when there was a water surplus in the soil (b) Number of crops in each country in excess of 1 per cent of total crop area, 1961–5
After M.D. Dennet, J. Elston and C.B. Speed, 'Climate and cropping systems in West Africa', Geoforum, 1981, vol. 12, pp. 193–202

There are, however, variations in the distribution of each crop, and particularly in the diversity of crops grown.

In the southern half of the region a wide variety of crops is grown, each country having at least six crops that occupy 1 per cent or more of the total area of cropland, and, in the case of Cameroon, fourteen (Figure 3.13). Diversity is far less in the north, where from three to six crops only are grown in significant amounts. This reflects differences in the number of days when there was a water surplus in the soil, which, as temperature is not limiting, is a crude measure of the length of the growing season. It was over 200 days in parts of coastal Cameroon, Nigeria, Liberia and Sierra Leone; it was less than twenty days in much of Mauritania, Mali, Niger and Chad, so that crop growth was confined to the southern most part of these states. Of the crops grown in West Africa, millet and sorghum are the food crops most capable of giving a yield in a very short growing season. Hence they dominate the crop combinations of the northern states, occupying over 30 per cent of the cropped area. Further south, farmers have a wider range of possible choices, and rice, yams and maize are all important food crops, but one crop never occupies such a high proportion of the total cropped area as in the north, where the extreme climatic conditions greatly limit both the food crops that can be grown and also the cash crops. Groundnuts is the major cash crop in these regions, although cotton is grown with irrigation. In the south, a wider choice of crops is available to the farmer, and forces other than environment become important.

CONCLUSIONS

Establishing the optimum climatic conditions for the growth of a crop is important for understanding the present distribution of crops, but it is by no means the only factor involved. First, not all the suitable areas are necessarily occupied by a crop. For example, O. Jonasson has estimated that 0.7 per cent of the earth's land surface is suitable for the cultivation of *arabica* coffee, but only one-tenth of that area was in coffee in the early 1960s. This was because of the limited demand for coffee; the area then in cultivation could meet the current demand. Second, many parts of the earth's surface have environmental conditions which are optimum for several crops that are in competition for the land. Factors other than environment then determine its use. Third, some crops are grown in sub-optimal conditions, when the price of a crop is high enough to justify significant modifications of the environment (such as irrigation), or when local price protection allows higher production costs. But, for all these qualifying remarks, climatic differences are the main determinant of differences in crop distribution on a world scale.

SOURCES AND FURTHER READING

O.E. Baker, 'The potential supply of wheat', *Economic Geography*, 1925, vol. 1, pp. 15–52.

C.J. Barrow, *Water Resources and Agricultural Development in the Tropics*, Harlow, Longman, 1987.

T. Bayliss-Smith, *The Ecology of Agricultural Systems*, Cambridge, Cambridge University Press, 1982.

D.J. Briggs and F.M. Courtney, *Agriculture and Environment, The Physical Geography of Temperate Agricultural Systems*, London, Longman, 1985.

D.K. Britton, *Cereals in the United Kingdom: Production, Marketing and Utilization*, Oxford, Pergamon Press, 1969.

A.H. Bunting, M.D. Dennett, J. Elston and C.B. Speed, 'Climate and crop distribution', in Sir Keith Blaxter and Leslie Fowden (eds), *Food, Nutrition and Climate*, London, Applied Science Publishers, 1982, pp. 42–75.

Jen-hu Chang, 'The agricultural potential of the humid tropics', *Geographical Review*, 1968, vol. 58, pp. 333–61.

L. Curry, 'Regional variation in the seasonal programming of livestock farms in New Zealand', *Economic Geography*, 1963 vol. 39, pp. 95–118.

D.H. Davies, 'Observations on land use in Iraq', *Economic Geography*, 1957, vol. 33, pp. 122–34.

M.D. Dennett, J. Elston and C.B. Speed, 'Climate and cropping systems in West Africa', *Geoforum*, 1981, vol. 12, pp. 193–202.

R. Dudal, 'Land resources for development', *11th International Congress of Soil Science, University of Alberta Plenary Session papers*, 1978, vol. 2, pp. 314–40.

D.B. Grigg, *The Harsh Lands: A Study in Agricultural Development*, London, Macmillan, 1970.

M.N. Hough, 'Mapping areas of Britain suitable for maize on the basis of temperature', *ADAS Quarterly Review*, 1975, vol. 18, pp. 64–8.

S. Huang, G. Li, C. Zhou, X. Fan and C. Shen, 'A climatological study of injury to citrus trees from freezing weather in China' *Agricultural and Forest Meteorology*, 1993, vol. 65, pp. 129–38.

International Rice Research Institute, *Symposium on Potential Productivity of Field Crops Under Different Environments*, Los Banos, Laguna, Philippines, 1983.

O. Jonasson, 'The potential areas of coffee growing and their relation to the settlement of the white man', *Geografiska Annaler*, 1958, vol. 30, pp. 89–100.

K.H.W. Klages, *Ecological Crop Geography*, New York, Macmillan, 1942.

H.H. McCarty and J.B. Lindberg, *A Preface to Economic Geography*, Englewood Cliffs, New Jersey, Prentice Hall, 1966.

J.L. Monteith, 'Climate and the efficiency of crop production in Britain', *Philosophical Transactions of the Royal Society of London*, B, 1977, vol. 281, pp. 277–94.

M. Parry, *Climatic Change and World Agriculture*, London, Earthscan, 1990.

L.P. Smith, 'Meadow hay yields', *Outlook on Agriculture*, 1962, vol. 3, pp. 219–24.

L.P. Smith, 'Meteorology and the pattern of British grassland farming', *Agricultural Meteorology*, 1967, vol. 4, pp. 321–8.

L.P. Smith, 'Assessment of the probable dates for return to soil moisture capacity in the autumn', *ADAS Quarterly Review*, 1971, vol. 2, pp. 71–5.

L.P. Smith, 'The effect of weather, drainage efficiency and duration of spring cultivations on barley yields in England', *Outlook on Agriculture*, 1972, vol. 7, pp. 79–83.

J.A. Taylor, *Climatic Resources and Economic Activity: A Symposium*, Newton Abbot, David & Charles, 1974.

J. Tivy, *Agricultural Ecology*, Harlow, Longman, 1990.

J. Tricart and C.J. Krewiet de Jonge, *Ecogeography and Rural Management*, Harlow, Longman 1992.

U. Varjo, 'Productivity and fluctuating limits of crop cultivation in Finland', *Geographical Polonica*, 1979, vol. 40, p. 225–33.

P.F. Wareing and J.C. Cooper, *Potential Crop Production: A Case Study*, London, Heinemann, 1971.

Chapter 4

Soils and the farmer

Soil has been succinctly described as 'the stuff plants grow in'. It provides not only the material for the plants' roots to grow in, but the water essential for transpiration and most of the sixteen chemical elements necessary for growth and development. Soils vary considerably in their characteristics—in structure, depth, texture, plant nutrient content and acidity – and this affects both the range of crops that can be grown, and the level of crop yields which can be reached. Spatial variations can occur both on the macro-scale (between, for example, the humid tropics and the Arctic) and on the micro-scale, when soil type may vary in one field. It is, however, possible to think of an edaphic – or soil – optimum that is analogous to the climatic optimum discussed earlier.

THE EDAPHIC OPTIMUM

In the optimum soil a wide range of crops can be grown, and high yields are obtained without the need for expensive modifications of the soil. Away from the optimum area, adverse soil characteristics increase, and so fewer crops can be grown and yields are lower. Thus the need to modify the soil by using fertilizers to increase the plant nutrient supply or liming to reduce acidity, increase the cost per unit of output. As with climate (see above, pp. 19–23) an economic margin is reached and later an absolute margin where, for example, excessive acidity, acute waterlogging or a low level of plant nutrients precludes crop growth. Although most crops thrive on deep, well-drained loams with a good supply of plant nutrients, some crops do have optimum soil requirements that differ from the general, and so it is possible to envisage a soil optimum for each crop. Thus rice, unlike virtually all other soils, requires an impermeable subsoil so that the water in the *padi* does not drain away, while cranberries require a very acid soil. As with climate, crops vary in their ability to withstand adverse soil conditions, and this may often explain their distribution. Flour for bread can be obtained from wheat or rye. Over the last hundred years demand for rye has fallen as incomes have risen, and most rye is now fed to livestock. Rye is also an inferior fodder, yet it is still widely grown in northern Europe. This is partly because of its tolerance of a shorter growing season, but in the Netherlands and northern Germany, where climatically either crop could be grown, rye is still found. This is explained by the presence of sandy, acid soils: rye will tolerate acidity; wheat will not.

Good soils – those which are deep, well drained, neutral and retain sufficient soil moisture for crop growth – are not common. In England and Wales, only 17 per cent of the improved agricultural land is without moderate or severe limitations, and only in eastern England is a high proportion of land in this category. On a world scale, a mere 11 per cent of the total land area is without marked limitations to crop growth, while only 24 per cent of the total area is thought to be capable of growing crops at all.

CRITICISMS OF THE EDAPHIC OPTIMUM CONCEPT

The idea of the edaphic optimum is of less value in interpreting crop distributions than the climatic optimum, partly because of the lack of information on soils. Until recently, soil scientists were concerned primarily with the origin and field properties of soil profiles, regardless of whether these were relevant to crop growth. Few parts of the world have soil maps based upon field survey, as distinct from inference based on geology and climate. It is thus difficult to seek correlation between soil type and crop distribution. It is also difficult to distinguish the effect of soils in *sensu stricto* upon crop growth from other environmental variables.

Texture is thought to be a major determinant of crop yields in England because it influences the amount of moisture available in the soil, yet this is clearly ultimately a function of rainfall and evaporation, not simply texture. The soil is more easily modified than climate or slope. Modern farming methods make it possible to supply plant nutrients to an inherently infertile soil, acid soils can be treated with lime, and waterlogged soils can be improved by underdraining. However, it does not follow from this that good soils are of less importance than in the past. Inputs of fertilizer obtain a better yield response on good soils than upon poor soils. Thus, in the USA corn production has been slowly concentrating in the regions with optimum soil and climate, and declining elsewhere. This requires not only fertilizers but good conditions that allow such regional specialization.

SOIL CHARACTERISTICS AND AGRICULTURE

An important characteristic of a soil is its *depth*. Many parts of the world suffer from too shallow soils, both in arid regions and in areas such as the Canadian Shield where glaciation has removed the soil, leaving only bare rock. A shallow soil is often unable to carry sufficient moisture for growth, and the supply of plant nutrients may be inadequate. For some crops, shallow soils may be insufficient for root development. In England this is particularly true for potatoes and sugar-beet. Potatoes are rarely grown on the thin limestone soils of the south and south-east, although these soils give excellent crops of the shallower-rooted cereals. It is often argued that potatoes in England are grown either near the major markets (see below p. 117) or, in the case of early potatoes, in the warmer south-west. But in fact the major areas of production are found in areas of deep loams – on the silt of the fenland, on the warp soils of the Humber and on the mosses and sands of Lancashire.

The *texture* of a soil is a measure of the relative importance of particles of different sizes. Soils made up of large particles have many pores, and so water passes through the soil rapidly; these sandy soils may suffer from drought in dry periods and are susceptible to wind erosion. On the other hand, they warm up rapidly in spring, and may be good sites for the cultivation of early vegetables. In contrast to these are the clay soils, which are fine-textured, with a predominance of small particles through which water has difficulty in moving. They may suffer from excess water, which depresses plant growth. In addition, poorly-drained soils are easily damaged by the hooves of animals and compacted by heavy machinery. In spring the sun's energy is used drying-out the wet soil rather than warming it, so that the beginning of the growing season is retarded. In autumn, clay soils are difficult to cultivate in wet years (see above, p. 34). Clay soils have two advantages which, however, are of less significance under modern farming conditions. The large clay fraction slowly releases potassium so that they suffer less than other soils from potash deficiencies, and their water-retaining capacity means that they give above average yields in very dry years. The drainage of clay soils can, of course, be improved by under-drainage with pipes or mole-ploughing, but the texture of a soil cannot be altered. The ideal soil is one which has a predominance of neither clay nor sand. These loam soils suffer neither from excess water nor a low moisture content. Under modern farming conditions in Britain, texture is the main edaphic determinant of yield.

Soils may be classified as either *acid* or *alkaline* on a pH scale running from 0, the most acid, to 14, the most alkaline, with neutral at 7. Acidity is a function of the chemical composition of the parent material and the rate of leaching, which in turn is closely related to the amount of rainfall. In temperate climates soil acidity is greater in areas of heavy rainfall. Thus in the USA acidity increases eastwards of 95°W longitude; to the west soils are predominantly alkaline. In Britain, acid soils are found in the west and the upland areas. As acidity increases the nitrogen-fixing bacteria in the soil are reduced, and so are the soil organisms that improve structure and texture. Crops vary in their optimum pH requirements, but there are few

Table 4.1 Soil pH below which growth may be restricted on mineral soil

Rye	4.9	Wheat	5.5	Barley	5.9
Potatoes	4.9	Maize	5.5	Beet, Sugar	5.9
Oats	5.3	Rape	5.6	Peas	5.9
Swedes	5.4	Clover, Alsike	5.7	Trefoil	6.1
Turnips	5.4	Mangels	5.8	Lucerne	6.2

Source: Alan Wild (ed.) *Russell's Soil Conditions and Plant Growth*, 11th edn, Harlow, Longman, Scientific and Technical, 1988, p. 878

that thrive in highly acid or highly alkaline conditions; most prefer a neutral or slightly acid soil. Of the crops grown in the British Isles, oats, rye and potatoes are the most tolerant of acidity, and lucerne, barley and sugar-beet the least tolerant (Table 4.1). However, acid soils can be limed and the drawback overcome. Highly alkaline soils are rare in temperate regions but common in semi-arid areas and those irrigated areas which have water-logged soils. The date palm, barley and cotton are the more important of the few crops that have a high tolerance of alkalinity.

PLANT NUTRIENT AND FERTILITY

Plants require some sixteen chemical elements for successful growth and development, of which nitrogen, phosphorus and potassium are the most important. These nutrients are derived from the decomposition of rocks, the decay of organic matter and, in the case of nitrogen, by the fixation of atmospheric nitrogen by bacteria in the soil. Under natural vegetation, nutrients are taken up by the roots of plants and returned to the soil when the plants die and decompose, or through the urine and excreta of herbivores. There is thus a closed cycle of nutrients between soil and vegetation, and little loss from the system. However, once the natural vegetation is cleared and crops planted, there is loss. When crops are grown the removal of the seeds, roots and straw at harvest is a heavy loss of nutrients, while the natural vegetation is no longer present to replenish the soil. If crops are planted continuously, then crop yields will fall to a very low level and the soil will be liable to erosion. Farmers have to devise a system which will allow the removal of nutrients in the harvested crop and also maintain the soil nutrient content. It must also be recalled that crops have different requirements; some remove far more nutrients than others. The essence of successful farming is to find a way to harvest crops, which removes nutrients, while maintaining the soil-plant nutrient status.

FARMING SYSTEMS AND FERTILITY

When natural vegetation occupies an area, there is a cycle of plant nutrients between the soil and the vegetation with little or no loss from the system;

soil and vegetation are in equilibrium. Man can collect the fruits and nuts, but this requires no modifications. Once the vegetation is removed then some means of restoring fertility must be found. There are several ways in which this can be achieved.

The natural fallow

In the humid tropics shifting cultivation is still to be found. A small part of the forest is cleared, and the trees and lianes burnt. A variety of crops including cereals, roots and bushes is planted intermixed in the clearing, protecting the soil from high temperatures. After two or three years weeds become difficult to remove and crop yields fall. The tribe move their huts to another area and repeat the process. The original clearing is colonized by bush and, later secondary forest. After twenty years or more the vegetation has restored the soil fertility, and it can be cropped again. Such a system assumes a very low population density. In Africa, shifting cultivation is now rare, and bush fallowing, where fallows are only long enough for grass or bush to be established, is more common. Reduction of the fallow period, without some means of maintaining plant nutrients, makes soil exhaustion likely. Fallowing, although rare now, was once a common method of maintaining soil fertility in both temperate and tropical regions: increasing population density caused other methods to be adopted.

Nitrogen-fixation and legumes

In most farming systems the limiting factor to crop growth is nitrogen. Nitrogen is fixed in the soil by bacteria, which live under two sets of circumstances. First are free-living bacteria, which are not associated with any plant and occur in nearly all soils. They fix very little nitrogen. An estimate made in the USA puts the annual increments as low as 6.7 kg per hectare. However, there is one important exception to this, the blue-green algae which are found in the submerged soils of wet-rice *padi* fields. These free-living bacteria can fix up to 78 kg of nitrogen per hectare. The rivers that provide the irrigation water for wet-rice also deposit plant nutrients brought in solution and suspension from the upper reaches of rivers. This has allowed wet-rice cultivation to produce reasonable rice yields over very long periods, and is still the basis of maintaining soil fertility in much of Asia.

Second, and more important, are the nitrogen-fixing bacteria living symbiotically with the nodules that occur on the roots of all legumes. The temperate legumes include peas, beans and clover. The latter, when grown in southern England, fix between 112 and 224 kg per hectare per year, and lucerne is also as efficient. The growth of clover in rotation with cereals and root crops has been an important traditional method of maintaining the nitrogen level of West European soils and was one of the methods of sustaining crop yields on the mixed farms of Western Europe.

Tropical legumes, such as soybeans, groundnuts and chick peas, are less efficient fixers of nitrogen than the temperate legumes, and have been grown as a protein-rich food rather than for their abilities to maintain the soil's nitrogen content.

Livestock and manure

When human beings or livestock eat plant foods, their bodies absorb some of the plant nutrients, and some of the nutrients are rejected in the urine and faeces. Human excreta has been widely used as a manure, but most notably in southern China. Livestock are everywhere used to provide the manure, but particularly in Europe. In medieval farming systems much of the manure was deposited upon the common grazing land, and only on arable crops when cattle were grazed on the straw left standing after harvest. However, in the nineteenth century and in the first half of the twentieth century, cattle were fed in stalls and their dung mixed with straw. Farmyard manure, which contains nitrogen, potassium and phosphorus, was sufficient to maintain cereal yields at quite a high level. This system requires that much of the farmer's land be in grass or fodder crops, such as turnips; in combination with the growth of legumes it was the basis of mixed farming in Western Europe.

Chemical fertilizers

Inorganic fertilizers have been widely used in traditional farming systems. Thus bones have been crushed to give phosphorus, and clays have been mixed with sands to improve texture and add potassium. The modern fertilizer industry dates back to the 1840s, but it was not until after the Second World War that fertilizer production became cheap enough to allow its intensive use. The consumption of fertilizers has greatly increased in all parts of the world since 1945, but particularly in Europe and European settled areas. This has allowed some farmers to abandon mixed farming – the keeping of livestock and the cultivation of crops on the same farm – and specialize in cereals, for fertilizers can replace farmyard manure entirely.

All farming systems need some means of maintaining the soil's plant nutrients. Without this, the cultivation of crops leads eventually to soil exhaustion, declining yields and soil erosion. Although it was argued that there is an edaphic optimum analogous to the climatic optimum, it is apparent that there are few 'natural' agricultural soils, for their original properties have been greatly changed by ploughing, draining, liming and by using fertilizers.

SOIL TYPE AND THE DISTRIBUTION OF ARABLE LAND

As was noted earlier, soil type can vary both on the world scale and within a field; some illustrations of the significance of soil variations must now be given, beginning with the world scale.

Only a small proportion of the world's land area is used to grow crops – some 11 per cent in 1989. Large proportions are unsuitable for climatic reasons, particularly in the drier and colder regions, but soil type is also a factor in some areas. It should be noted, however, that of the principal soil types only the tundra areas entirely lack arable land. In contrast the chernozem, alluvial and grumusol groups have the highest potentially cultivable proportions. Some of the principal soil types have considerable limitations. In arid regions shallowness of soil is a significant problem, as is salinity, some 7 per cent of the world's land area suffering from this defect. In hot, arid regions, ground water moves to the surface by capillary action, and evaporation causes salts to be deposited in the upper parts of the soil profile and on the surface. This can be a problem in areas of rainfed agriculture – some 40,000 ha were withdrawn from cultivation in western Australia between 1962 and 1970 – but is often a greater problem in irrigated areas. In the lower Tigris and Euphrates and in the Indus valley, irrigation over long periods without adequate drainage has led to a permanent rise in the water table, and much land has had to be withdrawn from cultivation.

In the cooler, wetter regions of the world, once covered by coniferous forest, podzols are the dominant soil. Although large areas of podzols are cultivated, particularly in the eastern USA and northern Europe, they require careful cultivation, for they are acid and plant nutrients are easily leached away. In southern podzol areas, such as England, podzolization is only weakly developed, occurring mainly on sands. In the northern podzol regions with long, cold winters, the subsoil is permanently frozen; only the upper layers of the soil melt in summer and so are waterlogged and thus difficult to cultivate. Large areas of northern Russia and Canada are uncultivable for this reason.

The soils of the tropics are less well understood than those of the temperate regions; until recently they were though to be inherently infertile and characterized by the presence of laterite. However, recent research shows that there is a far greater variety of soil types in the tropics, that a high proportion are potentially cultivable, and that the presence of true laterite is unusual. On the recent FAO Soil Map of the World, only 5 per cent of Africa contains laterites. None the less, the soils of the humid tropics, which experience high temperatures and high rainfall throughout the year, do present particular problems. The natural vegetation – of which little is left – is rainforest. This gives some protection to the soil, with the shade reducing soil temperatures. But once this is removed, the very high temperatures and the continuous supply of moisture leaches plant nutrients below the roots of crops. There are farming systems that can overcome this problem; shifting cultivation, for example, only uses the soil for two or three years, and the cleared patches of land are sown with a mixture of cereals, root crops and bushes, which provides protection from the sun and rain. In wet-rice cultivation – which is comparatively rare in the *humid* tropics – the water in the *padi* fields reduces the soil's exposure to the sun. Plantations grow trees or bushes or a mixture of the two, and thus, like shifting cultivation, simulate the rainforest. But in countries where the high cost of fertilizer prevents this method of maintaining soil fertility, a high premium is put upon areas where soil material is continuously being replenished.

Deltas and volcanoes

Areas where soils are constantly being replenished are comparatively rare, but two outstanding cases are the deltas and lower reaches of rivers and regions of recent volcanic activity. In Asia – and particularly in South-East Asia – there is a marked contrast between the population density of the rivers and deltas, and the non-riverine areas. The latter are subject to the problems of leaching and soil erosion touched upon above. The lower rivers, however, gain plant nutrients brought from the catchment basins. These are flat, comparatively easily irrigated, and provide ideal conditions for wet-rice cultivation. The deltas of the Ganges-Brahmaputra, the Mekong, the Irrawady and the Chao Phraya, therefore, all have very high rural population densities. But it does not follow that all deltas have such high densities. Few of the deltas of Africa have been developed agriculturally, and in the Americas farmland is rare in the Amazon basin. Approximately 5 per cent of the Amazon basin is made up of riverine deposits, which are potentially fertile, but four-fifths of these soils are under water for part of the year, and as yet these problems have not been overcome. The upland areas of the Amazon basin present considerable problems to farmers, and the recent attempts to clear and settle the Amazon basin have not been very successful. Probably less than one per cent of the total area has been cleared in the last thirty years, and most farmers have reverted to grazing cattle after failing to grow crops.

The other replenished soils are those near to active, or recently active, volcanoes. Indonesia illustrates their significance. Kalimatan (or Borneo) has a very low population density; so too does most of Sumatra. In contrast, Java, and particularly central and eastern Java, has some of the highest rural population densities in the world. There are several possible explanations for this, but the presence of volcanoes is very important. A chain of active volcanoes, emitting ash and less commonly lava, runs down the west coast of Sumatra and through the centre of Java and Bali; these latter islands have 130 active volcanoes. Kalimatan, however, has no volcanoes. Ash is not confined to the immediate areas of the volcanoes. In Sumatra it is carried by eastward flowing streams and forms the alluvial coastal plain while the northern plains in central Java have a similar origin. There is, however, an important regional difference in the type of volcanic deposits. West of the volcano Gunang Slamet, in central Java, they are acid and give infertile soils in Sumatra and western Java; eastwards they are basic and the soil is more fertile. In addition, central and eastern Java have a dry season, unlike the rest of Indonesia, and leaching is less intensive. So the presence of arable land, and indeed differences in rural population density, can be at least partly attributed to soil type.

Soil type and farming in Britain

In an area the size of Britain, climate is the principal physical factor determining the broad pattern of farming types; soil, however, is the factor of most significance over short distances. Yet there are comparatively few studies which examine the influence of soil type on the distribution of crops and upon their yields. This is not surprising; there are few published maps of British soils, and they for the most part are concerned with soil morphology, not agricultural characteristics. Further, British soils have been farmed for some thousands of years, and their natural characteristics are much changed. Differences in management – in the use of fertilizers, lime, or draining – may be more important in deciding what and how much is grown, than the inherent characteristics of the soil.

None the less, a number of studies have shown the importance of soil type in agricultural geography. C.J.W. Edwards has analysed the relationship between soil type and land use in the area around Glastonbury in Somerset. This is dominated by four upland areas, including the Mendips, and two lowland areas, one on Lias Clay, the other on the organic soils of the Somerset Levels (the latter being very difficult to drain). Edwards identified four principal soil types – the calcareous soils, the Brown Earths, the gley and the organic soils. Three land-use regions were identified. In the upland areas between 30 per cent and 60 per cent of the agricultural land was in crops, in the eastern lowlands less than 20 per cent, while in the badly drained Levels there was no arable land; all was in grass. A series of correlation coefficients was then calculated for relationships between the land use of parishes and the predominant soil type. It was shown that there was a positive correlation between the percentage of a parish in permanent grass and in organic or gley soils; an inverse relationship between the ratio in calcareous soils and in grass; and a positive correlation between barley and calcareous soils. This investigation was repeated using point samples of land use and soil type, and the initial correlations were confirmed, while an analysis of hay and barley yields demonstrated why there was this difference in soil type and land use.

Some of the problems of relating soil type and the type of farming are revealed in D.A. Davidson's study of Lower Deeside in Scotland, an area of predominantly livestock production but with varying emphases upon the rearing, feeding and fattening of beef cattle and sheep raising. He identified morphological units upon a sample of farms, and then for each unit measured slope angle, soil depth, drainage and texture. Each unit was given a score based upon these measures, so that the units could be ranked in order of land capability. Eleven types of farming were identified, and the data were examined to see if there was any correlation between type of terrain and type of farming. This only occurred for the best and the worst land. On the poorer land farmers could only rear beef cattle and sheep, selling them to others for feeding and fattening. On the best land, however, a farmer could rear, feed and fatten cattle. Sheep – an extensive use of land – were not kept on the better land.

CONCLUSIONS

It is rare that the geographical distribution of a crop can be attributed solely to one factor, whether it be physical or economic. This is particularly so with soil type, for soils are the result of interaction between the climate, natural vegetation and parent materials, and so it is difficult to distinguish the importance of soil from that of climate. Moreover, soils have been greatly changed by farmers, and differences in management practices may often explain more of the agricultural geography of an area. However, soil type is not be neglected; it is likely that the growing number of soil surveys adapted to agricultural requirements will reveal more associations between farming and soil type.

SOURCES AND FURTHER READING

F.A. von Baren, 'Soils in relation to population in tropical regions', *Tijdschrift Voor Economische en Sociale Geografie*, 1960, vol. 51, pp. 230–4.

N.C. Brady, *The Nature and Properties of Soils*, New York, Macmillan, 1974.

E.M. Bridges and D.A. Davidson, *Principles and Applications of Soil Geography*, London, Longman, 1982.

C.A. Charlton, 'Problems and prospects for sustainable agricultural systems in the humid tropics', *Applied Geography*, 1987, vol. 7, pp. 153–74.

A.J. Conacher and I.D. Murray 'Implications and causes of salinity problems in the Western Australian Wheat belt; the York Mawson Area', *Australian Geographical Studies*, 1973, vol. 11, pp. 40–61.

J.G. Cruickshank and W.J. Armstrong, 'Soil and agricultural land classification in

County Londonderry', *Transactions of the Institute of British Geographers*, 1971, vol. 53, pp. 179–94.

D.A. Davidson, 'Terrain evaluation: testing a technique in Lower Deeside', *Scottish Geographical Magazine*, 1976, vol. 92, pp. 108–19.

D.A. Davidson, *The Evaluation of Land*, Harlow, Longman Scientific, 1992.

R.L. Donahue, J.C. Shickluna and L.S. Robertson, *Soils: An Introduction to Soils and Plant Growth*, Englewood Cliffs, New Jersey, Prentice Hall, 1971.

C.J.W. Edwards, 'The assessment of the quality of agricultural land in Central Somerset', in R.W. Steel and R Lawton (eds), *Liverpool Essays in Geography: A Jubilee Collection*, London, Longman, 1976, pp. 461–77.

M.G. Jarvis and D. Mackney, *Soil Survey Applications*, Harpenden, Technical mongraph no. 23, 1979.

J. Kirby, 'Agricultural land use and the settlement of Amazonia', *Pacific Viewpoint*, 1976, vol. 17, pp. 105–32.

B. Lynch, *Indonesia: Problems and Prospects*, Malvern, Victoria, Sorret, 1977.

Ministry of Agriculture, *Modern Farming and the Soil*, London, HMSO, 1970.

E.W. Russell, *Soil Conditions and Plant Growth*, London, Longman, 1973.

J.A. Taylor, 'The relation of crop distribution to the drift pattern in south west Lancashire', *Transactions of the Institute of British Geographers*, 1952, vol. 18, pp. 77–91.

J. Tivy, 'Nutrient cycling in agro-ecosystems', *Applied Geography*, 1987, vol. 7, pp. 93–113.

J. Tivy, *Agricultural Ecology*, Harlow, Longman, 1990.

P. Woodhouse, 'Farming a wetland ecosytem: rice cultivation in Asia', in P. Sarre (ed.), *Environment, Population and Development*, London, Hodder & Stoughton with the Open University, 1991, pp. 85–122.

A. Young and P.F. Goldsmith, 'Soil survey and land evaluation in developing countries: a case study in Malawi', *Geographical Journal*, 1977, vol. 143, pp. 407–38.

Chapter 5

Slopes, altitude and agriculture

The morphology of the earth's surface has a profound influence upon the type of agriculture which can be carried on. Mountainous areas for the most part offer few opportunities to the farmer; conversely, most of the great farming regions are found in lowland plains. In this chapter some of the reasons for this are explored.

ALTITUDE

Mean annual temperatures decline with height above sea level. The lapse rate averages, in temperate regions, 6°C for every 1000 m above sea level. The consequences of this are dramatic, but differ greatly between temperate and tropical regions.

Altitude and agriculture in the temperate regions

In most temperate regions, an increase in altitude has adverse effects upon farming. As mean annual temperatures decrease with increasing altitude, the growing season – the period with mean daily temperatures above 5.6°C – shortens, commencing later in the year and ending earlier, and so the amount of energy received from the sun is less. With increasing height and falling mean annual temperatures, summer temperatures become more variable and the risk of harvest failure greater. Rainfall and cloud increase, reducing the amount of sunshine received, and retarding ripening. Higher windspeeds are found, giving lower sensible temperatures, and in some cases grains may be shaken from the stem of the plant. These conditions require animals specially bred to utilize the poor fodder and cold winters; in Britain some breeds of sheep are adapted to the uplands, others only to the lowlands. Higher rainfall precludes the growth of many crops, and also causes leaching so that soils are often highly acid. In flat, poorly drained areas in the uplands, peat bogs are formed; indeed they occupy 6.5 per cent of the total area of the United Kingdom.

Thus, an increase in altitude in the temperate regions has much the same disadvantages for the farmer as an advance towards the poles. The yield of crops falls, the variability of harvest increases, and the range of crops that can be grown diminishes. Grass growth also declines with increasing altitude as temperatures fall; the growing season begins later and the rate of dry-matter production is less. For example, in Scotland the onset of grass growth in spring is delayed 4.3 days for every rise of 100 m above sea level. On the lower flanks of the British uplands, dairy cattle can be kept if feeds are purchased; with increasing altitude only beef cattle can be reared, for sale to lowland farmers who will fatten them for market upon better pastures. Higher still, only sheep will survive on the poor grazing, and they too are bred for sale to lowland farmers. The range of crops that can be grown diminishes with altitude; in Britain oats, with its tolerance of greater rainfall, is grown higher than other crops.

A study of the Lammermuir Hills, south-east of Edinburgh, illustrates some of the relationships between crops and altitude. Almost the full range of British field crops can be grown at sea level, but the land surface rises from sea level to 533 m in a few miles. M.L. Parry has distinguished an area

Figure 5.1 The limits of oats cultivation in the Lammermuir Hills, Scotland
The upper limit is the absoloute limit for oats cultivation. The lower limit is the line below which the commercial cultivation of oats is possible
After M. Parry , 'Secular climatic change and marginal agriculture', *Transactions of the Institute of British Geographers,* 1975, vol. 64, pp. 1–14

marginal for oats cultivation (Figure 5.1), and has identified the climatic variables that define these limits: accumulated temperatures over a base of 4.4°C, in day degrees C; a measure of end of summer potential water surplus (PWS); and average windspeed. The absolute upper limit to the cultivation of oats occurs when accumulated temperatures fall below 1050 day degrees, PWS exceeds 60 mm and average windspeed exceeds 6.2 m/s (Figure 5.1). At lower altitudes, where there is greater warmth, lower windspeeds and it is less wet, there is a another limit *below* which yields are high enough for oats to be sold off the farm as a cash crop; between the upper and lower limits oats can be grown, but yields are lower and variable, and the crop can be grown only for consumption on the farm. The decline of oats with increasing altitude is not simply a result of the linear decline of temperatures with height. Although mean annual temperatures fall at a constant rate with height above sea level, the chances of a complete crop failure increase at a quasi-exponential rate. At 215 m above sea level, there is a probability of failure only once in 20 years; at 250 m about once in 10 years, at 300 m once in 5 years and at 330 m once in 3.3 years.

Agriculture and altitude in the tropics

In the tropics temperature is rarely a limiting factor for crop growth, and it is more commonly lack of moisture that prevents cultivation. However, as in temperate regions, increasing altitude leads to a decline in mean annual temperatures. At approximately 3500 m above sea level, temperatures are too low for even the hardiest of temperate crops. Such altitudes are common in the Andes, rare in the Asian tropics, and in Africa are confined to the east. However, areas above 2000 m occupy significant parts of Central and Southern America, Ethiopia, Tanzania and Kenya. Thus, in the tropics altitude only rarely prevents any crop growth, but the changes in temperature greatly influence the type of crop that can be grown. This is most noticeable in the Americas.

In Central America, half the total area lies over 770 m above sea level, with a substantial modification of sea level temperatures, while 10 per cent lies over 1700 m above sea level and has frost frequently between December and February. In South America the Andean plateau areas have agricultural economies substantially different from those found at sea level at the same latitude. Five altitudinal zones are recognized in Latin America. The *tierra caliente* is the lowland area up to about 1000 m. On the Caribbean and Amazonian slopes of the mountains the climate of this zone is humid tropical, the natural vegetation rainforest; on the Pacific coast there is a dry season, and vegetation and crops are different. Between approximately 1000 m and 2000 m, in the *tierra templada*, warm temperate crops such as maize, cotton, sugar-cane and coffee can be grown, but not the crops of the *tierra caliente* such as cocoa. It was the *tierra templada*, which lacks both frost and also the high temperatures and humidities of the lowlands, which attracted European settlers in Central and Southern America, as did the 'White' Highlands in Kenya. Above 2000 m lies the *tierra fria*, in which frost occurs from December to February, and the crops of neither the *tierra caliente* nor the *templada* can be grown; instead the staples are potatoes and barley. Above 3500 m is the *tierra helada*, where no cultivation is possible. A transect across Ecuador demonstrates how altitude influences the growth of crops, with the difference between the lowlands and the Andean intermontane zone being most noticeable (Figure 5.2).

SLOPES AND AGRICULTURE

The shape and slope of the earth's surface is a neglected but important determinant of land use. At the micro-scale, the angle and direction – the aspect – of slope may influence the type of farming. For example, in the Alps and other mountain areas of the northern hemisphere, valleys that are aligned east-west may have quite different land uses on the valley sides, owing to the different amounts of insolation received on the south-facing – *adret* – slope and the north-facing – *ubac* – side of the valley. In Britain there may be a difference of 20 days in the length of the growing season between a south-facing slope of about 20° inclination, and a level site in the same locality. But slope has wider significance, for it limits the use of machinery and determines the rate of run-off and hence soil erosion.

In developed countries most parts of the farming routine have been

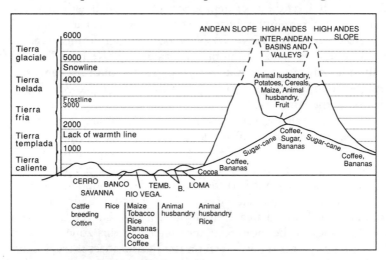

Figure 5.2 A land use transect through Ecuador
After W. Manshard, *Tropical Agriculture: A Geographical Introduction and Appraisal*, London, Longman, 1968

mechanized, and much of the machinery is heavy and costly to move. On steep slopes such machines are not only difficult and expensive to operate, but may be hazardous. Thus, areas with a predominance of steep slopes have a limited agricultural value. In addition, areas with very steep slopes may be liable to soil erosion if cultivated. In Britain, slopes above 11 to 13° are rarely sown to crops, although grass and afforestation are possible. Tree crops are indeed a useful way of utilizing slopes too steep for ordinary crops, for the soil is not ploughed each year and the trees or bushes give some protection to the soil from very high temperatures in subtropical and tropical regions. In the Mediterranean regions, tree crops such as olives and grapes often occupy the steeper slopes, while the plains are under cereals. The olive thrives on the plains but can grow on steep slopes; cereals cannot. The occurrence of large areas of flat land is thus a necessary (if not sufficient) condition for the mechanized cultivation of cereals, for it reduces cost and avoids the problem of soil erosion that may occur on steeper slopes. A study of farming in eight states of the American Midwest confirms this. Grain production in the USA is highly mechanized, and can profitably be carried on only if machines can be used, whatever the suitability of other factors. An American geographer calculated the proportion of each county that was in cash-grain farms, and then estimated the proportion of the total area of each county that had slopes of less than 3°. There was a high correlation between the two, but flatness explained only half the distribution. In two areas of predominantly flat land, cash grains were not important. In one soils were too thin for wheat and barley, while in the other, on the good soils of the Mississippi flood-plain, more valuable subtropical crops could be grown.

SLOPES AND WATER

Water will flow very rapidly over even shallow slopes, but in some very flat areas heavy rainfall or the floods of rivers cannot be removed easily, and waterlogging prevents their agricultural use or reduces yields. This was the case in the English fens until the introduction of steam-pumping. Parts of the fenland lie below sea level, and the remainder is very flat; hence the gradient of the rivers that flowed across the plain was very low, and rain falling on the fens was difficult to remove. The construction of dykes and the scouring of the outfalls improved the removal of water, and the building of embankments prevented the rivers overflowing or the sea encroaching. But it was not until power – first steam and later electricity – was available to pump water that this area could be converted to arable land. The English fenland now constitutes the largest area of first-grade land in the country. Similar problems have been met and overcome in other regions, notably the Netherlands.

Conversely, on very steep slopes water moves rapidly, and if there is no

Table 5.1 Slope and soil erosion at Sefa, Senegal (7 year means)

	Slope angle (%)		
	1.25	1.5	2.0
Annual rainfall (mm)	1235	1235	1186
Run-off (%)	16.5	21.9	30.0
Erosion loss (tonne/ha)	4.75	8.62	11.81

Source: J.M. Kowal and A.H. Kassam, Agricultural Ecology of Savanna: West Africa, Oxford, 1978, p. 170

natural vegetation cover sheet erosion may remove the top soil and later gullying will destroy the land. Such erosion is particularly likely in the tropics, where the intensity of rainfall (and hence also the impact of rain drops on the soil) is high, while the combination of high temperatures and heavy rainfall accelerates chemical weathering, predisposing the soil to erosion. Many parts of Africa have been subject to soil erosion where the natural vegetation has been removed, particularly where traditional farming practices have been abandoned.

In shifting agriculture and bush fallowing in savanna and forest regions in Africa, land that is not in crops is under a natural fallow: the natural vegetation is allowed to regenerate, and, whether secondary forest or bush, protects the soil. When the land is cleared for cultivation, it is not as thorough as in most European farming, and only the hoe or the digging stick are used. Further, intercropping is practised instead of single stands of one crop; a mixture of crops is grown on the same patch of land. This often includes root crops, cereals and bushes, so that again some protection against high temperatures and heavy rainfall is provided. When such practices are abandoned, then soil erosion becomes more likely, particularly on the steeper slopes. Although slope angle is not the only determinant of erosion, it is a powerful cause of spatial differences in erosion rates. Under natural vegetation in the African savanna, soil erosion occurs but at less than the rate at which new soil is formed. Once the natural vegetation is removed, erosion exceeds soil formation. A study of soil erosion at Sefa, in Senegal (Table 5.1) with a comparatively high annual rainfall, showed that run-off increased with slope, and this greatly increased the rate of erosion. The amount of soil lost on land with 2.0 per cent slopes was more than twice that on 1.25 per cent slopes.

SLOPES, WATER AND WET-RICE

As has been seen, the mechanized production of cereals is closely associated with flat land in the USA, and indeed in the other leading cereal-producing regions in the former Soviet Union, Canada, Australia and

Argentina. Wheat and barley form the principal crops in these regions, and oats and rye are also grown. But rice, the leading cereal in the world (together with wheat), is absent from these regions. Like wheat, but for quite different reasons, rice requires flat land.

Two principal varieties of rice can be distinguished: dry-rice is sown and cultivated like any other cereal; wet-rice, however, is grown in slowly moving water which reaches an average of 100–150 mm on the stalk for three-quarters of the growing season, the water being withdrawn for the ripening stage, harvesting, and to allow weeding. This requires an elaborate system of water control to direct water which comes as rainfall, river floods or from reservoirs. To ensure that the water is the same height upon the stalk demands that fields be level and surrounded by small earthen bunds to contain the water. Such fields, generally called *padi* fields, but in Indonesia *sawah*, must be made upon flat land. The production of wet-rice in Asia is thus found overwhelmingly in the deltas and lower reaches of rivers. This location gives not only flat land which can be turned into *padi* with only rudimentary levelling, but it also, of course, provides easy access to water. In some areas, flat land for *padi* fields has been created on steep slopes by terracing, but this requires enormous labour; terracing is by no means common in Asia. It is most noteworthy in southern China, where a quarter of the cultivated land is terraced, Japan, and in some of the islands of South-East Asia, especially Java. It is rare in the Indian subcontinent and mainland South-East Asia.

The unusual circumstances of wet-rice cultivation provide other favourable conditions for growth. The rivers bring plant nutrients, in solution and suspension, removed by erosion from the upper reaches of the rivers, and so each annual deposition of silt helps maintain soil fertility. In the lower reaches of rivers the heavier silt carried by water is finally deposited; and this forms clay soils, often impermeable, which are necessary for the *padi* fields. On sandy, light-textured soils, the water in the *padi* would drain away. Finally, the presence of blue-green algae in the *padi* fixes nitrogen in the soil, and this helps maintain soil fertility.

CONCLUSIONS

The morphology of the earth's surface has been neglected in the study of agricultural geography. Yet a combination of high altitude and steep slopes make much of the earth's surface unsuitable for farming. Conversely, the commercial production of cereal crops requires not only a suitable climate, but flat land. On the micro-scale, slope may be significant; aspect influences the location of frost-susceptible crops, and on many British farms the steeper slopes are left in grass.

SOURCES AND FURTHER READING

A. Garnett, *Insolation and Relief*, Institute of British Geographers, no. 5, 1937.

D.B. Grigg, *The Agricultural Systems of the World: An Evolutionary Approach*, Cambridge, Cambridge University Press, 1974.

J. Hidore, 'The relationship between cash grain farming and landforms', *Economic Geography*, 1963, vol. 39, pp. 84–95.

J.M. Kowal and A.H. Kassam, *Agricultural Ecology of Savanna: West Africa*, Oxford, Clarendon Press, 1978.

D.R. MacGregor, 'Some observations on the geographical significance of slopes', *Geography*, 1957, vol. 42, pp. 167–73.

G. Manley, 'Topographic features and the climate of Britain', *Geographical Journal*, 1944, vol. 103, pp.241–63.

W. Manshard, *Tropical Agriculture: A Geographical Introduction and Appraisal*, London, Longman, 1968.

W.T.W. Morgan, 'Altitude and crop zones; a transect in the Kenya Highlands', *Die Erde*, 1977, vol. 108, pp. 124–8.

M.L. Parry, 'Secular climatic change and marginal agriculture', *Transactions of the Institute of British Geographers*, 1975, vol. 64, pp. 1–14.

L. Symons, *Agricultural Geography*, Boulder, Colorado, Westview Press, 1979.

J.A. Taylor, 'The British upland environment and its management', *Geography*, 1978, vol. 63, pp. 338–83.

J. Tivy, *Agricultural Ecology*, Harlow, Longman, 1990.

K. Utaaker, 'Local climates and growth climates of the Sognefiord region', *International Journal of Biometeorology*, 1980, vol. 24, pp. 13–22.

R.C. West and J.P. Augelli, *Middle America: Its Lands and Peoples*, Englewood Cliffs, New Jersey, Prentice Hall, 1966.

Chapter 6

The demand for agricultural products

Agricultural geographers have concentrated upon supply conditions when studying spatial variations in agricultural activity, yet the pattern of demand is of great importance. Agriculture provides a wide range of products. Crops provide not only foodstuffs but also fibres, perfumes, drugs, oils for lubrication and paint, dyes and alcoholic and non-alcoholic drinks. Livestock provide not only meat and milk, but hides, bristles, wool and fats, and in much of the world they are the main source of draught power on the farm. But although agriculture provides a wide range of goods for industry, foodstuffs are by far the most important products. In the USA 90 per cent of the value of farm produce is consumed as food, and 93 per cent of the farmland is sown with food crops. No comparable figures are available for other parts of the world, but even in countries often thought of as mainly producers of industrial raw materials, food crops are dominant. In Bangladesh, for example, jute occupies only 7 per cent of the arable area.

HUMAN FOOD REQUIREMENTS

The minimum food requirements for a healthy life vary a great deal according to sex, climate, age and occupation. All, however, need an energy intake, measured in kilocalories, to maintain the metabolic rate and to allow the body to work. Energy intake per capita in 1986–88 averaged 3398 kilocalories in the developed countries, but only 2434 in the developing countries. The human body also requires protein, which is necessary for healthy growth and development. Protein is made up of 22 amino-acids, of which some 10 or 11 are essential. These can be derived from two sources. Eggs and most meats provide all the essential amino-acids, but animal products are expensive, and few people in the developing countries can afford them in adequate amounts. Protein is also found in most plant foods, although generally in low quantities. Further, no one crop contains all the essential amino-acids. However if a combination of plant foods is eaten, this drawback can be overcome. This explains why most traditional diets contain both a cereal and a legume. In Western Europe in the past wheat was grown in combination with peas or beans, in the Americas maize and beans are still grown together on many farms, and in eastern China rice is grown with soybeans or peanuts.

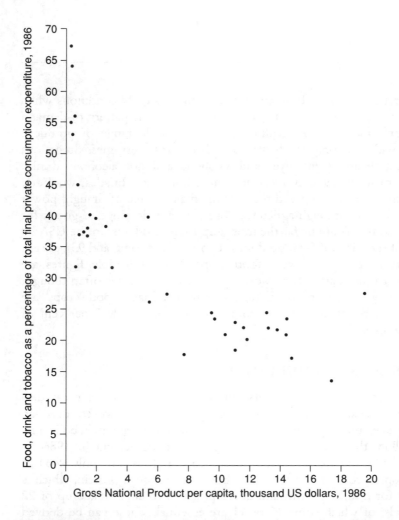

Figure 6.1 The relationship between food, drink, and tobacco as a percentage of consumption expenditure and gross national product per capita, US dollars, 1986
Sources: Food and Agriculture Organization, *Food Balance Sheets 1986–88*, Rome, unpubished; World Bank, *World Development Report, 1988*, Oxford, Oxford University Press, 1988

INCOME AND FOOD REQUIREMENTS

The two major determinants of the demand for food are, over time, the growth of the population and changes in income.

Many studies of the relationship between household income and expenditure on food show two constant relationships. First, the poorer the household, the larger the proportion of total income spent on food; as income increases so the proportion of total income spent on food declines. Second, the absolute amount spent on food increases. Thus in India in the 1960s, the poorest 20 per cent of a sample survey spent 72 per cent of their monthly income on food, the richest 51 per cent spent 41 per cent. But the richer group none the less spent nearly six times as much upon food as the poor.

Much the same relationships hold if countries rather than families are considered (Figure 6.1). In the poor countries of the developing world, with national incomes per capita of less than US $4000, between 32 per cent and 67 per cent of all consumption expenditure is upon food and drink, but in the richer countries, with national income per capita over US $10,000, between 27 per cent and 13 per cent of consumption expenditure is on food. But as with family expenditure, the *amount* spent per capita on food is far higher in the developed than the developing countries.

Table 6.1 Proportion of all calories derived from specific foods, 1986–8

	Developed Countries	Developing Countries	All Countries
All plants[1]	69.7	89.4	81.2
Cereals and roots	33.3	65.7	52.5
Pulses	0.7	3.5	2.8
Oil bearing crops and vegetable oils	11.3	8.0	9.5
Sweeteners	12.7	6.8	9.2
Vegetables and fruit	4.8	3.6	4.3
Alcohol	5.1	1.1	2.5
All plants foods other than cereals and roots	36.4	23.7	28.7
All livestock[2] products	30.7	10.6	18.8
Meat	12.7	4.0	7.1
Milk[3]	8.2	4.5	6.8
Animal fats[4]	6.5	0.9	2.8

Notes: 1 Includes beverages, spices, nuts and miscellaneous not recorded separately in this table.
2 Includes eggs, offal and fish not recorded separately here.
3 Milk and all milk products except butter.
4 Includes butter.
Source: Food and Agriculture Organisation, *Food Balance Sheets 1986–8*, Rome, FAO, 1989

LOW INCOMES AND THE STARCHY STAPLE RATIO

These two facts have very important consequences for the demand for food and for the geography of its production. Poor families and poor nations have to try and meet their minimum requirements for calories by buying the foods that give the most calories for the least money.

In most countries the cheapest source of calories are cereals and root crops, such as potatoes and yams, because they give a high yield of calories – and protein – per hectare. Thus the major food crop in much of Asia is rice, in parts of Latin America and tropical Africa it is maize and in the drier regions of Africa it is sorghum or millet. In parts of West and Central Africa manioc or yams are the chief source of energy. As a consequence most of the countries with low national incomes per capita get a high proportion of their calorie intake from the starchy staples, cereals and roots. (Table 6.1;

Figure 6.2 The relationship between the percentage of total calories per capita per day derived from cereals and roots and gross national product per capita, US dollars, 1986–8
Source: Food and Agriculture Organization *Food Balance Sheets, 1986–88*, Rome, unpublished; World Bank, *World Development Report, 1988*, Oxford, Oxford University Press, 1988

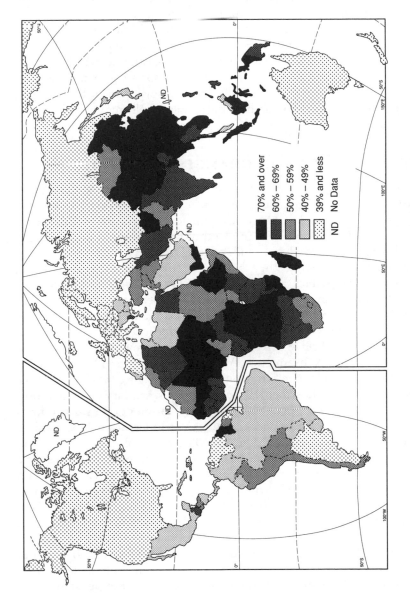

Figure 6.3 Percentage of all calories derived from cereals and roots, 1986–8
Source: Food and Agriculture Organization, *Food Balance Sheets 1986–8*, Rome, unpublished

Figures 6.2 and 6.3). In the developed countries, with higher incomes, more of the expensive livestock products can be eaten, and the starchy staples are consequently a much smaller percentage of all calories consumed. Livestock products are expensive because they give a very low calorie and protein output per hectare, for reasons that have been explained earlier (see Chapter 2). As a result of these variations in consumption, and hence demand, food output in the developing countries is dominated by cereals and roots (Figure 6.3); exceptions occur, where crops are grown for export. Livestock may be numerous, but production is a small part of total output, for few people can afford to purchase more than small amounts of meat or dairy products.

HIGHER INCOMES AND CHANGING DEMAND

When very poor people get an increase in their incomes, they spend it upon the cheapest cereals and roots to satisfy their hunger. This once done they begin to buy a preferred staple: in the nineteenth century as Europeans became better off they switched from rye flour to wheaten flour and the area under rye declined. Later, and once Europeans were receiving an adequate intake of energy, they began to buy more expensive foods, including fresh vegetables and fruit, but above all livestock products – meat, milk, cheese and butter. For a variety of reasons (see Chapter 2) livestock products are far more expensive per calorie than cereals or roots. In most developed countries there has been a decline in the consumption of potatoes and bread since the 1920s, and an increase in the consumption of animal foods. In North America, Australasia and Western Europe over a third of all calories are derived from animal foods (Figure 6.4) but in Africa and Asia the figure is less than 10 per cent. This has far-reaching consequences for the world's agricultural geography. In the developed countries there is a high demand for livestock products, and they make up two-thirds or more of the value of farm production. These animals are fed partly on grass, but increasingly upon grain. In contrast, in the poor countries little land is devoted to growing crops to feed animals, and livestock production is a small part of total output, which is dominated by staple food crops.

When countries reach the levels of affluence in North America and Western Europe in the last thirty years, there are yet further changes in the demand for food (Table 6.2). An increasing proportion of food is consumed not at home but in restaurants and cafés; bread and potatoes decline in consumption; above all foods are increasingly processed before they are bought. Thus in Britain the consumption of fresh vegetables has declined while that of frozen and processed vegetables has increased. In the last twenty years, the consumption of carcase meat from butchers has declined but more processed and packaged meats have been eaten. The growth of the intensive feeding of pigs and poultry has cheapened their

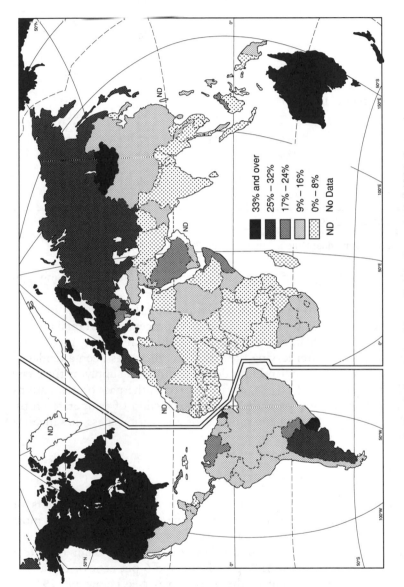

Figure 6.4 Percentage of all calories derived from livestock products, 1986–8
Source: Food and Agriculture Organization, *Food Balance Sheets 1986–8*, Rome, unpublished

33% and over
25% – 32%
17% – 24%
9% – 16%
0% – 8%
ND   No Data

Table 6.2 Purchase of selected foods for home consumption
(Indices of average quantities per person per week, 1986=100)

	1961	1971	1981	1990
Bread, white	218	181	132	89
Fish	110	100	95	98
Potatoes	146	127	108	91
Fresh vegetables[1]	103	100	99	93
Sugar	225	197	138	75
Other Vegetables and vegetable[2] products	51	65	87	95
Cheese	74	87	94	96
Eggs	155	151	122	73
Beef and veal	138	121	106	80
Mutton and lamb	224	180	141	97
Pork	54	84	105	82
Poultry	33	67	100	109
Milk and cream	125	124	107	92

Notes: 1   Excluding potatoes.
          2   Excluding fresh vegetables.
Source: Central Statistical Office, Social Trends 22, London, 1992, p. 128

meats relative to those from cattle and sheep with consequent changes in consumption.

There have been two important results of these latter trends. First, at least half the price of food in the shops goes to processors and retailers; the farmer gets less than half. Second, because such an increasing proportion of food is processed after leaving the farm gate, there has been a tendency for food processors to buy land in order to control the supply of their raw materials. This system, of course, always existed in the past on plantations in the tropics. It has now extended to the production of temperate crops, particularly in the USA, where the rise of the agribusiness has been a distinctive feature of the last twenty years.

TASTES AND PREFERENCES

The growth of numbers and incomes are not the only determinants of demand for food or of spatial variations in diets, although they are most important. Religious taboos are a powerful factor in regard to some products. Thus neither Jews nor Muslims eat pork; although the Near East has 5 per cent of the world's population and 6 per cent of the arable land, it has only 0.04 per cent of the world's pigs (see below, pp. 191–2). The Muslim prohibition on alcohol also has an effect upon demand, consumption and thus land use, although perhaps only in a minor way. It accounts for the decline of viticulture on the eastern and southern shores of the Mediterranean between the seventh and nineteenth centuries. The present vineyards to the south of the Mediterranean are French and Spanish introductions of the nineteenth century. Other differences in demand have less obvious explanations. For example, in Europe until recently only the British consumed lamb and mutton in significant amounts, while within Britain there is no obvious reason for the higher consumption of mutton in Wales and the west of England.

INDUSTRIAL DEMAND FOR AGRICULTURAL PRODUCTS

Although most of the world's agricultural land is used to produce food, crops for industry may locally be very important, and often dominate the export trade, as does jute in Bangladesh and rubber in Malaysia. The expansion and contraction of the areas under non-food crops is influenced by industrial demand and the development of alternative raw materials.

The growing of fibres has been much influenced by the development of synthetic fibres, beginning in the 1930s and widely used since 1950. This has principally influenced the cheaper fibres, and the output of sisal, hemp, wool and flax has declined over the last ten years, while jute output has increased only slowly. Initially the introduction of nylon had a disastrous effect upon the Japanese silk industry, but the growing prosperity of the 1960s and 1970s led to a renewed if limited demand for it. Cotton output has held up better than most fibres, for there is no satisfactory synthetic substitute.

Rubber had little value until the invention of vulcanization; initially used for weatherproofing, demand for rubber grew as the electrical and motor vehicle industries got under way in the early twentieth century, and there was a remarkable spread of rubber-growing in South-East Asia, leading to much overproduction in the 1920s. Synthetic rubber was first made in the 1930s, and its output expanded enormously during the Second World War. It might be thought that this would have had disastrous consequences for the rubber industry, but the boom in motor vehicle production allowed natural rubber and synthetic rubber to share a growing market.

The industrial recession of the 1970s and 1980s has also had an impact upon demand for agricultural products. However, although this had a severe impact on some economies, agricultural products for industry remain a small proportion of total agricultural output.

THE IMPLICATIONS OF VARIATIONS IN DEMAND

The most fundamental differences in demand are between the high incomes of the developed world, and the low incomes of the developing world. In the latter the poverty of the mass of the population means that a very high proportion of the area in crops has to be devoted to cereals and root crops that give a cheap supply of energy. Little land can be spared for horticulture or fodder crops, and the limited demand for livestock products means that such products are rarely a significant part of farm income. Paradoxically, this does not mean that livestock are not numerous in these countries. Livestock are kept as a source of draught power on the farm, and their manure often forms the supply of plant nutrients, although in some countries it is also used as a fuel. In some areas livestock dominate the farm economy, as in parts of Africa and the Middle East where pastoral nomads occupy considerable areas. In the developed countries high incomes mean that livestock products provide a high proportion of farm income; in much of Western Europe two-thirds or more of total farm income is derived from livestock products. Yet this does not mean that cereals are unimportant in Europe and North America; a high proportion of cropland is in cereals but much of this is fed to livestock, while in addition Europe imports grain and other fodder crops for this purpose. Horticultural products are also of importance locally in the developed countries.

Although lack of demand greatly influences the agriculture of the developing world, it does not follow that livestock production or horticulture are entirely absent. Even in the poorest countries there are some people with high incomes, while some high value products, although too expensive for the local population, are grown for export.

SOURCES AND FURTHER READING

M. Capstick, *The Economics of Agriculture*, London, George Allen & Unwin, 1970.

D.B. Grigg, *The Dynamics of Agricultural Change: The Historical Experience*, London, Hutchinson, 1982.

D.B. Grigg, *The World Food Problem 1950–1980*, Oxford, Basil Blackwell, 1985.

D.B. Grigg, 'International variations in food consumption', *Geography*, vol. 78, 1993, pp. 251–66.

H.G. Kariel, 'A proposed classification of diet', *Annals of the Association of American Geographers*, 1966, vol. 56, pp. 68–79.

R.L. Kohls and W.D. Downey, *Marketing of Agricultural Products*, London, Collier, 1972.

J.W. Mellor, 'Food price policy and income distribution in low income countries', *Economic Development and Cultural Change*, 1978, vol. 27 pp. 1–26.

M. de Nigris, 'The impact on demand of changes in income distribution', *Monthly Bulletin of Agricultural Economics and Statistics*, 1972, vol. 21, pp. 1–11.

D. Oddy and D. Miller, *The Making of Modern British Diet*, London, Croom Helm, 1976.

E. Oughton and P. Baron, 'Regional consumption patterns of meat in the UK', *Oxford Agrarian Studies*, 1980, vol. 9. pp. 115–28.

W.N. Peach and J.A. Constantin (eds), *Zimmerman's World Resources and Industries*, 3rd edn, New York, Harper & Row, 1972.

E.H. Whetham, *The Economic Background to Agricultural Policy*, Cambridge, Cambridge University Press, 1960.

Chapter 7

The economic behaviour of farmers

Demand determines why farmers produce food and fibres; the supply of these goods and why there are spatial variations in the production of different crops and livestock is the concern of the rest of this book. It is, however, important to note that the production of farm products differs substantially from the production of manufactured goods or the provision of services, largely because of the biological basis of farming and certain social characteristics of agricultural populations.

THE ECONOMIC DISTINCTIVENESS OF AGRICULTURE

The role of land

In the location of manufacturing industry land is of little importance on the macro-scale, although the availability of land for building warehouses, blast-furnaces or assembly lines is important within a particular locality. In contrast land is a fundamental part of agriculture. The total amount of land that is available is fixed in quantity, as is that of any one nation, save for exceptional cases such as the reclamation of the Zuider Zee. It is also fixed in position. Labour, entrepreneurial skills and inputs such as fertilizer or machines can all be moved from one place to another; land cannot. Land also differs greatly in quality as has been seen (Chapters 3, 4 and 5): some land has abundant rainfall and a long growing season, and will grow a wide range of crops and give high yields; other land is too cold or dry to grow any crops except at prohibitively high costs. These differences will help determine what crops can be grown in any particular region.

It follows from this that there is a fundamental difference between the study of location in agricultural geography and in other branches of economic geography. In the study of industrial location it is the optimum location for a new plant that is sought. The entrepreneur seeks the best location with reference to the assembly of raw materials and access to market. But in agricultural geography the location and environment of the farm is given, and the farmer has to decide what combination of crops and livestock will give the most profit or, in the case of the subsistence farmer, what crops will satisfy most of his or her consumption needs. It is rare that a farmer will decide to raise a particular crop and then seek the optimum location.

Dependence upon nature

Because farmers deal with living things they are more dependent upon nature than industrialists. First, as has already been noted, climate limits the crops the farmer can grow. Second, the time between the decision to grow a crop and the time when it is available for sale is rarely short; it may be as little as six months, but in the case of some perennial crops several years. Third, farmers have a limited control over the quantity they produce, for the size of the harvest varies with fluctuations in rainfall or temperature, and is liable to loss from disease and pests. Fourth, farmers do not have complete control over the quality of their product; thus the timing of a grape harvest influences the quality of wine, while frosts may damage fruit. Lastly, all foodstuffs are perishable. Milk must be drunk within a day or two of milking, and vegetables once harvested soon become unpalatable.

Smallness

Agriculture, unlike manufacturing industry, has a very large number of small producers. Although in the developed countries big farms account for an increasing proportion of total production, output is rarely dominated by a few large-scale producers. Thus, the behaviour of a few farms cannot influence total output, and as the output of individual farmers is such a small part of total output, response to price changes is apt to be slow. As most farms are small there are few workers on a farm, and this limits the possibilities of the division of labour. Indeed most farmers, unlike the managers of industrial firms, combine management with manual labour. The smallness of farms also makes it difficult to raise capital or benefit from economies of size.

Multi-products

In manufacturing industry most plants produce only one good with perhaps an incidental by-product. In agriculture most farms produce several different crops. The subsistence farmer needs a variety of crops to produce an adequate diet, and to avoid the risk incurred if one crop fails. Some crops or livestock yield more than one product; sheep, for example, give mutton and wool. There are also advantages in combining livestock and crops on the same farm rather than specializing; livestock provide manure for the crops, and also draught power. For these reasons and in spite of trends towards specialization most farms still raise a number of products.

Farming and social life

For most people in the developed world there is a physical difference between home and place of work; manager and employee both commute to work. This is not so for farmers in either the developed or the developing world; family household and business are the same. On a majority of farms in the world the family provides all or most of the labour on the farm, and on many the family consumes most of the produce. Thus, more than in most forms of economic activity, the cultural, economic and social characteristics of the family determine how the farm is run.

For the preceding reasons many would argue that there are fundamental differences between the economic behaviour of farmers and people in other sectors of the economy, and that further, there is a difference between the economic behaviour of commercial farmers and subsistence farmers.

THE ECONOMIC BEHAVIOUR OF COMMERCIAL FARMERS

Economic theory has provided a number of principles that help to understand the rational farmer who aims to maximize profit. First the farmer has to decide which crops and animals to produce, and this will be determined by prices.

The laws of supply and demand

Farmers produce agricultural products to be consumed as food and raw materials, and the demand for these commodities is determined by a variety of factors. Typically, a demand curve is downward sloping, showing how much of a product will be purchased at a given price at any time, with the quantity purchased increasing as the price falls (Figure 7.1). A supply curve shows how much farmers are prepared to market at a given price. Typically this will slope upward so that as the price offered increases the amount marketed by farmers increases. Supply and demand are equated at the equilibrium price, A. Generally farmers are prepared to produce more of a crop or livestock products as prices rise, less as prices fall, but the biological and economic peculiarities of farming mean that this relationship does not always hold.

Farmers should change their products as prices change, for they are

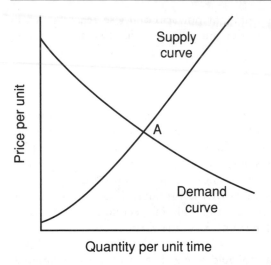

Figure 7.1 The determination of the equilibrium price: supply and demand curves

assumed to be aiming to maximize their profits. If so, then they must adjust their inputs and outputs towards this aim. They have to decide how much of a single input to use, how to combine two or more inputs to produce a given amount of produce at the least cost, and what combination of products to raise so as to maximize their profit.

Intensity of farming

When a farmer decides to produce a crop or livestock he or she has a fixed amount of land, but can use varying amounts of labour or capital, such as

Table 7.1 Measures of intensity of type of farming in England and Wales (£ per hectare)

	Labour costs	Capital inputs	Total inputs	Net farm income
Horticulture	152	432	585	277
General cropping[1]	55	222	277	166
Specialist dairying	49	348	397	144
Specialized cereal production	35	169	204	77
Sheep and cattle	22	114	136	60
Sheep	6	33	39	21

Note: 1   Includes cereals, sugar-beet and potatoes.
Source: Ministry of Agriculture, *Farm Incomes in England and Wales 1975–76*, No. 29, London, HMSO, 1977

fertilizers and pesticides. The amount of inputs used per hectare is described as the intensity of production; in *intensive* production a large number of inputs per hectare are used and give a high return per hectare; in *extensive* production relatively few inputs are applied, and returns per hectare are consequently relatively low. One way of measuring intensity is in terms of the cost of all the inputs applied to the land, but often either labour or capital alone are measured, so that production is described as labour or capital intensive or extensive. Types of agriculture can also be described as intensive or extensive. In England there is an

Figure 7.2 Increasing, diminishing and negative returns

obvious distinction between intensive horticultural production and extensive sheep rearing (Table 7.1). It should be noticed that net farm income per hectare is related – with the exception of specialist dairying – to the level of inputs, but the increase in income is not linear with the increase of inputs. This is because of the law of diminishing returns, or as it is usually described, the law of variable proportions.

The law of variable proportions

It is a matter of observation that the increasing application of an input – of labour-hours or fertilizer, for example – to a unit area of land will increase output, but that output does not increase proportionally to the increase in the number of inputs. Doubling fertilizer application, for example, will not necessarily double crop yields.

At first (Zone 1) (Figure 7.2 and Table 7.2), an increase in the number of input units applied not only increases total output, but the additional or marginal output which results from adding an input also increases, as does the average output (Table 7.2). In Zone II the addition of extra inputs leads

Table 7.2 Inputs and total, average and marginal output

1 Input (x)	2 Total output (y)	3 Average output (y/x)	4 Marginal output (x)	
0	0	–	–	
			5	Zone
1	5	5		I
			9	
2	14	7		
			7	
3	21	7		
			5	
4	26	6.5		
			4	
5	30	6		Zone
			3	II
6	33	5.5		
			2	
7	35	5		
			1	
8	36	4.5		
			0	
9	36	4		
			−1	Zone
10	35	3.5		III

Source: C.E. Bishop and W.D. Toussaint, *Introduction to Agricultural Economic Analysis*, London, Wiley 1958, p. 37

to further increases in total output, but the marginal product begins to diminish: each extra input brings a smaller increment of output. The average output also declines. A third zone occurs when the addition of an extra input leads to a decline in total output; the marginal product becomes negative.

These data suggest that the rational farmer will not operate in Zone I or III. In Zone III using extra inputs will *reduce* total output. Such instances are rare in practice. However, excessive inputs of irrigation water applied to arable land may cause waterlogging and reduce crop yield (total output), while allowing too many cattle to graze pasture may reduce fodder supply and hence the output of milk or meat per unit area; this would seem to be common in Africa. In Zone I farmers can gain in both total output and marginal output by adding an extra input, so it is equally irrational to operate in this zone. Again, instances of this are rare, although it is thought that many dairy farmers in Britain apply too little fertilizer to their grass, and would gain increases in the marginal output of fodder supplies by applying extra fertilizer. Most farmers operate in Zone II where marginal returns are diminishing. However, it is necessary to know the prices of products and the cost of inputs to calculate what the optimum input per unit area should be. If inputs are assumed to cost £5 each, and the price received for each unit of output is £2, then the optimum point is where the maximum total net revenue is obtained (Table 7.3, column 8). This is £36, and is reached when the marginal cost, £5 (column 6a), equals the marginal value of the product (column 5), which is obtained when between 5 and 6 physical units are applied.

The optimum number of inputs will vary if the price of inputs or the product changes. Thus, if the price of each input doubles, to £10 (Table 7.3, column 6b), the maximum net revenue becomes £12 which is obtained when the marginal cost of £10 equals marginal product, with between three and four physical inputs. Thus if the cost of inputs rises, the farmer must reduce inputs to maximize net revenue.

If the price of the product increases and there is no change in the cost of the input, then to obtain the highest net revenue (the point where marginal cost and marginal product are equal) will require an increase in the number of inputs; conversely, a fall in prices without a change in the price of inputs will mean that the optimum input will be lower. Thus, as product prices increase, to obtain the greatest net revenue more inputs should be applied; when they fall fewer inputs are needed. The cost of inputs includes the cost of purchasing an input such as fertilizer, and also the cost of transporting the fertilizer from the factory to the farm. Thus, input prices can fall if technological advances make them less costly to manufacture, or if advances in transport reduce the cost of moving them. If farmers buy their inputs from the same place as they sell their products then inputs will be cheaper for those farmers near the market and more expensive for those

Table 7.3 Total revenue, marginal cost and net revenue

1 Inputs	2 Total product	3 Total revenue	4 Value of average product	5 Value of marginal product	6a Marginal cost a when inputs cost £5	6b Marginal cost b when inputs cost £10	7 Total cost	8 Total net revenue when inputs cost £5	9 Total net revenue when inputs cost £10
0	0	0	–	10	5	10	0	0	0
1	5	10	10	18	5	10	5	5	0
2	14	28	14	14	5	10	10	18	8
3	21	42	14	10	5	10	15	27	12
4	26	52	13	8	5	10	20	32	12
5	30	60	12	6	5	10	25	35	10
6	33	66	11	4	5	10	30	36	6
7	35	70	10	2	5	10	35	36	5
8	36	72	9	0	5	10	40	32	–8
9	36	72	8	–2	5	10	45	27	–18
10	35	70	7		5	10	50	20	–30

Note: In columns 4–8 each input costs £5 and each unit of product receives £2. Column 3 shows net revenue when each unit of input costs £5. Column 6b and column 9 show marginal cost and net revenue when each input costs £10. The other columns have not been altered for this case.

Source: C.E. Bishop and W.D. Toussaint, *Introduction to Agricultural Economic Analysis*, London, Wiley, 1958, p. 47.

who are remote. This explains why farmers near the market will maximize revenue by farming *intensively*, and those in more remote situations will maximize revenue if they farm less intensively, or *extensively* (see pp. 114–19).

Combining two inputs

Farmers also have to decide how to combine two or more inputs to produce a given output. How this is achieved depends upon the technical feasibility of substituting one input for another, and the relative costs of the inputs. Some inputs can be combined only in *fixed proportions*; if one unit of an input is added, then another unit of the other input must also be added (Figure 7.3a). Thus, if one tractor is added then an extra man must be hired to drive it. Such instances are rare in agriculture. Inputs may also be combined at a *constant rate* (Figure 7.3b); here one input bears a direct and unchanging ratio to another input. Thus, in feeding cattle one bushel of maize gives the same feed value as a specified amount of sorghum or barley. Under these circumstances the farmer chooses either one or the other of the two feeds, depending upon their price, not a combination of the two. The most common condition in farming, however, is where inputs combine at a *varying rate* (Figure 7.3c). Here the farmer has to calculate what is the least cost combination which will give a given output. Farmers thus have to be aware of divergent trends in the cost of their inputs; wages, the price of fertilizer, the cost of purchasing and maintaining machinery, and the cost of energy to drive their machinery are all important.

Choosing a combination of products

Farmers have to decide how many products they will produce to maximize their revenue with a given number of inputs. In some cases the farmer automatically produces two products; examples of such *joint products* are

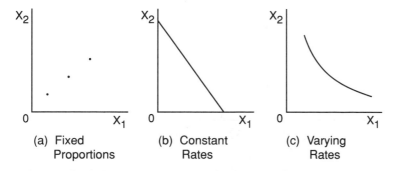

Figure 7.3 Input substitution at differing rates

beef and hides, wool and mutton, or cotton lint and cotton seed. There is
no decision to be made about the product combination in the short run,
although in the long run a farmer may shift to breeds of sheep that yield
mainly wool or meat.

A second class of products can be described as *complementary.* Here some
of the fixed quantity of inputs can be transferred from one product to
another; both increase in output as a result. An example of this is the
introduction of a legume crop into a continuous rotation of grains. Thus, if
a year of soybeans is introduced after several years of sorghum the farmer
gains the soybean output and an increased yield of grain from the fixation
of nitrogen that occurs during the cultivation of the leguminous soybean.
The introduction of clover into a course of wheat crops may have the same
result.

More commonly, however, farms grow *competitive* crops. With a given
quantity of inputs available, if some of the inputs are transferred from one
crop to another, the output of the latter will increase, the former decline. If
the farmer is operating in the zone of diminishing marginal returns, the
more of Y_1 that is produced, the greater the number of units of Y_2 that
must be given up (Figure 7.4). The farmer has to decide what combination
of Y_1 and Y_2 will give the maximum revenue, and thus requires knowledge
of the price of the product. Suppose a farmer can produce either sheep or
steers or a combination of the two; the production possibility curve is
shown in Figure 7.5. If sheep fetch £7.20 and steers £80, it is possible to
draw *isorevenue lines* linking all combinations of sheep and steers which

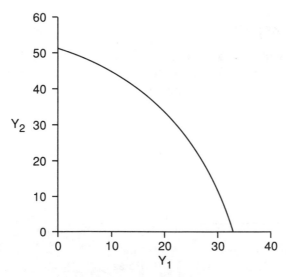

Figure 7.4 Production possibilities curve for a given input level for competitive
products substituting at a given rate

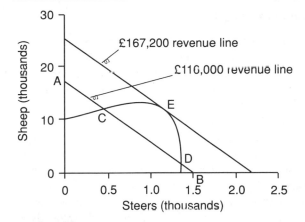

Figure 7.5 The combination of sheep and steer output that maximizes net revenue

produce an equal total revenue. One such case is the line AB. The sale of 1450 steers would fetch £116,000, but so would 16,100 sheep or any combination of sheep and steers on the line AB. The farmer could choose one of the two points C or D, where the isorevenue line cuts the production possibility curve. But the farmer's profit is not then maximized, for any isorevenue line cutting the curve between CE and DE will give a greater return. The highest net revenue is the line which is tangential to the curve at E, giving a revenue of £167,200.

Specialization and diversification

Under the farming conditions of the developed countries, there has been a trend towards specialization. Farmers may concentrate upon one crop because this is the optimum 'combination'. However, there are reasons why diversification may take place even though the solution to the optimum 'combination' of products suggests one crop only. First, if the work on one crop is concentrated in clearly defined seasonal peaks, then the labour force will not be utilized in other parts of the year. If a second crop has different seasonal requirements, it can be grown without reducing labour inputs for the first crop. Second, there may be agronomic reasons for combining a number of products. Thus in areas where chemical fertilizers are too expensive for farmers to purchase, livestock may be kept to provide manure. Third, farmers may be reluctant to risk growing only one crop. The fear of unexpected falls in price, or the risk of disease and weather hazards may cause farmers to diversify even though the production of one crop would maximize net revenue (see below, p. 82).

Criticisms of the profit maximizing model

There have been many criticisms of the idea that farmers are profit maximizers who respond automatically to changes in prices. Studies in Britain have attempted to identify the economic aims of farmers, and they suggest that there are two other motives which are as important as maximum profit. First, farmers aim at security and stability in their incomes; maximization is less important. There are good reasons for this. Although England has a temperate climate with few extremes, the income of farmers varies from year to year more than that of firms in other sectors of the economy. Under these circumstances farmers are loathe to take risks with new crops or methods, and reluctant to switch into new enterprises. Second, farmers value the independence that farming as a livelihood gives them, in contrast to most other occupations. This is particularly relevant to the farmer with a small amount of land. Under modern technological and economic conditions small farmers cannot produce as efficiently as large farmers; indeed many in Britain and especially in Western Europe earn less than they would as farm labourers or as industrial workers. One of the reasons why such farmers stay in agriculture is that they value independence.

Economic theory assumes that farmers will adjust their inputs in response to price changes, and shift from one enterprise to another as relative product prices change. But there are good reasons why this may not always hold. In post-war Europe and North America new technologies that give higher yields have become available to farmers at comparatively low cost. Increased output combined with the limited increases in demand have caused prices to fall or stagnate. Farmers responded, not by reducing inputs or reducing output, but adopting further new technologies that reduced costs – a process described as the treadmill. Falling prices do not always lead to a reduction in supply for other reasons. Some farmers may increase supplies in order to increase their aggregate income, thus compounding the decline in prices. Not all farmers can switch into alternative enterprises. Thus, the small farmers of much of the west of England lack the area or a suitable environment to become large-scale cereal producers, and continue to produce milk. Most of the problem regions of agricultural Europe are in areas of poor soils and small farms, where alternative enterprises are difficult to find (see below, pp. 108–10).

Nor, might it be said, is it easy to define the maximum profit. Farmers have to calculate two types of cost. *Fixed costs* are those they would have to bear even if they sowed no crops and kept no livestock, such as rent, taxes and interest on the capital borrowed to buy machinery or buildings. *Variable costs* are those that arise in actual production, such as the purchase of seed, fertilizer and feeds. It is not always easy to allocate fixed costs to specific enterprises and calculate their profit. The farmer must also differentiate between *long-run* and *short-run* profits. Thus, profit may be maximized in the short run by growing cereals continuously without break crops; in the long run this may lead to soil exhaustion, falling yields and falling incomes. This happened in the Great Plains in the USA in the 1930s, and is a common occurrence in parts of the tropics when no effort is made to protect the soil from high temperatures and high rainfall impact.

THE ECONOMIC BEHAVIOUR OF SUBSISTENCE FARMERS

The economic behaviour of farmers described above applies to farmers who sell most of their production off the farm, and are thus dependent upon changes in price over time, and also spatial differences. Further, they purchase many of the inputs they use, and differences in the price of these will effect whether they use labour or machines, or large or small amounts of fertilizer. But many farmers in the developing world purchase few inputs, and sell little off the farm: their main aim is to provide food for their family. They are thus less influenced by price changes, and so their behaviour may differ from that of commercial farmers.

First, if subsistence farmers seek to provide their families' consumption needs they will aim to maximize gross output rather than profit, and yield per hectare rather than output per head. As land and labour are the main inputs, it is unlikely that the onset of diminishing returns will affect their behaviour. Farmers will work until they have achieved a sufficient supply of food; it is a point on the total output curve that is important, not maximizing returns by equating marginal cost and revenue. Second, they are not likely to specialize in one product. An adequate diet requires cereals, legumes and preferably a source of animal food. Thus, traditional farmers in every part of the world grow a combination of crops. This has agronomic as well as dietary advantages. In Western Europe farmers in the past kept livestock and grew crops, the livestock being fed on rough grazing and stubble. Manure maintained crop yields, and peas and beans – legumes – both provided food and helped maintain nitrogen supplies in the soil. In many parts of the tropics in shifting agriculture and bush fallowing systems a variety of crops are grown; these are grown intermixed, and a combination of tree crops, bush crops and cereals provide a cover to the soil that protects it from soil erosion. Even in the densely-populated regions of East and South Asia the monoculture of rice is rare. The need to grow a variety of crops means that some crops may be grown on soils to which they are unsuited.

Third, subsistence farmers try to produce as much of their own food as they can, with the minimum of risk. Their farms are small, and in many parts of Afro-Asia fluctuations in rainfall lead to considerable annual variations in crop yields. The result of harvest failure may be starvation

Table 7.4 Income and weather conditions

	1	2	3	4	Average income
A	£45	£55	£60	£50	£52.5
B	£70	£30	£90	£34	£56
C	0	£100	0	£300	£100

Note: A, B and C are different crops or crop combinations: 1, 2, 3 and 4 are years each with different weather conditions.
Source: After Gould, 1963

or the forced sale of their land. They are thus averse to taking chances with new crops or methods. Further, if they sell some of their crops, they may choose to grow a combination of crops that is likely to give them a *secure* income rather than maximum profit. Thus, farmers may have a choice of growing three different crops or crop combinations A, B and C (Table 7.4). In four consecutive years there are very different weather conditions. The profit maximizer might choose, on the basis of this experience, combination C, for it gives an average profit of £100. The next best profit is combination B, with £56, but suppose a farmer needs £40 a year for the family's needs. The farmer will not then choose B, for in two of the four years income falls below this amount. Instead the farmer will choose A, with the lowest average profit, but which gives £40 in each year.

CONCLUSIONS

The economic behaviour of farmers in the developed countries is for the most part rational, and a body of economic theory exists both to describe and predict their actions. In recent years, however, it has been shown that farmers may prefer stability and security to profit maximization, but this for the most part does not invalidate the general principles. Yet, economic theory as developed in the West has limited value in explaining the behaviour of farmers in the command economies of socialist countries. More important, the assumption of profit maximization as the prime aim in the subsistence economies of much of the developing world may have to be modified.

SOURCES AND FURTHER READING

K.C. Abercrombie, 'The transition from subsistence to market agriculture in Africa south of the Sahara', *Monthly Bulletin of Agricultural Economics and Statistics*, 1961, vol. 10, pp. 1–7.

C.E. Bishop and W.D. Toussaint, *Introduction to Agricultural Economic Analysis*, London, Wiley, 1958.

C. Clark and M. Haswell, *The Economics of Subsistence Agriculture*, London, Macmillan, 1970.

S.H. Franklin, *The European Peasantry: The Final Phase*, London, Methuen, 1969.

P.R. Gould, 'Man against his environment: a game theoretic framework', *Annals of the Association of American Geographers*, 1963, vol. 53, pp. 290–7.

J.B. Hardaker, J.N. Lewis and G.C. MacFarlane, *Farm Management and Agricultural Economics: An Introduction*, London, Angus & Robertson, 1970.

E.O. Heady, *Economics of Agricultural Production and Resource Use*, Englewood Cliffs, New Jersey, Prentice Hall, 1952.

B.E. Johnston and P. Kilby, *Agriculture and Structural Transformation: Strategies in Late Developing Countries*, New York, Oxford University Press, 1975.

W.B. Morgan, *Agriculture in the Third World: A Spatial Analysis*, London, Bell, 1977.

T. Shanin (ed.), *Peasants and Peasant Societies*, Harmondsworth, Penguin, 1971.

J. Singh, 'Commercialization of agriculture in Punjab, 1971–2: a spatial analysis', *Geographical Review of India*, 1979, vol. 41, pp. 1–8.

C.R. Wharton (ed.), *Subsistence Agriculture and Economic Development*, London, Cass, 1970.

Chapter 8

The modernization of agriculture

Over the last century and a half agriculture in the developed countries has been profoundly altered. Output and productivity have greatly increased and there have been major changes in technology. Farmers who once produced mainly for home consumption now sell nearly all their produce, and whereas the inputs used were once produced on the farm, most are now purchased from industry. In addition much of the farmers' produce is sold not directly for consumption, but to food processors. These great changes, which can be described as modernization, are closely related to the progress of industrialization and the general process of economic development. Not surprisingly there are striking spatial differences in the degree of agricultural modernization, which give rise to great differences in agricultural productivity. The principal difference is between the developed and the developing regions, although modernization has been experienced in some regions within developing countries, such as in the Indian Punjab or parts of Brazil.

THE EXTENT OF SUBSISTENCE FARMING

Some of the differences between traditional and modern farming are shown in Table 8.1. The degree of commercialization is of first importance, but it is not easy to define or measure the extent of subsistence farming. Farmers who sell nothing off their farms are rare; on the other hand those whose first aim is to provide their family's food and other necessaries, and for whom sales for cash are secondary are dominant in much of Asia, tropical Africa and parts of Latin America; they may be described as semi-subsistence farmers.

In tropical Africa three-quarters or more of all food crops are consumed upon the farms where they are grown, and in India two-thirds of all the grain. In China in the 1970s four-fifths of total food production was consumed by the families that produced it, although this proportion has since fallen. In Latin America agriculture is more commercialized. For

Table 8.1 Differences between subsistence and commercial farmers

	Traditional, subsistence	Modern, commercial
1 Proportion of output sold off the farm	Low	High
2 Destination of foods	Local direct consumption and some processed locally	High proportion processed and to food manufacturers
3 Origin of inputs		
i Power	Draught animals, human labour	Petroleum, electricity
ii Plant nutrients	Legumes, ash, bones, manure	Chemical fertilizers
iii Pest control	Crop rotations, intercropping	Insecticides, fungicides, break crops
iv Weed control	Rotations, hoeing, use of plough	Herbicides
v Implements and tools	Hoe, plough, sickle, scythe.	Machinery, often self-propelled combine harvesters
vi Seed	From own harvest	Purchased from seed merchants
vii Livestock feeds	Grass and fodder crops grown on farm or common land	Purchased from compound feed mixers
4 Economic aims	i Prime aim to provide family food	Profit maximization
	ii Land and labour main inputs; few capital inputs	Capital and land major inputs; labour a declining input
	iii Diversity of crops grown	Specialized production
	iv Aims at maximizing gross output and yield per acre	Aims at maximizing output per head and minimizing production costs.
	v Prime aim avoidance of risk; reluctant to innovate	Innovation

about half the farm population the first aim is to grow their own food, but these small peasant farms also contribute food for the home market and some export crops. In the past the now developed countries also had a semi-subsistence agricultural economy; in the 1820s about three-quarters of food production in the USA was consumed on the farm but today virtually all food output in developed countries is sold off the farm; commercial farmers, like non-farmers, buy their food from shops.

A number of factors explain the degree of commercialization. First, the size of the urban population, where no one grows their own food, determines the size of the market for farmers. In tropical Africa towns are a small proportion of the total population, and so little of the total output is sold off the farms. Similarly, before 1800 three-quarters of the population of Western Europe were employed in farming, so the market was limited. Now less than 5 per cent work in farming and most of the population has to buy its food.

Second, is the size of farm. In Asia and Africa a majority of farms are only a few hectares in size, and most of this land is needed to provide the family's food, so little can be marketed. Third is location; farms that are remote from towns, and where the cost of transport to market is high, find it difficult to sell crops or livestock upon a regular basis, unless their products have a very high value per unit weight.

THE PURCHASE OF INPUTS

Traditional subsistence farmers produce most of the inputs they use on their farms (Table 8.1). Seed for the next crop is taken from the current harvest; livestock provide manure; human labour and draught animals – oxen, water buffaloes and horses – provide all the power; livestock are fed grass or fodder crops grown upon the farm. In the 1860s purchased inputs in Swedish agriculture were only 5 per cent of the gross value of output; today they form over 50 per cent, and this is so in nearly all developed countries. Far fewer inputs are used in the developing regions, particularly

Table 8.2 Share of the value of inputs in the value of gross output (per cent)

	1982/4
Developed countries	c.50
Near East and North Africa	36
Latin America	25
Asia (excl. China)	24
SubSaharan Africa	10

Source: N. Alexandratos, World Agriculture: Toward 2000. An FAO Study, London, Belhaven Press, 1988, p. 135

in Africa (Table 8.2). The use of these purchased inputs is a key to international differences in agricultural productivity.

POWER AND MACHINERY

One of the most notable innovations of the industrial revolution was the application of steam-power to machines. This was long delayed in agriculture, but since the invention of the internal combustion engine, petroleum and also electricity have replaced human labour and draught animals. However, there is great spatial difference in the amounts of energy used in agriculture, as can be seen in Figure 8.1. Here energy includes not only that used on farms but also in the production of chemical fertilizers.

North American consumption is nearly seven times that of Western Europe, but Western Europe uses much more commercial energy than any of the developing regions. Indeed in the developed world nearly all power is now provided by petroleum and electricity, and draught animals and human labour make only very limited contribution. This is not so in the developing regions where the labour force does nearly three-quarters of the work and tractors are of significance only in Latin America (Table 8.3). The distribution of tractors corresponds quite closely to the level of economic

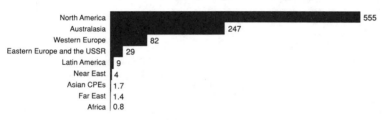

Figure 8.1 Use of commercial energy in agriculture production, per agricultural worker: 10^9 joules

Table 8.3 Contribution to total power use on farms, 1982–4 (per cent)

	Labour force	Tractors	Draught animals
Sub-Saharan Africa	89	1	10
Near East and North Africa	69	14	17
Asia (excl. China)	68	4	28
Latin America	59	22	19
All developing countries	71	6	23

Note: Total power use in man-day equivalents is obtained by converting estimated tractor hours and work days of draught animals into labour-day equivalents.
Source: N. Alexandratos, World Agriculture: Toward 2000. An FAO Study, London, Belhaven Press, 1988, p. 145

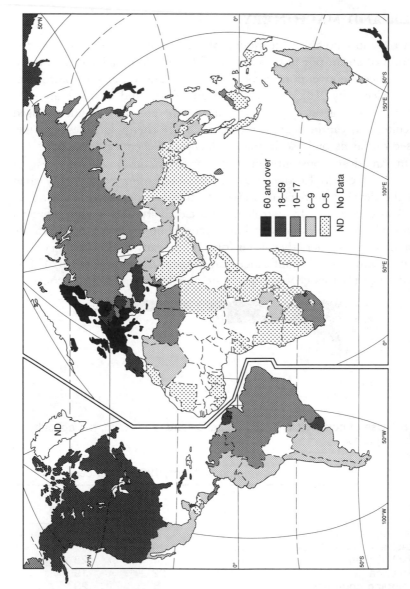

Legend:
- 60 and over
- 18–59
- 10–17
- 6–9
- 0–5
- ND No Data

Figure 8.2 Number of tractors per 1000 hectares of arable land, 1986
Source: Food and Agriculture Organization, *Production Yearbook 1989*, vol. 43, Rome, 1990

development (Figure 8.2). There are more tractors per 1000 hectares of arable land in Europe than anywhere else, although this underestimates their importance in the USA. Tractors in the USA are larger and more powerful than in Europe; if data on horsepower per hectare were available rather than simply numbers of tractors, North America would rank higher, as would Australia and Argentina.

Tractors are not, of course, the only machinery used by commercial farmers (Table 8.4) who have a wider range of machines, implements and tools than the traditional farmer. It is in the industrialized parts of the world that the use of machinery has been widely adopted, and power used so liberally. This is first because in most of these regions migration from the countryside to the towns in search of higher wages has reduced the

Table 8.4 Different methods of farming

	Semi-subsistence	Commercial
Power	Human muscle, oxen, horses, water buffaloes	Electricity and internal combustion engine
Machinery	Implements and tools only. Machete, axe. Simple ploughs. Hoes, spades. Sickle, scythe or knife for harvesting. Flail or oxen hooves for threshing	Machines, tractors cultivators, drills, pesticide spreaders, combine harvesters
Weed control	Weeding by hand or hoe during fallow or with row crops during growth	Herbicides before and during growth
Disease control	Rotations, fallow, mixed cropping, immune varieties	Break crops, rotations, immune varieties, pesticides, fungicides and insecticides
Livestock	Used for draught; meat and milk incidental. Little selective breeding. Limited veterinary services	Selective breeding, specialized for meat or milk. Veterinary services, antibiotics preventive health measures, immunization. Intensive feeding, factory farming of pigs and poultry
Livestock feeds	Grass, some fodder crops. Little feed purchased	Grass, cereals, purchased concentrates. Balanced rations

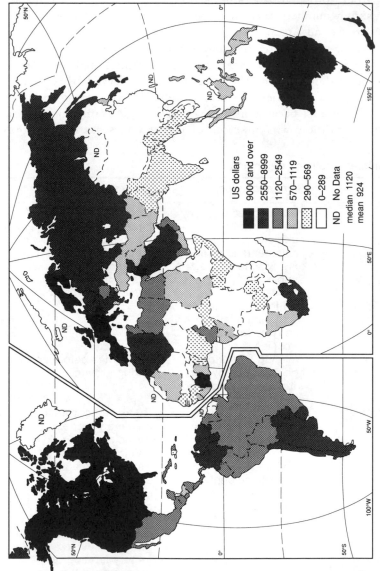

Figure 8.3 Agricultural gross domestic product per capita of the agricultural labour force, US dollars, 1988

Source: D. Grigg, 'World Agriculture: production and productivity in the late 1980s', *Geography*, 1992, vol. 77, pp. 97–108

US dollars

9000 and over
2550–8999
1120–2549
570–1119
290–569
0–289
ND No Data

median 1120
mean 924

availability of agricultural labour, and farmers have had to substitute capital – machinery – for labour (see below, Chapter 12). Second, industrial countries have the capacity in their engineering and vehicle industries to produce machinery, which the developing countries for the most part have not. Third, farmers in the developed countries are more prosperous than those in the developing, partly *inter alia*, because they have larger farms and because prices are subsidized by the state, and they can therefore afford to purchase machines. Fourth, farms in much of the developing world are generally too small to justify the use of machines, whilst the low cost of labour makes the use of machinery of dubious value. The substitution of power and machinery for labour has greatly increased output per head in the industrial countries; there remain, however, great differences in output per capita between the developed and developing countries (Figure 8.3). Labour productivity is highest in North America, Australasia and Latin America; it is lowest in tropical Africa, South, South-East and East Asia.

COMMERCIAL FERTILIZERS

Traditional farmers have a variety of means of maintaining soil fertility and hence crop yields. Fallowing, the growth of legumes, and the use of livestock manure are all practised (see Chapter 2). Since the middle of the nineteenth century these methods have been supplemented by the use of factory-made chemical fertilizers, compounds of nitrogen, potassium and phosphorus. Until 1950 fertilizers were only intensively used in north-western Europe, but since then their application has increased both there and in the rest of the world. Differences in fertilizer usage are not, unlike the use of tractors, a simple function of the level of economic development. The lowest levels of application are found in Africa, Latin America and mainland South-East Asia (Figure 8.4), the highest are found in Europe and the USSR, but also in China, Korea and Japan, whilst quite high levels obtain in South and South-West Asia. But the usage of fertilizers in Australasia and North America falls below what might be expected. This is because much of the crop production is extensive: the farmers grow large areas in wheat and other cereals, with few yield-increasing inputs but with the use of machinery. In Asia in contrast, with notably high densities of population, farmers strive to maximize output per hectare, and the liberal use of chemical fertilizer is one way in which this is achieved.

MODERN CROP VARIETIES

In the past the farmer obtained the seed for the next sowing by retaining part of the crop just harvested. Over very long periods many varieties evolved adapted to local micro-conditions, and were often selected to give

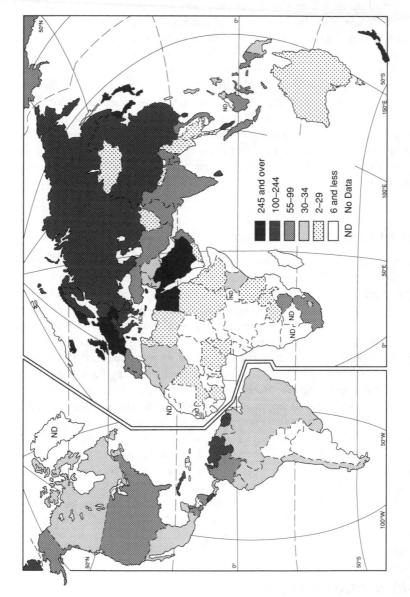

Figure 8.4 Chemical fertilizers, kilograms per hectare of arable land, 1986
Source: Food and Agriculture Organization, *The State of Food and Agriculture 1989*, Rome, 1989

an adequate yield under poor environmental conditions. Farmers would improve their seed by buying it from other farmers, but until there were advances in plant genetics it was not possible to breed specific characteristics into new varieties. This has been possible since the beginning of this century, and since then plant breeders have been able to breed into new varieties immunity to specific diseases, an ability to mature in a shorter growing season, allowing the extension of the crop into cold areas, a greater tolerance of drought, and above all a greater response to chemical fertilizers, giving much higher yields. New varieties have been constantly provided by plant breeding institutes and adopted by farmers. Between the 1930s and the 1970s cereal yields doubled in the USA and Great Britain, and half of this increase was due to the adoption of new varieties, the rest to the use of pesticides, fertilizers and other improved practices. Most seed in the developed world is purchased from seed-merchants and is of improved modern varieties.

Far less progress in breeding new varieties had been made in Afro-Asia or Latin America, except with some export crops such as sugar-cane and bananas. In the 1960s new high-yielding varieties of wheat and rice were introduced into Asia; with shorter stems than traditional varieties, they gave much higher yields, provided that fertilizers, pesticides and irrigation were used. At much the same time improved maize varieties, first developed in the USA in the 1920s, began to be adopted elsewhere. By the 1980s modern varieties occupied half the sown area of maize, wheat and rice in the developing countries, and contributed to the very substantial increase in cereal output between the 1960s and 1980s (Table 8.5). Africa has gained least from these advances, for wheat and rice are very little grown there and sorghum, millets and root crops, that make up a substantial proportion of the total food crop area, have not experienced much improvement in their seed.

Table 8.5 The adoption of modern crop varieties in the developing countries, (per cent of area in crop sown with modern varieties, mid-1980s)

	Wheat, 1982–3	Rice, 1982–3	Maize, 1983–6	All three crops
Asia (non-Communist)	79.2	44.9	35.5	49.3
Asia (Communist)	30.6	81.0	71.1	63.2
Near East	30.6	8.4	46.4	32.5
Africa	50.6	4.7	14.9	45.5
Latin America	77.6	32.9	27.3	55.4
All LDCS	50.7	72.6	79.4	49.3

Source: M. Lipton and R. Longhurst, *New Seeds and Poor People*, London, Unwin Hyman, 1989, p. 2

INSECTICIDES, FUNGICIDES AND HERBICIDES

Traditional farmers can control weeds by careful cultivation, but this requires a very substantial use of labour for frequent ploughing and hoeing. The use of herbicides which destroy weeds reduces this labour input. This has revolutionized farming in developed countries, where the use of herbicides, available only since the 1940s, has been largely confined. Traditional farmers had very little control over pests such as insects, rodents, bacterial disease and fungi, although the use of rotations, mixed cropping and frequent ploughing between crops could effect some reduction. Since the 1940s there has been a considerable increase in the use of insecticides and fungicides. Expenditure upon pesticides increased 15 fold in the non-Communist world between 1955 and 1978, most of this increase being in the developed countries. In developing countries spraying is limited mainly to export crops.

IRRIGATION

The provision of water for crops other than from rainfall has a long history in Asia, but most of the present irrigated area has been established comparatively recently. In 1800 the world's irrigated area was only 8 million hectares, but had increased to 40 million by 1900. Between 1900 and 1950 a

Table 8.6 Irrigated areas of the world, 1988

	Irrigated area (million hectares)	Total arable (million hectares)	Irrigated area as a % of total arable
Developed	63.2	674.1	9.4
North America	18.9	235.9	8.0
Western Europe	11.5	94.4	12.2
Australia	2.1	47.4	4.4
USSR	20.7	232.4	8.9
Eastern Europe	5.8	45.7	12.7
Other developed	4.2	18.2	23.2
Developing	165.3	801.2	20.6
Africa	5.3	156.2	3.3
Latin America	15.6	179.8	8.7
Near East	19.5	82.4	23.7
Far East	76.8	271.4	28.3
India	41.8	169.5	24.7
Pakistan	15.7	20.9	75.1
Asian CPEs	48.1	110.0	43.7
China	44.9	96.6	46.5

Source: Food and Agriculture Organization, Production Yearbook 1989, vol. 43, Rome, FAO, 1990

further 80 million hectares were added, and between 1950 and 1988 the figure rose from 120 million to 228 million hectares.

Irrigation has three benefits. First, it allows the cultivation of land where rainfall is insufficient for any crop growth, such as in Egypt, much of Pakistan or the oases of the Peruvian coast. Second, it is an important supplement in regions where rainfall in the growing season is variable; and third, it allows water to be stored in the wet season and used in the dry season, thus allowing two crops to be obtained during the year. A controlled water supply allows much higher yields, and also ensures that fertilizers can be fully utilized; in dry areas a low proportion of fertilizers that are applied are actually taken up by the plants roots. As a result the world's irrigated area, 14 per cent of the total arable, provides 35 per cent of the value of the world agricultural output.

But whereas the inputs so far considered are most intensively used in the developed countries, nearly three-quarters of the world's irrigated land is to be found in the developing countries, half of it in China and South Asia. (Table 8.6). There is little in Latin America; in tropical Africa, where half the continent has insufficient soil moisture for crop cultivation only 3 per cent of the arable land is irrigated.

DIFFERENCES IN LAND PRODUCTIVITY

Regional variations in output per hectare are different from those of output per head. They reflect not only differences in crop yield, which in turn reflect the relative intensity with which inputs are applied to land, but also whether high value crops, such as fruit or vegetables, or low value crops, such as cereals, are grown and also whether land is farmed intensively or extensively, and whether it is in crops or livestock. The highest values per hectare are found in Europe, and in East and South Asia, the lowest in tropical Africa (Figure 8.5). In Australasia, the USSR and North America values are low because so much of this land is devoted to extensive crop production or extensive rearing of livestock.

It is not possible to measure output per unit of *all* resources of land, labour and capital. However, a grouping of countries, according to whether they stand above or below the median figure for output per hectare and output per capita does produce a grouping of countries into four classes (Figure 8.6):

1 Those below the median for both land and labour productivity; this includes most of tropical Africa.
2 Those above on both counts, which include Europe, Japan, South Korea, Egypt and New Zealand.
3 Those with below median values per hectare but high output per capita: this includes the USSR, North and Latin America, and Australia.

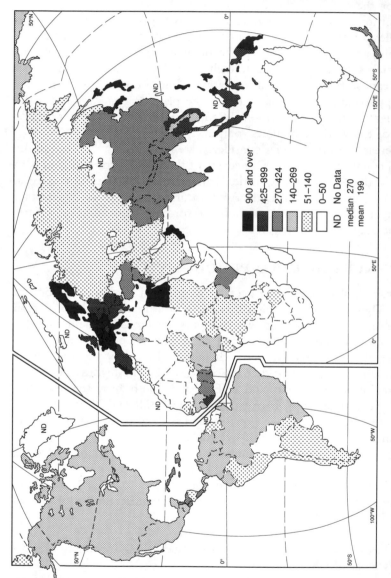

Figure 8.5 Agricultural gross domestic product per hectare of arable land and permanent grass, US dollars, 1988

Source: World Bank *World Development Report, 1990*, Oxford, Oxford University Press, 1990; Food and Agriculture Organization, *Production Yearbook 1989*, vol. 43, Rome, 1990

Legend:
- 900 and over
- 425–899
- 270–424
- 140–269
- 51–140
- 0–50
- ND No Data

median 270
mean 199

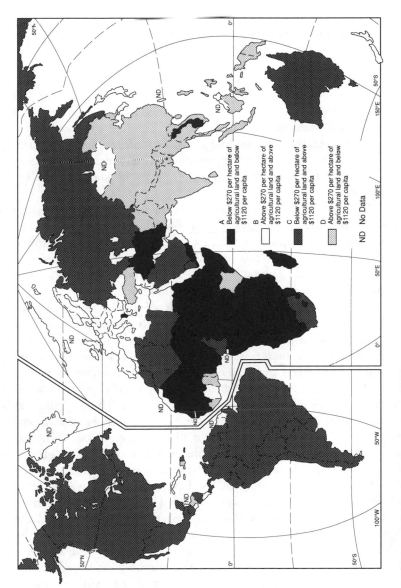

Figure 8.6 Productivity classes, 1988
Source: D. Grigg, 'World agriculture: production and productivity in the late 1980s', *Geography*, 1992, vol. 77, pp. 97–108

4 Lastly the countries with low labour productively but comparatively high output per hectare which include nearly all of east, south-east and east Asia.

THE PROCESSING OF FARM AND FOOD OUTPUT

So far it has been shown that there are two salient characteristics of the modernization of agriculture: the increasing proportion of output which is sold off the farm rather than being consumed by farm families, and the intensification of production, with a sharp increase in the purchase of inputs from the industrial sector. The latter also includes the purchase of services – of accountants, veterinary surgeons, and information from farm advisory services; indeed in some countries farmers can have special contractors to undertake parts of the farm operations such as spraying or even harvesting.

A third characteristic of modernization is said to be the increasing proportion of farm produce which is processed by food manufacturers. The processing of farm produce is not new; grain has always been ground in flour mills, sugar-beet sold to factories that refine sugar, barley converted into malt or distilled into spirits. Three features, however, characterize modern agriculture in contrast to traditional agriculture.

First has been the introduction of methods of preserving perishable foods, such as canning and freezing. Second, much of the processing of products has moved from the farm to factories. Until the 1850s cheese and butter were produced only on farms; now they are largely made in factories. In addition products which were once processed off the farm in a large number of small, local firms are now dealt with by a small number of large-scale processors, which benefit from economies of scale. Thus in Britain as elsewhere in northern Europe, breweries were found in most small towns until this century, but beer output is now highly concentrated. Whereas once every village had a miller, now a small number of firms, mainly in coastal locations, undertake the milling of home produced and imported wheat. Third, much of the increase of food processing has resulted from the transference of activities which were once performed in the kitchen, to factories. These range from the washing and packaging of potatoes to the production of pre-cooked foods, the mass production of cakes or the preparation of sauces. Indeed in many developed countries the numbers employed in food processing now exceed the numbers employed on the land, as do the numbers employed in the industries supplying inputs. In short the farmer has become increasingly a supplier of raw materials; the food production system has benefited from the increasing specialization of all those involved in the chain, thus leading to the long-term decline in the real price of food in shops.

ECONOMIC DEVELOPMENT AND AGRICULTURAL PRODUCTIVITY

One of the paradoxes of the world pattern of agricultural productivity is that it is lowest in those countries where agriculture employs the highest proportion of the labour force, and contributes the highest proportion of the agricultural Gross Domestic Product; and that it is highest in the developed, or industrialized countries, where agriculture plays only a small part in employment or the value of total output. This leads to a further paradox: the developed countries, with only 5 per cent of the world's agricultural labour force, only a quarter of the world's total population and only 41 per cent of the total agricultural area produce more than half of the world's agricultural output. There are a number of reasons for this.

First, nearly all the developing countries lie within the tropics, and so a high proportion of their total area is arid or lies within the humid tropics, and there are agronomic difficulties in farming these areas. Yields are higher for crops grown in the temperate areas than in tropical areas, and this is not simply due to differences in the intensity of inputs. Furthermore, livestock production in the tropics is hampered by the greater prevalence of animal diseases and the inferior yields of forage crops grown there (see Chapters 2 and 3).

Second, in the industrial countries the growth of urban employment with higher wages than in agriculture has led to outward migration, a decline in the rural population and hence a fall in the agricultural labour supply. Machinery has been substituted for labour with consequently greater output per capita. In contrast in developing countries the agricultural population in spite of outward migration, continues to increase, and there is much surplus rural labour, so reducing output per capita (see Chapter 12).

Third, the industrial nations have engineering and vehicle industries and chemical industries that produce most of the world's agricultural machinery, pesticides and chemical fertilizers, and so these inputs are available more cheaply in real terms, than to farmers in developing countries.

Fourth, in developed countries non-farmers have high incomes which enable them to purchase livestock and horticultural products that have a higher price than cereals, roots and pulses, which make up most of the demand for food from the much poorer populations of the developing countries. Hence gross income of farmers is higher in the developed countries (see Chapter 6).

Fifth, over the last fifty years in the developed countries, farmers have been protected by the state, maintaining artificially high prices; in contrast developing countries have, for political reasons, protected consumers rather than farmers, and the often low prices for foodstuffs have reduced the incentive to increase output.

Sixth, in developed countries the process of industrialization has been accompanied by the spread of an elaborate transport network; the real cost of moving agricultural products and inputs has been falling, and is lower than in developing countries.

Finally the basis of modern agriculture has been the application of advances in science and technology; only the developed countries have educational institutions capable of carrying out this research. Furthermore most developed countries have agricultural advisory services that help farmers to use new crops and methods, whilst the farmers are better educated than those in developed countries.

CONCLUSION

It was shown in the first part of this book that differences in environment profoundly influence the location of crop and livestock production. In this chapter an equally important factor has been discussed – the level of economic development – for the growth of manufacturing industries, the improvement of transport, the spread of urbanization and the increase of effective demand all influence the commercialization of agriculture, and the intensity of production, and hence differences in agricultural productivity.

SOURCES AND FURTHER READING

N. Alexandratos, *World Agriculture: Toward 2000*, London, Belhaven Press, 1988.

D. Goodman, B. Sorj and J. Wilkinson, *From Farming to Biotechnology; a Theory of Agro-Industrial Development*, Oxford, Basil Blackwell, 1987.

H.F. Gregor, *Industrialization of US Agriculture, an Interpretive Atlas*, Boulder, Colorado, Westview Press, 1982.

D. Grigg, *The Dynamics of Agricultural Change: The Historical Experience*, London, Hutchinson, 1982.

D. Grigg, *The Transformation of Agriculture in the West*, Oxford, Blackwell, 1992.

M.J. Healey and B.W. Ilbery, *The Industrialisation of the Countryside*, Norwich, GeoBooks, 1985.

B.F. Johnston and P. Kilby, *Agriculture and Structural Transformation*, London, Oxford University Press, 1975.

T. Marsden, P. Lowe and S. Whatmore (eds), *Rural Restructuring, Global Processes and their Responses*, London, David Fulton, 1990.

Chapter 9

The state and the farmer

The economic laws that effect the farmer (Chapter 6) only operate if there is a free market for products, land, labour and capital. Yet governments in most parts of the world, but particularly the developed countries, intervene in nearly every aspect of farming life. They try to encourage the growth of particular crops by supporting or increasing prices; conversely, they may try to reduce output of others by limiting the area which can be cultivated. New technologies can be encouraged by subsidizing the use of fertilizers, new seeds or machines. The distribution of landownership can be changed by the expropriation or purchase of land and redistribution to the landless; in some countries ceilings have been placed on the amount that one person can farm. Trade in agricultural produce is limited by tariff barriers and encouraged by export subsidies. In many countries the marketing and export of cash crops is organized by the state, while in others farmers are provided by the government with expert advice on how to grow crops. In nearly all countries fundamental research on agriculture is financed by the state, and its results are freely available to farmers. In short, there are few parts of the world in which the state is not a potent force in the farmer's life. Thus the role of the state may be of major importance in determining spatial variations in agricultural activity.

REASONS FOR GOVERNMENT INTERVENTION

There are a variety of reasons for the wide-scale intervention of the state in farming matters. First is the need to ensure a secure home-grown supply of food in time of war. Most countries do in fact provide 95 per cent or more of the minimum food requirements for their populations. Few leading countries import any substantial proportion of their needs, Japan and the United Kingdom being notable exceptions. In the mid-nineteenth century the United Kingdom abolished duties on the import of grain, and later of other foods; by the eve of the First World War the country was importing about two-thirds of its food consumption. During the war, U-boats put the nation's food supply at risk. However, little protection was afforded to agriculture after the end of the war in 1918, and British agriculture was in a parlous state between the wars; food supplies were again at risk in the war of 1939–45. Thus, the 1947 Agricultural Act, which introduced an elaborate system of government support for agriculture, was prompted by (among other things) a need to secure home food supplies. British agriculture now provides 62 per cent of consumption needs. Although self-sufficiency is not an explicit aim of the Common Agricultural Policy of the European Community, the system of protection has made the member states far less dependent upon food from outside.

Second, farmers in all countries suffer from the instability of the prices of agricultural products. Crops are subject to unpredictable variations in output, owing to fluctuations in climate from year to year, and the ravages of disease and pests. Such variations in supply give rise to marked fluctuations in prices, which are accentuated because farmers find it difficult to store their produce and large quantities are marketed simultaneously. The problems of instability are particularly marked in the case of perennial crops. A period of short supply prompts plantings that begin to yield some years later. Periods of over-supply and under-supply thus alternate. International associations have attempted to stabilize the prices of products such as sugar, cocoa and coffee.

Third, most developing countries have problems in producing enough food for their populations, and in those countries where agriculture still employs a majority of the population, in providing land for those who want it. To assist in the former aim, many developing countries have encouraged the adoption of new farming methods. So the spread of the Green Revolution through Asia – the adoption of new high-yielding wheat and rice varieties – has been encouraged by government distribution of seed and the subsidizing of fertilizers. Equally important has been the creation of new farms. Governments in many developing countries have expropriated or purchased land and allocated it to landless people, while much – indeed most – reclamation of new land has been promoted by the state.

Fourth, and of most importance, over the last fifty or sixty years the agricultural sector has become of declining importance in the economies of the developed countries; at the same time the gap between farm and non-farm incomes has grown larger. Most governments have attempted to give some form of support to farmers to try and diminish this gap, or at least to prevent farm incomes falling further behind non-farm incomes, prompted partly by the power of the farm vote, partly by the feeling that this gap, which exists in developed and developing countries, is inequitable. Yet few of these policies have been successful in closing the gap. There are many reasons for this but three deserve attention.

First, in the developed countries consumer incomes are high, and most needs for food and drink are satisfied. As a result little of any increased income is spent upon food, and so the farmers' market is increasing very slowly. Second, the improved farm technologies of the post-war period have greatly increased food output in North America and Western Europe. Indeed output has run beyond demand for many products, creating the familiar surpluses of the European Community and preventing any free market increase in price. Third, improved efficiency has caused the real price of food to fall continuously for much of this century but the cost of inputs like fertilizers and machinery has risen, so that farmers' real incomes have fallen. Overproduction has been compounded by the fact that there are many small producers in farming, and they frequently respond to falling prices by producing more to maintain incomes, and so depress the price even more. Indeed it is the presence of so many small producers that depresses average agricultural incomes. In most other economic activities small inefficient producers go out of production or are absorbed by larger firms. In the European Community the number of small farmers has fallen dramatically since the 1950s, but not fast enough to lead to parity of incomes with the non-agricultural sector.

As result of these and other causes farm incomes are lower than non-farm incomes, generally between a half and three-quarters (Table 9.1). Parity is most nearly achieved in developed countries, where government protection bolsters farm income; incomes are lowest relative to non-farm incomes in agrarian countries with, however, a valuable non-agricultural export, such as petroleum in Saudi Arabia.

METHODS OF INTERVENTION

Government intervention in farming in the developed countries has two main purposes: first to maintain farm incomes and second to contain or reduce farm output.

Several methods have been used to maintain farm incomes. In the past tariff protection was the most common; a commodity entering a country

Table 9.1 Agriculture's share of total employment as a percentage of agriculture's share of total gross domestic product, 1990

Denmark	1.1	Ethiopia	0.6
France	0.8	Pakistan	0.5
Australia	0.8	China	0.4
Greece	0.7	Mexico	0.3
Tunisia	0.7	Saudi Arabia	0.2
Germany	0.6	Peru	0.2
Nigeria	0.6		

Note: Where shares are equal, index is 1.0.
Source: Food and Agriculture Organization, Production Yearbook 1990, vol. 44, Rome, 1991; World Bank, World Development Report 1992, Oxford, 1992

was subject to a levy that raised the cost of the imported food above the home produced commodity. The Common Agricultural Policy of the European Community currently imposes a levy on a wide range of temperate agricultural imports, but not on those products not grown in the community.

A second method is that of parity prices. Prices of foods are allowed to fluctuate within the country, but each year the government establishes a parity price; if farmers sell below this price, they are given the difference between the sale price and the parity price. This method is used in the USA and the European Community. In both areas there is a further protection if the farmer cannot sell; government will buy at a threshold price below parity and store the commodities. This gave rise to the celebrated butter mountains and wine-lakes in the European Community.

A third method of protection is indirect; governments in many countries, including the European Community, are prepared to subsidize farm improvements by paying part of the capital costs of new buildings, under-drainage and reclamation, and even inputs such as fertilizers.

Since 1950 the combination of new technology and government protection of farming has led to periodic surplus production of many farm commodities, and governments have tried several ways of reducing output. The most obvious is to dismantle the elaborate apparatus of price support, but this has proved politically impossible. In the European Community two methods have been tried. First, in the 1980s the parity price − known as the target price − was not increased as fast as inflation; indeed in 1992 the Community was prepared to cut target prices by one-third. Second, farmers have not received the target price on quantities produced above a given threshold.

More common have been physical methods to limit output. In the European Community each country cannot plant more than a given quota of sugar-beet or potatoes, and dairy farmers have been limited in the volume of milk they can produce. In the USA in the 1930s the government introduced schemes whereby farmers were paid to withdraw land from cultivation for crops such as cotton and wheat that were in surplus. These schemes have continued intermittently to the present day. In 1987 68 million acres, 18 per cent of the total cropland, was temporarily withdrawn from cultivation.

At the heart of the problem of low farm incomes, however, is the existence of large numbers of small farms that cannot produce enough to provide a satisfactory income, which are too small to utilize fully the labour available, and too small to benefit from the economies of scale in the utilization of labour. The European Community has therefore employed rather half-hearted schemes to reduce the number of uneconomic holdings by providing pensions for farmers who retire early, and paying part of the costs of farm amalgamation.

The best way to deal with the spatial impact of government policy upon farm production is by example. Two commodities, sugar and cotton, are discussed below, and then the effects of European Community efforts to limit output are examined.

SUGAR-BEET AND SUGAR-CANE

The history of sugar production illustrates the importance of two centuries of political intervention in agriculture. Europeans obtain their sugar from either sugar-cane or sugar-beet. Sugar-cane was introduced into the Mediterranean basin by the Arabs after the seventh century AD, and taken in the sixteenth century to the Americas. Sugar was not commercially extracted from beet until 1799, and as late as the 1850s sugar-cane still provided 85–90 per cent of world consumption. There are three problems. First, sugar-cane is a subtropical crop produced mainly in the developing countries; sugar yields are generally higher than those obtained from beet, and production costs lower. Second, sugar-beet is grown mainly in cool temperate regions, in developed countries, and owes its origin to state subsidies and tariff protection. Third, most of the sugar in world trade comes from sugar-cane and moves mainly to the developed world. There has thus been a constant problem of over-production since the beginning of this century. International conferences, beginning in Brussels in 1903, have attempted to resolve this problem, but without much success.

The sugar-beet industry in Europe can be traced back to the Napoleonic Wars. Britain's blockade of the Continent limited the import of cane-sugar from the Caribbean, which was then the major source of supply. Napoleon encouraged experiments with sugar-beet factories, which had been first established in Silesia in 1799, but at the end of the wars cane-sugar was again available. However, sugar-beet production became well established in Germany with the aid of subsidies upon home-produced beet and duties on imported sugar. Such a system spread to other European states, and the growth of beet-sugar production was rapid in the late nineteenth century, so that by 1900 it provided 47 per cent of world consumption.

Sugar-beet was then grown in considerable amounts in every West European state except Great Britain, which continued to rely upon sugar from its cane-growing colonies in the West Indies, Mauritius, Natal and Fiji (although West European beet growers were also supplying the British market). Attempts had been made to grow sugar-beet in Britain in the nineteenth century, but these had failed. However, the problems of securing supplies in the First World War, and the depressed conditions in British agriculture in the 1920s encouraged the government to introduce a subsidy on British beet-sugar in 1925. Sugar-beet not only provided sugar, but also the residue of the plant could be sold back to farmers as cattle feed. Sugar-beet fitted easily into rotations in eastern England, and the need for fertilizers and intensive cultivation benefited following crops. After 1925 there was a rapid expansion; in 1924 there were only three factories, by 1928 there were seventeen. The area in sugar-beet rose from 8855 ha in 1924 to 139,568 in 1930, and by the late 1980s was not far short of 200,000 hectares. In Western Europe, Britain's area is exceeded only by Germany and France.

EEC policies on sugar-beet have included both tariffs on imported sugar-cane (except from former British colonies and some French colonies), and quotas which decide how much each country can grow. This has led to considerable surpluses of sugar, both from high production at home and quota imports of cane-sugar. Exports from the EEC, mainly by France, are only possible with export subsidies. The British sugar-beet industry, largely a result of state protection (as indeed were the other beet-sugar producers), is now vulnerable, as yields are the lowest in the EEC and annual variability the highest.

COTTON IN THE USA

In the 1920s, the USA produced about 12 million bales of cotton a year, half of which was exported. Two-thirds of this output was grown in, or east of, the lower Mississippi valley, much of it on small farms. The depression, beginning in 1929, reduced demand for cotton at home and overseas, and the price of cotton fell. Subsequently, the introduction of synthetic fibres further reduced demand, and the expansion of cotton production elsewhere in the world, often at much lower cost than in the USA, further exacerbated the problems of over-production of cotton. In 1933, the United States Congress passed an Agricultural Adjustment Act, the first of a series of measures which tried both to maintain the incomes of small cotton producers and also to reduce output. From 1933, the government annually announced a parity price, usually well above the world price; the government was obliged to buy cotton not sold at parity, and so accumulated stocks. But the government also annually announced a quota, the total area of cotton that could be grown; each individual farm received a quota, normally a percentage of previous years – a system abandoned in 1971. Other measures included payments to farmers who planted land to hay, pasture or legumes.

The result has been a remarkable decline in the United States cotton area, from over 16 million hectares in the 1920s, to an average of 4.5 million in the mid-1980s. This has not been entirely due to government action. Soybeans has proved a profitable alternative to cotton in the south, and the decline of the labour supply, a result of migration to northern cities, has made it increasingly difficult for many farmers to grow cotton. However, although the area planted with cotton has contracted, output has fallen far less. When farmers had to withdraw land from cotton, they abandoned the poorer land, concentrating its cultivation on better soils, while there have been considerable increases in cotton yields due to increased use of fertilizer. Thus output is not far short of the level of the 1920s, although the location of production has radically changed. Three-quarters of the area under cotton now lies west of the valley of the Mississippi, and is grown on large, mechanized and irrigated farms. In the traditional south cotton is no longer king. Ironically, state intervention did little or nothing to reduce stocks. Not until price support was reduced in 1971 did stocks begin to fall substantially.

THE COMMON AGRICULTURAL POLICY OF THE EUROPEAN COMMUNITY

The Common Agricultural Policy came into effect in 1967, when there were only six members, and still applies in 1994, much modified with twelve members. More radical changes will occur in the 1990s as a result of new policies established at the GATT agreement of 1993. For many years the European Commission established annually target prices high enough to provide the least efficient producers with a living and large farmers with considerable profits, for lower priced foreign products were excluded by a levy on imports. The Commission also undertook to buy and store any produce that could not be sold. Not surprisingly many commodities were in surplus, but it was not until the 1980s that any serious efforts were made to constrain output.

Milk quotas

In the 1970s milk yields rose throughout the European Community, and by 1983 milk output was 111 million tonnes, of which 25 million tonnes was surplus. The European Commission therefore decided to control output by allocating each country a quota of milk on which target prices were to be paid; surplus product was penalized. In the United Kingdom each registered milk producer was given a quota, which was 1 per cent below 1983 output, and the quota has since been progressively reduced. This has had widespread implications, for 30 per cent of all the European Community farms keep dairy cows. Farmers reacted in a number of ways. Some cut the feeding of concentrates to reduce milk yields; others culled their older cows, yet others left milk production altogether. But some produced more, for the quota allocated to a particular farm could be sold to others, and many large, efficient producers bought the quota of small farmers. In the 1980s the European Community's dairy herd fell by 17 per cent; this was mainly due to the decline of the number of small herds. Herds under 20 cows accounted for nearly four-tenths of all herds in 1979, but by 1987 accounted for only one-quarter. But yields did not fall in the long run, and milk is still in surplus, albeit not on the scale of the early 1980s.

Set aside

Milk and cereals were the principle surpluses in the European Community; various attempts to curtail cereal output by manipulating prices failed, and in 1988–89 a policy of acreage contraction based on the United States set-aside scheme was introduced. Farmers were to be paid £200 per hectare if they were prepared to withdraw 20 per cent of their land in supported crops for five years. The initial reaction was limited in the European Community; only 1 per cent of the total arable area was withdrawn in 1988–89, generally on poor land or near towns. American experience suggests that set aside will not necessarily reduce output, for farmers withdraw their poorer soils and use more fertilizers on their better land.

Regional policies

Very few state agricultural policies are confined to one region, but, in 1975 the European Community, which has attempted to encourage modernization, farm amalgamation and the retirement of older farmers on small farms, asked member countries to identify poorly-endowed regions which deserved subsidies, to be allocated on the basis of either the area in crops or head of livestock. Member countries were to make the payment, but the European Community would refund 25 per cent of the subsidy. Three types of region were identified (Figure 9.1). First, mountain areas with problems of steep slopes and high altitudes. Second, areas threatened with depopulation, and with farm incomes below the national average. This included upland regions in southern Germany and areas of sandy soil on the North European plain, while in Britain this zone encompassed the upland areas of Wales, Scotland and northern England. A third category embraced areas where support for farming was necessary to preserve the countryside for tourism, or for other special reasons. The million farms in these three regions occupied one-quarter of the agricultural land of the European Community but produced only one-tenth of its output.

The upland regions of Britain have long presented problems, and in the last half-century the British government has provided some support for hill farmers. Since the middle of the nineteenth century, out migration of the young has led to depopulation; sparsely populated, it has been costly to provide services, and as numbers have fallen so services have been even more difficult to sustain. The essential problem has been, however, the poverty of the environment. High rainfall, acid soils and a short growing season preclude the growth of all but the hardiest crops for fodder, while even permanent pasture is rare (see Chapter 4). Three-quarters of the agricultural area of British sheep farms is in rough grazing. Farmers are thus limited, except in the lower hill areas, to hill sheep farming. The flocks of ewes produce lambs which are sold to lowland farmers for fattening,

Figure 9.1 Types of agricultural problem region in the European Community
After I. Bowler, 'The CAP and space economy of agriculture in the EEC', in R. Lee
and P.E. Ogden (eds), *Economy and Society in the EEC*, London, Saxon House,
1976

■ Areas with specific
handicaps

▦ Areas threatened
by depopulation

□ Areas of mountain
and hill farming

mutton from ewes past lambing, and wool, which, however, is in competition with imported wool. Hill sheep farming gives the lowest net return per
hectare of any English farming type, and although farms are large –
averaging 200 ha – farm incomes are low. Thus half of Welsh sheep
farmers in the 1970s had *less* than a farm labourer's wage to live on, and
with which to pay interest on any capital borrowed, while a further quarter
had incomes only equal to a farm labourer's wage.

The British government has in effect implemented regional subsidies
since the Second World War. Since 1940, a subsidy has been paid annually
on each ewe kept on rough grazing, while after 1943 subsidies were paid on
hill cows (cows kept on poor land over 100 m above sea level). In addition,
the state financed half the capital improvements made on farms above

244 m. These payments have not greatly improved the standing of upland farmers; subsidies were rarely more than one-third of gross income, although a much higher proportion of net income. Without subsidy, however, there would be fewer hill sheep farmers.

LAND COLONIZATION AND LAND REFORM

In the developing countries the central problem is to produce more food, and so the state has often provided assistance to increase production. But there is a further problem. In most developing countries a large proportion of the population relies upon farming for a living; these numbers are rapidly increasing, and there are few opportunities for employment outside agriculture. A need exists, therefore, to provide farms for the landless, and there are two ways in which this can be done. First, where much of the land is owned by a small number of landlords and farmed in large units, this land can be purchased or expropriated by the state and divided up into smaller farms for the landless. Second, land not used for agriculture can be reclaimed and the landless settled upon new farms. The state has played such a role in many countries in Afro-Asia and Latin America since 1950.

Since the Second World War, there has been a considerable increase in the area sown to crops in the developing countries. In some cases this has been achieved by increasing the amount of land double cropped; sometimes it has involved reclaiming poorer land on the edge of villages. But substantial areas have been added by the colonization of hitherto unpopulated or sparsely populated waste land. Such schemes invariably require the support of the state, for on poor land the cost of clearing the land, providing irrigation and building roads is beyond the individual. There are a variety of reasons for state support of such schemes. In some cases it is to provide a cash crop to export, as in the case of the Gezira cotton scheme in the Sudan, and in many of the irrigated projects in the savanna interiors of west Africa. Elsewhere the reclamation of new land is for welfare reasons. For example, in India after Independence there was a need to provide land for the refugees of partition, and the Indian government has continued to try and supply farms for the landless. About half those settled on state colonization schemes in India between 1947 and 1971 had been landless. But in most of the developing countries, a fundamental reason for colonization schemes has been to increase food output for a rapidly growing population. Government-sponsored colonization schemes have had an apparently important contribution to make in Asia. Thus, between 1950 and 1963, 200,000 colonists from Java were settled in Sumatra; in Malaysia over half a million were resettled during the Emergency, 1949–53, and a further 20,000 in more peaceful conditions, 1956–64. In Ceylon 128,823 ha were reclaimed, mainly in the Dry Zone, between 1947 and 1966. By far the largest schemes have been in India where, from Independence to 1971, 600,000 ha were brought into cultivation, providing homes for 800,000 people. But however large this may seem, it is a minute fragment of India's cultivated land, and an even smaller fraction of rural population growth in this period. Some have argued that the extension of the cultivated area is too expensive, and that money would be better spent supporting the more intensive farming of existing cropland. But this of course neglects the welfare aims of colonization schemes.

Immediately after the Second World War, it was thought by many that a better standard of living and higher productivity in agriculture were only possible if land reform was carried out. There were several strands of thought behind this contention. First was the obvious injustice of the unequal distribution of landownership in many countries. In many Latin American states much of the land was – and still is – concentrated in a small number of large estates, while the bulk of the rural population had too little land for a reasonable living, or none at all. Even where land ownership was not so inequably distributed, it was argued that tenancy was unjust, and that farmers who owned their land would be more efficient and productive. Thus the last fifty years have seen wholesale changes in landownership in the developing world.

The most radical changes have come in those countries which have come under Communist rule, most notably China and Eastern Europe. Here, the landlord was first expropriated, and the peasant given the land. Then the peasant farms were grouped in collectives. But there were almost as radical changes elsewhere, for example in Iran beginning in 1951, or in Kenya after independence. Some of the most impressive results of land reform can be seen in Taiwan. Reform began with Acts in 1951 that provided the tenant with security and controlled rents. In 1953 the government compulsorily purchased private land in holdings above 6 ha of wet-rice land and 12 ha of dry land, and provided purchasers with comfortable credit terms. As a result the proportion of farm land cultivated by owner-occupiers rose from 56 per cent of the total in 1948 to 86 per cent in 1959. Taiwan has achieved a remarkable rate of productivity increase in agriculture since the Land Reform.

CONCLUSIONS

It is impossible in such a short space to do more than touch upon the widespread influence of the state in agriculture. There are few parts of the world where the state has not influenced the spatial pattern of farming, either by encouraging land settlement in particular regions, protecting particular products, or encouraging new farming methods. It is a factor that cannot be neglected by the agricultural geographer.

SOURCES AND FURTHER READING

W.H. Bailey, 'Government policy and the location of cotton production', *Southeastern Geographer*, 1978, vol. 18, pp. 93–101.

I.R. Bowler, 'The CAP and the space economy of agriculture in the EEC', in R. Lee and P.E. Ogden (eds), *Economy and Society in the EEC*, London, Saxon House, 1976, pp. 235–55.

I.R. Bowler, *Government and Agriculture: A Spatial Perspective*, London, Longman, 1979.

I.R. Bowler, 'Government agricultural policies' in M. Pacione (ed.), *Progress in Agricultural Geography*, London, Croom Helm, 1986, pp. 124–48.

I.R. Bowler, 'The geography of agriculture under the CAP', *Progress in Human Geography*, 1987, vol. 11, pp. 24–40.

A. Burrell, *Milk Quotas in the European Community*, Wallingford, C.A.B. International, 1989.

C.J. Downs, 'EC agricultural policy and land use. Milk quotas and the need for a new approach', *Land Use Policy*, 1991, vol. 8, pp. 206–10.

D.E. Erwin, 'Set-aside programmes: using US experience to evaluate UK proposals', *Journal of Rural Studies*, 1988, vol. 4, pp. 181–91.

B.H. Farmer, *Agricultural Colonization in South and South-East Asia*, Hull, Hull University Press, 1969.

B.H. Farmer, *Agricultural Colonization in India since Independence,* London, Oxford University Press, 1974.

G. Fielding, 'The Los Angeles milkshed: a study of the political factor in agriculture', *Geographical Review*, 1964, vol. 54, pp. 1–12.

J.S. Fisher, 'Federal crop allotment programs and responses by individual farm operators', *South Eastern Geographer*, 1970, vol. 10, pp. 46–58.

D. Gillmour, 'EEC scheme for farming in less favoured areas', *Irish Geography*, 1977, vol. 10, pp. 101–8.

D. Goodman, *The International Farm Crisis*, London, Macmillan, 1989.

S. Harris 'US and EEC policy attitudes compared towards the 1977 International Sugar Agreement', *Journal of Agricultural Economics*, 1980, vol. 3, pp. 351–67.

B.W. Ilbery, 'Adoption of the arable set-aside scheme in England', *Geography*, 1990, vol. 76, pp. 69–73.

A.J. Rayner, 'The regional pricing policy of the Milk Marketing Board and the public interest', *Journal of Agricultural Economics*, 1977, vol. 28, pp. 11–25.

H.A. Reitsma, 'Crop and livestock production in the vicinity of the United States border', *Professional Geographer*, 1971, vol. 23, pp. 216–23.

H.A. Reitsma, 'Agricultural changes in the American–Canadian border zone, 1954–1978', *Political Geography Quarterly*, 1988, vol. 7, pp. 23–38.

G.M. Robinson, 'EC agricultural policy and the environment: land use implications in the UK', *Land Use Policy*, 1991, vol. 8, pp. 95–108.

I. Smith, 'Europe's sugar dilemma', *Journal of Agricultural Economics*, 1980, vol. 31, pp. 215–27.

J.R. Tarrant, *Food Policies*, London, John Wiley, 1980.

M. Tracey, 'Fifty years of agricultural policy', *Journal of Agricultural Economics*, 1976, vol. 27, pp. 331–48.

H.D. Watts 'The location of the beet sugar industry in England and Wales, 1912–36', *Transactions of the Institute of British Geographers*, 1971, vol. 53, pp. 97–116.

A. Winegarten, 'British agriculture and the 1947 Agricultural Act', *Journal of the Royal Agricultural Society of England*, 1978, vol. 139, pp. 74–82.

Chapter 10

Markets and transports

The first model of agricultural location was put forward by a German economist, J.H. von Thünen, in his book *The Isolated State*, published in 1826. He argued that distance from the market was the main determinant of what combination of crops a farmer should grow and with what intensity. His model has been much criticized by later writers, and attempts have been made to modify it.

VON THÜNEN'S RINGS

Von Thünen's book contained two theories, the intensity theory and the crop theory, and to demonstrate them he devised an imaginary state in which all the other factors that might influence land use patterns were held constant. The isolated state was a plain without any climatic or soil variations; farm produce could be marketed in only one place, a town in the centre of the plain. The plain was bounded by a wilderness and there were no imports or exports. The price of farm goods was set in the town; farm produce was transported by waggon to this central point, and the cost of movement was paid by the farmer and was directly proportional to the weight of the produce and the distance it travelled. As the farmer paid the cost of transport to market, the amount a farmer received for produce diminished with increasing distance from the market. Farmers were assumed to be attempting to maximize their profits, and made prompt responses to changes in prices.

Von Thünen used two terms in his analysis which need explanation. He did not refer to profit but to land rent, usually called economic rent by modern writers. This was the total revenue received by the farmer for the sale of his or her goods minus production costs on the farm, interest on the capital invested in the land and buildings, the cost of the farmer's own labour and a wage for the farmer's managerial skills. Land rent was thus a residual, a return due to the land alone as a factor of production. Von Thünen also used the term *intensity*, and by this meant the cost of labour per hectare. At the time when he wrote, land and labour were the most important farming inputs. Production with few labour inputs per hectare was called extensive; that with many labour inputs per hectare, intensive. The terms were used in a relative sense rather than on an absolute scale, and are now also used to describe types of agriculture or farming system, as well as the production of one crop (see above, Chapter 7).

THE INTENSITY THEORY

Von Thünen began by imagining that only one crop was grown in the isolated state. By using farm accounts he showed that growing the crop without a fallow, and thus using much labour, would give a high economic rent near the town, but with increasing distance from the market the price received by farmers fell, for the price at the market was reduced by the cost of transporting the crop to market. Consequently economic rent would also decline with increasing distance from the market (Figure 10.1a and 10.1b, Crop I in 10.1c).

If the crop was grown in a rotation which had a fallow – a year when no crop was grown – then fewer labour inputs were necessary. This would give a lower economic rent near the market (Figure 10.1c, Crop II) but economic rent would decline less steeply with increasing distance from the market. Eventually the more extensive system would give a greater economic rent than the intensive system (Figure 10.1c, at E). The rational farmer who wished to maximize profit would switch from intensive methods to less intensive beyond E.

Von Thünen came to this conclusion by studying farm accounts of two different farms, but it can be justified by marginal analysis (see above, Chapter 7). Farmers who wish to maximize profit, revenue or economic rent will increase or decrease inputs until the price of the marginal input equals the marginal revenue. A farmer who is near the market has little to pay for transporting grain to market and will use much labour to maximize revenue. The farmer at a distance receives less for his or her grain because of the cost of transporting it to market. This farmer will maximize revenue by using fewer inputs than the farmer near the market (Table 7.3, p. 76).

THE CROP THEORY

It is von Thünen's second theory, the crop theory, that is best known today. He argued that the farmer who wished to maximize economic rent would change the combination of crops and animals that he or she kept – or type of agriculture – as distance from the market increased, and hence the price received at the farm gate declined. As prices declined at an equal rate in all directions from the town, this gave rise to a series of rings of different land uses around the market. However, the intensity of these different land uses,

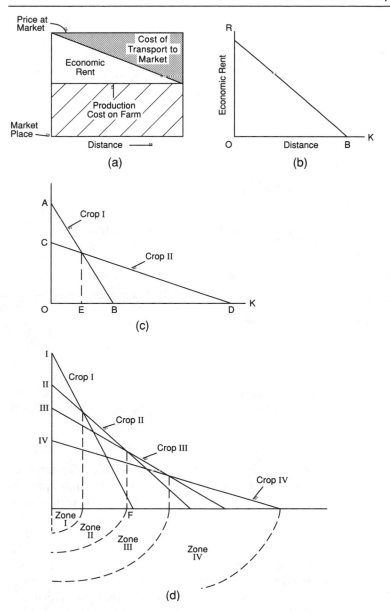

Figure 10.1 The formation of land use rings around a central market

or farming systems, did not necessarily diminish with increasing distance from the market, as is often stated.

In the free cash cropping zone (Figure 10.2) two types of commodity were produced: those which were highly perishable, like milk or fresh

VII | VI | V | IV | III/ II/ I
371 | | 234 183 | | 70 52 30
Kms | | Market Town | | Kms
100 | 200 | 300 | 400

I   Free cash cropping: horticulture, milk, hay, straw, fattening cattle, potatoes, no fallow,
no fixed rotation, town manure.

II   Forestry: firewood and building timbers.

III   Crop alternation system: potatoes, rye and beet, oats, clover, wheat, no fallow.

IV   Improved system: rye, barley, oats, cattle, sheep. Seven-year rotation including fallow.

V   Three field system: rye, barley, cattle, sheep. One year in three is bare fallow.

VI   Stock farming: butter, meat, grain for distilling, rape, tobacco, clover, seeds, flax.

VII   Wilderness: forests, hunting, hides.

Figure 10.2 Von Thünen's land use zones
After W.B. Morgan, 'The doctrine of the rings', *Geography*, 1973, vol. 58, pp.
301–12

vegetables, and those with a very low value per unit weight, like straw or
potatoes. The second zone was devoted to forestry; the inner part to
firewood, the outer to timber. Timber was, of course, more widely used
in von Thünen's time. It was not, however, an intensive system, for there
were few labour inputs per hectare, and its location was due to its low value
per unit weight of product, which could not be profitably marketed in the
town if grown a great distance away. This zone was followed by three
farming systems with a progressive increase in fallow outwards, and hence
fewer labour inputs. In these cases intensity did diminish with distance
from the market, and this sequence was justified by the intensity theory.
The outer zone was described by von Thünen as one of stock farming; it
certainly produced wool, store cattle for fattening near the town, and
butter, but cereals were also grown for distilling into alcohol, rape-seed
for oils, and tobacco.

It is in fact difficult to discern the principles that determine the zones,
but four can be inferred from von Thünen's analysis.

1 Highly perishable commodities like milk must be produced near the market.
2 Products with a low value per unit weight, such as wood or straw, must be produced near the market because the cost of transporting a unit will equal the price received at the market after only a very short distance.
3 Products with a high value per unit weight, such as wool or tobacco, *may* be produced at some distance from the market, for they *can* tolerate the high cost of transport to market.
4 Some goods which are perishable may be processed into less perishable commodities which also have a higher value per unit weight, and can then be produced at a distance. Milk for fresh consumption must be produced near the market, but at a distance it can be converted to butter or cheese, which are less perishable and more valuable. Similarly, low-value products can be processed to give more expensive products; thus grain can be converted to alcohol.

CHANGING TECHNOLOGY AND VON THÜNEN'S MODEL

When von Thünen wrote, there were few effective ways of preserving foods for long periods, and freight rates were high and a large proportion of the total cost of producing and marketing agricultural produce. Since then there have been significant changes. The introduction of bottling, canning and refrigeration have made it possible to move perishable products long distances, and railways, lorries and aeroplanes have allowed perishable produce to be moved much faster as well as much further. The consequence of this is that, while the production of fresh milk and vegetables is still found near cities, it is possible for both to be produced at some considerable distance away from the major markets.

In the United Kingdom, London's milk supply, once limited to the city's immediate hinterland, can now be drawn from as far away as Cornwall and Derbyshire, areas whose better grass growth gives a comparative advantage in dairying. Similarly, crops of low value per unit weight such as the potato are no longer confined to areas near the market. Much of England's potatoes are now grown in the Fens, with its deep loam soils, while early potatoes and other vegetables are grown in the south-west where milder temperatures allow early production. In North America the principal market for vegetables and fruit was and remains the north-east, but the adoption of canning, refrigeration and the spread of the railway in the late nineteenth century have allowed California and Florida, with their climatic advantages for the production of fruit and vegetables, to compete in the north-east. In the nineteenth century, fruits and vegetables were widely grown in the Mediterranean but were consumed only locally, even though the large urban population of north-west Europe provided a potential market. The introduction of refrigeration on ships, and the replacement of sail by steam and later oil made it possible to send citrus fruits as well as vegetables northwards, and have led to horticultural specialization in many areas on the Mediterranean shores.

※ Since the 1820s there has been continuous decline in real freight rates and the cost of moving agricultural produce has become a decreasing proportion of the combined cost of farm production and transport. However, this decline has not removed two important transport differentials. First, the transport of most farm produce is still cheaper by water than overland, as indeed von Thünen recognized. One of his modifications of the Isolated State was to allow a river to cross the plain to the market; then all the rings extended further out. Second, the reduction of freight rates has not removed the differences in the value per unit weight of agricultural products. There is still a limit to the distance that a cheap, bulky product can be moved, while in contrast high value goods can be moved much further.

Some writers have argued that transport costs have fallen so low that they are no longer of much significance for the location of agricultural production. Farm products will now be grown where there is an advantage in terms of good soils, a favourable climate, or a cheap labour supply. Unfortunately there is little information on the cost of moving farm goods. In the USA in the 1950s the cost of transporting farm products from the farm to the first point of consumption was 10 per cent of the combined cost of farm production and transport, and this proportion has declined since. In New South Wales in the 1960s transport costs were less than 5 per cent of gross returns for wheat, lambs, wool and beef; only for milk, where the figure was 15 per cent, was location near to market likely to have been a significant factor.

MODERN MODIFICATIONS OF VON THÜNEN

Some modern writers have attempted to improve the theoretical structure of von Thünen's model. They have confined themselves to the crop theory, and have shown, using the following formula, how farmers will try to maximize economic rent at given distances from the market:

R = E (p − a) − Efk
R = economic rent per unit area of land
k = distance from the market
E = yield of crop
p = market price per unit of commodity
a = production cost per unit of commodity
f = transport cost per unit of distance for each commodity

The relationship between economic rent and the market place O is demonstrated in Figure 10.1b. At O, transport costs to market are zero and the farmer receives the full market price. But for farmers anywhere between O and K, economic rent declines as transport costs increase and the price received at the farm gate declines, until at B economic rent becomes zero and cultivation ceases. If, however, the price of the good increases, the margin of cultivation can extend outwards; similarly if the price declines, then the margin of cultivation contracts towards O. Farmers are assumed to be commercial farmers, and will not grow crops beyond B, although subsistence farmers may do so. It is the absence of transport that explains the persistence of subsistence farming in parts of South-East Asia and Africa (see above, Chapter 7).

In Figure 10.1c two crops are considered. Crop I produces the higher economic rent near the market, and is therefore cultivated in preference to Crop II. However, the gradient of the economic rent line of Crop I is steeper than that of Crop II. Hence the farmer aiming to maximize economic rent will change from Crop I to Crop II at E. A similar transfer from Crop II to Crop III will take place at F (Figure 10.1d) and for the same reasons. This gives rise to the sequence of rings and differing land uses around the central market place. Clearly, the precise nature of these rings will depend upon the figures fed into the formula $R = E (p - a) - Efk$. This exposition also depends upon the assumption that the higher the economic rent per hectare a crop gives on the farm, the more rapidly transport costs will reduce this. There are few empirical studies that support this contention.

TESTING VON THÜNEN

There have been many attempts by modern geographers to test von Thünen's belief that crop combinations and crop intensity change with increasing distance from the market, but this testing is far from easy to carry out.

First, there are few parts of the world where the conditions of the Isolated State are to be found. Few large areas have no internal variations in climate or soil type, nor are there many states or large regions where there is only one market for agricultural produce. There are, however, some approximations to this condition: the north-east of the USA has a high proportion of the non-rural population of the country, but a low proportion of the agricultural land. Several writers have argued that land values, land use and net farm income per hectare change with increasing distance from the north-east, and that the great metropolitan region of the north-east influences United States agriculture in much the way that von Thünen envisaged.

Second, von Thünen assumed that there were no spatial variations in soil type and climate within the Isolated State. Not only is such uniformity rare over large areas but, as the real cost of transporting farm products has fallen, so the advantages offered by optimum climates or soils have increased the concentration of production in such areas.

Third, it is difficult to test von Thünen by comparing the location of types of farming in relation to market because some of his types of farming are no longer found in Europe: the three mixed farming systems with fallow which occupy so much of the Isolated State no longer exist in their early nineteenth-century form, while few of his types are to be found in the tropics.

Fourth, it is difficult to test using von Thünen's measures of economic rent and intensity. Economic rent is not easily measured: the value of land and buildings, and contract rent, which have been used as surrogates by some writers, are certainly not the equivalent of economic rent. Nor is von Thünen's measure of intensity applicable today. Labour has greatly declined as an input; in modern Britain it accounts for only one-fifth of total agricultural production costs, excluding horticulture, pigs and poultry. There are, however, still considerable variations in intensity between types of farming (Table 7.1, p. 72). Horticulture, dairying and general cropping, which includes the cultivation of sugar-beet and potatoes, are all intensive whether measured by the number of man-days worked in a year, the cost of labour per hectare, or the cost of *total* inputs per hectare. In contrast, specialized cereal production and livestock rearing are extensive types of farming by all three measures of intensity, and net farm income per hectare is much lower than in the intensive types of farming.

DISTANCE AND FARMING TODAY

Although it is difficult to show that distance from the market is the exclusive or even dominant factor in determining spatial variations in agriculture today, it is none the less important not only at the scale that von Thünen considered, the national scale, but at the farm level and on the world scale. Many such examples are documented in Michael Chisholm's book *Rural Settlement and Land Use*, and only a few examples are considered here.

Villages and farms

In parts of Western Europe, Australia and North America farmers live in isolated farmsteads, with their fields surrounding the farm house and at some distance from other farms. Elsewhere the homes of farmers and their farm buildings are grouped together in villages and their fields lie some distance away. Either way farmers have to spend time travelling to the more distant fields to cultivate them. Where tractors are available and the fields are compact these costs may be small. But where fields are remote – research suggests over 2 km – and there is no cheap farm transport, it is likely that less time will be spent on the outer fields. Thus, the nearer fields will be farmed intensively, the remoter fields will be farmed extensively or be in less time-consuming crops.

A good example of the latter case comes from the area around Agogo, a small town to the east of Kumasi, which in 1946 was in Ashanti Crown Colony, now part of Ghana. The natural vegetation of the area was rain forest, but most of this had been cleared for cultivation; on land abandoned to fallow the natural vegetation was recolonizing. Two types of crop production were found. Small patches of forest were cleared for food crops, including cocoyams, maize and cassava; after two or three years in crops the land was abandoned and left to be colonized by trees and grass. In contrast there were quite large areas in cocoa bushes. Once this land had been cleared the bushes would yield cocoa beans for several years, requiring little attention. Food farms, in contrast, required frequent attention. Thus,

Figure 10.3 Land use in Agogo, 1946
After M. Fortes, R.W. Steel and P. Ady, 'Ashantia Survey, 1945–6; an experiment in social research', *Geographical Journal*, 1947, vol. 110, pp. 149–79

most of the food crop farms were within 1.5 km of Agogo, a majority of the cocoa farms beyond this (Figure 10.3).

✻ In modern farming capital inputs are more important than labour, and intensity should perhaps be measured in terms of total inputs. This is not always easy to do. A study of farms around the three small towns of Bega,

Figure 10.4 Intensity in dairy farming in New South Wales
After E. Dayal, 'The present pertinence of Von Thünen theory in an advanced economy: a case from south east Australia', *Proceedings of the International Union Regional Conference 1974*, Hamilton, New Zealand, 1975

Barraga and Bemboka in New South Wales used livestock units per hectare of farmland as a measure of intensity (Figure 10.4), on the grounds that the number of cattle which could be supported was a function of capital inputs such as fertilizer, improved seed and purchased feeds. In this area of dairy farming, intensity did decline away from the towns.

Zones within a country

Uruguay appears to conform quite closely to the conditions of the Isolated State. Most of the country is a low-lying plain with uplands only in the east. There is little trade westwards across the Rio Uruguay, or northwards with

Figure 10.5 Land use regions in Uruguay
After E. Griffith, 'Testing the von Thünen theory in Uruguay', *Geographical Review*, 1973, vol. 63, pp. 500–16

Brazil, and most of Uruguay's trade flows through Montevideo, which has 43 per cent of the country's population and is the dominant market. A rail network extends radially outwards from the capital; there are no east-to-west lines. Uruguay has a warm subtropical climate, with no significant internal contrasts. Under these circumstances a zonation of land use around Montevideo might be expected, and indeed at first sight this is borne out (Figure 10.5). Viticulture and orchards are found to the north of Montevideo; the town is surrounded by an arc of intensive crop production, to the north of which lies a zone of dairying. Beyond this, but not in concentric circles, lie cereal and livestock production. But these zones are aligned north–south, not east–west. Most of northern, central and eastern Uruguay is devoted to sheep rearing and cattle ranching. This is largely explained by the distribution of soil types, the good and medium soils being confined to the south and west, where the more intensive farming is found.

Value, perishability and trade

In von Thünen's model, perishability and the value of the produce were important determinants of location, and there was no trade outside the state. It may of interest to see if either of these factors influence present-day trade in agricultural products. In Figure 10.6 the value per unit weight of products is plotted against the proportion of world output entering world trade, the assumption being that the higher the value per unit weight, the more that could move long distances; conversely the lower the value, the shorter distances that can be moved and hence the lower the amount in world trade.

In the case of high value non-perishable commodities (Figure 10.6) a high proportion of total product does enter the world trade. It is of course the high value that allows countries as remote from the major markets as Australia and New Zealand to export wool. Coffee also illustrates this point. Some of the leading coffee producers are not only remote from Western Europe, but some distance from the coast and the cheaper sea routes. The interior of West Africa and Kenya are cases in point. Uganda's exports also illustrate this. Uganda is a leading producer of bananas, for which there is a high demand in Europe, yet none are exported. Not only is Uganda remote from Western Europe, but it has no coastline, and the need for bananas to reach market within fourteen days precludes their export. Cotton on the other hand is not perishable and has a higher value per unit weight, and thus is exported. A low percentage of the total output of low value commodities such as rice, oats and barley enter international trade. However, wheat and maize, despite their relatively low value per unit weight do enter international trade in large quantities. In the case of wheat this is partly explained by the elaborate systems of handling and marketing grain that have been developed over the last hundred years; special bulk

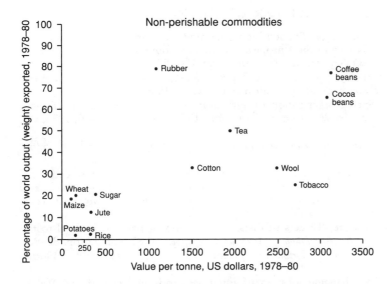

Figure 10.6 The value per unit weight of agricultural commodities plotted against the proportion of world output exported for perishable and non-perishable commodities
Source: Food and Agriculture Organization, *Production Yearbook 1981*, vol. 35, Rome, 1982; *Trade Yearbook 1981*, Rome, 1982

carriers on land and sea have greatly reduced freights, and grain is easy to handle in bulk.

Although the preservation of foods has been greatly improved by the development of canning, refrigeration and rapid transport, only a small proportion of the world output of perishable commodities enters world trade, regardless of their value (Figure 10.6). This is the most apparent with fresh milk, although dried and canned milk is exported. Since the 1880s chilled and frozen meats have entered world trade in increasing quantities; none the less a comparatively small proportion of all the meat produced is exported. Thus, in spite of the advances in food preservation and falling transport costs, perishability and value still influence the nature of world trade.

CONCLUSION

The cost of moving agricultural products is clearly an important factor in explaining the location of different types of farming. But the fall in real transport costs has reduced its significance; in the last twenty years geographers have perhaps exaggerated its importance, just as before then they exaggerated the importance of climate and soil type.

SOURCES AND FURTHER READING

R. Belding, 'A test of von Thünen locational model of agricultural land use with accountancy data from the European Economic Community', *Transactions of the Institute of British Geographers*, 1981, vol. 6, pp. 176–87.

E.T. Benedict, H.H. Stippler and M.R. Benedict (eds), *Theodor Brinkmann's Economics of the Farm Business*, Berkeley, California University Press, 1935.

P.M. Blaikie, 'Spatial organization of agriculture in some north Indian villages', *Transactions of the Institute of British Geographers*, 1971, vol. 52, pp. 1–40; 1971, vol. 53, pp. 15–30.

M. Chisholm, *Rural Settlement and Land Use: An Essay in Location*, London, Hutchinson, 1979.

E. Dayal, 'The present pertinence of von Thünen theory in an advanced economy: a case from south east Australia', *Proceedings of the International Geographical Union Regional Conference and Eighth New Zealand Geography Conference, Palmerston North, 1974*, Hamilton, New Zealand, 1975, pp. 43–52.

D. De Garis De Liste, 'Effects of distance on cropping patterns internal to the farm', *Annals of the Association of American Geographers*, 1982, vol. 72, pp. 88–98.

E.S. Dunn, *The Location of Agricultural Production*, Gainesville, University of Florida Press, 1954.

R. Gasson, 'The changing location of intensive crops in England and Wales', *Geography*, 1966, vol. 51, pp. 16–28.

E. Griffin, 'Testing the von Thünen theory in Uruguay', *Geographical Review*, 1973, vol. 63, pp. 500–16.

P. Hall, *Von Thünen's Isolated State*, Oxford, Pergamon, 1966.

R.J. Horvath, 'Von Thünen's Isolated State and the area around Addis Ababa,

Ethiopia', *Annals of the Association of American Geographers*, 1969, vol. 59, pp. 308–23.

A. Kellerman, 'The pertinence of the macro-Thünian analysis', *Economic Geography*, 1977, vol. 53. pp. 255–64.

A. Lösch, *The Economics of Location*, New Haven, Yale University Press, 1954.

G.T. McDonald, 'The fellowship of the ring', *Proceedings of the International Geographical Union Regional Conference and Eighth New Zealand Geography Conference, Palmerston North 1974*, Hamilton, New Zealand, 1975, pp. 33–42.

T.L. Martinson, 'Economic rent and selected changes in agricultural production along the Western Highway of Honduras, 1952–1965', *Revista Geographica*, 1969, vol. 71, pp. 65–74.

W.B. Morgan, 'The doctrine of the rings', *Geography*, 1973, vol. 58, pp. 301–12.

P.O. Muller, 'Trends surfaces of American agricultural patterns: a macro Thünian analysis', *Economic Geography*, 1973, vol. 49, pp. 228–42.

P. Scott, 'Population and land use in Australia: an analysis of metropolitan dominance', *Tijdschrift voor Economische en Sociale Geografie*, 1968, vol. 59, pp. 237–44.

J.R. Shaw, 'The location of main crop potato production in Britain – an application of linear programming', *Journal of Agricultural Economics*, 1970, vol. 21, pp. 267–82.

R. Stevens and Y. Lee, 'A spatial analysis of agricultural intensity in a Basotho village of southern Africa', *Professional Geographer*, 1979, vol. 31, pp. 177–83.

Chapter 11

Agriculture in peri-urban regions

At the time when von Thünen wrote not only could perishable products be transported only short distances, but a very small proportion of Europe's population lived in towns and so very little farmland was directly influenced by cities. Now, however, a much higher proportion of the population live in towns, which have expanded physically to cover much greater areas than was possible in the early nineteenth century. In some regions, such as the West Midlands of England, the Randstadt region of the Netherlands and the Ruhr in Germany, a number of towns have grown towards each other, leaving only patches of farmland between. Not surprisingly this has profoundly influenced the agriculture of these areas. But the influence of the city has spread further into the countryside. Improvements in transport have allowed an increasing number of city workers to live in villages and small towns and commute to work. As the city physically expands, the zone on the edge of the city becomes more urban in its nature. The social and demographic characteristics of this zone are distinctive and it has been described as the urban fringe. A rather larger area is influenced by the city and this has been called the peri-urban region, although it has not been satisfactorily defined. A report by the Organization of Economic and Cultural Development (OECD) stated the peri-urban region to be that area 'whose structure and activities are modified by the presence or extension of one or more agglomerations'. This is clearly difficult to define in practice, but none the less would seem to include a substantial part of the total farmland of the developed countries.

In France, those communes defined by the census as industrial or urban contain one-fifth of the total farmland and one-quarter of the active agricultural population. Such areas have increased rapidly in the last fifty years; in West Germany there were marked changes between 1950 and 1970 (Table 11.1). In Belgium and the western Netherlands, few farms are any great distance from a town, while in the USA there is a remarkable urban sprawl, called Megalopolis by Jean Gottman, from Boston to Baltimore. In England, London has expanded dramatically; its physical area doubled between 1918 and 1939.

Table 11.1 Share of peri-urban areas in land and population in West Germany

	1950	*1970*
Land area		
Urban	3.0	4.2
Peri-urban	8.9	21.8
Rural	88.1	74.0
Population		
Urban	31.4	36.0
Peri-urban	14.7	27.3
Rural	53.9	36.7

Source: OECD, *Agriculture in the Planning and Management of Peri-Urban Areas*, vol. 1, *Synthesis*, Paris, 1979, p. 13

The physical encroachment of urban areas has given rise to distinctive features in the farming of these zones (Table 11.2). However, some qualifications must be made about the generalizations listed. First, not all the changes taking place in the agriculture of the peri-urban regions are due solely to urban influence. Thus, the loss of farm labour is part of a national trend. Second, not all farmers in the zone react alike to the anticipation of urban development.

THE LOSS OF FARMLAND

The loss of farmland is obviously a distinctive feature in areas of urban expansion. Land under urban uses gives a far higher economic rent than any agricultural enterprise, and so farmland has been bought up on the edge of cities and converted to residential or industrial purposes. The urban fringe has steadily advanced in the last fifty years, except where checked by zoning regulations such as the United Kingdom's Green Belt policy. The loss of farmland in England and Wales was at its highest in the 1930s, when 240,000 ha of farmland were lost each year; between 1945 and 1965 the loss was 15,000 ha a year, with the rate at its highest in Lancashire, the West Midlands and the south-east. Other parts of the world have lost farmland to urban expansion. In California half a million hectares of farmland were built upon between 1940 and 1950. In Germany the Ruhr did not experience industrialization until the second half of the nineteenth century so that in 1893 85.5 per cent of the core area was still farmland or forest, but by 1960 this had fallen to 47.7 per cent.

THE ANTICIPATION OF URBAN EXPANSION

The expansion of towns into surrounding farmland means those farmers within a few miles of the city edge may soon have the opportunity to sell

Table 11.2 Agricultural characteristics of peri-urban regions

Land use
 1. Percentage of total area in farmland is high
 2. Percentage of land in crops is high
 3. Percentage of land in fallow is low
 4. Percentage of land in multiple cropping is high

Farm types
 5. Percentage of all farms that are horticultural is high
 6. Percentage of all farms that are dairying is high
 7. Percentage of all farms that are pigs and poultry is high

Inputs
 1. Labour inputs per hectare are high
 2. Capital inputs per worker are high
 3. Wage rates are high
 4. Total inputs per hectare are high
 5. Price of agricultural products are high
 6. Net income per hectare is high
 7. Rent per hectare and value of land sales are high

Structure
 8. Percentage of small farms is high
 9. Percentage of farms that are tenanted is high
10. Percentage of part-time farms is high
11. Percentage of farms that are fragmented is high

Note: 'High' is relative to regional or national average.

their land at very high prices; they may be subject in some countries to compulsory purchase. It has been argued that anticipation of this sale will influence the intensity with which the land is farmed. Farming types will become more extensive, and less attention will be paid to preserving soil fertility or maintaining buildings and fences. Farmers are unlikely to start long-term improvements or plant orchards or other perennial crops. There are other reasons for a shift to more extensive practices. On the edge of cities the decline in the agricultural labour force is particularly strong, and it may become insufficient for some labour-intensive crops. Further, there are many part-time farmers near cities, and they are less likely to farm intensively. In some places land is left idle because the building of roads or houses has cut off a field from the main part of the farm.

This is, of course, all contrary to von Thünen's argument that farming would be most intensive near the city and decline with distance from it. There have, however, been few attempts to test the hypothesis that intensity is low in the urban fringe, increases in the zone away from anticipated building, and then declines with increasing distance. Some instances have been noted. Around Rockford, Illinois, labour inputs are lower in the more urban counties than in the rural counties, and extensive cash grain farming more common than intensive dairying. East of Belfast, in Northern Ireland, much land is given over to extensive beef fattening; dairying, a more intensive activity, only occurs further away from the town.

LAND USE AND FARM ENTERPRISES

Most peri-urban regions are still dominated by specialized and intensive farming systems. In 1982 the Metropolitan Statistical Areas of the USA contained only 16 per cent of the total farmland, but produced three-quarters of all the sales of nursery and greenhouse products, and nearly 70 per cent of the vegetables, fruits and nuts. Thirty years earlier, in 1950, this effect was already pronounced. Megalopolis, Jean Gottman's term for the urbanized north-east of the USA, had only 1.8 per cent of the total farmland but produced 5 per cent of the total farm sales. The dominant production in this region was of high value goods with high labour and capital inputs. Fresh vegetables, fruits, cut flowers and nursery plants for urban gardens were typical. Livestock enterprises included the production of poultry and milk for fresh consumption. Poultry were fed not on locally grown feed, but grain imported from further west. Nor is such a pattern atypical. A wide range of enterprises is to be found around London, but horticulture, poultry, and pig production are the dominant types.

In recent years, two other trends have become noticeable. Nearness to towns has been a declining advantage for farmers for some time because of the increased ease of transport. However, in the last twenty years the high cost of harvesting fruit, flowers and some vegetables has led farmers to invite the public to pick their own produce, while farm gate sales have also increased. In both cases proximity to a large urban market is an advantage. In a sample of farmers north-east of London in Essex, 29 per cent had farm gate sales, providing 19 per cent of their income.

FARM SIZE AND LANDOWNERSHIP

In many countries there are marked spatial variations in farm size and landownership. It has often been noted that farms near towns are smaller than the regional or national averages, that a relatively high proportion of the farmers are tenants, and that part-time farming is common. There have, however, been few surveys to substantiate these assertions. In some areas – around Sydney, for example – farms near the town are small, and they increase in size with distance from the town. The reasons for the small size of farms is unclear. It is true that the expanding town may lead to the sale of part of the farm, and that land is expensive and therefore few farmers can increase their holding. The small size of farms may also provide an alternative explanation of the intensity of farming near the town; occupiers of small farms must choose enterprises with high net returns per unit area in order to make a living, and such farming is usually intensive – horticulture, pigs, poultry, or dairying.

Similar reasons have been offered to explain the prevalence of tenancy in some peri-urban regions. Farmers who wish to increase the size of their farm cannot afford to buy high-priced land, and have to rent instead. Historically, urban dwellers have often bought land around the town both as a long-term investment and as a way of controlling the town's food supply, and have rented this land to tenants. But perhaps more noteworthy is the growth of part-time farming in peri-urban regions. The importance of part-time farming depends very much upon its definition, and can easily be exaggerated. Thus, in 1980, 92 per cent of all US farm families had some non-agricultural income, but the fact that one member of the family had a job off the land hardly makes it a part-time farm. In 1955 in England and Wales there were 370,000 holdings of agricultural land. On 49 per cent of these, less than 275 man-days were worked in a year. As this means that they failed to occupy one person for a year, they could be defined as part-time farms. It does not follow, however, that half English farmers only work part-time upon their farms.

However difficult it may be to define part-time farmers, they are clearly divided into two types. There are those with land who take another job to increase their income, and those with a full-time job who buy land as an investment, as a tax loss, to provide themselves with a pleasant home, or as a hobby. The former category, called worker-peasants in Europe, has a long tradition. In the nineteenth century many smallholders in the new coal-mining areas in France, Poland and the Ruhr became miners, but the greatest expansion has come since 1945. The rapid growth of industrial employment with its comparatively high wages combined with the difficulty of obtaining an adequate living on a small farm led many small farmers in Europe to work in a factory during the day and on their land in the evenings and weekends. Worker-peasants reached their zenith in the 1960s when one-quarter of all the farms in Germany were so defined and one-third of those in Poland. Since then the number of worker-peasants has declined. As farms become vacant due to retirement or death, few young people are willing to begin such a hard life.

Of increasing importance in the peri-urban regions of Western Europe and North America is the person with a full-time – and usually well-rewarded – job who buys a farm as a hobby. In some areas such farmers are quite numerous. Of a sample of farmers in Essex, on the outskirts of London, 20 per cent were part-time; and in a sample near London, Ontario, 13 per cent were hobby-farmers. Such farmers are often different from full-time farmers. Their farms are smaller than the local average and, with limited time at their disposal, they adopt less intensive farming methods and avoid livestock with its need for regular and long hours.

THE DISADVANTAGES OF PERI-URBAN FARMING

Although proximity to large urban markets is thought to be advantageous to farmers, there are disadvantages. The high cost of buying or renting land has already been noted, and this makes it difficult for successful farmers to expand their business. Wages for farm workers are high, for the attractions of employment in the town are more apparent. Indeed, it is often said that the decline of the agricultural labour force, which is common throughout the developed countries, is most marked in the peri-urban regions, although this has rarely been substantiated. But nearness to towns has other drawbacks. The purchase of land for building roads and houses may divide farms and make access to fields difficult. Industrial pollution may lower crop yields, and open land may be used for dumping rubbish. Vandalism may damage growing crops, and dogs worry livestock, particularly sheep. In parts of North America, farms incorporated into towns have to pay much higher taxes than those in rural areas, although in England rates on agricultural land are lower than on urban land, Yet, whatever the hazards they rarely drive farmers away.

PERI-URBAN FARMING IN THE USA

Most of the generalizations about farming near urban areas rely upon sample surveys of farms around a few cities in many different countries. However, in the USA the collection of agricultural data includes information upon farms in the Metropolitan Statistical Areas, which include not only densely populated areas on the edge of cities, but also less densely

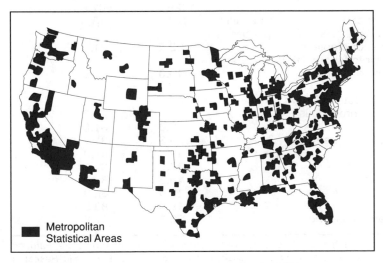

Metropolitan
Statistical Areas

Figure 11.1 Metropolitan Statistical Areas in the USA

populated areas where urban occupations, habits and attitudes predominate. In 1982 farmland in these areas accounted for some 16 per cent of all
US farmland. They are of particular importance in the north-east and
California (Figure 11.1). The statistics bear out many of the generalizations
made about peri-urban farming (Table 11.3). Farms are smaller than in the
non-Metropolitan areas, and there are more part-time farmers, reflecting
the greater opportunities for off-farm employment; farmland values are
twice as high. Farming intensity is higher than in non-Metropolitan areas,
whether measured by the use of fertilizers or labour, or by the type of
farming; the value of farm sales per acre is twice that of the non-
Metropolitan areas, and the Metropolitan areas have a disproportionate
share of the output of more intensive crop production, such as vegetables
and fruits, whereas grain production is less important. Of the livestock

Table 11.3 Farming in the Metropolitan Statistical Areas of the USA, 1982

	Metropolitan	Non-Metropolitan
Percentage of all land in farms	16.1	83.9
Percentage of all farms	28.7	71.3
Average farm size, acres	247	518
Percentage of farms under 100 acres	71.4	44.3
Percentage of farmland owner operated	57.7	62.2
Percentage of farmland tenant operated	41.2	38.0
Percentage of farmers for whom farming is the principal occupation	47.5	58.2
Value of land and buildings, US dollars per acre	1429	661
Value of farm sales, US dollars per acre	243	113
Commercial fertilizers, US dollars per 1000 acres of cropland	32.5	21.4
Cost of all hired labour, US dollars per 1000 acres of cropland	10.6	1.7
Percentage of total US farm sales:	29.3	70.7
Nursery and greenhouse	76.0	24.0
Vegetables	69.0	31.0
Fruits, nuts and berries	68.3	31.7
Hay and silage	49.0	51.0
Dairy products	37.9	62.1
Hogs and pigs	16.3	83.7
Cattle and calves	18.0	82.0
Grains	19.8	80.2
Sheep, lambs and wool	22.8	77.2

Source: R.E. Heimlich and D.H. Brooks, *Metropolitan Growth and Agriculture. Farming in the City's Shadow*, United States Department of Agriculture, Economic Research Source, Agricultural Economic Report 619, 1989 enterprises dairy products are important near to urban areas, but the others – pigs, beef, cattle and sheep – far less so.

CONCLUSION

The very rapid extension of urban areas in the last forty years, combined with much greater mobility, means that an increasing part of national farm areas is directly influenced by cities. Because of the differing reactions of farmers to this expansion, it is difficult to make generalizations about the structure and land use of such regions, but it is clearly a condition that will increase, and one that merits further study.

SOURCES AND FURTHER READING

D. Berry, 'The sensitivity of dairying to urbanization; a study of north eastern Illinois', *Professional Geographer*, 1979, vol. 31, pp. 170–6.

R.H. Best, *Land Use and Living Space*, London, Methuen, 1981.

A.M. Blair, 'Urban influences on farming in Essex', *Geoforum*, 1980, vol. 11, pp. 371–84.

F.W. Boal, 'Urban growth and land value and patterns: government influences', *Professional Geographer*, 1970, vol. 22, pp. 79–82.

C.R. Bryant, 'The anticipation of urban expansion', *Geographia Polonica*, 1974, vol. 28, pp. 93–115.

C.R. Bryant, 'Agriculture and urban development', in M. Pacione (ed.), *Progress in Agricultural Geography*, London, Croom Helm, 1986, pp. 167–94.

C.R. Bryant and T.R.R. Johnston, *Agriculture in the City's Countryside*, London, Bellhaven Press, 1990.

C.R. Bryant, L.H. Russworm and A.G. McLellan, *The City's Countryside. Land and its Management in the Rural–Urban Fringe*, Harlow, Longman, 1982.

H.D. Clout, 'Part-time farming in the Puy de Dôme department', *Geographical Review*, 1972, vol. 62, pp. 271–3.

A.B. Cruikshank, *Where Town meets Country; Problems of Peri-Urban Areas in Scotland*, Aberdeen, Aberdeen University Press, 1982.

I. Davies, 'Urban farming: a study of the agriculture of the city of Birmingham', *Geography*, 1953, vol. 38, pp. 296–303.

R. Gasson, 'The influence of urbanization on farm ownership and practice', *Studies in Rural Land Use*, No. 7, Wye College, 1966.

R. Gasson, 'Part-time farming and farm-size', *Sociologia Ruralis*, 1967, vol. 7, pp. 176–89.

R.G. Golledge, 'Sydney's metropolitan fringe: a study in urban rural relations', *Australian Geographer*, 1960, vol. 7, pp. 243–55.

J. Gottman, *Megalopolis: The Urbanized North Eastern Seaboard of the United States*, London, MIT Press, 1964.

P.F. Griffin and R.L. Chatham, 'Urban impact on agriculture in Santa Clara county', *Annals of the Association of American Geographers*, 1958, vol. 48, pp. 195–208.

P.G. Hall, *The World Cities*, London, Weidenfeld & Nicolson, 1977.

R.E. Heimlich, 'Metropolitan agriculture. Farming in the city's shadow', *American Planners Institute Journal*, 1989, vol. 55, pp. 457–66.

R.E. Heimlich and D. H. Brooks, *Metropolitan Growth and Agriculture. Farming in the*

City's Shadow, United States Department of Agriculture, Economic Research Service, Agricultural Economic Report, 619, 1989.

H.W. Lawrence, 'Changes in agricultural production in Metropolitan Areas', *Professional Geographer*, 1988, vol. 40, pp. 159–75.

R.L. Leyton, 'The operational structure of the hobby farm', *Area*, 1978, vol. 10, pp. 242–6.

N. Low, 'Farming in the Inner Green Belt', *Town Planning Review*, 1973, vol. 44, pp. 103–16.

P.F. Mattingly, 'Intensity of land uses near cities: a case study', *Professional Geographer*, 1972, vol. 24, pp. 7–10.

W. Moran, 'Spatial pattern of agriculture on the urban periphery: the Auckland case', *Tijdschrift voor Economische en Sociale Geografie*, 1979, vol. 70, pp. 164–76.

R.J.C. Munton, 'Farming in the urban fringe', in J.H. Johnson (ed.), *Suburban Growth: Geographical Processes at the Edge of the Western City*, London, John Wiley, 1974, pp. 201–24.

R. Munton and S. Whatmore, 'Reconsidering urban-fringe agriculture: a longitudinal analysis of capital restructuring on farms in the Metropolitan Green Belt', *Transactions of the Institute of British Geographers*, 1988, vol. 13, pp. 324–36.

Organization of Economic and Cultural Development, *Agriculture in the Planning and Management of Peri-Urban Areas*, 2 vols, Paris, 1979.

R. Sinclair, 'Von Thünen and urban sprawl', *Annals of the Association of American Geographers*, 1967, vol. 57, pp. 72–88.

Chapter 12

Population, labour supply and agriculture

Much has been written on the relationships between population growth and food supply, rather less on the influence of population growth and regional differences in density upon farm structure and land use. Yet differences in the amount of labour used in agricultural production are of paramount importance in determining spatial differences in the way farming is carried on. In this chapter a brief account of world differences in agricultural densities is given, followed by an outline of Ester Boserup's theory that links changes in land use intensity to population increase. Some empirical relationships between population density and agricultural characteristics are then discussed.

AGRICULTURE AND ECONOMIC DEVELOPMENT

Two centuries ago, four-fifths of the working population of most countries in the world were engaged in agriculture. Since then, Europe, North America, Japan, the Soviet Union and Australasia have experienced industrialization. During this process the absolute numbers working in manufacturing industry and the services have increased, and the proportion engaged in agriculture has fallen to below 15 per cent in most of these countries, and to less than 3 per cent in the United Kingdom, Belgium and the USA. Elsewhere, industrialization is in its early stages, and the proportion engaged in agriculture remains high, particularly in Asia and tropical Africa (Figure 12.1). In all the developed countries, the numbers employed in agriculture are now in rapid decline (Figure 12.2); industry has offered higher wages than agriculture, and the introduction of labour-saving machinery has reduced the need for labour on farms. But this is a relatively recent trend. In the early stage of industrialization, Phase I, the agricultural population increased (Figure 12.3), for rural natural increase was higher than the rate of migration from country to town. Then, in the middle stages of industrialization, migration and natural increase were much the same, and the agricultural labour force stagnated or slowly declined (Phase II).

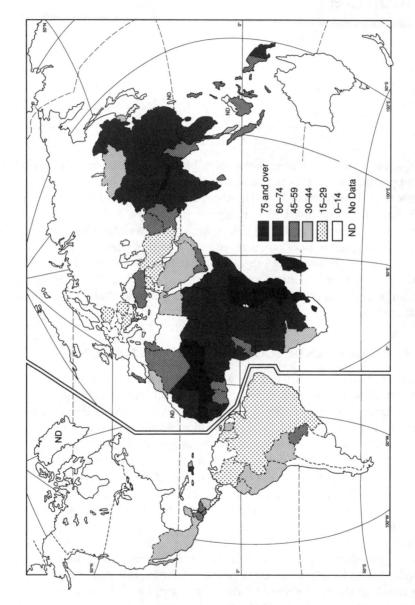

Figure 12.1 Percentage of the economically active population engaged in agriculture, 1990

Source: Food and Agriculture Organization, *Production Yearbook 1991*, vol. 45, Rome, 1992

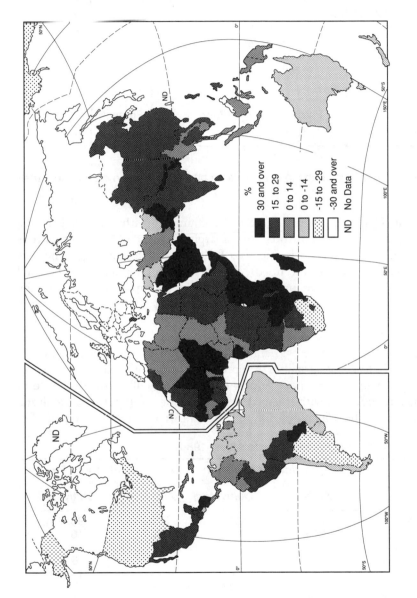

Figure 12.2 Changes in the numbers economically active in agriculture, 1975–90
Source: Food and Agriculture Organization, *Production Yearbook 1991*, vol. 45, Rome 1992

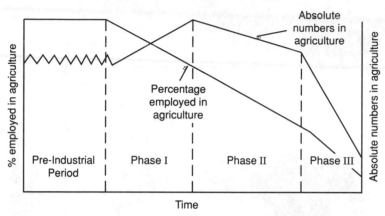

Figure 12.3 A model of changes in the agricultural population during industrialization

Finally, in Phase III migration from the country greatly exceeded natural increase, and the labour force fell sharply. Most developing countries remain in Phase I of this model of development. Although there is substantial migration to the towns, the rate of natural increase in the rural areas is very high, often over 2 per cent per annum. Consequently, the numbers dependent upon agriculture are increasing. Indeed, in some parts of Africa the agricultural population increased by over 30 per cent between 1975 and 1990 (Figure 12.2).

Regional differences in agricultural population densities are shown in Table 12.1. However agricultural population density is measured, whether by using the agricultural population (which includes all those employed in agriculture together with their dependants), or simply the agricultural labour force (which includes only those employed in agriculture), the Far

Table 12.1 Agricultural population densities, 1989

| | Agricultural population per Km² | | Agricultural labour force per Km² | |
	Arable	*Cultivated*	*Arable*	*Cultivated*
Far East	444	196	216	96
Africa	216	40	88	16
Near East	127	27	42	9
Latin America	66	16	23	5
Europe	32	20	16	10
USSR	17	2	9	7
North America	3	2	2	1
Oceania	2	0.2	1	0.1

Source: Food and Agriculture Organization, *Production Yearbook 1990*, vol. 44, Rome, 1990

East and Africa have the highest densities, and North America, the former Soviet Union, and Oceania (or Australasia) the lowest. However, these figures conceal important differences within continents.

When figures for each state are examined (Figure 12.4) it can be seen that the highest densities are to be found in East, South-East and South Asia, but there are also very high densities in much of tropical Africa and in the irrigated areas of the Middle East. The lowest densities are in North America, Australasia, temperate South America, the former Soviet Union and parts of north-west Europe. Densities in Latin America are higher than in Europe, but low compared with Afro-Asia: the highest densities in this area are found in the upland areas of the Andes and Central America. Within Europe there are still differences between the north-west, where densities are lowest, and the east and south. This is partly related to the date when industrialization began. It was earliest in the north-west, and the agricultural labour force there has been in decline for a century; industrialization was later in the east and south, and the decline began only some thirty years ago.

It is important to note that there is a considerable difference in density between Western Europe and the European settlements overseas. Europe has a long history of settlement, and agricultural densities had reached a high level by the early nineteenth century before the age of labour-saving machinery; out-migration has since reduced these densities. In contrast, much of western North America, temperate South America, southern and eastern Russia and Australasia were not settled until after 1850, by when machinery was available. Thus, densities in these regions were never as high as in Western Europe.

AGRICULTURE AND POPULATION IN DEVELOPING COUNTRIES

Many writers have asserted that population growth and density influences agriculture, but the only theory relating the two is that put forward by Ester Boserup. Her theory demonstrates how population growth over time forces changes in land use and farming methods, but she also believes that spatial variations in population density explain current geographical differences in farming practices.

Her model makes a number of assumptions:

1 It is confined to subsistence societies, where the aim is to preserve leisure once basic needs are satisfied, rather than to maximize profit.
2 Modern agricultural technologies are not available to farmers.
3 Farmers are thought to be aware of a wide range of traditional farming methods, but use only extensive methods. They will only adopt methods that need more labour if population increases.

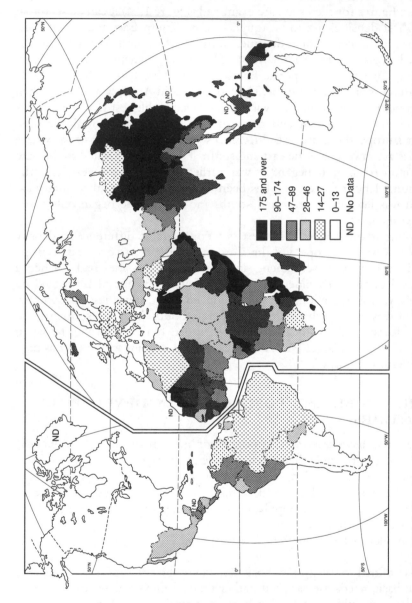

Figure 12.4 Number of persons economically active in agriculture per 100 hectares of arable land, 1989

Source: Food and Agriculture Organization, *Production Yearbook 1990*, vol. 44, Rome, 1991

Legend:
- 175 and over
- 90–174
- 47–89
- 28–46
- 14–27
- 0–13
- ND No Data

4 Population increase is assumed to be due to external factors such as improved public health conditions, and is not dependent upon an increase in the food supply. It is in fact the growth of population that requires extra work to be done in order to increase the food supply.

5 Variations in soil type and climate are assumed to have no influence on the intensity of farming. The theory thus applies to parts of developing countries with both low and high densities, but not to developed countries.

Boserup argues that in a sparsely settled area, with abundant land per capita, shifting agriculture or forest fallow will be practised (Table 12.2). This system requires few labour inputs other than those needed to clear the forest for cultivation, and output per capita is high. Farmers can obtain an adequate food supply with little work, and there is ample leisure time. If, however, population increases farmers need to increase their food supply. This they do in two ways. First, they reduce the amount of land in fallow between crops: thus a series of types of farming defined by the length of fallow results from each successive increase in population density (Table 12.2). Second, as the fallow is reduced, so the ability of the natural fallow to restore fertility diminishes. Farmers then have to increase labour inputs to maintain crop yields by preparing the seed-bed more carefully, carting manure and, in the later stages, by irrigation and terracing. Although crop yields are maintained or even increased in each stage, this does not compensate for the extra labour involved, and so output per capita falls at every stage. Increasing intensity of cultivation also requires changes in the implements used. In forest fallow no seed-bed is prepared, and the axe and the digging stick are all that is required. When the length of fallow is reduced, secondary forest is not re-established and a grass cover invades the fallow. Thus, a hoe is needed to remove the roots when the land is cropped again, and later a plough becomes necessary.

Boserup believes that all parts of the world have experienced these changes owing to increasing population density, and that present spatial variations in intensity are a function of density. But nowadays annual cropping is common in most regions outside Africa, and fallowing is practised for reasons other than conserving soil fertility. Thus, in many semi-arid regions two years' moisture is necessary for a crop, and land is alternately under crop and fallow. Purely subsistence societies are rare, and even in developing countries some modern inputs are purchased. In most developed countries the labour force is declining, and so the theory is not applicable. Thus, it is only in Africa and limited areas of Asia and Latin America that the early stages in the sequence are found. At the other end of the sequence multiple cropping may be a function of density, but it is only possible where irrigation and a long growing season allow it. Some contemporary examples of the relationship between density and intensity are now considered.

Table 12.2 Type of farming and population density

Type	Typical densities (per km²)	Cropping length	Fallow length	Frequency[1] of cropping (%)	Type of fallow	Tools in use	Fertilizer	Labour needs	Labour productivity
1 Forest fallow	0–4	1 to 2 years	15 to 25 years	0–10	Secondary forest	Axe, fire, digging stick	Ash	Land clearance with axe and fire. No cultivation or weeding	High
2 Bush fallow	4–64	2 or more years	8 to 10 years	10–40	Small trees, bush	Hoe	Ash, vegetation, turfs mixed in soil	Less land clearance but some weeding	Falls as yields fall and extra weeding needed
3 Short fallow	16–64	1 to 2 years	1 to 2 years	40–80	Wild grasses	Plough	Manure and human waste	Extra preparation of seed bed. Extra weeding and carting manure	Falls as extra cultivation, extra weeding, collecting and distributing manure, care of draught animals needed
4 Annual cropping	64–256	One crop each year	A few months	80–100	Legumes and roots	Plough	Manure, human waste, green manure, marling and silting, composts	Extra cultivation, weeding, terracing, irrigation, and water control	Falls as extra cultivation and weeding, collecting and distributing manure, constructing and maintaining irrigation, terracing, water-control, etc. needed
5 Multi-cropping	256 and over	Two or more crops in each year	Negligible	200–300	–	Plough			

Note: 1 Average area in crops as a percentage of crops plus fallow.

Source: E. Boserup, The Conditions of Agricultural Growth, London, Allen & Unwin, 1965

SUBSISTENCE COMMUNITIES IN THE TROPICS

Three American geographers have tested the assertion that population density determines agricultural intensity. They collected data from twenty-nine studies of simple village communities in the tropics on population density, cropping frequency, the principal food crops, the presence of livestock and on three variables of environmental quality. Linear regression and correlation techniques were used to test a number of hypotheses. Their conclusions can be summarized as follows. They found that agricultural intensity – the ratio of the area in crops to the sum of the area in crops plus the fallow – did increase with population density. The best fit for the regression line was an exponential model, suggesting that as density increased so intensity had to increase more rapidly to overcome the problems of diminishing returns. They went on to distinguish between farmers who grew root crops and those who raised cereals, and found that for any given population density agricultural intensities were higher for cereal growers than those cultivating roots. This is because the root crops such as yams, sweet potatoes and manioc give a higher calorific yield than cereals (see above, pp. 10–12). There is thus a greater need for cereal growers to reduce fallow. In those communities that kept livestock, agricultural intensities were higher than in those communities with similar population densities but no livestock. This was because these communities had to keep some of their land for grazing; arable expansion was limited and fallow had to be reduced earlier than in villages without livestock.

DENSITY AND FARMING IN WEST AFRICA

West Africa has islands of high population density separated by very large areas of low density. Several geographers, independently of Ester Boserup, have argued that land use intensity in this region is a function of population density.

Shifting agriculture is distinguished by a very long fallow during which time secondary forest is established, which restores soil fertility. After two or three years in crops the land is abandoned, and the settlement itself moved, to clear another patch of forest. Such a system is only possible where there are very low population densities and abundant land. Although it is now found in only a few places in West Africa, it was more common in the past. When population densities reach about 10 per km^2, settlements become fixed and fallows much shorter.

Rotational bush fallowing has shorter fallows and longer periods in crops. Typical densities are from 2 to 20 per km^2 in the drier north where cereals are the staple crops, but from 27 to 77 per km^2 in the south where root crops, with their higher yields, can be grown. This farming type, the most common in West Africa, has fallow periods that are longer than the periods in crops. Unlike shifting agriculture, however, the land in fallow remains in the possession of the family that cultivated it, and the settlement is not moved.

The third type of farming, *permanent cultivation*, has longer periods in crops than in fallow, and is found in regions of very high density such as the Kano area of northern Nigeria. In this area farming practices are intensive. Land is frequently hoed, manure carted from the town, and Fulani pastoralists are encouraged to graze their stock on the stubble. In other high density regions, similar practices designed to increase yields and avoid soil erosion are found.

There are other possible explanations for these areas of high density and intensity. The spread of commercial agriculture has encouraged farmers to sell crops for profit rather than simply to feed their families, and this leads to increased intensity. Nowhere in the high density zones, it should be noted, has the plough replaced the hoe (except on experimental farms), and multiple cropping is confined to the state-financed irrigation zones of the savannah interior.

MULTIPLE CROPPING

Multiple cropping is rare in the high density areas of Africa, and is uncommon in the cool temperate areas where the growing season is too short for more than one main crop in the year. Multiple cropping may be related to population density in peasant societies, but even in the tropics and sub-tropics, where temperatures are not limiting, it depends upon a year-round supply of water, normally only available with irrigation. There is a weak positive correlation between density and double cropping (Figure 12.5). The more striking residuals are related to the availability of irrigation, which is low in both North and South Vietnam and very high in Taiwan and Egypt. However, the data does bear out a difference in population density between South Asia and East Asia. The lower densities in India, Pakistan, Thailand and Burma are reflected in the low indices of multiple cropping in these countries when compared with East Asia.

A more detailed study – of Assam – has shown a close relationship between population density and the intensity of cropping. Assam was sparsely populated in the nineteenth century, but the development of tea plantations attracted immigration which has continued since 1947 (during which time there has also been a high rate of natural increase). Two-thirds of the workforce are engaged in agriculture, and nine-tenths of the total population live in rural areas; there are few opportunities for work outside farming. M.M. Das has shown that there is a positive correlation of $r^2 = 0.69$ between rural population density and the percentage of the net sown area cropped more than once a year; a regression analysis showed that half

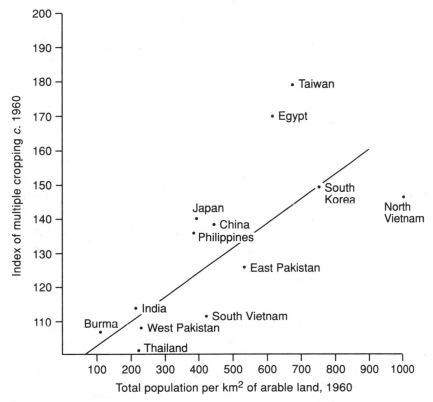

Figure 12.5 Population density and multiple cropping in selected countries, *c.* 1960

The index of multiple cropping is the proportion of the arable area sown twice or more during the year

Source: D.G. Dalrymple, *Survey of Multiple Cropping in Less Developed Nations*, Washington DC, US Department of Agriculture, 1971

the changes in the intensity of cropping could be explained by a change in population density.

CHARACTERISTICS OF AREAS OF HIGH POPULATION DENSITIES

Boserup's theory states that in subsistence societies population growth requires more intensive farming to provide the extra food supply needed by population increase, but although gross food output increases, output per capita declines as density increases. However, there are other changes as density increases, largely adverse. Most agricultural areas with very high population densities and without modern agricultural technology are areas of poverty and distinctive agricultural features. Nor can Boserup's theory be applied to most of the developed world, for here not only are modern technologies – such as fertilizers and machinery – in use, but the agricultural population is declining. These two contrasting regions are now discussed.

AGRICULTURAL CHARACTERISTICS OF REGIONS OF HIGH POPULATION DENSITY AND GROWTH

Areas of high density and rapid growth have distinctive agrarian features, some of which are shown in Table 12.3 In areas of dense and increasing agricultural population, farms are subdivided. Not only are they small, but frequently many of them are *too* small to provide sufficient food for the family, and additional sources of income have to be sought by working as labourers on larger farms, by temporary migration to the towns, or by home crafts. In much of the densely populated Far East farms are remarkably small. In Sri Lanka in 1971, 65 per cent of all farms were less than 1 ha, and 96 per cent less than 5 ha; in Bangladesh in 1974, 95 per cent of all farms were less than 3 ha. However, a predominance of small farms may not be due simply to high population densities. In Colombia the smaller farms, averaging 3 ha, constituted 60 per cent of all farms, but they occupied only 4 per cent of the farmland. Holdings of 100 ha, which constituted only 3

Table 12.3 Characteristic features of agriculture in areas of high population density

 1 Very small farms; often too small to provide minimum diet.
 2 High degree of fragmentation.
 3 Large proportion of rural population are without land.
 4 Labour force on family farms are underemployed.
 5 Landless labourers have low real wages and are often unemployed.
 6 Abundance of cheap labour retards the adoption of labour-saving machinery.
 7 Scarcity of land gives high rents and high land values.
 8 Farmers concentrate upon food crops and can spare little land for fodder.
 9 Livestock are relatively unimportant except as draught animals.
10 Cereal crops replaced by high yielding but nutritionally inferior crops e.g. cassava.
11 Expansion of arable land at expense of grazing leads to overgrazing and soil erosion.
12 Low incomes and variable harvests lead to indebtedness, bankruptcy, forced sale of farms, growth of tenancy and share-cropping.
13 Lack of capital means farmers are unable to purchase inputs such as seeds, fertilizer and irrigation water.
14 Although abundant labour inputs give high crop yields in the traditional context, farms are unable to reach the high yields that are possible with modern technology.
15 Low incomes, poor diet.

per cent of all farms, accounted for 60 per cent of the cropland. Much of Colombia is held in very large units of landownership, to which small farmers do not have access. Thus the pattern of landownership, as well as density, is of great importance in determining farm size.

As farms are subdivided over time the fields of a farm become scattered among the fields of neighbouring farms, and one farm may consist of widely scattered plots. Fragmentation, as this is called, means that farmers spend much time walking from plot to plot, land is wasted in a plethora of field boundaries, and plant disease is hard to control. Population, however, is not the sole cause of fragmentation. In some localities farmers want scattered plots to ensure that their farm has a variety of soil types (see below, pp. 165–8).

When farms are small and families large it is not possible for all children (sons) to acquire land, and so the landless populations of most parts of Asia have increased over the last thirty years, for it has not been possible to create enough new farms for them, nor has industrial growth been rapid enough to provide alternative jobs. At the beginning of this century landless labourers were a small proportion of the population of India, but by 1951 they were a third of the rural population. When the landless are so numerous real wages remain low, and there is much unemployment. On the very small farms that characterize much of Africa and Asia the family labour available is rarely fully utilized and so underemployment as well as unemployment is common. Thus, it has been estimated that 30 per cent of the labour hours available to farmers in South Korea are not used; in the Maghreb the figure has been put at 58 per cent. Similar conditions were found in Eastern Europe in the 1930s, although industrial growth and a falling rate of natural increase has since eased the problem. Even so, in 1953 31 per cent of the farm population of Yugoslavia was thought to have been surplus to requirements. This, combined with the low wages of farm labourers, provides little incentive to farmers to adopt labour-saving machinery.

With an acute shortage of land, few farmers can afford to grow crops other than those for direct consumption. Forage crops are rare and few livestock are kept, except those like pigs and poultry which can be fed the residue of human foods (although some oxen or buffalo are kept for draught purposes). In some very densely populated regions the preferred staple crop, usually a cereal, has to be replaced by nutritionally inferior but higher-yielding root crops. The continued increase in population may lead to the expansion of cropping on to physically marginal land, and this in turn, to soil erosion. In parts of Africa the growth of arable land has reduced the grazing area, and this in turn has caused overstocking and overgrazing.

Thus poverty is endemic in high density regions, and this very poverty prevents increased output. The high labour inputs in these areas mean that by the standards of traditional agriculture the yields are high, although output per capita may be low. Further increases in yields require not further labour inputs but new inputs such as fertilizers and improved crop varieties, like those used in the Green Revolution. But poverty prevents the smaller farmer purchasing these inputs.

Java

The problems of Java illustrate graphically the problems of high density agricultural areas. In 1980 the population of Indonesia reached 150 million, of which Java, with only 6.3 per cent of the area, had 95 million. The population of the island had doubled since the end of the Second World War. Not surprisingly 70 per cent of the total land area is in crops, and the area left in forest is now thought to be less than that necessary to prevent soil erosion and accelerated run-off in the upland regions. There is little land left that could be brought into cultivation. Both during Dutch rule and since efforts have been made to move farmers from Java to Sumatra and the other Outer Islands, but with limited success.

Farms in Java are remarkably small, four-fifths being less than 1 ha. Yet it has been estimated that a family needs 0.7 ha of wet-rice land or 1.4 ha in dryland crops to feed itself. Nor is this acute subdivision of farms due to any gross inequalities in landownership; less than 1 per cent of all farms are larger than 5 ha. At the other extreme, half Java's rural population has either no land or less than 0.1 ha. Nor is much land devoted to non-food crops.

Most of Indonesia's plantation crops are grown on the Outer Islands; only 7 per cent of Java's arable is occupied by these crops. Wet-rice is the most important of the food crops, grown with elaborate terracing and irrigation systems. Until the introduction of high-yielding rice varieties in the 1960s, much of the harvest was gathered in with a hand knife, although now that these varieties occupy about half of the island's rice crop the sickle is more common. Not surprisingly, with such high densities, much of the land is double cropped. Double cropping is found not only on the irrigated wet-rice land, called *sawah*, but also on dryland, or *tegalan*, on which maize is the main food crop.

Livestock necessarily play a small part in the agricultural economy, accounting for less than a tenth of the value of gross agricultural output. Arable per capita has halved since the 1930s, so that the problems of feeding the population have been acute. The typical Javanese spend four-fifths of their income on food. Even so the diet of many is inadequate: average daily consumption was less than 2000 calories per capita in the 1960s, although it has improved since. High population densities may not be the only cause of Java's poverty, but they are a significant contributor.

AGRICULTURAL CHANGE IN REGIONS OF DECLINING AGRICULTURAL LABOUR FORCE

In all the countries of the developed regions the agricultural labour force is in decline (Figure 12.2). In Western Europe this decline began in the later nineteenth century, in Eastern Europe not until after the end of the Second World War; since 1950 it has been dramatic. A combination of the attraction of higher wages in industry, and the adoption of labour-saving machinery upon farms has led to very large reductions in the labour force. In the USA the labour force in 1980 was less than a third of what it was in 1950, and in the United Kingdom it is less than a half. In Western Europe there has been no marked change in the agricultural area since 1950, so the density of the agricultural labour force has fallen and the amount of land per worker has doubled in nearly all countries since 1960 (Table 12.4). However, there is still a marked difference in the amount of land per worker between Western Europe and the Soviet Union on the one hand, and the overseas European settlements of Canada, the USA, New Zealand and Australia on the other. Hence differences in population densities help to account not only for differences between the developed and developing regions, but for some of the differences in farming practice between the low density regions of European settled areas overseas, and the higher densities of Europe itself.

Changes in farm size

Until the Second World War, the decline in the agricultural labour force was largely accounted for by the migration of hired agricultural labourers to the towns. Thus in Britain the number of labourers fell from 2,100,000 in 1851 to 1,110,000 in 1951, but there was little change in this period in the

Table 12.4 Agricultural land per capita of the agricultural labour force, 1960 and 1989 (hectares per capita)

| | Arable | | Cultivated area | |
	1960	1989	1960	1989
Italy	2.5	6.9	3.3	9.7
West Germany	2.2	6.6	3.8	10.5
France	4.9	13.7	7.9	22.0
USSR	4.9	11.8	12.8	30.7
United Kingdom	7.5	11.6	20.2	30.8
Canada	49.3	100.4	74.1	173.5
USA	39.5	63.8	94.3	145.0
Australia	68.7	118.2	1011.0	1127.0

Source: Food and Agriculture Organization, Production Yearbook, 1963, vol. 17 Rome, 1964; 1973, vol. 27, Rome, 1974; 1990, vol. 44, Rome, 1991 number of farmers. Since the end of the Second World War, not only have labourers continued to leave farming, but many small farmers have also left the land. On small farms it is difficult to make a living comparable to that of an industrial worker. In addition, with advances in agricultural technology there are considerable economic advantages in farming large units. The result has been that in nearly every country in Western Europe and the European settled areas overseas, the number of farms has declined. In the USA there were 5.6 million farms in 1950, in 1970 only 2.6 million. In the EEC the number of farms over 1 ha fell by one-fifth between 1960 and 1970; at the same time the number of larger farms increased. While the number of farms in all size categories below 20 ha declined in the same period, the number in all categories over 50 ha increased in every one of the nine member states. In England and Wales since 1950, the number of farms

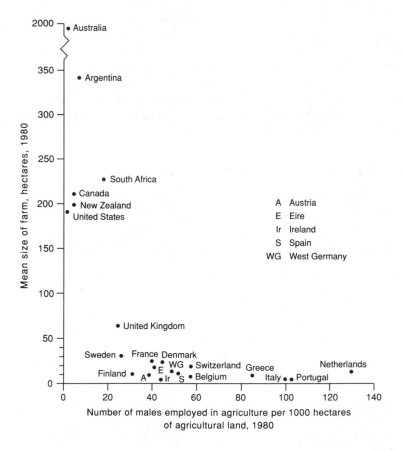

Figure 12.6 Mean size of farm and agricultural labour density, 1980
Source: Food and Agriculture Organization, *Production Yearbook 1981*, vol. 35, Rome, 1982

in each size category over 120 ha has increased, the number in each category below 120 ha has declined.

Although the number of small farms in Europe has greatly decreased since 1950, there is still a marked difference in farm structure between Western Europe and North America. Europe still has a greater proportion of its farms in the smaller size categories, and little of its land is occupied by very large farms (see Chapter 13). Such differences are difficult to represent either statistically or cartographically, for national censuses of agriculture use different size categories to record farm numbers, and differ in the minimum size that is to be recorded as a farm. There are also differences in the area counted as farm area; some censuses include woodland and rough grazing, some do not. Thus, the mean size of holding is a far from accurate measure. None the less, there are very substantial differences between Western Europe, and North America and Australasia. In 1980 none of the countries in the latter area had a mean size below 200 ha, none in the former area (except the United Kingdom), a mean size over 35 ha (Figure 12.6). Although there is no linear relationship between farm size and agricultural density, size is clearly partly a function of agricultural density. In the future it is likely that further decline in the agricultural population, and the continuance of the advantages of economies of scale for large farms will lead to further increases in the mean size of holding in both Europe and North America, but the difference in size between the two regions is likely to persist for some time.

Other studies of farm size covering countries in the developing world, suggest that population density is an important, but not the sole, determinant of farm size. Mean size of holding in the major regions is loosely related to population density (Table 12.5). Asia has the smallest farms, Australasia and the Americas the largest. But as noted earlier, population density is not the sole determinant of farm size. In Latin America, the original allocation of very large land grants to the early Spanish and Portuguese settlers has been a major significant factor determining farm size. In Africa, the mean size of holding is below the figure population

Table 12.5 Mean size of holding, 1960 and 1970 (hectares)

Australia and New Zealand	195.0
Canada and the USA	185.0
South America	68.0
Central America	14.5
Western Europe	13.1
Eastern and Southern Europe	7.7
Africa	3.7
Asia	2.7

Source: Food and Agriculture Organization, *Production Yearbook 1973*, vol. 27 Rome, 1974, p. 8

density might suggest. This may be because the simple implements most African farmers still use make it difficult for a family to cultivate more than a few hectares. It should also be recalled that in many parts of the developing world, in contrast to the developed, the mean size of holding is declining.

Land supply and the choice of technology

The great difference in the amount of land available to farmers in Western Europe and the European areas overseas has often been noted; many have argued that this difference will influence the farmers' economic aims and their choice of technology. In the more densely populated countries land is costly and labour relatively abundant and cheap. The farmer will thus select

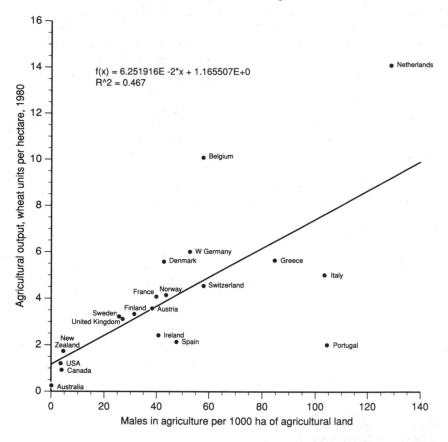

$f(x) = 6.251916E\,\text{-}2^{*}x + 1.165507E+0$
$R^2 = 0.467$

Figure 12.7 Agricultural output per hectare and the density of the agricultural labour force, 1980 (number of males employed in agriculture per 1000 hectares of agricultural land)
Source: Y. Hayami and V.W. Ruttan *Agricultural Development: An International Perspective*, Baltimore, Johns Hopkins University Press, 1985

those enterprises that give a high return per hectare, and will spend much on inputs that increase crop yields, such as fertilizers, pesticides and herbicides. In contrast, farmers with large areas of land at their disposal can gain large total incomes even if they practise enterprises with a low return per hectare. They concentrate on maximizing output per capita, spend much on labour-saving machinery and less on yield-increasing inputs. This is to some extent borne out by present conditions, for there is a positive, if weak, relationship between the value of output per hectare and agricultural population density (Figure 12.7).

There is a substantial difference between output per hectare in the USA, Canada and Australia, and the more densely populated parts of Europe. The United Kingdom, with the largest farms and one of the lowest

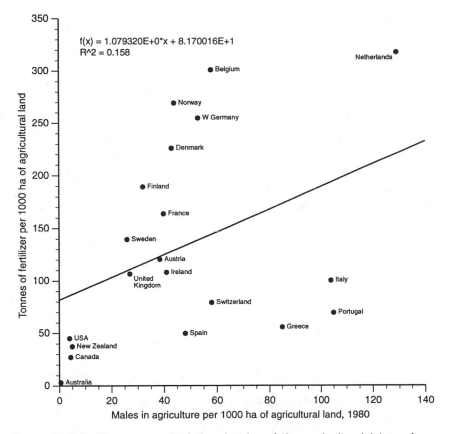

Figure 12.8 Fertilizer usage and the density of the agricultural labour force, 1980
Source: Y. Hayami and V.W. Ruttan *Agricultural Development: An International Perspective*, Baltimore, Johns Hopkins University Press, 1985

densities in Europe, lies nearer the extensive farming of overseas settlements than the intensive farming of the Netherlands. The major yield-increasing input in agriculture is fertilizer. Fertilizer usage is certainly low in the overseas countries, and higher in every European country, but there is only a very weak relationship with density (Figure 12.8). This relationship is least close in the poorer (in 1980) economies of the Mediterranean basin where fertilizer consumption is much less than density would predict.

It might be expected that in more sparsely populated countries the value of agricultural output would be high per capita of the workforce, and in densely populated countries it would be low, and this is borne out by the data for 1980 (Figure 12.9). Output per capita is higher in Canada, New Zealand, Australia and the USA than anywhere in Europe, and the lowest

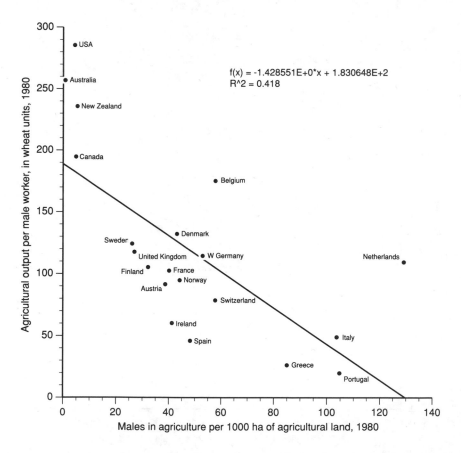

Figure 12.9 Agricultural output per capita and the density of the agricultural labour force, 1980
Source: Y. Hayami and V.W. Ruttan, *Agricultural Development: An International Perspective*, Baltimore, Johns Hopkins University Press, 1985

outputs are found in the more densely populated countries of Greece, Italy and Portugal, although the Netherlands is anomalous.

High outputs per capita have been obtained by the adoption of labour-saving machinery. The amount of tractor power per capita is inversely related to the density of the male agricultural labour force (Figure 12.10). However, although the USA and Canada with among the lowest densities, have the greatest tractor power per worker, Australia and New Zealand although much more sparsely populated than Europe, have less tractor power available than a number of more densely populated countries. This may be partly explained by the fact that tractors are only one of a great range of machines used on modern farms. But it also reflects the fact that since the 1950s the differences in agricultural productivity between Europe

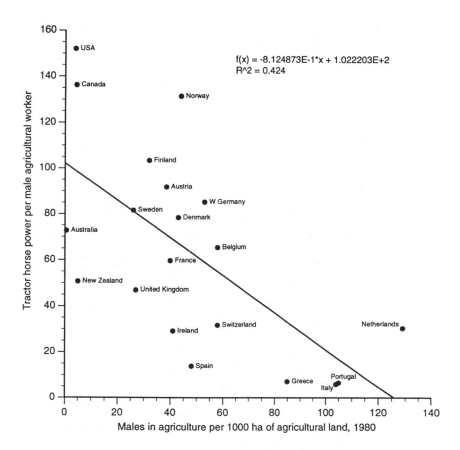

Figure 12.10 Tractor horsepower per male agricultural worker and male workers in agriculture per 1000 hectares of agricultural land, 1980
Source: Y. Hayami and V.W. Ruttan, Agricultural Development: An International Perspective, Baltimore, Johns Hopkins University Press, 1985

and its overseas settlements have diminished. In North America there has been an increase in yield-increasing inputs, in Europe there has been an widespread adoption of machinery in spite of the prevalence of small farms. With a long period of state subsidy European farmers have striven not only to increase inputs per acre, but with the decline in labour, have had to adopt machinery to increase output per capita.

CONCLUSIONS

Clearly, population density – or more exactly agricultural population density – has a marked effect upon the type of farming. In the densely populated areas it encourages intensification but has adverse consequences for structure and land use, and the densely populated agricultural regions of the world are for the most part regions of poverty. In the developed world the declining agricultural labour force has led to changes in farm size and the type of technology that can be related to the differences in density.

SOURCES AND FURTHER READING

H. Beguin, 'Densité de population, productivitié et développement agricole', *L'Espace Géographique*, 1974, vol. 3, pp. 267–72.

E. Boserup, *The Conditions of Agricultural Growth: The Economics of Agrarian Change under Population Pressure*, London, George Allen & Unwin, 1965.

E. Boserup, *Population and Technological Change: A Study of Long Term Trends*, Chicago, Chicago University Press, 1981.

H.C. Brookfield, 'Intensification and disintensification in Pacific agriculture', *Pacific Viewpoint*, 1972, vol. 13, pp. 30–48.

R. Calmes, 'L'évolution des structures d'exploitation dans les pays de la CEE', *Annales de Géographie*, 1981, vol. 90, pp. 401–27.

D.G. Dalrymple, *Survey of Multiple Cropping in Less Developed Nations*, Washington, DC, United States Department of Agriculture, Foreign Economic Development Service, 1971.

M.M. Das, 'Population pressure and intensity of cropping in Assam', *Geographical Review of India*, 1979, vol .41, pp. 105–14.

B.A. Datoo, 'Relationship between population density and agricultural systems in the Uluguru mountains, Tanzania', *Journal of Tropical Geography*, 1976, vol. 42, pp. 1–12.

B.A. Datoo, 'Towards a reformulation of Boserup's theory of agricultural change', *Economic Geography*, 1978, vol. 54, pp. 135–44.

F. Dovring, 'The share of agriculture in a growing population', *Monthly Bulletin of Agricultural Economics and Statistics*, 1959, vol. 8, pp. 1–11.

F. Dovring, *Land and Labour in Europe in the Twentieth Century: A Comparative Survey of Recent Agrarian History*, The Hague, Nijhoft, 1965.

J.F. Eder, 'Agricultural intensification and the returns to labour in the Philippine swidden system', *Pacific Viewpoint*, 1977, vol. 18, pp. 1–21.

Food and Agriculture Organization, *Agricultural Structure Study No. 1*, Rome, 1961.

M.B. Gleave and H.P. White, 'Population density and agricultural systems in West

Africa', in M.F. Thomas and G.W. Whittington (eds), *Environment and Land Use in Africa*, London, Methuen, 1969, pp. 273–300.

D.B. Grigg, 'Trends in the world's agricultural population', *Geography*, 1971, vol. 56, pp. 320–5.

D.B. Grigg, 'Agricultural populations and economic development', *Tijdschrift voor Economische en Sociale Geografie*, 1974, Vol. 65, pp. 414–20.

D.B. Grigg, 'Population growth and agrarian change', *Progress in Geography*, 1976, vol. 8, pp. 135–76.

D.B. Grigg, 'Ester Boserup's theory of agrarian change: a critical review', *Progress in Human Geography*, 1979, vol. 3, pp. 64–85.

D.B. Grigg, 'Agriculture in the world economy: an historical geography of decline', *Geography*, 1992, vol. 77, pp. 210–222.

A.T. Grove, 'Population densities and agriculture in Northern Nigeria', in K.M. Barbour and R.M. Prothero (eds), *Essays in African Population*, London, Routledge & Kegan Paul, 1961, pp. 115–36.

Y. Hayami and V.W. Ruttan, *Agricultural Development: An International Perspective*, Baltimore, Johns Hopkins University Press, 1985.

Y. Huang, 'On some determinants of farm size across countries', *American Journal of Agricultural Economics*, 1973, vol. 55, pp. 89–92.

J.S. Levi, 'Population pressure and agricultural change in the land intensive economy', *Journal of Development Studies*, 1976, vol. 13, pp. 61–78.

B. Lynch, *Indonesia: Problems and Prospects*, Malvern, Victoria, Sorret, 1977.

L. Manderson, *Overpopulation in Java: Problems and Reactions*, Canberra, Australian National University, Department of Demography, 1974.

W.B. Morgan and J.C. Pugh, *West Africa*, London, Methuen, 1969.

J.E. Schwartzburg, 'Agricultural labour in India: a regional analysis with particular reference to population growth', *Economic Development and Cultural Change*, 1963, vol. 16, pp. 337–52.

Sie Kwat Soen, *Prospects of Agricultural Development in Indonesia with Special Reference to Java*, Wageningen, Centre for Agricultural Publishing, 1968.

N.V. Sovani, 'A comparative study of population growth and agricultural change in some countries of the ECAFE region', in A.J. Coale (ed.), *Economic Factors in Population Growth*, London, Macmillan, 1976, pp. 273–92.

B.L. Turner, R.O. Hanham and A.V. Portaro, 'Population pressure and agricultural intensity', *Annals of the Association of American Geographers*, 1977, vol. 67, pp. 384–96.

W. Zelinsky, L.A. Kosinski and R.M. Prothero (eds), *Geography and a Crowding World*, Oxford, Oxford University Press, 1970.

Chapter 13

Farm size and landownership

Spatial differences in farm size and landownership are one of the most distinctive features of the agricultural geography of the world. Not only are there marked differences between continents in average size of holding (Table 13.1), but also within countries. For example, in England and Wales, large farms are more important in the east and the south-east than in the west; yet within the region dominated by large farms lies the fenland with its much smaller farms. Differences in landownership are also often a prominent feature of the agricultural landscape. Thus in the USA share-croppers are still found in the south, while in the north-east occupier-owners predominate. In Africa, there is a great difference between the systems of communal ownership found among the indigenous peoples, and (where they survive) the holdings of Europeans. Farm size and ownership must be considered when comparing two areas; they also affect other variables, influencing the type of crop chosen, the intensity with which it is grown and the efficiency of production.

THE SIZE OF FARMS

The size distribution of farms can be measured either by the percentage of the total *area* occupied by each size class, or by the percentage of the total *numbers* in each size class (Table 13.1). Invariably a small proportion of the number of farms occupy a disproportionately large proportion of the area, whilst even when small farms form a great majority of all farms, they often occupy a small proportion of the area. This discrepancy is at its most extreme in Central and South America where the landownership system imposed by the Spanish and Portuguese in the sixteenth and seventeenth centuries survives. Most of the land is divided into relatively large estates, occupying most of the agricultural land, but the majority of the farms are smallholdings that account for a very small proportion of the land. Although this discrepancy is found in every region, it is less marked in Europe, Asia and Africa where farms of under 10 hectares are

Table 13.1 Farm size distribution by regions, *c.* 1970, percentage of total

	Under 5 ha	5–10	10–50	50–100	100–500	500–1000	1000 & over
Africa							
Area	48.6	14.4	14.7	2.1	3.3	1.4	15.5
Numbers	91.5	5.6	2.7	0.1	0.1	–	–
Central America							
Area	1.8	1.1	4.6	3.9	11.3	7.1	70.2
Numbers	73.3	8.5	11.1	2.6	2.8	0.5	0.8
South America							
Area	2.0	2.0	11.7	7.7	23.5	10.8	42.3
Numbers	48.7	13.7	25.3	5.3	–	0.8	0.6
Asia							
Area	46.5	20.6	26.0	4.6	1.0	0.3	1.0
Numbers	89.6	6.7	3.6	0.1	–	–	–
Europe							
Area	13.7	15.4	36.4	9.4	14.7	2.2	8.2
Numbers	65.9	16.4	15.8	1.2	0.6	–	–
Australasia							
Area	–	–	0.4	0.7	4.8	4.1	90.0
Numbers	13.1	7.1	19.3	13.1	28.7	8.5	10.2
North America							
Area	0.1	0.25	5.5	10.2	40.0	9.5	34.4
Numbers	7.0	5.5	31.7	23.1	28.9	2.3	1.5

Source: Food and Agriculture Organization, *1970 World Census of Agriculture: Analyses and International Comparison of Results*, Rome, 1981

a large majority of all farms, but also occupy a substantial proportion of the land.

Very large farms – over 500 hectares – dominate the farm size distribution of Central and South America, Australasia and North America, accounting for more than half the agricultural land. The very large farm – state and collective farms – occupies an even greater proportion of the agricultural land in Eastern Europe and the former Soviet Union (not included in Table 13.1). Small farms – under 10 hectares – occupy half or more of the agricultural area in Africa and Asia, and nearly a third in Europe. However, in Europe it is the small medium-sized farm that is dominant, occupying a third of the area; very large farms account for only a tenth.

A rather different pattern emerges if the distribution by farm numbers is considered. In Asia and Africa nine-tenths of all holdings are less than

5 hectares, three-quarters in Central America, nearly two-thirds in Europe and a half in South America. In China since the abolition of the communes in 1985, it is estimated that there are 180 million farms averaging only 0.5 hectares in size. Only in Australasia and North America is the smallest category unimportant.

It might be thought then that the world's land use pattern is dominated by the very large farm, but its social structure by the farmer with a very small holding. Certainly farms over 1000 hectares occupy half the total land in farms (Table 13.2). However, very considerable proportions of the larger holdings are grass or rough grazing, particularly in Australasia and Latin America. If farms are measured by their arable land only then 70 per cent is on farms of less than 50 hectares, 45 per cent on farms of less than 10 hectares. Thus it is comparatively small farms that account for most of the world's crop production.

The reasons for the wide regional variations in farm size – which occur within countries as well as between continents – are numerous, and can only be touched upon here. Population density is a prime factor, with the lowest average sizes in the more densely populated regions. Land tenure is important, as already noted in the case of Latin America and the Soviet Union. Inheritance systems may be significant. Where owner-occupied farms are passed on at the death of a farmer, primogeniture, where only the eldest son inherits, gives rise to larger farms than partible inheritance, where the land is divided amongst all the children. This is a partial explanation of the greater average size of farm in England than in the rest of Western Europe, and the marked difference in size between West and East Germany.

Table 13.2 Distribution of total land and arable land by size of holding, 42 countries

	Total land in holding %	Arable land %
Under 1 ha	1.7	5.6
1–2 ha	2.3	7.4
2–5 ha	5.8	16.2
5–10 ha	6.3	15.6
10–20 ha	6.3	14.3
20–50 ha	6.8	11.8
50–100 ha	4.5	5.7
100–200 ha	4.8	4.2
200–500 ha	6.2	4.6
500–1000 ha	5.1	4.4
1000 ha & over	50.2	10.1

Source: Food and Agriculture Organization, World Census of Agriculture: Analyses and International Comparison of Results, Rome, 1981

The size of farm has a number of important effects upon agriculture. First, it affects the farmer's standard of living. In many parts of Asia a large proportion of the farms, however intensively farmed, are too small to provide an adequate supply of food for the farmer's family (see Chapter 12), and they have to seek other sources of income by working upon larger farms or in nearby towns. In Western Europe, the problem of the small farm is not one of providing enough food, but of producing an income comparable with that obtainable in other parts of the economy. In the last thirty years the incomes of small farmers have fallen below the incomes of those employed in industry. In Britain, many farmers with less than 40 ha, particularly those on poor soils, earn less than an agricultural labourer. In 1989, the farm with less than 5 ha was a considerable proportion of all farms in most parts of the EEC and only in exceptional circumstances can such farms provide an income comparable to that obtained in other parts of the economy (Table 13.3).

Second, farm size influences the type of farming practised. In the developing countries, occupiers of a hectare or less are rarely able to buy their food, and have to use all their land for growing crops. They are unable to spare land for cash crops or for fodder crops. Consequently such livestock as they have are poorly fed and give low yields of milk and meat. In Western Europe, the problem of the farmer with little land is different. To obtain an adequate income the farmer must choose an enterprise with a high net return per hectare (such as dairying or horticulture), yet soils or location may make this difficult (Table 7.1, p. 72). On large farms, however, farmers can generate a good income even with

Table 13.3 Farm size distribution in Western Europe, 1989

	Number of farms in each class as a percentage of all farms			
	1–5 ha	5–20 ha	20–50 ha	50 ha and over
UK	13.5	27.7	25.4	33.3
Luxembourg	18.9	22.3	32.5	26.2
Denmark	1.7	41.6	39.4	17.2
France	18.2	30.8	32.8	18.1
Ireland	16.1	44.4	30.3	9.0
Netherlands	24.9	43.4	27.3	4.4
Belgium	27.7	42.6	23.9	5.8
West Germany	29.4	39.7	24.8	6.1
Italy	67.9	25.6	4.6	1.9
Greece	69.4	27.6	2.5	0.5
Spain	53.3	31.3	9.4	6.0
Portugal	72.5	22.2	3.4	1.9
European 12	49.2	30.3	13.7	6.8

Source: Commission of the European Communities, *The Agricultural Situation in the Community, 1992 Report*, Brussels, 1993, pp. T122/123

enterprises with a comparatively low net return per hectare, such as cereals. For some enterprises, such as sheep rearing, returns per hectare are so low that few British farms are large enough to give an adequate income. However, in many sparsely occupied areas, such as Australia and Latin America, very large holdings are devoted to sheep or cattle. Although returns per hectare may be very low, total farm income is high.

Third, farm size in both the developed and the developing countries is an important determinant of intensity. On small farms in Kenya labour inputs per hectare increase as farm size decreases (Table 13.4). In India the index of multiple cropping and the proportion of land irrigated is higher on small than larger farms (Table 13.5), and on both the value of output per hectare diminishes as farms increase in size. However, generally the value of output *per capita* declines with an increase in farm size. High labour intensities are found on the small farms of Asia and Africa, because the use of labour is the main means of increasing output per hectare; farmers will utilize their labour force to maximize total gross output per hectare. They do not cease to work when marginal input equals marginal revenue (Chapter 7). In developed countries, small farmers have to select those enterprises that have a high net return per hectare, and these are invariably the more labour-intensive types of farming.

Fourth, efficiency of output is related to the size of farm. Efficiency is difficult to define, but is commonly measured by relating the value of total output to the value of all inputs. This ratio is held to increase as farms become larger, because of economies of size. Thus, overheads such as the cost of maintaining buildings are lower per hectare on a large farm than on a small one. Machinery can be more fully utilized; there is little point in having a combine harvester for a hectare of wheat, or a milking parlour for

Table 13.4 Farm size, output and labour intensity on settlement schemes in Kenya, 1967–8

Farm size class (acres)	Gross output (Kenyan shillings per acre)	Labour inputs (Men equivalent per 1000 acres)
Less than 10	635	808
10–19.9	250	399
20–29.9	156	234
30–39.9	161	159
40–49.9	113	124
50–59.9	98	111
60–69.9	98	109
70 or more	111	70

Source: W.M. Senya, 'Kenya's agricultural sector', in J. Heyer, J.K. Maitha and W.M. Senya, *Agricultural Development in Kenya. An Economic Assessment*, Nairobi, Oxford University Press, 1976

Table 13.5 Farm size and intensity in India, 1970–1

	Value of output (rupees per hectare)	Cropping index	Percentage of area irrigated
Under 2 ha	2026	151	50
2–6 ha	1651	139	51
6–10 ha	1253	128	38
10 ha and over	924	121	29

Source: G. Etienne, *India's Changing Rural Scene*, Delhi, Oxford University Press, 1982

a couple of cows. Farmers with large farms can often negotiate lower prices for the purchase of fertilizers or feeds in bulk; the small farmer, with more modest requirements, has to pay a higher price. He or she may well also find it more difficult to obtain credit. On the large farms found in some parts of Britain, the labour force is large enough for individual workers to specialize in a particularly activity, and so become more efficient, while the farmer has no need to do manual labour and can improve his or her management techniques. On very large farms, however, the costs of supervision and the difficulties of controlling very large areas and labour forces may reduce efficiency; this undoubtedly occurred on the very large state farms in the former USSR. On the smaller farms in Britain and elsewhere the principal cause of low efficiency is that the farmer does not have enough land to occupy his or her labour and that of the family throughout the year, so that labour costs per unit of output are high. The optimum size of farm – that which maximizes efficiency – varies for different types of farming: it is smaller for dairying than for cereal cropping, and for some types of farming the advantages accruing to size diminish beyond a certain point (Figure 13.1). It should be noted, however, that most of the economies of size potentially available to farmers can be obtained on comparatively small farms. In the USA in the 1970s 90 per cent of the possible economies of size were available on farms of just over 300 acres.

THE LAYOUT OF FARMS

In Britain and the USA, most farms consist of a house and buildings surrounded by land divided into separate fields, the block of land being clearly distinguished from adjacent farms by a fence, hedge, wall or wire. This is not so in much of Western Europe or Asia. Here the farm buildings are in a central village which is surrounded by many small fields, and the fields of each farmer are not next to each other, but are intermixed with those of other farmers (Figure 13.2). This dispersal or scattering of the plots or fields that make up a farm is called fragmentation. It was more common in the past in Europe when the open-field system prevailed. In

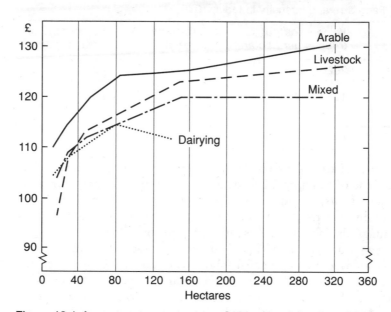

Figure 13.1 Average gross output per £100 of input by size of farm and by type
of farming
After Office for the Minister of Science, *Scale of Enterprise in Farming*, London,
HMSO, 1961

the nineteenth century, land in Britain, Denmark, southern Sweden and
northern Germany was enclosed, and the scattered plots of an individual
farmer consolidated, so that he received a compact block of land. However,
consolidation was slow in the rest of Western Europe – and indeed Eastern
and Southern Europe – so that as recently as the 1950s much of Europe's
farmland was still held in scattered, small and narrow fields.

The reasons for fragmentation are not clear. It is not simply a result of the
fossilization of the open-field system, for it is also found in Asia and Africa.
One possible explanation is partible inheritance. Where, at the death of a
farmer, the land is divided among the sons or all the children, not only does
the farm become subdivided, but the heirs may share the better and poorer
land equally, so causing scattering. In periods of rapid population growth
both the subdivision of farms and the fragmentation of plots increases.
Fragmentation may also occur because farmers want a share of soils of
different types; a farmer may want some good well-drained arable land and
also wetter land, near a river, for meadow. In Asia, where irrigated land is of
great value, and where not all the village land is irrigated, it is likely that each
farmer will have a share of both irrigated and dry land. Thus, scattering may
be a conscious insurance against risk. If a farmer's land is on different soils

Figure 13.2 The fragmentation of farms in a Belgian community, 1949
After W.S. and E.S. Woytinsky, *World Population: Trends and Outlook*, New York,
The Twentieth Century Fund, 1953

and in different parts of the village land, the farmer may avoid complete
disaster if there is flooding, localized frost, hail, or plant or animal disease.

Whatever the reasons for fragmentation, it has drawbacks for modern
farming, retarding improvement and reducing efficiency. A farmer with
widely spaced plots wastes time travelling from plot to plot, and the cost of
moving machines and fertilizers is high. Most fragmented farms consist of
small and often narrow fields, and the difficulties of moving machinery are

considerable; not only is time wasted moving from field to field, but in small fields much time is spent simply turning tractors round. A notable feature of modern British agriculture is the removal of field boundaries to reduce this loss of work-time. This is not possible, of course, if the farm is highly fragmented, as is still the case in some parts of Europe. The desire to use machinery is probably the most powerful motive for consolidation. The intermixture of fields also makes it more difficult to prevent the spread of plant and animal disease, and also weeds, for farmers are victims of the least efficient neighbour. A further drawback is the loss of potential crop land in the proliferation of field boundaries and paths.

In the last thirty years, there have been attempts to consolidate fragmented holdings in many parts of the world, but particularly in Europe. Ironically, fragmentation now seems to be on the increase in Britain and the USA, where it has not hitherto been a problem. Modern farming in both countries needs machinery, which must not be under-utilized, thus farmers are constantly seeking to add to their land. Farm size in both countries – and indeed elsewhere – has been increasing, but farmers are not always able to buy or rent land adjacent to their existing farm, and have often acquired land at some considerable distance from it. This of course increases fragmentation; some argue that the benefits which accrue to the use of larger amounts of land with the stock of machinery are offset by the costs of movement and the increased difficulties of supervision.

LANDOWNERSHIP AND FARMING

There are few reliable statistics on the world pattern of land tenure. However, a survey based on the 1950 World Agricultural Census (which excluded the Communist countries) estimated that 68 per cent of the 988 million ha surveyed were farmed by occupier-owners, and 26 per cent by tenants. Since then the numbers who are occupier-owners have increased. In the developed countries, greater prosperity has allowed some tenants to buy their land. In England and Wales, for example, occupier-owners now hold 60 per cent of the farmland, compared with only one-tenth in 1900. In many developing countries in the 1950s and 1960s, notably in Iran, Japan and Taiwan, land reform schemes made tenants into freeholders by compulsory purchase or expropriation. However, in Communist countries, both occupier-owners and landlords have lost land; private property has been largely extinguished, and all agricultural land is the property of the state. Some 28 per cent of the world's total agricultural area is now in Communist or ex-Communist countries.

Although many believe that land tenure is a primary barrier to agricultural progress, and the redistribution of land is necessary for social justice, it is less easy to point to any obvious effects upon the type of crops grown or livestock kept. The principal consequences of land ownership differences are upon the control of decision-making and upon the farmers' willingness to innovate. In areas where the occupier-owner predominates, the decisions are made by the farmer and in most areas of tenancy the occupier is in control of the majority of decisions upon the farm. Where share-cropping is practised – a system where the landlord provides land and sometimes part of the seed, fertilizer and equipment, in return for a share of the harvest – the landlord may decide what is grown. But it is in the former Communist countries that many decisions about what, and how, to grow were taken not on the farm but in central planning offices. The system of agriculture in the former Soviet Union illustrates this.

Two types of farm were found in the Soviet Union: the collective and the state farm. The former was run by a committee of members of the collective, the latter by a manager with hired agricultural workers. National targets for agricultural output were established by the Ministry of Agriculture in each of the Five Year Plans. The targets were allocated to major regions, and then to lesser administrative regions, until eventually each farm received its targets. Both state and collective farms were required to deliver grain quotas to the state at fixed prices, any surplus above quota being sold to the state marketing system at more flexible prices. A third component of the system was the private plot to which all members of collectives and state farms were entitled. Although these occupied only 3 per cent of the sown area of the Soviet Union, they produced in 1988 26 per cent of total output. This is perhaps not surprising for the private plots produced a high proportion of vegetables, milk, meat and eggs, and accounted for 40 per cent of all the hours worked on Soviet land.

The centralized nature of Soviet agriculture has had numerous consequences for its agricultural geography. Three only are noted here. First, Soviet economists believed that farms could produce economies of scale comparable to those obtained in industry. As a result, the average size of farms has steadily risen since the 1930s; collectives in 1986 averaged 6360 ha and state farms 15,640 ha. Except for the private plots, there are no small or medium-sized farms, comparable with the family farms of Western Europe, or even with the larger family farms of the USA. Second, planners have always argued that there are few natural drawbacks to the expansion of the cultivated area in the Soviet Union, and so increases in output were obtained by bringing more land into cultivation; the Virgin Lands scheme of the 1950s added 40 million ha in a few years, but in areas with very low rainfall. As a result, measures to increase output per hectare have received less attention. This is in marked contrast to Western Europe where, in the last thirty years, the growth of output has been almost entirely due to yield increases; marginal land has been abandoned and land lost to urban expansion. Third, the centralized system has made it difficult to establish regional specialization, growing crops in those regions most suited to them. This is partly because national targets tend to be divided among regions in proportion simply to their area, rather than their climatic suitability, and partly because the state and collective farms pay no rent. There is thus no way in farm accountancy to allow for differences in environment, although attempts have been made to produce land classification maps to promote regional specialization.

The collapse of Communism in Eastern Europe and the former Soviet Union has not yet led to any radical change in the system; some private farms have been formed, generally only on the poorer land. However, in the late 1970s there were radical changes in the organization of farming in China. The commune was replaced by the household as the unit of direction, and farmers were allowed to sell their produce rather than deliver it to the state. The result was a great increase in output and productivity.

Differences between tenancy and occupier-ownership in the rest of the world produce less marked economic consequences. Where tenants are protected from excessive rents, and are compensated for improvements if they give up the lease of a farm (as they are in most of North America and Western Europe), then there are few differences in productivity or the type of farming followed. However, where tenancy systems leave the tenant prey to exorbitant rents or eviction, as they still do in parts of Asia and especially in Latin America, then there is little incentive for the tenant to improve farming methods, and tenurial conditions are a primary cause of backward agriculture. In some types of tenancy – notably share-cropping – the landlord rather than the tenant may decide what is grown and how it is grown.

Communal agriculture is far less common that it was, but is still found in parts of Africa. Here, land is the property of the group; each member of the tribe or village has the right to some land, and the land cannot be sold. Although such systems may ensure the well-being of all in the group, they do not work satisfactorily when population pressure increases, or when farming becomes commercialized. Thus in much of Africa such systems are being replaced by individual property rights, just as common land was in nineteenth-century Europe.

THE MODERNIZATION OF AGRICULTURE AND THE ORGANIZATION OF PRODUCTION

One of the most striking features of the past forty years has been the farmers' growing dependence upon inputs purchased from industry, and the greater proportion of farm output that is processed in some way in the food manufacturing sector. Indeed by the 1970s the agricultural input and the agricultural processing and distribution sectors produced a greater proportion of gross domestic product than production on the farm. This might be expected to lead to changes in the organization of production, and certainly most developed countries have experienced a decline in the number of small farms and an increase in the number of large. What also might be expected is the growth of vertical integration, where food manufacturers own and manage the land which produces the crops or animals that are processed. Sometimes firms such as these are referred to as agribusinesses, and it has been argued that they will eventually control large proportions of the farm output of US agriculture. This was already true of particular commodities such as broilers in the early 1980s. Another apparent sign of vertical integration was the growth of corporate farming, but most of these farm corporations are in fact family companies, which can benefit from tax and other allowances as companies rather than as individual proprietors. In 1979 only 6 per cent of US farm receipts went to true corporate farms; this type of farming is even less important in Western Europe. In most developed regions, however, contract farming is common, where particular crops such as peas or sugar-beet are grown by farmers under the fairly strict control of a food processor, but this is hardly a measure of vertical integration.

In the developing world corporate farming has perhaps made more progress. Many plantation crops have been produced by companies that own both the farm that produces the crop and the factory that processes it, generally for export to the USA or Western Europe. Such companies have been absorbed by large transnational agribusinesses that grow, process and market an increasing proportion of developing country agricultural exports.

CONCLUSION

It is perhaps easier to show how differences in ownership, farm size and layout affect productivity, rather than the selection of different types of crop or livestock. None the less, it is a factor that must always be considered when comparing one farming area with another.

SOURCES AND FURTHER READING

R.A. Berry and W.A. Cline, *Agrarian Structure and Productivity in Developing Countries. A Study prepared for the International Labour Office*, Baltimore, Johns Hopkins University Press, 1979.

D.K. Britton and B. Hill, *Size and Efficiency in Farming*, London, Saxon House, 1975.

R. Calmes, 'L'évolution des structures d'exploitation dans les pays de la CEE', *Annals de Géographie*, 1981, vol. 90, pp. 401–27.

W.J. Carlyle, 'Farm layouts in Manitoba', *Canadian Geographer*, 1983, vol. 27, pp. 17–34.

C.J.W. Edwards, 'The effects of changing farm size upon levels of fragmentation; a Somerset case study', *Journal of Agricultural Economics*, 1978, vol. 29, pp. 143–54.

B.H. Farmer, 'On not controlling subdivision in paddy-lands', *Transactions of the Institute of British Geographers*, 1960, vol. 28, pp. 225–35.

Food and Agriculture Organization, *World Agricultural Structure, Study No. 1*, Rome, 1961.

D.B. Grigg, 'Large and small farms in England and Wales; their size and distribution', *Geography*, 1963, vol. 48, pp. 268–79.

D.B. Grigg, 'The geography of farm size: a preliminary survey', *Economic Geography*, 1966, vol. 42, pp. 205–35.

B. Hill, 'The myth of the family farm: defining the family farm and assessing its importance in the European Community', *Journal of Rural Studies*, 1992, vol. 9, pp. 359–70.

Y. Huang, 'On some determinants of farm size across countries', *American Journal of Agricultural Economics*, 1973, vol. 65, pp. 89–92.

R. King, *Land Reform: A World Survey*, London, Bell, 1977.

R. King and S. Burton, 'Land fragmentation; notes on a fundamental rural spatial problem', *Progress in Human Geography*, 1982, vol. 6, pp. 475–94.

R. King and S. Burton, 'Stuctural change in agriculture: the geography of land consolidation', *Progress in Human Geography*, 1983, vol. 7, pp. 471–501.

A. Lambert, 'Farm consolidation in Western Europe', *Geography*, 1982, vol. 48, pp. 31–48.

D. Mazumdar, 'Size of farm and productivity: a problem in Indian peasant agriculture', *Economica*, 1965, vol. 32, pp. 161–73.

W. Morgan, G. Blunden and J.C. Greenwood, 'The role of the family farm in agrarian change', *Progress in Human Geography*, 1993, vol. 17, pp. 22–42.

J. Naylon, 'Land consolidation in Spain', *Annals of the Association of American Geographers*, 1959, vol. 49, pp. 361–73.

Office for the Minister of Science, *Scale of Enterprise in Farming*, London, Her Majesty's Stationery Office, 1961.

J. Pallot and D.J.B. Shaw, *Planning in the Soviet Union*, London, Croom Helm, 1981.

C.W. Pannell, 'Recent Chinese agriculture', *Geographical Review*, 1985, vol. 75, pp. 170–85.

F. Pope, *Agriculture in the United States and Soviet Union*, Washington DC, US Department of Agriculture, Foreign Agriculture Economic Report no. 92, 1977.

F.L. Pryor, 'An international perspective on land scattering', *Explorations in Economic History*, 1982, vol. 19, pp. 296–320.

D.J. Shaw, 'The problem of land fragmentation in the Mediterranean area: a case study', *Geographical Review*, 1963, vol. 53, pp. 40–51.

W.C. Thiesenhusen and J. Melmed-Sanjuk, 'Brazil's agrarian structure: changes from 1970 through 1980', *World Development*, 1990, vol. 18, pp. 393–415.

I. Wallace, 'Towards a geography of agribusiness', *Progress in Human Geography*, 1985, vol. 19, pp. 491–514.

Chapter 14

The diffusion of agricultural innovations

Most analyses of agricultural distributions concern themselves with the present alone, and this may be misleading. In Figure 14.1, the limit of a crop distribution lies at AB, some 50 km east of the coast on which there are a number of small ports. One possible explanation is that rainfall declines eastwards, and at AB yields are too low for its profitable cultivation. Alternatively, it may be that the product is perishable and, in the absence of refrigeration facilities on local trains and lorries, cannot be transported in fresh condition more than 50 km. But a consideration of earlier distributions of the crop might suggest a quite different reason for the present limit. Twenty-five years ago the crop was unknown, but was then introduced into the ports by immigrants. Farmers near the ports rapidly adopted the crop, and five years later its eastern limit was up to 10 km away (Figure 14.1). Its continued adoption by more distant farmers, who saw their neighbours growing the crop, explains its present limits. In ten years, if demand continues to grow, the eastern limit may lie 60 km from the coast. The crop, a cash crop for export, rarely occupies more than 30 per cent of a farmer's land. As the crop spreads eastwards, a transect from west to east (Figure 14.1) shows that farmers near the towns are the first to plant 30 per cent of their land in the crop. At some future time, all farmers may plant 30 per cent.

The diffusion of plants, animals and other agricultural innovations has long been a matter of interest to geographers, botanists, sociologists and anthropologists. More recently others have asked why it is that some farmers adopt a new method before others, and how the innovation spreads. Two distinct approaches have been adopted.

SOCIAL DIFFUSION

Rural sociologists and economists have asked why some farmers (a small percentage of the total) are always the first to adopt a new crop or method, while others are always last (Figure 14.2). It is argued that an adoption

Figure 14.1 Models of diffusion

curve, over time, shows a slow cumulative rate of adoption at first, when the innovators are the only ones to adopt it. Then the rate of adoption accelerates and finally slows when only the laggards are left.

Sociologists believe that this rate of adoption is a function of the flow of information. Innovators and some early adopters hear of the innovation from the radio, in farming magazines, from agricultural extension officers or from agents selling the new seed or fertilizer; late adopters, in contrast, hear of the innovation only from their neighbours, and adopt the innovation only after watching their neighbours' experience. The early adopters have a number of social characteristics in common. They are younger than average, better educated, have larger farms, are more business-like, have a high social standing, and mix more widely in the local community. Such

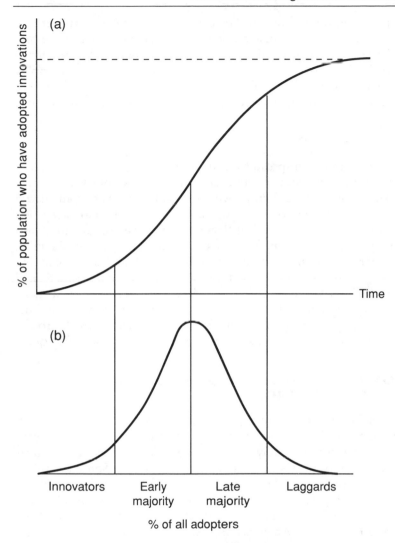

Figure 14.2 The adoption of an innovation (a) The adoption curve showing the cumulative percentage of all adopters who have adopted an innovation over time (b) Innovators and laggards as a percentage of all adopters

views have been much criticized by economists, who argue that adoption is determined primarily by a farmer's economic assessment of an innovation; if it will increase profit, it will be adopted. It has also been noticed that in developed countries most farmers, and not a minority, hear of an innovation directly rather than from neighbours, so that the information lag assumed by sociologists does not exist.

The characteristics of the innovation may also prove important in the rate at which an innovation spreads. For example, new seed or fertilizers are divisible, and can be tried in small amounts at low cost to see if they work. Combine harvesters or new buildings are costlier and have to be brought in one lump. Simple innovations are likely to be adopted before complex machinery, and innovations that fit easily into the existing farming system will be adopted before those that require major changes in farming routine.

SPATIAL DIFFUSION

A new crop or method can spread from its source region in two ways. First, it can be taken by farmers or others migrating to a new country. Much of North America's livestock and crops were brought by settlers from Britain and other West European countries, while the Spanish merino sheep was taken to Australia via South Africa. Second, new crops or methods also spread through an existing, settled population. One farmer grows the crop, neighbours observe and then adopt it themselves and so, like a ripple in a pool when a stone is dropped, the innovation spreads outwards. Spatial diffusion is rarely as simple as this: in particular, if a majority of farmers, rather than a minority, hear of the innovation and adopt it at the same time, there will not be the slow spread from farmer to farmer outwards from a limited source area that is assumed in most models of spatial diffusion.

THE DOMESTICATION OF PLANTS AND THEIR PRESENT DISTRIBUTION

All agricultural plants were originally wild; the earliest domestications took place some nine or ten thousand years ago. The places where they were domesticated were comparatively limited. Only a few regions have contributed domesticated plants to the farmer, South-West Asia, South-East Asia and Central America being the most important. Since then, crop plants have spread from their areas of domestication throughout the world. Much the same is true of the major domesticated animals, which were all indigenous to Eurasia; the Americas and Australasia had no horses, cattle or sheep until these were introduced by European settlers.

The principal farming regions now have a remarkable mixture of crops from different source regions. This is a result of several thousand years of diffusion which, however, was greatly accelerated by European expansion that began in the fifteenth century (Table 14.1). Only one-quarter of the crops grown in Europe north of the Alps are from plants indigenous to the region. The most important crops acquired from elsewhere were the cereals wheat, barley and oats – all indigenous to South-West Asia – which spread into Europe several thousand years ago. The most important subsequent introductions were the potato and maize, which are indigenous to Latin America. The potato was brought to Europe in the sixteenth century,

Table 14.1 Crop combinations of major regions by area of plant domestication (percentage of area in major crops)

	Indigenous	South-West Asia	South-East Asia	Latin America	Africa	Northern Europe	China	Other
South-West Asia	79.5	I*	3.2	9.1	1.9	4.1	–	0.2
South-East Asia	69.9	0.4	–	22.3	2.6	–	1.7	–
Latin America	48.0	14.4	14.4	–	9.1	1.7	0.9	2.1
Africa	41.8	3.7	7.0	39.7	–	0.2	–	4.0
Northern Europe	24.2	47.9	0.1	21.4	0.1	–	0.1	4.0
China	16.9	29.1	22.2	12.0	12.5	1.4	–	2.0
India	1.2	21.7	28.8	14.6	26.2	–	–	–
Mediterranean	1.6	67.6	0.6	16.8	–	7.5	–	–
North America	0.1	40.9	1.4	26.1	5.7	9.2	14.3	0.5
Australia	–	84.3	0.3	1.7	0.3	10.6	–	–

Note: *I = Indigenous
Source: D.B. Grigg, The Agricultural Systems of the World: An Evolutionary Approach, Cambridge, Cambridge University Press, 1974, p. 27

although it did not become an important food crop until the nineteenth century. Neither North America nor Australasia had indigenous crops of any significance. When Europeans first settled in the USA and Canada, they brought with them the crops of Western Europe, but they later adopted some of the crops grown by the Indians in the east, which in turn had been acquired from Central and Southern America. Of these crops, maize was by far the most important. African crop patterns were profoundly changed by the discovery of the Americas. American food crops such as manioc and maize were taken from Brazil to Africa in returning slave-ships, and in the nineteenth century the two crops spread inland to become staple crops. Rice was probably domesticated somewhere in mainland South-East Asia, and was carried north into China and west into India at a very early date.

The exchange of non-food crops has also been important. Rubber is indigenous to Central and South America, but was little used until the nineteenth century. The demand for rubber in Europe after the discovery of vulcanization was initially met by the collection of latex from rubber trees growing wild in the Amazon basin. Seeds of the tree were smuggled to Kew in London, and taken from there to Singapore, where they formed the basis for the remarkable expansion of rubber planting in the early twentieth century.

THE DIFFUSION OF HYBRID CORN IN THE USA

Until 1918, all corn sown in the USA was of the open pollinated variety. In that year it was shown that a cross between genetically unlike varieties was possible, and these hybrid varieties became commercially available by the 1930s. Hybrids could be bred for a specific locality, and they gave yields 15–20 per cent above open pollinated varieties. By the 1950s hybrid varieties had largely replaced the older varieties.

Hybrid corn was marketed by seed merchants. They first sold their seed in the heart of the Corn Belt, where a high proportion of total farm land was in corn, yields were highest and the potential profit to both farmer and merchant was greatest. It was here, too, that hybrids were most rapidly adopted. Iowa, for example, had only 6 per cent of its corn area in hybrids in 1934, but 80 per cent by 1939; Alabama, in contrast, did not have 5 per cent until 1947, and reached 80 per cent only in 1957. The spread of hybrid corn can be seen in Figure 14.3, where the date when a county first had 10 per cent of its total corn in hybrids is shown. Although the map indicates a slow spread outwards from the core area in the Corn Belt, as theory would suggest, there are some exceptions. First, the initial spread was more eastwards and westwards than southwards. This was because hybrid varieties were adapted to a particular growing season. Thus, it was easier for the early hybrids, bred for Iowa, to spread east and west, where the growing season was the same, than south, where the growing season was longer.

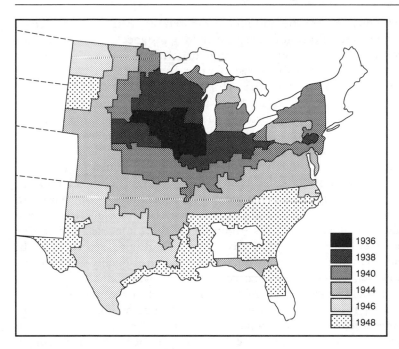

Figure 14.3 The diffusion of hybrid corn in the USA, 1936–48 The map shows
the year that a county first had 10 per cent of its total area in corn sown with
hybrid seed
After Z. Griliches, 'Hybrid corn and the economies of innovation', *Science*, 1960,
vol. 132, pp. 275–80

Second, between 1940 and 1944, hybrids spread rapidly south-west but not
south-eastwards. This seems to have been owing to the presence in the
south-west of efficient agricultural experimental stations that rapidly bred
seed adapted to local conditions. In the south-east, in contrast, there were
problems with plant disease and insects, while not only was a small
proportion of farmland in corn, but yields were low, so that potential
profit to both farmer and seed merchant was lower than elsewhere. So,
although the outward expansion of hybrid corn approximates the simple
model of spatial diffusion, there were important exceptions.

THE DIFFUSION OF CATTLE: HEREFORDS AND THE ABERDEEN ANGUS

Cattle, sheep, goats and pigs were all domesticated in Eurasia, and spread
slowly to other parts of the world. There were no sheep or cattle in the
Americas until Europeans arrived. The Portuguese and Spanish introduced
Longhorn cattle, which formed the basis of cattle stocks in much of North

and South America until the mid-nineteenth century. Although adapted to dry conditions, and tolerant of being driven long distances, they gave a poor quality meat. In the USA in the second half of the nineteenth century, Texas Longhorns formed the basis of great herds that grazed the open range from Texas northwards. These animals were driven to railheads and thence taken to the more humid Midwest where they were fattened for market. In the 1880s, Longhorns were replaced or crossbred with an imported English breed, the Hereford, to give a better quality beef.

A similar sequence occurred in Argentina. Before 1876, cattle in Argentina were predominantly of Longhorn or creole origin, and valued primarily for their hides (although some salted beef was exported). The introduction of refrigeration into ships gave Argentina an opportunity to send beef to Britain, the leading export market at the time. But creole cattle gave a poor quality beef. From the 1870s Argentine ranchers imported Shorthorns (and to a lesser extent Herefords) from Britain, and upgraded their herds. These cattle fattened more quickly and gave a better quality beef. Shorthorns, however, gave a great deal of fat, which was then acceptable in Britain as it could be made into suet and dripping. But the rise of incomes in Britain after 1918 saw an increased preference for lean and tender meat; at the same time, animal fats, which had been used as ingredients in the manufacture of soap, cooking oils and margarine, were increasingly replaced by synthetic detergents and vegetable oils. Since 1945, Argentina has ceased to rely upon Britain as a market, but similar trends are apparent in its other export markets where there is a similar preference for lean beef. The response in Argentina has been to increase the number of Aberdeen Angus in the national herds, for the Angus matures more rapidly than the Shorthorn, has less fat and a more tender beef. In 1930, the Angus represented only 4 per cent of the nation's cattle, by 1947 10 per cent, and by 1970 40 per cent. The Angus, essentially a beef animal, has made no progress in the dairying region near Buenos Aires, nor in the drier and cooler regions, where the hardier Hereford still predominates, but in the south-east of the pampas – the breeding region on which other rearing and fattening regions rely for their supply of stock – it made up 40 per cent or more of all cattle by 1960.

THE GREEN REVOLUTION IN ASIA

Most studies of the adoption of agricultural innovations have emphasized the lag in adoption between innovators and laggards, and the slow spatial diffusion – from neighbour to neighbour – outwards from a source area. Yet not all farmers wish to adopt all innovations, nor are all innovations suitable to all areas. The introduction of a new milking parlour is of little interest to cereal growers, and combine harvesters have no value to horticulturalists. Similarly, many innovations can only be adopted in suitable physical environments. Tropical crops cannot be transferred to the Arctic, not do animals bred for the cool, moist climates of Western Europe thrive in tropical regions. The adoption of improved hybrid wheats and rice in Asia since 1965 well illustrates that many agricultural innovations are specific to a particular type of environment.

New hybrid wheats from Mexico and hybrid rice bred in the Philippines were introduced into Asia in 1965. The new rice varieties had a number of advantages.

1 They were semi-dwarf, with a short, strong stalk that could carry a heavy head of grain. The long-stalked indigenous *indica* varieties collapsed under heavy grain yields, and could not be harvested.
2 They were more responsive to fertilizer than *indica*, giving a greater increase in output for each unit input of fertilizer.
3 They matured in a shorter time than most traditional varieties, allowing double cropping and hence an increase in the area sown in a year.
4 Unlike the traditional varieties they did not flower in response to day length; because they were photo-insentitive their sowing dates could be more flexible. If sown in the dry season (assuming irrigation was available) when cloud cover was less and the radiation received was greater, they could give higher yields than traditional varieties, which had to be grown in the monsoon which has extensive cloud cover.

The new varieties did not always give higher yields than traditional varieties if solely traditional methods of cultivation were followed. If, however, fertilizer and pesticides were used, and the water supply was adequate, they did perform dramatically better than the traditional varieties. Although there was a considerable increase in production cost, there was also a marked increase in net return per hectare.

There was a dramatic rise in the area under wheat and rice sown to the

Table 14.2 Percentage of area in crop sown with modern varieties

	1970–1	1976–7	1982–3
Rice			
China	n.d.	80.4	81.0
Rest of Asia	13.1	30.4	44.9
All Asia	n.d.	45.7	56.8
Wheat			
China	n.d.	25.0	30.6
Rest of Asia	39.1	72.4	79.2
All Asia	n.d.	48.4	48.7

Sources: D.G. Dalrymple, *Development and Spread of High Yielding Varieties of Wheat and Rice in the Less Developed Nations*, Washington, DC, 1978; M. Lipton, *New Seeds and Poor People*, London, Unwin Hyman, 1989

hybrid varieties between 1965 and 1977. By the latter year, 72 per cent of the wheat in Asia (excluding Communist countries) (Table 14.2) was sown to the new high-yielding varieties, as was 30 per cent of the rice: in the whole of Asia the figures were 45.7 per cent and 48.4 per cent respectively. However, in 1976/7 there were marked differences in the rate of adoption between countries, and between regions within countries (Figure 14.4). In Burma, for example, only 7 per cent of the rice area was sown with the new varieties; in the Phillipines, where the first successful hybrid rice, IR8, was bred, over two-thirds of the sown area was in the new varieties. Although the date of introduction was later in some countries (none was sown in South Korea until 1971/2), this was not the sole cause of the differences in the proportion sown in 1976/7.

Government influences were important: in India, for example, not only were extension agencies established to advise farmers, but fertilizers were subsidized, and the seed, initially, was free. Furthermore, India, unlike most

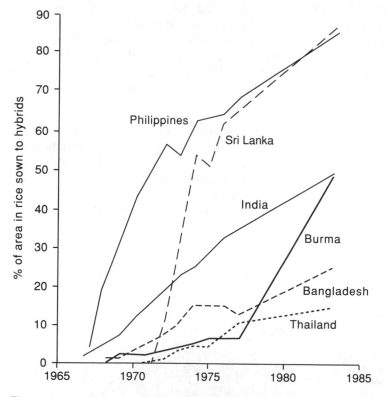

Figure 14.4 Increase in the area in hybrid rice in Asia, 1965–77
Source: D.G. Dalrymple, Development and Spread of High Yielding Varieties of Wheat and Rice in Less Developed Nations, Washington DC, US Department of Agriculture, 1978

Asian countries, had agricultural scientists who could breed varieties adapted to local conditions. Farm size may also have influenced the rate of adoption. Although in theory the new varieties could be as economically adopted on small farms as large – for there were no great economies of scale, and the inputs could be purchased in small amounts – there is some evidence that in the 1960s and early 1970s those with large farms were prepared to adopt the new package of inputs because they could borrow money to purchase it. Small farmers, on the other hand, could not bear the risk of borrowing. However, in the later 1970s there was little difference by farm size in the rate of adoption.

Of paramount importance was the availability of irrigation. Nearly all rice

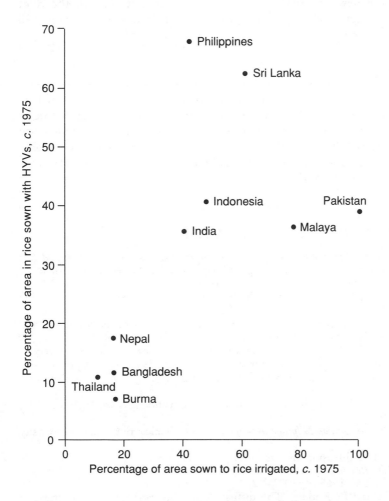

Figure 14.5 New high-yielding rice and irrigation in selected countries, 1975

in Asia is wet-rice, but only a third of it has reliable supplies of water during the growing season. Two-thirds rely upon rainfall from the monsoon, or the flooding rivers, and therefore are erratic and difficult to control. In these regions, the new varieties could not easily be adopted. In the flooded deltas, such as in Bangladesh or Thailand, only long-stalked varieties could be grown; the short-stalked hybrids would be drowned. Thus the adoption of hybrid rice shows a positive relationship to the proportion of the total rice area that is irrigated (Figure 14.5). This means that many of the more densely populated deltas and lower reaches of rivers, in most need of increased yields, have been slow to adopt the new varieties. In India on the lower plains and deltas of the Ganges, with problems of flooding in the monsoon, the new varieties were adopted less rapidly than in the drier middle and upper reaches – particularly in the Punjab – where tube-well irrigation was available.

CONCLUSIONS

Patterns of farming are constantly being changed by the adoption of new crops and new methods. The rate of adoption of innovations varies among farmers, according to their perception of the potential profit which will result. The spatial diffusion of an innovation takes some time to complete, so that at any one moment geographical limits of a crop or implement may be a result of the rate of diffusion, rather than of any climatic or economic factor.

SOURCES AND FURTHER READING

D.G. Dalrymple, *Development and Spread of High Yielding Varieties of Wheat and Rice in Less Developed Nations*, Washington, DC, United States Department of Agriculture, Foreign Economic Report no. 95, 1978.

D.G. Dalrymple, 'The adoption of high yielding grain varieties in developing nations', *Agricultural History*, 1979, vol. 53, pp. 704–26.

B.H. Farmer, 'The Green Revolution in South Asian rice fields: environment and production', *Journal of Development Studies*, 1979, vol. 15, pp. 304–19.

A. Findlay and D. Maclennan, 'Innovation diffusion at the micro-scale: a reconsideration of information and economic factors', *Area*, 1979, vol. 10, pp. 309–14.

R.D. Garst, 'Innovation diffusion among the Gusii of Kenya', *Economic Geography*, 1974, vol. 50, pp. 300–12.

Z. Griliches, 'Hybrid corn and the economics of innovation', *Science*, 1960, vol. 132, pp. 275–80.

T. Hägerstrand, *Innovation Diffusion as a Spatial Process*, Chicago, Chicago University Press, 1967.

G.E. Jones, 'The diffusion of agricultural innovations', in I. Burton and R.W. Kates (eds), *Readings in Resource Management and Conservation*, Chicago, Chicago University Press, 1965, pp. 475–92.

A.E. Joseph and P.D. Keddie, 'The diffusion of grain corn production through Southern Ontario, 1946–1971', *Canadian Geographer*, 1981, vol. 25, pp. 335–49.

C. Lado, 'Peasant farmers, rationality and the diffusion of agricultural innovations in Maridi district, Southern Sudan', *Malaysian Journal of Tropical Geography*, vol. 20, 1989, pp. 20–9.

M. Lipton, *New Seeds and Poor People*, London, Unwin Hyman, 1989.

J. Rigg, 'The Green Revolution and equity – who adopts the new rice varieties and why', *Geography*, 1989, vol. 74, pp. 144–50.

J. Rigg, 'The new rice technology of agrarian change: guilt by association', *Progress in Human Geography*, 1989, vol. 13, pp. 374–99.

A.B. Shaw, 'Approaches to agricultural technology adoption and consequences', *Geoforum*, 1987, vol. 18, pp. 1–19.

J.R. Tarrant, 'Maize: a new United Kingdom agricultural crop', *Area*, 1975, vol. 7, pp. 175–9.

T. Unwin, 'Household characteristics and agrarian innovation adoption in north-west Portugal', *Transactions of the Institute of British Geographers*, 1987, vol. 12, pp. 131–46.

M.D. Winsberg, 'The introduction and diffusion of the Aberdeen Angus in Argentina', *Geography*, 1970, vol. 55, pp. 187–95.

Chapter 15

The cultural framework of farming

In recent years there has been much criticism of economic determinism in agricultural geography and economics. It was seen earlier (Chapter 7) that many doubt that farmers are all profit maximizers. In developed countries farmers may prefer a secure and stable income to the risks of profit maximization; many farmers with smallholdings and low incomes choose to remain poor and independent, rather than leave farming to take a better paid job with an urban employer. In the developing countries many farmers aim to provide as much of their own food as possible, and thus aim to maximize output per hectare, not profit. But factors other than economic or environmental restraints may influence the farmer's behaviour.

In many parts of the world the traditional culture or way of life may require farmers to behave in an apparently non-rational (in the eyes of Western economists) manner. Such cultural factors have been much emphasized by anthropologists and sociologists who have worked in the developing countries, for they are thought to explain why there is relatively slow progress in agricultural productivity. In Africa, for example, kinship obligations rather than the market may determine the production of food crops. In India, caste may decide who works upon a farm or at a particular task, and in both Africa and Asia there are traditional agricultural roles for men and women which may impede efficiency and progress. The family and its needs are a powerful factor in traditional agricultural societies, and the way property is passed on to the next generation may have a profound effect upon the size of farms, their layout and their prosperity. In this chapter our concern is with how such cultural features may determine spatial variations in agriculture. Two examples only are considered: the influence of ethnic differences and of religion.

ETHNIC FACTORS AND FARMING

In countries where immigrant groups have settled on the land, they may bring with them techniques and crops that differ greatly from those of the indigenous population. This, rather than environment or the market, may account for features of the agricultural geography.

Malaysia

In the Malay Peninsula the indigenous Malays were primarily rice producers. In the late nineteenth century the British established rubber plantations and tin mines, and indentured labourers were brought from India and China to work in these enterprises. Many of these immigrants did not return to their countries, and some of their descendants have become farmers. The Malays remain primarily rice producers or rubber growers. The Chinese have not unnaturally become rice and also rubber growers, but they have additionally developed two types of production rarely pursued by Malays or Indians: intensive vegetables and pigs – both part of the Chinese agricultural tradition. The Malays, who are Muslims, will not keep pigs, and neither the Malays nor the Chinese milk livestock (see below, pp. 193–5). In both Malaysia and Singapore, the great majority of cows and water buffaloes are kept by people of Indian origin; the cows were originally imported from India. Goats are even more ethnically specific, being mainly kept for milk by Tamils.

The Americas

Ethnic origins are also a significant force in the agricultural geography of the Americas. In the USA, many historians have stressed the importance of different European immigrants in the rise of particular types of farming; the role of Scandinavians in the dairy industry has been emphasized. Although such factors have little contemporary significance, ethnic origins have great importance in understanding the broad pattern of farming in the Americas.

First, the original peoples, the Amerindians, had no plough, wheel, cattle, sheep, pigs or horses; their staple crops were maize, squash and beans in North and Central America, potatoes in the Andes, and manioc in the Amazon lowlands. Traditional agricultural systems, based upon the crops and methods the Amerindians practised before 1500, are still found widely.

Second, in North America, both the French in Quebec and the English in New England brought with them the idea of mixed farming, traditional European crops and livestock, and their initial systems of land holding, farm layout and village types were those of their homelands.

Third, further south, the English in the West Indies and in Virginia and the Carolinas at first tried to work smallholdings themselves, or with indentured labour from the British Isles. Later, however, slaves were imported from Africa, and the plantation system became established in the south of the USA, the West Indies and Brazil. At the abolition of slavery some plantations survived, with blacks becoming wage labourers; elsewhere share-cropping became the predominant mode, while in some regions freed slaves took up smallholdings to produce food crops and small amounts of cash crops. What was conspicuously absent from the plantation regions was the substantial middle-sized farm worked by its owner. However, this was typical of much of the northern USA.

Fourth, in Central and Southern America most of the land was seized by the Spanish and Portuguese in the sixteenth century. Two features of sixteenth-century Iberia were transplanted.

First, land was allocated in very large holdings; in addition the existing indigenous Indian population was used as a workforce, although they were not necessarily evicted from their own land. Thus a form of feudalism took root that has persisted to the present day.

Second, the Spanish and Portugese imported cattle from the south of Spain; they also brought methods of raising cattle which were typical of southern Spain in the sixteenth century but which were very different from the rest of Europe at that time. Cattle were allowed to run free on the open range for much of the year. Periodically each cattle owner rounded up his cattle, branded the calves and cut out older cattle for slaughter. The herders were mounted on horses, wore the bolero jacket, spurs, low-brimmed hats, and used a saddle based on the Moorish saddle introduced into southern Spain by the Arabs. Such a system of ranching was well established in northern Mexico – where the lasso was added – and in Texas, then part of Mexico, when immigrants from the USA arrived in large numbers in the 1830s. When the distinctive ranching of the Great Plains and the Rockies developed after the end of the Civil War, these methods were the basis of the system. Since then, the advance of agricultural settlement, the introduction of barbed wire, the use of irrigation for supplementary feeding, and the spread of motor vehicles and railways have destroyed the Hispanic nature of the American ranching industry, and it is now a blend of Spanish and Anglo-American methods.

RELIGION AND CROPS

Religion has had a powerful influence upon farming, in both a positive and negative manner. Two positive influences can be seen in the distribution of viticulture and citrus fruits.

Viticulture

In the earliest references to wine in Eygpt and Mesopotamia, it was associated with religion. Much later, the development of the cult of Dionysus in Greece seems to have encouraged wine consumption and viticulture; as Greek influence and settlements spread westwards through the Mediterranean, so did viticulture. By the time of Roman hegemony in the Basin, wine was widely consumed and conspicuous in trade. It was the Romans who were influential in the spread of viticulture northwards into Europe. With the collapse of Roman power in the middle of the first millennium AD, viticulture declined except in monasteries, where the use of wine as a sacrament ensured its survival. In the high Middle Ages, viticulture revived and again became an important element in trade. By the sixteenth century, the grape and viticulture were taken overseas by the Spanish, and viticulture developed in suitable climates in the Americas. Indeed, with the exception of Australia and South Africa, the main wine producing countries outside Europe – Argentina, California and Chile – are all of Spanish origin.

Viticulture remains almost exclusively a product of European settled areas. In the Near East, the home of the domestication of the grape and of the first wine production, very little wine is now produced, for much of this region has been under Muslim influence since the seventh century AD, and alcohol is forbidden to Muslims. In Morocco, Tunisia and Algeria, viticulture was reintroduced by the Spanish and the French in the nine-teenth century, and has persisted since the end of colonial times (although mainly for export). Indeed in the former Soviet Union the Muslim Republics of Central Asia have become leading producers of wine. The grape itself has not, however, been banished from Muslim areas. Raisins are an important product of Egypt, Iraq and Iran, and especially Turkey, and have replaced viticulture in some parts of Algeria.

Citrus fruits

Of the eight citrus fruits grown commercially, all – with the possible exception of the grapefruit and the citron – were domesticated in mainland and archipelago South-East Asia, yet there is very little commercial produc-tion of these crops in that region today. Although the citrus fruits were found wild in a hot, humid region, they are now widely grown in the tropics and the sub-tropics, and indeed some of the main areas of production are found on the margins of the natural limits, where frost is a threat. Two-thirds of world output (two-thirds of which is oranges) is found in only three regions: in the countries bordering the Mediterranean, both north and south of the sea; in the USA, principally in Florida and California; and in south-east Brazil. Other producers include Japan, South Africa and Central America.

Citrus fruits were grown at an early date in India, and from there taken to the early civilizations in the Near East. At the time of Christ, they had not spread westwards from the Levant. There are two explanations of their subsequent spread throughout the Mediterranean. One argument is that the crops and the techniques were taken westwards by the Jews in the Diaspora of the first four centuries after Christ. At some time in the late first millennium BC, the citron (now the least important of the citrus fruits) was used by the Jews in a religious festival, and naturally grown by them in Palestine. By the fourth century AD, Jews were found in large numbers in many cities around the shores of the Mediterranean, and there was also considerable Jewish rural settlement, particularly in North Africa, Turkey, Sicily and Corsica. The citron would have been cultivated, and Erich Isaac argues that it is likely that the Jews would also have taken other citrus fruits with them. So the initial distribution of citrus fruit occurred during the Diaspora.

A second, and more usual, explanation of the spread of citrus fruits also has an indirect religious basis. From an early date there was trade between the Red Sea, the Persian Gulf, Arabia and India, and citrus fruits were brought to the Near East at an early date, along with other crops and new techniques of irrigation. After the death of Mohammed in 632 AD, the Arabs expanded to convert peoples by force or persuasion to Islam. Within two centuries, the area of Muslim domination had reached Spain in the west and India in the east. Not surprisingly, citrus fruits and the techniques of growing them spread throughout the Mediterranean. Thereafter Christian Europe reasserted itself, and Spain was freed from Muslim rule in the fifteenth century. With the discovery of the Americas, it was natural that the Spanish should take citrus fruits to the New World. In the USA Spanish explorers probably brought the orange to Florida, for it was found growing wild there when settlement began, and in California it was Spanish missionaries who introduced the fruit.

RELIGION AND LIVESTOCK

Pigs and Islam

Of far more importance than the positive influence of religion on crops, is the negative influence upon the present distribution and utilization of livestock. The pig is absent from parts of the world today because the Koran declares it to be unclean – as do the Jews. In India, *ahimsa*, the reluctance to harm animals, has had a significant effect upon the cattle industry.

Although Jews and members of other religious sects in the Middle East and North Africa believed the pig to be unclean, and forbade its keeping, it was the similar prohibition found in the Koran that has led to the exclusion of the pig from large areas. By the seventh century AD Muslim power had spread through North Africa to Spain, east into Central Asia and India, and later was to include the Sudan zone of West Africa, Mongolia, Malaysia and Indonesia. In these regions the pig is now of negligible importance (Figure 15.1). In most countries where Muslims predominate, the pig forms less

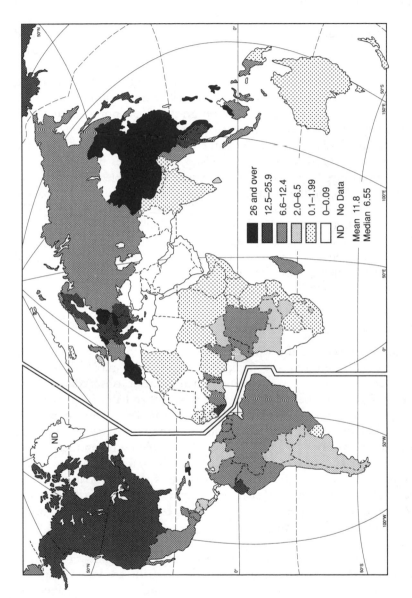

Figure 15.1 Pigs as a percentage of all livestock units, 1980
Source: Food and Agriculture Organization, *Production Yearbook 1981*, vol. 35, Rome, 1982

than 0.1 per cent of all livestock units, and is kept only by non-Muslims, for example the Chinese in Malaysia and Indonesia.

Religious taboo is probably not the only reason for the unimportance of the pig in some parts of the world, including the Muslim regions. The pig was independently domesticated in China and Europe, and was not found in Africa south of the Sahara until the arrival of Europeans. It remains unimportant in most of tropical Africa, although there is little Muslim influence there, outside the north. The pig has disadvantages compared with other domesticated livestock. It is not easily herded (and certainly not over long distances), and cannot graze on grass, as it is not a ruminant. It has no advantages for the nomadic pastoralist, and could not survive easily in drier regions. Unlike the ox or water buffalo, it cannot be used for draught purposes, the sow cannot be milked, and it gives no wool.

The pig has always been associated with sedentary arable civilizations. In Europe it was fed upon the residues of human foods and allowed to forage in forests. As the latter dwindled the pig became confined to its sty. In China it has been a scavenger, fed largely upon kitchen waste. In modern times it is of greatest relative importance in China, Europe and the European settlements overseas. Its advantage now is its high biological efficiency in producing meat (see Chapter 2); the modern pig is fed on skimmed milk and grain.

Cattle in India

India has 15 per cent of the world's cattle and half of the world's water buffaloes. Cattle densities are high compared with most developing countries, and indeed in the opinion of many outside observers, far too high. Yet this large number of cattle produces less than half of 1 per cent of the annual world output of cattle and buffalo meat. This is not to say that cattle have no role in the Indian agricultural economy. They still provide most of the draught power on Indian farms – buffalo are confined to the wet-rice areas – and supply one-third of India's milk output, the water buffalo providing most of the rest. Their dung is the principal source of manure, and is still used as a fuel in many rural areas. Cattle that die naturally provide some meat and hides, but less than 1 per cent of all cattle are slaughtered each year.

Thus, India's cattle provide very little meat, and there are several explanations for this. First, the low incomes of most Indians means that there is a limited demand for meat. Second, the cattle are very badly fed, relying upon waste land for their fodder, for in such a densely populated country little land can be allocated to forage crops, and the indigenous grasses are of poor quality. There has been little selective breeding among the zebu cattle, and they put on weight very slowly. However, the main reason for the small meat industry is the Hindu and Buddhist belief in *ahimsa* – that it is wrong to kill living creatures, and in particular cattle. This belief is not held by the lower castes or the hill tribes, but widely held by most other Indians. Indeed, in some states the slaughter of cattle is illegal, and homes for elderly cattle have been established.

Dairying and its distribution

Religious scruples do not limit the milking of cattle in any part of the world, but some peoples have an aversion to milk. Milk is obtained from sheep, goats, camels and water buffalo, but nine-tenths of the world's milk output comes from cows. Fresh milk is drunk as such or converted into products such as butter, cheese, ghee, ice-cream, and dried, powdered and evaporated milk. Dairy products are a major source of farm income in the European parts of the world, and not surprisingly it is these regions that produce much of the output. North America, Europe, the USSR and Oceania have half the world's cows but produce three-quarters of the fresh milk and butter and 85 per cent of the cheese. This remarkable concentration of dairy output in the European-settled areas is not due simply to the distribution of livestock. Cattle are widely distributed throughout the world – Asia alone has one-quarter of the world's cattle – and they are numerous in Africa and Latin America as well.

At first sight, this distribution may be explained in economic and ecological terms alone. First, dairy products are expensive because the production of milk requires more land than the production of an equivalent amount of calories or proteins from crops (see Chapter 2). Few people in the non-European areas can afford dairy products in any quantity. In the high income countries, however, dairy products make up a significant part of the diet.

Second, cows feed primarily upon grass. In the cool, temperate regions, grasses of high quality give a very high dry matter yield, and provide grazing in spring and summer and hay for winter feed. In contrast, grasses do not grow in deserts or in the shade of tropical forest, and if the forest is cleared the land is soon invaded by low quality grasses. Even the better tropical grasses give poor fodder. In Malaysia it requires 4 ha to give the feed equivalent of 1 ha in England. Consequently, in most tropical regions cows are badly fed and therefore give a low yield of milk.

Third, cows in most developing countries are not from specialized dairy breeds, unlike those of the developed regions, and thus milk yields are low. European breeds imported into the tropics do not easily adapt to the higher temperatures, and milk yields and reproduction rates are lower than in their homelands.

These reasons might be thought to explain satisfactorily the comparative unimportance of dairying in much of the tropics, but there may be other factors. Until recently, there were substantial areas in Africa and Asia where milkable animals were kept but not milked. This seems to be related to the origins of milking and the spread of the practice from its source. The first evidence of milking is found in the Near East in the fourth millennium BC. Subsequently the practice spread into Europe, North Africa, Central Asia and India (the latter in about 1500 BC). In 1500 AD, before the age of European expansion, the practice of milking was unknown in the Americas (which lacked domesticated livestock that could be milked), tropical Africa, China and South-East Asia (Figure 15.2). In Asia the line was between India and the countries of South-East Asia, including the archipelago, and in East Asia between the Mongol peoples of northern China and the sedentary Han Chinese. Such a distinction existed until comparatively recently, although milk consumption has increased in recent years in parts of Asia (notably in Japan). Why there should be such a non-milking zone in Eurasia is far from obvious. Among some African tribes milk is regarded as unclean as urine; in others it is thought suitable only for priests and chiefs. Among Buddhists it is thought unkind to deprive the calf of its sustenance – although such a view, though it could be linked to the belief in *ahismsa*, is not held among Indians. In China, the long conflict between the milk-drinking Mongols and the Han Chinese farmers may explain the distribution.

More recently a biological explanation for non-milking practices has been

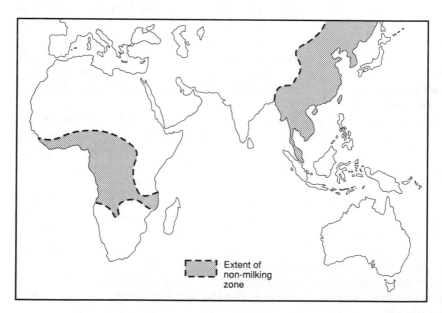

Figure 15.2 The traditional non-milking zones of Asia and Africa
After F.J. Simoons, 'The non-milking area of Africa', *Anthropos*, 1984, vol. 49, pp. 58–66; 'The traditional limits of milking and milk use in southern Asia', *Anthropos*, 1970, vol. 65, pp. 547–93

suggested. Milk contains lactose or milk sugar that is hydrolized in the small intestine. If this does not occur, vomiting and diarrhoea will follow. Tests on populations in various parts of the world suggest that only a small number of the sample suffer from adult lactose malabsorption in Europe, North Africa and India, a much higher proportion elsewhere. How such a genetic difference arose is unclear. As dairying has a long tradition in the Near East and its borders, it may be that natural selection has reduced the proportion suffering from lactose malabsorption. Whatever the explanation, it does suggest a further reason for the lack of milking in parts of Africa and East and South-East Asia.

CONCLUSIONS

It is not suggested here that environmental and economic reasons for spatial differences in agriculture activity are unimportant; simply that cultural features cannot be ignored. It is true, of course, that such explanations are of less importance in the developed world, for the process of modernization during the last two centuries has reduced the influence of religion and other traditional beliefs. None the less, it is unwise to ignore the possibility that some non-economic or non-environmental reasons may explain features of the agricultural geography of the Western world; while in the developing countries it would be unwise in the extreme to ignore the many cultural differences from the West.

SOURCES AND FURTHER READING

M.K. Bennett, 'Aspects of the pig', *Agricultural History*, 1970, vol. 44, pp. 223–35.
M. Debysingh, 'The cultural geography of poultry keeping in India', in D.E. Sopher (ed.), *An Exploration of India: Geographical Perspectives in Society and Culture*, London, Longman, 1980.
P. Deiner and E.E. Robkin, 'Ecology, evolution and the search for cultural origins: the question of Islamic pig prohibition', *Current Anthropology*, 1978, vol. 19, pp. 493–540.
M. Harris, 'The cultural ecology of India's sacred cattle, *Current Anthropology*, 1966, vol. 7, pp. 215–38.
R. Hoffpauir, 'The water buffalo: India's other bovine', *Anthropos*, 1982, vol. 77, pp. 215–38.
E. Isaac, 'Influence of religion on the spread of citrus', *Science*, 1959, vol. 129, pp. 179–86.
E. Isaac, 'The citron in the Mediterranean: a study in religious influences', *Economic Geography*, 1959, vol. 35, pp. 71–8.
W. Neville, 'Singapore: ethnic diversity and its implications', *Annals of the Association of American Geographers*, 1966, vol. 56, pp. 236–53.
Jin-Bee Ooi, *Peninsular Malaysia*, London, Longman, 1976.
C.O. Sauer, *Agricultural Origins and Dispersals*, New York, American Geographical Society, 1952.
F.J. Simoons, 'The non-milking area of Africa', *Anthropos*, 1954, vol. 49, pp. 58–66.

F.J. Simoons, *Eat not this Flesh: Food Avoidance in the Old World*, Madison, University of Wisconsin Press, 1961.

F.J. Simoons, 'The traditional limits of milking and milk use in southern Asia', *Anthropos*, 1970, vol. 65, pp. 547–93.

F.J. Simoons, 'Questions on the sacred cow controversy', *Current Anthropology*, 1979, vol. 20, pp. 467–93.

F.J. Simoons, 'Dairying, milk use and lactose malabsorption in Eurasia: a problem in culture history', *Anthropos*, 1979, vol. 74, pp. 61–80.

D. Stanislawski, 'Dionysus westwards: early religion and the economic geography of wine', *Geographical Review*, 1975, vol. 65, pp. 427–42.

K. Sutton, 'Algeria's vineyards: an Islamic dilemma and a problem of decolonisation', *Journal of Wine Research*, 1990, vol. 1, pp. 101–20.

Chapter 16

Agriculture and the environment

Over the last forty years world agriculture has been remarkably successful in increasing the output of food and fibre. This has been particularly noticeable in the industrialized countries, but many developing countries have also had rapid increases. To a large extent this has been due to the adoption of new inputs purchased from industry, such as chemical fertilizers, pesticides and high-yielding seeds, petroleum and machinery. Greater output has been mainly due to increased crop yields per hectare, although expanding the area in cultivation has been important in some areas, notably in Latin America and tropical Africa. Not only has the output per hectare risen, but so too has output per capita, particularly in North America and Western Europe, where power in the form of the tractor and self-propelled machines have replaced the horse, oxen and human labour. These advances has not been regionally uniform. Output per capita is at its highest in North America, Australasia and Western Europe, and at its lowest in tropical Africa, East, South and South-East Asia (Figure 8.3 p. 90).

But all is not well in agriculture. First, although famines are now confined to tropical Africa, malnutrition is still widespread in many parts of the developing world. However, this cannot be attributed solely, or indeed mainly to the ineffectiveness of food production. Only in Africa has food output per capita fallen consistently over the last thirty years. Most writers now believe that low incomes amongst the purchasers of food is the main cause of malnutrition.

Second is the condition of agriculture in the developed countries. All the developed countries protect farmers in some way, principally by guaranteeing prices above the world level (see Chapter 9). This has had numerous consequences. It has meant that the prices paid by consumers are above those which would occur if free trade was permitted. The levies imposed by the Common Agriculture Policy have excluded would-be exporters from the developing countries, and also the traditional exporters of temperate crops and livestock in North America, Argentina and Australasia, leading to farm bankruptcies in the USA and Australasia in the 1980s. The subsidizing of exports from the European Community has penalized other exporters. Within the European Community and in North America public resentment at food surpluses and the high bill for agricultural protection has forced politicians to re-examine agricultural policies. Paradoxically farm real incomes have fallen for much of the last decade.

Third is the damage modern farming has caused to the environment. Since the 1960s there has been much research and much public comment on the damage to soil, water, flora and fauna caused by the use of agricultural chemicals; in the developed countries farmers have lost their status as guardians of the countryside. However, it is important to note that environmental damage is not new and not a product solely of the impact of industrial farming. Salinity was a major problem in the farms of the Euphrates and Tigris valleys in the second millennium BC, whilst over-grazing and other factors led to the deforestation of the hills surrounding the Mediterranean Sea over two thousand years ago. In this chapter an attempt is made, first to review some of the worldwide aspects of land degradation caused by farmers, and second, to consider those that are specifically a result of the adoption of modern farming methods.

DEFORESTATION

Few examples of environmental damage have aroused more interest in the last two decades than the destruction of the tropical rainforests, particularly those in the Amazon basin; about one-tenth of the Amazon forest in Brazil has been cleared, mainly in the last few decades. There have been many criticisms of this: it is destroying the last large area of rainforest, which contains a rich flora and fauna; it is destroying the habitat and way of life of the indigenous Amerindian population; by removing the protective cover-ing it exposes the soil to the impact of raindrops and high temperatures increasing leaching of soil nutrients and making the soil more susceptible to water erosion; furthermore much of the clearance is for products such as cattle or timber that are exported rather than directly benefiting the home population; efforts to settle landless from the rest of Brazil have had very limited results; finally there are fears that deforestation may have adverse effects upon the local and possibly the global climate.

It is certainly true that the rate of deforestation of the moist tropical forests has accelerated in the last three or four decades, not only in the Amazon basin, but elsewhere. One much cited example is in Central America (Figure 16.1) where much of the Caribbean coastal forest has been cleared since 1950, mainly for the ranching of cattle. In the Philippines 57 per cent of the total land area was covered by forest in 1972, only 38 per cent in 1980, and in Thailand in the same period the proportion fell from a half to a quarter. Indeed one estimate is that half of the world's original tropical rainforest has been cleared for timber, fuel and to create agricultural

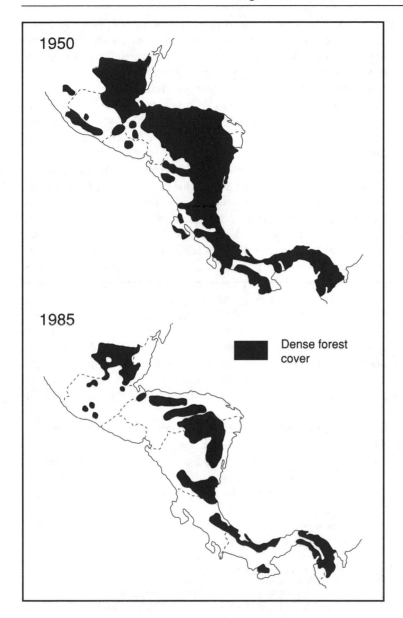

Figure 16.1 Deforestation in Central America, 1950–85
After M.C. Brady, 'Making agriculture a sustainable industry', in C.A. Edwards,
R. Lal, P. Madden, R.H. Miller and G. House (eds), Sustainable Agricultural
Systems, Ankeny, Iowa, Soil and Water Conservation Society, 1990, pp. 20–32

land. If a broader definition of tropical rainforest is taken (Table 16.1 and Figure 16.2), it can be seen that substantial proportions of the world's tropical forest have been destroyed. Nor is this surprising. Although the tropical forests of Latin America are sparsely populated – except for that of the Brazilian coastal areas where the rainforest has been almost entirely removed since the sixteenth century – in Asia and tropical Africa much of the former forest areas are now densely populated; deforestation has been mainly for cultivation and has been going on for at least seven or eight thousand years.

Nor has deforestation been confined to the tropics. The existence of much of the arable land that sustained the major civilizations of the eastern USA, Europe, India and China has been possible only because of the slow removal of woodland by populations which have expanded steadily for five thousand years, and rapidly for the last two centuries. Not only was the clearance of woodland essential for cultivation, but until the nineteenth century wood provided fuel for domestic and industrial purposes, timber for houses and for ships, waggons, furniture and a wide range of other goods which are now made from metals or plastics. The removal of the European forest was a slow process, with a major period of deforestation in the Middle Ages. However, in the USA it was rapid. In 1620 the forest covered 170 million hectares; it is now less than 10 million. Much of the deciduous woodland of the northern hemisphere has gone, and the more substantial forest areas are now to be found in the boreal forests of Scandinavia, Russia and North America, for the most part too cold for cultivation.

Estimating the extent and rate of deforestation, whether global or tropical is exceedingly difficult. Quite apart from the absence of accurate maps or air photos of much of the world at suitable intervals, there is difficulty in distinguishing different types of forest; are tropical forests to include only rainforest, for example? In many estimates secondary growth is excluded. Hence some writers believe that the extent of deforestation has been exaggerated. However, it is clear that without deforestation there would have been no agriculture, no food and no people. This does not

Table 16.1 Rainforest and moist deciduous forest

	Percentage of original forest cut down	Area surviving (million hectares)
Africa	49	180
Latin America	63	400[1]
Asia	60	250[2]
World	60	830

Notes: 1   Amazon forests.
       2   Indo-Malaysia forests.

Figure 16.2 Original and 1986 extent of tropical rainforest
After C.J. Barrow. *Land Degradation. Development and Breakdown of Terrestrial Environment*, Cambridge, Cambridge University Press, 1991, p. 74

Approximate extent 1986

Probably forested before clearance

preclude of course, the need for a sensible and planned control of forest removal, and of forest replanting.

LAND DEGRADATION: SOIL EROSION

Soil is continuously removed from the surface of the land by wind and water; new soil is continuously but slowly created by the decomposition of the regolith and the activities of plants, animals and microbes. Soil erosion occurs when there is a significant net loss of soil. What is difficult to measure is the intensity of soil erosion and its agricultural significance. In many parts of the world, particularly in semi-arid areas, large gullies caused by storms on highly friable soils lead to the abandonment of the land; it is a total loss to agriculture. On the other hand gentle sheet erosion may slowly remove plant nutrients in the soil which would lead, after many decades, to a fall in crop yields of a few percentage points, but that will almost certainly be masked by the use of chemical fertilizers. Thus it is difficult to describe the geographical distribution of soil erosion, because estimates rarely distinguish the intensity of erosion in different places. One exception to this is in the USA where soil scientists have measured soil losses against the T-factor; soil erosion is significant if it exceeds 0.4 tonnes per hectare per year on shallow soils, 2.02 tonnes on deep soils. Currently the rate of erosion in the USA exceeds 2 tonnes on 46 million of the 170 million hectares of cropland, 27 per cent of the total.

Soil loss has two consequences for crop production. First it reduces plant nutrients, the water holding capacity and organic matter, and so reduces crop yields. Second, it makes soils shallower and so restricts the type of crop that can be grown to shallow-rooted crops such as cereals; deep-rooted crops such as potatoes or sugar-beet cannot be grown. Such effects often take a long time to occur. The United States Department of Agriculture has estimated that if current rates of erosion continue, without any advances in agricultural techniques, crop yields will have fallen by 5–10 per cent in one hundred years time.

Estimates of the extent of soil erosion over larger areas must be treated with some caution. It has been estimated, for example, that over the last 7000 years 430 million hectares in the world as a whole have been 'severely degraded', about 29 per cent of the present world arable land. In India half of the total land area is said to be degraded by erosion, although the intensity of erosion is not distinguished, nor is it in the estimate that one-sixth of the total area of China is subject to soil erosion; in Australia 30 per cent of the usable land is 'significantly eroded'.

However debatable some of these estimates may be there is no doubt that soil erosion is a threat to farming, both by causing the abandonment of land and by reducing crop yields. The causes of soil erosion are various, but removing the natural vegetation for cultivation immediately increases the risk of soil erosion, for the soil is no longer protected from the wind or the impact of raindrops, or in tropical climates from high temperatures and greater rates of chemical decomposition. Ploughing the land further increases the risk, as does the creation of a fine tilth in which to sow the seed. Agricultural soils are most prone to erosion when the soil is bare; in England for example much of the water erosion occurs in autumn, and wind erosion is most likely in spring before crops become established.

The ideal farming system is, therefore, where the soil is covered by secondary vegetation or crops for as much of the year as possible. Thus in the humid tropics the farming system most successful in reducing soil erosion is shifting cultivation. Land is cleared for crop production in small plots, which are surrounded by forest. The soil in not ploughed, and a digging stick is used to plant a mixture of cereals, root crops and bushes, so that the soil is covered for most of the year. The plot is abandoned after two or three years, and secondary forest becomes established, until it is cleared again after twenty years or more, when soil fertility has been restored. Such a farming system protects the fragile soils from rain and high temperatures, but it is possible only in areas of low population densities.

There are a number of factors influencing variations in the susceptibility of soils to erosion. First is the nature of rainfall; although wind may locally be a powerful erosive agent, most soil erosion is due to the action of running water, either in rills and gullies, or in slower mass movements over the surface of the soil, causing sheet erosion. The physical impact of raindrops is important; potential erosion is greatest in the violent storms of the tropics, least where the rainfall mainly falls in gentle drizzle, as in Western Europe. Second is the amount of vegetation cover. In the hilly watersheds of the Mississippi the loss of soil on land still forested is a few hundredths of a tonne per hectare per year, on land in pasture 4 tonnes, on land in corn 54 tonnes, and on land abandoned because of gullying, the rate reaches 450 tonnes a year.

Third is slope: the steeper the slope, the faster the water travels as run-off, and so the greater the capacity for erosion. In the last thirty years population growth in many developing countries has caused the expansion of settlement from the plains into upland areas where much of the land surface is in high angle slopes. In Colombia slopes of over 45 per cent have been cultivated and soil loss has reached 370 tonnes per hectare per year. Clearing the vegetation for crop production leads to soil erosion, destroying not only the soil on these slopes, but depositing the silt in down-stream areas, often causing flooding. In Britain the high prices for cereals has led some farmers to plough areas with high slopes. It is generally assumed that 11° is the maximum slope for crop production, yet slopes of up to 20° have been ploughed on the South Downs.

Soil texture is a fourth factor influencing the rate of erosion. Generally the most easily eroded soils are sand and gravels, which have large spaces between soil particles; in contrast soils with a high clay content are less susceptible. Thus in England the soils most likely to be eroded by wind are not those in the areas of highest average wind speed in the west, but on the areas of sandy soils in the east and south-east, such as the Bunter Sandstones, the Lower Greensand and the chalk. A fifth factor is the occurrence of semi-arid climates. Although rainfall is low and evaporation high in these regions, the vegetation cover is thin, even where not cleared for cultivation, and overgrazing has reduced the vegetation cover and so exposed the soil to the impact of rare but violent rainfall. These regions are considered separately (see below, pp. 205–7).

Soil erosion is clearly a significant problem for farmers. Its precise extent is difficult to establish: it is not a new phenomenon, but the rate of erosion has greatly accelerated in the last one hundred years. To some extent it is a result of modern farming methods (see below, pp. 207–9) but for the most part it is due to the rapid growth of population, and the adoption of unwise farming methods, either in response to greater subsistence needs or the search for greater profits.

LAND DEGRADATION: SALINITY AND ALKALINITY

Soil erosion is a mechanical process, but there are also adverse chemical effects upon soil. Change in the environment or in farming methods can lead to more acid or more alkaline soils (see Chapter 4). Although the removal of the European forest cover may have increased the acidity of soils since the Middle Ages, the most notable and most debated current cause of increased acidity is from acid rain. Industrial pollutants lead to the increase of sulphur dioxide and nitric oxides in the atmosphere, which reach the earth in rainfall as sulphur or nitric acid. The latter may increase soil acidity, and it is claimed that this has reduced crop yields in parts of eastern Canada by 10 per cent.

Of far greater importance, however, is the occurrence of saline and alkaline soils in the arid and semi-arid parts of the world. Saline soils occur under two circumstances. First, many semi-arid areas are naturally saline; ground water with a large salt content reaches the surface and the high rates of evaporation lead to the crystallization of salts which, according to their degree of concentration in the soil, can limit the type of crop that can be grown, reduce crop yields or cause the abandonment of land. There are over 5 million hectares of saline soils in Western Australia and salinity has led to the abandonment of some 260,000 hectares.

Second, and of far greater significance, is the salinity that occurs in irrigated and semi-arid regions. Irrigation causes the water table to rise to within a short distance of the surface. In the Punjab, for example, irrigation has raised the water table 7–9 feet since 1895. This has been the result of over application of water by farmers, leaks from canals and a lack of underdrainage to remove surplus water. Capillary action raises water and salts form in and on the surface of the soil. In the 1980s it was estimated that between a third and a half of all irrigated land was affected by salinity to some extent. Although only 14 per cent of the world's arable land is irrigated, it produces one-third of the value of world agricultural output and so salination may have serious consequences for world food output. In the long established agricultural settlements of South-West Asia and north Africa, half the irrigated land in Iraq is salinized, a third in Egypt, a quarter in Pakistan and 15 per cent in Iran. Nor is salinisation confined to the developing countries or ancient civilizations; it is a major problem in the areas of recent irrigation in the south-west of the USA. Salinization can be cured by draining the land; the use of tube-wells and pumping has been successful in parts of Pakistan.

DESERTIFICATION

In the 1930s it was claimed that the Sahara desert was creeping southwards; the droughts in the Sahel in the 1970s renewed the belief that the desert was expanding, and in the following years it was asserted that desertification was to be found in many other parts of the world. The causes of desertification and its precise definition have been a subject of considerable debate. It seems now agreed that the term should be applied to the degradation of ecosystems in arid and semi-arid regions which leads to a loss of plant productivity and species diversity. Thus on the edge of deserts the vegetation of semi-arid areas is reduced to the status of desert vegetation, and the subhumid areas to semi-arid. This is due not to any long-term climatic change, although prolonged drought may be a powerful contributor, but to human mismanagement of fragile environments. The main forms of land degradation in the drylands are the deterioration of vegetation, soil erosion and salinity. Thus desertification is not a climatic process but simply a term used to describe land degradation in the drylands.

The world's drylands – arid, semi-arid and subhumid – occupy 47.2 per cent of the world's land surface. Of this nearly twenty per cent is defined as arid – already desert – so that it is the semi-arid and subhumid areas that are at risk, a quarter of the earth's land surface (Figure 3.9, p. 30). About one-fifth of the drylands are experiencing soil erosion by water and wind, and much of the natural vegetation is experiencing degradation. The main cause of this is poor land management which in turn is a result of population growth and the increasing commercialization of agriculture.

The United Nations Environment Programme work upon desertification provides some estimates of the distribution and intensity of soil degradation. Surprisingly the largest proportion of the total land area lies in Europe, but this includes the subhumid grasslands of the former Soviet Union

Table 16.2 The extent of soil degradation by region

	Total land area (million hectares)	Total area experiencing soil degradation (million hectares)	Area experiencing soil degradation as a percentage:		Percentage of area susceptible to erosion experiencing:		High and very high degraded (million hectares)
			Total land area	Area of drylands susceptible to erosion	Low and medium degradation	High and very high degradation	
Africa	2966	319	10.8	24.9	19.1	5.8	74.0
Asia	4256	370	8.7	25.0	22.0	3.0	43.7
South America	1768	79	4.5	15.0	13.8	1.2	6.3
North America	2191	79	3.6	9.6	8.7	0.9	7.1
Europe[1]	951	100	10.5	33.1	31.5	1.6	4.9
Australasia	882	88	10.0	13.0	12.8	0.2	1.6

Note: 1 Including European Russia.
Source: N. Middleton and D.S.G. Thomas, *World Atlas of Desertification*, United Nations Environment Programme, London, Edward Arnold, 1992

(Table 16.2). In absolute terms Africa – particularly North Africa, the Sahel and south-west Africa – and Asia, notably the Middle East, Western India and northern China – have the greatest areas subject to erosion (Table 16.2). By far the largest areas suffering from severe degradation are to be found in Africa and Asia.

There are numerous causes of land degradation in drylands. Overgrazing is a prime cause. In much of the drylands the only possible utilization of the meagre natural vegetation is pastoralism. The increased human populations, together with advances in animal hygiene, have greatly increased livestock numbers, and this has led to overgrazing. This reduces the palatable species, encourages invasion by the less palatable, and increases the proportion of bare land; all this increases the possibility of soil erosion.

Two forms of crop production have encouraged land degradation. First is the expansion of cultivation into pastoral areas. In the Sahel a series of years with above average rainfall in the 1960s encouraged expansion into land once left to pastoral nomads. The droughts since the early 1970s have led to falling yields, soil damage and land abandonment. In Rajastan, in India, marginal land was ploughed in the 1960s and 1970s with comparable results. Second is the intensification of crop production, which has also had adverse results. In Africa, rainfed traditional agriculture requires a number of years in fallow to maintain crop yields but increasing population has led to a reduction of the period of fallow, and hence reduced soil fertility, crop yields, and an increased likelihood of erosion.

Deforestation has led to the deterioration of the vegetation and accelerated erosion. In Africa trees are cut primarily for fuel; wood is the only source of fuel for cooking, heating and other purposes for most of the rural population.

MODERN FARMING AND THE ENVIRONMENT

Since 1945 farming in North America, Australasia and Western Europe has been radically changed by new agricultural technologies: the tractor has replaced the horse, machines have replaced men and women, chemical fertilizers have replaced farmyard manure; herbicides are sprayed to weed, where harrows and hoes were once used; and insecticides and fungicides are used to control plant disease. But these developments have had undesirable effects upon the landscape, the soil, flora and fauna, and the water supply, although it must be said that the extent of these effects is still controversial.

The use of pesticides to destroy weeds and plant diseases accelerated in the 1950s; most of the sprays also affected plants and fauna other than the pest, and delivery by spray meant that only a small proportion of the pesticide affected the pest. It was soon discovered that sprays and seed dressings could kill birds. Seed-eating birds died from seed-dressings and hawks from eating infected birds, whilst egg-thinning led to later losses. Mammals do not seem to have been affected by pesticides. Butterflies have declined in the last forty years, but this has been due more to the destruction of their habitats than to the direct effect of sprays. Residual pesticides have found their way into groundwater and surface waters, but at low levels of concentration. Legislation to control the safety levels of pesticides has led to the withdrawal of some sprays and work in the USA has led to doubts as to whether chemical spraying has been an effective economic or physical control of pests.

Before the Second World War most of the nitrogen, potassium and phosphorus added to the soil came from farmyard manure. Since then there has been a rapid increase in the use of chemical fertilizers, mainly in the form of straight nitrogen. This has led to a great increase in crop yields but also to an increase in the nitrates in surface and groundwater. In surface waters the increased nitrogen has caused eutrophication, a rapid growth of plants such as weeds that clog rivers, and encourage algae on the surface that cut out light, and so indirectly reduce the oxygen supply for fish. Nitrates have also reached very high concentrations in groundwaters which provide human water supplies, particularly in the east and south-east of England, which is where most of the fertilizer is used. In a number of areas nitrates in drinking water exceed the European Community safety levels; as yet, however, the connection between nitrites in drinking water and stomach cancer and the blue-baby syndrome is unproven. Nitrate levels have also been increased by the ploughing of grassland in the 1940s and 1950s, and the continued use of farmyard manure.

Before 1939 most farms in England kept livestock and crops, and the manure was used as fertilizer. Since then the use of chemical fertilizers has replaced farmyard manure, and the number of livestock in eastern England has fallen as farmers have specialized in crop production. Increasingly livestock have been kept in the west, crops grown in the east, and it has been too costly to move farmyard manure from the livestock areas to the crop areas. Large amounts of animal waste have had to be disposed of, and leaks from storage tanks and the use of slurry have added to nitrate levels, as have leaks from silos in which grass is made into silage.

The mechanization of agriculture has also led to much criticism; machines can be used more efficiently in large fields, and hence hedgerows have been uprooted, particularly in the arable east, reducing the habitat of birds and small mammals. The use of heavy machinery, in combination with other new practices has increased the risk of soil erosion. Heavy machines compact soils, and wheels leave rills that channel water. Finer seed-beds increase the risk of wind erosion, the increase in autumn sowing crops has left more land bare in winter, and the reduction of rotations which include grass and legumes has reduced the organic content of soils, and so increased the potential for erosion.

Finally, the combination of new technologies and the high guaranteed prices of the last forty years have encouraged farmers to increase the area under crops, and particularly cereals. This has led to the destruction of land with particular habitats for wildlife. Since the end of the Second World War a number of distinctive habitats in England and Wales have been destroyed (Figure 16.3)

TOWARDS SUSTAINABLE AGRICULTURE

The adverse effects of modern farming have been dealt with by piecemeal legislation. Attempts have been made to control the safety of pesticides; in Britain Environmentally Sensitive Areas have been designated in which farmers are paid to adopt less damaging practices; and some rare habitats have been declared Sites of Special Scientific Interest. But there have been advocates of much more decisive changes in farming practice. These new approaches have been described as organic farming, sustainable agriculture, low-input agriculture, alternative agriculture or radical agriculture. The general argument is that before the use of agro-chemicals farming practices were designed – as a result of centuries of experience – to maintain crop yields over the long run without damage to the environment. Thus in the mixed farming of Western Europe before 1945 livestock and crops were produced on the same farm; farmyard manure provided plant nutrients and organic matter for the soil, crops were partly sold as cash crops, partly retained to feed livestock, and the straw from cereals was

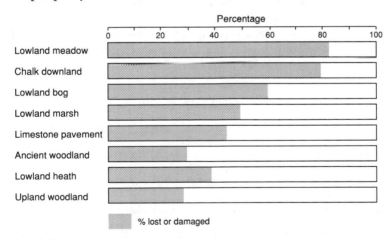

Figure 16.3 Percentage area of selected wildlife habitats destroyed in England and Wales since 1945
After T. O'Riordan, 'Agriculture and environmental protection', *Geography Review*, 1987, vol. 1, pp. 35–40

used to make farmyard manure. Crops were grown in rotation and not continuously, and most rotations included leys of grass and clover, the latter adding nitrogen to the soil, the grass improving soil structure. Root crops such as sugar-beet, potatoes and fodder roots allowed thorough weeding during growth by hoe. Growing crops in rotation limited the build up of disease in the soil, for most diseases are specific to one crop.

The use of herbicides has greatly reduced the amount of labour necessary for weed control, and fertilizers have lessened the need to keep livestock, and so the basis of mixed farming has been undermined. Organic farmers have argued that pesticides and artificial fertilizers are unnecessary and that traditional farming methods produce a healthier and more palatable food. Some extreme advocates of organic farming would also eliminate the use of purchased energy in the form of tractors and electricity, on the grounds that non-renewable resources such as petroleum should be conserved for other purposes. In the USA low-input farming has been advocated, where agro-chemicals are not spurned, but used in much reduced and at safer levels. Thus Integrated Pest Control envisages the much more careful and less intensive use of sprays combined with crop rotations and biological control of pests.

As yet these new – or revived forms of agriculture – have been adopted by few farmers, and the evidence on their performance is limited. However, yields are generally lower, and although inputs are less, net returns per hectare are also lower than in chemical farming. At the moment the continuation of food surpluses and the challenges of limiting environmental damage may make these farming methods attractive to farmers in the developed world. They are less likely to appeal in the developing countries where continued rapid population growth requires continued increases of crop yields which are unlikely to be obtained with the traditional agriculture still practised in much of Afro-Asia and Latin America.

SOURCES AND FURTHER READING

T.M. Addiscott, A.P. Whitmore and D.S. Powlson, *Farming, Fertilizers and the Nitrate Problem*, Wallingford, C.A.B. International, 1991.

D. Baldock, *Agriculture and Habitat Loss in Europe*, CAP Discussion Paper no. 3, Gland, Switzerland, World Wildlife Fund, 1990.

C.J. Barrow, *Land Degradation. Development and Breakdown of Terrestial Environments*, Cambridge, Cambridge University Press, 1991.

P.M. Blaikie, *The Political Economy of Soil Erosion in Developing Countries*, London, Longman, 1985.

T. Clunies-Ross and N. Hildyard, *The Politics of Industrial Agriculture*, London, Earthscan, 1992.

G.R. Conway and J.N. Pretty, *Unwelcome Harvest: Agriculture and Pollution*, London, Earthscan, 1991.

P. Crosson and J.E. Ostrov, 'Sorting out the environmental benefits of alternative agriculture', *Journal of Soil and Water Conservation*, 1990, vol. 46, pp. 34–41.

C.A. Edwardes, (ed.), *Sustainable Agricultural Systems*, Ankeny, Iowa, Soil and Water Conservation Society, 1990.

S.A. El-Swaijy, W.C. Moldenhaver and A. Lo, *Soil Erosion and Conservation*, Ankeny, Iowa, Soil Conservation Society of America, 1985.

A. Goudie, *The Human Impact on the Natural Environment*, London, Basil Blackwell, 1990.

A. Grainger, *The Threatening Desert. Controlling Desertification*, London, Earthscan, 1990.

N. Hanley (ed.), *Farming and the Countryside*, Wallingford, C.A.B. International, 1991.

R.D. Hodges and C. Arden-Clarke, *Soil Erosion in Britain: Levels of Soil Damage and their Relationship to Farming Practices*, The Soil Association, 1986.

N. Middleton and D.S.G. Thomas, *World Atlas of Desertification*, United Nations Environment Programme, London, Edward Arnold, 1992.

T. O'Riordan, 'Agriculture and environmental protection', *Geography Review*, 1987, vol. 1, pp. 35–40.

M.H.R. Soper and E.S. Carter, *Modern Farming and the Countryside*, Ipswich, Farming Press Books, 1991.

Chapter 17

Conclusions

It was stated at the beginning of this book that the aim of agricultural geography is to describe and explain spatial variations in agricultural activity, and that the heart of the problem is the extraordinary diversity of agriculture.

That there is such diversity is not surprising. There are far more people involved in farming than in any other human economic activity. They are found in every physical environment, from the Arctic to the Equator, they speak every language, and vary in economic standing from great riches to abject poverty. This diversity is further emphasized by the fact that farmers deal with living things, with different environmental needs, which they manipulate to produce economic products, subject to the laws of economics. Yet at the same time, the farm is not only the farmer's workshop but also a home, so that the farmer's job and family life are often one and the same.

These conditions suggest that the explantions of spatial diversity are unlikely to be simple. Yet there are further complications. Agriculture attracts the attention of many academic disciplines; agronomy, botany, soil science, hydrology, climatology and biology all concern themselves with aspects of farming. So too do geographers, sociologists, anthropologists and economists. Not surprisingly there are many views on the behaviour of farmers.

It follows from the complexity of agriculture that it is unlikely that there will be one key factor that explains all spatial variations in agricultural activity in all parts of the world. This book has emphasized the many different variables which help explain why farmers do what, and where. But it is only a beginning, and it is not suggested that there are no other approaches to the subject. The main aim of an introductory text is to suggest that the subject of agriculture is of remarkable interest, and to encourage the student to find out more about it, in the field, the laboratory, the computer room and in the library.

Index

DATE DUE
